JOURNEY TO THE EAST

Journey to the East

The Jesuit Mission to China, 1579–1724

Liam Matthew Brockey

THE BELKNAP PRESS OF
HARVARD UNIVERSITY PRESS
Cambridge, Massachusetts
London, England
2007

Printed in the United States of America

Design by Annamarie McMahon Why

Library of Congress Cataloging-in-Publication Data

Brockey, Liam Matthew.
Journey to the East : the Jesuit mission to China, 1579–1724 / Liam Matthew Brockey.
p. cm.
Includes bibiographical references (p.) and index.
ISBN-13: 978-0-674-02448-9 (alk. paper)
ISBN-10: 0-674-02448-6 (alk. paper)
1. Jesuits—Missions—China. 2. China—Church history. I. Title

BV3417.B76 2007
266′.251—dc22 2006049695

For J.S.A.E.

Contents

Preface

Like the chain of events recounted in the chapters that follow, this book started with a journey. But in contrast to the voyages of missionaries four centuries ago, mine was a journey to the West. Although I did not know at the time what my future would hold, I first began to think about the China Jesuits at the old Imperial Observatory in Peking in 1996, when I stood before a statue of Matteo Ricci. I had visited the ruins of St. Paul's at Macau only weeks before but had not made the connection between the two places. It was not until a few years later in Portugal that I would return to thinking about missionaries in East Asia. By that time it was no coincidence that I turned up traces of Ricci and his colleagues. Over the past several years I have traveled far to uncover evidence relating to their story, and I have incurred many debts of gratitude along the way that I would like to repay here.

This book first took shape under the careful guidance of Philip Benedict of Brown University. Diogo Curto and Jerome Grieder also provided invaluable assistance. My colleagues Huihung Chen, Henrique Leitão, and Joshua Zeitz all lent their support to this project at that early stage. Since coming to Princeton I have received assistance from several colleagues in the History Department. In particular, I thank Peter Brown, Bob Darnton, Nicola Di Cosmo, Ben Elman, Tony Grafton, Martin Heijdra, Bill Jordan, Peter Lake, Philip Morgan, Sue Naquin, Willard Peterson, Ted Rabb, and Peter Silver for their insights and encouragement. Others beyond New Jersey also offered their expertise, especially Ad

Dudink, Noël Golvers, Ronnie Hsia, Tom McCoog, Eugenio Menegon, Ken Mills, John Russell-Wood, Nicolas Standaert, and Ines Županov. Yet I made no greater friend on this journey than Jurgis Elisonas, whose academic rigor is surpassed only by his warmth. It was he who read draft after draft of this book, never ceasing to improve my writing and analysis, and so I dedicate it to him in friendship.

Over the years I have tried the patience of numerous archivists and librarians. I am grateful to two of them in particular, Dra. Conceição Geada of the Biblioteca da Ajuda in Lisbon and Father Thomas Reddy of the Archivum Romanum Societatis Iesu. Without the help of Dra. Conceição, I might never have learned to read the Jesuits' handwriting during my first months at Ajuda. And without Father Reddy's generosity and assistance, I would have had to spend far longer in the Eternal City than I did. Of course, I never would have visited either place if not for the foundations that sponsored my research. I thank the Instituto Cultural de Macau and the Fulbright Program for the grants that I received for study in Portugal and Italy. I am also grateful for a series of grants given to me by the University Committee on Research in the Humanities and Social Sciences at Princeton. Most important, I must thank Luís dos Santos Ferro and the Fundação Luso-Americana para o Desenvolvimento for their unfailing support of my research.

It is a tiring business keeping one's focus trained on a single subject for years at a stretch. I doubt that I would have been able to summon the endurance needed for this project if not for the loving support of my family in America and in Portugal. My wife, Mónica, has been my most careful and discerning editor, reading every line of this book in its formative and its final stages. With her company, and that of our children, Beatriz and Leonor, this journey has been a pleasant one. My only regret is that my friend and mother-in-law, Maria do Céu, passed away before seeing this book published. It was in her house that I learned Portuguese and that I wrote the pages that follow, looking out from her patio over the rooftops of Lisbon. From that inspirational perch I could see a blue sliver of the Tagus River, where the India fleets once lay at anchor awaiting their turn to make a journey to the East.

Note on Translations and Orthography

This book is based on archival and published materials in several languages, including Portuguese, Latin, Spanish, Italian, French, and Chinese. All translations into English were done or commissioned by the author, who alone accepts responsibility for any inaccuracies. Quotations from the Latin Vulgate Bible have been rendered into English using the Rheims-Challoner translation (Baltimore, 1899). I have attempted to standardize the spelling of the names of the European and Asian protagonists in this study. As a general rule, first names are indicated according to the modern spelling in each individual's native tongue (such as Matteo for Mateus, or João for Joam). I have made an effort to respect the contemporary spelling of surnames as indicated by each individual writing in his own language (such as Ricci instead of Rixio, or Gouvea instead of Gouveia). There are, however, a number of instances in which the individuals in question did not write their names in a consistent fashion or else used abbreviations. In these cases, the most appropriate form of the name has been selected in light of the individual's native tongue (such as Alfonso Vagnone for Affonso Vanhoni and João Rodrigues for Joam Rōīz). Chinese terms and the names of Chinese individuals are given in pinyin romanization. Since Portuguese was the lingua franca of the China Jesuits, the baptismal names they gave to Chinese men and women are provided in that language (such as Paulo Xu Guangqi or Miguel Yang

Tingyun). The standard reference employed for names, as well as dates and other biographical information, is Joseph Dehergne, *Répertoire des Jésuites de Chine de 1552 à 1800* (Rome and Paris, 1973). Readers should be aware that the French- or Latin-based spellings of Portuguese, Spanish, and Italian names found in Louis Pfister, *Notices Biographiques et Bibliographiques sur les Jésuites de l'Ancienne Mission de Chine,* 2 vols. (Shanghai, 1932–1934), are thoroughly outdated. I have chosen to use some more recognizable forms of Chinese place-names (such as Peking and Canton) for ease of readability. The names of most of the places within China mentioned here, however, appear in pinyin romanization.

JOURNEY TO THE EAST

Introduction

As night fell on December 2, 1621, a solemn procession wound its way through the streets of Macau, a Portuguese enclave on the southernmost extremity of the Chinese mainland. It was the eve of the feast of Francis Xavier, the recently beatified Jesuit priest who had been the first European since the Middle Ages to attempt spreading the Christian message among the peoples of East Asia.

In the two weeks leading up to the anniversary of his death, the city had conducted lavish celebrations in his honor. They began with the sounds of blaring trumpets, pealing bells, and exploding fireworks, while a banner bearing the future saint's likeness was raised in front of the church of São Paulo, the sanctuary at the headquarters of the missions of the Society of Jesus in Japan and China. These celebrations culminated with the procession that proclaimed Xavier Macau's new patron. Carrying a silver reliquary case containing one of the missionary's arm bones, Bishop Diogo Correa Valente led a train of priests, friars, local nobles, and other laymen through streets bedecked with flags and tapestries. Singing children followed close behind, escorting carriages that portrayed Xavier's virtues. The procession paused at impromptu theaters erected in squares where students of the Jesuit college reenacted episodes from his life. On one of these stages China appeared in the company of Shangchuan Island. The great Ming empire was regally dressed, her clothes adorned with gold and silver ornaments and precious stones, yet she bore a lament in her mouth. She complained bitterly that when Blessed Francis Xavier stood before her gates, bearing a treasure greater than all others, she had obstinately refused him entry. By contrast, the humble island reveled in the fact that the Apostle of the Orient had passed on to greater glory in a hut on one of his beaches. As Shangchuan exhorted his shepherds and their flocks to dance and sing praises in the flickering light of torches and luminaries, China was left with her empty riches to weep at her misfortune.[1]

Francis Xavier had died sixty-nine years earlier, in 1552, not far from the site of this commemorative procession. He was born in Spanish Navarre into the lower ranks of the Basque nobility in 1506 and spent part of his formative years at the University of Paris. While studying at the French capital, he met Ignatius Loyola and joined the group that would become recognized by the papacy in 1540 as the Society of Jesus. Soon after that, he embarked for Asia at the behest of King João III of Portugal. As the first overseas missionary of a dynamic young religious order, Xavier represented a new breed in contemporary Catholicism—the aggressive seeker of gentile souls to baptize, the energetic laborer in the "vineyard of the Lord." Following in the steps of the colonists, traders, and soldiers who had built the fortresses and trading entrepôts that constituted the Portuguese Estado da Índia, Xavier spent ten years shuttling across Maritime Asia between India, Southeast Asia, and Japan attempting to open new mission fields.

During his travels in Asia, Xavier benefited from the presence of other Europeans, who gave him crucial protection and support, and the interest of numerous local intermediaries, who at least gave the appearance of understanding his religious motivations. But these individuals merely helped him over the first hurdles in his race for a heavenly prize. The evangelic conquests sought by Xavier lay beyond the new hybrid worlds established by the Portuguese in their coastal settlements; he aimed at the heart of the kingdoms and empires of Asia. By his own optimistic reckoning, the missions he had started on the Malabar and Fishery coasts, in the Moluccas and Malacca, and on Honshu and Kyushu had all made inroads for the implantation of the Catholic faith into indigenous cultures. Yet according to the hagiographical tradition that was later constructed about his apostolic endeavors, Xavier died with his greatest prize just out of reach when he expired on Shangchuan Island right outside the gates of the Ming empire. The challenge of establishing a mission in the cultural heart of East Asia lay before those who would respond to his call for missionaries from Europe. The story of the men who picked up the standard of the Apostle of the Orient and pursued the enterprise in China that he had only imagined is the subject of this book.

As Francis Xavier's reputation for holiness and missionary vigor was completing its spread from Portuguese Asia to the last corner of Catholic Europe in the late sixteenth century, one of the greatest works of Chinese literature was being produced. *Journey to the West,* or *Xiyou ji,* a prose masterpiece derived from centennial folk traditions, was first printed in 1592. It is a book of disputed authorship, most frequently attributed to Wu Cheng'en (ca. 1500–1582), a minor scholar-official with a taste for the supernatural. The plot reworks the historical journey made by Xuanzang, a seventh-century monk, to India in order to acquire the Buddhist scripture, elaborating on the trials undergone by a group of adventurers to bring a foreign religion to China. What rendered this tale so compelling to the generations of storytellers who had passed it on, embellished it, and made it an appropriate subject for a former mandarin to write down was that it combined adventure and religion in epic fashion set against the boundless landscapes of Inner Asia.

In *Journey to the West,* Xuanzang must travel across deserts and mountain ranges, confront the perils of the fabulous and the unknown, and defeat monstrous foes on his way to far-distant India. The perilous road trodden by this seeker allegorically represents the Buddhist path to enlightenment.[2] Fortunately for Xuanzang, he is escorted and protected from harm by three companions with supernatural powers, of whom the best known is the monkey Sun Wukong. While the religious quest of the wandering monk provides the central motif of the fabled journey, the tale of the monkey with his extraordinary ingenuity and wit has made this one of the canonical works of Chinese fiction. Coincidentally, the supposed author of *Journey to the West* died in the same year that Francis Xavier's missionary successors acquired their first residence within the Ming empire.

At first sight, no analogies appear between the late Ming period's *Journey to the West* and the story of the Jesuit mission to China as it is told here. After all, no parallels are drawn between the founder of the mission, Matteo Ricci, and Pigsy, the voracious pig, in the account that follows; the dispositions of the missionary-astronomer Ferdinand Verbiest and the monk Sandy are not subjected to comparison. Important elements of the Ming tale do, however, resonate clearly with the central themes of this book. In both cases, the sequence of events features dramatic actions leading to the introduction of a new religious tradition into the Chinese social and cultural context; attention is drawn to the challenges faced by individuals as they traveled vast distances and tried to equip themselves with the tools required for making sense of the complexities of a civilization radically different from their own.

It is the adventurous progress of the Jesuits' journey to the East, rather than the content of the religious dogma transmitted by them, that forms the core of this work. The peril of travel in the premodern world, the danger of entering a foreign land alone and unarmed, the difficulty of vanquishing the real or imagined foes who stood in the way, and the challenge of understanding a wholly unfamiliar culture constitute episodes of high drama in a script that includes several reversals of fortune for its protagonists. But unlike *Journey to the West,* this account of the China Jesuits in the sixteenth and seventeenth centuries is not a fairy tale. It should not be confused with the familiar Western story which treats the Jesuits' mission as an epic encounter between East and West. Not all adventures are epics, and the fate of the Society of Jesus in late imperial China is not told here in either heroic or hagiographic terms.

This book is about a handful of missionaries who believed that they could, with little more than firm conviction and divine assistance, convert the Chinese to Christianity. Its main characters are Jesuit priests and brothers, as well as indigenous men and women who became Christians (and whose numbers reached 200,000 by 1700). These figures are set against such diverse backdrops as the imperial court at Peking, the dusty villages of Shanxi Province, the bustling cities of the Yangzi delta region, and the mountain hamlets of Fujian. But their gestures reach across continents and at times the action takes place far beyond the confines of China. It moves over thousands of miles and years of travel from the headquarters of the Society of Jesus in Rome to the order's colleges in Portugal and onward to the missionaries' staging posts at Goa and Macau. The story begins in this European settlement on the rim of the Ming empire in 1579, where the first Jesuit set about studying the Chinese language. As it progresses over the span of the seventeenth century, the missionaries establish a network of residences and Christian communities across China. It ends when, after sustaining a sprawling enterprise for over a century, the missionaries' efforts were fatally checked by the combination of a disastrous visit by a papal envoy to Peking in 1705 and the proscription of Christianity in China by imperial fiat nearly two decades later.

The story of the China Jesuits' enterprise is no simple tale of rise and fall. A complex set of factors, born of both European and Chinese circumstances, was behind the vicissitudes of the missionaries' fortunes, and this book explores a considerable variety of political, cultural, and scientific encounters. Given the complexities of the subject, an author must choose. I have accorded pride of place here to an examination of the religious practices that the Jesuits imported into Chinese society and an inspection of the forms that Christianity acquired in that context. At the broadest level, this study traces the development of a mission church, that is, the collectivity of Christian communities created under the Jesuits' auspices and sustained through their pastoral efforts. I discuss the missionaries' strategies for proselytizing in China, the techniques they relied on to group together the individuals who submitted to baptism, and the methods they used to foster spiritual progress among Chinese Catholics. The book therefore tells the story of the mission church "from the ground up."

The Jesuit mission to China is deliberately treated here as a component of early modern Catholicism. This sweeping notion encompasses the parallel, complementary, and at times contradictory strands of individual piety, group devotion, and institutional development that characterized Catholic Christianity as a whole from the sixteenth to the eighteenth centuries.[3] The China mission was not some exotic experiment cut off from the rest of the world. The priests who traveled to China were full members of a religious culture, and their work in Asia bore the mark of their European academic, devotional, and social backgrounds. In short, although the events discussed here took place in China, they are part of a larger European story about Catholicism. While the Jesuits were busy bringing this complex of religious doctrines, attitudes, and institutions to China, Catholicism was being transformed by various political and social forces in Europe. The panorama of Catholic culture changed greatly during the mission's span, between the 1580s and the 1720s; consider that this enterprise, begun during the age of Luis de Granada and Philip II, ended shortly after that of Bossuet and Louis XIV. It is therefore not surprising that as generation after generation of missionaries journeyed to Asia, the cultural baggage they carried with them shifted along with movements within the Roman Church and Europe itself.[4]

For this reason, this is also a book about religion in early modern Europe. For as one looks through the prism of the China mission, certain hues on the wide spectrum of Catholic experience in that period appear with remarkable clarity. At one end lies the devotional dynamism of the sixteenth century in southern Europe that sparked the creation of institutions such as the Society of Jesus and initiated a burst of activities including the overseas missions. In the middle of the spectrum lie the varieties of regional and national Catholic practice which, when mixed with the strong corporate identity of the Society of Jesus, helped shape the attitudes of the missionary priests. And at the far end appears the repressive force of the institutional church, born of the Counter-Reformation and intent on imposing orthodoxy and asserting papal primacy. Eventually, it is this force that would be brought to bear against the China Jesuits. So the most distant (and, in many ways, the most revealing) mirror of early modern Catholicism was to be found at the farthest fringe of the Catholic world, among the missionaries and their Chinese Christians.

The Society's China enterprise had its genesis in the general reinvigoration of piety in southern Europe at the start of the early modern period. Often called the Catholic Reformation, this movement originated in Italy and Iberia, where reforming bishops, observant nuns and friars, and male and female mystics began to change the tenor of religious life. The Society of Jesus itself emerged from this trend in spiritual renewal, springing from the personal charisma and organizational genius of a Basque nobleman, Ignatius Loyola. The order's exponential increase in membership—from the original band of ten at its founding in 1540 to almost a thousand by the time of Loyola's death sixteen years later, and five times that number by 1580—is a testament to the magnetism that its vocation and character had on contemporary men.[5] These first Jesuits enabled the Society to establish itself across Catholic Europe. And, riding on the crest of the Spanish and Portuguese expansion to Africa, Asia, and the Americas, some of this burgeoning number of priests and brothers opened residences in the new colonial cities. It was from vantage points such as Macau that the men of the Society looked out beyond the boundaries of empire and contemplated expanding Catholic Christendom by claiming conversions.

If one kind of zeal powered the Society's drive to establish residences throughout Europe and its empires, it took a different degree of pious commitment to launch missionary efforts in non-Christian lands. The China Jesuits were motivated by a firm belief in the universal applicability of Christian teaching and by a conviction that the Christian language had an elasticity that permitted it to conform to the contours of even the most widely disparate cultures. In contrast to the worldly pretensions of secular agents of empire, such as merchants and mercenaries, the missionaries' spiritual ambitions knew few limits. Indeed, many of the Jesuits headed for Asia with the express goal of earning their passage to paradise through martyrdom. The men who requested missionary assignments in China were well aware that they would have to carry out their apostolic activities without the protection of colonial arms and that no coercive force would come to their aid in the face of indigenous hostility. Once they sailed up the Pearl River toward Canton and points north, they knew that the only discernible prize they could hope for beyond their satisfaction at occasioning conversions was the recognition they might gain from mandarins and emperors. Moreover, the Chinese Christians, the treasured rewards of the missionaries' efforts, had to remain in their home locales; they could not be transported overseas like spices or bullion. It would thus appear that the lure of souls was stronger for some Europeans than the scent of gold.

The missionary fervor that flourished among the Jesuits during the Catholic Reformation did not result, however, in scattershot attempts at evangelization. It was tempered by long reflection on proselytizing strategies and years of academic training, two legacies of the Society's twin vocations for missions and education. By the time Jesuit priests entered China, their order had developed effective techniques for conducting missionary work that aimed at sparking a renewal of popular piety in Europe.[6] To be sure, the Society's techniques built on the models created by older religious orders, such as the Franciscans and Dominicans, and served to channel their pastoral energy toward teaching doctrine, preaching sermons, hearing confessions, and seeking to reconcile feuding parties. From the sixteenth century until the eighteenth, itinerant Jesuits traveled to cities and towns across Europe exercising a vocation that combined rhetoric, theatricality, casuistry, personal fortitude, and, for its most renowned practitioners, the odor of sanctity. Although the young men who were sent to Asia are unlikely to have had much personal experience as missionaries, they were certainly aware of how their older confreres conducted their missions in Europe.[7] The pastoral efforts of the China Jesuits were therefore an exercise in emulation. In that sense the scattered communities of Chinese Christians were vivid patches of baroque piety set in a vast and largely indifferent land.

Education was also a major factor in shaping the Jesuits' missionary efforts. The order was heir to the tradition of piety and scholarship, known as Christian humanism, which had flourished since the late fifteenth century, and it placed considerable emphasis on the academic formation of its members. By the time the China mission began in the 1580s, the Society had started a program for standardizing the methods that were used in its schools for teaching grammar, rhetoric, philosophy, and theology. With the exception of the very first missionaries, most of the China Jesuits passed through this uniform academic program twice, first as students and later as teachers. The communal life of the men of the Society of Jesus in their colleges was therefore as much a life of the mind as a life of the spirit.[8] Their academic habits would be crucial in China, where the Jesuits faced the challenge of being the first Europeans to attempt to understand the Chinese language as well as Confucian philosophy. The study of native traditions, they knew, was essential for making their religious message fit into the Chinese cultural register. But knowledge was not all. Without rhetorical skills and a predisposition for debate—further legacies of their academic training—how could the Jesuits have hoped to convince the Chinese of the validity of Christian doctrine? After all, one of the first lessons they learned in China was that the keys to the gates of social legitimacy remained firmly in the hands of mandarins, men who had gained powerful positions within the state bureaucracy by virtue of being learned. Yet this book moves the Jesuits past that barrier and relates their actions beyond elite circles in the realms of Chinese society where they found willing converts.

Many of the high contrasts across the spectrum of early modern Catholicism that become visible through the prism of the China mission are caused by the tension between two factors: the corporate identity of the Society of Jesus and the variations in regional and national religious practices. Like other religious orders of the early modern period, the Jesuits had a very strong sense of group cohesion—although to a far lesser degree than the oft-repeated clichés depicting the Society as a "military-styled order" that served as the "shock troops of the Counter-Reformation" might suggest.[9] Because of the individual charisma of its members and the order's institutional character, not to mention the sheer number of Jesuits, the Society stood out among the panoply of other Catholic groups. Moreover, the fact that the Society was founded at a time of spiritual renewal, when older orders were seeking to redefine their specific vocations, gave the Jesuits an added impulse to insist on what they called "our way of proceeding." The use of common vows, procedures of governance, educational norms, devotions, and pastoral practices all contributed to forging the Society's institutional identity. These shared habits were especially meaningful for the Jesuits, since, in contrast to monastic religious orders, their activities were not dominated by communal prayer routines and their range of movement was not restricted to the confines of their residences. If an adherence to the Society's customs was important for its members in Europe, so much more so was it in China, where, scattered in cities hundreds of miles apart, priests often lived alone or in the company of only one or two other men.

It bears repeating that the Society of Jesus was an international religious order. It had colleges and residences throughout the vast space identified with the Roman Church and in lands that were predominantly Protestant and Orthodox as well. As a consequence there was also a wide variety of nationalities represented in the order's membership. Just like the Society itself, the China mission drew on a multinational recruitment pool for its priests and brothers. The largest fraction of Jesuits in East Asia was from Portugal, with Italy and the Southern Netherlands supplying significant numbers of men as well. But in contrast to many other missions, the ranks of the China Jesuits were very diverse in terms of national origin. Their priests and brothers hailed from places as distant from each other as Lombardy and Lithuania or Castile and Croatia. This diversity made the Society's corporate unity doubly important, because outside their institutional identity and shared vows of obedience there was little to bond the missionaries together across the vast expanses of Chinese territory that separated them. It also meant that the China Jesuits did not share a political loyalty—despite their nominal allegiance to the king of Portugal, the patron of their mission, and the emperor of China, the direct master of those who served at Peking—a factor which might have stimulated what contemporaries considered a natural sense of unity.

There is a stubborn (often polemical) scholarly custom of ascribing an ironclad uniformity to the structures of the Roman Church. Yet not all bishoprics and cardinalates, much less parishes, were created equal. In actuality, local traditions of piety and political prerogatives exercised a strong influence over the practice of Catholicism in early modern Europe. This tension between universality on the one hand and particularity on the other was evident among the ecclesiastical hierarchy of the day, as well as among religious orders such as the Society of Jesus. It is imperative to avoid explaining the fortunes of the China mission in reductionist terms based on the national characters of its priests, but it is equally important to recognize that distinct regional forms of Catholic life and Jesuit attitudes influenced the development of the missionary enterprise. Two examples will suffice to alert the reader to these tensions. One is the appearance of fault lines according to nationality among the China missionaries in the mid-seventeenth century, as the devotional (and political) center of gravity in Catholic Europe shifted from Spain to France. Many of the French, Flemish, German, and Italian missionaries who arrived in China after 1650 brought with them different attitudes toward the combination of political sentiment and piety which had caused distress among their brethren who had traveled from Europe at the time of Habsburg ascendancy. And the most glaring example of this tension occurred when the Society's members in China became embroiled in a bitter intramural dispute with a band of French Jesuits sponsored by Louis XIV who arrived in 1687. The newcomers insisted forcefully on their independence from their confreres, whom they labeled and dismissed as "Portuguese."

If at one end of the spectrum of early modern Catholicism can be found the forces of spiritual renewal, at the other lay the instruments of ecclesiastical control associated with the Counter-Reformation. Whereas the zealous dynamism of the Catholic Reformation period created the centrifugal spiritual energy that impelled the Jesuits to travel from Europe to Asia, the centripetal forces of the ecclesiastical hierarchy generated in response to the Protestant challenge also acted as a decisive brake on the China mission. In particular, two processes that had their origins in the mid-sixteenth century at the time of the Council of Trent eventually came to intrude on the Jesuits' activities in Asia: a repressive effort that sought to check innovation in theological matters; and the push toward papal primacy, accompanied by exertions to reduce independence among the regular clergy. It was the combination of these forces, rather than the difficulty of translating Catholic Christianity into Chinese, that eventually brought the mission to an end.

The Counter-Reformation was a late arrival in China. To be sure, by the time its effects were felt in distant Asia, it was no longer the same phenomenon that had given rise to the Holy Office of the Inquisition or the Index of Prohibited Books. By the time the Thirty Years' War came to an end, the Counter-Reformation had entered its maturity, drawing its strength from decades' worth of experience accumulated by the official organs of institutional repression.[10] At that time, these church bodies were kept busy primarily by the adjudication of disputes between Catholics, such as the conflict between the Jesuits and the Jansenists, rather than the persecution of heretics or those who practiced Judaism or Islam, which had preoccupied them in times past. Nevertheless, the sheer distance between Europe and the Asian mission fields meant that it took decades before the Jesuits' policies in China began to cause concern among the theology faculty of the Sorbonne or to the Roman Inquisition. The social standing and religious dynamism of the Society of Jesus during its first century had by and large shielded the order from censure—if not from suspicion—for heterodoxy, even if the Jesuits produced perhaps more than their share of controversial theologians. Their detractors, many of them members of other religious orders, rarely stopped insisting that the Society's positions on matters divine were less than orthodox. After becoming embroiled in polemics over their stances on regicide, free will, and moral theology, the Jesuits had to face bitter and persistent criticism in Europe and Asia about their missionary practices in China.

Readers familiar with the history of the Jesuits in China or that of the Enlightenment will already be aware of the controversies over the Chinese Rites, and the causes for contention will be discussed at several points in the following chapters. Still, it is worth noting here that the ferocity of this debate played an important role in galvanizing anti-Jesuit sentiment at the highest levels of the ecclesiastical hierarchy in the late seventeenth century. At issue was where the men of the Society situated the divide between idolatry and orthodoxy among their Chinese Christians. Could Catholic scholar-officials participate in the state ceremonies linked to Confucianism? And what was the appropriate way for Christians to honor the dead in a culture that observed ancient funerary traditions? In the eyes of some of the other European missionaries who arrived in China in the 1630s, the Jesuits had expanded the limits of acceptable Catholic practice so far as to be abetting paganism among their flocks. These critics took their impressions of the practices of the Society's neophytes back to Europe and submitted their findings to the highest theological tribunals. After decades of polemics on both sides of the thorny issue of the Chinese Rites, the papacy decided against the Jesuits and set out to impose its will on the missionaries in China.

The expansion of papal power in the wake of the Council of Trent was a process that spanned the early modern period. Despite the obvious differences between the nature of the power possessed by popes and kings, the centralizing forces within the church were as strong as they were in Europe's secular monarchies.[11] The papacy's drive to assert its primacy over church institutions included the demand that all Catholic rituals conform to the Roman standard, as well as the insistence that independent bodies such as religious orders be brought more firmly under Rome's control.[12] The Jesuits, for example, would be forced toward stricter observance of their vows of obedience to the Holy See. The overseas missions, and in particular the China enterprise, were key battlegrounds in this struggle. In the late seventeenth century, the Society of Jesus increasingly came into conflict with the cardinals of the Congregation for the Propagation of the Faith, or Propaganda Fide, the church body created in 1622 to supervise missionary work.

For the papacy, the main issue was control over Asian Catholics and their missionary pastors. In an attempt to circumvent the loose jurisdiction of the archbishop of Goa, whose expansive see, created in the early sixteenth century, stretched from East Africa to Japan, late-seventeenth-century popes began to appoint Propaganda bishops to administer the nascent Christian communities in lands such as Vietnam, India, and China. Yet the China Jesuits were no more ready to cede control over their mission church than popes and cardinals were willing to brook insubordination from the members of a religious order. In the wake of a disastrous embassy to the Kangxi emperor, during which a papal legate unsuccessfully attempted to negotiate control over China's Catholics, the Jesuits were faced with the impossible choice of obeying the papacy or remaining among their Christians. This dilemma proved fatal. Among its consequences were the expulsion of several missionaries from China and a change in relations between the Jesuits and indigenous authorities that ultimately led to the proscription of Christianity. In the end, Rome destroyed what it could not possess.

This is in the main a European story, even if the Jesuits' efforts in China have traditionally been set down as part of a Chinese tale. It goes without saying that the social, political, economic, and religious contexts of the late Ming–early Qing era were important to the development of the missionary project, and they form the backdrop to this account. While the reader will no doubt gain a greater knowledge of European religious culture than of its Chinese counterpart, I have made a concerted attempt to provide a balanced depiction not only of the missionaries and the Chinese but also of aspects of Christianity that impinged on China. Such a safeguard is meant to keep the central elements of this story from being reduced to caricature, a fate they have suffered on occasion in missionary history when Jesuits were depicted as uniformly heroic and China as unchanging. By the same token, I have chosen to avoid the polemical themes that have preoccupied many previous scholars who pondered the role of the Jesuits within Chinese history. It is assumed in this book that there is no urgent need to celebrate missionary triumphs, to provide apologetics for the perceived failures of Christian churches in China, to denounce subtle (or direct) forms of Western imperialism, or to lament the corruption of Chinese culture by foreign taint.

How has the history of the Jesuit mission to China been written? For generations, scholars relied on the narrative established by the missionaries themselves in the early modern period. Since the Society of Jesus actively publicized its overseas missions for the purposes of celebrating its triumphs and attracting recruits, reports from Ming China began to be printed in Europe shortly after the order acquired its first residence within that empire. Following thirty years of brief statements on missionary valor and achievement, the first substantial history of the mission appeared in 1615, when a version of mission founder Matteo Ricci's diary was translated into Latin and published as *De Christiana Expeditione apud Sinas,* "The Christian Expedition to China"—the title an unwitting parallel to its contemporary, *Journey to the West.*[13] Subsequently translated into a number of European languages, this text enshrined Ricci at the heart of the mission's history. In effect, it made the chronology of the early progress of the mission largely identical to that of his journey from outsider in Canton in 1582 to insider in Peking in 1610. Later Jesuit authors, as well as external commentators, seized on this narrative thread and developed it further over subsequent decades by adding episodes about the missionary-astronomers who served at the imperial court.[14] Scholars who drew uncritically from these sources continued to recapitulate this story until the middle of the twentieth century, presenting the Jesuit mission to their readers in the same way Ricci himself had done.

Certain aspects of the image and actions of the missionaries highlighted in early European publications—their use of silk robes, their attraction to the study of pagan arcana such as Confucian philosophy, and their willingness to serve a non-Christian emperor by purveying the profane sciences (all topoi rooted in the reality of their working conditions at the Imperial Astronomical Bureau)—were powerful rhetorical weapons used by the detractors of the Society of Jesus. The Jesuits countered with volume upon apologetic volume to defend their reputation at Paris and Rome, but the polemical interpretations of the China mission produced first by Jansenists and later by philosophes proved to be longer-lived. Translations of texts in the latter vein bequeathed to the Anglo-Saxon public a vision of the Society's enterprise that was awash in commonplaces and merged easily into the nineteenth century's rising tide of anti-Jesuitism. The mission was primarily metropolitan, as the polemic vision would have it; it was focused on the imperial court of China. The Jesuits had little interest in preaching to commoners; naturally, their enterprise must falter as soon as Chinese elites grew weary of them. Of course, this argument continued, the Jesuits sought to forestall the demise of their project. Their overweening concern to avoid offending their hosts led them to embark on a vain search for parallels between Chinese antiquity and Christian revelation, to the point that they maneuvered themselves into obscuring crucial doctrinal, such as the Incarnation and the Passion. These notions melded with a broader set of stereotypes that labeled the Jesuits as devious, cunning, and laxist. A wealth of clichés about the China mission resulted.

When it was not merely an object of praise or derision, the Jesuits' mission was often presented as part of a larger history either of the spread of the Christian faith in China or of Sino-Western relations. Echoes of an older apologetic tradition could still be heard in the works of scholars in the early twentieth century who treated the Jesuits' enterprise in late Ming and early Qing China as a logical starting point in charting the implantation of Christianity in that country. This expansive view resulted in a sectarian interpretation lacking in analytical rigor. Since a significant part of modern scholarship on China grew out of Protestant and Catholic missionary experiences in the late Qing and Republican periods, it was only natural for historians in this tradition to inscribe their own efforts within the centuries-old tradition of evangelizing the Chinese. For Catholic scholars, a salient topic for discussion emerged after the final resolution of the controversy over the Chinese Rites in 1939. For reasons having to do with the unenviable position of Japanese Catholics at a time of strident nationalism in the run-up to the Pacific war, a papal brief ruled in favor of the interpretation of Confucian ceremonies as political rather than religious. By doing so, the papacy legitimated the standpoint of the early modern Jesuits, which had previously been condemned.

This change in official policy, coupled with the increasingly global concerns of the Catholic Church in the 1950s and 1960s, sparked reevaluations of the China Jesuits—but often for polemical ends in the theological debate over the limits of inculturation that continues to the present day. Scholars engaged in this debate over the degree of cultural accommodation that may be necessary in spreading Christianity to non-Western cultures, often members of religious orders themselves, frequently saw the China Jesuits as forerunners of "modern" or "tolerant" attitudes. A sharp and restricted focus on missionaries who had been deeply engaged with native philosophical traditions was especially useful for these authors. Those Jesuits of long ago, they maintained, had possessed an enlightened ability to distinguish between essential and nonessential cultural and doctrinal concerns.[15] Since their chief aim was to argue this position to a theologically minded audience, these scholars neglected to analyze other aspects of the mission. Topics such as how the Jesuits organized their enterprise, how the mission church developed, or what forms of Catholic piety they fostered were left untouched, leaving much ground for future historians of religion to cover.

The place of the Jesuit mission within the grand interpretive theme of the history of Sino-Western relations has been another topic of debate among historians, one that continues to inspire new contributions. Scholars writing from this perspective tended to focus on how European science and technology were transmitted to China via missionary publications. Primarily concerned with the modern technological and industrial divide between East and West, they presented the Jesuits as the standard-bearers of superior technological skills that were eagerly received by indigenous intellectuals. To be sure, the Jesuits who went to China were not, for the most part, the cutting-edge natural philosophers of their day; moreover, they had ulterior religious motives for engaging in translations of scientific texts. Nevertheless, yet another vision of the China mission emerged, one centered on the Imperial Astronomical Bureau at Peking.

Although this vision was devoid of a religious content, it tracked the same chronology and focused on the same individuals as the story told by Christian missiologists. As did their predecessors, scholars following this new approach lingered at certain determinate way stations, showing that Matteo Ricci secured access to the mandarin bureaucracy by virtue of his first philosophical treatises in Chinese and that his successors Johann Adam Schall and Ferdinand Verbiest continued his work by producing texts on European mathematics and astronomy. Instead of being appraised for their attempts to pass on religion, the Jesuits and their Chinese interlocutors were evaluated on the basis of their level of success at transmitting modernity through science.[16] Against the backdrop of nineteenth- and twentieth-century relations between China and the West, it appeared that the missionaries had failed the Chinese on both accounts: they had given them neither faith nor reason.

Altogether the Jesuits have been freighted by historians, surely against their original intentions, with the task of building a bridge between civilizations, one that would serve as a long-lasting conduit between East and West. Only the surge of interest since the quatercentenary of Matteo Ricci's arrival in China in 1982 has lifted something of this burden from the missionaries' shoulders by calling into question many of the suppositions undergirding earlier analyses. Much of the dynamism behind this new wave of scholarly production has come from the field of Chinese studies, where experts have looked away from the corpus of Western sources used by earlier generations of historians, turning instead to materials in Asian languages.[17] When seen from a perspective conceived within a Chinese cultural frame, that is, through an analytical lens shaped by the dynamics of internal historical development, attempts to explain China—itself a vague term—exclusively in relation to the West or to Christianity come to seem particularly futile. Similarly, the assumption that Chinese intellectuals quickly recognized the inherent superiority of Western technology or religion is rendered somewhat absurd when confronted with the variety of textual responses to the Jesuits found in both print and manuscript sources. The move away from missionary texts to Asian sources has produced a concomitant reconceptualization of the Jesuits and their role in Chinese history.

As a result, numerous new avenues for research have been opened and new paths of inquiry illuminated. One of the most fruitful lines of inquiry focuses on how Chinese thinkers responded to the missionaries' texts, whether religious or scientific, and on the ways in which they incorporated aspects of Western thought into their own worldviews.[18] Another analyzes the texts produced by the Jesuits in Chinese to sound the depths of their engagement with indigenous philosophical traditions and to examine how they chose to represent Western concepts in Chinese terms. My own book is deeply indebted to the historians, linguists, and philosophers who have contributed to reshaping this field in recent years. But I seek to pursue my own path and recount the story of the missionaries in a fresh light, presenting a new chronology of the Jesuit enterprise and charting the trajectory of its development according to new criteria. Surely the contours of the mission's history will emerge more distinctly if many of the heroic attributes conventionally ascribed to the Jesuits in the past are first erased and the priests reinserted into their proper, early modern European context. Only by uncoupling their actions from the long chain of events related to the expansive—often teleologically conceived—phenomenon of the spread of Christianity in China can the missionaries' intentions and motivations be revealed.

The resources necessary for this reconsideration of the Jesuits' China mission were hidden in the proverbial broad daylight. The shift to Chinese-language documents has greatly enriched the field; but the return to previously neglected Western-language sources can also bring new understanding to the history of the mission. Despite the number of early modern and contemporary works on the China Jesuits, very little attention has been paid to the large corpus of descriptive accounts, correspondence, and administrative documents written in Portuguese and kept in European archives. This fact is all the more surprising because the number of these sources, compared with those in Latin or other Romance languages and Germanic tongues, is disproportionately large.

That Portuguese should be so important ought to astonish no one familiar with the history of Catholic Europe and the European expansion to Asia and the Americas. The China mission was supported in more than one way by the Portuguese crown and was staffed primarily with men from continental and insular Portugal. It formed a part of the Portuguese Assistancy, the Jesuit administrative unit that roughly overlapped the most optimistic Portuguese pretensions to imperial authority—all lands between Brazil and Japan.[19] Hence the lingua franca of the China Jesuits was perforce Portuguese. The missionaries also used other European languages to communicate with one another and with their superiors in Rome, but far less often. In the wake of the collapse of the Portuguese empire and the suppression of the Society of Jesus, the documentary legacy of the China mission made its way back to Europe and eventually came to rest in large part in the royal and ecclesiastical archives of Lisbon and Rome. While the durability of the Black Legend in Anglo-American historiography is a likely partial explanation for the lack of English-language studies based on these sources, it remains puzzling why generations of French, Belgian,

German, and Italian scholars—many of whom were Jesuits or members of other Catholic religious orders—largely ignored these Portuguese documents.[20] This study of the Jesuit mission to China is based primarily on archival research in Western-language sources. It draws heavily on the collections of the Biblioteca da Ajuda in Lisbon and the Archivum Romanum Societatis Jesu in Rome. The sources now in the Ajuda Palace library are copies of documents once found in the Society's archives at Macau. They contain documents pertaining to the Jesuit administrative units known as the Province of Japan (which covered the missionary efforts in that country, as well as those in Southeast Asia and parts of southern China after 1657) and the Vice-Province of China (founded in 1619). Between about 1742 and 1748, the Jesuits José Montanha and João Álvares were commissioned by the Real Academia da História in Lisbon to transcribe the contents of their order's repository at Macau. The sixty-two bound volumes of the Jesuítas na Ásia collection they produced are faithful copies of many texts that were lost after the suppression of the Society of Jesus. This invaluable archival resource contains records of internal and external affairs that passed through the Portuguese colony of Macau, the nexus of Jesuit communications between Europe and Asia. From yearly reports on the mission's advances and setbacks to insider accounts of the missionaries' labors and private correspondence between Jesuits and their superiors on a host of sensitive issues, the Ajuda collection gives unparalleled insight into the Society's China enterprise.

The best complement to the Ajuda sources is the extensive collection of missionary materials at the Roman archive of the Society of Jesus. This central administrative repository, dispersed after the 1773 suppression of the order and subsequently reconstructed, contains documents addressing broader institutional concerns relating to the Society's enterprises around the globe. Sources found in the Japonica-Sinica, Goana, and Lusitanica collections (those dealing with the affairs of the Jesuit provinces of Japan and China, Goa, and Portugal, respectively) cover issues reserved for the Society's highest administrative levels. These documents include items such as yearly personnel catalogues used for assigning positions within the mission hierarchy, annual letters relating the mission's progress, copies of the Jesuits' Chinese compositions, and petitions to Superiors General for binding decisions on missionary policies. The combined analysis of this double set of archival sources affords a view of the Jesuits and their mission from the inside, revealing how the missionaries themselves understood their efforts and opportunities as well as how they evaluated the outcomes of their strategies and actions in the mission field. It is hoped that linking these documents to recent studies by scholars who have mined Chinese-language sources as well as to newly translated Chinese materials will be helpful in producing a balanced account of the Jesuits' enterprise.

This book is divided into two parts, the first consisting of an extended chronological narrative and the second analyzing specific aspects of missionary education and the components of the mission church. Part I reconsiders the mission's development, following a chronology that departs somewhat from the norm. Its five chapters address the initiation, consolidation, and disintegration of the Society's enterprise, with the aim of presenting a new framework for the discussion of the Jesuits' China mission and constructing a contextual backdrop for the analyses of its internal dynamics. The main protagonists in this section are the Jesuits, their converted Christians, and other Chinese figures whose paths intersected with that of the mission. At times, Europeans other than Jesuits are mentioned, but only in regard to their interactions with the Society and its Chinese flock. Since this book is not a general history of Christianity in China, the endeavors of the Dominicans, Franciscans, Augustinians, Vicars Apostolic, and members of the Missions Étrangères de Paris are relegated to the background.[21] This was a conscious decision, and the reader should not assume that it was taken in defense of the Jesuits' position in their well-known conflicts with members of other religious orders. Rather, it was part of my design to examine the Society's missionary efforts from an internal perspective. Accordingly, I consider the French Jesuit mission, founded in 1687, to be of secondary importance as well, for these priests saw themselves as separate from the Vice-Province, that is, from the enterprise that had been initiated by Matteo Ricci.

In keeping with my desire to envision the Jesuit mission as a whole, this chronology concentrates on the events that took place in the centers of proselytizing activity in the Chinese provinces rather than on the interactions between missionaries and mandarins at the court. As a result, a host of previously marginal Jesuits come to be seen as the primary force behind the construction of the mission church. Figures such as Rodrigo de Figueiredo, Francesco Brancati, José Monteiro, and Étienne Faber—men who plowed the fertile mission fields of the lower Yangzi valley, the coastal areas of Fujian, and the Yellow River basin in Shaanxi and

Shanxi—appear in high relief, an elevation usually granted only to the likes of Matteo Ricci, Johann Adam Schall, and Ferdinand Verbiest. The story of these priests and the communities of Chinese men and women that formed in response to their message and developed largely under their guidance is the core of the narrative chapters of Part I.

The central argument developed in the first, narrative section about the nature of the mission church is that it had been fashioned by the Society of Jesus in its own image; that the religious practices of the Chinese Christians reflected Jesuit ideals of lay piety; and that the mission church was built according to the Society's organizational templates. To support this claim, the second part of this book presents analyses of the elements that combined to form the missionary enterprise and its Christian communities, namely, the Jesuits and their Chinese flock.

Part II asks how the Society of Jesus was able to imbue successive generations of its members with the skills necessary for creating and sustaining a mission church in a cultural context vastly different from the European one. Its first two chapters address dimensions of Jesuit education in Europe and Asia, starting from grammar school and ending at the mission station. In the Society's European and, at times, colonial colleges, future China Jesuits received a standard academic formation and participated in teaching duties that gave them important intellectual and organizational skills. During their years in the order's novitiates, the young men learned the elements of Jesuit spirituality and pastoral techniques. In this academic and devotional climate, they developed the desire to spend the rest of their lives as overseas missionaries. After setting sail for Asia, missionary hopefuls began to exercise their vocations, practicing their order's primary spiritual ministries in the harsh environment of the ships of the Portuguese Carreira da Índia. Once in China, new recruits to the mission took part in the first standardized program for learning the Chinese language and Confucian thought elaborated by Europeans with the goal of making the trainees into efficient, culturally sensitive communicators. Armed with the skills acquired over an average of seventeen years of study, the Jesuits ventured into the mission field with arguably the best possible preparation for meeting the challenges that lay before them.

The last three chapters of this book are dedicated to examining the interactions of these highly trained missionaries with their Chinese interlocutors. They deal with the creation and maintenance of the Christian communities that formed the mission church, assaying the lived religion of the Chinese Christians within the context of the forms of spiritual expression transmitted to them by their Jesuit pastors. This portion of the book also seeks to evaluate the importation of elements of early modern Catholic piety into the late imperial Chinese context, yet another form of intercultural communication determined by both European and indigenous factors.

These final chapters examine the building blocks of the mission church, starting with the conditions of conversion and proceeding through the various forms of communal organization, cohesion, and mutual spiritual development. The first step in the process of making Christians was active proselytizing, with Jesuits moving about urban and rural areas and presenting their religious message to prospective converts through rhetorical agility, amplified by ritual gestures aimed to impress. As substantial numbers of people responded to them, the missionaries set up new communities by employing Jesuit educational techniques that fostered group cohesion and regular devotions. When the numbers of the faithful began to exceed the missionaries' pastoral capacities, they began to enlist male and female catechists as auxiliaries in the maintenance of their dispersed "parishes," assigning them duties that ranged from basic supervision to the teaching of doctrine.

Like any other religious institution, the mission church was made up of individuals with varying degrees of religious commitment, from members in name only to lukewarm adherents to fervent believers. The last group included those Christians who adhered most faithfully to the Jesuits' vision of the rewards of effective missionary work. These men and women demanded new forms of spiritual expression that would set them apart from the mass of other believers, and the missionaries responded by helping them to elaborate forms of group piety. Special brotherhoods for prayer, penance, and charity eventually spread to all the provincial centers of the mission church, creating loci of fervor where a new Catholic elite engaged in increasingly complex forms of devotion—practices that came to equal the rigorous lay devotions recommended at the time by the Society of Jesus for its most pious European followers. Empowered by the spiritual intensity bequeathed to them by their pastors over decades, these individuals were responsible for maintaining Christianity in China during the eighteenth century, as the Jesuit mission faded into memory.

I

CHARTING THE COURSE

I

An Uneasy Foothold

In the three decades that followed Francis Xavier's arrival in East Asia in 1549, Jesuit priests attempted to establish a mission in the Ming empire without success. But after a change of tactics in 1579, a handful of missionaries from the Society of Jesus began to attract the attention of influential figures in Guangdong Province. The friendships forged between these two groups enabled the Jesuits to emerge from the undifferentiated tides of traders that swept up the Pearl River delta each year to visit the Canton fairs. Unlike other foreign emissaries, these new arrivals would be permitted to remain in China.

During their first years in the Ming empire, the pioneers of the China mission made contacts with important political figures by projecting an image of erudition and moral austerity that appealed to their interlocutors. They thereby garnered fame and, more important, the possibility of summoning their missionary brethren from Macau. The early China Jesuits devoted themselves primarily to learning the language and observing local customs, which in turn allowed them to solidify their social contacts and convert some of their hosts to Christianity. While their initial tactical move was to don the attire of the Buddhist clergy and present themselves as religious figures, the missionaries at length adopted the dress and attitude of the secular authorities—the mandarins. By creating a new image for themselves, one echoing the Chinese cultural register, the Jesuits gained acceptance among members of the late Ming elite. They saw this type of recognition as the necessary prerequisite for their missionary work.

Maritime Asia

MONGOLIA

TIBET

Tsaparang

Yellow River

CHINA

Ganges River

Yangzi River

Pearl

LAOS

INDIA

BURMA

TONKIN

Bassein

Goa

SIAM

Ayutthaya

Cochin

Fishery Coast

Malacca

Indian Ocean

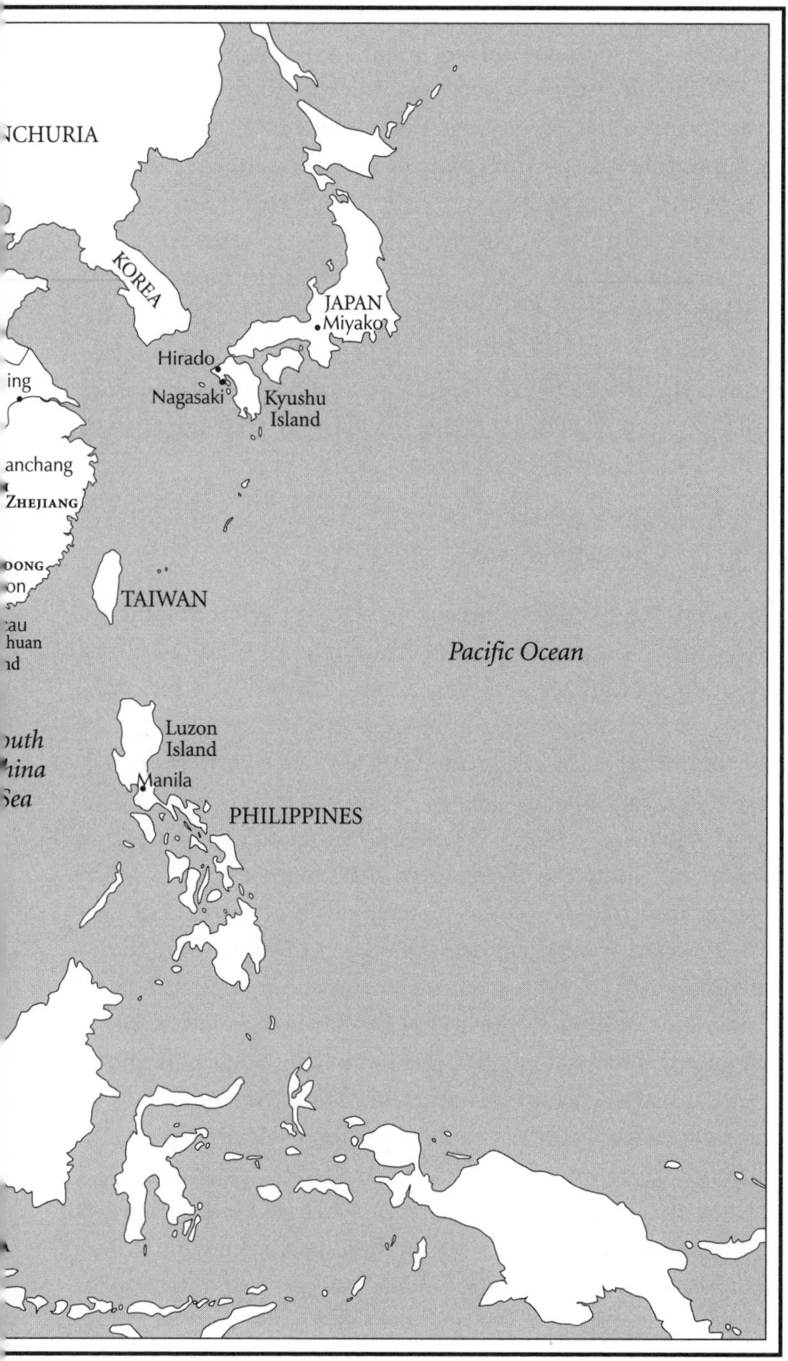
KOREA
JAPAN
Miyako
Hirado
Nagasaki
Kyushu Island
ZHEJIANG
TAIWAN
Pacific Ocean
Luzon Island
Manila
PHILIPPINES

The Jesuits' enthusiasm at this early stage in their enterprise was not reciprocated, and its development did not follow a linear progression. In fact, the mission's first foundations rested on the acceptance of their public image rather than on making a significant number of converts. Although they attracted attention from many levels of society, they claimed few adherents to their religion. Moreover, the Jesuits were far more successful at transmitting Christianity to commoners than to members of the elite, despite the time they spent currying the favor of the literati. To be sure, after twenty years of work, their reputation for erudition had enabled them to establish residences in four cities, including Nanjing and Peking. In time, the nuclei of the Jesuits' first Christian communities would be formed in these cities, where the mission sank roots deep enough to withstand the winds of adversity.

Opening the Door, 1579–1594

According to Jesuit lore, the China mission grew from Francis Xavier's dying wish. While the Apostle of the Orient had originally bypassed China in 1549, heading instead for Kyushu, he was aware of the need for establishing a mission in the Ming empire in order to ease the spread of Christianity elsewhere in East Asia. His possibilities for action were restricted, however, by the fact that Xavier—like all of his successors—was dependent on others for transportation and political legitimation. His range of options was therefore limited by the rhythms of Portuguese trade in Maritime Asia and the imperial logic of the representatives of the king of Portugal. By 1551, however, Xavier had decided on a plan to get beyond the ephemeral trading entrepôts of the Portuguese on the coastal islands off southern China. Responding to the pleas of merchants held captive at Canton, he arranged to be appointed to the train of an embassy from the viceroy of the Portuguese Estado da Índia to the Ming emperor.

Unfortunately for him, Francis Xavier's hopes for a splendid entry into China were dashed when his embassy was disbanded by order of the admiral of Malacca, Álvaro de Ataíde, the son of Vasco da Gama. Not easily deterred, the missionary tempted fate by heading to the China coast on his own initiative in 1552, trusting in his ability to find a Chinese merchant willing to smuggle him into the empire. He got as far as Shangchuan Island, a rocky outcrop not far from the mouth of the Pearl River, but the Portuguese who had carried him thus far left him behind and sailed away at the end of the trading season. Likewise, all the (traders had retreated homeward, fearful of being implicated in breaking the laws against foreigners' entering the empire, which had been imposed to curb the piracy that was rampant along the Chinese littoral. Weakened by hunger and disease, Xavier died in the early hours of December 3, 1552.[1]

In his last letter he wrote about his great hopes of going to China even as he uttered the concern that Satan was "greatly disturbed" at the prospect of the Jesuits' starting a mission there.[2] The numerous difficulties encountered by this Basque priest and by his successors in the course of the next thirty years of attempts to settle in China seemed to validate his claim. The first of Xavier's successors to return to the Guangdong coast was his former colleague Melchior Nunes Barreto (1520–1571), who had gathered information about the Ming empire from a Portuguese merchant in Malacca. The account he wrote for his Jesuit brethren in Europe touched on issues such as the riches of China's cities, the intensity of its commerce, the justice of its mandarins, and the omnipotence of its emperor. In short, Barreto's report spoke of a stable society where civil structures resembled and even surpassed their European equivalents—the ideal conditions for Jesuit missionary activity.[3]

Yet the fortunes of Xavier's first successors were no better than his own. Venturing beyond where Xavier had been stalled, Barreto sailed to Canton in 1555 in the company of a Portuguese trade embassy. He remained in that city for ten months, but when the biannual trade fair ended, he had to leave China with his compatriots. Frustrated by the intransigence of the Guangdong mandarins, who insisted on enforcing the Ming laws prohibiting foreigners from residing in China, Barreto and his confreres turned their attentions to Japan. The wisdom of their choice to focus their efforts across the sea was confirmed in the late 1560s, when the schemes by Juan Bautista Ribera (1525–1594) to remain in Canton beyond the end of the trade fairs were all stymied in similar fashion.[4]

The Jesuits' prospects for gaining entry into China were greatly enhanced when the agents of the Estado da Índia negotiated the creation of a permanent Portuguese trading outpost at the mouth of the Pearl River. The founding of the city of Macau in 1557 was more than beneficial for the China mission, however. It was of crucial importance for all missions of the Society of Jesus in East Asia. In this tiny hybrid European-Chinese settlement the Jesuits had a safe haven, for even though the Guangdong mandarins retained final authority in the city, they delegated effective rule to the Portuguese. This arrangement permitted the European merchants who constituted the city's elite to use Macau as a launching point for their periodic journeys between Canton and Japan. The Jesuits accordingly followed them, benefiting from the regular trading runs to ports such as Hirado and Nagasaki to consolidate the fledgling mission that Xavier had founded in western Japan. As conditions in Japan permitted Portuguese trade in silks and silver to grow, so too did the missionary effort there. But in light of the considerable advances of the Jesuits in Kyushu in the 1570s and the Society's position as the most important religious order in the Portuguese empire, its lack of engagement in China was something of an embarrassment.

This situation changed when the path of missionary expansion in Asia was redirected under the leadership of a forceful new policymaker, Alessandro Valignano (1539–1606), whom the Society's Superior General appointed as his plenipotentiary Visitor to the Asian missions in 1573. Valignano, a native of southern Italy trained in law, joined the order soon after it had metamorphosed from a band of charismatic priests into a highly articulated and structured institution that considered missionary and educational activities its primary vocations. After serving as the director of the Jesuit novitiate in Rome, he was sent to the Indies to verify that the changes instituted in the Society in Europe were carried out overseas. This weighty task fell on the shoulders of a man of uncommon ability, for the Visitor had remarkable talent for political and organizational matters. Valignano's initial assignment was to inspect all Jesuit missions between Mozambique and Miyako, requiring him to shuttle between East Africa, India, Southeast Asia, China, and Japan. When in the 1590s the Society's mission fields had grown too large for any one man to monitor, the Visitor's bailiwick was limited to East Asia. With regard to the challenge of China, he insisted on the importance of overcoming the hurdle of language—just as the Jesuits in Japan had done. If the Chinese authorities permitted unlettered Portuguese merchants who spoke only through interpreters to co-opt a slice of their territory, Valignano reasoned, they would surely allow educated men trained in local customs and language to penetrate further into their empire.

Valignano therefore wrote to the superior of the Province of India at Goa and requested that a qualified individual be sent to Macau for the purpose of learning Chinese. The Visitor specifically mentioned Michele

Ruggieri (1543–1607), whose qualities, he said, included the "age, virtue, ability," and dedication necessary for the undertaking.[5] Ruggieri, also from southern Italy, was distinguished not only by his religious zeal but also by doctorates in canon and civil law. He had served the Spanish crown in Naples before joining the Society and becoming one of Valignano's novices in Rome. Ruggieri was sent to India in 1578, finished his theology studies in Goa, and was then assigned to the Fishery Coast in southern India, where he began to learn Tamil. For Valignano, however, Ruggieri's most important quality was his age. The Visitor understood that a mature Jesuit would likely enjoy a better reception in China than a young one, and had originally sent for an older missionary.[6] Nevertheless, in 1579 Ruggieri's thirty-five years still made him almost a decade older than his peers on the voyage to Asia.[7]

After traveling overland from his mission station to Cochin and then by ship to Macau, Ruggieri found instructions from Valignano regarding his future assignment. He was told to immerse himself in the study of Chinese language and culture. At the Visitor's behest, special accommodations set apart from the rest of the community were provided for him at the local Jesuit house so that he might not be distracted from his studies.[8] Valignano instructed Ruggieri to acquire the Nanjing dialect of spoken Chinese used by the literati elite rather than the Cantonese of the populations in Macau and Guangdong. He likened the use of Mandarin to that of Latin in Europe, justifying his choice to his superiors in Rome by remarking that "neither do the mandarins speak any other tongue, nor can others speak another language with them. Mandarin is so widely spoken that everyone more or less understands it."[9] These comments did nothing to diminish the difficulty of Ruggieri's task, since he had no local interpreters to explain Chinese to him. Rather, during the three years he lived in the Portuguese colony, he struggled to learn the written and spoken language in the manner of Chinese children—something, he reminded his superiors, that took schoolboys between fifteen and twenty years to do. When he began to show progress, Ruggieri complemented his studies by composing tracts on Christian doctrine so the Chinese would "gain a liking for this holy law."[10]

The hopes of Jesuits throughout Asia were pinned to the outcome of Ruggieri's efforts to "open the door" to China.[11] They were rewarded when his studies began to produce fruit in the early 1580s. Just like the previous missionaries who had tried to gain access to China, Ruggieri traveled to Canton in the company of Portuguese traders from Macau. But unlike his predecessors, he appealed to the local mandarins in their own language for permission to stay in Canton—something that quickly aroused their curiosity. His linguistic ability soon gained him an edge over the Portuguese merchants, who were obliged to lodge aboard their ships, for an official granted Ruggieri a small house in which to reside for the duration of the trade fair.[12] The Jesuit repaid his fellow Europeans by turning part of his quarters into a chapel where they could attend his daily masses, and he offered his services to them as an intermediary. During the months that he spent in Canton from 1580 to 1582, Ruggieri became a minor celebrity, drawing curiosity seekers from throughout the city. In his own words, "There were people all day long at my doorstep until midnight simply to see me, with nothing I could do to make them go away."[13]

This show of curiosity, however, did not necessarily imply that Ruggieri received a warm welcome in Canton. In fact, he claimed that a passerby had one day rushed into his house and bloodied his forehead with a stone—a more direct attack than the subtler vexations he suffered at the hands of others. Thankfully for Ruggieri, he won the friendship of important mandarins such as the governor of Guangdong Province, the chief naval mandarin, a military mandarin, and several retired officials. These men were drawn to Ruggieri for the European curiosities such as clocks and prisms that he had brought from Macau and for his unique ability to speak to them about foreign lands in their own tongue. Ruggieri curried favor with them, judging that if he gained the friendship of the mandarins, "the other heathen subjects would show respect." And even if not from genuine respect, the residents of Canton might at least leave him alone and unharmed out of fear of reprisals from the city's authorities.[14] By entering the shadow of local officials for protection, Ruggieri inaugurated a strategy for protecting the mission that would endure until the last China Jesuits of the early modern period died at Peking in the late eighteenth century.

Although tradition holds that Matteo Ricci, Ruggieri's first companion, was the founder of the China mission, that honor rightfully belongs to Ruggieri himself. It was due to his diplomacy at Canton that the Jesuits were not only permitted to reside within the Ming empire in 1582 but also granted a temple in Zhaoqing, the capital of Guangdong Province. Making his desire to remain in China known along with his Western curiosities, Ruggieri appears to have bargained for his first residence with a clock. In December 1582 the Jesuit was summoned from Macau by the governor general, who had earlier shown interest in the timepiece while at the same time indicating two residences in Zhaoqing where Ruggieri might reside. Although Ruggieri was skeptical about the outcome of this encounter—"because the promises of these heathens are of little worth, since they ordinarily lie and are not bestirred except in their own interest"—Valignano insisted that he go "to tempt fate."[15] For his part, Ruggieri went to the provincial capital "to conserve the friendship" that he had established with this mandarin.[16] The governor made good on his offer, and the missionary was allowed to live at an old temple. There, he told his patron, he would continue his language studies "so as to be able to communicate our knowledge and learn of the good things of China."[17]

Not only did Ruggieri get a residence at Zhaoqing from the governor, but also he secured permission for two companions to enter China. When it appeared that the Jesuit was making progress with his diplomatic overtures, Valignano summoned two other missionaries from India to Macau to join him. These two Italians, Matteo Ricci (1552–1610) and Francesco Pasio (1554–1612), had attended the Society's novitiate in Rome during the Visitor's tenure. On finishing his studies at the order's college in Goa, Ricci taught grammar and rhetoric in Goa and Cochin; Pasio served as mission procurator at the capital of the Estado da Índia. The latter accompanied Ruggieri to their new house in late 1582, with Ricci heading into China in early autumn of the following year. Although Pasio would not remain with them for long, Ricci and Ruggieri stayed in Zhaoqing for the next six years, continuing their studies and devising ways of spreading their religious message.

Making the adjustment to life in a Chinese city far from the comforting presence of other Europeans was difficult for the missionaries, but they saw their best chance for starting a new enterprise in the adaptation to local customs. At the urging of the governor general, Ruggieri chose to dress in the fashion of the Buddhist clergy. He claimed that this garb was "slightly different" from his sober soutane, insisting in early 1583, "Now the robes are being cut and soon we will be made into Chinese."[18] While this change in attire would create ambiguities about the nature of their message, something the missionaries would later correct, it no doubt made their exotic presence more palatable to the local literati. Yet even dressed in this fashion, the missionaries at Zhaoqing decided to keep a low profile. According to Ruggieri, they had two goals for the first years of their stay among the Chinese: to edify them by their lifestyle and "to learn characters with all possible diligence in order to read their books well and confound their errors" while acquiring "the language for explaining our concepts."[19]

Even if he had gained a residence inside the Ming empire, Ruggieri remained doubtful about how long the Jesuits would be welcome in Zhaoqing. His fears of provoking popular unrest were somewhat allayed by the good relations he maintained with the educated elite of the region, including the provincial mandarins. Through their conversations on European philosophy, morality, and, most important, mathematics and technology, the missionaries piqued the curiosity of these Late Ming literati. In turn, their Chinese acquaintances spread the word about the foreigners to their friends and patrons, contributing to the Jesuits' meager store of *guanxi* (that is, a personal relationship or connection understood as a form of social capital). Most famously, Ruggieri and Ricci discoursed on Euclidean geometry to their visitors, showed them maps indicating China's place in the wider world, explained the functions of armillary spheres and glass prisms, and displayed oil paintings of Jesus and the Virgin. Only after they had captured the attention of their listeners did they broach the subject of the primary cause behind the perfect order of the universe demonstrated by mathematics. By late 1584 they had printed up translations of the Paternoster, the Ten Commandments, and the Ave Maria to reinforce the interest of the curious.[20]

By 1585 Valignano felt confident enough to tell Claudio Aquaviva, the Superior General in Rome, that the decision he had made six years earlier to call Ruggieri to Macau had not been in vain. Nevertheless, the Visitor found himself defending the fact that there had been no reports of Chinese conversions to Christianity—in contrast to the substantial tallies that kept arriving from Japan. He asserted that the missionaries at Zhaoqing were obeying his orders to "exercise much caution in making Christians . . . until they became well known and recognized," so as to avoid being expelled from Guangdong Province. His exhortations for restraint notwithstanding, Valignano reported that his subordinates had claimed some conversions, "and the mandarins had shown no disgust."[21] These neophytes included the first individual baptized by the Jesuits in China, a man with an incurable illness who had been abandoned by his relatives in a field to await death. When the missionaries took this man in, he gladly agreed to learn about their religion and accepted baptism shortly before dying.[22]

According to Valignano, the missionaries at Zhaoqing had also baptized a literatus, an individual "who was learned and important, and was going to receive the degree of mandarin."[23] The Jesuits knew that conversions among the ranks of the literati could provide social legitimation for the mission, and those from within the mandarinate could afford political protection. But rather than the fruit of any overall strategy to preach to the elite, this specific conversion (if it was more than merely a reflection of missionary optimism) was a fortunate side effect of the Jesuits' sustained contacts with educated individuals. In fact, missionary writings—Matteo Ricci's in particular—make it clear the Jesuits knew that their converts were likely to come from the "very lowest rank of the people." These included outcasts, the destitute, the terminally ill, illiterate rustics, and uncultured artisans whom the missionaries encountered in the course of their charitable works. As was evident from the fact that the first Chinese Christian was destitute, wrote Ricci, building a mission church in the Ming empire would take patience, as "God clearly wanted such a great project to commence from the smallest beginning."[24] Other conversions sparked in the Jesuits' first years of spreading their religious message came from the same humble milieu, a pattern initiated here that repeated itself for the rest of the mission's history.

As the Jesuits made themselves more visible to the inhabitants of Zhaoqing by claiming converts in plebeian circles, they also brought lingering popular suspicions about them to the fore. Lacking the knowledge of the Cantonese language that might have helped them explain their message to a larger percentage of the population, and hampered by orders to exercise discretion, the missionaries were open to all manner of rumor and speculation. For instance, Matteo Ricci claimed that the news of the first conversion "was poorly received by the Chinese," who ventured that there was a jewel in the dying man's head and that the missionaries would extract it after his death.[25] In Guangdong Province, where an exposure to coastal piracy and contraband as well as the constant presence of a variety of foreigners at the Canton fairs bred resentment, the missionaries were in an especially precarious position. On more than one occasion in the 1580s, inhabitants of Zhaoqing aired their ill feelings by pelting the missionaries' house with stones.[26] Perhaps more seriously for the Jesuits, several local mandarins were fearful of the missionaries' links to Macau, where the Portuguese remained a potentially dangerous presence on Chinese soil.[27] The fact that the officials who had befriended the Jesuits were constantly being rotated to assignments elsewhere in China merely compounded the insecurity of the missionaries' situation. Obviously, there was no guarantee that they would be able to win over all newly arrived officials.

In spite of these difficulties, the Jesuits felt confident about the prospects for the mission in the late 1580s. Ruggieri informed Valignano of his need for more men, including "someone with prudence" to come to the mission as its superior, and the Visitor responded by posting António de Almeida (1557–1591) and Duarte de Sande (1547–1599) to China.[28] Unlike Almeida, a young man who had only recently arrived from Portugal, Sande had been in India for seven years by 1585 and had served as the rector of the Jesuit College of Bassein. The reason for choosing Duarte de Sande as mission superior, beyond the fact that the Society of Jesus tended to promote older, more experienced priests to positions of leadership, was that Ruggieri had never held such an administrative post within the Society.

Another reason for Sande's appointment as mission superior was that Ruggieri had engineered a project for expanding the Jesuit enterprise farther into the empire. He had been invited by Wang Pan (*jinshi* degree 1572), the circuit intendant for Guangdong and Jiangxi provinces, to accompany him on his journey to Peking, or at least as far as the official's home in Zhejiang Province. In order to ensure the safety of the mission, Ruggieri left on his journey northward in November 1585 with Almeida, leaving Sande and Ricci at Zhaoqing. Although his mission ultimately proved fruitless, it impressed upon Ruggieri the immense scale of China and the possibility that he would be able to enlarge his circle of elite friends elsewhere.[29] This opinion would be confirmed during the missionary's two other trips to Guangxi and Huguang provinces in 1587.

Although in their later recollections the China Jesuits would gloss over the setbacks that they encountered during their first two decades of trying to get their mission established, the late 1580s were a time of crisis for their fledgling enterprise. Their labors were not made any easier by such ventures as those launched by the imprudent Spanish Jesuit Alonso Sánchez (1545–1593), who twice visited China and circulated rumors and projects in Macau, Manila, Madrid, and Rome about a Spanish embassy to Peking (with the figment of a Spanish invasion of the Ming empire looming in the background).[30] In order to dispel notions about the feasibility of such endeavors in Europe, Valignano sent Ruggieri to the Roman curia with a petition to have this most informed of all Jesuit China hands appointed papal ambassador to the Wanli emperor (r. 1572–1620). But Ruggieri never returned to China after his departure for Italy in late 1588, and with the death of four popes in quick succession, his project never got off the ground. Luckily for the China mission, neither did the schemes of Sánchez.[31]

Further difficulties arose when popular resentment toward the missionaries and their contacts with the Portuguese boiled over at Zhaoqing in 1589. The new officials who had come to replace the Jesuits' friends in positions of local authority decided that it was preferable for the missionaries to leave than for the city to face the prospect of civil unrest.[32] Matteo Ricci, by that time the most experienced missionary, then decided to petition the new governor for another residence within Guangdong Province. His audacity was rewarded by an offer to reside in any city except Canton or Zhaoqing. Ricci chose Shaozhou in the northern part of the province, where the missionaries apparently got a warmer reception than in the provincial capital. Ricci claimed that they successfully avoided trouble: "Since we say we come from Zhaoqing, no one mentions Macau." Soon they had been visited by "all of the important people of the city."[33] While the attitude of the Shaozhou elite seems to have been one of mild acceptance, the same cannot be said of the Jesuits' reception by the city's commoners. The missionaries suffered random acts of violence and saw their residence vandalized repeatedly in the 1590s.

Sporadic friction with the local populace was not the only problem that confronted the Jesuits at their new residence. A decade after the mission had managed to establish itself inside the Ming empire, it was still an enterprise of modest dimensions. Only Ricci and Almeida moved to Shaozhou in 1589; Sande returned to Macau to take up the post of rector at the Society's college. Matters were further complicated by the untimely death of Almeida in 1591 and that of his replacement, Francesco de Petris (1562–1593), two years later.

Staffing their enterprise was a chronic problem confronting the missionaries. It should come as no surprise that sending men from Europe to China in the early modern period was a tremendous challenge; the sea voyage alone caused the deaths of half the prospective missionaries who embarked. Of those who reached Asia alive, very few were sent by their superiors into China. On their arrival in India, most of them first had to complete their academic training in the Society's schools in that country and were then reassigned to Indian mission stations. Moreover, as the Japan mission continued to grow in the late sixteenth century, almost all of

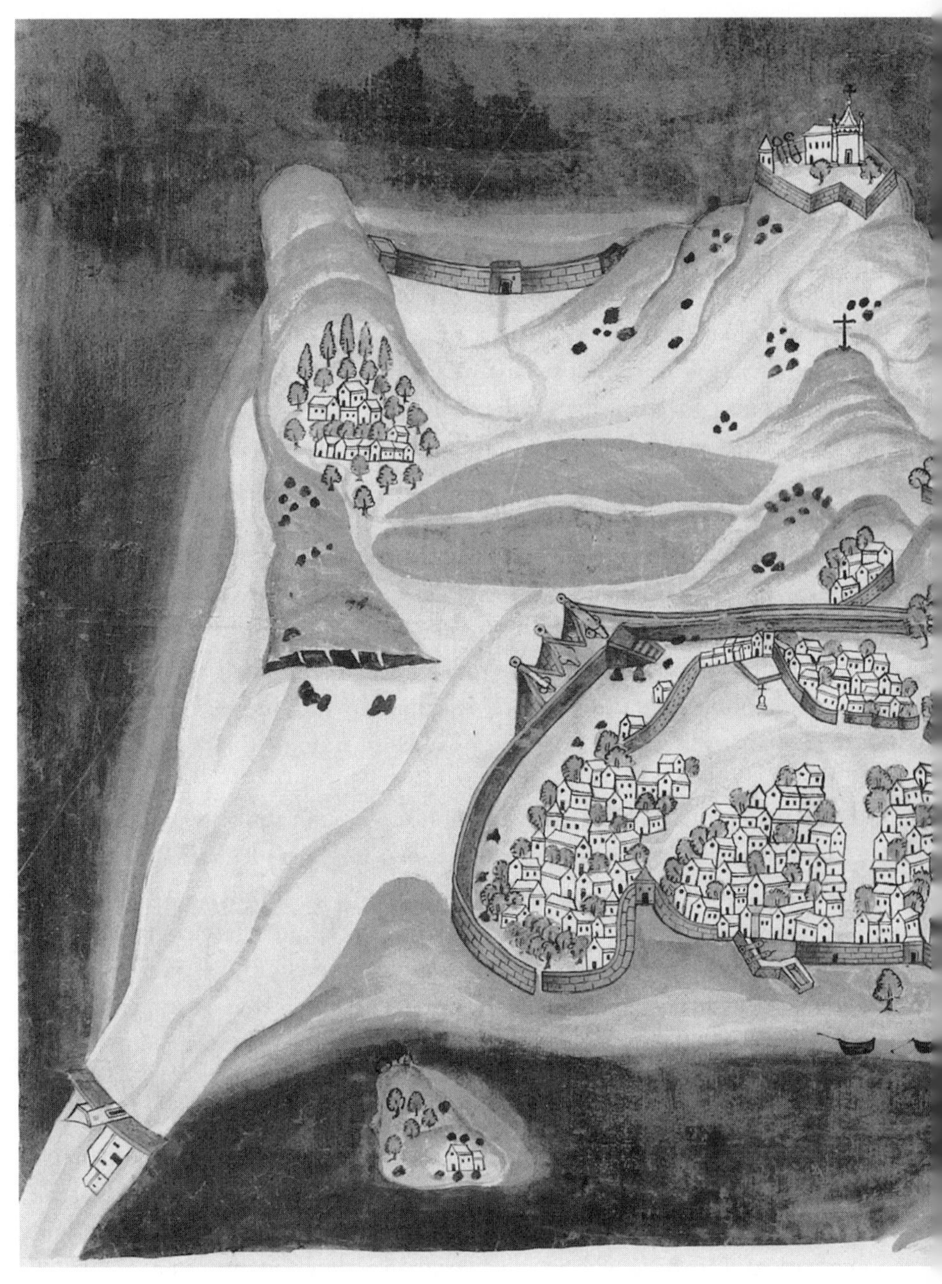

View of Macau in the early seventeenth century, by Pedro Barreto de Resende. The Jesuits' Church of São Paulo and College of Macau are shown atop a staircase next to the fortress at the center of the map. From António Boccaro, *Livro das Plantas de Todas as Fortalezas, Cidades e Povoações do Estado da Índia Oriental* (1635).

the Jesuits who reached Macau were directed onward to Nagasaki rather than into China.

Moreover, rising tensions between the Portuguese and the Ming authorities magnified the distance between Shaozhou and Macau, making it difficult for new recruits to enter China. Knowing that the Europeans maintained close contacts with the Japanese, Guangdong officials tried to keep watch in order to prevent the infiltration of spies into the empire—especially in light of Toyotomi Hideyoshi's invasion of Korea in 1592.[34] As the Jesuits knew well, the invitation that had been extended to Ruggieri was not a general permission for any and all Jesuits to enter the empire. Those seeking to rendezvous with Ricci therefore had to enter illegally, evading the patrols in the Pearl River delta to get past Canton to relative safety. By the mid-1590s, one Italian and two Portuguese priests who would assist in the mission's later geographic expansion, Lazzaro Cattaneo (1560–1640), João Soeiro (1556–1607), and João da Rocha (1565–1623), had managed to reach Shaozhou.

Further help came from the recruitment of Chinese Catholic men, typically born in Macau of Chinese or mixed parentage. Taking his cue from the experience of the Japan Jesuits who had made considerable use of native auxiliaries, in 1591 Duarte de Sande assigned two Macanese men, Sebastião Fernandes (1562–1621) and Francisco Martins (1545–1604), to Shaozhou for training as temporal coadjutors.[35] This degree of membership within the Society of Jesus meant that they were sworn by vows of poverty, chastity, and obedience like the rest of their brethren. These coadjutors were not, however, destined for the priesthood but were charged primarily with carrying out domestic tasks or catechetical work. While all members of the order were identified as coadjutors (and referred to as "brothers") upon joining, those who would later become priests were typically referred to as "scholastics" in light of the fact that they were engaged in studying at least moral theology (or at most the Society's complete curriculum in grammar, rhetoric, philosophy, and both moral and speculative theology). One should not, however, infer a value judgment against these Macanese Christians as a result of their terminal designation as coadjutors. In Europe, most of the temporal affairs at the Society's colleges and professed houses were run by coadjutors, and the range of duties that fell to them was even greater in China. Given the language barrier between the missionaries and Chinese commoners, the Macanese coadjutors were in a unique position to help the mission in its apostolic endeavors as catechists. Furthermore, in light of the dangers faced by Europeans traveling to and from Macau, Martins and Fernandes were invaluable as couriers. Indistinguishable from other southern Chinese, they easily evaded border guards on the lookout for foreigners.

Taking the Name of Literati, 1595–1600

In the absence of Michele Ruggieri and mission superior Duarte de Sande, Matteo Ricci took the lead in managing the affairs of the Jesuits' China enterprise. Ricci had shown mettle in avoiding expulsion to Macau when conditions deteriorated at Zhaoqing and had made progress in learning the Chinese language and Confucian philosophy. Paradoxically, the slow pace of conversions had created favorable conditions for him to observe his hosts, and especially the members of the educated elite. By the mid-1590s he felt secure enough in his observations of Chinese society to attempt new ways of carrying out his mission. His biggest challenge lay in somehow ensuring that the Jesuits would not be permanently on the run from one residence to another when their mandarin friends moved on. Ricci wanted to enable the mission to sink deeper roots, and that necessitated not only reevaluating the strategies employed by the Jesuits in the preceding fifteen years but creating new ones as well based on their accumulated knowledge. That, he wrote, was the only way to endow the mission with a "good foundation," considering that, in his well-informed view, he and his colleagues had from the beginning been "treated and regarded as the scum of the earth."[36]

One part of Ricci's plan aimed at gaining more durable political protection. Because the Ming era mandarinate constantly shuffled its members from one posting to another in order to avoid political entrenchment, the missionaries could not count on friends who were officials in any one place for very long. Ricci would therefore have to head to the imperial court and appeal to the center of Chinese political power in an attempt, if at all possible, to submit a petition directly to the Wanli emperor. To be sure, Ricci was not the first to come up with this idea; Michele Ruggieri's original intention in going to Zhejiang Province in 1585 was to travel from there onward to Peking. Nor was this strategy born out of any desire to concentrate exclusively on preaching the Christian message to the educated elite.

As a member of the Society of Jesus, a religious order that had been founded only in 1540 but had quickly set up scores of residences across western Europe and in the European overseas colonies, Ricci was using a proven method for implanting a new Jesuit presence in a society with amenable political and social institutions. His idea was to seek out the highest level of political patronage possible by appealing directly to the emperor and, failing that, to obtain protection from important individuals within the highest ranks of the state bureaucracy. Here Ricci borrowed from Francis Xavier and Simão Rodrigues, who traveled to the court of King João III of Portugal under the protection of Pedro de Mascarenhas, a member of the high aristocracy who had served his king as ambassador to Rome. Xavier, in turn, had been sent on to Goa at the request of the king himself, thereby cementing the links between the crown and the Jesuit missions in Asia. If Ricci could do the same in China, he and his fellow missionaries would have free rein to carry out their proselytizing enterprise there.

Lacking the common religious ground for establishing new friendships with potential protectors which had worked so well among Europeans, Ricci was forced to adjust these familiar Jesuit tactics to new circumstances. Instead of relying on shared faith, he appealed to the moral sensibilities of the mandarin elite and to their taste for the exotic with his rhetorical skills. In some respects, this was what Ruggieri had done in the first years he had spent in China. By the mid-1590s, however, Ricci was already a very accomplished linguist whose command of Chinese learning made him a more skillful communicator than his former companion. In fact, in 1595 he translated a series of aphorisms from "Western Sages" such as Cicero and Seneca and published it under the title *Jiaoyun lun* (On Friendship).[37] Ricci hoped that those literati who read his book would take a liking to him, and that amity would in turn lead to protection and patronage. Most important, Ricci was ready to exploit the connections he had made with his mandarin friends, willing to gamble the fate of the mission on his ability to win new allies, and able to deploy linguistic sleight of hand to his advantage. Thankfully for the Jesuits, the prevailing intellectual climate among the educated elite of late Ming China was propitious for such a risky venture. That Ricci combined moral austerity, erudition, and technical skills with the capacity to make himself understood made him an attractive figure to his literati interlocutors.

Matteo Ricci's chance for carrying out his plan came in early 1595, when one of his mandarin acquaintances headed to the capital to receive a higher bureaucratic dignity. This official is referred to in missionary sources as "Scielou" (alias "Xeije"), a senior military mandarin whose true identity has eluded scholars.[38] In this official's journey north, Ricci saw "such a good occasion to be able to lean on such a great and powerful mandarin." The Jesuit even told his escort that "we other literati" had a strong desire to see the imperial court, but that the mandarin had warned him against proceeding beyond Jiangxi Province (the first inland province north of Guangdong).[39] In light of the fact that Ricci was a foreigner, Scielou also told him not to attempt going to Peking or Nanjing. Yet Ricci was not daunted by this admonition since, as he explained in a letter to his superior, he knew the stakes were high: "Until we have a foothold in one of these two royal cities we will always live in fear of losing this mission to China."[40] With this conviction, he sailed through Jiangxi in early 1595 to establish a residence in Nanjing.

On his way north, Ricci made an audacious change in his visual appearance. At the suggestion of Qu Taisu (1549–1611), a lower-level literatus who would later become a convert, Ricci discarded his Buddhist robes in favor of dressing after the fashion of the mandarins. His primary aim was to leave behind any a priori association that might be made between himself and the Buddhist clergy because of his clothing—especially since these priests, the "bonzes," had reached the nadir of their public reputation during the Wanli era.[41] While the Jesuits would never sit for the state examinations, and thus never gain the *shengyuan* (bachelor), *juren* (licentiate), or *jinshi* (doctor) degrees of their literati peers, the keys to social status and political power in late imperial China, they wanted to be accepted on Chinese terms as learned men. Writing to Duarte de Sande, Ricci stressed that his gesture would enable the missionaries "to leave behind the name of bonzes, which among the Chinese is held as vile and lowly, and take the name of literati." In addition to donning the robes used by the elite when they went calling on one another, Ricci went on, he had grown his hair and beard *à la chinoise.* Attempting to relate his new garb to his superior in Macau, Ricci explained that his robes were made of dark purple silk lined with blue trim "very similar to what the Venetians use in Venice."[42]

Ricci's move to associate himself more closely with the public perception of the educated (not to say powerful) classes in Chinese society would have long-lasting repercussions for the mission. For one thing, it put him and the missionaries who emulated him in a new category for their Chinese observers. Seeking to avoid burdening their gospel and their lifestyle with negative associations, Ricci and his successors blurred the visual distinction between the religious and secular spheres of Chinese society. They attempted to benefit from the social prestige of the literati (and, ultimately, the mandarins) by talking and dressing like them; at the same time, they bore a religious message, something not ordinarily considered the province of *ru* (scholars). Although there is much debate over just how divided the religious and secular spheres were in late Ming China, it is undeniable that with this move the Jesuits created a sense of ambiguity about their social function. Their use of Confucian philosophy as an indigenous support for their religious teachings (that is, as a valuable moral complement to Christian revelation, in the mold of Greek and Roman thought) served to confuse established Chinese categories even more. While at least one scholar has argued that the image of the "missionary literatus" was a primary reason for the failure of the Jesuits' religious message to take hold in China in the way that Buddhism—another foreign religion—had done, Ricci's move to emulate an elite model paid off handsomely from the start.[43]

On another level, Ricci's change of clothes can also be seen as the culmination of a process of rationalizing missionary tactics to serve what the Jesuits understood as the ultimate goal of their mission: the conversion of the Chinese to Christianity. In this respect, the choices made by Ricci were characteristic of the new forms of Catholic pastoral activity being developed at the time in Europe. In China, Ricci was one of the farthest-flung representatives of a typically Jesuit or, more specifically, Ignatian spirit that subsumed the means of sparking conversions or spiritual invigoration to the ends—*ad maiorem Dei gloriam.* Defending his confrere's shift in strategy to the members of the Society of Jesus in Europe, Duarte de Sande wrote: "In truth, among these nations that are so distant from ours, and have laws and customs so different, it is necessary to enter with theirs to come out with ours, accommodating ourselves to them in what our Holy Faith permits, in this way to divulge and teach our holy doctrine, which they would receive in no other way."[44] Ricci's attempt to put himself fully into a Chinese frame of reference is one of the better-known instances of "accommodation," the modern name for a strategy of attracting converts to Christianity that would later be found at the center of the Chinese Rites controversy, both lauded and condemned.

Although Matteo Ricci's trip into the heart of the Ming empire in 1595 would later be seen as a great step forward for the mission, it did not seem so at the time. The Jesuit wrote how the handlers of his mandarin escort had repeatedly begged him not to enter Nanjing and, if he did, then "at least not to say that he had come with them or their mandarin." Yet Ricci was unfazed by their injunctions. As soon as he bid them adieu at the city gate, he found a place to stay and "did nothing else" than say that he had arrived with Scielou.[45] In his new courtesy clothing, he also sought out a mandarin he had known in Guangdong who was serving in the Ministry of Rites. But this reunion did not go as well as Ricci intended. After a cordial welcome, his host flew into a rage at the missionary's presence—"with such exasperation and fury that he seemed crazy"—insisting that he had considered the Jesuit a suspicious character ever since they first met in Canton. Without further ado, Ricci was expelled from the capital and forced to retreat southward. Chastened and "very confused" by the encounter with this mandarin, he headed to Nanchang, the capital of Jiangxi Province, where Scielou had first instructed him to go.[46]

At Nanchang, Ricci's new strategy worked better. His overtures to local officials were more successful there, and soon he declared to his superiors that he had secured "safe terrain" for the mission.[47] Choosing to remain in Jiangxi until another opportunity to head for the capital manifested itself, Ricci consolidated his efforts by summoning João Soeiro and Sebastião Fernandes from Shaozhou to man the residence he had acquired. The site of the new Jesuit house at Nanchang gave Ricci reason to be optimistic about the prospects of carrying out his original plan to pitch the Christian message to the emperor. Far away from the court, and close by to the missionaries, there lived a large population of distant imperial relatives, called *wangfu,* some of whom might recommend Ricci to their august kin. But his efforts among these men and women, like those among other segments of the city's population, did not meet with success.[48] As a somewhat embarrassed Ricci wrote to a Jesuit friend in Italy in late 1595, "Do not ask me how many thousands of souls I have converted, but only how many of those millions I have told for the first time that ancient news that in heaven lives a God, the creator of heaven and earth."[49]

But beyond the confines of coastal Guangdong, in one of the central provinces of the Ming empire, Matteo Ricci still harbored the desire to present himself to the highest levels of political power with the aim of winning new friends. The opposition encountered by the Jesuits at both Shaozhou and Nanchang convinced Ricci and his superiors of the need to seek more solid protection for the mission. As one Jesuit at Macau put it regarding the efforts of his confreres in Jiangxi Province, "The Christians are still very few and, speaking candidly, always will be until we have permission from the King of China to be in his lands without any interference."[50] Visitor Alessandro Valignano agreed with Ricci on the need to attempt another journey to Nanjing, the former Ming capital city still invested with the bureaucratic trappings of a metropolis. He named Ricci mission superior in 1597, and dispatched a shipment of European gifts to Nanchang for him to distribute to prominent mandarins on the occasion of a second trip to the southern capital. Ricci set out for Nanjing in 1598 in the company of Lazzaro Cattaneo but passed through that city and followed on to Peking. Rebuffed in this first sally to the northern capital, he returned to Nanjing to found the mission's third residence.

By the time Ricci settled in the former Ming capital, his investment in Chinese literati culture was paying substantial dividends. Building on the reputation he had gained in Jiangxi, he was able to attract the attentions of members of the provincial literati circles in the Jiangnan region, the area surrounding Nanjing. Attracted by his collection of maps, globes, prisms, European books and oil paintings, curious members of the elite as well as plebeians flocked to the Jesuit residence, where they heard Ricci discourse on things Western. His talks invariably ended with a reference to Christianity. Letters from the missionaries at the turn of the seventeenth century speak of their technique of attempting to convert educated Chinese by exposing them to an amalgam of European moral, scientific, and religious teachings that would become known among late Ming literati as *Tianxue,* Learning from Heaven.[51] The Jesuits quickly realized the value of their scientific ideas for their interlocutors and tried to attract converts "through the door of Mathematics."[52] With Cattaneo's help, Ricci preached to the visitors who came to their residence, solidifying his reputation as a scholar in the Chinese tradition. This was an extremely effective strategy in Jiangnan, where a dense network of rich cities boasted the highest concentration of mandarins, literati, and retired officials in the empire. The conversion of a handful of retired mandarins was the missionaries' reward for their efforts.

Buoyed by Ricci's growing fame at Nanjing, the Jesuits in Shaozhou and Nanchang tried to replicate his methods. They too adopted literati dress and set about studying Confucian philosophy with the aim of assuming a socially important identity that would at once win protection and impress prospective converts. But their conversations focused on *Tianzhu jiao,* the Teachings of the Lord of Heaven, the religious component of *Tianxue.* According to the tallies of baptisms that they recorded, this strategy worked with varying degrees of success. For instance, there were only about twenty Christians at Nanchang in 1603 despite the fact that a sickly João Soeiro had lived there for six years by that point. During his convalescence, the Jesuit composed a short tract in dialogue form on the basic concepts of Christian belief, titled *Tianzhu shengjiao yueyan* (Brief Introduction to the Holy Religion of the Lord of Heaven).[53] When Soeiro's health finally returned in 1604, his relations with the local mandarins improved and the "fire of conversion began to rage." That year, the missionary claimed close to three hundred converts.[54] The work of the Jesuits who stayed behind in northern Guangdong appears to have taken off earlier. The Sicilian Niccolò Longobardo (1565–1654), a recent arrival, recorded a harvest of two hundred converts as early as 1602, including a substantial number of villagers from the area outside Shaozhou. His report even noted that many of the Christians in that area were women, the wives of men who had submitted to baptism. The Jesuits were especially impressed that these women could "recite Christian doctrine from the beginning to the end" when examined on the subject.[55]

It is worth pausing to underscore these early efforts to convert ordinary Chinese men and women, since the notion that the Society of Jesus sought only mandarin conversions has long been a defining characterization of the mission. It is understandable why scholars have reached this conclusion, given that the Jesuits had to address the political necessity of projecting their message to the governing elite of China, not to speak of their equally exigent need to trumpet conversions to Christianity from the ranks of the mandarins to their superiors, aristocratic patrons, and the many other readers of their published correspondence in Europe. In fact, a superficial overview of the documents produced by the missionaries would lead one to assume that the Jesuits were almost exclusively interested in the Chinese literati. But if one reads the same materials more closely, it becomes difficult to draw the conclusion that the Jesuits defended a method of evangelization "from the top down." It is therefore incorrect to assert, as many scholars have done, that the Jesuits' strategy in China was to focus on the elite and that only the Mendicant friars who arrived in later decades aimed to convert the lower ranks of society.[56]

While it is clear from archival evidence that the few mandarin converts made by the Jesuits represented victories for the mission and as such were widely celebrated, the missionaries were not the upholders of a simplistic logic which dictated that if the elite converted, so too would the plebs.[57] At most, Matteo Ricci and his followers hoped that the image of Christianity in China would benefit from the conversion of literati or mandarins. In the words of Niccolò Longobardo, the presence of individuals of high social standing within neophyte communities helped both the priests and their Christians: "When something happens that calls our enterprise into question, it is a great shield and succor for us to say that so-and-so and so-and-so already follow this new law."[58] Yet these converts were merely the icing on the missionaries' cake. It is clear from their writings that the Jesuits sought to make new Christians from all ranks of Chinese society and that they proselytized the lower orders whenever it was possible for them to do so.[59]

The Jesuits knew better than to count on many baptisms among the elite. They realized that various social impediments prevented mandarins, gentry, and literati of whatever level from becoming Christians. Foremost among these obstacles was the practice of taking concubines as a symbol of status or to ensure producing an heir. The missionaries insisted that a Christian man could have only one wife. As virtually all Chinese men with sufficient wealth had concubines who had borne them children, this requirement meant repudiating these women for the new religion's sake. As mandarins were public figures who sought the estimation of their peers, they were wary of adopting a foreign religion at the cost of an adverse effect on their careers. Some Christian ritual practices, such as having to kneel before a priest in order to confess, also appear to have dissuaded members of the elite from baptism.[60] Given these constraints, many of the mandarins who were baptized during this early period were retired officials old enough to dispense with any concubines and persons no longer dependent on others who might not favor Christianity. Even so, the Jesuits were candid about their dealings with members of the Chinese elite, at times striking a defensive tone: "The fathers of the Society in China do not enjoy dealing with or befriending the Magistrates for any other reason except that it is necessary for the Christian community, because if they do not convert as we desire, at least we seek to build and cultivate the church in their shadow and with their help, since without their favor it is all built on sand."[61]

In the Classroom of Heaven, 1601–1607

By May 1600, Matteo Ricci had cultivated his persona as a *Xiru,* or Western scholar, at the southern capital for almost two years and was eager to present himself to the highest ranks of Chinese officialdom at Peking. When fresh orders arrived from Alessandro Valignano to attempt another journey northward, he was ready. To be sure, with eight Jesuits (including the two Chinese coadjutors) already inside the Ming empire, the Visitor was not taking a dangerous risk. Rather, he felt on the basis of Ricci's assessments that the time was ripe for his subordinate to gather his most precious European gifts and head to the capital to win new mandarin allies. Ricci set out in the company of Diego de Pantoja (1571–1618), a Spaniard who had reached Macau in 1597, and the two coadjutors, Fernandes and Martins. The party included an indispensable native escort, a respected palace eunuch. Thanks to Ricci's reputation, his escort was able to clear many of the obstacles created by other mandarins and eunuchs opposed to the Jesuits' journey to Peking. Yet despite the prohibitions against foreigners visiting the capital independent of fixed tribute embassies, Ricci continued northward. When he was imprisoned in Tianjin for his illegal progress, a command from the Wanli emperor secured his release in recompense for a clock and a set of oil paintings.[62] This show of imperial favor was the first in a series of tacit demonstrations of approval that culminated in the permission obtained by the missionaries to reside in Peking.

With the Jesuits' arrival at the imperial capital in late January 1601, a central goal of Matteo Ricci's strategy for securing the mission had been accomplished. With a Jesuit ensconced at Peking—by order of the emperor himself—the reputation of the Society of Jesus in China would improve along with that of Ricci himself. It is not easy to overstate the importance of Ricci's acceptance at court. The fact that he quickly became a minor celebrity at the capital was crucial for the safety of the mission and its future expansion. As soon as Ricci and Pantoja settled down, they drew a stream of mandarin and literati visitors curious to see the exotic goods they had brought to present to the emperor. According to one of the first accounts from the capital, the missionaries entertained a mandarin from the *Lipu* (Ministry of Rites, the agency in charge of dealing with foreigners) by demonstrating that "the Sun is larger than the Earth and the Moon smaller." Another mandarin who had been impressed by Ricci's

"On Friendship" visited the Jesuits and offered them help in securing a residence outside the quarters reserved for foreign delegations.[63] Ricci's colleague Pantoja contributed to the renown of the missionaries with his blue eyes alone: "The Chinese find them very mysterious, and normally say that my eyes spy where to find precious stones and the like . . . claiming even that they have characters written inside them."[64]

The fame of the Jesuits at the capital was essential for legitimizing the efforts of the missionaries in the southern provinces. As soon as news of Ricci's reception began to spread via the words and letters of his literati acquaintances, the fortunes of the missionaries in Nanjing, Nanchang, and Shaozhou improved. When they came under the suspicion of local officials, the other Jesuits invoked Ricci's name—or, rather, the name of his alter ego, Li Madou, their famous colleague. For instance, when Niccolò Longobardo was brought before the city magistrate in Shaozhou in 1605, he mentioned his contacts with Ricci to a visiting provincial official. Since this superior official had heard of Li Madou and knew how he had been received at court, he ordered the local magistrate to drop his case against the missionary.[65] Although Ricci's fame would not insulate the Jesuits from all attacks—including the verdict of a Nanchang magistrate in 1607 in favor of a group of literati who denounced Christianity as a heterodox sect—it certainly helped dampen some early flares of persecution.[66]

Beyond providing protection for the mission's established residences, Ricci and Pantoja's installation at the capital also permitted the geographic expansion of the Jesuit enterprise. Owing to the Jesuits' growing network of friendships at Peking and the constant motion of the mandarin cogs in the machinery of the massive Chinese bureaucracy, it was not long before news of the missionaries and their message reached the far corners of the empire. Ricci was helped in no small measure by the presence of throngs of metropolitan examination candidates who traveled to the capital every three years. These mandarins were eager to get copies of his books on Learning from Heaven.[67] Some of them chose to become Christians and implored the Jesuits to accompany them to their civil service postings in the provinces.

In the first years of the seventeenth century, there were too few missionaries on the ground in China for such requests to be considered. Even so, Ricci had scored a major coup by situating himself close to the beating heart of the late Ming state. As much as any one man could, he had harnessed the mission to the dynamism of the Chinese bureaucracy, establishing an expansive network of correspondents, allies, and converts. But this link to the motion of the civil service came at a price. A Christian mandarin's reassignment to an area with no priest could mean the potential loss of a proportionally large group of converts. As João da Rocha remarked at the departure of a converted military mandarin from Nanjing to Henan Province with his entire household, "We are left with one less parish."[68]

Matteo Ricci's success at Peking, however, was a double-edged sword, something that has not been adequately recognized by historians. By underscoring the importance of his arrival at the capital, scholars have rightly recognized his most important legacy but have missed its unintended consequences. For despite the high profile of the Peking house and the crucial role it played in securing the safety of the other mission stations, its locus at the heart of the Chinese state removed Ricci and his court Jesuit successors from contributing fully to the religious goals of their collective effort—the conversion of the Chinese to Christianity. Since most of the Peking missionaries' time was consumed by dealings with literati, including the various scientific projects that would emerge from Ricci's fame as a mathematician and astronomer, they spent less time preaching the gospel. This is not to say that the Jesuits saw their sacred and profane duties as mutually exclusive, but rather that it is very easy to arrive at a skewed vision of the Jesuit enterprise if one focuses only on the missionaries at the court. An exaggerated emphasis on Ricci and his successors in Peking, a view that has long characterized histories of the mission, has almost completely overshadowed the work of Soeiro, da Rocha, Longobardo, and Cattaneo, who were busy propagating Christianity at the Jesuits' other residences.[69]

The great interest generated by the adventures of the Europeans at the Ming court makes it understandable why the image of the Peking Jesuits became the mission's prevailing cliché. Their reputation, after all, was rooted in reality. In keeping with Matteo Ricci's impression that the Jesuits should do nothing at court, including any rigorous proselytizing, that might harm "the pleasant odor of our faith" or—perhaps more important—"la fama de' Nostri," the missionaries' first years at Peking were primarily devoted to improving their reputation.[70] Their primary activities consisted of receiving guests and entertaining visitors, as well as writing treatises on academic or religious topics. In addition to composing an introduction to the fundamental Christian teachings, *Tianzhu shiyi* (The

True Meaning of the Lord of Heaven, 1603), Ricci produced a further text which included references to teachings drawn from classical authors such as Epictetus, *Ershiwu yan* (Twenty-five Sayings, 1605), and a set of essays recording his debates with Chinese literati, *Jiren shipian* (Ten Essays on the Extraordinary Man, 1608). For all of his writings, the Jesuit received assistance from his literati acquaintances to make his texts as stylistically elegant as possible.

It was thanks to their knowledge of European science and technology that the Peking Jesuits gained their greatest renown among the late Ming literati. Ricci himself had studied under Christoph Clavius (1538–1612), the famed Jesuit mathematician in Rome, and regularly discoursed on scientific matters. But while neither Ricci nor his successors at the court were "scientists" in the modern sense, their education in European Jesuit colleges had provided them with a basic background in astronomy, mathematics, and natural philosophy. After all, the curriculum there included the likes of Aristotle, Euclid, and Sacrobosco. As the value of such scientific knowledge for the Peking residence—and, by extension, the whole China mission—became apparent to the Jesuits, they began to devote more of their time to scientific endeavors. Ricci first linked the missionaries to the sciences in Chinese eyes when he worked with Xu Guangqi (1562–1633, *jinshi* 1604) and Li Zhizao (1565–1630, *jinshi* 1598), two high-ranking mandarins who would become converts, on a series of mathematical treatises including a translation of Euclid's *Elements of Geometry* (*Jihe yuanben,* 1607). So important were these endeavors to the mission that by 1613 the Jesuits would candidly state to their superiors in Rome that the Peking residence served uniquely "to legitimize the Society in this kingdom." Therefore, its priests were to proselytize less and focus on "mathematics and similar things, which have been shown to be apt tools toward this end."[71]

Although the Peking Jesuits did attempt to form a Christian community at the capital, there were fewer converts at the court than in other cities. Ricci conceded that despite his efforts, "the number of baptized individuals was not what was desired."[72] Another Jesuit would claim, however, that while "the Peking natives are very difficult to convert," those who did become Christians showed considerable fervor.[73] Undistracted by large numbers of neophytes, the priests could dedicate whatever time they allotted to pastoral work to providing their flock with focused spiritual guidance. One result of this concentrated attention was the precocious establishment of the mission's first devotional confraternities. While it is clear that the initiative to form the first such association came from a Chinese Christian known as Lucas Li and that it was fashioned largely after the common forms of Chinese groups of Confucian or Buddhist inspiration, it is no less clear that Matteo Ricci guided the group's founder by providing him with information about Jesuit Marian sodalities popular in Europe at the time. When the group was inaugurated on September 8, 1609 (the feast of the Nativity of the Virgin), it provided a venue for the local Christians to display and encourage their piety.[74] So well received was this new form of lay devotion that a second Sodality of the Blessed Virgin *(Shengmu hui)* was founded the following year in Nanjing to structure the devotions of the southern capital's converts.

News of Ricci's reception at Peking bolstered Jesuit expectations for the mission while sparking rumors about missionary successes in China that spanned the globe. In the first decade of the seventeenth century, a combination of misunderstood insider reports and word-of-mouth exaggerations by Europeans in Maritime Asia led some as far away as Rome to believe that many important mandarins had submitted to baptism. The most far-fetched of these canards claimed that the Wanli emperor himself had accepted Christianity—obviously foreshadowing the mass conversion of the Chinese to Roman obedience. On the basis of letters from Ricci and the other missionaries, however, Jesuit superiors at Macau were wiser to the reality of the mission. The fruits of twenty years' labors in China were modest at best. To their credit, the Jesuits had established residences in the two imperial capitals, as well as in two provincial cities. They had also gained renown among the ruling class and had made important friendships with high-ranking mandarins. Yet by their own admission, the Jesuits could claim fewer than one thousand Chinese Christians in 1605.[75] When contrasted with the results achieved by the Jesuits in Japan, who reported hundreds of thousands under their spiritual care, including a large number from the warrior aristocracy, the China mission was worryingly unproductive. After all, even religious orders had to mind their balance sheets.

The provincial hierarchy in Macau was further disabused of any overblown assessments of Jesuit successes in China when it sent its first Visitor to inspect the southern residences. Knowing that Ricci could not leave Peking to review the work of his colleagues in person, Valignano assigned the task to Manuel Dias the elder (1559–1639), a senior Jesuit from Portugal who had served as rector at the College of Macau. The Visitor appointed Dias as the superior for the residences at Shaozhou, Nanchang, and Nanjing, and instructed him to verify the numbers and quality of Chinese neophytes.

After completing his initial tour of these houses in 1604, the inspector sent word to the highest authorities of the Society of Jesus in Rome that in fact there were few "important" converts. Even those mandarins who had accepted baptism along with the other members of their households accounted for only a handful of Christians. With regard to the spread of rumors, Dias assured his superiors that he would tell them no more about "what the priests here would do, but what really went on." Although he did find nascent communities of Christians frequenting the sacraments during his visit, Dias realized that it would require more effort for those churches to strike deeper roots. As for the emperor, he was neither "Christian, nor is there hope for this." Nevertheless, Dias wrote of the rumor, "God willing, it will prove a prophecy of what is to come."[76]

With such sobering warnings about the lack of results from the missionaries inside the Ming empire, it would have been possible for the hierarchy of the Society of Jesus at Macau to write off the China enterprise. After all, they were also responsible for the welfare of the Japan mission, which in 1600 counted 30 residences, 123 Jesuits, and 90 seminary students—not to mention scores of Christian communities.[77] To this serious if mundane concern was added the specter of bloody persecution. After the first anti-Christian edicts were issued by Toyotomi Hideyoshi in 1587, it would be only a decade before Japan's Christians and their priests would begin to receive the palms of martyrdom.

The amount of administrative attention lavished on the great Jesuit endeavor in Japan far outweighed that devoted to China, making it hard for Ricci, Sande, and Dias to attract financial donations from pious laymen or to lure new missionaries to join their efforts. The China Jesuits implored their confreres in Europe to consider missionary vocations in the Ming empire, and not to dismiss the prospect of working there because of what they might have heard about the exotic customs of the Japanese. Somewhat disingenuously, Manuel Dias insisted that potential recruits should be informed that China was "almost like Europe, because they eat the same meats and rations as there, sit in tall chairs, sleep on cots and other similar things."[78] Yet for the bulk of the zealous young Jesuits who petitioned to become missionaries, such claims of urbanity were apparently less persuasive than grim tales of dying for the faith in Japan—an attraction the China mission did not offer in the early 1600s.

The one Jesuit who had the greatest stake in making sure that the China enterprise did not languish was Alessandro Valignano. In 1604, just two years before his death, the Visitor made a set of decisions of enduring consequence for the mission. Perhaps the most critical was the removal of the China mission from the supervision of the rector of the College of Macau. This decision meant that the mission superior (then Ricci) became directly responsible to the head of the Society's Province of India, a step aimed at taking China out of the shadow of Japan and giving it greater institutional autonomy.[79] Valignano once again contributed to plans for the mission's future when he dispatched a group of priests, the Italian Alfonso Vagnone (1568–1640) and two Portuguese, Pedro Ribeiro (1570–1640) and Gaspar Ferreira (1571–1649), to Nanjing to begin studying Chinese.

The Visitor also sent a procurator to Rome to conduct business on behalf of the East Asian missions. This priest was to present himself to the Superior General of the Society of Jesus and the Portuguese Assistant (the Superior General's aide for affairs relating to the Portuguese Assistancy, the administrative unit comprising the provinces of Portugal, Brazil, India, and later Japan and China) and request the separation of the Japan and China missions from the control of the Province of India. While in Rome, the procurator was also to inform both the Superior General and the pope of the "great hopes" that the China mission inspired, using this prospect to advance the request for an endowment. He was, moreover, to visit Madrid to plead with Philip III of Spain and the Council of Portugal for further financial support.[80]

When Valignano died in 1606, after over thirty years as the Society's supreme official in Asia, the China mission bore the clear imprint of his foresight and leadership. Although his death cannot be seen as a definitive watershed in the mission's history, it was an indicator of how far the Jesuits' enterprise had come since the Visitor ordered Michele Ruggieri to study Chinese in 1579. By the second half of the first decade of the seventeenth century, the Jesuits—that is, the handful of men led by Matteo Ricci who presented themselves as Western scholars—were a known quantity in China. They manned residences in four cities and gained ever greater renown as more and more curiosity seekers sought them out. Their religious message had begun to attract adherents, though in smaller numbers than the Jesuits hoped and envisioned. Compared to other mission fields, gaining Christians in China required a considerable investment in time, money, and luxury goods. Even after much effort and expenditure, the results remained uncertain. Yet the Society of Jesus had an interest in seeing this endeavor through. That is why Valignano and his Roman superiors indulged Ricci in his long years of studying Chinese thought and entertaining the curiosity of literati, willing to wait and see whether their patience would pay off. Loath to write off the work of the missionaries in the provinces, the Society stomached the reports of a meager crop of converts, seemingly gained one at time. In fact, the mission's foundations in China were stronger than outside observers could discern. The Jesuits' labors to create a name for themselves and their religion had sunk deep into the Chinese soil, below the top layer of late Ming society. Soon enough, those efforts would bear more abundant fruit.

2

In the Shadow of Greatness

After seven years spent at Peking, Matteo Ricci and his companions could reflect on the merits of his strategy for establishing the mission in the political heart of the Ming empire. Their chief concern was whether they would reap their expected apostolic rewards. By the end of the first decade of the seventeenth century, it appeared that his predictions would be borne out, as the Jesuits recruited a few good men as converts—powerful scholar-officials who both legitimated their message and escorted the priests to new mission fields.

But the Jesuits' growing confidence in Ricci's achievement did not mean that they had been formally received into Chinese society by any explicit decree of welcome or tolerance. Actually, the missionaries' arrival at court raised the stakes in the gamble they had made to gain access to the highest levels of the Ming state. Whether or not they could transform the goodwill of their allies into an imperial edict in their favor remained a crucial challenge. To be sure, the Jesuits had latched on to individuals who were in the midst of their climb up the ladder of bureaucratic success; nonetheless, they remained exposed to shifting political winds. While the climate of political stagnation and institutional decay created the conditions for a moral and spiritual revival among the elite—a tenor of anxiety that benefited the missionaries in their apostolic endeavors—it intensified the rivalries between literati factions. As minor figures in a grand power struggle, the Jesuits suffered a major setback in the second decade of the seventeenth century, one that nearly cost them expulsion from the empire. Cast out of the imperial capitals and forced into hiding, they survived during the period from 1616 until 1623 thanks only to the aid of their Christian mandarin protectors.

This exile was a major setback, but it, too, showed that the missionaries had done well to enlist the support of influential members of the elite. Eventually the Jesuits regained their mission stations and founded new ones. When they emerged from hiding, they realized that their enterprise had more durable foundations than they had thought. Consequently, it demanded more institutional independence within the Society of Jesus, that is, further separation from its sister mission to Japan, achieved with the establishment of the Vice-Province of China in 1619. With renewed optimism, the missionaries passed on a vision of progress to the next generation of China Jesuits. Further justification for this change of mood came with the appointment of the Peking priests to a project for reforming the imperial calendar. This was a substantial step forward, because the formal integration of the Jesuits at the capital into the state bureaucracy permitted their colleagues in the provinces to adopt more aggressive proselytizing strategies. By the 1630s, growing threats of foreign invasion and rising levels of popular anxiety created a fertile ground for their message. The combination of these factors meant that the Jesuits could finally stand on their own, stepping outside the shadow of their mandarin friends.

The Power of Patronage, 1608–1612

Over the course of the mission's first decades, the Jesuits came to learn the value of the friendships forged with individual mandarins. But they had come to China to make converts, not friends. They knew from a tactical point of view that if they could make Christians of their elite allies, both their religious message and their enterprise as a whole would benefit tremendously. Still, there was no guarantee that they could bridge the divide between friendship and conversion. Matteo Ricci and his colleagues knew well that there were a few mandarins whose interest in *Tianxue*, or Learning from Heaven, surpassed that of their peers. These four men, Xu Guangqi (*jinshi* degree 1604), Li Zhizao (*jinshi* 1598), Yang Tingyun (1557–1627, *jinshi* 1592), and Wang Zheng (1571–1644, *jinshi* 1622), were members of the bureaucracy who had passed the metropolitan examinations. Of them, Li and Xu reached the highest levels of the civil service, with Xu becoming an Imperial Grand Secretary toward the end of his life. Crucially for the Jesuits, the men decided to embrace Christianity, receiving the baptismal names Paulo (1603), Leão (1610), Miguel (ca. 1611), and Felipe (1616), respectively.[1] These elite converts became the mission's primary protectors and promoters, publishing books in defense of Christian doctrine and Western learning, and displaying their friendship with the Jesuits.

More than just a stratagem for gaining political cover, Ricci's plan of winning mandarin allies had another purpose. He wanted Christianity to be carried around China in the luggage of traveling literati, and his first elite converts were ideal candidates. Like all members of the mandarinate, these men were only temporary residents of the capital. As bureaucrats, they took up posts in distant provinces; as filial sons, they were compelled by custom to return to their hometowns upon the death of their parents. Because their adoption of Christianity was made all the more significant by their high social standing, the Society of Jesus could not forgo the opportunity to accompany them on their travels. From their base at Peking, the Jesuits synchronized themselves with the internal dynamism of the Ming state. Fortunately for them, the end of the first decade of the seventeenth century was a propitious time for letting the movements of mandarin allies determine the paths of the mission's expansion.

The Jesuits' first chance came in 1608 upon the death of Xu Guangqi's father. In keeping with tradition, Paulo had to return to his home in Shanghai for three years of mourning. Knowing that Ricci could not leave the capital, Xu requested that one of his subordinates visit him and possibly open a residence. In September of that year, Lazzaro Cattaneo left Nanjing for Shanghai, where he stayed for two months receiving curiosity seekers, including many of Xu's literati friends, as well as common people and members of the Buddhist and Daoist clergy. Cattaneo found the local people to be "smart and happy," with the city folk more "wily" than their simpler counterparts in the surrounding countryside.[2] But although the Jesuit mission in Shanghai would later account for over a third of all Chinese converts, this initial stay yielded only a modest foretaste of later success. Cattaneo claimed forty-two new Christians—in his words, "very few for such a vast field." To explain his meager harvest, he acknowledged, among other obstacles, "the doubts and fears that circulate about us everywhere."[3]

While the Jesuits did not establish a new mission in Shanghai in 1608, they endeavored to open a residence somewhere in the Jiangnan area outside of Nanjing. They waited three years until, at the insistence of Yang Tingyun and Li Zhizao, they settled in Hangzhou, a thriving metropolis four days' journey from the smaller city of Shanghai. Both Miguel and Leão were from Hangzhou and readily proffered protection and financial support to the Jesuits. In order to strengthen the missionary endeavor in coastal Jiangnan, Ricci sent Nicolas Trigault (1577–1628), a newly arrived priest from the Southern Netherlands, together with a Chinese coadjutor to aid Cattaneo. After a bout of sickness forced the missionaries back to Nanjing, Cattaneo returned to Hangzhou with other companions in 1612 to lay firmer foundations there. In this way, the missionaries fulfilled the objectives that lay at the heart of Ricci's strategy for inaugurating missions in new areas. They established a small community of religious whose public association with influential figures granted them both legitimacy and visibility.

Once inside the complex world of late Ming literati social relations, the Jesuits became closely linked to the public identities of their patrons. Sympathizers with Learning from Heaven emerged from the ranks of the Jiangnan literati (as did critics), especially since the missionaries' message reached beyond the realm of intellectual affinities and into the domain of religious doctrine. Yang and Li's prestige brought the first Hangzhou Jesuits throngs of visitors predisposed to be impressed with their teachings. The mandarins were well-known supporters of *Tianxue;* accordingly, the greater the complexity of the teachings transmitted by Cattaneo and his colleagues, the better for Yang and Li. But this formula came at a price for the missionaries, since too many hours spent discoursing with their hosts distracted them from preaching the gospel. As a result, the Jesuits refused Li's initial offer of a set of apartments inside his palace, choosing a rented house instead. "We were afraid," wrote Feliciano da Silva (1579–1614), "that Doctor Leão would busy us with translating philosophy books and thereby upset the work of conversion that was the goal and primary fruit for which we had come."[4]

In their promotion of Learning from Heaven, these Christian mandarins at the same time implicitly and explicitly criticized Chinese religious traditions, exacerbating the antagonism between the Jesuits and the Buddhist and Daoist clergy. In late Ming Jiangnan, where gentry and mandarins lavished patronage on religious establishments, the newly forged bonds between the Europeans and rich members of the elite provoked clerical ire.[5] Moreover, ever since Matteo Ricci had come to his first unfavorable conclusions about the "bonzes" and the "tausus," the Jesuits spared no invective in their published writings on native religious traditions. And since this handful of renowned literati appended prefaces and dedications to such attacks, the missionaries' writings reached greater audiences. The Jesuits surely relished the chance to confront adversaries on religious matters, especially with mandarins in their corner. Their establishment in Hangzhou, according to a frank admission by Niccolò Longobardo, who took over as mission superior upon Ricci's death, was part of this struggle. When the Buddhist clergy boasted that the priests would abandon their converts and return to Nanjing, they felt obliged to stay.[6]

Matteo Ricci breathed his last in May 1610, but the radiance of his renown continued to be of service to the mission. Certain of the founder's fame—greatly increased at the moment of his passing by the crowds of visitors who came to pay their last respects—his assistants Diego de Pantoja and Sabatino de Ursis (1575–1620), with the help of some mandarin friends, submitted a petition to the Wanli emperor for a burial site near Peking.[7] When their request was granted, accompanied by a proclamation praising the virtues of this illustrious foreigner, the Jesuits had proof of imperial favor that they could broadcast throughout the empire—even if it was customary for the Chinese state to offer burial sites and boilerplate eulogies for ambassadors who died in China. From the Jesuits' perspective, this gesture signaled their firm establishment at the capital, since they could now refer to their—Confucian—duty to take care of an ancestor's tomb in seeking to justify their continued presence there. João Rodrigues (1561–1633), a veteran of the Japan mission, went so far as to assert that Ricci had accordingly done "more with his death than with his life."[8]

Scholars tend to see Matteo Ricci's passing as the end of the mission's foundational period. Such a view, however, has exaggerated the link between this prominent Jesuit and the China enterprise as a whole, distracted attention from the smooth transition of leadership to Niccolò Longobardo, and relegated to obscurity the growth in missionary numbers that followed quickly after 1610.[9] In 1613 alone, four arrivals brought the total of European missionaries in China to fifteen. This second generation would carry on the work that Ricci had begun, filling in when older missionaries died or could no longer bear the burdens of their tasks, and benefiting from the praise and protection bestowed on them as Li Madou's companions.

The change in leadership brought new energy and ideas to the China mission. It also adjusted the balance between the academic pursuits that had been the founder's forte and the proselytizing efforts of the missionaries in the provinces, shifting slightly in favor of the latter. In other words, upon Ricci's death the expansion of their Christian communities became the Jesuits' foremost concern. For the first time, official reports sent back from the mission to Europe began to record tallies of converts that passed the thousand mark.[10]

Just how many Chinese Christians were there? This question has plagued the Jesuits' enterprise since its early years, for many observers have taken numbers as the only true yardstick of success. If seen in this light, the mission was a splendid failure, as the total population of China grew from roughly 260 million in the late Ming period to roughly 310 million in the early Qing.[11] In order to gauge the fluctuations of the mission, it is necessary to have some means of measuring the relative size of the Jesuit enterprise in the different Chinese regions. Yet almost all of the relevant information comes from missionary pens. Depending on the type of report examined, the number of Christians varies, typically in proportion to the size of the intended audience in Europe. Modest estimates appear in internal Jesuit correspondence. Larger numbers are found in more public documents, such as the Annual Letters that were written to be read aloud at mealtimes in the Society's colleges in Europe. The biggest tallies appear in printed reports, since their circulation had the three-pronged aim of edifying the readers, boosting the Jesuits' fame, and attracting financial donations from pious laymen.

By taking the nature of the sources into account, one can estimate the size of the Jesuits' Christian communities at regular intervals. Frequently, they tell only of the numbers baptized each year, not the total number of Christians. Moreover, Jesuit sources rarely give figures for the apostasies that were part and parcel of any missionary enterprise. Nicolas Standaert's careful attempt to trace the Chinese church's growth by compiling the totals provided in both printed and manuscript sources nonetheless confirms accelerating growth in the numbers of Christians during these years: from 1,000 converts in 1606, to 2,500 in 1610, to 5,000 in 1615.[12] Although small in comparison with the rapid pace of expansion and the numbers previously achieved in Japan—or later claimed in China—the eagerly awaited improvement in the tallies from the Ming empire was greeted with much enthusiasm in Macau, the Estado da Índia, and Catholic Europe.

Facing the "Ministers of Satan," 1612–1618

With Matteo Ricci buried at Peking and mandarin converts openly patronizing the missionaries in Jiangnan, the Jesuits' fears of imminent expulsion had been allayed. Mission superior Longobardo went so far as to claim in the 1612 Annual Letter to the Superior General of the Society of Jesus (and all others who read or heard his words) that the missionaries would never be expelled from the Chinese empire.

In the fashion of a professor of logic at a Jesuit college, Longobardo gave three arguments to demonstrate why his prognosis was "very probable." First, Diego de Pantoja and Sabatino de Ursis were allowed to remain in Peking after Ricci's death and continued to receive the state pensions of their former colleague. As they were prized for their mathematical and technical knowledge, Longobardo could claim that "the King enjoys our being in China" and that "there are always favorable mandarins who assist and defend us." The mission superior's other reasons were based on his perception of the Jesuits' place in Chinese society. He pointed to what he took to be Chinese raison d'état, asserting that the Ming rulers were averse to expelling foreigners who had gained inside knowledge about the empire. Citing the fact that Muslim traders in Shaanxi Province were not permitted to leave China after nine years, Longobardo contended that the Jesuits' thirty-year stay would surely prevent their expulsion. Finally, at the most general level, he averred that the fruit of so many years' residence had given the Jesuits a fine-tuned sensitivity to Chinese "tastes and humors." Proof of this assertion could be seen in the missionaries' many friends who, Longobardo stated, "truly know, love, and favor" them. He confidently concluded that even if persecutions were to impede the course of preaching the gospel, at worst "they will only send us from one place to another, or put us in prison; but they will not throw us out of China."[13]

Despite Longobardo's confidence, the Jesuits still faced a serious problem that had dogged their mission since the 1580s. This was their necessary relationship with the Portuguese at Macau—a tie which ensured that not just mail but also money and manpower were funneled into China. After fourteen years of living at Shaozhou, Longobardo was well aware of the tensions between the colony's merchants and the Canton mandarins, who were wary of Portuguese smuggling activities and links to the Japanese. To be sure, dealing with the Europeans was a complex matter for the Ming government, since its primary aim was to exercise as much control as possible over an unruly trading zone. Neither permitting the Portuguese greater access to the Chinese interior nor destroying their settlement was a viable option to those officials most familiar with southern China. Sensing a climate of mandarin anxiety and popular suspicion—in part based on the fact that the colonists had armed ships and no qualms about dealing with unsavory merchants—Longobardo informed his superiors that "all of China is scared of the Portuguese."[14]

Whether or not Longobardo was aware of a plan outlined by the governor general of Guangdong and Guangxi provinces in 1612 to set strong restrictions on the coastal areas around Macau and apprised of the debates that it sparked in Peking remains unclear. It is also difficult to ascertain how many mandarins were sure of the Jesuits' connection to the Portuguese in the first fifteen years of the seventeenth century.[15] But in 1611, when Longobardo was at Peking, Xu Guangqi informed him on three occasions that some mandarins had denounced the Jesuits as "people from Macau." When the mission superior asked this friend if he should come clean about his links to the colony, he was advised against it, since the missionaries had everything to lose. Yet despite urging caution, Xu also informed the Jesuits that although a number of mandarins knew that they depended on Macau, they had chosen to dissimulate.

In the end, Longobardo instructed his subordinates to proceed with caution and secrecy, avoid going to Macau if possible, and have nothing to do with the colony in public. Trusting his own vigilance to avoid having the Ming authorities "close the door on us" and prevent more missionaries from getting into the empire, he returned to Guangdong in 1613.[16] In view of his fears of an official backlash and popular hostility, however, Longobardo decamped that same year from Shaozhou to Nanxiong, the last town inside the border with Jiangxi Province.

Given the administrative structure of the missionary enterprises of the Society of Jesus in East Asia, the China Jesuits faced a nearly impossible challenge when they tried to distance themselves from the Portuguese. For one thing, they were dependent on the Japan mission for their financial support (although this funding was unreliable). The China mission was an administrative appendage of its sister enterprise, meaning that its official business had to be approved by superiors in Macau and Nagasaki. During the foundational period, Ricci and Longobardo had been confronted with numerous situations that demanded immediate resolution, yet their subordinate position within the Jesuit hierarchy prevented them from taking many decisive actions. Only the high esteem they enjoyed in Alessandro Valignano's eyes kept their concerns visible to the Society's officers outside China, but this intercessor had died in 1606.

Faced with a grave political conjuncture in 1612, Niccolò Longobardo felt that the mission's only remedy was to sever its ties to the Province of Japan. To this end, he appointed Nicolas Trigault as procurator and sent him to Rome the next year with orders to petition the Society's Superior General to split the East Asian missions in two. Longobardo, frustrated by the lack of response on the part of the Visitor and the Japan Provincial, chose to address his order's highest authority directly in order to move out from the shadow of Japan. If that was to happen, the China superior claimed, the Superior General needed to learn of the true state of the mission, as seen from the inside, and create a new province.[17] This move would entail endowing the China enterprise in such as way that it could truly be independent of Macau. In other words, the procurator's trip was to be a fundraising and publicity tour of Catholic Europe.[18]

By sending Trigault, Longobardo also sought to expose how the China mission's subordination to its counterpart in Japan had positively hampered his and his colleagues' proselytizing efforts. He boldly claimed that despite years of neglect from its superiors in Nagasaki, the Chinese enterprise had grown to five residences and "could open another five in other provinces with the greatest of ease."[19] Longobardo further justified his idea of splitting the missions by reiterating his confidence about the Jesuits' status within China. In contrast to the sense of security he felt at Nanxiong, he uncannily ventured that a bright future was "not certain in Japan"—only two years before the onset of the bloody Tokugawa era persecutions.[20]

Longobardo's predictions about the precarious situation in Japan came to fruition with Shogun Tokugawa Hidetada's 1614 edict banishing all Catholic priests from that country. Adding to the difficulties that the China missionaries had with their superiors outside the Ming empire, there now came a flood of Jesuit exiles from Japan. The College of Macau became the Japan mission's headquarters in exile, and as a result, the concerns of Longobardo and his colleagues were shelved. By the summer of

1615, wrote Lazzaro Cattaneo, the affairs of the mission's five residences and eighteen Jesuits were "very poorly governed and provisioned even worse," all owing to the turmoil in Japan and Macau. In a letter to the Society's Superior General, he echoed Longobardo's sentiments by claiming that "it would be much better for this mission if our immediate superior were absolute."[21]

The expulsion of the Jesuits from Japan also spurred the China missionaries to reaffirm the terms of their stay within the Ming empire. Assuming that the principal weakness of his confreres had been the fragility of their relationship with the Japanese hegemons, Longobardo proposed that the Jesuits make a direct appeal to the Wanli emperor. Fearing that those he dubbed "the ministers of Satan" might also seek to expel the missionaries from China as they had done in Japan, he consulted with his colleagues about the viability of asking for more explicit terms for their stay in the empire. Longobardo's plan was to offer a set of luxurious European commodities and a synopsis of Christian doctrine (including a protestation about how the missionaries harbored no seditious intents) to the throne, and then to wait for some form of recognition.[22]

But while the mission superior looked south to Macau for problems and north to Peking for solutions, he glossed over the troubles brewing between missionaries and mandarins in the heart of the empire. The Jesuits were therefore caught off guard when Shen Que (1565–1624), the vice minister of the Nanjing Ministry of Rites, launched an attack against them. Much ink has been spilled in the attempt to explain the events known as the Nanjing affair (sometimes called the Nanjing persecutions), which occurred between 1616 and 1623, by Chinese brushes and European quills in the early modern period no less than by Western and Asian scholars in the modern age. Only recently have historians attained an understanding of these events that moves beyond presenting the views of the protagonists.[23] For the Jesuits, these events were a calamity, and their writings from the time in question clearly echo their worry over the fate of the mission. Conversely, in the view of their Chinese adversaries, the missionaries deserved nothing but derision and disdain. There was no sparing of derogatory names from the literati lexicon. If one looks beyond the surface and within the long-term conspectus of the Jesuit enterprise, however, it appears that Shen Que's attacks were not fatal to the mission. They do not seem to have had any effect other than to check its growth temporarily.

The initial accusations brought against the Jesuits at Nanjing contained a laundry list of complaints that decried them as unorthodox—that is, not adhering to the Confucian worldview—or as subversive. Seen through the prism of Chinese law, the missionaries were easy targets. To be sure, they had played fast and loose with the native symbolic register by passing themselves off as foreign literati who had come to learn China's moral teachings. The Jesuits also dealt in the soft currency of ambiguity when they tried to use secular skills and learning to achieve religious goals, thereby crossing a line that more than a few mandarins saw as a clear boundary. Their apologetic texts on *Tianzhu jiao* at times further obscured their foreign origins, with the Jesuits trying so hard to make their message palatable to Chinese scholars that it was stripped of much of its European savor—giving many literati readers and even some converted mandarins the impression that the Christian message differed only slightly from Confucian thought.[24] Although it had worked well, this strategy was not foolproof, as the Jesuits found out in 1616 at Nanjing, which was still a capital like Peking. The missionaries felt that they could comport themselves there as if in a provincial city, that is, without the reserve of their confreres at the northern court. It should come as no surprise, then, that if the contradictions about the Jesuits' Chinese persona were to be exposed, it would happen where adversarial political forces had the most power.

In spite of the institutional decay of the late Ming state, the disengagement of the Wanli emperor from the business of government, and the high degree of factionalism in the Jiangnan area, officials such as Shen Que who served at Nanjing could effectively impose their version of Confucian orthodoxy. The actions of this senior official from the Ministry of Rites (which was charged with maintaining orthopraxis, as well as managing the affairs of foreigners in China) can be understood as one of the variety of literati responses to the late Ming political situation. The same climate of anxiety that led men such as Xu Guangqi and Yang Tingyun to adopt the Teachings of the Lord of Heaven inspired some of their contemporaries to turn to stricter interpretations of Confucian orthodoxy or to encourage the reinvigoration of lay Buddhism.[25] That the Jesuits had become the allies of men who appeared to constitute a rival literati faction, the followers of *Tianxue,* or appeared to be seducing commoners like heterodox sects such as the White Lotus movement, made them worthy of official attention—especially as the missionaries became more antagonistic toward the Buddhist clergy or showed undue arrogance, born of a false sense of security, toward members of the Chinese elite.[26]

Shen Que submitted his first memorial denouncing the missionaries at the two imperial capitals in the summer of 1616. Historians have disputed his motivations, but it appears that he moved primarily with the intention of making a display of the proper way to uphold orthodoxy in the public arena. It is also likely that Shen harbored a personal resentment toward some of the Jesuits, their religious teachings, and their mandarin protectors. In his denunciations, found in three distinct documents, he charged the missionaries with illegally residing in Peking and Nanjing and "injuring the imperial influence."[27] It is worth recalling that when Matteo Ricci had first tried to settle at Nanjing two decades earlier, his mandarin friends warned him that foreigners could not reside at either capital.

Using stock phrases from the language of orthodoxy, Shen Que enumerated the ways the Jesuits menaced the Ming state. Most important, their novel teachings on astronomy threatened to corrupt Chinese traditions.[28] In addition, they elided the difference between Chinese and barbarians by adopting the manners and dress of the literati. They held secret meetings in the manner of proscribed groups. They gained conversions through bribes. They confused the common people. They practiced alchemy. They acted as spies on behalf of the Portuguese at Macau. They owned a residence close to the imperial palace and tomb of the Ming dynasty's founder at Nanjing, where they encouraged sedition. They had illegally acquired houses in other provinces for the same purposes. Finally, they had usurped the words "Heaven" and "Great" from the emperor to describe their God and their homeland.[29]

Shen Que contended that the best way to restore orthodoxy was to expel the Jesuits from the imperial capitals, denounce their pernicious influence, and undo the harm they had done to the social order. As soon as his memorial was favorably received at the Peking Ministry of Rites, he ordered the municipal authorities to seize the members of the foreign sect and their leaders. By September 24, twenty-three local Christians were imprisoned in Nanjing, along with Alfonso Vagnone, Álvaro Semedo (1585–1658), and two Chinese Jesuit coadjutors. Despite memorials written by Xu Guangqi and the Peking Jesuits in defense of Vagnone and Semedo, a final verdict came from the throne on February 3, 1617. It decreed that they and their confreres at Peking, Sabatino de Ursis and Diego de Pantoja, were to be shackled inside wooden cages and carted to Canton, from whence they would be sent to Macau and onward to the West.

As for their residences in the capital cities, the Peking house was shuttered and the Nanjing residence dismantled. The proceeds from the sale of its timbers were used for restoring the shrine of a set of Confucian martyrs and the tomb of a king of Brunei—Shen's statement of proper reverence to the state and the correct relationship between Chinese and foreigners.[30]

As soon as the missionaries in the provinces heard of the fate of their four colleagues at the two capitals, they went into hiding in their converts' homes. Once the expulsion edicts were made public, the provincial residences were also closed. One important measure of the limits of Shen Que's power—or perhaps of his will or motivations—was that his attack was not felt strongly beyond the city limits of the capitals. Fearful of further repercussions, however, the remaining Jesuits stayed underground. But in partial vindication of Niccolò Longobardo's earlier claim, they were not expelled from the empire. Nevertheless, the Society's superiors at Macau saw yet another baroque tragedy unfolding before their eyes to match the running drama of the Japan mission. Commenting on the extraordinary twist of fate that had befallen the Jesuits in both Japan and China, Visitor Francisco Vieira (1555–1619) wrote in 1617: "It serves Our Lord that of the 5 houses and 5 churches that we had in China, and the more than 120 that we had in Japan, today not one house nor one church do we have in which to gather and breathe."[31]

Despite the virulence of Shen Que's attack against the court Jesuits, the shadow of their mandarin allies was long enough to preserve the mission. While the Nanjing vice minister of rites was denouncing the Europeans, Yang, Li, and Xu were busy printing up defenses of *Tianxue* and its exponents. Yang confronted the accusation that Christianity was akin to heterodox sects like the White Lotus or Non-Action movements in a pamphlet titled *Xiaolun bu bingming shuo,* or "The Owl and the Phoenix Do Not Sing Together" (1616).[32] And beyond maneuvering to block the publication of the edicts against the missionaries in their Jiangnan hometowns, the Jesuits' friends offered to shelter them. In light of Visitor Vieira's order that no priest leave China alive unless captured and bound—the bit of wisdom gained from most Jesuits' willing departure from Japan—the missionaries secretly made their way to Yang's palace at Hangzhou by 1618.[33] For the next five years, while Shen remained in power, the fourteen Jesuits who stayed in China (eight European priests and six Chinese coadjutors) kept a low profile, seeking, as one Jesuit put it, "to avoid giving our accuser another reason to bark at us."[34]

New Portents from Afar, 1619–1623

The greatest immediate consequence of the Nanjing incident, seen from the Jesuits' perspective, was that the missionaries were largely cut off from their nascent communities of neophytes while they waited for the authorities' wrath to ebb. In their writings from the period until 1623, the year they left Hangzhou, the Jesuits saw their Christians reliving the trials of the Primitive Church. The missionaries lauded the "valor and constancy" of their followers, describing how they had retained their faith and aided their sequestered pastors.[35]

While the Christians in Hangzhou and Shanghai benefited from the proximity of priests, those at the capitals were not so lucky. In Peking and Nanjing, however, the devotional groups that had been founded in 1609 and 1610 served as the principal mechanism for ensuring the cohesion of the Christian communities. When the Jesuits regained Peking, they learned that the local Christians had held their confraternity meetings "all this time, gathering on their appointed days to discuss the things of God in order to conserve themselves in the faith."[36] At Nanjing, the city's converts had been divided up into neighborhood groups, each with its own chapel. Christians congregated there on holy days, wrote Álvaro Semedo, "and after having recited their devotions held discussions and inspired one another to virtue."[37] Seeing how effectively such groups could defend the fledgling church, the Jesuits went on to encourage their formation almost everywhere they sparked conversions.

Yet given the central importance of the figure of the priest in early modern Catholicism, with his crucial role in dispensing the sacraments, the Jesuits resisted being cut off from their neophytes completely. During the heat of the Nanjing affair, they made extensive use of the Chinese men who had joined their ranks as coadjutors and had served the mission as catechists and couriers. Since these men could "go out at any time without anyone's noticing," claimed Manuel Dias the younger (1574–1659), they were best positioned to bring the Eucharist to the sick or to those who could otherwise not visit the priests. Nevertheless, Dias noted, when circumstances merited—"such as when they are about to die, or if they want to confess, or receive some other sacrament"—the priests went out to their Christians under the cover of darkness in closed sedan chairs.[38] As time went by, the Jesuits at Hangzhou ventured farther and farther from their base. By early 1618, João da Rocha had taken another priest and two

Chinese coadjutors to Jiangxi Province to "visit and reassure" the Christians there, settling in Jianchang. Likewise, Gaspar Ferreira, who had lived in the northern capital in Ricci's last years, spent some time in a town "two days' journey from Peking" and went to Nanjing to tend to the Christians and administer baptisms while Shen Que was still there. Other Jesuits also left Hangzhou for Shanxi, Huguang, and Guangdong provinces.[39]

Three years after the start of the Nanjing incident, the Jesuits felt that their time of trial was ending. Shen Que's reputation as a defender of orthodoxy moved him swiftly to the summit of the bureaucratic ladder, and he was promoted to Imperial Grand Secretary at Peking in 1620. While he remained a threat to the Jesuits until his death in 1624, he and the rest of the late Ming mandarinate were far more preoccupied with the troubles newly affecting northern China than with any problems that might arise from a handful of Westerners. To be sure, an official crackdown against White Lotus sectarians and rebels in Shandong Province in 1620–21 briefly rekindled the fires of persecution in Nanjing.[40] A far greater challenge to the Ming state came with the Manchu incursions into China that began about 1618 and were to culminate in the capture of Peking in 1644. Soon after the invasion of the Liaodong Peninsula, an area within striking distance of the imperial capital, fear and rumors spread throughout China. According to a group of terrified Chinese merchants who came to Macau in 1618, one Jesuit wrote to a friend in Europe, "even the Tartars' horses eat Chinese people, and 100,000 Chinese arrayed against them are scattered in a flash."[41]

Not surprisingly, the Jesuits had an alternative reading of these Manchu raids. They were clearly a manifestation of divine justice, they claimed. From Macau, Alfonso Vagnone ventured that the Almighty "wants to give a great lashing to this kingdom for its many sins and, in particular, for having thrown out the preachers of the Gospel."[42] By coincidence, the new military menace was accompanied by a series of natural disasters and portents that exacerbated the climate of popular anxiety within the Ming empire. On top of famines and earthquakes, two comets appeared over China in November 1618. Seeing the nervousness of the Guangdong Province mandarins, Manuel Dias the elder at the College of Macau suggested that these signs could bode "something good for conversions." Elaborating the point, he claimed, "The Chinese are very quick to attribute similar portents to some fresh disorder in the kingdom, such as today's

banishment of the Law of God."[43] As a state of turmoil gripped the empire and its political and economic situation soured, the Jesuits regained confidence in their enterprise.

The missionaries' positive outlook was further brightened by the safe return of procurator Nicolas Trigault to Macau on July 22, 1619. His arrival heralded great changes for the mission in the form of new organization, manpower, and material support. Fortunately for Trigault, he had reached Europe before the worst news of persecution in Japan and China, so the tenor of his trip matched the optimism of the years before Shen Que's attack. Trigault disembarked with seven new priests, money for the cash-strapped residences, a cache of devotional objects for the Chinese Christians, costly presents for mandarin allies and the emperor, and a valuable European library to be used for making an impression on the literati. The most important elements, however, were the recruits from Portugal, Germany, and Italy. Together they formed a band that would be responsible for the mission for the next four decades: João Fróis (1591–1638), Rodrigo de Figueiredo (1594–1642), Simão da Cunha (1587–1660), Francisco Furtado (1589–1653), Johann Adam Schall von Bell (1592–1666), Johann Terrenz Schreck (1576–1630), and Giacomo Rho (1592–1638).[44]

Trigault also brought orders from the Roman headquarters of the Society of Jesus that created an administrative divide between the East Asian missions. From 1619 on, the China mission had greater independence from the withering Japan mission and was renamed the Vice-Province of China.[45] Because of its small number of priests, its lack of a central place built on the model of the Society's colleges, and its dependence on exterior sources of funding, it was not designated a full-fledged province. Rather, this change put a new hierarchy in place for the China mission without completely divorcing the two Asian missions. Most important, the finances of the Japan and China enterprises remained intertwined. The fact that many of the endowments of property or customs duties in Maritime Asia made by the Portuguese crown and European merchants before 1600 had been earmarked simply for "the missions in Asia" further complicated matters.[46]

Peter Paul Rubens, *Portrait of Nicolas Trigault in Chinese Costume.* This portrait was executed during Trigault's visit to Antwerp as mission procurator in 1617.

This separation gave the China mission a more coherent internal structure, one that would remain in place into the eighteenth century. By permitting direct governance by experienced missionaries familiar with China, it paved the way for the mission's subsequent growth. The new organization had a superior officer, the Vice-Provincial, who would rely on a number of consultors (typically four or five senior Jesuits) to run the mission's affairs, distributing supplies and salaries, visiting the residences to ensure that every Jesuit lived according to the Society's *Constitutions,* and making personnel catalogues that contained evaluations of each missionary for use in promotion decisions. The first priest appointed Vice-Provincial was João da Rocha, but his death in 1623, as the Jesuits moved to reestablish the mission, meant that the office was transferred to Manuel Dias the younger. These men were subordinate to the Visitors, the heirs to Alessandro Valignano's office, who resided at Macau and were typically drawn from the ranks of senior missionaries in East Asia.[47]

The news of this divide came as yet another crushing blow for the members of the Japan mission despairing in exile at Macau. Where Longobardo and the other China Jesuits saw greater administrative efficiency and missionary effectiveness, their confreres saw betrayal. In light of the Nanjing affair but also in defense of their corporate interests, the Japan Jesuits decried the separation as precipitous and potentially harmful—clearly the handiwork of audacious, inexperienced upstarts. According to the opinion of "all of the elder men of this province," wrote Visitor Francisco Vieira, the split would be "the total ruin of the China mission."[48] As the Society's Japan enterprise was slowly dismembered, leaving a richly endowed college filled with frustrated missionaries, the friction between the two sets of Jesuits acted as a brake on the China mission.

Their hands freed, the senior China Jesuits and the Visitors at Macau devised new regulations for the mission based on forty years of collective experience. The compendium of rules they issued in 1621 delineated the obligations of all members of the Vice-Province from the superior to the coadjutors. It addressed a range of issues from the use of trade to support the mission, to the proper way of writing Chinese characters, to how the priests should wear their hair. The duties of the Vice-Provincial were outlined, indicating when he was to defer to the Visitor or Japan Provincial in personnel and financial matters. Jesuits serving as residential superiors were instructed how to maintain their houses, allot food rations, and regulate communal spiritual life. Individual priests were exhorted to study local customs so as to avoid provoking scandal and were told to keep regular devotional schedules. Coadjutors were instructed to maintain a courteous rapport with the Christians in their communities and to catechize neophytes. The rules also obliged the Jesuits to elaborate a system for teaching Chinese language and thought to newly arrived missionaries.[49]

The 1621 rules for the Vice-Province also included recommendations intended to unify the Jesuits' methods for propagating Christianity. They standardized pastoral issues such as the proper way to conduct rural missions, the use of the Portuguese liturgical calendar, and the correct way to teach baptismal names to converts to avoid mispronunciation. One major point of contention that was resolved in the rules—as a result of negotiations between Rome, Macau, and the China Jesuits—was the use of science as a means not only for spreading Christianity but also for defending the mission.

According to Sabatino de Ursis, one of the missionaries at Peking, the Jesuits had been strongly divided over whether they should devote part of their time to composing books or holding discussions on secular themes. The flashpoint of this debate was the proper place of mathematics and morality—instead of the gospel—at the Peking residence. Well aware of how Western astronomical ideas had made it into Shen Que's litany of unorthodox Jesuit teachings, a group of priests at Macau led by Japan Provincial Valentim de Carvalho (1559–1630) and Visitor Francisco Vieira labeled Matteo Ricci's policies a distraction. Diego de Pantoja, one of the Peking Jesuits, seconded their opinion that such activities were unfitting for professed members of a religious order. With Ricci gone, however, the defense of *Tianxue* rather than *Tianzhu jiao* fell to Niccolò Longobardo and the other senior China missionaries. Despite the claims of several modern scholars, Longobardo encouraged the use of mathematics, cartography, and morality for attracting the Chinese to Christianity.[50] But he also had to manage his fractious subordinates at Peking, whose differences of opinion were laced with petty jealousy. According to de Ursis, Manuel Dias the younger, author of *Tianwen lüe* (Catechism on the Heavens, 1615), which included an appendix summarizing parts of Galileo's *Sidereus Nuncius* (1610), soured on the use of mathematics after a dispute over which men were assigned to live in the mission's two houses in Peking.[51] In his final adjudication, Superior General Claudio Aquaviva chose a middle path. The rules he approved contained provisions for the use of science, but with the caveat that it not consume a missionary's time entirely.[52]

The set of rules also shows how the Vice-Province's collective attitude toward the gradual creation of a Chinese church was formalized. The key elements of what has become known as the "Jesuit position" toward the Chinese Rites, in particular their approach toward Confucianism as a secular philosophy and their attitude toward ancestor worship, were decided by 1621. Understanding that it would take years, if not decades, to form Chinese Catholics who knew the boundaries between orthodoxy and "superstition," the Jesuits decided to raise the spiritual demands to be made on new converts incrementally. For instance, newly converted mandarins were permitted "for now" to perform the required ceremonies to Confucius, since these were merely "a sign of gratitude to a master." Likewise, when ordinary neophytes were given devotional images, they were to be instructed to display them "in another part far away" from any ancestor tablets in their homes. The Jesuits also agreed to refrain from telling the newly converted all of the spiritual obligations of European Catholics, such as the observances of feasts or fasts, "so as to not make our Holy Law very burdensome."[53]

In order to set the missionaries back on the path to legitimacy in late Ming society, the 1621 rules contained directives touching on the renewed promotion of *Tianxue,* or *Xixue,* Western Learning. One of the most important permissions was the right to publish books in Chinese. In Europe, Jesuit writings underwent a thorough process of revision, including inspections by the Inquisition and royal censors, before they appeared in print. In the absence of any external oversight capable of understanding Chinese, the missionaries were allowed to publish their writings after an internal review process.[54] By keeping control of the image of Christianity on the printed page in China, the Jesuits did much to make their translated version of Catholicism the familiar one that the Chinese knew in the early modern period.

Finally, the Vice-Province's founding statutes set out mechanisms to blunt the impact of future persecutions. Produced only five years after the outbreak of the Nanjing affair, they insisted on the creation of well-educated spiritual communities that could resist outside attacks. Although they conceded to Chinese lay catechists the right to baptize new Christians, they also ordered priests to examine new converts on basic doctrine. In light of the recurrent frustrations over the low numbers of Chinese Christians, it is somewhat surprising that the 1621 rules specifically warned the Jesuits against converting more people than the mission could handle.[55] By balancing the mission's limited manpower and financial resources, the superiors hoped that the Vice-Province would avoid the pitfall of simply increasing baptismal tallies at the expense of proper indoctrination.

A Difference from Times Past, 1623–1633

With new priests, fresh supplies, and a restored sense of unity and purpose, the Jesuits returned to the mission field in 1623 to bring to fruition the Vice-Province of China. The previous year, Shen Que retired from his post as Grand Secretary, and a reprise of the persecution in Nanjing ended, signaling to the Jesuits that they could emerge from hiding at Hangzhou to return to their communities and found new ones. Writing to Visitor Jerónimo Rodrigues (1567–1628) in April 1623, Manuel Dias the elder claimed that the time was ripe for the missionaries to spread out. It appears that their mandarin protectors were growing uneasy at the continued presence of so many Jesuits in their homes. Yang, Li, and Xu insisted on their departure, according to Dias, because of rumors of impending government crackdowns on literati factions in Jiangnan. "We are very noticeable," Dias wrote, "and whoever speaks against us, speaks against them for harboring us."[56]

In sending off their guests, the Jesuits' mandarin allies offered them advice for regaining the positions of respect they had once enjoyed. What they recommended is reminiscent of the main lines of Matteo Ricci's initial strategy for establishing the mission: Some Jesuits should try to establish themselves at Peking and form relationships with high imperial officials. The patronage of the powerful would encourage provincial authorities, who lived in fear of those higher up the bureaucratic ladder, to extend de facto tolerance to the Jesuits in their districts. As an added precaution, the rest of the eighteen Europeans and five Chinese coadjutors should fan out across the provinces "in the shadow of some local or retired mandarin, through whose intercession they can win friends."[57]

Li, Yang, and Xu also contributed materially to making this new strategy work. After the last flares of the Nanjing affair died down, Li Zhizao submitted a memorial to the Tianqi emperor (r. 1620–1627) proposing that the Europeans be summoned to the capital as technical advisers in the war against the Manchus. He lauded their abilities as mathematicians and experts in the design and construction of ordnance, and suggested that they bring with them a contingent of Portuguese infantry and artillerymen.[58] Although the Jesuits initially balked at this project's bellicose implications, Li conjectured that such a venture might win them commissions in the state bureaucracy. Manuel Dias the younger and Niccolò Longobardo therefore returned to Peking, where they discovered a new current of literati interest for both Learning from Heaven and the Teachings of the Lord of Heaven, in large part owing to Li and Xu's public praise for the Jesuits. Seizing the opportunity, some of Nicolas Trigault's recruits slipped into China from Macau "in literati costumes, with long beards, hair grown out and tied on their heads in Chinese fashion."[59]

Under the leadership of Vice-Provincial Manuel Dias the younger, who ran the mission from 1623 until 1635, the Jesuits returned to reinvigorate their old missions and begin new ones. To be sure, some new residences were opened before 1623—at Jianchang in Jiangxi Province in 1620, and at Shanghai two years later. The Jesuits' friendship with one of Xu Guangqi's disciples, Sun Yuanhua (1581–1632, *juren* 1612), led to his conversion in 1621 and the creation of another new mission station. When licentiate Inácio Sun invited Francesco Sambiasi (1582–1649) to his hometown of Jiading, he offered the Jesuits one of his palaces.[60] Owing to Jiading's proximity to Shanghai and its minute Christian community, the Vice-Province used this residence for training newly arrived priests in the Chinese language and Confucian philosophy during the 1620s.[61]

Outside of the Jiangnan region, Giulio Aleni (1582–1649) followed a converted literatus to Shanxi Province, where he founded a mission at Jiangzhou. The Christian community in this northern region was to become one of the largest in the Vice-Province after Alfonso Vagnone reentered the Ming empire in 1624 with a different Chinese name. Leaving northern China, Aleni headed to Fujian Province in the company of former Grand Secretary Ye Xianggao (1562–1627), a longtime friend of the Jesuits. Benefiting from Ye's prestige, he opened a residence at Fuzhou and began to preach in the coastal towns and cities. Nicolas Trigault headed to Henan Province in 1623 to establish a house at Kaifeng after visiting Wang Zheng in his hometown of Xi'an. Trigault's visit to the Chinese far west laid the foundations for a residence in that city as well.[62] In addition to setting up these new houses, the Jesuits also tried to enlarge their numbers of followers in the areas where they had been for years. From Hangzhou, they preached in rural Zhejiang Province, baptizing many and going so far as to christen the towns where converts lived with saints' names.[63] By spreading out its manpower, the Vice-Province expanded dramatically; by 1626 it counted ten houses, twice what it had prior to the Nanjing affair.

How was the nature of the China mission affected by the geographic expansion of the Vice-Province? As it distributed missionaries across the vast expanse of the Ming empire, the Society of Jesus placed an enormous amount of trust and responsibility in each. After all, Catholic religious orders in the early modern period were typically conceived of in terms of communal units. At one of the Society's colleges or professed houses, the constant presence of superiors kept the obligation to obedience forever before the eyes of their subordinates. Things were different in the overseas mission fields. But even when compared to the Jesuit enterprises in South America or India, the Chinese case was an extreme example of missionary independence. In order to staff the Vice-Province's far-flung residences, individual China Jesuits frequently lived alone, or with one other priest or coadjutor. Only at Peking and Shanghai were there ever under normal circumstances four or more Jesuits grouped together. Sheer distance and a lack of supervision meant that most of the priests were left to their own devices—and many of them doubtless preferred it that way. In fact, as will be seen, the most glaring examples of discord occurred when the Jesuits were forced to confront one another face to face. At those moments superiors could exercise authority directly, but their attempts to curtail the degree of independence encouraged by the very structure of the China mission were often futile. In this respect, the spread of the Vice-Province was a mixed blessing. While fulfilling the Jesuits' dream of propagating Christianity throughout China, it created administrative problems that later superiors would have to resolve if they were to bring about conformity among their subordinates.

The rapid growth of the mission also raised questions about how the Jesuits would be able to sustain their promising enterprise. Above all, they needed replacements, regular shipments of healthy, young priests. But the bad news from East Asia that had flowed to Europe starting in 1614 gravely affected the Vice-Province's supply chain, and the China mission continued to live in the shadow of Japan. Despite the rejuvenating effect of Trigault's recruits, by the 1620s its men were old by European standards. By 1626, in fact, eight of the mission's eighteen priests were older than fifty, and five were over forty.[64] Manuel Dias the elder put the situation of the Vice-Province to his superiors in stark terms: without new blood, the China mission would be "pierced through." At sixty-four, Dias could state unequivocally, "Here we are almost all old and dead."[65] Fortunately for the Vice-Province, some missionaries lived to prodigious ages; Manuel Dias the younger died at eighty-five and Niccolò Longobardo at eighty-nine.[66]

Why had the Jesuits been able to spread out so widely? Their erudite image, promoted via the printed word, was perhaps the main reason. Knowing the voracious reading habits of his peers, Xu Guangqi had recommended that the missionaries print "thirty thousand" copies of their works and distribute them throughout the empire. In this way, they would ensure that increasing numbers of literati found out about their teachings, helping the Jesuits to "win friends and credit." Publications could also change the minds of those mandarins who were aware of Shen Que's defamatory memorials but had never actually met any of the priests.[67] Acting on this suggestion, in the 1620s the Jesuits embarked on one of their most intense periods of composition and publication. Giulio Aleni, Francisco Furtado, Manuel Dias the younger, Alfonso Vagnone, and Niccolò Longobardo are the best known of the authors whose works appeared during this period, but almost all the China Jesuits were involved.

Yang Tingyun, Li Zhizao, and Xu Guangqi contributed to this publicity effort in various ways, writing prefaces and verifying that the Europeans' compositions had elegant style. Li helped them to spread the news about the discovery of the Nestorian Christian stele at Xi'an in the 1620s. By publishing the monument's inscription in 1625, the Jesuits hoped to counter their detractors' aspersions regarding the antiquity of Christianity and its acceptance in eighth-century China, during the Tang dynasty.[68] Other instances of collaboration included Yang's publication of a descriptive world atlas by Giulio Aleni, *Zhifang waiji* (Record of Countries Not Listed in the Record Office, 1623). Most important for the Jesuits' religious project, this book contained a lengthy description of Judea and "several chapters dealing with points of the holy faith."[69] Further publicity came from Wang Zheng, whose interest in mechanics spurred him to join Johann Terrenz Schreck in writing *Qiqi tushuo* (Illustrations and Explanations of Wonderful Machines, 1627).

The Jesuits also composed texts on Catholic doctrine and devotions to meet the spiritual needs of their neophytes. Perhaps the most important composition from this period was the *Tianzhu shengjiao nianjing zongdu* (Collection of Prayers for the Holy Teachings of the Lord of Heaven, 1628), a joint effort of many missionaries edited by Niccolò Longobardo. This book contained translations of many prayers as well as a number of spiritual essays adapted from the writings of the Spanish Dominican Luis de Granada (1504–1588).[70] In response to the elder Manuel Dias's claim that the Chinese Christians needed a guidebook "to know what and how" to confess, Giulio Aleni wrote his *Dizui zhenggui* (Correct Rules for Confession, 1627). Other treatises explained various elements of the faith, including the meaning of the mass, the lives of the saints, and the nature of the soul, matters about which Dias argued that the Christians knew "less than they should."[71] Texts such as Aleni's *Misa jiyi* (Explanation of the Mass, 1629), Alfonso Vagnone's *Shengren xingshi* (Lives of the Saints, 1629), and Francesco Sambiasi's *Lingyan lishao* (On the Soul, 1624) helped to remedy this lack while seeking to instill a desire for the sacraments.

With new printed reference texts available for distribution in the 1620s, the Jesuits moved to increase and diversify their followers' spiritual practices. During this first period of expansion, however, they were most successful at stimulating new forms of piety that most readily fit into established Chinese cultural categories. For example, the Jesuits encouraged the formation of charitable groups—a social phenomenon with deep Chinese roots that easily meshed with the Jesuits' brand of Catholic lay piety. From his residence at Jiangzhou in Shanxi Province, Alfonso Vagnone promoted forms of Christian charity as a complement to his preaching on the corporal and spiritual works of mercy. Pedro Duan Gun (d. 1641) organized a group to attend the funerals of his coreligionists. While the Jesuits claimed that he was moved to do this after hearing of European benevolent societies, such as the Portuguese Misericórdias or the Italian Monti di Pietà, Duan likely drew his inspiration from Buddhist or Confucian groups. He had mourning clothes made for twenty poor Christians, who processed "with lighted candles and rosaries in hand" to the local burial ground.[72] The nature of this group is revealed in its function: since they had renounced other religious practices, Christians had to invent new forms of piety that corresponded to Chinese cultural values, such as the importance of dignified funeral ceremonies.

Another example of the meshing of Chinese social and Christian religious practices can be seen in the missionaries' efforts to convert women. By printing up prayer books or doctrine manuals written in simple language, they hoped to project *Tianzhu jiao* into the domestic sphere—an area that by Chinese custom was off-limits to these foreign men. To this end, the Jesuits encouraged their female converts to recite prayers during their neighborhood work gatherings. Instead of gossiping while they spun, wove, and folded, reads the 1626 Annual Letter from the Vice-Province, the Christian women at Jiangzhou "go singing prayers to alleviate their labors." As a result, children also learned doctrine; even "three-and-a-half-year-old girls," the Jesuits contended, knew their prayers by heart "without mistaking a word." The vehicles for this progress included the prayer book just mentioned and João da Rocha's *Tianzhu shengjiao qimeng* (Instruction for the Young on the Holy Religion of the Lord of Heaven, 1619), a catechism in dialogue form. According to the Jesuits, the repetition of the prayers and lessons in these texts was frequent enough to make "the teachings of the Law of God so well known that even heathen women know them."[73]

Although the Jesuits spread their message with greater vigor than they had previously, their actions were conditioned by the contemporary political climate. As the decaying Ming state made its last attempt to impose its will on literati factions in the 1620s, the missionaries were forced to restrain their apostolic activities. In particular, they had to exercise caution when gathering Christians for mass or prayer meetings. To suspicious authorities, especially in the Jiangnan region, with its numerous secret societies and literati factions, such gatherings of foreigners and their followers might seem like seditious conventicles. That the Jesuits openly combined literati dress and religious ritual doubtless made them doubly suspect. Moreover, they had taken the term *hui* (association), used by literati factions and sectarian groups alike, to designate their prayer groups. The 1625 crackdown against the Donglin Academy, a large literati faction with a moralizing political agenda, therefore had the potential of destroying the mechanisms that powered the Jesuits' expansion.[74] In an attempt to root out the Donglin faction and other private groups deemed subversive, the missionaries reported, the Tianqi emperor forbade public gatherings and prohibited the unauthorized printing of "books on virtue, political or economic policy, or, in general, things that are new or strange to his kingdom."[75]

Even if the pace of the Ming state's collapse soon ran ahead of its repressive capacities, the Jesuits chose to err on the side of caution. Even as they sought to diversify the devotional habits of their Christians, they resisted the urge to form large new groups until the specter of official suspicion passed. At Jianchang in Jiangxi Province, for example, when Gaspar Ferreira founded a group, he called it simply "the Rosebush," avoiding the term *hui* in its name. He also tried to balance the Christians' desire for access to the sacraments with the thorny problem of attracting attention. Members of the group were required to pray the rosary daily, taking inspiration from the illustrated *Song nianzhu guicheng* (Method for Reciting the Rosary, 1619). In the manner of European Catholics who belonged to Jesuit devotional groups, they were to fast every Saturday and confess twice monthly. Those deemed worthy were invited to take the Eucharist once a month. As a defensive move, however, Ferreira instructed the group's members to visit his church by threes "so it cannot be perceived that many are coming."[76]

Although the men of the Vice-Province began to claim more converts in the late 1620s than at any previous time, the small number of missionaries, their wide geographic distribution, and their limited financial resources kept baptismal tallies low. To be sure, the Jesuits had only their powers of persuasion and the symbolic gravity of their public image as authority figures to win new adherents to *Tianzhu jiao.* Unable to produce scores of new Christians through coercion—as many of their counterparts could in areas under colonial dominion—the China Jesuits at best built their mission church one household at a time. They could not trumpet the triumphal march of the gospel that was expected by their superiors and supporters in Catholic Europe, especially in light of so much talk of mandarin allies and converts. At times the Jesuits' writings reveal the embarrassment they felt at their seeming ineffectiveness. In describing the newly founded Xi'an residence in Shaanxi Province in the 1628 Annual Letter, Rodrigo de Figueiredo reported disarmingly on Álvaro Semedo and Johann Adam Schall: "While we know that they have baptized some people, it seems it was such a small number that they did not dare to write any specifics about them for me to pass on."[77]

In far-off Rome and nearby Macau, Jesuit officials tabulated the Vice-Province's low numbers of converts with increasing concern. Their totals did little to balance the impression that many outside readers of the missionaries' reports came to: that, far from a religious enterprise, the China mission was an exercise in vanity, in which silk-robed Jesuits abandoned their vows of poverty and masqueraded as mandarins. The prescribed remedy for the ills of the young Vice-Province was an inspection. Visitor

André Palmeiro (1569–1635), a senior Jesuit with years of experience in Portugal and India, was sent to handle the task. In December 1628 he followed a contingent of Portuguese soldiers heading from Macau to northern China to assist the Ming army in its struggles against the Manchus. Beyond his intention to give the lie to the damning rumors and to resolve real internal problems, Palmeiro's goal was to discover why the Christian community remained so small "after so many years of work with such excessive expenditures."[78]

After visiting the residences at Nanxiong, Nanchang, Jianchang, Peking, and finally the houses in Jiangnan, Palmeiro arrived at his conclusions about the China enterprise. "The truth," he wrote to Superior General Muzio Vitelleschi, "is that there are few Christians, very few considering the many years during which so many priests have been occupied with them." In his estimation, after almost fifty years of missionary work, the total number of Chinese Christians did not reach six thousand. Yet Palmeiro was reluctant to blame the lack of adherents to his faith on either the priests' scant diligence or their "flight from trials." He averred that "they study, tire themselves, work, and seek occasions for making many Christians; for all that, they are few."[79]

The Jesuits' limited success, Palmeiro contended, was attributable to the latent xenophobia of the Chinese, which caused prospective converts "to be terrified and recoil from any foreigner." In his opinion, the type of relationship that the Jesuits had with their mandarin protectors was different from the bonds between the Society of Jesus and its patrons in Europe. In other words, the yawning cultural divide between China and Catholic Europe impeded the Jesuits from truly becoming part of Chinese society. Yet Palmeiro's claim rings hollow. If there had been such a degree of xenophobia against the Jesuits, they would never have attained the renown they enjoyed by the late 1620s. If they had not been able to overcome the hurdle of anti-foreign sentiment, they would certainly never have been granted permission to take part in the official project to reform the imperial calendar at Peking with Li Zhizao and Xu Guangqi in 1629. A better explanation for Palmeiro's conundrum may be that the recent memory of persecution and official crackdowns, coupled with the Ming state's frequent bureaucratic malfunctioning during the first three decades of the seventeenth century, created a climate of uncertainty about the future that led many to be suspicious of the Jesuits. The men of the Vice-Province would have to wait patiently until certainty returned—a realization about the inevitable collapse of the Ming dynasty and the ineluctable onslaught of the Manchu invaders—before the mission could expand in earnest.

At the end of his tour, in the summer of 1629, Visitor Palmeiro summoned the Vice-Province's consultors to Hangzhou to receive a new set of rules designed to update the 1621 regulations. These statutes touched on all aspects of Jesuit life, seeking to chart the course for the mission's future. With regard to the low tallies of conversions, Palmeiro offered words of encouragement. He recognized that "caution and circumspection in preaching the holy gospel" were essential but insisted that the Jesuits avoid "excessive fear." The Visitor also warned against antagonizing the Society's detractors or rivals in the religious arena. "Although such is good and necessary in the preaching of our holy law," he wrote, "do not attempt to refute the law of the idols [Buddhism] and that of the literati [Confucianism] with scandalous words." One should nevertheless not seek to cover up the uniqueness of the Christian message, Palmeiro maintained, by letting the Chinese believe that it is more or less the same as their native religions and philosophies. Instead, "they should be informed of their errors with modesty and prudence, so with new awareness they will give credit more quickly to the truth that we teach."[80]

The Visitor's decision to demand that his subordinates sharpen the dividing lines between Christianity and Confucianism was aimed at quelling a dispute that had been brewing among the missionaries for some time. In the years following the death of Matteo Ricci in 1610, Jesuits from the Province of Japan began to read through the published writings of their confreres in China. At the instigation of João Rodrigues, the foremost expert on Japanese language and culture among the missionaries, the Society's superiors in East Asia opened an inquiry into the Chinese terms employed to signify Christian concepts. Between 1613 and 1615 Rodrigues had traveled through China, visiting the mission's residences and speaking with literati Christians. These interviews, and other observations he made of the devotional practices permitted to Chinese Christians by some of his confreres, led him to the conclusion that the China Jesuits, even if unwillingly, were abetting idolatry.

The crux of Rodrigues's objections to the way that Ricci and his successors had promoted Christianity in the Ming empire rested on their use of dubious doctrinal terminology. The terms that caused the most problems were *Tian* (Heaven), *Shangdi* (Sovereign on High), *Tianzhu* (Lord of

Heaven), *Tianshen* (angels), and *Linghun* (soul). Writing to Superior General Claudio Aquaviva in 1616, Rodrigues made clear his view that his brethren in China had stumbled into error through their ignorance of the subtleties of Asian philosophy. He contended that the term employed for God (in this case *Tianzhu*) was "a very wicked one" that signified not the Almighty but rather "a famous deity among the Chinese." Rodrigues further argued that the terms for "soul" and "angel" were "pernicious and wicked," and that all of the books that had been printed by the missionaries up to that point should be emended or destroyed.[81] The only sure way to avoid ambiguity was to employ Latin terms with pronunciations transliterated into Chinese. This was the course of action that had been adopted in Japan, where an urge toward purity and orthodoxy led to the introduction of Latin or Portuguese terms into the Japanese doctrinal vocabulary in place of potentially ambiguous native terms. As far as their Japanese converts were concerned, "God" was "Deus," who was adored under that name by the baptized everywhere. In similar fashion, the Japanese word for "soul" was "anima" and the word for "Christian" was "Kirishitan."[82]

The Nanjing affair, following hot on the heels of the Jesuits' expulsion from Japan, presented the missionaries with an opportunity to discuss the issue of the controversial Chinese terms in greater depth. Among the four China Jesuits who were expelled to Macau there were strong differences of opinion. Ricci's erstwhile colleagues Sabatino de Ursis and Diego de Pantoja stood on opposite sides of the issue, and Alfonso Vagnone's forceful defense of the terms contrasted starkly with João Rodrigues's objections to them. Under the auspices of Visitor Francisco Vieira and the members of the Province of Japan at the College of Macau, the missionaries were invited to compose apologetic treatises in 1618. At that time, no final decision was taken on the issue because of the need to appeal to Rome for a conclusive judgment and on account of the recent split between the East Asian missions. In either case, once the substance of these debates became known to the missionaries at Hangzhou, they began to take sides on the basis of their appreciation of the Chinese literary canon.

When André Palmeiro reached Macau in 1626 to take up the office of Visitor, he found the tensions between the China Jesuits running high. Their disagreements over the disputed terms were not dictated by simple criteria such as nationality but rather arose from divergent readings of Chinese texts. The most important matter that divided them concerned the terms *Tian, Shangdi,* and *Tianzhu,* used to signify the Christian God. At issue was whether the references to *Tian* and *Shangdi* found in the writings of Chinese antiquity referred to more than the material heaven—and by extension, whether the Chinese had known of the existence of a creator God. As a result of the Macau debates over this issue, Superior General Muzio Vitelleschi wrote to the China Jesuits in August 1625 to prohibit the term *Shangdi*. The only priest permitted to reevaluate the controversy was his newly appointed Visitor.[83]

In order to repair the rifts between his subordinates, André Palmeiro gave his blessing to a conference held in 1627 at Jiading. But even this effort was to no avail. While almost all of the Jesuits agreed that the term *Tian* could not signify the Christian God, *Shangdi* presented more problems. In the opinion of several of the missionaries who were considered to be "most well read" in Chinese texts—Alfonso Vagnone, Giulio Aleni, Diego de Pantoja, Nicolas Trigault, and Rodrigo de Figueiredo—careful analysis had shown *Shangdi* to be admissible.[84] But the word's ambiguity, revealed in a series of interviews that Niccolò Longobardo had conducted with literati converts including Yang Tingyun and Li Zhizao (who showed confusion about the nature of their adopted Supreme Being), made it unacceptable to other missionaries.[85] Longobardo even insisted, with the backing of João Rodrigues and Brother Pascoal Mendes (1584–1640), that the term *Tianzhu* was freighted with idolatrous connotations and should also be banned.[86]

The Visitor stepped in to quell the controversy over the terms, but too late to avoid tragedy. The pitch of disagreement at the Jiading conference and afterwards had reached an extreme. João Rodrigues went so far as to upbraid Rodrigo de Figueiredo for his "most ardent" defense of *Shangdi*—an outburst that drove Palmeiro to impose a period of fasting on the interpreter from Japan. Rodrigues decided to take matters into his own hands by publishing a new doctrine primer at Canton, using different characters for Christian concepts.[87] On the other side of the dispute, Alfonso Vagnone contested Palmeiro's attempts to settle the issue. The Visitor reported to the Superior General in Rome that he felt tempted to recall Vagnone to Macau for insubordination but had stayed his hand in light of the mission's limited manpower.[88] As though this internecine strife were not enough, the dispute claimed one Jesuit's life. André Palmeiro discovered that the mentally unstable Trigault had committed suicide in 1628 in a fit of depression over his inability to defend conclusively the use of *Shangdi*.[89]

Jesuit Residences In China, 1630

• Cities with Jesuit Residences
○ Other cities

As a result of these events, the Visitor ordered that all discussion cease and the designation *Tianzhu* be used to signify God. The words *Tian* and *Shangdi* were to be struck from the Jesuits' lexicon of Chinese Christian terms.[90] Palmeiro also attempted to stifle any lingering discord among the missionaries by destroying all copies of Longobardo's report and Rodrigues's doctrine manual, imposing silence on Trigault's shameful death, and emending publications that had been marred by dubious terminology. To be sure, the Jesuits could not retrieve all the books they had distributed throughout China over the span of three decades. Instead, Palmeiro encouraged them to embark on a new publication effort in order to introduce approved texts into the corpus of Chinese writings by Jesuit authors. To this end, he expanded the Vice-Province's permissions with regard to revising and publishing books in China without outside ecclesiastical oversight.[91] These measures satisfied the China Jesuits, or so claimed Vice-Provincial Manuel Dias the younger in 1634, five years after Palmeiro's visit. Brimming with optimism at the new consensus, Dias declared that the controversy seemed completely resolved and that it would "never, or only in a long while, be spoken of again."[92]

André Palmeiro's 1629 reaffirmation of the China Jesuits' work augured well for the mission. During the following two years, six new missionaries entered the empire, bringing the total number of Jesuits to twenty-six. Twenty-one of these were European priests; five were Chinese coadjutors.[93] The recruits included Étienne Faber (1597–1657), Tranquillo Grassetti (1588–1647), Michel Trigault (1602–1667), Pietro Canevari (1596–1675), and Inácio da Costa (1603–1666). While the deaths of Johann Terrenz Schreck (1630) and Nicolas Trigault (1628) represented setbacks, the new arrivals brought fresh funding and provisions that enabled the Vice-Province to move forward. By 1631 the mission had eleven residences spread over eight of the fifteen imperial provinces: Peking, Jiangzhou (Shanxi), Xi'an (Shaanxi), Kaifeng (Henan), Shanghai (Jiangnan), Jiading (Jiangnan), Nanjing, Hangzhou (Zhejiang), Nanchang (Jiangxi), Jianchang (Jiangxi), and Fuzhou (Fujian). The Jesuits' tally of conversions also began to rise, with reports of larger groups asking for baptism. In 1630 Gaspar Ferreira claimed 260 baptisms in Jianchang alone, while in the Shanghai area Pedro Ribeiro recorded only 14 fewer.[94] The following year, the mission claimed a grand total of 1,786 baptisms, an increase of almost a third if Palmeiro's previous estimate of 6,000 Christians in the whole mission was valid.[95]

In the early 1630s, after half a century of missionary work, the China enterprise of the Society of Jesus finally came of age. Reflecting on the changes that had occurred since the crises of 1616–17, Álvaro Semedo noted that the mission's affairs had begun to proceed in a manner "very different from times past." In his opinion, the tumult of earlier years was the work of the Divine Gardener: "A mature tree is cut back so that it will spring forth again more vigorously, and more vibrantly."[96] Redoubling their efforts, the missionaries preached boldly and reaped the reward of more conversions. They strengthened their position at Peking by serving the throne through their assistance with the calendar reform project (1629–1635), burnishing their reputation as scholars who could make indispensable contributions to the welfare of the Chinese state.

The confidence and sense of security felt by the Jesuits at court were shared by their confreres in the provinces, enabling the Vice-Province to overcome the losses of almost all of the mandarin protectors who had repeatedly intervened to safeguard it. In 1627 both Yang Tingyun and Ye Xianggao died. Three years later Li Zhizao passed away. Caught in an imbroglio that ended with his condemnation for rebelling against the throne, Sun Yuanhua was beheaded in 1632. And in the following year Xu Guangqi died shortly after maneuvering to help the Jesuits get reestablished at Nanjing. All had used their influence at court, in the provinces, or in printed texts to protect and foster the mission in the preceding three decades. For the coming decades, the hometowns of these mandarins—Hangzhou, Shanghai, and Fuzhou—remained the centers of the Jesuit mission. But while the progeny of these illustrious men formed the cores of their local churches, the Jesuits would claim very few other high-ranking officials as converts in the future.

In the eyes of a number of modern scholars, the missionaries' failure to convert any more Grand Secretaries or other powerful figures was due to their inadequacy as Matteo Ricci's successors. They were neither diplomatic nor intelligent enough to win the hearts of the literati at the top of the cultural scale. One mode of argument tries to detect a series of national fault lines among the Jesuits, reasoning that the Portuguese priests who assumed control of the Vice-Province after 1623 were hampered by a "conquistador mentality" that prevented them from entering into meaningful dialogue with later mandarins.[97] This charge builds on another, the claim that the Jesuits had focused all along on converting the elite: "As the status of the literati converts dropped, the Jesuit effort began to falter."[98]

Another line of reasoning about the Jesuits' incapacity to produce a significant number of mandarin converts is rooted in explanations of the cultural climate among late Ming literati. To the scholars who support this view, the later years of the Wanli reign (roughly from 1590 until 1620) produced an openness to nontraditional thought systems, such as *Tianxue* or the Buddhist-Daoist-Confucian melding known as *Sanxue* (Three Teachings). During those three decades, disillusioned Chinese scholars were more willing to make a "desperate leap" into a foreign religion for the purpose of salvaging some of the fundamental values of Confucian teaching. Yet by the 1630s, as John Wills has claimed, that moment had passed.[99]

But if one looks at this phenomenon from a different perspective, it becomes apparent that by 1633 the Jesuits no longer needed the protection of such officials. Their strategy of winning powerful friends had achieved its purpose of legitimizing them in the eyes of the elite. During the mission's first fifty years, their reputation at Peking and throughout the empire had reached the point where they could dispense with courting individual mandarins. The Jesuits had concentrated on befriending authority figures primarily for the protection of their other, socially less important converts, who were at the mercy of potential persecutors. Once the missionaries themselves could guarantee the same protection by virtue of their standing at court, they focused on the more promising lower-class milieu in the provinces. Given the many impediments to elite conversions, this shift made sense. Although the Peking Jesuits would curry favor among successive emperors and eventually gain official recognition as directors of the Imperial Astronomical Bureau, they ceased counting on others for their protection. As the empire gradually descended into chaos and the Manchu forces loomed on the horizon, the Jesuits changed from protégés of the Ming elite into individuals capable of standing on their own.

3

Witnesses to Armageddon

In the 1630s, clouds of chaos swept across Ming China. In the words of António de Gouvea, a Portuguese Jesuit stationed at Hangzhou, God had sent "miseries, hardships, and calamities" to the empire as just punishment for its myriad sins. In the Vice-Province's Annual Letter for 1636, Gouvea alerted his readers in Europe to the dangers facing the mission. Hordes of bandits roamed the countryside, bloated "with the taste of loot." In the northern provinces, Manchu horsemen ran roughshod, "as if China were their homeland and property." These raiders carted off booty from towns and cities, telling the cowering officials "not to bother coming to look for them, because they would soon be back." Rebel armies sprang up across the empire. Hell-bent on exacting revenge from their mandarin oppressors, they left a swath of destruction behind them. In the ferocity and inhumanity with which these bands turned on their own countrymen, wrote Gouvea, they resembled "beasts more than men." The Ming forces marshaled to combat these threats were overwhelmed. In an opinion doubtless shared by other observers, the Jesuit declared that the mandarins in charge of the military were "better with brushes for writing than with lances for fighting." Upon hearing reports of military defeats, the Chongzhen emperor "turned many times to Heaven, offering sacrifices and gifts to calm it," but to no avail.[1]

In the midst of social unrest and upheaval that swallowed up the Ming dynasty, new problems and new opportunities were to be found for the Society of Jesus. During the dynastic transition period, the half-century from the first Manchu-led military raids inside the Great Wall in the 1620s until the pacification of the empire under the Qing in the 1670s, nearly every corner of China was touched by war, revolt, famine, and natural disasters. Paradoxically, the Jesuit enterprise experienced one of its steadiest periods of expansion while chaos reigned. From the early 1630s through the late 1650s, the Vice-Province spread into new regions and claimed ever greater numbers of conversions. It was a critical time for the Jesuits, who risked life and limb to lay stronger foundations for their mission church as the Ming state crumbled. In view of the political disintegration, they felt no fear of reprisals from Chinese authorities when they headed out to preach.

The Jesuits chose to ride out the tempest alongside their converts, and they suffered with them. As the last embers of conflict died, the missionaries tried to reassemble their dispersed communities amid the ruins. Too insignificant a social force to merit the attention of the Manchu conquerors, the Jesuits were again expanding the ranks of their followers by the time the new dynasty established control over its vast acquisitions. But in a changed climate filled with unknown perils, there remained a constant need: the Jesuits had to gain political legitimacy before the Qing. To achieve it, they stuck to their old strategy of offering their services at court. When a handful of Peking Jesuits became confidants of the first Manchu emperors, they won far greater rewards than they had gained under the Ming. In their shadow, the Vice-Province's expansion gained momentum, turning *Tianzhu jiao* into an identifiable, if minuscule, feature on the Chinese religious landscape.

Wiring the Mission's Circuits, 1633–1640

The 1630s witnessed the breakdown of the Ming state. In addition to the military menace that was amassing on the northern frontier, with increasingly daring raids by the composite army of Manchus, Mongolians, and Chinese in the service of the new "barbarian" dynasty that from 1636 called itself by the name of Qing, the Chongzhen emperor (r. 1627–1644) and his bureaucracy were beset with internal problems. The shift to a silver-based economy in the late sixteenth century had introduced tensions that, combined with perceived government failures and long-standing plebeian discontent, exploded in widespread peasant rebellions in the first decades of the seventeenth. In addition, a series of natural disasters including droughts and famines stretched the capacities of the Ming state to the breaking point. This string of catastrophes snapped the centripetal political pull of the empire, creating a vacuum of authority in the provinces. Reacting to the progressive collapse of the Ming body politic, some regional rebel groups metastasized into full-fledged armies with leaders who went so far as to anoint themselves with new dynastic titles. And the tremendous social upheaval of the years leading up to the Manchu capture of Peking in 1644 was but the prelude to the brutal conquest and pacification of the following decades.

Amid the unrest, the Jesuits redoubled their efforts to propagate Christianity. Their primary focus was on the rural areas that surrounded the urban centers where they kept residences. The villages around Peking saw visits by Niccolò Longobardo and Johann Adam Schall between 1636 and 1638, even as the Manchu banner armies drew closer to the city's walls. Alfonso Vagnone continued his work in the villages of Shanxi Province. He left Jiangzhou twice each year, "according to custom," and in 1639 claimed 388 new baptisms.[2] Inácio Lobo (1603–after 1638) was entrusted with the first missions to the Pescadores Islands in the Taiwan Strait, as well as in the coastal areas around Fuzhou in Fujian Province. Both Francesco Sambiasi and Manuel Dias the younger traveled from Nanjing around the Jiangnan area, visiting the cities where their acquaintances from the southern court resided. Trips to the outlying villages around Shanghai produced a wealth of new converts in the 1630s. According to the 1636 Annual Letter, these journeys around the coastal plain gave the missionaries a chance to encounter not only "the greatest number of Christians, but also the most fervent ones."[3]

It was during these rural missions that the Jesuits did the most to improve their previously poor baptismal tallies. While they were clearly aware of the rewards to be reaped among urban commoners and rustics as early as the 1590s, they had erred on the side of caution to avoid being labeled another heterodox sect that seduced unlettered peasants with dangerous dogmas. But with the mission on a firmer footing and copies of their religious writings freely circulated among the literati—not to mention the diminished threat of an official crackdown against them—the Jesuits established mission circuits in rural areas. Periodic trips to the villages where Christians were found served the dual purpose of delivering the required yearly sacraments and increasing the numbers of neophytes. By 1637, the circuit centered on Jianchang in Jiangxi Province had expanded to the point where Gaspar Ferreira visited "seven cities, and many villages."[4] In the southern districts of Fujian Province, the efforts of Giulio Aleni in the Quanzhou area had netted him three different routes to visit every year.[5] In Shanxi Province, Alfonso Vagnone and Étienne Faber (1597–1657) strung together a mission circuit that attempted to ensure regular visits to twenty churches where the Christians from "eight cities, some towns, and countless villages" gathered to receive the sacraments.[6]

What was responsible for the Jesuits' surprising amount of reported success among Chinese rustics? If these individuals did not engage with the missionaries on intellectual matters, what attracted them to their religious teachings? Moreover, if countryside converts had only a tenuous command of spoken Mandarin—and there is no evidence that the Jesuits were schooled in the Babylonian diversity of local dialects in the areas where they preached—what did they know about their adopted faith? To be sure, even the most thorough search of the Chinese documental record is not likely to turn up many testimonies by rural Christians in the seventeenth century. But the same can be said about their counterparts in early modern Europe. Yet by parsing the available sources to separate the elements of actual religious practice from the missionaries' idealized interpretations of their followers' piety, it is possible to speculate about what motivated rural converts to embrace *Tianzhu jiao.*

To rural folk, the Jesuits were powerful masters of ritual. Their manners and presence evoked awe and respect. Dressed after the fashion of the native elite, they exuded a recognizable form of gravitas. And like magistrates, they spoke the tongue of political power. Their aura surely endowed their foreign religious message with a great degree of symbolic legitimacy, far more so than if they had trekked from village to village with begging bowls in hand like the Buddhist clergy. Since the intricacies of Christian theology were beyond the ken of the rustics—and the missionaries were skilled enough at rhetoric to best any of them in a debate—it appears that the Jesuits' use of religious ritual made them and their message attractive. In this respect, they were similar to the native religious experts who relied on arcane texts or foreign utterances in their dealings with the supernatural. In the fluid religious climate of late imperial China, where men and women pragmatically drew on a host of devotions from Buddhist, Daoist, and folk traditions to meet their spiritual needs, the novel teachings of *Tianzhu jiao* found willing adherents. It was the perceived power of the Jesuits' rituals, such as exorcisms or the mass, along with their constant invocations of a supreme Lord of Heaven who trumped all rival deities that attracted converts in the countryside.

A good example of how the Jesuits deployed ritual in rural settings is found in a detailed account of Inácio Lobo's 1637 trip to the coast of Fujian Province. Traveling alongside a native Christian, the priest landed on an island where he had no "friends or acquaintances." The pair headed to the nearest village, where they encountered a crowd of the curious who had been alerted by the first frightened farmhands to see them. Lobo created a spectacle by marching straight to the town's clan temple and entering it without making the customary bows before the revered ancestral tablets. With his companion most likely acting as an interpreter, he declared that "there was only one God, the creator of all things, and that this Lord was worthy of being adored." After talking with the village headman, Lobo retired to a house that had been offered him as lodging and set up an altar. When a group came calling the next day, he ceremoniously unveiled a painting of Jesus ornamented with a red silk border. According to his report, the men of the village were so impressed by this Western-style icon that "they did not take their eyes from it." With incense and candles burning, he set the image above the altar and performed the mass. Lobo continued to say mass each day during his stay on the island. He even gained credit for bringing much-needed rain, he claimed, when one mass coincided with a storm—something that did not happen when sacrifices were made at the local temples. Twenty-six converts were the reward for Lobo's efforts.[7]

Another attraction of Christianity was that ordinary converts could co-opt some of the spiritual power of the priests through prayers and devotional objects. Such things were not novelties in late Ming China, since beads, images, and prayers were all used in the popular practice of Buddhism. Rather, the perception that devotional objects, items with a recognizable value within the Chinese religious system, were endowed with new meanings infused them with an unusual potency in the eyes of the people who used them. The centrality of devotional objects to Chinese popular piety was a fortunate coincidence for the Jesuits, and made it possible for the missionaries to substitute common European Catholic objects such as rosaries, nominas, veronicas, and Agnus Dei pendants for their indigenous counterparts without much explanation.[8] Holy water and symbolic gestures such as the sign of the cross were also elements of the spiritual arsenal that the Jesuits shared with their neophytes. In one account from the wilds of Shanxi Province, where Alfonso Vagnone went on mission in the 1630s, the sign of the cross was lauded as an effective protection against ravenous wolves—except, that is, in the case of two Christians "who were publicly held to be less than observant of the Ten Commandments." This pair saw their two children eaten before their eyes in spite of their holy gesticulations.[9]

Well aware of the limits of popular understanding of spiritual matters, the Jesuits hoped to instill a strong attachment between their converts and their new faith by insisting on the power of devotional objects and prayers. But the missionaries' reliance on symbolic rituals and their insistence on the power of objects meant that they ran the risk of spreading false notions about themselves and their message. Yet they agreed to pay this price to attract ever-greater numbers of people to *Tianzhu jiao.* As a result, they gained fame in the late 1630s as healers and exorcists. In Jianchang, Jiangxi Province, for example, Gaspar Ferreira was asked to visit a nearby village in order to attend to eight sick individuals who had exhausted their fortune by paying doctors and Buddhist priests to restore their health. The Jesuit received this request from a relative of the afflicted, a literatus who had heard that the Christian God was "all powerful" and hoped that the priest would perform a ceremony for them. But rather than go himself, Ferreira sent a group of Christians. He instructed them to "console the infirm, give them holy water to drink, put rosary beads around their necks, and pray."[10]

By delegating this task to a set of auxiliaries, Ferreira tried to dispel the notion that he was like one of the Buddhist or Daoist priests who made a living enacting rituals. Although he recorded his pleasure at the conversion of the sick men and women after they recovered their health, the missionary surely knew that he was treading a thin line between promoting devotions and magic. Yet in a land that held pragmatic views about the usefulness of religious practices based on their perceived effectiveness, Ferreira and his colleagues faced a formidable challenge. They were obliged by the tenets of their faith to focus attention on the spiritual rather than the material rewards of adopting their religion. To this end, they insisted on the proper use of devotional objects, stressed the indispensability of prayer, and intoned a continual refrain about the inscrutable judgments of the Lord of Heaven. But doctrine teaching at each stop on a rural mission circuit over the course of decades was the only sure way of making progress toward the Jesuits' goal. Eventually, the association between Christian rituals, devotional objects, and doctrine implanted in the minds of peasants merged to form a recognizable popular Chinese Christian identity, an alternative to the literati image of *Tianxue.*

Challenges Close at Hand, 1637–1640

The mission's expansion into rural areas and the development of mission circuits brought new burdens to the Vice-Province as it struggled to balance limited manpower resources with growing numbers of Chinese Christians. On the one hand, the Jesuits wanted to strike while the iron was hot, expanding their communities by converting as many people as possible. On the other hand, they knew that as the only Catholic priests in China, they were not there simply to baptize. For every baptism that did not occur in the shadow of death, the Jesuits looked forward to a lifelong commitment between priest and Christian, one centered on the yearly observance of confession and communion. This meant that all new groups of countryside converts had to be incorporated into ever more time-consuming mission circuits. While aggressive missionaries such as Alfonso Vagnone were capable of creating communities of almost eight thousand souls in the course of a decade, it took two or three priests to minister to them all afterwards.[11] And with reported yearly baptismal tallies by the late 1630s reaching the four thousand mark, the mission was beginning to feel the curious strain of success.[12]

The political conditions that accompanied the disintegration of the Ming state, however, created opportunities for expansion that were too good to pass up. New paths appeared for the Jesuits to expand the Vice-Province, even if such moves would overstretch their capacities. Since the Almighty had seen fit to encourage their efforts, they reasoned, He would surely send the reinforcements for which they ardently prayed. To be sure, they had not abandoned all caution. In 1635 Francisco Furtado, a Portuguese priest from Terceira Island in the Azores, became Vice-Provincial and brought renewed vigor to the mission's leadership at a decisive moment. He directed his men to logical new pastures, areas linked by transportation arteries to the Jesuits' other residences and locations where local mandarin allies could be found. These geographic concerns explain why the mission did not open new stations in the 1630s in the southwestern provinces of Yunnan, Guangxi, or Guizhou, the northwest beyond Xi'an, or the northeastern regions of Liaodong or Manchuria.

Instead, Furtado sent Inácio da Costa in 1637 to Puzhou in Shanxi Province, a city with a large Christian community that had been part of Alfonso Vagnone's mission circuits. There Costa was protected by the Han family, a prominent clan whose members included Tomé Han Lin (ca. 1600–1649, *juren* 1621). The Vice-Provincial sent Niccolò Longobardo up the Grand Canal to open a residence in Shandong Province. After two scouting trips in 1637 and 1638, the seventy-three-year-old veteran missionary settled in Jinan in 1640.[13] Furtado also ordered António de Gouvea up the Yangzi River in 1637 to reestablish the mission in Huguang Province that had been abandoned years earlier. With the help of the family of a mandarin at Peking, Gouvea purchased a house in Wuchang the following year.[14] Perhaps the riskiest venture of all was the expedition of Lodovico Bugio (1606–1682) in the autumn of 1640 to meet with literati patrons and open a mission at Chengdu in Sichuan Province.

The missionaries' enthusiasm, communicated in missive after missive, had a certain impact on Jesuit superiors outside China. Visitor Manuel Dias the elder forwarded requests from the Society's Roman curia for Furtado to evaluate launching new missions to Tibet, Mongolia, and Korea. With the exception of Mongolia, these areas had already seen the passage of Jesuit priests. In the 1620s António de Andrade (1580–1634) made journeys from India up into the Himalayas, reaching the capital of the Tibetan kingdom of Guge at Tsaparang. In the 1590s Gregorio de Cespedes (ca. 1551–1611) went to Korea in the train of Toyotomi Hideyoshi's invasion of that country, cheering onward the Christian samurai who played prominent roles in the assault divisions. But nothing came of this potential vanguard of a new mission, as the invasion was repulsed and the Jesuits' links to Korea from Japan were severed; to be sure, they converted a number of Korean slaves in Kyushu. Conceivably, China was a good springboard into new areas, but Furtado knew his mission could not afford the leap. "Men and silver do not suffice to undertake all this at once," he reminded his superiors, countering that the mission should spread first to all fifteen Chinese provinces.[15]

The burgeoning numbers of new Catholics weighed heavily on Furtado's conscience. He insisted that his subordinates find new ways to maximize their efforts while ensuring that new converts were not abandoned by their pastors. Groups such as the men and women of Changshu, a city in the Jiangnan region, repeatedly asked for a priest to be stationed there. The leader of that particular community, Tomé Qu Shisi (1590–1651, *jinshi* 1616), had given the Jesuits one of his study pavilions to serve as a church and residence. But there were only twenty-five European Jesuits and five Chinese coadjutors in China as of 1639. So the mission was forced to leave some neophytes adrift "in the midst of such a vast sea of heathens."[16]

Furtado also urged his subordinates to rationalize their pastoral methods. He insisted that a confraternity model of community organization be employed throughout the mission, building on the urge to form associations that was such an integral part of Chinese culture. In the Shanghai area, Christian men and women in villages were grouped into separate brotherhoods. The missionaries then drew up a calendar for ensuring that a priest, a brother, or a lay catechist would visit each group at least once monthly. A similar schedule coordinated each group's visits to the Jesuits' residence church for the purpose of assisting at mass. Much of the legwork for managing these communities was delegated to the more fervent Christians, many of whom were deputized as catechists. One instance illustrating how the missionaries coordinated and supervised their activities occurred when Rodrigo de Figueiredo instituted a catechist brotherhood at Kaifeng in 1640. The members of this Confraternity of St. Thomas gathered twice monthly to discuss doctrine teaching techniques as well as "the means to further the Christian community and spread the Law of God."[17]

For all the Jesuits' enthusiasm about expansion, their meager financial resources restrained them. New residences required investment in real estate. When Xu Guangqi, Li Zhizao, and Yang Tingyun were alive, they gave generously to the mission, donating land, buildings, and money. In the late 1620s, the mission used this money to decorate its churches and transform homes into sanctuaries. While the daughters and sons of these wealthy benefactors continued to give money to their local churches, these pious legacies could not be stretched infinitely to fund new ventures. The mission therefore suffered materially when these wealthy Christians passed on. The Jesuits knew better than to expect their peasant converts or even their lower-level literati followers to pay for new church buildings.

There were other factors in the Vice-Province's financial struggles. Beyond the costs of maintaining their public image—importing gifts for local authorities, keeping their residences in good repair, paying for the publication of their compositions—the Jesuits had to gain legal rights to the properties they were given. For instance, when the Chongzhen emperor rewarded Johann Adam Schall and Giacomo Rho with real estate for their work on the imperial calendar in 1635, the Vice-Provincial lamented this stroke of good fortune. Not only was the snail-like pace of the bureaucracy a vexation, but also, Furtado knew, lots of silver would be necessary for paying bribes, "without which the king's ministers do nothing." After two years, he recorded, the missionaries still had not received the deeds to these properties, adding that as foreigners, they had no lack of "jealous rivals" at court who sought to extort money from them at every turn.[18]

Without cash in hand, the Vice-Province needed its troublesome link to Macau more than ever. Upon the dissolution of the Ming defenses on the southern coast, it became easier for missionaries to communicate with the Portuguese colony, but payments from there came with no greater frequency than before. First of all, the mission's endowments in the Estado da Índia never produced a continual stream of revenue. The China mission's primary external source of income was a yearly payment from the customs house at Malacca, but the predations of the Dutch East India Company on Portuguese trade—not to mention the diversion of shipping traffic to Batavia—meant that this sum rarely reached Macau. When the Dutch captured Malacca in 1641, the axe finally fell on this income source.

Closer by, the Vice-Province relied on the generosity of the Macanese merchants, who redirected their pious donations from Japan to China upon the downfall of the Japan mission. In keeping with the time-honored tradition of religious orders in Europe, the Jesuits invested in real estate in Macau and inside China. But the banishment of all Portuguese traders from Japan in 1639 caused this source of funding to dry up as rental properties in the Portuguese colony became worthless.[19] The mission's other real estate holdings in China were reduced to ashes in the fury of the Manchu invasions.

The disasters and unrest of the last years of the Chongzhen reign compounded the Jesuits' financial woes. The yearly salaries that made it into the empire were insufficient to keep pace with the skyrocketing costs, and everyday necessities became scarce. The missionaries—along with the Chinese population as a whole—were reduced to poverty and, in some places, starvation. In their misery, China Jesuits turned a jealous eye toward what they considered to be the riches of the Province of Japan. They bitterly complained about the imagined luxury of the College of Macau, and how both Provincials and Visitors seemed deaf to their cries. Once again the China Jesuits sought remedy in a publicity tour of Europe. In 1636 Francisco Furtado sent Álvaro Semedo to visit Portugal, Spain, and

Rome, but it would be nine long years before he returned to China. By 1641 Furtado was imploring the Superior General for some new form of support: "I only ask that in your prayers to Our Father, Your Paternity remembers at the *'panem nostrum quotidianum da nobis hodie,'* to ask Him for this for your sons, so that they may work in this vineyard of the Lord."[20]

The 1630s also saw the arrival of another set of problems for the Vice-Province when the first Franciscans and Dominicans from Manila disembarked on the shores of Fujian Province. After many years of preaching to the Chinese diaspora in the Philippines, the Mendicants were spurred to start their own enterprise by news of missionary successes across the sea.[21] From the perspective of the Society of Jesus, these rivals might destroy the mission they had worked for so many years to build. The Jesuits resisted what they considered an unfair intrusion into their territory—even if the Ming empire was patently far too big for any one order to handle, and despite the fact that it was standard procedure in lands under European colonial rule for different religious orders to work in separate mission districts. There was no guarantee, they feared, that the new arrivals would adopt the Jesuits' carefully cultivated public image or adhere to their rules for missionizing.

The Society also read the history of the Mendicant presence in East Asia as a series of calamities. The Jesuits put the blame for the wrath of Toyotomi Hideyoshi and the Tokugawa shoguns in Japan squarely on the shoulders of the imprudent Spanish friars. In previous years, Mendicant expeditions from Manila had been turned away at Canton and elsewhere. "They were bursting to enter and do there what they had done in Japan," wrote Alfonso Vagnone in 1619, "but the Chinese watch freed us from these fears."[22] By the 1630s, however, this Argus had lost sight of the far inlets of the Fujian coast.

The friction between the China Jesuits and the Mendicant friars was exacerbated by the national rivalry between the Portuguese and the Spanish. Although the Iberian Peninsula had been politically united since 1580 under Philip II and his Habsburg successors, tensions ran high along the East Asian fault line dividing the Spanish and Portuguese empires. Within the Society of Jesus, the Vice-Province was part of the Portuguese Assistancy, and its principal chain of supply and command passed through Goa and Lisbon to Rome. To be sure, the Jesuits were not free of divisions along national lines; for instance, Visitor Francisco Vieira had denounced Nicolas Trigault's journey to Rome in 1613 as part of an Italian cabal created by Niccolò Longobardo to reduce Portuguese influence.[23] By the 1630s, however, the corporate interest of the Society of Jesus had won out over the national rivalries of its members. For their part, the Jesuits in Manila, linked to the Spanish Assistancy through Mexico and Madrid, had kept out of Chinese affairs since the Sánchez episode in the 1590s. Their Mendicant compatriots felt no such compunction about respecting the Jesuits' internal divisions or about the artificial political and economic divide between the two Iberian empires. Seemingly, however, they were not aware that in the short sail from Luzon to Fujian they had slipped from under the mantle of colonial power into a realm of unfamiliar social and political forces. Just like the Jesuits, the friars thought, they went in search of fertile ground for planting the gospel. God would surely reward them if the crown did not.

Between 1631 and 1634 a handful of Dominicans and Franciscans made their way to Fuzhou and requested that Giulio Aleni assign them mission districts in Fujian Province. When Aleni declined, the Dominicans accompanied a group of minor literati whom the Jesuit had baptized to their hometown of Fu'an. In this remote region on the province's northeastern coast, the friars founded a mission that would prove a thorn in the Vice-Province's side for decades to come. Even in this far corner of China, the Jesuits saw their control over the image of Christianity at stake. Their corporate persona, after all, was virtually synonymous with their religion in the Chinese mind. The possibility that Chinese authorities might have reason to question the intentions of all missionaries on account of the actions of Spanish Mendicants in Fujian was very troubling indeed. When the first anti-Christian incident in Fu'an involving mandarins and friars occurred just six years after the Dominicans' arrival, the Jesuits' fears were confirmed.[24]

If the presence of friars on the Fujian coast gave the Jesuits cause for concern, their attempts to penetrate further into the empire in the late 1630s raised cries of alarm. According to Antonio de Santa Maria Caballero (1602–1669), the first Franciscan to reach Fu'an, Vice-Provincial Manuel Dias the younger had arranged for him to be kidnapped by a team of Chinese Christians and Jesuit domestic servants when he headed inland in 1634.[25] Two other Franciscans from Manila did better than their confrere: They reached Peking in the summer of 1637. There they contacted Johann Adam Schall and Francisco Furtado to ask for help in getting safe conduct passes and permission to open churches in Fujian. They also wanted a cash advance. Schall chastised them for their temerity, insisting that their presence had put the whole mission at risk. He informed a fellow Jesuit that the Franciscans had shown themselves to be "all swelled up with desires either to be martyrs or to convert the king and all the Chinese right away." Schall further noted that neither friar could speak Chinese, but that both were ready to "jump up on benches with their crucifixes in hand" to preach the gospel.[26]

Vice-Provincial Furtado's first concern was to make the friars disappear unnoticed from the capital. For this he enlisted the aid of two Christian mandarins, Li Zhizao's son and one of Schall's assistants. The pair went to the friars' lodgings in high official dudgeon to inform them that their petitions had been denied and that they had to be escorted back to Fujian for expulsion to Manila. The ruse worked; the Franciscans did not return to northern China for over a decade. Furtado also worried that the friars had discovered the Jesuits' secret: that the mission was hopelessly understaffed for its ambitious apostolic task. If the Mendicants knew how strapped the Vice-Province was, they would have greater grounds for appealing to the royal court in Madrid and the Papal Curia in Rome for permission to preach in the Ming empire. More ominously, Furtado heard the Franciscans ruminating about the chances for success of a Spanish invasion of China from the Philippines. He urged his superiors in Macau to warn the city's authorities to petition Philip IV if they wanted to preserve their settlement, asking the king to stifle such public speculations—"because we all know the humor of the Castilians when it comes to conquests."[27]

When these friars returned to Manila, they set in motion a struggle for spiritual authority over Christianity in China that lasted for over a century. Paradoxically, the theological battles known as the Chinese Rites controversy would have little bearing on the development of the Jesuit mission within China for the next seventy years. To be sure, this affair produced such massive quantities of polemic and apologetic in Europe that scholars can be forgiven for assuming that it cast a shadow over the China mission from well before the beginning of the eighteenth century.[28] But the issue of the Chinese Rites was primarily debated in Manila, Paris, and Rome. And although it created problems within the Vice-Province at several later junctures and was debated in China itself by Jesuits, Chinese

Christians, literati, and even emperors, it did not monopolize the missionaries' attentions.

The basic contours of the dispute are as follows. As early as 1635, the Dominican Juan Baptista de Morales (1597–1654) and the Franciscan Caballero made inquiries in Fu'an into the meaning of a number of common Chinese rituals. These missionaries especially objected to seeing Christian literati participate in Confucian ceremonies and ordinary Christians keep tablets inscribed with their ancestors' names in their homes. In the friars' opinion, both were intolerable manifestations of idolatry and not, as the Jesuits claimed, merely political and social customs. From Manila they sent warnings to European ecclesiastical authorities of the Jesuits' permissive attitude, with the goal of bringing their missionary rivals to heel.

By transporting the issue of the Chinese Rites from Asia to Europe, the Mendicants delivered a sizable store of ammunition to the Jesuits' detractors. One should recall that in 1640, just three years before Morales and Caballero arrived in Rome, the Society of Jesus celebrated its first centennial, basking in the glow of unrivaled prestige among the Catholic elite of early modern Europe. But this was the high-water mark of the Jesuits' dramatic rise. Many observers—especially at the Papal Curia and in other religious orders—considered the Society of Jesus to be dangerously independent and potentially subversive to the institutional church. After all, the decades that had passed since the conclusion of the Council of Trent in 1564 had seen the gradual uniformization of Catholic practice across Europe and the curbing of liberties of the church's diverse component parts under the Roman standard. Sooner or later the papacy would have to deal with the Society of Jesus as well. The scandalous reports supplied by Mendicant informers about the Jesuits' China enterprise would at length prove to be an ideal starting point for Rome's project of subduing all of its subordinates.

Secular affairs in Europe also played a role in the rites controversy. Roughly by the end of the Thirty Years' War, as France assumed its place at the center of European culture, the order that had spouted from the twin Iberian springs of mysticism and imperialism found its influence on the wane—even if the Society's total membership continued to increase until the early eighteenth century. Other currents within Catholicism were also intertwined with political power and social prestige in France, despite the undeniable importance of the place held by the Society of Jesus in the hearts and minds of the French elite. So the rites controversy was also a French theological dispute between the ascendant Jansenist rigorists and the still formidable Jesuits. And as French power spread to the Papal Curia, displacing the weight of the Spanish monarchy, the Society of Jesus saw its claims to be the vanguard of Catholic culture challenged. This historical development eventually caused the European battles that ensued over the rites to be brought back to Asia by the fleet of Louis XIV. Then the Chinese (no less than the missionaries) would be surprised to learn that the Jesuit face was not the primary reflection to be seen in the mirror of Catholic Europe.

But though the rites controversy concluded in Europe, it began on the shores of Fujian Province in the 1630s between rival subjects of Philip IV of Spain. To the Mendicants who had been trained in Mexico and the Philippines, where the crown's agents were ready and willing to impose belief through coercion, accepting Christianity was a transformative experience that superseded all cultural concerns. While it would be too much to brand the friars as completely blinkered Eurocentrics, by and large their view was that religious matters which raised doubts should be resolved by theologians, not by neophytes—meaning in this case that the Chinese Christians should not be allowed to decide for themselves whether or not they were approaching the rites as civil or religious ceremonies. Those who had only recently slipped the shackles of paganism through baptism, the friars reasoned, could not be fully aware of the differences between idolatry and true religion. For the sake of their own souls, Chinese Christians must not participate in any seemingly idolatrous ritual.

From the Jesuits' point of view, the Mendicants had jumped to conclusions based on an imperfect knowledge of Chinese customs. The Portuguese superiors who penned the statutes of the Vice-Province agreed with Matteo Ricci's contention that Confucianism, the "sect of the literati," was a political philosophy that was atheistic at its core. In the manner of the Humanist scholars, Ricci maintained that Confucian thought was compatible with Christianity, if only one could get past the Buddhist-influenced metaphysical coating of the Song period's Neo-Confucian commentary and read the sage's original texts. Unlike the friars, the Jesuits spent years studying Confucian thought before adopting this approach. Consequently, they had no difficulty in perceiving the yearly participation of Christian literati in rituals at Confucian temples as a solemn expression of remembrance for a revered master. To be sure, the Jesuits saw the only possibility for promoting Christianity in China in the accommodation of their religious message to the dominant political orthodoxy. Moreover, they owed the safety of their mission to the protection of men who were, by profession, committed Confucians. This is why Francisco Furtado's hackles were raised when he learned of friars roaming the streets of Peking, preaching that "the king was wrong and Confucius was in Hell."[29]

The Jesuits also saw the second main issue in the rites controversy, the suggestion that they turned a blind eye to ancestor worship, through the same prism. They were aware of the high importance of the cult of the dead in Chinese culture and insisted that Christians needed to approach it with the correct attitude. In their opinion, the presence of ancestor tablets in Christian homes was again merely a sign of respect. The Jesuits felt that they had made it sufficiently clear to their spiritual charges that the souls of the dead did not reside in these stone markers. It was obvious that the departed could not come to receive the sacrifices that other Chinese placed before their ancestral tablets. Here again, the missionaries adapted the practice of their religion to the local cultural context, giving new meanings to age-old customs—many with clear counterparts in Catholic Europe—instead of forcing their converts to divorce themselves from their society. To be sure, the Jesuits harbored doubts about these ceremonies and published their objections in their Chinese writings. But they contended that their neophytes would gradually give up these dubious practices of their own accord. If they viewed the Mendicants' all-or-nothing approach toward conversion as vinegar, the Jesuits hoped that their gradualist view on attracting swarms of Christians would prove to be honey. They felt that their attitude was vindicated by every new Chinese baptism.

A Preview of the Day of Judgment, 1641–1650

As the Jesuits and the Mendicants fired the opening salvos in a protracted propaganda war, another engagement reached its climax on the battlefields of northern China. For men who saw the world through a biblical lens, the collapsing Ming empire that they beheld in the 1640s was nothing short of Armageddon. For their Chinese peers who saw the natural disasters and social unrest of the day as signs of impending political change, it was clear that Heaven had forsaken the reigning dynasty and was about to usher in a new order. In the Vice-Province's Annual Letter for 1641, João Monteiro (1602–1648) conveyed the epic scale of the destruction that overcame China even before the great wave of the foreign invasion:

> Who can describe the calamities and misery that China has suffered this year without pain in his heart and tears in his eyes? It appears that heaven, earth, and the other elements have entered the lists against these heathens so that we can truly say *et pugnavit pro eo Orbis contra insensatos.* God has closed the doors to His treasury of rain and clouds, the seedbeds dry up, the wheat and the rice die, and weeds do not satisfy the need for rations. An infinite number of people evidently go hungry, the airs are corrupted, a plague grows all over the kingdom, and one cannot count the dead. Such cruel bandits rise up in so great a number, sparing nothing, robbing all, devastating all. Men roam with death before their eyes, dazed and astounded. Some do all they can to preserve their lives; others, tired of life, hang themselves. Once the rations are eaten, they eat weeds and tree bark, and finally are reduced to eating human flesh.[30]

In Monteiro's judgment, God was sending a very clear message to the Chongzhen emperor: he must mend his ways and recognize his creator. If the Ming ruler would accept baptism from the missionaries so close to the throne, Monteiro contended, "God Our Lord would surely sheath the sword of His Divine Wrath and extend the arm of His infinite mercy."[31] Yet while the sovereign dallied, the missionaries gave thanks for the opportunity to baptize scores of souls in imminent danger of damnation.

In Shaanxi and Shanxi provinces in northwestern China, peasant revolts followed hot on the heels of famine and a void of government control. Yet the Jesuits there informed European readers that they "always culled good fruit in a time of so many calamities."[32] As the news of impending invasions and roving bands of rebels spread across the empire, the missionaries used the rising tide of fear to diffuse their message of divine protection and, failing that, personal salvation. One vignette shows how the missionaries rejoiced in the widespread reputation of Christianity in Shanxi Province, where "even the thieves respect it and recognize its truth." To prove their point, they told of a baptized merchant who fell in with bandits as he traveled in the company of non-Christian traders. When the cutthroats found his rosary beads, they asked what purpose they served and learned that the man was a follower of *Tianzhu jiao.* For this, the bandits released the Christian but slew his companions. Yet they took his beads, informing him that if they had "the opportunity to change their trade and way of life," they would no doubt become Christians.[33]

While the mood of anxiety that preceded the dynastic transition was helpful for the Jesuits' conversion efforts, the reality of uprisings and military campaigns cost the mission dearly. With the empire's communication network disrupted, the Vice-Province was forced to split itself in two so that a superior could always respond to new crises. Francisco Furtado therefore became Vice-Provincial for northern China and deputized Giulio Aleni in Fujian as Vice-Provincial for southern China. Neither superior, though, could help Rodrigo de Figueiredo at Kaifeng in Henan Province in 1642. This Jesuit perished along with his Christian community when retreating Ming armies cut the dikes along the Yellow River in a desperate attempt to crush the rebel forces of Li Zicheng (1605–1645). The ensuing flood that swept across the area resulted in the drowning of three hundred thousand people. In the words of one Jesuit commentator, Kaifeng was razed like ancient Troy, and even two years later no trace of the city or its surrounding countryside could be seen "except the water with which it was flooded." Hoping to save another Jesuit from a similar fate, Aleni ordered António de Gouvea to abandon Wuchang in 1643. Under the cover of darkness, this missionary fled from the sight of "dead people in piles" by boat, sailing down the Yangzi River and out of the reach of rebels and bandits.[34]

During this turmoil, the Vice-Province focused on preserving its most vital resources, its priests. Residences like the ones at Kaifeng or Wuchang could later be recovered, but the mission's manpower problems were chronic, and the Society's enterprise could not bear the loss of too many trained men like Figueiredo. It does not appear that rebels, bandits, and Manchus made a special target of the Jesuits, and the Vice-Province escaped largely intact. At Xi'an, Inácio da Costa and José de Almeida (1612–1647) hunkered down in their church while Li Zicheng's army stormed the city in 1643. Although about a hundred soldiers entered the sanctuary, "stealing some things that pleased them," they did not harm the priests. Francisco Furtado encountered the same type of trouble during a trip that he made across northern China in 1642 to deliver salaries to his subordinates. On two occasions he came across thieves, who stole his chalices and silver.[35]

Some missionaries were not so fortunate. When Gabriel de Magalhães (1610–1677) traveled to Sichuan in search of Lodovico Buglio in 1642, both men initially enjoyed the protection of important literati. But when the warlord Zhang Xianzhong (1601–1647) conquered the province and proclaimed himself in 1645 ruler of a new polity, *Daxi guo,* the Great Western State, he pressed the pair into service as astronomers. They complied and even claimed a few conversions among Zhang's retainers; but the ruler's paranoia and his campaign of wanton destruction in Sichuan made them fear for their lives. Dragged along under heavy guard in the warlord's train as he abandoned the land he had devastated and decamped for Shaanxi Province, the pair were captured by Manchu soldiers after Zhang's defeat in 1647. But a Qing commander who had known Johann Adam Schall at Peking recognized them and took them along with his victorious army on its return to the court the following year.[36] In 1644 Michael Walta (b. 1606) met his death in Puzhou in Shanxi Province at the hands of soldiers who mistook him for a scion of the imperial family "hiding under the cloak of religion." His assassins arrived at this conclusion because they found him in a church that had once been a mandarin's palace.[37] Two other priests, Tranquillo Grassetti and José de Almeida, were killed in 1647 along with a Chinese coadjutor, Manuel Gomes (b. 1608), during the Manchu capture of Nanchang in Jiangxi Province.

The violence of the dynastic transition could not but take its toll on the Jesuits' baptismal tallies. In 1644, the year the Manchu army captured Peking, the Vice-Province recorded 188 new Christians for all six northern residences, "quite a small number," in the words of one missionary. Yet this Jesuit expected as much in the midst of such tumult, when the "blind heathens" had time only "to seek ways to escape death and save their lives," not to think about their souls.[38] In some areas, however, conversions continued apace. At Shanghai, Francesco Brancati (1607–1671) claimed 966 new Christians that same year. This tally was impressive, the Jesuits contended, in light of the "many revolts that obliged the priest to refrain from making trips to the neighboring Christian communities."[39] The missionaries at Nanchang also claimed success amid danger. They recorded 220 baptisms in 1643, which they deemed "a great number." These Jesuits further congratulated themselves on creating two new confraternities, which took the lead in assisting Christians impoverished by drought or affected by the revolts in nearby Huguang Province.[40]

The proclamation of a new dynasty at Peking in 1644 did not significantly alter the Jesuits' strategy for conducting their mission. Once again, however, they had to establish their legitimacy in the eyes of the new sovereigns and secure political protection for the mission. To be sure, it was not until the late 1650s that the Qing emerged victorious in the long struggle for control over China.[41] While the question of sovereignty was in doubt, the Jesuits proclaimed loyalty to whichever party was in power. In Peking, Johann Adam Schall was quick to offer his scientific abilities to the Manchu rulers. His overtures met with approval, and the new overlords gave him a decree to post on his church prohibiting any attacks on the building or its residents.[42] The missionaries took this as a favorable portent and were pleased to note that the new rulers "leaned more toward atheism than to any particular cult of false gods." The start of the Qing rule at Peking therefore gave them reason to hope for "some notable good for the faith and the Christian community."[43]

To be sure, they did not wager all on the Qing horse. In the uncertain political climate of the late 1640s, they thought it wise to hedge their bets by having the Jesuits in South China make overtures to the rump courts of the Southern Ming. They established relations with both the Longwu and the Yongli emperors to ensure the survival of the mission in the (however unlikely) event of a resurrection of the Ming empire.[44] During his time in Nanjing, Francesco Sambiasi became a friend of the favored son of the Wanli emperor, the Prince of Fu, Zhu Changxun, and the Prince of Tang, Zhu Yujian. When, in the summer of 1645, the successor to the Prince of Fu, Zhu Yousong, was installed as the Hongguang emperor (r. 1644–1645) at Nanjing, he appointed Sambiasi as his ambassador to Macau to petition the Portuguese for military aid.[45] Unfortunately for the Ming, the Jesuit did more for the Europeans than for the Chinese. With imperial pomp, Sambiasi sailed to Canton, where he negotiated trade concessions from the local authorities for the destitute colony. His arrival at Macau aboard imperial ships bedecked with flags bearing Christian crosses caused quite a stir. According to one eyewitness, many Portuguese averred that "either the world would surely end or else be born anew."[46] In spite of Sambiasi's empty-handed return to the exiled court in Fujian, the Prince of Tang, named the Longwu emperor (r. 1645–1646), gave him a decree praising Christianity and conceded him the right to establish a church at Canton. As the Jesuit headed off to open his new residence, Longwu asked his friend where they might meet again. To the doomed emperor's delight, Sambiasi replied, "at the court of Nanjing."[47]

Another set of Jesuits fostered relations with the Yongli court, first in Guangdong and then in Guangxi Province. The story of how Michael Boym (1612–1659) and Andreas Xavier Koffler (1612–1652) followed the fleeing courtiers across southwestern China is well known. After baptizing the Empress Dowager Wang as Helena and the infant heir to the throne as Constantine, Koffler ordered Boym to travel to Rome in 1651 with a request for military aid addressed to Pope Innocent X.[48] By the time the Polish Jesuit returned to East Asia in 1659, however, it was too late for anyone to raise the Ming standard. In a matter of three short years a battalion of Manchu soldiers would overtake Yongli (r. 1646–1662) in northern Burma. While the missionaries' work among the Southern Ming loyalists may have resulted in no more than Pyrrhic apostolic victories, they did help ensure the survival of Macau and the start of a new mission at Canton.

By the 1650s the Peking Jesuits had confirmed that the star of the Qing was in the ascendant, and as good astronomers, they followed its course. Johann Adam Schall's initial overtures toward the Manchu sovereigns garnered prestige for the mission. As early as 1645 the Macau Jesuits communicated their optimism to the Society's Roman curia, asserting that Schall enjoyed greater favor in Peking than Sambiasi did with Longwu in Fujian.[49] Moving to capitalize on the new regime's need for legitimacy, Schall presented a version of the calendar that he had helped calculate for the Chongzhen emperor. This gesture earned him a position as one of the mandarin supervisors at the Imperial Astronomical Bureau in 1645, with the title of director and a corresponding salary within the state bureaucracy. He also won the friendship of the Shunzhi emperor (r. 1644–1661), facilitating the political protection necessary for his colleagues to conduct missionary work in the new Qing domains.

Despite the links of amity forged by Schall at Peking, the men of the Vice-Province had mixed emotions about the Manchu conquerors. Even though the might of the invaders had succeeded in pacifying the empire, they left a tremendous swath of devastation in their wake. In the opinion of Francisco Furtado, the tragedy he had seen played out before his eyes seemed like a full dress rehearsal of "the state of the world on the last day of Judgment after the War of the Elements." Another missionary could think of no greater calamities that might occur at the end of time: "What more vivid image could there be of a finished world but grassless fields and devastated cities with all their inhabitants gone?"[50] António de

Gouvea contrasted the dynasty's symbolic name, Qing—in his definition, "pure kingdom, clear like a sky without clouds"—with the brutality of the invasion. "Much ado and very little reality" could be sensed in the "names and pomp signifying the virtues" of the conquerors, he claimed, given what "one sees with his eyes and feels with his hands."[51] But at least one Jesuit retained his optimism, averring that "the conquerors only desire to lord over the land and to take from the rich; they do not seek to offend the poor"—in this case, the missionaries and their Christians.[52]

Rebuilding over the Ruins, 1651–1663

As the fires of the Manchu invasion died down and a fearful calm spread over China, the men of the Vice-Province again renewed their apostolic endeavors. But after so many years of war and privation, the Jesuits were older and fewer in number. Only a handful of young missionaries headed into the ravaged empire from Macau, and there they encountered a corps of Jesuits who, by early modern standards, were the living dead: of the twenty-three European priests and four Chinese coadjutors listed in the 1645 personnel catalogue, twelve were over fifty years old. These included men of venerable age, such as Manuel Dias the younger at seventy-one, Gaspar Ferreira at seventy-three, and Niccolò Longobardo at eighty-one. Only six of the China Jesuits were under forty years old, and two of these would be killed by 1647. Thirty-one-year-old Martino Martini (1614–1661), a Tyrolean from Trent, was but a babe by comparison.[53]

To make matters worse, by the early 1650s the mission was in dire financial straits. Johann Adam Schall's pension was sufficient only for supporting the Jesuits in northern China. The rest of the Vice-Province still depended on Macau, a settlement whose sources of revenue had run dry. Even after it resumed trade with Canton, the colony remained a shadow of its former self. The protracted wars of the Portuguese Restoration (1640–1668) meant that Macau, along with the rest of the Estado da Índia, was left to fend for itself. But while King João IV rallied his troops against the Castilian army in Europe, the Dutch East India Company kept up its attacks on Iberian possessions half a world away. The Dutch presence in Southeast Asia severed the China Jesuits' links to Goa, depriving them of rental revenues from their properties in India. In the estimate of Álvaro Semedo, the man who had managed the mission's temporal affairs for over a decade, the combination of high prices, scarce goods, and no revenues in 1650 made the state of the mission "the most miserable that it could be."[54] In a move of desperation, Martino Martini was sent to Europe that same year to secure new funds.

Lacking money, the Vice-Province was sorely restricted in its ability to reestablish older Christian communities and expand to new areas. Few patrons could be found inside the empire to meet the needs of the missionaries, who were left to beg, borrow, or steal. Choosing the second option, they incurred substantial debts with Chinese lenders in the hope that their fortunes would soon increase. Simão da Cunha, who had lived in the upland districts of Fujian Province for twenty years, put the situation to his superiors quite plainly: "One makes war on the devil with silver also." He lamented having to abandon important activities, such as "printing books, going on missions, and augmenting the numbers of Christians."[55] A remark made by Feliciano Pacheco (1622–1687), a Portuguese priest who worked primarily in the Jiangnan region, gives a further indication of the severity of this crisis. Writing to his European colleagues, he conceded that the mission's woes had become so great that the Vice-Province no longer sought "to acquire and invite new men and workers." Sustaining the men in the field became more important than promoting the mission, since "one can hardly attend to things spiritual while lacking the temporal."[56]

Pacheco's alarmed claims notwithstanding, the Jesuits reported substantial missionary activity between 1650 and 1663. In the aftermath of the Manchu conquest, the number of new Chinese Christians increased steadily. As long-distance traders in "divine merchandise," the missionaries benefited from the quelling of banditry and the resumption of commerce.[57] Their financial lot improved with the resurgence of the Chinese economy. In the cotton-growing region of coastal Jiangnan, the spread of Christianity recommenced along with cloth production in the villages around Shanghai. In 1647, just a year after Qing forces had subjugated the area, Francesco Brancati claimed 1,162 converts.[58] The following year, the Sicilian reported that his duties included ministering to forty-five confraternities in different towns, twelve of which maintained their own churches. To be sure, by designating these groups of Christians as confraternities, each with a *huizhang,* or leader, Brancati (and his colleagues elsewhere in China) in effect created a system of parish units. By adopting the Chinese social impulse of forming common-interest groups, the Jesuits were able to endow their newly founded Christian communities with a strong element of internal cohesion. In the Shanghai area the outcome of this strategy was readily visible. As early as 1653 Brancati claimed the number of Christians had multiplied so fast that he was responsible for over seventy rural brotherhoods.[59]

The Jesuits in Fujian Province garnered similarly abundant fruit. Building on the previous efforts of Giulio Aleni and António de Gouvea in the coastal districts, Simão da Cunha launched new missions in the mountainous interior. There he set up stations at strategic points on the province's river network, at the cities of Yanping, Jianning, Shaowu, and Dingzhou. Attempting to make the weight of his pastoral burdens understood by his superior, Cunha claimed that he alone had to deal with enough Christians to keep busy all the Jesuits at "the colleges of Rome, Coimbra, Évora, Goa, and Macau." By his own count, he visited twelve churches, four chapels, and a host of household oratories during his mission circuits.[60]

By the 1650s, some of the Vice-Province's Christian communities were more than fifty years old. In several cases, three generations had passed since the first members of a clan had been baptized. The fact that the Jesuits' church was no longer made up solely of neophytes brought changes to the mission, as some of their lifelong Christians began to demand initiation in more complex forms of Catholic expression. The missionaries responded to this spiritual need by assisting their followers in the introduction of new types of collective piety. Membership in these groups typically involved the observance of more rigorous devotional schedules. At Hanzhong in southern Shaanxi Province, for instance, Étienne Faber founded a penitential confraternity that included fasting, flagellation, and sexual abstinence among its requirements. A similar group that he formed in Xi'an met at the local church on Saturday nights to perform flagellation after saying prayers and hearing an excerpt from saintly exempla.[61]

The passage of time witnessed the gradual transformation of *Tianzhu jiao* from a religion of converts to a faith of families. This change created a need for qualified individuals to teach doctrine to the children who had been born into their religion. In Shaanxi Province, Faber attempted to meet this challenge by starting a "Confraternity of the Angels," a group modeled on the doctrine classes held outside the gates of nearly every Jesuit establishment in Europe. Actually, Faber was borrowing a technique from Francesco Brancati, who had used such groups to indoctrinate children since the 1640s. Similar assemblies were formed elsewhere in China by the end of the 1650s in regions such as Jiangnan, Shandong, and inland Fujian.

As the Jesuits' communities grew in size, so did the amount of time each priest needed to allot for celebrating the mass and distributing the sacraments. This increase in pastoral duties necessarily meant scaling back proselytizing efforts. But by the 1650s, men and women able to take up the task of spreading their religious message and catechizing converts could be found among the mission's Christians. In order to coordinate the efforts of his catechists at Changshu in the Jiangnan region, Girolamo Gravina (1603–1662) founded a "Brotherhood of the Twelve Apostles." Members of this group, selected from among the most fervent in the community, were obliged by the brotherhood's statutes to attend mass, receive communion regularly, and confess at least once a month. Their most important task, however, was to carry out the work of conversion in the missionary's stead. They were obliged to "either reinvigorate a cold Christian or convert some heathen" every month.[62]

Their advances in the first years of the Qing regime gave the Jesuits the impression that they had been successfully integrated into Chinese society. To be sure, it was crucially important to the mission that some of the dust kicked up during the invasion should have settled on their churches, suggesting to the invaders that they had been a part of the landscape for a long time. While it is unlikely that the Manchus fell for the ruse, the Jesuits felt confident enough to relinquish their previous discretion about proclaiming their religion. Tangible manifestations of this new attitude could be found in the fact that in the mid-1650s, their churches went from being discreet gathering points to clearly marked public buildings, at least in some cities. Since the priests' confidence rose quickest at the imperial court in Peking, so too the new standards of *Tianzhu jiao* rose first in that city. In 1655 the Shunzhi emperor granted a residence to Gabriel de Magalhães and Lodovico Buglio, complete with a gilt sign in his own calligraphy proclaiming the edifice a gift from the emperor.[63] The two Jesuits commissioned a stone cross flanked by kneeling angels for the gable of its façade, and claimed that the sight of it compelled "all those who passed by, even those on horseback or in carriages," to stop.[64] Although the cross could barely be glimpsed above the high walls of the missionaries' compound, Magalhães declared it to be the first publicly visible Christian monument erected by the Vice-Province in China.

Excited by the prestige that the Peking Jesuits had gained for the mission, their confreres in the provinces also moved to make their churches into more visible marks on the urban fabric of the cities where they lived. For example, the church that Simão da Cunha opened in 1657 in Yanping, Fujian Province, mirrored the public orientation of the new court edifice. In contrast to Cunha's old church with its discreet entrance, this building was palatial, the former residence of a Christian mandarin who had donated it to the community of his local coreligionists. It sat in the heart of the city, "in such a manner that when the main door is opened in the daytime, it is known to all people, Christians and heathens alike." At the inauguration ceremony, on November 1, 1657, Cunha staged a procession to transfer the sacred images from the old church to the new one. A literatus led the way, bearing the banner of the Holy Cross, while two pairs of other literati processed with paintings of a guardian angel and the Blessed Virgin. The priest marched behind the images, leading a train of Christians who carried incense and rosary beads. In their wake came a clutch of non-Christian musicians who had been hired for the occasion, "celebrating their creator on that day without knowing Him." What most impressed Cunha, however, was that a Chinese city had witnessed a public procession which included literati making an unembarrassed profession of the faith they had "learned from a European man."[65]

The public recognition of the place of *Tianzhu jiao* among the other religions in some areas of China was accompanied by an increased rivalry between the Jesuits and the Buddhist and Daoist clergy. Simão da Cunha bragged to his superiors that he had pulled off his procession in plain sight of the "bonzes" and their lay sympathizers without fear of reprisals. There as elsewhere, the Jesuits' attitude to these rivals shifted from fear to competitiveness—in addition, of course, to a strong sense of contempt—as they increasingly saw themselves in a struggle for new adherents. On this battlefield, rumor was a powerful weapon. During the Chinese New Year in 1660, Michel Trigault and Albert d'Orville (1621–1662) overheard gossip in Jiangzhou, Shanxi Province, about the severity of their religion. At the time of the Lantern Festival, typically celebrated on the fifteenth day of the first lunar month, they learned of a rumor claiming that "in the Holy Law, there is no such feasting or happiness." To quiet their detractors and reassure their followers, on February 2 the Jesuits instituted the celebration of Candlemas, the feast of the Purification of the Virgin. They instructed their Christians to build a platform in the city's church and decorated it with silk, candles, incense, flowers, and paper lanterns. On the night of the feast they opened the doors of their church to passers-by, inviting them to see the "lanterns dedicated to the Lord of Heaven and His most holy Mother."[66]

At Jinan in Shandong Province, Jean Valat (ca. 1614–1696) promoted another festival to stem the tide of rumors about Christian customs. In the days after *Qingming,* the springtime grave-sweeping festival, outsiders remarked that the followers of *Tianzhu jiao* did not take part in what one Jesuit termed "bacchanalias that more often end in drunkenness, brawls, and riots than piety or reverence for the dead." Within the Chinese cultural context, the obvious conclusion to draw was that Christians had no respect for their deceased forebears. So in order to display their observance of the precepts of filial piety, Valat decided to hold a public celebration of All Souls' Day. This gesture was also intended to encourage the local Christians to use consecrated cemeteries instead of burying the dead according to Chinese custom in clan tombs scattered about the countryside. In 1660 Valat organized a procession to the communal burial plots "with the solemn pomp of carriages, flutes, and flags." The priest led the congregation in responsorial prayers for the dead, conducting "the rest of the rites and ceremonies required by the Holy Church for that day."[67]

It was only in 1659 that Martino Martini returned from his perilous round trip to Europe. During the nine years of his absence, the Vice-Province had made great strides in promoting its message despite being reduced to a skeleton crew. By 1651 there were only eighteen European priests and three Chinese coadjutors in China, and many of these did not have long to live.[68] It appears that the old guard hung on just long enough for the first new blood to reach the Vice-Province. The arrival at Macau of a few new recruits, such as Manuel Jorge (1621–1677) from Coimbra and Giandomenico Gabiani (1623–1694) from Nice, gave the first signals that the mission's fortunes might improve. By 1660, however, many of the veteran missionaries who had built the Vice-Province of China were in their graves, including Manuel Dias the younger, Simão da Cunha, Francisco Furtado, Álvaro Semedo, Étienne Faber, and Niccolò Longobardo.

These aged missionaries could have taken greater comfort at the hour of their death had they known of the success of Martino Martini's voyage. From the Norse port of Bergen through Amsterdam, Antwerp, Rome, and Lisbon, the procurator rekindled European interest in China and gave fresh impetus for young Jesuits to request assignments to the Vice-Province. His widely translated account of the Manchu invasions, *De Bello Tartarico* (Antwerp, 1654), and his descriptive atlas of China, *Novus Atlas Sinensis* (Amsterdam, 1655), played no small role in this propaganda effort. Martini's passage through the Society's colleges in the Southern Netherlands inspired the vocations of at least three well-known Flemish priests: Philippe Couplet (1622–1693), François de Rougemont (1624–1676), and Ferdinand Verbiest (1623–1688). Martini had a similar effect in France, encouraging the departures of Jacques le Faure (1613–1675), Humbert Augery (1618–1673), Louis Gobet (1609–1661), and the brothers Claude (1618–1671), Jacques (1619–1692), and Nicolas Motel (1622–1657).

By sailing from Lisbon to Goa and Macau, these men ran the risk of being captured by hostile Dutch forces in Maritime Asia. The fact that Martini himself had been imprisoned briefly at Batavia spurred the leadership of the Society of Jesus to seek an overland route to China. The Austrians Johann Gruber (1623–1680) and Bernhard Diestel (1623–1660) left Rome in 1656 for the Levant, but were forced to sail from Ormuz to Macau when the route across Persia was blocked. Gruber trekked back to Europe from Peking in the company of Albert d'Orville just two years after arriving at the Qing capital. François de Rougemont and Philippe Couplet also tried to find an overland route from India to China after their arrival in Goa in 1656. After two years of travel the Jesuits had only reached Siam, from whence they sailed to Macau. The road to China, as it turned out, was paved with good intentions but was too arduous to constitute a reliable alternative to the Cape route.

Martino Martini's safe return to China was a rousing triumph for the Vice-Province. In addition to escorting a set of new missionaries, he had ensured that another group was waiting in the wings for their turn to head for China. These were the eight priests and one coadjutor whom Martini had left at Goa to complete their studies. Moreover, while at Rome he scored what the Jesuits thought was the definitive resolution of the controversies that had been started by the Spanish Mendicants. In the wake of the papal condemnation of the Chinese Rites as they had been presented by Friar Juan Baptista Morales in 1645, the Society sought to present its own interpretation. Martini's arrival offered a prime opportunity for a skilled China hand to explain these practices to the ecclesiastical authorities. Convinced by his explanation, Alexander VII issued another decree in 1656 allowing the rites to be observed by the Jesuits' Chinese Christians. The existence of two contradictory papal statements on the rites,

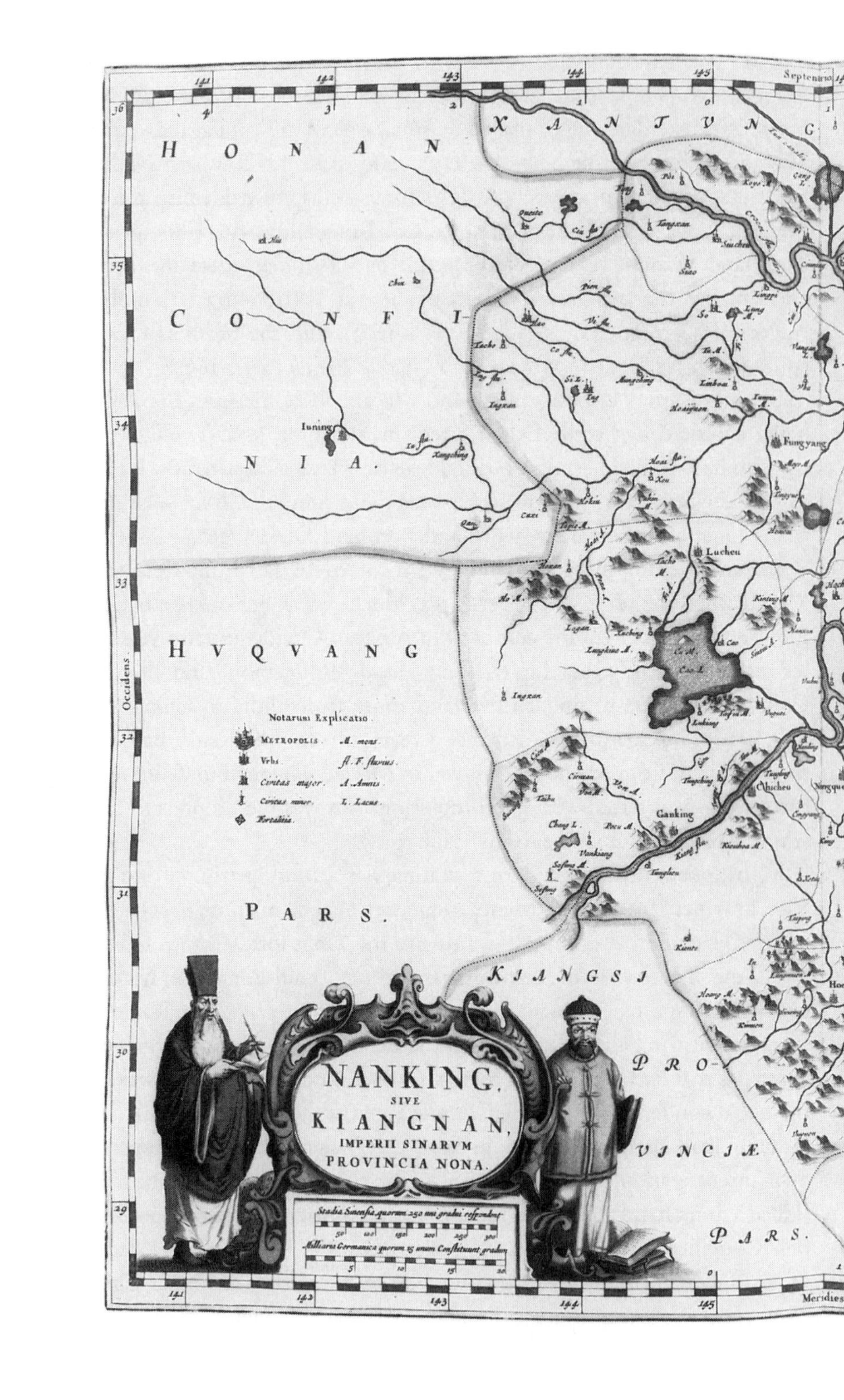
NANKING, SIVE KIANGNAN, IMPERII SINARVM PROVINCIA NONA.
HONAN CONFINIA.
XANTVNG
HVQVANG PARS.
KIANGSI PROVINCIÆ PARS.
Notarum Explicatio
Metropolis.
Vrbs
Civitas major.
Civitas minor.
Fortalitia.
M. mons.
fl. F. fluvius.
A. Amnis.
L. Lacus.
Occidens.
Septentrio
Meridies
Fungyang
Lucheu
Ganking
Chicheu
Iuning
Hoeicheu

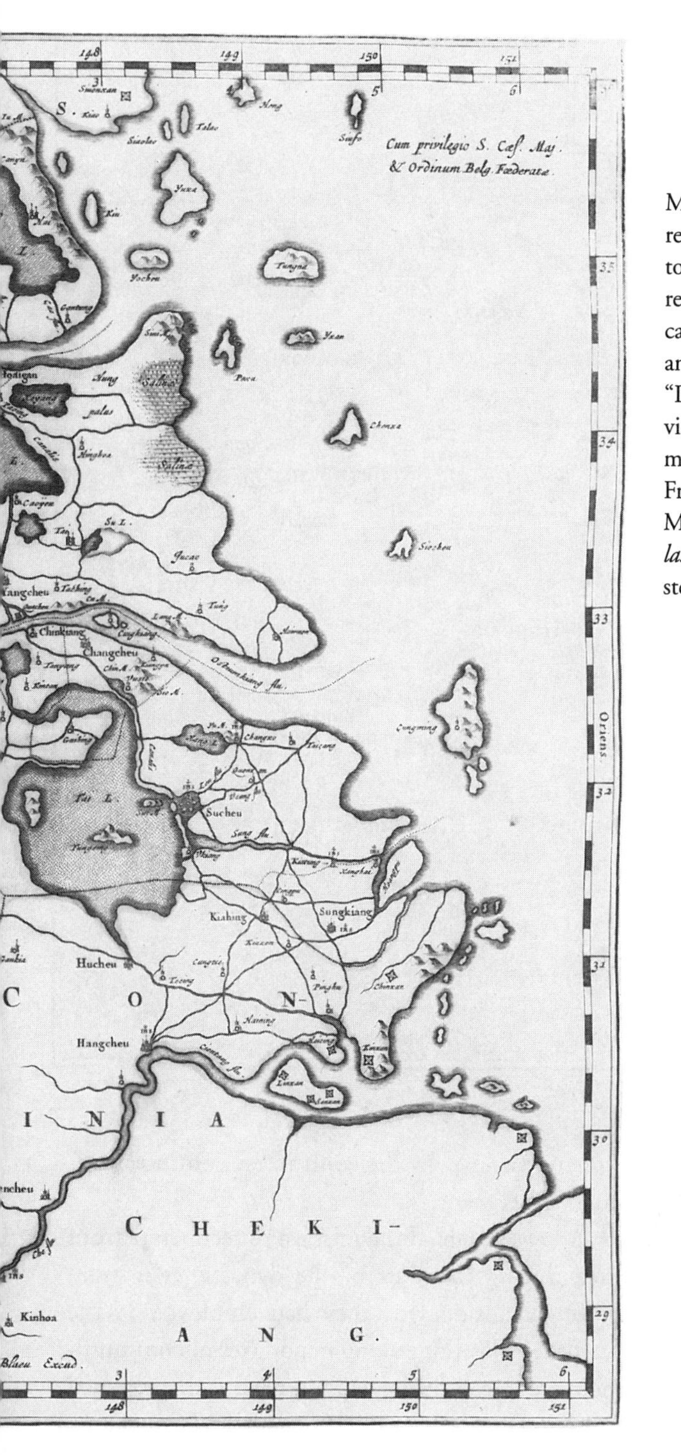

Map of Jiangnan region. Cities and towns with Jesuit residences are indicated with a cross and the monogram "IHS," not fully visible here (see map on page 122). From Martino Martini, *Novus Atlas Sinensis* (Amsterdam, 1655).

however, was one of the main reasons why the controversy continued unresolved for at least another eighty years.

The infusion of new manpower enabled the mission to recuperate from the losses it had sustained during the wars of the dynastic transition. Using the same criteria for expansion that they had employed in the 1630s, the Jesuits reinforced their positions along major axes of communication. To consolidate their presence in the Jiangnan region, they opened residences in cities such as Yangzhou, Changshu, Huai'an, and Songjiang, places that had previously been visited by itinerant missionaries. From

Jiangnan, the Vice-Province resumed its work in Henan Province, sending the Austrian Christian Herdtrich (1625–1684) to Kaifeng to find and build on the vestiges of Rodrigo de Figueiredo's efforts.

In an attempt to reestablish a presence in Jiangxi Province after the destruction of the Nanchang residence and its Christian community, Jacques le Faure was sent to petition the governor general for permission to reside there. After meeting with this mandarin in Ganzhou, the seat of the southern military garrison, Faure chose to settle in that city.[69] From the strategic perspective of the Vice-Province, he had made an excellent choice. Not only was Ganzhou situated on the main north-south route from Guangdong to Jiangnan, but it sat at the confluence of rivers leading east out of Jiangxi into Fujian as well. From here missionaries could travel south to Canton and Macau and east to Dingzhou, Shaowu, or Yanping. The mission fully resumed its work in Jiangxi Province in 1661, when Inácio da Costa opened a house at Nanchang and helped Prospero Intorcetta (1625–1696) get settled at Jianchang.

Another example of the Jesuits' efforts to regain lost ground was the reopening of their Huguang Province residence. In 1661 Jacques Motel accompanied Basilio Xu Zuanzeng (1627–1700, *jinshi* 1649), the great-grandson of Xu Guangqi, on his journey up the Yangzi to take up a post in Sichuan. News of uprisings to the west gave Xu reason to tarry at Wuchang, where he insisted that Motel settle. The French Jesuit purchased a house with a large garden in the center of the city, using funds that Xu had given him. Motel informed his superiors that his new residence was situated on the principal street that led from the quayside to the palaces of the important provincial mandarins. All of the officials who arrived at Wuchang therefore had to pass in front of his church on their way to visit the governor, "seeing it, learning about it, and taking news of it all over the province." This strategic position, Motel claimed, made this new sanctuary known to far more Chinese than other churches "that had been open for many years."[70]

By 1663 the men of the Vice-Province were confident about their future in the Qing empire. Their warm relations with the Peking mandarins even led Gabriel de Magalhães to exclaim, "Never during the previous dynasty had the mission reached the state in which it is now."[71] Despite the fact that their ranks comprised only twenty-four European priests and three Chinese coadjutors, they had nearly doubled their number of mission stations in the face of tremendous social unrest. Whereas in 1631 they had just eleven houses, by 1663 they could count twenty residences spread across ten provinces. Moreover, the Vice-Province also had another eleven churches in different cities, each with living quarters for itinerant priests. Although it did not have enough men to staff all of the houses, the Jesuits knew that new recruits would shortly arrive from India and Europe.

In one estimate from 1663 the China Jesuits stated that they administered the sacraments to over 105,000 Christians every year. This number represented close to 100,000 more adherents of *Tianzhu jiao* than the mission had claimed at the time of André Palmeiro's 1629 visit. Logically, the focal points of the Vice-Province were the areas where the highest concentrations of Christians were to be found. These included Peking with three residences and 13,000 Christians, Shaanxi Province with two residences and 24,000 Christians, and the Jiangnan region with ten residences and 51,000 Christians. Of all of these residences, the mission station with the greatest pastoral burden was at Shanghai, where a lone priest and coadjutor ministered to more than 40,000 Christians. The only significant loss of Chinese Christians had occurred in the Yellow River valley in Shanxi and Henan provinces. In the Jiangzhou-Puzhou area, war, famine, and revolt had reduced the number of Christians from almost 8,000 at the time of Alfonso Vagnone's death in 1640 to just over 3,300 in the early 1660s, while Kaifeng's community appears to have been destroyed entirely.[72]

After eighty years of missionary work in China, it seemed that the Jesuits' patience and effort had begun to pay off. Clearly the passing of the Ming order, under which Matteo Ricci and his early colleagues had found their first interlocutors in China, had not hampered the men of the Vice-Province from making converts to Christianity.[73] They were starting to fulfill the hopes of their Roman superiors, to the point where Superior General Goswin Nickel decided in 1658 to attribute the southern regions of Guangdong, Guangxi, and Hainan Island to the withered Province of Japan. This act imposed an administrative boundary on the Jesuit map of China at the place where the Vice-Province had always encountered problems. It also reinvigorated the Society's work at Macau, turning the city's Jesuit college into a new hub of missionary activity radiating out across southern China, Tonkin, Cochin China, Laos, Siam, and Cambodia. While this gesture removed a set of burdens from the collective shoulders of the China Jesuits, it did not meaningfully resolve the disparity between the number of Chinese Christians and the number of missionaries. As it happens, all the efforts of the men of the Vice-Province had sufficed to build a massive house of cards that would come tumbling down if a strong wind blew against it.

4

The Problem of Success

In the spring of 1664 the China Jesuits went from the heights of optimism to the depths of despair. Looking back over the series of misfortunes that had befallen them in such a short span, the missionaries could only express astonishment. The initial years of Qing rule had been good for them, wrote Manuel Jorge, but this "peace was not peace, it was a traitorous silence, a feigned calm, a dubious mildness, a sea of milk soon to be changed into a sea of tears." Suddenly, the Peking Jesuits were carted off to prison bound with "nine long and thick chains of iron, all with iron locks; three around the neck, three on the arms, and three on the feet." By early 1665, all of the priests had been summoned to the capital to hear the sentence brought against them by the Ministry of Rites: Johann Adam Schall was to be executed and the others were to be exiled to Manchuria. Before leaving the capital, each priest was to receive forty lashes with a bamboo cane—"cruel blows, which kill those on the first strike who cannot hold on to receive the second one." The ministry further ordered their churches shuttered and their books and images about the Lord of Heaven and His teachings consigned to the flames.[1]

The events known as the Calendar Case and the Canton exile caught the Jesuits off guard and very nearly ended their missionary enterprise. Only a stroke of luck in the form of a natural disaster prevented the harsh verdicts against them from being carried out in full. Instead, the missionaries were banished to Guangdong Province to await deportation to Macau. This, too, they were spared; they instead spent seven years in Canton under house arrest. When the political winds at Peking shifted after the enthronement of the Kangxi emperor, the court Jesuits were restored to their positions, and their colleagues were permitted to return to their provincial residences.

The missionaries who fanned out across the empire in the early 1670s encountered a different set of pastoral tasks than they had known before. Their primary challenge shifted from proselytizing to managing their ever-expanding Christian communities. Moreover, they had to find some way to alleviate the substantial pastoral burdens that had accumulated during their absence. The Jesuits had three options: to delegate more of their tasks to native auxiliaries; to ordain a Chinese clergy; or to request help from other religious orders. Since they believed that their past and future successes hinged on the efforts of a carefully trained and unified corps of missionaries, they eventually rejected all three. Yet while the Jesuits deliberated, events that would bring them new worries continued to develop beyond their control. A tide of rivals from Manila, Rome, and France gathered on Chinese shores; soon it would crash against the Vice-Province. The new arrivals had come to partake of the apostolic glory that the Society of Jesus had long touted in Europe. The Jesuits' claim to sole proprietorship over Christianity in China was fast coming to an end.

"No Lack of Vexations," 1664–1670

The crackdown that began in 1664 came as a near-total surprise to the missionaries tending to their Christian communities outside Peking. This attack, launched at court by one of Johann Adam Schall's competitors, hit the mission at its most vulnerable point. Over the years since the late 1620s, with the integration of the court Jesuits into the imperial bureaucracy, they began to take over responsibility for the safety of the mission from their first mandarin allies. After Schall became director of the Imperial Astronomical Bureau in 1645, the critical task of cultivating goodwill among the governing elite fell to him personally.

The German Jesuit had carried out his assignment with considerable aplomb, befriending the Shunzhi emperor and receiving the material displays of respect befitting any important court mandarin. He was, however, anything but unaffected by his prestige and by the realization that it was his skills that made him the linchpin of the Jesuits' China enterprise. He had no shortage of detractors even within the ranks of his religious order. Gabriel de Magalhães and Lodovico Buglio, Schall's companions at Peking, felt that the lifestyle of a Chinese official was unbecoming to a member of the Society of Jesus. They criticized Schall's willingness to serve a non-Christian emperor in ways that seemed to make him instrumental in the propagation of idolatry. After all, what was the purpose of the imperial calendar? Buglio and Magalhães, as well as other Jesuits, knew that that Qing state relied on Schall's astronomical data to draw up a schedule of lucky and unlucky days for imperial ceremonies.[2] Other missionaries such as Jacques le Faure and Francesco Brancati defended Schall, noting the tangible benefits that the Vice-Province had received because of his service at court.[3] To their Jesuit superiors, however, the Vice-Province could not suffer the loss of either Schall's pension or his standing at court. They chose instead to stomach the contradiction between the image of a mandarin and that of a missionary, *ad maiorem Dei gloriam.* Nevertheless, they censured his court lifestyle, seeking to stifle rumors about Schall's flamboyance and arrogance.

If Schall was a controversial figure within the Society, he was even more so outside it. The central problem, however, was that his entry into Qing court politics involved the fate of the Vice-Province. As yet another rider jockeying for position within the new foreign dynasty's court, Schall inevitably left disgruntled rivals behind. Perhaps the most important of these Chinese detractors were the Muslim astronomers at the Astronomical Bureau whose dismissal Schall had requested and obtained in 1657. These rivals caught up with the mandarin missionary and the rest of the Jesuits soon after his imperial patron—the Vice-Province's de facto protector—died in 1661.

The primary instigator of the Calendar Case was a minor court figure, Yang Guangxian (1597–1669), an acquaintance of one of the Muslim astronomers sacked at Schall's instigation. Primed by personal dislike and an objection to the German's exclusive control of the official methods of practicing astronomy, Yang began to spew forth accusations in 1659. He composed a set of books that attacked Western scientific methods and mocked aspects of Christianity.[4] He then submitted memorials to the throne, denouncing Schall as a threat to the Qing state. Employing the register of literati discourse in his writings, Yang cast himself in the role of a defender of Confucian orthodoxy who sought to restore the proper balance between Chinese and foreign influences at the imperial court.

It was only after 1661, while the Oboi regents governed in the stead of the future Kangxi emperor (r. 1661–1722), that these attacks began to receive a favorable reception at the highest levels of imperial power. In an ironic vindication of Magalhães, Yang offered proof in one of his memorials that the bureau run by Schall had calculated an inauspicious day and place for the burial of an infant from the imperial household, using faulty science. The Jesuit had thereby brought on the deaths of Shunzhi and his consort, who expired in the following months. Surely this treasonous act merited investigation, Yang maintained, since these foreign agents were likely plotting even greater rebellious acts. By late summer 1664 the regents had delegated the case to the Ministry of Rites, which moved immediately to detain the court Jesuits and seven of their Chinese Christian assistants from the Astronomical Bureau, including Li Zubai (baptized 1622, d. 1665), a prominent astronomer. As Schall, Buglio, Magalhães, and their younger colleague Ferdinand Verbiest sat in jail alongside their native collaborators, news of a major crisis for the Vice-Province left the capital.[5]

Unlike the swift flow of communications throughout China, the wheels of imperial justice turned slowly enough for the Jesuits to escape severe punishment. Edicts summoning the provincial missionaries to the capital went out soon after the imprisonment of their colleagues at Peking on September 15, 1664. When word reached Jiangxi Province, Prospero Intorcetta, Adrien Grelon (1618–1696), and Pietro Canevari were harassed by authorities and jailed before being sent on their way. The four Dominicans and one Jesuit, Humbert Augery, found in Zhejiang Province were also imprisoned. But not all of the men in the provinces received the harsh treatment reserved for those accused of treason. For instance, the mandarin who expedited Manuel Jorge from Huai'an let the Jesuit decide the date when he would be carried to Peking—in a sedan chair, though with an armed escort. Inácio da Çosta and António de Gouvea likewise traveled freely from Fujian Province to the capital, traveling north "without soldiers, without guards, and even without an edict from the mandarins." Similarly, François de Rougemont, Philippe Couplet, Francesco Brancati, Feliciano Pacheco, and Jacques le Faure were called to Suzhou before being sent north, but the local mandarins treated them cordially, letting them stay in the city's mission station and meet with Christians.[6] By the midsummer 1665, twenty-one Jesuits (along with four Dominicans and a Franciscan) had arrived at court.

In April 1665 the Ministry of Rites issued its sentence against Schall and his accomplices: the ringleader and his Chinese auxiliaries from the Astronomical Bureau were to be executed by dismemberment, while the rest of the foreigners were to be exiled with forty lashes as viaticum. Yet just as the authorities prepared this pronouncement, Heaven apparently showed its displeasure in the form of a comet. Then, shortly after the verdict came out, an earthquake struck the capital, splitting one of the walls of the imperial palace. These coincidences led to the issuance of a general pardon, but it did not extend to those guilty of treason. Li Zubai and four of Schall's other Chinese assistants suffered the harshest fate of all the condemned; they were beheaded in mid-May.

The amnesty was more valuable to the Europeans, and especially the court Jesuits. The sentence against Schall was downgraded to house arrest. Magalhães and Buglio were sent back to their residence, Peking's Eastern Church, where Verbiest and later Schall joined them. It remains unclear why the condemned Jesuits were allowed to stay on at the capital, although Manuel Jorge claimed that Schall and Verbiest were summoned in chains in 1665 to predict an eclipse for the young Kangxi emperor—throwing doubt on Yang's abilities as an astronomer.[7] To be sure, Yang did not see himself as Schall's replacement; during his first year as court astronomer, he submitted five memorials requesting permission to resign his post.[8] One of the Dominicans called to Peking, Friar Domingo de Navarrete (1618–1689), suggested that they had been kept at court for "Chinese reason of state" since they had been pensionaries. As such, they either were still useful or knew too much about the workings of the Qing government to be sent away.[9] In any case, the main offender, the seventy-four-year-old Schall, expired within a year of the verdict.

The other missionaries fared somewhat better. To start with, they were permitted to stay at the Vice-Province's Peking residences instead of in jail. In the final verdict of September 12, 1665, their punishment was reduced to exile to their native lands via Macau. Clearly seeing the hand of the Almighty in the mission's affairs, Jorge described how the earthquake caused a cross to fall to the ground from the façade of one of the Peking churches: "Thus Heaven told us that all of the priests would have to go in procession to Canton bearing the cross." It was indeed a Via Dolorosa. The priests sailed slowly down the Grand Canal in the cold Chinese winter, without adequate provisions, in vessels that failed to protect them from the elements. A little over a month after their arrival in Canton on March 25, 1666, Inácio da Costa succumbed to an illness provoked by the rigors of the journey.[10]

Just as during the Nanjing affair, the verdict of expulsion against the Jesuits was not carried out. Once at Canton, they were confined to the residence owned by the Society of Jesus. But the Guangdong authorities were not uniformly averse to the missionaries; moreover, they did not stand to gain great rewards if they diligently carried out the order to expel the missionaries to Macau. As François de Rougemont recorded, the Europeans initially encountered "no lack of vexations" from some magistrates. But the "damnable intents" of these "relics of the persecution," he noted, were curbed by the provincial governor, who treated the missionaries kindly.[11] According to Domingo de Navarrete, this mandarin stated that he was in the midst of a dispute with the Portuguese colony and so would take the prisoners under his personal care.[12] The governor's benevolence included sending money to the Europeans twice for expanding their cramped quarters—enough to build twenty-two cubicles in a house that originally had room for just two men.[13] Confused about their fate, the missionaries whiled away their time in study and prayer. "We passed from the life of the world," wrote Navarrete, "which was very sad and melancholic, to that of God, which was good since we had lost our liberty for the sake of His law."[14]

The combination of official favor and bureaucratic inertia eventually helped undo the strictures placed on the Jesuits and their coreligionists. Less than two years after they had arrived at Canton, they found themselves with considerable liberty to move about the city. They could even make daylong journeys unimpeded.[15] Such freedoms enabled them to return to the business of cultivating their Chinese Christians as well as the communities of African and Indian slaves who had escaped from their Portuguese masters at Macau to Canton. In September 1668, taking advantage of their relative lack of supervision, the Jesuits secretly sent Prospero Intorcetta to Europe to report on the state of the Vice-Province to their Superior General. In order to avoid raising suspicions, the missionaries replaced the Sicilian under the cover of night with a Frenchman, Germain Macret (1620–1676), who had been smuggled into the empire from Macau.

During their confinement, the Peking Jesuits had ample opportunity to reflect on recent events and plan their return to prestige. Since the Calendar Case had started at court, they hoped that it would end there with a vindication of their scientific skills. The fact they had stayed on at Peking meant that there were men ready to return to the Astronomical Bureau when Yang left the stage. Their opportunity came a few years after Yang

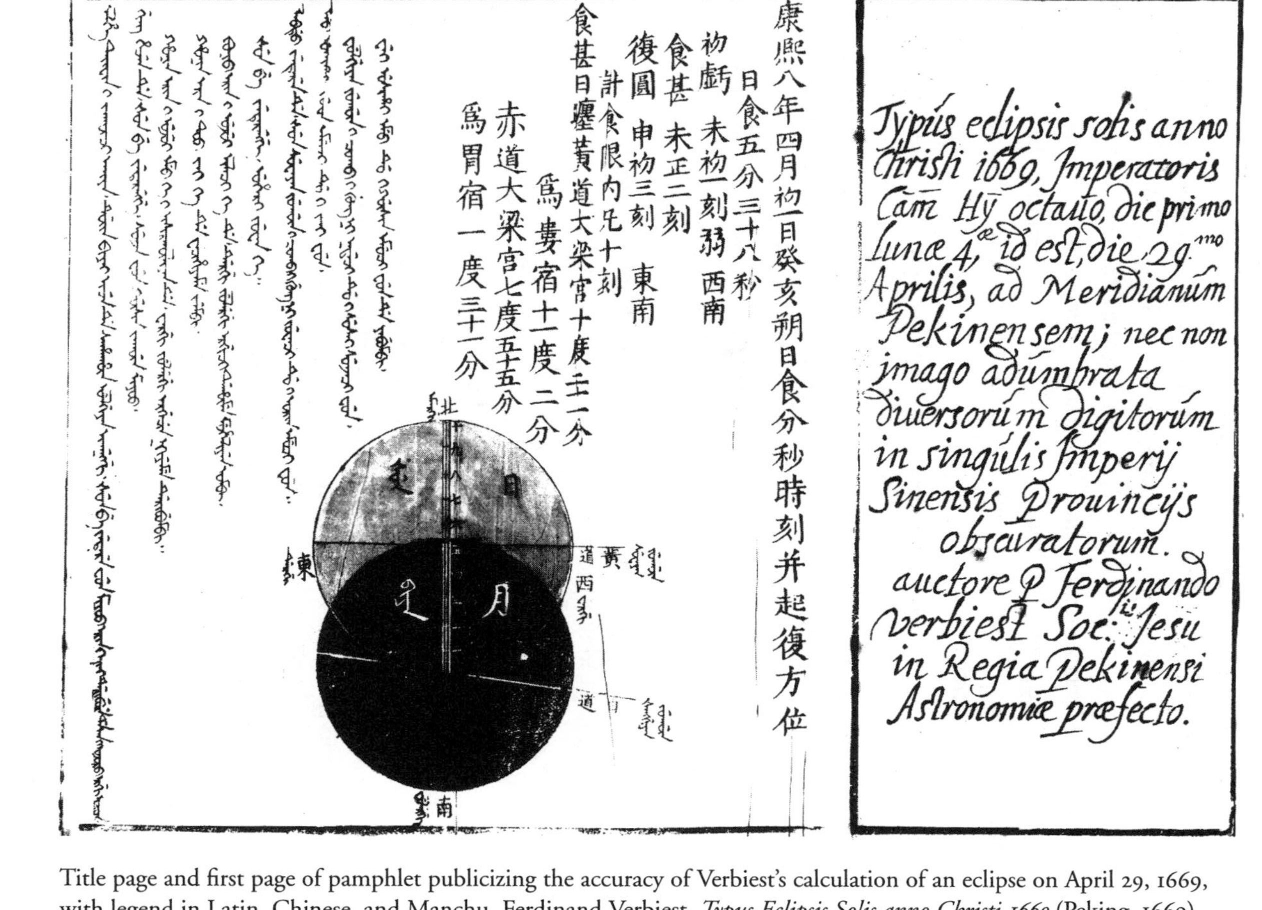

Title page and first page of pamphlet publicizing the accuracy of Verbiest's calculation of an eclipse on April 29, 1669, with legend in Latin, Chinese, and Manchu. Ferdinand Verbiest, *Typus Eclipsis Solis anno Christi 1669* (Peking, 1669).

and his Muslim colleagues were entrusted with calculating a new calendar. By 1668 Ferdinand Verbiest had assumed the role of chief scientist among the Jesuits at court. He had demonstrated his competence in astronomy to the future emperor at several reprises, and in 1668 revealed the inaccuracy of Yang's calendar. In his first act of personal rule the following year, Kangxi dismissed Yang from government service, citing his incompetence as an astronomer and his false accusations against the deceased Schall. The Qing sovereign then installed Verbiest as director of the Astronomical Bureau. This event inaugurated a new period of friendship between Kangxi and the Peking Jesuits, with the Flemish priest serving as one of the young emperor's personal tutors.

In the late 1660s the priests at Canton turned their attention to reviewing their missionary strategies. Much had changed since the last time a sizable number of Jesuits had gathered in one place, three decades before. Most important, the Vice-Province had spread its men throughout the empire and started Christian communities that had grown significantly. New methods were required for dealing with the large numbers of Chinese men and women who needed to receive the sacraments every year. It was also necessary to devise new ways of teaching doctrine and a standardized pastoral practice so that new recruits could take over smoothly when their colleagues died or were transferred. In addition to their pastoral concerns, the Jesuits confronted the reality that they were no longer the only European clergy in China. By the late 1640s, a pair of Franciscans had set up a mission in Shandong Province, and the Dominicans continued their efforts in the Fu'an area and southern Zhejiang Province. In fact, only three Dominican friars were present at Canton because five others were undetected or overlooked by the authorities in Fujian Province.

Hoping to reach an agreement among the three religious orders about a new general strategy for propagating Christianity in China, the priests held a conference. Between December 18, 1667, and January 26, 1668, they discussed such topics as the caution that was necessary when administering to women those sacraments which required a priest's touch, the want of able catechists and of competent doctrine teachers for children, the phrases to be used when baptizing, and the need to ensure that those converts who had practiced Buddhist vegetarian fasting abandoned it entirely. Other concerns dealt with the divisions among the missionaries. One point asked for common assent that no group denounce the others to the Qing authorities. On the last day of the conference, the assembled missionaries gave their unanimous assent that Saint Joseph be proclaimed the patron saint of China.[16]

According to Visitor Luís da Gama (1610–1672), the missionaries at Canton enjoyed a favorable consensus on most of the forty-one points discussed. The greatest stumbling block, however, was the divergence of opinions over the Chinese Rites. For their part, the Jesuits insisted that the 1656 bull secured by Martino Martini in favor of these ceremonies be observed by all three orders. But the lone Franciscan and the Dominicans objected. Domingo de Navarrete and Antonio de Santa Maria Caballero even attempted to persuade da Gama to command his subordinates to change their minds, presenting him with written explanations of their views, but to no avail. Nevertheless, the Visitor did express concern that the Mendicants might still cause the Jesuits trouble over this issue. "I fear that they will send their treatises to Rome," da Gama wrote to the Society's Superior General in 1668, "and that the ceremonies for Confucius and the deceased will again be abolished."[17] Little did the Visitor know that Santa Maria had already dispatched to Rome a partial copy of Niccolò Longobardo's banned text from the 1620s about the disputed terms as evidence against the supposed uniformity of the Society's position, and that Navarrete was soon to leave for Europe to vilify the China Jesuits in print.[18] In light of the rupture over the rites, the consensus on mundane pastoral matters at Canton was of little value. Soon the divisions between the religious orders would grow as each side took turns presenting its views on this contested issue to ecclesiastical authorities and the European public in the hopes of receiving another pronouncement in its own favor.[19]

The discord revealed at the Canton conference did not stop the men of the Vice-Province from developing new uniform procedures for their Christian communities. The variety of Catholic devotions spread across the Qing empire by priests of different nationalities was one of their central challenges. This diffuse spectrum of practices was the natural consequence of the chronology of the mission's expansion, since the last set of Vice-Provincial statutes was composed in the early 1630s, just before the numbers of Chinese Christians began to grow in earnest. During private consultations, the Canton Jesuits decided to reduce the diversity of devotional confraternities found in their communities to four: one penitential, one doctrinal, one charitable, and one more broadly devotional. These groups would use the standard appellations Brotherhood of the Passion,

Confraternity of the Angels, Brotherhood of Mercy, and Confraternity of the Blessed Virgin, respectively. Vice-Provincial Feliciano Pacheco issued other new rules, including a restriction on preaching, which was to be reserved for priests (not catechists or other Christians), the obligatory use of the special hat to be worn while saying the mass (priests celebrated the Eucharist with bare heads in Europe), and a prohibition on permitting converts to eat in the Society's residences after being baptized. The Jesuits also drew up a set of rules to be sent to their Christians, spelling out the obligations of lay Catholics and the new uniform pastoral practices to be used in China.[20]

The Jesuits' forced seclusion allowed them to reinvest in the intellectual undertaking that had gained them access to Chinese culture in the first place. Seeing knowledge of indigenous philosophy as their most formidable weapon in the battle for souls, they set about translating the main works in the Chinese canon for the benefit of future missionaries. Since the growing numbers of Christians made it unlikely that new missionaries would have the luxury of formal study in these texts, they produced their own editions with romanized text and commentary. It was also an opportunity to preserve the Society's acquired insights into Confucian thought. The Jesuits consequently decided to supplement Prospero Intorcetta's 1662 translation of the *Analects* and the *Great Learning,* titled *Sapientia Sinica,* with a larger edition called *Sinarum Scientia Politico-Moralis* for the use of missionaries throughout East Asia. The first of this work's two volumes was printed at Canton in 1667, while the second appeared in 1670 at Goa, a year after Intorcetta passed through India bound for Europe.

As their stay in Canton lengthened from months to years, the Jesuits grew uncertain how their tribulations would end. The news from Peking was encouraging, but they still needed Ferdinand Verbiest to be promoted to Johann Adam Schall's old position. Word reached Canton that the missionaries' sanctuaries and residences were intact, in accordance with an imperial decree requiring "that they not be knocked down but closed and guarded by the mandarins in each town."[21] Their mandarin acquaintances at the court insinuated to them that the Oboi regents had resisted destroying their churches out of fear of harsher reprisals from the young Kangxi emperor when he assumed the throne.[22] Only Peking's churches appear to have suffered at all: the Eastern Church was closed, and Yang Guangxian had taken over Schall's residence to use it, as one Jesuit wrote, for "parties, comedies, and other things unfitting a sacred place."[23]

An even more important concern for the missionaries was the spiritual welfare of their Christians. The lax conditions of their confinement at Canton permitted them to forward correspondence to the leaders of their communities, as well as copies of the new rules.[24] But from the perspective of this group of Catholic priests, five years was an intolerably long time for their flocks to be cut off from the sacraments. There was one priest, however, who could continue to circulate around China visiting the Jesuits' Christians. This was Gregorio López Luo Wenzao (1617–1691), a Chinese Dominican who had been born in Fujian Province at Fu'an and educated in Manila. Luo gained the Jesuits' gratitude for his repeated calls to their followers in the Jiangnan area. But even a superhuman effort exerted by one priest was far from sufficient for maintaining the faith of the thousands whom the missionaries had baptized throughout China—not to mention the children who had been born to Christian parents during their absence.

In addition to the indispensable service provided by Luo, the Jesuits counted on their lay auxiliaries for help. It was during the Canton exile that the catechists and local Christian leaders *(huizhang)* began to play increasingly important roles within their communities. Because of the growing numbers of adherents of the *Tianzhu jiao* and the stagnant numbers of priests, the Jesuits were forced to delegate an ever greater proportion of their pastoral responsibilities to auxiliaries such as these. To be sure, it was because the auxiliaries had performed well at such important tasks as doctrine teaching or overseeing the moral and spiritual progress of their peers that the priests so readily handed over duties which would under other circumstances have been incumbent on themselves. Reporting to Rome in 1667, Visitor da Gama noted how the *huizhang* had proved crucial to maintaining the devotional schedules instituted by the missionaries, especially in larger communities such as Shanghai. By 1670 the Jesuits could trumpet to Europe the news that their church had survived the rigors of the recent persecution: "Throughout the empire, the neophytes live in peace, fervor, and constancy. They gather in their confraternities with great modesty. And the industriousness of the local leaders makes the number of Christians grow daily."[25]

So the Canton exile had definitively shifted the responsibility of proselytizing from the foreign Jesuits to the Chinese Christians. In their role as catechists, these individuals took the initiative to claim converts, baptize new Christians, and oversee the publication of new editions of texts on Christian themes. When the Jesuits returned to their residences after receiving a pardon in December 1670, they found that their communities had increased in size during their absence. The change was most evident in the Jiangnan area. At Changshu, François de Rougemont claimed that his catechists had been responsible for three hundred new baptisms. Those at Shanghai had been even more active, with Francesco Brancati recording the addition of almost a thousand new Christians to his flock.[26] These were the first signals of a great shift in the nature of the Jesuits' relationship to the propagation of *Tianzhu jiao.* In the relatively short span of forty years since the mission church had begun to grow in earnest—including five years of exile—the Jesuits had been transformed from the primary propagators of a new religion into the overburdened managers of far-flung and ever-expanding Christian communities.

Straining at the Seams, 1671–1687

The signs of imperial favor toward Ferdinand Verbiest and the other court Jesuits that appeared in the late 1660s presaged the end of the Canton exile. In March 1671 the detained priests were permitted to leave Guangdong Province and return to their mission stations. To the Jesuits, the imperial proclamation that confirmed Verbiest's sciences and their liberty was a great triumph, a victory to be celebrated and publicized. But the document stopped short of either proclaiming tolerance for Christianity or declaring that the missionaries were free to preach their religion. In fact, it stated that they could practice their religion with the followers they had already made, but were barred from making new converts. A further condition prohibited Chinese Christians from holding meetings and from wearing devotional objects such as Agnus Dei, nominas, or veronicas.[27] While this combination of restrictions and liberty initially left the Jesuits perplexed about their status vis-à-vis authorities in the provinces (they were aware that such restrictions were typically placed on religious sects considered heterodox), they soon learned the benefit of the display of imperial favor. With Kangxi himself acting as their patron, no concerted attempt was made to enforce the less favorable clauses of this edict.

The Jesuits suffered from no illusions about how they had gained their freedom. They knew that the fate of the Vice-Province hinged on the emperor's goodwill in an obvious way. The unease that had arisen among certain members of the Society of Jesus over their confreres' scientific service to a non-Christian ruler dissolved in the face of this new reality. The Jesuits therefore placed even more of their limited resources at the court in order to cement their links to the Qing sovereign. In 1671 Claudio Filippo Grimaldi (1638–1712), a Piedmontese missionary who had traveled to Canton to take the place of Domingo de Navarrete when the Dominican left for Europe, went to Peking to join Buglio, Magalhães, and Verbiest. Tomé Pereira (1645–1708), a Portuguese priest, was sent to the capital two years later to entertain the emperor with his musical abilities.

The Peking Jesuits' overtures toward Kangxi brought them handsome rewards, helping them overcome the lingering stigma of the recent exile. Important gestures of imperial favor marked the emperor's visit to their residence on July 12, 1675. Accompanied by family members and retainers, Kangxi first toured the church and afterwards visited the missionaries' quarters and their garden. According to Gabriel de Magalhães, he exclaimed, "Great Harmony! Great Purity!" upon entering the compound's sanctuary. There Kangxi read the inscriptions of the Ten Commandments and the Works of Mercy which hung on the walls. Outside, he was taken by the way Grimaldi had engineered the perspectives in the gardens, "truly, a very curious and ingenious layout." But the greatest indication of Kangxi's patronage came when he presented the missionaries with an honorific inscription. While this gesture was in keeping with the emperor's attitude toward holy men—in the same year he also wielded the imperial brush for the Fifty-fourth Celestial Master, the Daoist priest Zhang Jizong—the Jesuits considered it a major display of respect.[28] Standing before the priests in Lodovico Buglio's room, he wrote *Jing Tian,* "Revere Heaven." The following day he sent the missionaries another copy of his Confucian-inspired motto in large calligraphy for them to hang on the façade of their church and invited the priests to join him for a horseback ride through his palatial gardens.[29]

The Jesuits moved quickly to ensure that potential rivals knew of their close contacts with the emperor. No sooner was the *Jing Tian* inscription displayed at the Peking residence than replicas were made for installation on their churches throughout the empire. Here was yet another instance of the predicament in which the Jesuits found themselves when they resumed their positions at the court. It had been over four decades since the missionaries had abandoned *Tian* as an acceptable term for the Christian God, but they could not resist publicizing Kangxi's favor. Similarly, they could not refuse his bequest of regal funeral pomp on the occasion of Gabriel de Magalhães's death in 1677. Even if, as a Jesuit, Magalhães was bound by a vow of poverty, his confreres had to use the gift of two hundred taels to conduct an elaborate burial. Once again, the Jesuits had been forced to reconcile the necessity of display with their pastoral obligations, to the detriment of the latter. Emblems of court ceremonial, including yellow banners decorated with a portrait of Magalhães and a copy of Kangxi's elegy, took pride of place over the dozens of poor Christians who came to pray for the soul of their priest.[30]

The Vice-Province's efforts to win Kangxi's favor came at a heavy cost. By placing five men at the court, the Jesuits diluted their capacities in the provinces and stretched their enterprise almost to the point of rupture in the 1670s. It was during this decade and the next that the ratio of priests to Chinese Christians reached its lowest mark. By 1675 the Vice-Province had at its disposal no more than seventeen European priests and three Chinese coadjutors to tend to more than 110,000 Christians, only a fraction of whom lived near Peking.

News of the Canton exile caused the Vice-Province's manpower supply line to run dry. The recruits left at Goa by Martino Martini in 1657 for the purpose of completing their schooling had been redirected to other assignments when word of the persecution reached India. Worse still, reports of the missionaries' confinement—regrettably, to their minds, not martyrdom—that reached Europe helped to shrink the pool of candidates who considered petitioning for service in China. Despite their release from Canton in 1671, the men of the Vice-Province were desperately few. In 1678 they numbered fifteen; in 1680, with the return of procurator Prospero Intorcetta, their numbers rose to twenty. By 1688 the total was once again down to seventeen, far too few to staff the vast expanses of the mission fields they had plowed.[31] As a stopgap measure, the Vice-Province requested men "on loan" from the amply staffed Province of Japan.

How did the chronic lack of priests affect the mission's development during the 1670s and 1680s? For one thing, it further distanced the Jesuits from the project of propagating Christianity through preaching, engaging in apologetics, or baptizing. Zealous Christians took up the task of proselytizing during the Canton exile, and that trend progressed during this period, leading to a general shift in the channels through which *Tianzhu jiao* reached new ears. The Jesuits' existing pastoral burdens rendered the task of writing new texts for prospective converts an unaffordable luxury—except for the Peking Jesuits, whose lifestyle was more conducive to literary composition. The provincial missionaries exhausted themselves trying to keep track of whether their burgeoning numbers of Christians were receiving a bare minimum of spiritual guidance.[32] But by and large the religious message once disseminated by the Jesuits alone was now spread through kinship networks and among acquaintances. Rather than traveling along the paths trod by the missionaries or being dilated through printed matter, Christianity passed from father to son, mother to daughter, and friend to friend.

Where the missionaries ceded control, the leaders of their Christian communities took over. By the 1670s these individuals were no longer neophytes but the descendants of converts. Their most important function in their communities was the coordination of devotional schedules in the absence of a priest. The communal spiritual life of the mission church therefore consisted primarily of prayer routines rather than daily or weekly masses. Even when a Jesuit was present, the recitation of responsorial prayers was the most widely used form of lay devotion. To be sure, by the standards for lay Catholic piety set at the Council of Trent and promoted by the Society of Jesus, prayer meetings were a sorry substitute for regular reception of the sacraments and close pastoral supervision. The China Jesuits were well aware of this fact, but they realized that such lay-run groups were their best means of preserving their communities while they waited for reinforcements. Yet from the perspective of less enthusiastic church authorities, such unsupervised manifestations of lay piety could be construed as a dangerous abdication of priestly responsibility—a hallmark of the Jesuits' risky habit of conceding spiritual responsibility to men and women who were neither trained in theology nor members of the clerical estate. Whereas in Europe the untiring eye of secular ecclesiastical oversight could spot the perceived excesses of the Society's lay devotees, no such church body existed to monitor the Chinese Catholics ministered to by the men of the Vice-Province.

According to a description of the Jiangnan-area Christians during the 1670s, in each city a male leader was elected to organize communal prayers. When the congregants were assembled, this individual would make the sign of the cross, and then "slowly pray the litanies of the saints following the usage of the Universal Church." For the Jesuits, these invocations were particularly useful because they inculcated points of doctrine and kept the Chinese Christians mindful of the principal mysteries of the faith with their repeated references to the Trinity, the Virgin, the angels, and the saints. The litanies were followed by prayers "for the emperor, for the magistrates, for peace within the empire, and for the fruits of the earth." Further petitions were made for "the emperor of the Holy Law" (the designation for the pope), the propagation of Christianity, the extirpation of heresy, the clergy, the Chinese Christians, and the souls of the deceased. These ceremonies ended with the recitation of the Paternoster and the Ave Maria, followed by five kowtows accompanied by short prayers to the Lord of Heaven and the Virgin.[33]

Although the identities of most of the lay leadership remain shrouded in obscurity, a clear image of at least one has survived. This was Candida Xu (1607–1680), the granddaughter of Paulo Xu Guangqi and mother of Basilio Xu Zuanzeng. In the biography written by Philippe Couplet, Candida's confessor during his ten years of residence in her hometown of Songjiang and nearby Shanghai, she is presented as the embodiment of the Jesuits' ideal of Chinese Christian lay piety. Candida, we are told, never appeared without rosary beads and other outward signs of her devotion. She always showed due respect for holy water, crosses, Agnus Dei pendants, blessed palm fronds, and relics. Personally ascetic, she practiced flagellation in her home, most likely in the company of other female Christians. According to Couplet, she applied such rigor in her devotions that he felt obliged to prohibit her austerities "because of the frailty of her advanced age."[34]

In addition to her pious example, Candida also made generous financial donations to the mission from the 1650s through the 1670s. She helped spread *Tianzhu jiao* among women in the Songjiang area by paying for new editions of Jesuit writings, which she gave to female catechists to distribute. Couplet referred to her as the "mother of all the confraternities" in coastal Jiangnan because she purchased rosary beads, sacred images, and other devotional objects to be given to the local Christians. Candida also paid for the decoration of the area's churches, commissioning paintings for the main church in Shanghai from "the most famous artists in the cities of Macau and Goa." And when Couplet went to Europe as procurator in 1680, she gave him a gold chalice for the Chapel of Saint Ignatius in the Gesù in Rome, as well as silk embroideries for the tomb of Saint Francis Xavier at Goa and the Society's churches in Lisbon, Mechelen, Paris, and Rome. These were gestures befitting a Catholic noblewoman—not surprisingly, the same type of woman to whom Couplet dedicated his treatise when it was published in Europe.[35]

Benefactors as munificent as Candida were rare among the Jesuits' Christians in early Qing China. Community leaders typically had a greater abundance of religious zeal than secular wealth, although they were often of slightly higher social stature than their coreligionists. Yet by sharing their spiritual riches, they made what the Jesuits considered to be the most important contribution to their fellow Christians. In the 1670s and 1680s the Jesuits detected the hand of their community leaders in stimulating a greater general desire for the sacraments of penance and the Eucharist. To be sure, this increased demand for access to Catholic rites was in part a result of the scarcity of priests who could administer them.

This desire for the sacraments was no doubt stimulated by the increased importance of collective piety in the mission church. Membership in all devotional groups, ranging from penitential brotherhoods to the "parishes" called Confraternities of the Blessed Virgin, required regular reception of the sacraments. During the middle decades of the seventeenth century, as these associations assumed a central role in the articulation of Catholic piety in China, their associated pastoral needs took center stage. For example, in the late 1640s Martino Martini noted that taking the Eucharist was "something not normally done, except by older, better-instructed Christians."[36] By the 1680s, however, reception of the sacraments was far more generalized. For one Jesuit in Jiangxi Province in the early part of that decade, this general determination and desire to partake in Catholic rituals, especially at the hour of death, was "a manifest proof that the faith of the greater part of the Christians was not faked but solid and true."[37]

Such expressions of lay piety on the part of their followers surely warmed the hearts of the China Jesuits. But each new Christian who yearned for the Eucharist was yet another pastoral burden bearing down on the fewer than twenty priests in the whole of the Qing realm (excepting the southernmost provinces). By one estimate, the Jesuits' church nearly doubled in size in the span of thirty years, from 105,000 in 1663 to approximately 200,000 in 1695.[38] This presented the Vice-Province with a logistical challenge of tremendous proportions, one that demanded the maximum rationalization of priestly effort. For example, in the late 1680s on Chongming Island near Shanghai, Simão Rodrigues (1645–1704) consolidated the numerous Christians into groups centered on eight oratory chapels and two churches. In this way he could make the most of his six-week stay on the island in 1688, when he baptized 250 Christians and administered communion to 1,300 in the company of another priest, François Noël (1651–1729).[39]

Indoctrination efforts had to be handled in similar fashion. Relying on their collective experience as students and schoolmasters before they had come to the mission field, the Jesuits divided up their flock as they might have structured classes in one of their order's European colleges. For example, when José Soares (1656–1736) spent three days in a village in Shanxi Province in 1687, he found that many Christian children did not know their prayers. He therefore exhorted their parents to gather in the local chapel "so that as some were being taught, all would learn together."[40] In coastal Jiangnan, however, such a task was beyond the Jesuits' individual capacities. In the Songjiang area, Emanuele Laurifice (1646–1703) appointed eight members of each of his forty confraternities to visit all of the Christians in their areas every few months.[41] Admitting the impossibility of going to all of the villages every year, Laurifice assigned these individuals to teach doctrine, baptize children, console the infirm, and exhort only those who were in extreme need of the sacraments to come to his residence.

Fathers and Sons, 1672–1690

Over the course of the decades since the Jesuits first complained about their lack of manpower, a few solutions did emerge. The most obvious one was to start ordaining a Chinese clergy. Native auxiliaries had assisted Jesuits from the time Matteo Ricci had secured a presence in the empire, accompanied by Macanese coadjutors. These indigenous Jesuits had taken vows as brothers, not scholastics; in other words, they were not destined to study for the priesthood. The role they accepted upon joining the order was largely restricted to performing tasks related to the mission's temporal affairs. In the aggregate, not many Chinese brothers served the mission between the 1580s and the 1680s; at any given moment, however, there were two or three. Surely the priests could supplement their paltry numbers with a few good men plucked from the ranks of their zealous catechists, not to speak of their thousands of male followers across the Qing empire.

The possibility of ordaining Chinese priests was something that the Jesuits considered at several junctures. The question was first raised in the 1610s in light of the precedent set by the Japan Jesuits in ordaining a handful of indigenous priests. But although things seemed to be going well for the mission at that time, missionaries in China did not see their enterprise developing in the same dramatic fashion as its East Asian counterpart. When asked by the Society's superiors in Rome if they needed permission to accept Chinese members, the China Jesuits replied that the limited numbers of converts obviated this necessity. Most important for the mission in the 1610s and 1620s was having sufficient "sons of Macau," men of either Chinese or mixed parentage who had been born in the Portuguese colony and schooled by the local Jesuits. While the Vice-Province depended on their courier service and assistance at various residences, no sustained push was made to have them ordained as priests.[42] The enthusiasm originating at the Society's Roman curia for an indigenous Chinese clergy was dampened when the Jesuits perceived the hand of native apostates and saboteurs who had served in their ranks in the wreckage of the Japan mission.[43]

For decades, the question why the China Jesuits dithered so long about creating a native clergy has vexed historians. Given the high esteem that virtually all of the members of the Vice-Province had for China's culture and morality, it appears strange that they did not move more swiftly. In the opinion of one set of scholars, the reason could only be found in the racist outlook of the mission's Portuguese superiors—curiously, the same ones who had carried out the ordination of Japanese priests.[44] Other analyses have insisted on a cleavage between the Jesuits at Macau and those at Peking, with the former being more open to the idea.[45] Yet no such absolute divisions among the missionaries along national or situational lines can be found in extant documents that address the issue.

The most plausible explanation is found in the public image that the Jesuits had cultivated for themselves. In late Ming and early Qing China, the terms "Catholic clergy" and *Tianzhu jiao* were virtual synonyms for the Jesuits of the Vice-Province and their message. Naturally, whether native men could join the Society as priests without compromising that image was a central issue. At stake was the order's exclusive control over the definition of essential terms within the Chinese cultural context. Would the strategies that the missionaries had employed to establish their public reputation and spread their religious message still be viable if Chinese men joined their ranks? How would their group identity and the potency of their rituals be affected by the integration of indigenous—that is, less exotic—members into their ranks? Would familiarity breed contempt? And what would happen to the reputation of the priests if a Chinese Jesuit decided to leave the order or disobey his superiors?

The twin issues of identity and obedience became flashpoints for debate in the 1670s, when the strain of pastoral burdens reached a critical point. For the men of the Vice-Province, the notion of identity was directly related to missionary education. Schooling played a crucial role in the corporate persona of the Society of Jesus. Since all of the China Jesuits had been educated in the order's colleges, it was unthinkable that they could accept men into their ranks who had not undergone such experiences. (The lack of proper training possibilities had first been raised by Francis Xavier with relation to candidates for the priesthood in India and repeatedly used by his successors as a reason to avoid creating a native clergy there.)[46] First of all, the years that the European Jesuits had spent in school had provided them with a common education in classical languages, Aristotelian philosophy, and scholastic theology. This formational path gave them the skills, in particular a knowledge of Latin, essential for church rituals, and a familiarity with "cases of conscience," indispensable for assigning the proper penance after hearing confessions. Second, the Society did not have a complete academic apparatus in East Asia. The College of Macau expanded during the boom years of the Japan mission but contracted considerably after its fall.[47] There was simply no demand among the colony's residents for an institution that taught the sacred and profane arts, so the Society scheduled classes for its members on an ad hoc basis. How and where, then, would the missionaries train their Chinese recruits as Jesuits?

This concern about priestly formation encountered further obstacles when the matter was considered against Chinese notions of maturity, wisdom, and education. As foreigners, the European priests could be implicitly understood as learned by virtue of the proven erudition of their peers who had composed sophisticated tracts. Chinese Jesuits, however, would first be held to the intellectual standards of their compatriots. In order to preserve the missionaries' studied gravitas, their native priests would therefore have to be mature men with literati pedigrees. But how could such individuals opt to return to the status of mere boys and subject themselves to the Society's standard curriculum? The two educational paths seemed mutually exclusive since both demanded years of effort. On the one hand, a Chinese man who completed the two tracks would be too old to handle the rigors of missionary life by the time of his ordination. On the other, social conditions in China made it impossible for a young native priest schooled only in the Jesuit curriculum to assume a position of authority over his designated flock or within the community where he resided. Moreover, his ritual dealings with his Christians might raise suspicions about him similar to those associated with other clergy such as Buddhist or Daoist priests.

Perhaps the greatest educational stumbling block was that, before becoming priests, the Chinese men would be obliged to learn Latin. Nicolas Trigault had pondered this perceived difficulty as early as 1615. While serving as procurator, he obtained a dispensation from Paul V, who permitted the celebration of the Eucharist in classical Chinese. He also got approval for the Jesuits to translate the Bible into that erudite language. But the Vice-Province never acted on these permissions. By the 1670s, when the question of a native clergy arose again, the earlier dispensations were under review for revocation in Rome, while in China many of the Jesuits despaired of the language abilities of the prospective priests. Lodovico Buglio was convinced that it was impossible for mature Chinese men to learn Latin, so he set about translating a series of liturgical and sacramental texts.[48] By that time, however, the last vestiges of Roman enthusiasm for divergent liturgies, whether in Europe or overseas, had eroded in the face of the standardizing project of *unam sanctam catholicam et apostolicam ecclesiam.* Moreover, suspicions about the Society's practices in China had waxed and Jesuit influence at the Papal Curia had waned. The Sicilian missionary's texts were therefore left to gather dust.[49]

Besides education, the other component of the Vice-Province's image was its internal cohesion. This was the result of the priests' shared loyalty to the Society of Jesus, a bond that had been forged by common experiences and reinforced by individual vows. The Jesuits' staunch defense of their order, a key piece of the cultural baggage they had brought with them from Europe, made it possible for their superiors to insist on discipline and impose punishments on those who strayed from established behavioral norms. In China, however, there was no way for native priests to learn such forms of loyalty and obedience. Most of those who were for the idea of a native priesthood no less than those who were against it shared the opinion that future Chinese priests had to be trained in some European or colonial environment.[50] In Portugal, Goa, Macau, or Manila, these seminarians would come to understand such key European concepts as the distinction between civil and ecclesiastical law. Moreover, they would acquire the discipline proper to members of a religious order. Jacques Motel raised this point in the 1670s. He was concerned about what the mission would do if one of the Chinese priests broke his vows

IHS
MISSALE
ROMANVM
auctoritate
PAVLI V. PONT. M
Sinicè redditum
A
P. LVDOVICO BVGLIO
SOC. IESV
Panormitano
PEKIM
In Collegio eiusd. Soc.
AN. M.DC.LXX.

and married. Here he contested a claim by Ferdinand Verbiest that the Society could rely on its internal disciplinary powers: "What power is this, I ask? By chance, are we in Europe?" Motel insisted that any mandarin would rule in favor of a renegade Chinese priest, just as the mandarins did for Buddhist monks who abandoned their monasteries. "In China," he asserted frankly, "all live as they please, entering or changing their religious profession at will."[51]

Discipline not only was necessary for maintaining the cohesion of the Vice-Province but also was crucial for ensuring that *Tianzhu jiao* retained its ritual purity. While the missionaries knew full well that the behavior of their Christians would never be an exact reproduction of European Catholicism, they sought to draw some boundaries that would prevent their flocks from sliding into syncretism. Men such as Jacques Motel objected to the ordination of Chinese priests because he saw it as a step too far over the cultural divide—at least until Christianity was legally recognized in China. Beyond blaming the Chinese in general for inconstancy, greed, and lust, the French missionary doubted that they could be counted on to guard Catholic orthodoxy. How could they, Motel maintained, when they were notorious for "saying and doing what they want, taking off in their own direction"? Most likely, they would mix in "what they choose from the sects of the Moors and Bonzes." Motel cited his own experience as grounds for his claim, noting that when he first arrived in Wuchang in 1661, he found a literatus who had been baptized long before by Rodrigo de Figueiredo "passing himself off as a master of the Holy Law." There was nothing this man would not do in trying to win over disciples, Motel wrote, including "telling fortunes, permitting polygamy, saying mass and offering communion of both wafer and wine, making holy water, baptizing in a new way, and changing the prayers." In short, this false priest tried to ape Figueiredo, "without even knowing how to mimic well."[52]

So there were strong disagreements among the Jesuits on this issue. The cleavage fell between two groups that can be called the Elders and the Moderns. Although it was not absolute, this divide was the distant

---

Title page of the translation of the Roman Missal prepared by Buglio for use in celebrating the liturgy in Chinese. From Lodovico Buglio, *Missale Romanum . . . Sinicè redditum* (Peking, 1670).

shadow of the great cultural shift that took place in the middle of the seventeenth century as France rose to cultural preeminence in Europe. Documents from the 1660s reveal a growing discomfort among those missionaries from the lands under Habsburg influence (Portugal, Spain, southern Italy) at what they considered the pretensions of the new French and Flemish arrivals. The differences between the missionaries became clearer under the circumstances of forced cohabitation at Canton. The nouvelle vague, which had begun to arrive in the wake of Martino Martini's trip to Europe in the 1650s, saw no insurmountable barriers to the ordination of an indigenous clergy. Moreover, its representatives felt obliged by the mission's weighty pastoral duties to get more priests into the field quickly—and resented the reluctance of their Portuguese superiors.[53]

The sense of self-assurance and initiative of the Moderns unnerved the Elders. Domingo de Navarette revealed as much in his published intrigues against the China Jesuits, in which he claimed that António de Gouvea had laid the blame for the Calendar Case and ensuing exile on the "French Fathers."[54] Francesco Brancati confirmed this tension in a 1668 missive to the Superior General of the Society with veiled references to the excesses of some priests "who had lately entered the mission." These men, the Sicilian claimed, did not want to "follow the customs introduced by the old priests and used for so many years."[55] Jacques Motel seconded this opinion, asking, "Could it be that these Moderns surpass so many saintly Elders in their zeal, virtue, prudence, and knowledge of doctrine?"[56]

With the passage of time, the Moderns gained the upper hand on the subject of Chinese priests. One of their number, Prospero Intorcetta, laid the groundwork for this plan during the Canton exile. When this Sicilian priest traveled to Rome as procurator in 1672, he carried with him suggestions drawn up by the Peking Jesuits (Buglio, Magalhães, and Verbiest) for the preservation and growth of the mission church. The first proposal was that Chinese men be ordained after being trained at a seminary somewhere in Asia.[57] It is possible that these ideas were discussed at Canton but that the differences of opinion between the Elders and the Moderns prevented them from reaching a consensus. A strong proponent of the ordination of a native clergy, Intorcetta made sure that the issue did not die. While he was in Rome, he acted on his own initiative to secure permission from Superior General Giovanni Paolo Oliva to open a college in Macau where the Vice-Province would train Chinese priests. In addition to this, the procurator received an endowment for the new institution from Pedro II of Portugal.

To be sure, the Roman curia of the Society of Jesus did not mandate the ordination of Chinese priests in 1672. No plan of action accompanied the funds secured by Intorcetta. Instead, the endowment and the permission he obtained served as the pretext for a new round of consultations. The procurator began a campaign to persuade the superiors of the Province of Japan to open the new seminary upon his return to Macau in August 1674. Both the East Asian Visitors and the Provincials of the Province of Japan had to agree to the plan since they were responsible for Jesuit affairs in the Portuguese colony. Intorcetta therefore cast his plan in the most favorable light. He explained that Chinese men, "literati of ripe age and virtue," would be brought to Macau for ordination and admission to the Society of Jesus as spiritual coadjutors. This title was given to priests in the order who professed the three vows of poverty, chastity, and obedience. In addition to sharing the pastoral burdens of their European confreres, these priests would share in the courier duties and language-teaching functions that had long been the responsibility of the mission's coadjutors. His most trenchant argument—the one that had won him recognition in Rome—was related to the mission's uncertain future. With the memory of the Dominican Luo Wenzao's efforts during the Canton exile fresh in his mind, Intorcetta argued that the native priests would be able to minister to the Chinese "in all times of peace and persecution, conserving the Christian community in perpetuity."[58]

In the summer of 1677, three years after Intorcetta's return from Rome, deliberations over the ordination of Chinese priests began. Visitor Feliciano Pacheco sent a circular to all of the China Jesuits ordering them to submit their opinions on two separate questions: if native priests should be ordained and whether the endowed seminary should be located in Macau or elsewhere in China. Although Pacheco's personal stance is unclear, the fact that he dragged his feet for so long before holding this consultation suggests that he was not keen on the idea. What is clear is that by the late 1670s the majority of the missionaries who sent their responses to Pacheco's successor, Sebastião de Almeida, agreed that it was time to begin accepting Chinese men into their ranks. By that, even Jacques Motel understood that the Moderns had won; in 1678 he claimed that he was offering his opinion "in vain, since all, or almost all, of those who were against this ordination are dead."[59] The only younger respondent who sided with Motel was Tomé Pereira, a court Jesuit. Although this Portuguese priest's response was not as straightforward as that of his French confrere, his meaning was clear. It would be a good idea to open a seminary with

Intorcetta's endowment, Pereira contended, "if there were anybody worthy of living in it."[60]

The missionaries who backed the idea took their cue from Vice-Provincial Ferdinand Verbiest. Yet although there was general consent for the plan, varied opinions were expressed about its specifics. For Verbiest, the proposed seminary would be best situated somewhere inside China (that is, not in Macau), and the new priests should be admitted to the Society. In this way, he claimed, they would be "shackled by their vows" to obey their European superiors.[61] Claudio Filippo Grimaldi and Lodovico Buglio, the two other court Jesuits, as well as Giandomenico Gabiani, at that time in Xi'an, all agreed with Verbiest's ideas. Buglio, however, added that Chinese seminarians should be literati and should be trained as priests in Hangzhou.[62] The other Jesuits whose responses have survived insisted that the new seminary would be best situated in Macau. Simão Rodrigues, Christian Herdtrich, Philippe Couplet, Jean Valat, and Prospero Intorcetta all felt that the likelihood of future persecutions was sufficient justification for opening the institution in the Portuguese colony.[63] For men such as Valat, Macau was ideal because, unlike Chinese cities, it was free of "so many bad examples from heathens, or so many occasions for distraction or growing cold in the faith." Viewing the Portuguese outpost through distinctly rose-tinted glasses, Valat concluded that it was the best place for Chinese priests to "imbibe the ways and customs of Catholics."[64]

Even with the stars aligned in their favor, the dream of the Moderns did not become a reality until the late 1680s. The Society's curia in Rome took years to respond to the outcome of the 1677 consultations. Two events, though, did help accelerate the pace of the plan's realization: the consecration of Luo Wenzao as bishop of Nanjing in 1685 and Prospero Intorcetta's assumption of the post of Vice-Provincial in 1687. The continued lack of priests and a desire to see his old plans come to fruition gave the Sicilian the impetus to request that Visitor Francesco Saverio Filippucci (1632–1692) send three of the mission's coadjutors to the bishop for training as priests. After spending over a year in Macau completing their novitiate, Simão Xavier da Cunha Wu Yushan (1632–1718), Bras Verbiest Liu Yunde (1628–1707), and Paulo Banhes Wan Qiyuan (1631–1700) left for Nanjing in early 1688. All three had achieved some degree of social prestige: Liu had been a director of the Astronomical Bureau at Peking, Wu (also known as Wu Li) was a renowned painter and poet, and Wan held a low-level degree.[65] During their training they learned how to say the mass and administer the sacraments by intoning the necessary Church Latin. By the time these Chinese deacons had taken up residence in Nanjing, the die had been cast. The local Jesuit superior, Giandomenico Gabiani, insisted that the Vice-Province could not renege on the ordinations "without provoking a great scandal in the Christian community and even among the heathens who knew the priests, as well as serious discredit and prejudice against the Society."[66] As a result, the Vice-Province accepted the three priests after their ordination on August 1, 1688.

Although some Jesuits received this news warmly, others found the ordinations a premature move whose repetition was to be resisted at all costs. These detractors exercised a strict vigilance over the new priests, seeking evidence from their behavior to confirm their suspicions. They were doubtless disappointed by the faultless service that both Wu Yushan and Liu Yunde gave the Vice-Province. On the basis of their work, Prospero Intorcetta informed Visitor Filippucci that he had other candidates who could be ordained as priests.[67] But the case of Wan Qiyuan presented problems. In the early autumn of 1689, Wan "disappeared one night, jumping over the wall" of the Jesuit residence in Shanghai.[68] In February of the following year, he appeared in northern Fujian Province asking for shelter and pardon from the local Jesuits.[69] This curious turn of events sparked a wave of criticism against Intorcetta. Tomé Pereira and José Monteiro (1649–1720) wrote of being scandalized by Wan's indiscretion and expressed their fears for the Society's reputation.[70] Even Intorcetta felt chastised, admitting that the affair was "such a disastrous case that it will urge caution in the future."[71] As a result, the Vice-Province became so hesitant to accept Chinese priests that it would take over four decades and another round of harsh persecutions before native Jesuits formed a significant portion of the missionary group.

The Arrival of Rivals, 1680–1692

While the Jesuits debated the ordination of native priests, the number of Chinese Christians continued to grow and the Jesuits' own to stagnate. This state of affairs forced the superiors of the Vice-Province to turn once again to the time-honored method of securing new manpower. In 1681 Philippe Couplet sailed from Macau for Europe in the post of procurator. His primary task was to publicize the mission, visiting kings and courts to solicit financial donations and passing through Jesuit institutions across the continent to identify new recruits for China. Couplet was also charged with publishing new tracts that would help in the debates taking place in Europe over the Chinese Rites.

As propaganda for the mission, Philippe Couplet's tour was highly successful. The procurator skillfully brought the apostolic affairs of the China Jesuits before the eyes of Europe, amply informing his numerous interlocutors about the Vice-Province. Couplet spent nine years on his travels from the Southern Netherlands through France and Italy and on to Spain and Portugal, and he was received by Louis XIV at Versailles and Innocent XI in Rome. He took news of the China mission beyond the usual paths trodden by its procurators, visiting the Northern Netherlands as well as the court of James II in England. Couplet's tour was part theater, since his train included a Chinese assistant, Miguel Shen Fuzong (ca. 1658–1691), and an array of Asian curiosities.[72] Where he made his greatest impression, however, was in the Republic of Letters. There Couplet introduced his learned peers to a pair of his Chinese acquaintances, Candida Xu and Confucius, the former figuring in his diminutive biography and the latter in the weighty tome containing the first translations of the Chinese classics printed in Europe, *Confucius Sinarum Philosophus* (Paris, 1687). But unfortunately for the men of the Vice-Province, Couplet's books and displays did little to strengthen their position. Instead of provoking widespread appreciation for their efforts, his tour cemented the resolve of the Jesuits' rivals to claim all or part of China for themselves.

A new surge of European interest in China started to develop in earnest in the 1680s, the years of Couplet's tour. It had been building for roughly a century but began to affect the men of the Vice-Province only as the cultural panorama shifted in Europe. In many respects, however, it was the Jesuits who had been stirring the waters with their triumphalist texts for decades in the hope of attracting the gaze of outsiders to their efforts and support for their enterprise. With so many splendid visions of Cathay spewing from European presses in the seventeenth century, the real marvel was that it took the Society's rivals so long to start paying attention. Once others fell under the spell of the siren song that the Jesuits had composed, it was only a matter of time before they themselves washed up on China's shores.

One way to gauge the impact of the Jesuits' propaganda efforts is to imagine an empty European bookcase from 1590 and watch it fill up with books large and small over the course of the following hundred years. The first works on the Jesuits in China would be the printed Annual Letters from the East Indies, which contained sections on Macau and the Guangdong Province residences. These small books would be dwarfed by Nicolas Trigault's account of the heroic deeds of Matteo Ricci and his colleagues, *De Christiana Expeditione apud Sinas* (Augsburg, 1615). Seven other editions of this work appeared in just over a decade in translations into French, German, Spanish, Italian, and English.[73] Next on the shelf, after another handful of shorter excerpts from Jesuit correspondence, would be Álvaro Semedo's account of the mission and the Nanjing affair titled *Imperio de la China, i Cultura Evangelica en él por los Religios de la Compañia de Iesus* (Madrid, 1642). This work made a far bigger splash in its subsequent Italian, French, and English translations.[74]

By the middle of the seventeenth century, the pace of publication of Jesuit texts on China quickened. Where Trigault and Semedo each published one account, Martini left four treatises on different aspects of the new Qing empire and the spread of Christianity there. His tale of the Manchu invasions, *De Bello Tartarico* (Antwerp, 1654), was translated from Latin into French, German, Spanish, Portuguese, and Italian. For more erudite readers, Martini wrote an account of the Chinese ruling dynasties, *Sinicae Historiae* (Munich, 1658), and a descriptive atlas, *Novus Atlas Sinensis* (Amsterdam, 1655). In order to correct earlier impressions of China as infertile soil for the gospel, he presented an exaggerated balance sheet of the Vice-Province's triumphs, *Brevis Relatio de Numero et Qualitate Christianorum apud Sinas* (Rome, 1654).[75] These works supplied the raw material for other Jesuits to produce new tomes for the already burdened bookcase. After digesting numerous manuscript and print accounts in the Society's Roman archives, Danielo Bartoli compiled a massive chronology of the mission, *Dell'Historia della Compagnia de Giesu: La Cina, Terza Parte dell'Asia* (Rome, 1663). The polymath Athanasius Kircher continued this effort by turning the celebration of his confreres' knowledge of the Qing empire into pictorial art with his *China Illustrata* (Amsterdam, 1667).

The tumultuous events of the 1660s gave the men of the Vice-Province plenty of reasons to add still more texts to the creaking stacks of European libraries. Rumors of their comportment, spread by Mendicant rivals, and actual attacks on the mission, launched by the Qing authorities, demanded that entire batteries of new apologias be rolled out lest the Society's supporters lose faith in its endeavors. Johann Adam Schall wrote a history of the mission, titled *Historica Narratio de Initio et Progressu Missionis Societatis Jesu apud Chinenses* (Vienna, 1665), which included a defense of his use of astronomy for the cause of religious orthodoxy.[76] Other texts, such as François de Rougemont's *Relaçam do Estado Politico e Espiritual do Imperio da China* (Lisbon, 1672; Leuven, 1673) and Adrien Grelon's two-volume *Histoire de la Chine sous la Domination des Tartares* (Paris, 1671–72), recounted events prior to the Canton exile. To reassure the reading public, one that no doubt despaired of the mission's prospects, Prospero Intorcetta wrote his *Compendiosa Narratione dello Stato della Missione Cinesi dall'anno 1581 fin all'anno 1669* (Rome, 1672).[77] Giandomenico Gabiani's *Incrementa Sinicae Ecclesiae Tartaris Oppugnatae* (Vienna, 1673) also gave a positive evaluation of the Vice-Province, while Ferdinand Verbiest's *Astronomia Europea* (Peking, 1678; Dillingen, 1687) explained how the science he employed at the Qing capital helped safeguard the mission. By the time Gabriel de Magalhães's *Nouvelle Relation de la Chine* (Paris, 1690) came off the presses, its translator felt compelled to insist on the novelty of the book's contents compared to the flood of other texts that had appeared in recent memory.[78]

But the Europe that received these Jesuit relations was not the same as the one left behind by the missionaries when they had departed for Asia. Even the first group of Moderns to arrive in China in the 1650s, the authors of the books published in Europe in the 1670s and 1680s, had never beheld the glory of the Sun King. On the whole, the China Jesuits had an outdated knowledge of the political situation in their homelands. Because communications between Europe and Asia were sporadic, the certainties they held dear—such as the Society's exclusive privilege to preach in China or the ecclesiastical jurisdiction of the archbishop of Goa, and by extension the king of Portugal, over South and East Asia, known as the Padroado—bore little resemblance to reality in the last quarter of the seventeenth century. With a new political tune from Paris drowning out the ever fainter drone from Madrid and Lisbon, the grandiose donations made by former popes to former kings seemed irrelevant at best and obstructionist at worst. And with the Spanish and Portuguese monarchs embroiled in a protracted war of succession, one that lasted from 1640 to 1668, they were in no position to hold firm over all the imperial dominions previously claimed by them. To make matters worse, forceful Spanish diplomacy at Rome had stifled any influence that the Portuguese crown could have exercised over the papacy. But by the 1680s Spain had ceded its sway over Rome to France, and a new wave of French and Francophile Italian prelates had little taste for the overblown claims and incessant quarrels of their Iberian counterparts. They had their own agenda to pursue, one that projected an increase of papal power in lockstep with the increase in French royal power.

One discordant riff that was picked up by attentive listeners in Rome, however, was that produced by the Dominicans and Franciscans from Manila. The friars had seen the China mission field firsthand and knew that the Jesuits were not telling the whole truth about their capacities for spreading Christianity there. The staffing problems, internal divisions, and dubious practices of the Vice-Province reached the European reading public when Domingo de Navarrete published his *Tratados Historicos, Politicos, Ethicos, y Religiosos de la Monarchia de China* (Madrid, 1676).[79] So filled with venom was this work that the Spanish Inquisition denied the author permission to print a second volume. Despite their differences, the Jesuits had sought peace with the Mendicants by ceding to them in 1671 the Christian communities they could no longer staff in southern Fujian Province. Missionaries from the Vice-Province also worked alongside the Franciscans in relative harmony at Jinan in Shandong Province. While there were never many members of the Mendicant orders in China, the mere presence of men who were not bound to conform to the Jesuits' practices was seen as a grave threat. The expansion of the Dominicans' efforts into Jiangxi Province and those of the Franciscans into the provinces of Guangdong, Fujian, and Jiangxi spurred the Jesuits to fight tooth and nail to defend from further encroachment what they considered to be their exclusive mission fields.

The central geopolitical weakness—to use an admittedly exaggerated term—of the Vice-Province was that it was shackled to the fortunes of the Portuguese Estado da Índia. Just as the Jesuits had risen to prominence in the shadow of Habsburg power and had expanded their efforts aboard Portuguese ships, so they paid the price when the kings at Lisbon and their viceroys at Goa could no longer muster the strength to defend their possessions. From the lofty vantage point of Versailles in the 1670s, the Estado da Índia looked like an overripe fruit ready for picking by Europe's most glorious sovereign. But the Portuguese empire in Asia would not fall of its own weight. Rather, it had to be plucked delicately with a combination of diplomacy and arm-twisting. Apparently out of respect for the English, Louis XIV did not move to seize the possessions of their Portuguese clients by invading the Estado's Indian colonies. Instead, he aimed at Goa's ecclesiastical monopoly over Asia, confident that he could smash it by supplying the men necessary for Rome's project to reduce the Padroado to the limits of Portuguese rule and not an inch beyond. The cardinals of the Sacra Congregatio de Propaganda Fide, the Holy Congregation for the Propagation of the Faith (hereafter called simply Propaganda), had started to carve up the vast jurisdictions of the archbishop of Goa in the 1650s. In 1657 they separated three new bishoprics from the diocese of Macau: Tonkin, Cochin China, and Nanjing. Each was governed by a Vicar Apostolic, a secular priest with the ecclesiastical powers of a bishop. Since these men had no Christian secular lords, they owed allegiance only to Rome.

As the Asian ambitions of Louis XIV grew, the Sun King found that he had a surfeit of zealous clergymen whom he could sacrifice to spread the Catholic faith *in partibus infidelium.* If they also paved the way for the arrival of French commercial and colonial interests, so much the better. The first Vicars Apostolic to make their way to Asia were members of the Société des Missions Étrangères de Paris, a congregation of secular priests that had been formed in 1658 for the purpose of missionary work. The initial locus of their activities in the 1670s was in Siam, the center of French commercial ambitions at the time. The Jesuits of the Province of Japan who had been working at Ayutthaya soon sent word to their superiors of the impending danger to their mission. These cries of alarm became more strident as the Vicars Apostolic branched out into Tonkin and Cochin China in the late 1670s and early 1680s. As bishops, these new arrivals were empowered to make demands on all clergy in their appointed territories. By virtue of their vows, the Jesuits had the choice to obey or leave. Filippo de Marini (1608–1682) urged the Portuguese crown to respond to these impositions on its jurisdiction. He demanded confirmation of the rumors circulating in Macau that "India has been sold to the Most Christian King" and asked whether it was true that the Jesuits were "no longer necessary."[80] Marini gave a more somber account to the royal confessor at Lisbon, a confrere in the Society, telling how the French gained "footholds in these missions of ours every day, in order to kick us out."[81]

The French push to establish a colonial presence in East Asia reached Chinese shores in the 1680s with Vicars Apostolic in tow. Ever fearful of repercussions from Qing authorities, the China Jesuits saw their delicately balanced enterprise teetering with the arrival of this new force. The missionaries at Peking had long served as the intermediaries between Kangxi and the European powers in Maritime Asia, advancing primarily the interests of the Portuguese crown and its representatives at Macau. This task had not been terribly difficult because the array of European participants in the China trade had evolved little over the course of the seventeenth century. Macau, Batavia, and Manila were all known quantities to the Qing rulers. The brusque arrival of the French in Fujian Province, outside the standard channel of communication stretching from Canton to Peking, not to mention their forceful relations with Chinese client states such as Siam, immediately put the Vice-Province on edge.

As far as the Jesuits were concerned, the arrival of the Vicars Apostolic was the start of a slow-motion replay of the events that had taken place in Siam and Vietnam. The papacy had cleared the way in 1673 when it declared China open to evangelization by secular priests, in addition to members of any Catholic religious order. Not only did this move aim to enhance Roman control over the mission by adding a layer of loyal oversight, but also it sought to dilute the predominance of the Jesuits as church representatives in China. For the Jesuits, the most pressing issue was the question of obedience, especially since the French Vicars Apostolic were not predisposed to accept the Society's view on the Chinese Rites. They also feared that the bishops would inform the Qing authorities of their precedence over any Jesuits working in their jurisdictions—in apparent confirmation of the oft-repeated Chinese claim that the Jesuits and their Western allies had secret designs to conquer China.

Luckily for the Vice-Province, François Pallu (1626–1684), the first Vicar Apostolic to reach China, disembarked in Fujian Province, where local officials were at least partially aware of the differences between the Europeans. It is likely for this reason that the presence of one more group of priests did not cause much of a stir among provincial mandarins. Pallu's arrival did, however, upset the Jesuits. His demand that they submit to his authority by swearing an oath of loyalty was rejected, even in the face of excommunication.[82] Vice-Provincial Ferdinand Verbiest was reported to have summed up the Jesuits' position by declaring that it would be a "mortal sin to swear such an oath." Verbiest reasoned that since the recently arrived bishop was unaware of Chinese actualities, he was liable to "ordain things prejudicial and destructive to the mission."[83] Claiming obedience to the archbishop of Goa and denouncing the uninformed policies of the Vicars Apostolic, the Jesuits referred their case to Rome. With the death of Pallu in 1684 and the revocation of the oaths imposed by the Vicars Apostolic in 1689, they were able to postpone their conflicts with the agents of the Propaganda for another few years.

If all of these challenges to the Vice-Province's position in the Qing empire were distant annoyances, the arrival of a group of French Jesuits destined for service at the imperial court in 1687 was a grave crisis close at hand. This was the other major policy initiative of the Moderns, the ones who had insisted on the ordination of Chinese priests. And just like that move, it caused severe internal divisions. The origins of this crisis can be traced back to the 1670s, when the Vice-Province confronted a lack of serious candidates to take over at the Imperial Astronomical Bureau after the death of Ferdinand Verbiest. During his tenure as Vice-Provincial in 1678, Verbiest had dispatched a series of letters to the Jesuit colleges in the Germanic lands, hoping to spark missionary vocations among his mathematically minded junior confreres.[84] His Flemish colleague at the court, Antoine Thomas (1644–1709), seconded these efforts, suggesting that recruits set out for China from Europe by any route, overland or by sea on Dutch, English, or French ships. Philippe Couplet had made similar appeals to his confreres during his visit to Paris in 1684, reiterating Verbiest's call for Jesuit savants to come to the Qing empire. These requests played no small role in Louis XIV's decision to appoint five Jesuits as "Mathématiciens du Roy" in 1685 with the charge of setting up a French academic outpost at Peking.

Modern scholars have reserved a major place within the history of the Society's China enterprise for the French missionary-scientists. To be sure, the sheer mass of printed propaganda that they produced at the cultural capital of late-seventeenth-century Europe was enough to collapse even the most sturdy of bookshelves. But one should not lose sight of the fact that these five Jesuits were sent to China as royal emissaries, the representatives of the Sun King to his counterpart on the far side of the globe. Though members of the Society of Jesus, they were not sent to Peking through the standard channels traveled by generations of missionaries. That means they did not travel first to Lisbon, then on to Goa and eventually to Macau, in order to be integrated into the Vice-Province of China. These French missionaries had no desire to join the efforts of their confreres in the Portuguese Assistancy and did not feel obliged to obey any non-French superiors. Rather, they saw themselves as an independent

French effort in the service of the crown. In this respect, most of the events surrounding their stay at Peking or elsewhere in the years after their arrival fall outside the scope of this book.

When Jean de Fontaney (1643–1710) and his four colleagues disembarked at Ningbo in Zhejiang Province on July 23, 1687, the Vice-Province's hierarchy found itself in an extremely complicated position. Not only had the French been detained by local mandarins, to whom they insisted that they were friends of Ferdinand Verbiest, but also they had come from Siam, a Chinese client state embroiled in a revolt against its king and his French allies. Vice-Provincial Intorcetta, feeling overwhelmed by the string of crises facing the mission, confessed to his superiors in Rome, "I do not know if there has ever been a time when this Vice-Province has faced such serious affairs as those which have transpired during my time governing."[85] Intorcetta's fears about a backlash against the mission as a result of these new arrivals were partly allayed when the Kangxi emperor personally summoned the French to Peking, brushing aside the objections of the Ministry of Rites.[86]

Shortly afterwards, as the French Jesuits began their trek to the court, Intorcetta naïvely ruminated on where the new missionaries would be of most help to the Vice-Province. During the autumn of 1687 and the winter of 1688, he wrote to Visitor Simão Martins (1619–1688) at Macau and his successor Francesco Saverio Filippucci in defense of the recent arrivals. After they had been received at Peking, Intorcetta proposed sending them to the most vulnerable mission stations, those in Hanzhong or Xi'an in Shaanxi Province, or to Hangzhou, where the Vice-Provincial himself required help. He also suggested sending one to Jinan in Shandong Province, where the ailing Jean Valat needed someone to minister to the local Christian communities, "and not leave them for the three Franciscan friars to take."[87] In light of their technical expertise, Intorcetta thought that at least one of them should stay at the capital to assist the aging Verbiest. He felt compelled to add that if the old Flemish astronomer did not have a substitute on hand, the Imperial Astronomical Bureau might "pass into the hands of the Moors," leading to the downfall not only of the mission "but also of the city of Macau."[88]

Despite Intorcetta's best-laid plans, the French Jesuits had no intention of leaving Peking for the provinces. At first, however, they chose to dissimulate their will to be independent of the Vice-Province. Writing from Ningbo in August 1687, Jean de Fontaney told Ferdinand Verbiest that their royal commission was to "give all of the necessary aid to these missions."[89] Taking the French Jesuits at their word, some of their more sympathetic confreres, such as Giandomenico Gabiani and Antoine Thomas, made sure that they were swiftly brought before the emperor. Kangxi indicated his desire to see Joachim Bouvet (1656–1730) and Jean-François Gerbillon (1654–1707) enter his service. It was likely because of the efforts of the Peking Jesuit Tomé Pereira, a fierce opponent of Thomas and the French missionaries, that Kangxi gave Fontaney, Claude de Visdelou (1656–1737), and Louis Le Comte (1655–1728) leave to work in the provinces.

When Visitor Francesco Saverio Filippucci seized the chance to direct the French Jesuits to where the Vice-Province most needed them, he unmasked Fontaney's true intentions. As the highest-ranking member of the Society in East Asia, the Visitor ordered the three Frenchmen to head for Shaanxi and Henan provinces, where they would help minister to the local Christians. Fontaney countered by requesting assignments in coastal areas, a suggestion that Filippucci rejected out of hand. It was plain to the Visitor that the French Jesuits would attempt to open a port of entry into China for their compatriots, creating an unsupervised channel of communication with Europe.[90] Fontaney chafed at this rebuke, informing Filippucci in the summer of 1688 that he and his colleagues had come to China not for missionary work but to inquire into "many matters of science in the Indies and China." He claimed that their work was to be similar to that which "the secular mathematicians from the Royal Academy had already done in Africa, America, England, Denmark, etc." To compound his insubordination, Fontaney threatened the Visitor and the rest of the East Asian Jesuits who opposed him with infamy in Europe. Fontaney remarked that he hoped they would not acquire a "monstrous reputation" by dint of having offended both "the Supreme Pontiff when he sent them bulls and decrees [with the Vicars Apostolic] and the Most Christian King as well."[91]

The position of the French Jesuits was greatly enhanced by the public reception they were given by Kangxi, and the Visitor had no choice but to allow them to create an independent mission. So the French did not resolve the problems facing the Vice-Province. In fact, their presence at the capital and in the provinces helped to exacerbate the divisions between the missionaries. The former split between Elders and Moderns took on a distinctly nationalist coloring, since the *mathématiciens* defended their autonomy on the grounds of their allegiance to the French crown. They foisted the designation "Portuguese" onto all of the members of the Vice-Province regardless of either their nationality or their feelings toward the French mission.

Despite attempts by many scholars to detect enduring nationalist divides among the missionaries from the start of their enterprise, there is little evidence that a strong cleavage existed among them on this issue before the 1680s.[92] It was then that a clear demarcation emerged on account of the transparent nationalist rhetoric of the French, not the multinational "Portuguese." To be sure, this latter set of Jesuits did include Portuguese who felt compelled to respond in kind to the denunciations they faced from the French—much scandalizing outside observers. The other missionaries from the various parts of Italy, Germany, and the Netherlands responded with varying degrees of sympathy toward their new confreres, betraying a departure from the cosmopolitan unity that had bound the Society of Jesus in earlier times. Admittedly, that same Jesuit unity carried an implicit recognition of southern European, and more specifically Iberian, cultural dominance.

Tensions ran highest at the court, where the Jesuits sought to maintain a semblance of unity in the presence of the emperor. In order to quell his fractious subordinates, Visitor Filippucci ordered the "Portuguese" Jesuits to cede one of their residences to the French. Likely greeting the chance to leave Tomé Pereira with joy, Antoine Thomas moved across the capital to join Gerbillon and Bouvet. But knowing of the growing resentment between the two groups, Filippucci also forbade them to speak "directly or indirectly with the Emperor or his ministers of the qualities, power, grandeur, victories, magnificence, or other qualities of the King, or Prince, of his homeland."[93] Under the surface, however, there was no peace. As Jean de Fontaney exclaimed, "If Saint Francis Xavier returned today, the Portuguese priests would surely teach him a lesson for having thought of writing to the University of Paris to ask for help."[94]

News of the arrival of the five French Jesuits prodded the Superiors General of the Society of Jesus to take a more active role in guarding its institutional integrity by protecting the Vice-Province. After the situation with the French Jesuits stabilized in 1690, Visitor Filippucci wrote to the royal confessor in Lisbon (a Jesuit) to declare that the China mission's problems stemmed from the fact that it had been run for over a decade by men with questionable loyalty to the Portuguese Assistancy. He insisted that new recruits for the Asian missions should be "mostly Portuguese," including a number of men with the aptitude for governing these enterprises in the future.[95] Acting with the approval of the Society's Roman curia, the Jesuit procurator in Lisbon responded that year by sending twenty-six men to Asia. He contended that there had been no want of willing candidates in earlier years but simply a lack of anyone to escort them to China. Previous procurators, he maintained, had only sought to take "their own," as was the case with Intorcetta, Couplet, and, in the late 1680s, Claudio Filippo Grimaldi.[96]

The Portuguese crown also understood what was at stake in the two-pronged French attempt to seize its Asian domains. It mounted a defense of the Vice-Province by devoting resources in Europe to preparing future missionaries and defending its Padroado. In order to stem the tide of complaints that there were not enough Portuguese Jesuits schooled in science, a qualification essential for service at the Qing court, Superior General Tirso González sent men to staff the chairs of mathematics that King Pedro II had endowed at the universities of Coimbra and Évora. The crown also pursued diplomatic initiatives in Rome that paid off handsomely for Portugal but created no small degree of confusion in China. In 1690 Alexander VII created two new Padroado bishoprics at Peking and Nanjing, removing both sees from the jurisdiction of the Vicars Apostolic. These new episcopal dignities offered the crown the chance to repay the Jesuits who had served Portuguese interests in Asia for so long. Here was the opportunity to name members of the Province of Japan or of the Vice-Province of China as bishops, and thereby retain their long-standing ecclesiastical authority over the missions.

This new set of ecclesiastical appointments added a further, ephemeral level of church control over the Chinese Christians, but the real influence over the adherents of *Tianzhu jiao* remained firmly in the hands of the Jesuits. For all of the grandiose claims of the Vicars Apostolic and the Propaganda, the Vice-Province was still synonymous with Roman Catholicism in China in 1691. Even the most developed Mendicant missions were small-scale affairs compared to the tens of thousands of Christians who formed the Jesuits' mission church in regions such as coastal Jiangnan. Moreover, from a strategic perspective, the activities of a handful of friars in the remote corners of Fujian or Shandong paled in comparison with the Society's presence in the heart of the Qing empire. Although the numerous conflicts with internal and external rivals had detracted the China

Jesuits from the business of managing their flocks, these crises had finally spurred their allies in Europe to send help. In 1691 the Vice-Province counted twenty-six priests and three coadjutors, with a number of promised new recruits on the way. Apart from the "five French priests who do not want to be subjects of this Vice-Province nor obey its superiors like the rest," the Jesuits were spread over nine provinces from Shaanxi to Fujian.[97] Years of hardship had taught them how to economize, and the wise stewardship of their imperial pensions had helped wean them from their dependence on Macau. At the start of the 1690s, the mission drew a large part of its revenues from rent-producing real estate holdings within the empire. If there was to be a final showdown between the Jesuits and their European adversaries over the fate of the China mission, at least the men of the Vice-Province would be prepared to fight.

5

Between Tolerance and the Intolerable

When the storm provoked by the arrival of the French Jesuits had died down, the men of the Vice-Province turned their attentions more fully to the daunting task of ministering to their tens of thousands of Christians. In the provinces, the missionaries redoubled their efforts to provide regular pastoral care by traveling continuously about their rural circuits, encouraging communal devotions through confraternities, and coordinating doctrine-teaching efforts. The Peking Jesuits continued to curry favor with the Kangxi emperor by presenting themselves as loyal servants of the throne. In 1691 they realized the value of decades' worth of service when a minor episode of official harassment flared up in Hangzhou. The missionaries there turned to their colleagues at court to seek imperial intervention to stop the depredations of local mandarins against the priests and their Christians. Acting on his high estimation of the Jesuits, Kangxi ordered an end to the persecution and issued a declaration of tolerance for the Society's religious activities—a reward the missionaries celebrated as their greatest victory.

The Jesuits were quick to trumpet their 1692 Edict of Toleration in Europe with the hopes of drawing new attention to their enterprise. Yet the mission benefited little beyond the renewal of confidence in the apostolic effort within the Qing empire. The missionaries were sure that Kangxi's gesture would spark a massive surge in conversions and a concomitant increase in the public stature of *Tianzhu jiao,* but they were unaware of a potentially harmful side effect: it encouraged their European rivals to claim the Chinese church for themselves more aggressively. Simultaneously, the debates taking place in Europe over the Chinese Rites reached their climax, spurring the papacy to assert its supreme spiritual authority and rein in the Jesuits' perceived aberrations. These decisions from Rome would fatally compromise the mission once they were made public in China. The disastrous fallout of the papal legation led by Carlo Tomasso Maillard de Tournon to Peking in 1705–6 found the Jesuits caught between two masters, both of whom they were obliged to serve. But neither the pope nor the emperor would compromise in his views on how Chinese Christians (and their priests) should respect orthodoxy.

In the wake of the Tournon legation, the forces that had enabled the Vice-Province to expand its numbers of Chinese Christians rapidly weakened. The Jesuits could not count on their stature at court as a safeguard for their work in the provinces, if only because their imperial protector was no longer convinced of the purity of their motives. The arrival of an ecclesiastical dignitary at great odds with the Jesuits forced the emperor to reconsider the assertions that the missionaries had made to him about European sovereigns, rivalries between different missionary groups in China, and structures of authority within Roman Catholicism. The clouds that gathered at court naturally cast their shadows over the empire, raising suspicions about *Tianzhu jiao* and stifling its expansion. The Vice-Province shifted to a defensive footing, seeking to preserve for as long as possible the mission church it had built. But as Kangxi created a new system for licensing priests that demanded adherence to his view of the Chinese Rites, and Jesuit after Jesuit left Peking at his behest to demand that Rome reconsider its interpretations of Chinese culture, the number of workers in the mission field dropped, leaving scores of Christians without priests. If the Jesuits had any hopes that the papacy would change its stance, they were dashed by the arrival of another legation in the early 1720s. In the end, the Jesuits paid the price for having made the throne their source of protection. The advent of the Yongzheng reign witnessed an abrupt volte-face in the policy of tolerance. Edicts issued in 1724 ordered the closing of all churches in the provinces and the expulsion of their resident Jesuits, sounding the death knell for the Vice-Province of China.

The Specter of Japan in China, 1691–1693

In late August 1691 a minor mandarin in Hangzhou posted notices around the city denouncing *Tianzhu jiao.* When the news reached Prospero Intorcetta, the local Jesuit superior, he took action in provincial courts, accusing his opponent before higher-ranking authorities. Intorcetta's case was based on imperial edicts that prohibited calumnies against his religion, but his strategy backfired on him. After a two-month delay, the governor of Zhejiang issued a severe criticism of Christianity and its preacher. He demanded to know who had permitted Intorcetta to come to Hangzhou from his original residence in Jiangxi Province and asked on what authority the Jesuit printed religious books. After upbraiding the missionary, the mandarin issued an edict to be displayed throughout the province, prohibiting any Chinese from adhering to Christianity. Local Christians were forbidden to wear their veronicas or carry relics and were to remove any sacred images from their homes. If Intorcetta was found with his followers, or if the Christians assembled by themselves, the edict ran, they would be punished by lashings and sentenced to "two months of wandering the public streets wearing a very heavy and very painful cangue around their necks." Although orders to destroy the religious images at the Hangzhou church were not carried out, Intorcetta was frightened enough to lament, "We already have Japan here in Zhejiang Province."[1]

By the late fall of 1691 the Jesuits had learned that this mandarin's bark came with a bite. First, a list of known Christians in Hangzhou and elsewhere in Zhejiang was compiled. Second, agents from the mandarin's *yamen* closed a chapel used for ministering to women. Not only did they pull down a cross from the building's roof, but they also confiscated its bricks so that the Christians would not rebuild it. Third, a Christian doctor was seized for distributing a calendar of Catholic feast days. On January 28, 1692, the man paid for his crime with forty lashes and "much flowing of blood." Fearing that the situation was worsening, Intorcetta made another appeal to the highest authority he could think of. He wrote to Tomé Pereira at Peking to ask the emperor to intervene on behalf of the missionary and his Christians.[2]

Intorcetta's request was a test of the strategy pursued by the Jesuits since the 1630s for defending the mission. Over the sixty years since the deaths of Xu Guangqi and their other elite protectors, the Vice-Province had placed its fate in the hands of the emperors. While the policy of maintaining a continual presence at court cost the mission a significant percentage of its manpower, it gained public standing with every display of imperial benevolence. After the death of Ferdinand Verbiest, one of Kangxi's former tutors, Tomé Pereira and Antoine Thomas had assumed important roles at court. By 1692 Pereira and Jean-François Gerbillon from the

French mission had earned praise from Kangxi for their service as Qing representatives in the border negotiations with the Russians at Nerchinsk three years earlier.[3] All of the Peking Jesuits were regularly received in the palace and often dealt personally with the emperor. When Pereira learned of the situation at Hangzhou, he therefore submitted a memorial that quickly made its way to the throne.[4]

The response, in the form of two decrees issued on March 17 and 19, 1692, far surpassed the Jesuits' expectations. These decrees came to be known as the Edicts of Toleration. The missionaries considered them to be the most important proclamations imaginable, short of a profession of faith by the emperor himself. Moreover, they claimed to spy Kangxi's hand in the specific wording of the edicts, quite different from bureaucratic boilerplate. That the first edict, which permitted the Jesuits to practice their religion in their churches by themselves, should have been supplemented by a second edict conferring the same privilege on male and female Chinese Christians was taken as proof of the emperor's personal intervention. In the March 19 edict—coincidentally issued on the feast of Saint Joseph, the patron saint of China—Kangxi asserted that *Tianzhu jiao* posed no threat to the state and that the Jesuits had contributed to the Qing dynasty with their scientific and linguistic skills. Yet this view fell far short of an endorsement of Christianity. At best it can be described as a display of "positive neutrality."[5] The edict was more direct about the Jesuits themselves. Perhaps referring to his meeting with Prospero Intorcetta at Hangzhou in 1689, Kangxi declared that the Westerners living in the provinces had "not committed crimes or behaved badly." He thus decreed it unfair to proscribe their religion.[6]

Scholars who have analyzed these edicts in light of Kangxi's other pronouncements have correctly noted that they did not concede permission to propagate *Tianzhu jiao*. Rather, they admit tolerating the practice of Christianity as it had been before 1691, with the assumption that its preachers would continue to behave like other religious professionals and remain inoffensive to the Confucian orthodoxy of the Qing state.[7] But the nuances were lost on many of the Jesuits, who were unused to reading the fine print of imperial edicts. One missionary summarized the second edict by noting that it ordered all of the Jesuits' churches to be returned to their former state, "and that all who wish to do so be left to venerate God." The same writer did not fail to note that the imperial pronouncement contained praise for the "many merits of the Europeans" and (according to his optimistic interpretation) declared that they "should not be impeded from preaching their doctrine."[8] Other Jesuit writings averred that the decrees permitted Kangxi's subjects to "freely receive our holy faith."[9] The emperor's domains, the missionaries claimed, were therefore officially open to the spread of Christianity.

The news quickly spread via official and Jesuit channels, giving the missionaries and their Christians cause for celebration. When word reached Zhejiang Province on April 7, the governor's decisions were reversed. The local Christians used their vindication to demand the return of the bricks that had formed their confiscated symbol, "giving the holy cross its own victory." Prospero Intorcetta embarked for Peking the following month to express his gratitude in person. On June 23, Kangxi received him with "kindness and honor," reportedly serving the Jesuit a ceremonial cup of tea.[10] In the following years, reports of the momentous events that had transpired in China reached Europe in tracts written by members of both the Vice-Province and the French mission. Glossing over the edicts' ambiguities in favor of their chosen interpretation of Kangxi's statements, these short books heralded the triumph of the Jesuits and the *Libertas Evangelium Christi annunciandi et propagandi in Imperio Sinarum solemniter declarata anno Domini 1692.*[11]

No celebration of the Edicts of Toleration, however, matched the festivities held in Macau. After all, the colony had heard nothing but bad news since the severing of its commercial links with Japan in 1639. The aggressive arrival of other European trading interests in Maritime Asia only exacerbated Macau's woes. The city fathers hoped that Kangxi's endorsement of things European would reinvigorate their stagnant trade with Canton. They joined with the local Jesuits to prepare a period of feasting, choosing first an auspicious date—May 11, the eighty-second anniversary of Matteo Ricci's death. Artillery salvos rang out from the ramparts of Macau's fortress, concerts were held across the city and aboard ships in the harbor, and fireworks lit the skies for three nights. The climax of the celebrations came during the procession of the Blessed Sacrament through tapestry-bedecked streets. Once again, the senior secular priest led the way for the nobility, the Jesuits, and the rest of the colony's clergy. In their wake came carriages bearing statues of the saints, as well as floats carrying players dressed to represent the lands that benefited from the pious heroism of the Society of Jesus. But in contrast to the celebrations on the same streets in 1621, where the figure of the Ming empire lamented its misfortune, during this procession all of the actors "applauded the triumph and congratulated China."[12]

The End of the Vine, 1693–1704

Despite the din created by the missionaries' trumpeting their elation, Kangxi's pronouncements did not significantly alter the way they conducted their enterprise. The changes that did occur to the Vice-Province during the 1690s resulted instead from earlier policies designed to increase the number of missionaries in the field. The Jesuits' Christian communities continued to expand as they had since the early 1670s, but with slightly more missionaries on hand to minister to them. Thanks to the dire reports from China in the 1680s, new priests arrived to expand the ranks of the Vice-Province from twenty-six members in 1692 to thirty-four in 1699.[13] In addition, men such as Manuel Rodrigues (1638–1698), Francisco Simões (1650–1694), and Francisco Pinto (1662–1731) pleaded with their superiors in India to let them leave for China upon hearing of that mission's renewed prospects.

This influx of priests was channeled toward the tasks of trekking around rural mission circuits, consolidating Christian communities that had survived without pastoral care, and staffing residences in strategic areas to forestall the arrival of other religious orders. The last of these projects was crucial if the Jesuits were to maintain any semblance of control over their mission church. In order to keep other missionary groups from splitting China into halves or quarters that they might claim as their own, the Vice-Province sent its men to consolidate its presence in as wide and as central an area as possible. The Jesuits therefore reinforced their numbers in Jiangnan and up the Yangzi valley, along the main north-south axis from Canton to Peking, and the region around the capital. These areas were the Qing empire's population centers and lay along its primary communication routes. With this move the Vice-Province reinforced the rationale for pushing its competitors to the margins of China. It gave the Jesuits firm grounds for insisting that their rivals start new missions in remote Sichuan, the far coasts of Fujian, the mountains of Jiangxi and Shanxi, and the rough rural districts of Shandong.

Part of the Vice-Province's project to consolidate its mission fields was the expansion into exposed nearby areas. With more men available, priests were sent to previously untouched areas such as the rural districts of

North Zhili, the northern reaches of Shanxi Province, and the cities of Changsha and Xiangyang in Huguang Province. New missionaries were allowed to put their zeal to work in these fresh pastures, relying heavily on catechists and other pious individuals to help communicate *Tianzhu jiao.* For instance, Tomé Pereira sent a series of younger Portuguese priests from Peking to consolidate the Jesuit presence in North Zhili. Visits by Miguel de Amaral (1657–1730), Francisco Simões, and Francisco Pinto to Zhending led to the growth of the area's Christian community, but it is likely that Pereira's aim was to curb the reach of the missionaries who settled in the company of the (Franciscan) bishop of Peking, Bernardino della Chiesa (1644–1721), at Linqing in northern Shandong Province.

From Jiangzhou in southern Shanxi the Jesuits headed for Taiyuan in the northern part of that province. While they did not have enough men to settle in this area, the Piedmontese Antonio Provana (1662–1720) and the Macanese Francisco Xavier Rosario Ho (1667–1736) visited the local Christians each year, "going in continuous circles, confronting thousands of hardships in voyages of a hundred or more leagues."[14] In Huguang, Pieter Van Hamme (1651–1727), a Flemish priest who had spent five years in Mexico before reaching China, set to work at Wuchang soon after his arrival in 1690. Just two years later, Van Hamme reported baptizing 437 people.[15] His colleagues, the Frenchman Simon Bayard (1662–1725) and the Spaniard José Ramón Arxó (1663–1711), worked in the province's southern parts and used their base at Changsha as a stepping stone into northern Guangxi Province as well.

As these numbers suggest, the Jesuits' reports from the 1690s reveal an attitude of wholesale renewal of their enterprise. Older Christian communities continued to expand, with a handful of new priests encouraging further growth. This was especially true in the Jiangnan region, where the Jesuits of Shanghai, Songjiang, and Changshu reportedly cared for tens of thousands of followers. In Changshu, Simão Rodrigues worked to consolidate his expansive mission district, an area including three churches in the city itself, one church each in Suzhou and on Chongming Island, and forty-eight chapels scattered about rural villages.[16] His task was made especially difficult, however, by the fact that many of his Christians had no fixed residences but lived on boats in the region's innumerable canals. The growth of the local community—967 baptisms were claimed in 1692 alone—led Rodrigues to encourage his flock to have their floating chapels "jump onto dry ground," leading to the creation of a new church building.[17] Similar gains were also recorded in Jiangxi Province, with Juan Antonio de Arnedo (1660–1715) tallying 500 baptisms at Nanchang in 1692, and François Noël continuing his efforts by baptizing 1,280 more people in the same city by the end of 1696.[18]

Concomitant with this expansion came a heightened desire on the part of some Chinese Christians to practice more sophisticated forms of group piety. This change came most readily among the missionaries' urban flocks, which enjoyed the luxury of relatively frequent access to the sacraments, since their pastors lived close at hand. Various types of devotional sodalities, such as prayer groups, penitential brotherhoods, and charitable confraternities, had been established throughout China since the 1630s. But they only reached their maximum evolution of the early modern period in the 1690s, when they began to adopt organizational statutes that were not merely ad hoc compilations of rules drawn up by the local Jesuits but direct translations of the statutes that structured confraternal devotions in Europe. At Peking in 1694, José Soares founded the first Chinese section of the Congregation of the Annunciation, an organization that had branches in all of the Society's colleges in Europe and the European colonies. The following year, José Monteiro and Giampaolo Gozani (1659–1732) founded a similar sodality at Fuzhou, "emulating that of the court." The missionaries in both cities petitioned their order's superiors to have their Chinese groups listed on the Roman register of Congregations of the Annunciation so that their members would be eligible to receive its prized indulgences.[19]

Despite the Jesuits' enthusiasm, they could not ignore the crushing weight of their pastoral obligations. Although new men arrived each year, they could not tend to all of their Christians. Nowhere was the pastoral challenge more overwhelming than in Shanghai. Even with three priests and one coadjutor working in concert, caring for the thousands of Christians who converged on the city's three main churches and more than eighty smaller sanctuaries in the countryside was an enormous burden—not to mention their followers in another thirty hamlets that lacked chapels, and a yearly minimum of 1,800 baptisms. According to Manuel Mendes (1656–1741), the residential superior at Shanghai, by 1697 the number of Christians exceeded 100,000. Others offered the more conservative estimate of 70,000, disregarding those individuals who "neither confess, nor care for their salvation." But rather than blame the Society of Jesus for its incapacity to care for all whom it baptized, Mendes accused

Christian parents of spending more time teaching their children "letters and trade rather than the knowledge and observance of divine precepts."[20]

Descriptions of the Shanghai church from the 1690s tell how throngs of Christians who sought to receive the sacraments overwhelmed the Jesuits. The missionaries attempted to rationalize their efforts by spending part of the year circulating around their district to tend to women, children, and the elderly. The rest of the time they spent at Shanghai while a constant flow of men's groups from the countryside coursed through their church to say their confessions, hear a sermon, and receive the Eucharist. While local Christians flocked continually to the city's Church of the Savior, the Christmas and Easter seasons drew the faithful from across the coastal plain. According to the Jesuits, on these occasions "five hundred, six hundred, and at times many more Christians" arrived wanting to confess. But even if they spent the night in the confessional, the missionaries claimed, it was impossible to satisfy all comers. So many converged on Shanghai, wrote the Jesuits, that the soldiers posted at the city gates were no longer surprised by the crowds coming to town wearing rosary beads. By this display, rural Christians could enter the city without having the watch ask their business. If they arrived without rosaries, the guards submitted them to a "rigorous examination"—apparently the challenge of correctly making the sign of the cross, a gesture that served them as "a guarantee and passport."[21]

This generalized swell of Christians meant that rural mission circuits were also more demanding for the Jesuits. One of the best descriptions of the typical pace of these countryside visits can be found in an account of Francisco Simões's travels around North Zhili in 1693 in the company of a catechist. "Normally," wrote Simões, "the priest arrives in a new village in the afternoon." He first greets the leaders of the Christian community, giving them devotional tracts or images and inquiring after any sick individuals or catechumens. After these preliminaries, the priest begins hearing men's confessions. Meanwhile, the catechist explains to "the uneducated" how they should confess their sins. Hearing confessions typically lasts until dinnertime, wrote Simões, after which the priest leads the Christians in praying "the rosary, litanies, and other devotions and prayers of the Church." Then, either the missionary or the catechist gives a sermon, inviting all, including "the heathens," to attend. Common topics were points of doctrine, subjects that the catechist would be able to explain in detail. The priest would attempt to hear all men's confessions, Simões explained, before retiring for the night.

Mass and baptisms of new converts were usually reserved for the following day. While the missionary heard women's confessions, the catechist would give final instruction to those who were to be baptized. Often other local Christians would assist in this process. At around eleven o'clock in the morning, Simões related, the priest said mass, gave another sermon, and led the Christians in "prayers sung in chorus, with men on one side and women on the other." Since rural oratories were frequently equipped with nothing more than a religious image, some incense, and crude benches, the Jesuits often brought portable altars. It was only after the missionary had offered communion and heard all confessions that he administered baptisms. According to Simões, the priest examined the village's catechumens after lunch, asking them about points of doctrine to see if they were ready to receive the sacrament. Those who passed muster were baptized; a brief sermon followed. Then the priest departed for the next village to start the process all over again.[22]

As this description makes obvious, Chinese catechists played a central role in supporting the Jesuits' pastoral activities. For decades these native auxiliaries had been primarily responsible for gaining new converts to *Tianzhu jiao.* To be sure, it would have been nearly impossible for the missionaries to master all of the dialects in the Chinese countryside in order to bring in by themselves the numbers of rural converts that they claimed. But the proselytizing work of these catechists was not limited to their efforts when in the Jesuits' company. Their zeal sparked scores of conversions that the priests would later have to verify. For example, Pieter Van Hamme reported that a Christian doctor in Huguang Province had not just delivered but baptized many children born to non-Christian parents—some seventy-three in 1692 alone. Van Hamme also noted that in areas far away from his residence, local Christians had baptized another 222 people of their own accord that same year.[23] In Jiangnan, an elderly catechist named Paulo delivered a notebook to Simão Rodrigues with the names of some thirty-two people whom he had baptized in the town of Taicang.[24] And in the villages near Hangzhou, Francisco Pinto recorded that a Christian named Lucio Xu baptized more than three hundred individuals in one year, in addition to "casting demons out of many bodies."[25]

This last comment touches on a central problem created by the Jesuits' move to concede certain ritual powers to a select group of laymen. While baptisms performed by ordinary Chinese men and women using the proper formula and ritual gestures were valid, other rites such as exorcism were, by Catholic tradition and law, reserved for priests. Yet the Jesuits' delegation of one ritual power seems to have blurred the boundaries, at least in Chinese eyes, between the role of the clergy and that of ordinary Christians. To be sure, the missionaries were caught between their desire to propagate Christianity and their status as the sole legitimate masters of Catholic ritual. What they lacked was an effective means of disciplining the thousands of unsupervised and often poorly indoctrinated members of the mission church. Undeniably, their actions ran counter to the dominant line of Catholic practice in Europe, where exaltation of the figure of the priest drew clear boundaries between laymen and clerics. In China, however, the Jesuits had none of the mechanisms that existed in Europe—ranging from the exhortations of parish priests to the judicial wrath of the Inquisition—to ensure that they remained the sole purveyors of Catholic rituals. Their only means for reining in exuberant catechists was the threat of excommunication, even if such a move might cast a pall over the pious efforts of their other auxiliaries. But the fact that the Jesuits recorded incidents of laymen performing rituals other than baptism indicates that by the end of the seventeenth century, control over *Tianzhu jiao* was slipping from their grasp. One indication of the severity of this problem arose when the Visitors of the Vice-Province requested that residential superiors keep close watch on all of their copies of the missal in Chinese. These books, the order explained, were not to circulate among the Christians or even among coadjutors, tempting them "to want to be priests."[26]

At the turn of the eighteenth century, the Vice-Province reached its greatest extent. Between 1699 and 1702, the corps of missionaries grew from thirty-four priests and three brothers to its largest number of Jesuits: thirty-six priests and six coadjutors (including both Chinese and European men).[27] Save for earlier sallies by Jesuits to the remote fringes of China, these men were spread out as far geographically as they had ever been during the seventeenth century. A glimpse at a report prepared by Vice-Provincial Antoine Thomas in 1703 for his Roman superiors gives a snapshot of the Jesuits' enterprise at its high-water mark.

Thomas began his report by defining the terms of the mission's organization: colleges, residences, churches, chapels, and oratories. He started by listing the four primary residences, or "colleges," that is, the houses at Peking, Nanjing, Hangzhou, and Ganzhou which had been so designated in 1681 in order to bring the structure of the Vice-Province into line with the Society's other provinces. This distinction was of little practical consequence since none of these residences—with the exception of a few math-

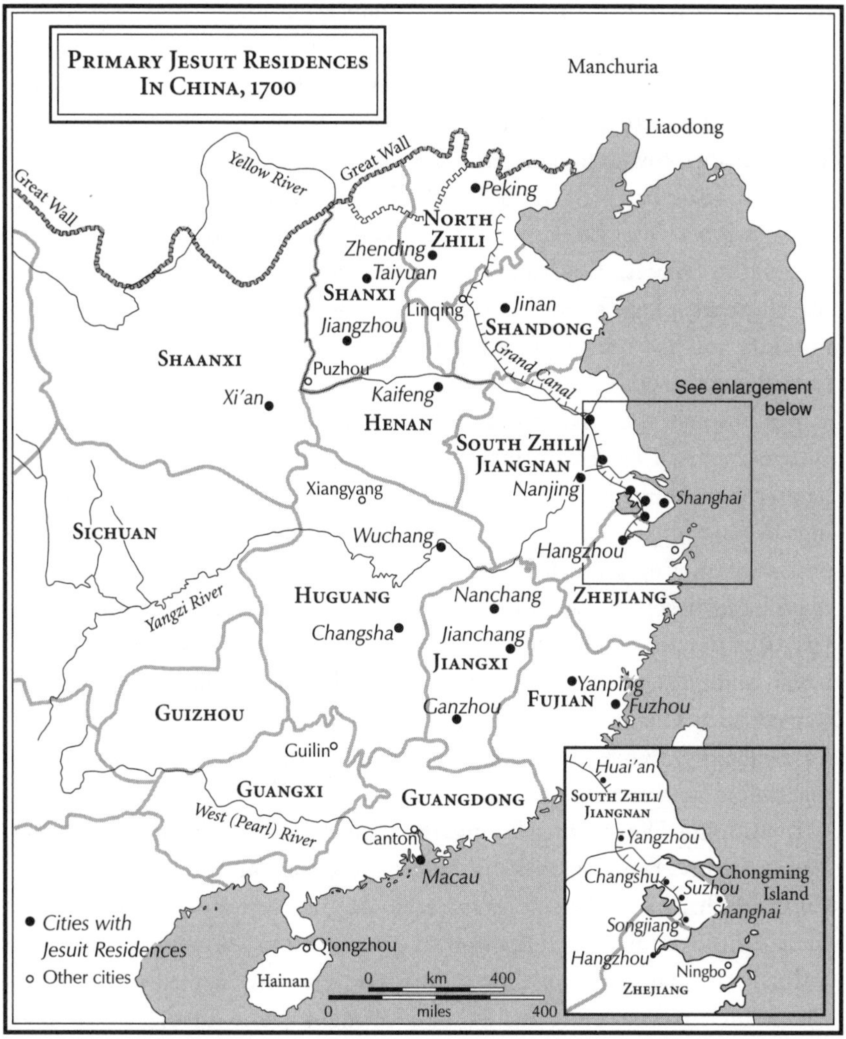

Primary Jesuit Residences in China, 1700

ematical lessons given to Chinese members of the Astronomical Bureau at Peking—aspired to present the slate of academic offerings available at other Jesuit colleges. And although all of the other residences were administratively dependent on one of these colleges, the entire mission was small enough to be directly controlled by the Vice-Provincials and Visitors. The thirty-six priests were divided among thirty-three residences, though not all of these residences were staffed at all times. Because six priests were stationed at Peking and three at Shanghai, the remaining twenty-seven Jesuits had to divide their time between residences in order to minister to all of their Chinese Christians.

The next order of mission organization in Thomas's report dealt with the physical structures of the mission church. By the 1703 accounting, the Vice-Province was responsible for 266 churches, 14 chapels, and 290 oratories. A residence—a building with living quarters and a sanctuary—was a structure that belonged to the Vice-Province, but the other buildings did not necessarily belong to the mission per se. Instead, many of the churches, chapels, and oratories were owned by the Christian communities and had been acquired by purchase or by donation from wealthy church members or sympathetic non-Christians. Thomas defined churches as places where the missionaries had space for lodging but where a catechist rather than a priest normally resided. Chapels were specifically designated rooms in large homes that were reserved for saying masses and holding confraternity meetings, while oratories were spaces in Christian homes that were only occasionally used for such activities. Typically, the size of the Christian community and the wealth of its members determined the size of a sanctuary, but some donations enabled the Jesuits to acquire larger buildings for poorer communities. The small number of chapels suggests that Christians wealthy enough to reserve space in their homes for religious activities were also sufficiently well off to donate properties that would be designated as churches.[28]

By Antoine Thomas's reckoning, the Vice-Province claimed a yearly average of 14,600 baptisms and administered the sacraments to over 196,000 Chinese Christians. This substantial flock, he asserted with pride, was spread throughout the Qing empire, excepting the remote provinces of Sichuan, Yunnan, and Guizhou. Moreover, Thomas claimed his tally of Christians was a conservative estimate of the outcome of the Jesuits' efforts. He informed his readers that he employed the phrase "more or less" because he did not want to "overestimate anything."[29] For this reason, the Vice-Provincial did not include the thousands of foundlings who were baptized each year by missionaries as well as laymen.

As had been the case over the course of the mission's history, the size of the individual Christian communities varied from region to region, and some of the designations used by the Vice-Province for its residences bore little correlation to the size of their local churches. For instance, the four Jesuits at Shanghai and the two priests at Songjiang lived in mere "residences" while caring for more than 110,000 Christians, well over half the mission church. By contrast, their lone confrere at the College of Hangzhou ministered to 1,000 men and women, and their two colleagues at the College of Nanjing cultivated a paltry 500 souls. Despite this disparity, Thomas described the Jiangnan region—stretching from Huai'an on the banks of the Grand Canal in the north, to Nanjing proper in the west and Chongming Island in the east, and to Songjiang in the south—as the place where the fervor of the Christians was "clearly greater and more ardent than any other in the whole of China."[30]

Outside of Jiangnan, substantial numbers of Christians (ranging from 1,000 to 10,000 in each area) were found at Peking; around Jinan in Shandong Province; along the Yellow River and its tributaries passing through Kaifeng, Jiangzhou, and Xi'an; and in the river basins of Huguang and Jiangxi. Some of these communities, such as the ones in Shanxi and Shaanxi provinces, had shrunk considerably during the dynastic transition but had begun to grow again by the 1690s. According to Thomas, only the missions in southern Zhejiang and Fujian provinces were on the defensive against what he considered encroachment by rival religious orders. In other areas, most notably Shandong and Shanxi, the Jesuits worked smoothly alongside Franciscan missionaries. But on China's southeast coast, relations between the Jesuits and other European clergy were tense. Perhaps the Society of Jesus was envious of the numbers of Christians that the Dominicans claimed in Fu'an district in Fujian Province. More likely they sought to avoid jurisdictional conflicts with the Vicars Apostolic and their French assistants, on the one hand complaining vociferously about the dangers of these bishops' policies and on the other ceding the coastal mission stations to them. Abandoning Christian communities that dated back to the late 1620s, the Jesuits retained only their residence at Fuzhou and focused instead on their inland churches.

Thomas's report intended to make a clear case for the need for more men. It was evident that the Jesuits' thirty-three residences needed to be staffed by more priests if the mission was to meet its pastoral obligations and stave off its rivals. Although the previous decades had witnessed the experiments with a native clergy, by 1703 there were still only eight Chinese Jesuits—five priests and three coadjutors—and the Society did not appear inclined to admit any more. Instead, Thomas reminded his superiors that China was a vast but highly fertile vineyard of the Lord that needed tending by Europeans. Curiously, he kept his request modest, asking for only twenty-four more priests. This number would nearly double the mission's personnel, and with sixty men, Thomas maintained, the Vice-Province would easily be able to meet the needs of its far-flung churches and maintain its steady pace of expansion.[31]

For all of the Vice-Provincial's optimism, his overview omitted a crucial element that gravely restricted the mission's potential: its perilous financial situation. The China Jesuits had never received enough money to meet their needs from either Europe or the Portuguese in Asia despite their incessant pleading. This chronic lack of money had kept the missionaries on a starvation diet for most of the seventeenth century, and it may have been out of resignation that Thomas neglected to ask for funds. Yet by 1700 the Jesuits did not face the same acute degree of penury that they had once confronted. One report by Thomas's predecessor, Vice-Provincial José Monteiro, shows that the mission had made strides toward securing stable sources of income by investing in land and buildings. In the 1690s the Jesuits had benefited from the thrift of Tomé Pereira, who skillfully managed the pensions earned by his confreres at the Astronomical Bureau. In addition, as the Christian communities in the provinces grew and larger sanctuaries were needed, older properties were either converted into women's churches or rented out. The China Jesuits had also accumulated a cash reserve at Macau from decades' worth of donations from Portuguese benefactors. Beyond helping to pay the missionaries' yearly salaries, this money endowed the colleges at Nanjing, Hangzhou, and Ganzhou with rental properties. The same strategy had been employed at Shanghai and Songjiang, where donations from wealthy Christians, especially the Xu clan, had enabled the Jesuits to acquire rental houses and farmland that contributed to meeting the mission's annual expenses.[32]

Despite these attempts at self-sufficiency, the Vice-Province still relied heavily on the funds it received from outside China. In a budget report from 1700 sent to the Portuguese crown with the obvious purpose of seeking donations, Visitor Carlo Turcotti (1643–1706) claimed that the mission required 2.3 million reis per year. This sum included salaries of 60,000 reis per year for Jesuits living by themselves and 50,000 annually for those who shared lodgings with others. In addition to covering the missionaries' living expenses, these disbursals paid for making devotional objects, maintaining residences and churches, paying catechists, and granting alms to poor Chinese Christians. According to Turcotti, the Vice-Province's revenues from its landholdings in India could potentially supply 700,000 reis, less than a third of the annual budget—but often the

Province of Goa claimed part of this cash as payment for training China missionaries. Without the court Jesuits' pensions and the Macau reserve, the Visitor contended, the mission could not survive.[33]

Even the combination of these streams of revenue was not enough to support the Vice-Province every year. Oftentimes the cost of life at court—and the missionaries' need to keep up appearances among their mandarin peers—curtailed the Peking Jesuits' ability to succor their colleagues. As José Soares noted in 1705, his surplus was sorely depleted by an inflation of prices at court.[34] The fragility of the mission's finances begged for caution, flying in the face of Antoine Thomas's requests for more men. In fact, one of the first things that Thomas's 1703 report mentions—with a vague hint of surprise—is that few recruits had recently arrived from India. What he did not realize was that the view from Peking of the mission's finances was very different from the view from the provinces. Knowing the general poverty of the other Jesuits, Visitor Turcotti had cut off the supply of new priests. Not only had he ordered that "no more men come to the Vice-Province," as he wrote in 1700, but also he sent some prospective candidates back to Macau. Turcotti had further suggested the prospect of reducing the number of Jesuits who staffed the mission "according to the possibilities of the present revenues."[35] Without a substantial influx of cash from Europe, the Visitor concluded, the Vice-Province had no chance of expanding further and stood at risk of losing control over what it had already gained.

"Terrible, Scandalous, and Diabolic," 1700–1704

From the perspective of the mission hierarchy at the beginning of the eighteenth century, the China Jesuits faced a number of temporal challenges. Surely, just as the mission's superiors had long maintained, their enterprise would flourish if only it had enough men and enough money. Their optimism appears to have blinded them to the imminent dangers posed by their European rivals. Although various Jesuits had sounded the alert to this peril at earlier junctures, the men of the Vice-Province were powerless to stop their competitors at the Qing empire's borders. They themselves had played no small role in attracting other Europeans to China by crying for help and publicizing the advance of the faith in that exotic setting. Their success at public relations was their undoing. By shouting the news of the Toleration Edicts from the rooftops, they attracted to China a new wave of missionaries who hoped to find there the ideal conditions for claiming their own apostolic victories. Once confronted with the difficult reality of carrying on in that country, these rivals blamed the Jesuits, accusing them of duplicity, obstructionism, and worse.

The first signs of the challenges that lay ahead for the Society came in the early 1690s. Cynically inclined observers, such as Tomé Pereira, remarked that the Edicts of Toleration had brought no great wave of Chinese conversions but only an onslaught of misguided European clergy. Assessing the "spiritual state" of the China enterprise in August 1693, this Peking Jesuit saw only an increase in the "great fervor with which members of other orders multiplied their number of residences without adding to the number of Christians." In the city of Canton alone, Pereira noted, they had proceeded with "such excess" that seven or eight new churches had sprung up.[36] By 1701 the Vice-Province's superiors estimated that there were sixty-five Europeans in China who did not belong to the Society of Jesus. This count included the Vicars Apostolic and their retinues of notaries and assistants.[37] Pereira and others of like mind understood that Kangxi's edicts were valid only for the *Yesu hui,* the Society of Jesus, and that such a profusion of non-Jesuits was bound to cause grave problems. One admittedly partisan observer went so far as to claim that as the number of priests from different orders increased, "the heathens started to shut their ears to the Catholic truths and the neophytes started to cool down and backslide in the faith."[38]

For most of seventeenth century, the Jesuits' rivals had been restricted to the fringes of the Qing empire. During the waning years of the Ming era, the combined strength of Iberian maritime power and official vigilance ensured that only recruits for the Vice-Province made their way into China. News of hardship and persecution served as a deterrent for other would-be missionaries until the last quarter of the century. Yet by the 1680s and 1690s, the reinvigoration of European trade in Maritime Asia brought a constant stream of vessels to the coasts of Fujian and Guangdong provinces in search of Chinese commodities. The same ships enabled Mendicants as well as Vicars Apostolic to disembark wherever their captains found welcome.

Along the southern Chinese coast, these missionaries found that the Jesuits had prepared the spiritual soil; they had planted the seeds that eager Franciscans, Augustinians, Dominicans, Propaganda priests, and Vicars Apostolic could cultivate. By 1701 there were six Franciscan residences, three Augustinian houses, and three churches run by French priests of the Missions Étrangères in Guangdong Province. In Fujian, Propaganda missionaries worked in concert with Dominicans, Franciscans, and Vicars Apostolic along with their retinues at eleven residences. The high concentration of priests in these areas prompted some missionaries to seek pastures in nearby provinces, with the Friars Minor setting up four houses in Jiangxi and the Order of Preachers opening two houses in southern Zhejiang.[39]

In the last decades of the seventeenth century, relations between the Society of Jesus and its fellow religious orders in southern China became openly adversarial. Since the Province of Japan was responsible for Guangdong Province, the battleground for the China Jesuits became Fujian Province. The Vice-Province swallowed a bitter pill in the 1690s, opting to vacate most of its residences there in order to avoid conflicts with the Vicars Apostolic, who, as bishops, could demand obedience from the Jesuits. It may have been wishful thinking on the part of Tomé Pereira that the local Christians "conserved a filial love" for the Jesuits, who had first brought them the gospel, in the face of "an inundation" of French priests.[40] It may also have been the case that those Catholics longed for the Society's brand of pastoral care after Charles Maigrot (1655–1730), the Vicar Apostolic for Fujian and member of the Missions Étrangères, on March 26, 1693, issued a series of prohibitions against the Chinese Rites. Either way, the Jesuits' frustrations at the changes wrought on their southern mission fields manifested themselves in short order. Just four years after Maigrot's decree, José Monteiro claimed that Fujian Province was "very sterile in conversions where before it had been very fecund."[41]

As if these jurisdictional problems were not enough, the turn of the eighteenth century also witnessed renewed tensions between the different national groups of Europeans in China. Visitor Francisco Nogueira (1632–1696) called attention to this problem when he decried the apparent scramble for bragging rights over the Chinese church. Blind to the fact that their presence could spell the end of all missionary activity in the Qing empire, he claimed, "Many enter just so those of their nation or religious order might prevail." Nogueira conceded that the Society, too, had fallen prey to this surge in chauvinism. He admitted that the Jesuits had reacted poorly to their rivals' rhetoric, losing the sense of cosmopolitanism that had bound their order for over a century and a half. To be sure, the Vice-Province had long worked under the assumption that if it owed an allegiance to any particular nation, it was to Portugal. This allegiance was reflected in the fact that Portuguese missionaries had traditionally outnumbered the Jesuits from other lands. But by the 1690s, Nogueira claimed, the Italians were clamoring to have equal numbers with the Portuguese, along with the Germans, the Flemings, and the French, who all wanted equal representation. The Visitor anticipated a scene of déjà vu. History would soon catch up to the Society if it did not cool these nationalist passions, he predicted, drawing a direct parallel to the fate of the Japan mission after the arrival of Castilian missionaries from Manila: "As soon as many other missionaries began to enter, the Japanese threw them out and us as well, bringing about the loss of all of those Christians that we are still bemoaning today."[42]

The primary rift among Jesuits in China had occurred as a result of the French mission's insistence on independence from the Vice-Province. In an attempt to mask internal divisions before the Kangxi emperor, the "Portuguese" Jesuits were forced to accept the French. A period of uneasy cohabitation ensued as the French ran their own affairs at odds with the will of the Vice-Province's superiors, opening new residences instead of assisting their confreres in need. Tomé Pereira, their most ardent foe, denounced the "scandalous intents" of the French at Peking and their "diabolical plan" to petition the Society's Superior General to divide China between the two groups of Jesuits.[43] Resentments reached over national lines, with Italians and other non-Portuguese Jesuits from the Vice-Province decrying the "incredible excesses" committed by the French at court. Alessandro Cicero (1639–1703), a Milanese Jesuit who had been consecrated bishop of Nanjing in 1696, intimated to a Belgian confrere that they had brought "perpetual infamy to the Society, perturbation and danger to the whole mission, scandal to Christians and heathens, and discredit to the missionaries and the holy faith."[44]

Making good on their earlier threats, the French Jesuits vilified Pereira and those of his opinion in their letters to Rome and included thinly veiled criticisms of the "Portuguese" in their Parisian publications. An attentive reading of Louis Le Comte's *Nouveaux Memoires sur l'État Présent de la Chine,* published in two Paris editions in 1699 and 1701, reveals clear attacks on the Vice-Province projected back onto the early history of the mission. Here, the figure of Matteo Ricci meets his toughest challenges not from the Chinese but from "his own brothers, European Christians." In this retelling of the story, it was the Portuguese who resolved to betray the early Jesuits, "whatever it might cost the faith (and also possibly the order)." Le Comte did not mince words. "Doubtless," he wrote, "many will find the gall of these false brothers amazing, since it was they who, for all their faithful engagement in giving their blood to support God's work, were determined to destroy the mission with such atrocious calumnies."[45] But in Rome at the headquarters of the Society of Jesus, where news of the Jesuit-Jansenist battles in France arrived daily, Superior General Tirso González could not afford to rebuke his French subordinates and risk insulting the order's powerful patron, Louis XIV.

Once ensconced at Peking and allowed to settle in the provinces, the French Jesuits moved to create their independent China mission. New missionaries arrived from France in 1698, 1699, 1700, 1702, and 1703, and were directed to residences in Jiangxi, Fujian, and Zhejiang.[46] Jean de Fontaney was frank with the Society's Roman curia when it came to justifying the actions of his subordinates. He asserted that the Portuguese "dream too often of expanding," to the neglect of their abandoned churches. Fontaney further argued that the French Jesuits should be given jurisdiction over the Society's missions across a swath of central China, including Fujian, Zhejiang, Jiangxi, Huguang, Shanxi, and Shaanxi provinces. His reason was that he preferred his men to be subject to the Vicars Apostolic rather than to the bishops of the Portuguese Padroado; the former were fellow French nationals while the latter were often drawn from the Vice-Province's ranks. Fontaney declared that his "Portuguese" confreres had enough on their plates in the six provinces under the jurisdiction of the Padroado, that is, the bishoprics of Peking, Nanjing, and Macau. He mocked their claims to the whole of China by using the example of their work in Henan Province, where their man at Kaifeng was responsible for a densely populated area. "Is this," Fontaney asked, "what they call creating and taking care of a true mission?"[47]

Bowing to French pressure, González institutionalized the division of the Society's China enterprise in 1700. Jean-François Gerbillon was named the first official superior of the French mission and accorded powers equal to those of the Vice-Provincial. González attempted to retain a degree of unity among the Jesuits in East Asia by making all of them subordinate to the Visitors, but to little avail. Not only did Gerbillon and his confreres resist this imposition, but they moved to petition the papacy as well to have several Chinese provinces designated as their exclusive mission territory. Upon hearing the news, even those members of the Vice-Province who had been sympathetic to the French began to denounce them. Claudio Filippo Grimaldi implored the Society's Portuguese Assistant in Rome to stop their "terrible attempt" to create a new "*patronatus* of France in China." Grimaldi recalled that Kangxi had not granted permission for any specific nation to reside in China but only the "successors of Father Li Matheus, meaning Father Matteo Ricci of happy memory."[48] If the emperor learned of the Jesuits' divisions and conflicting loyalties, he implied, the mission would be in grave danger.

Such appeals did little to ameliorate the bad blood in the Vice-Province. The resentment between the two groups was transparent, and their mutual suspicions gave rise to many rumors. Unconfirmed (and probably false) reports that reached Macau in the first years of the eighteenth century claimed that Kangxi was "very averse" to the French Jesuits at court. It was said that in 1702 he refused to accept the gifts that Fontaney had brought from France.[49] On November 21, 1701, according to news perhaps leaked to scandalmongers in the Portuguese colony by Tomé Pereira or someone like him, the emperor had called Jean-François Gerbillon "dirty, sleepyheaded, and lazy."[50] Such petty rivalries serve to illustrate the depth of the divisions between the Jesuits at a time when they were confronted with external threats of equal or greater danger. Perhaps Giampaolo Gozani gave the best summation of the Jesuits' inability to close ranks when he delivered the Vice-Province's residence at Fuzhou, Fujian Province, to the care of the French mission in June 1707. Commenting to a Portuguese colleague on how he had handed over the house to Claude de Visdelou, a French Jesuit and future Vicar Apostolic who would denounce the Vice-Province's position on the Chinese Rites, Gozani wrote, "I know that our enemies will triumph, but what remedy is there?"[51]

"A Cruel Tragedy," 1704–1709

Rent by internal divisions, the Society of Jesus had difficulty mustering the strength to defend the China mission in Europe, from whence any binding resolution on the Catholic missions would necessarily come. For the Vice-Province, the central question was whether it would be allowed to retain control over the vast regions that it had cultivated since the 1580s. But since this exclusive mission field covered all but the outlying Qing provinces, there was little hope that Rome would fully endorse the claims of the "Portuguese" Jesuits. The papacy had no compunction about confirming the privileges of the Vicars Apostolic to set the tone for missionary work in their appointed sees. After all, its primary purpose in sending the Vicars eastward was to shatter the Portuguese monopoly over Asian Catholicism. The overweening importance of the Society of Jesus in East Asia, linked directly as it was to the Padroado, needed to be downgraded if Rome was to assume true control over the Universal Church. If all the Vicars could establish themselves in their appointed areas as Charles Maigrot had done in Fujian, they would be in a position to assume direct control over the missions. If not, the Jesuits would remain in de facto control over the Chinese Catholics.

The flashpoint for this jurisdictional battle was the Chinese Rites. The theological disputes over these practices were used as a wedge in the struggle for control of the mission church. Despite the fact that both sides in the debate had been granted papal dispensations in the middle decades of the seventeenth century, Innocent XII appointed a set of theologians to reconsider the issue in the 1690s. By then, the mountains of polemical literature that had accumulated in Europe in support of one camp or the other begged for some final resolution to end the debates that pitted Catholic against Catholic, Jesuit against Jansenist.[52] In China, the Vicars Apostolic had aligned themselves with the Dominicans and some of the French Jesuits to condemn the rites, declaring the ceremonies to be superstitious and demanding that the men of the Vice-Province be censured for permitting idolatry. The Franciscans were divided on the issue, with some friars agreeing with the Jesuit position—though none too vociferously. The cardinals of the Propaganda Fide also entered the lists, confirming the decision taken by the Sorbonne theologians in 1700 to prohibit the rites. And after seven years of pondering the issue, the Roman Inquisition issued a negative verdict. In the face of so many condemnations, Clement XI sealed the issue on November 20, 1704, by publishing a brief that prohibited some of the Jesuits' policies—including their tolerance of the rites and the display of the *Jing Tian* tablets on their churches.

The tangle of episcopal jurisdictions in China made it difficult for Clement to make his decrees known to the priests there. Only fifteen years earlier, in 1690, Alexander VIII had confirmed the jurisdiction of the three Padroado bishops, and they were generally well disposed toward the rites. Moreover, the archbishop of Goa still chafed at the idea of Vicars Apostolic usurping his traditional jurisdictions. Neither the Jesuits nor the secular clergy of the Portuguese Padroado were likely to trust—or obey—

any pronouncements from French bishops. As late as 1702, Padroado bishops could insist to the Portuguese crown that the controversies stirred up by the Vicars Apostolic appeared to have died down. As the bishop of Nanjing, the Jesuit Alessandro Cicero, wrote that year to Pedro II, "There is no longer the fear here that a Vicar or two, set on perturbing the Christian community, will bring about the condemnation of the old missionary fathers."[53] If the papacy truly wanted to exert its power over Catholicism in China, it would have to circumvent the established ecclesiastical channels. The solution was to appoint a plenipotentiary legate who would travel to China to sort out matters with the various missionary orders, the Vicars, and Kangxi himself.

Clement's representative for this sensitive mission was Carlo Tomasso Maillard de Tournon (1668–1710), a priest of noble extraction from Turin. The legate was consecrated patriarch of Antioch and Apostolic Visitor of the Indies, titles that carried sufficient weight to ensure that his decrees would be respected, even if his youthful age of thirty-six did not. Tournon's arrival at Canton on April 8, 1705, and his subsequent audiences at Peking set off a chain of events that radically altered the conditions for missionary activity in China. Although he made his way to the court with ambassadorial pomp, his receptions by Kangxi in December 1705 and June 1706 were unmitigated diplomatic disasters. What began as a cordial entente at the first encounter ended with Tournon's public disgrace and exile after the second, the fruit of mutual misunderstandings and conflicting agendas.[54] The legation's fallout had disastrous consequences for the Vice-Province. To stretch a point, Tournon was the deus ex machina who appeared on the Chinese stage amid all of the Jesuits' missionary gains to announce the beginning of the end of their enterprise. In the words of one observer, the "triumphs of the Catholic faith" that Tournon had come to recognize officially "degenerated in such a cruel tragedy that the most prudent onlookers saw a catastrophe looming similar to that of Japan."[55]

In his capacity as ambassador, Tournon was charged with inaugurating a relationship between the Holy See and the Qing empire and designating one of the European priests to serve as the superior for all Catholic missionaries in China. While the first of these tasks seems to have been a formality, the second was of paramount importance, because it would enable the papacy to rein in the Society of Jesus and assume greater control over the mission church. At Tournon's first reception, on December 31, 1705,

Kangxi had shown himself amenable to the idea of creating a missionary administrator. According to contemporary testimonies, he had been shocked by the profusion of European missionaries in China during his southern tour in 1703 and annoyed at the court Jesuits for neglecting to inform him about the total number of foreign priests in his domains.[56] But it was at this point that Tournon's and Kangxi's positions diverged. The emperor insisted that such a supervisory role could be assigned only to one of the Jesuits whom he trusted and who had long years of experience in China. Speaking through Jesuit interpreters from the Vice-Province and the French mission, Tournon refused this condition. Rather, he made it clear that any such superior would be of his own choosing. Since the legate's plan was tantamount to creating a shadow bureaucracy beyond Qing control, it was clear that no easy compromise would be struck.

The issue of the Chinese Rites was conspicuously absent from Tournon's initial discussions with the Qing sovereign. It had been half a decade since Kangxi first heard from the Peking Jesuits about the European controversies over these practices. By Chinese tradition, the emperor was the final arbiter in ethical matters, and it was not surprising that he confirmed the Vice-Province's positions. In a statement that he gave in 1700 to members of the French mission with the intention of having them publicize it in Europe, Kangxi wrote about the secular nature of the Confucian ceremonies required by members of the state bureaucracy and the purely memorial nature of the Chinese ancestor cult.[57] He further asserted that the term *Tian,* proudly displayed on the Jesuits' churches in the emperor's own calligraphy, denoted the Supreme Being. Eager to discuss the rites, Kangxi summoned Vicar Apostolic Charles Maigrot to Peking to be present at Tournon's second audience. The pair were received on June 29, 1706, and made to defend their opposition to the rites. Unable to speak Mandarin and incapable of citing passages from the Confucian classics to support their arguments, they failed to convince the emperor. And when Maigrot was again summoned on July 26, Kangxi chastised him for his temerity in condemning customs that the emperor had defined, explained, and approved.[58]

Kangxi sealed the fate of the Tournon legation by ordering the legate and his retinue, along with Maigrot, to be sent back to Europe via Macau in August 1706. Things had not gone well at Peking, and someone had to take the blame. Unsurprisingly, Tournon was convinced that the misunderstandings at court were the result of the Jesuits' machinations. After all,

Pereira and Grimaldi could hardly be trusted with faithfully translating negotiations that would be prejudicial to the Society of Jesus and the Padroado. The fact that they were the emperor's chosen interpreters only made matters worse—especially since Tournon and Maigrot had been unable to speak for themselves and had not brought along attendants who could speak for them. As a result, when Tournon departed Peking, he rained down a shower of censures and threats of excommunication upon the Jesuits.

Both the emperor and the legate left their final meeting determined to take control over the Catholic missionaries in China. Kangxi was well aware that the issues of the rites and control over the missions were intertwined and needed to be resolved together. He was also convinced that the Roman pontiff would never have condoned the disgraceful comportment of his legate. The emperor therefore appointed two representatives to inform Clement personally of Tournon's insubordination, António de Barros (1657–1708) from the Vice-Province and Antoine de Beauvollier (1657–1708) from the French mission. Although the choice of two Jesuits for this task greatly reduced its chances for success, all hope was lost when the two men, sailing on different vessels, died in shipwrecks before reaching Europe. Of more immediate importance for the Vice-Province was Kangxi's decree of December 17, 1706. This proclamation declared that all missionaries had to obtain a license, or *piao,* if they wished to remain in the empire. The precondition for taking the *piao* was aimed at separating the good missionaries from the bad in Kangxi's eyes: the Europeans had to swear to accept the Chinese Rites.

Although Tournon had failed in his diplomatic mission, he was determined to succeed in imposing his authority on the Jesuits. By the time he reached Nanjing in late summer 1706, he still had not announced the 1704 papal brief prohibiting the rites. Tournon had also resisted summoning up the full flourish of his powers in order to demand obedience from the members of a religious order who had all professed vows of subordination to the Holy See. While at Nanjing, the legate met with Vice-Provincial José Monteiro to discuss how best to publish the papal brief. Knowing that such a move was likely to have catastrophic consequences, Monteiro pleaded with Tournon to wait for the return of Barros and Beauvollier before acting. The Vice-Provincial predicted a best-case scenario of the "exile of all of the missionaries without any hope of ever returning to China." The worst case, he claimed, would be the execution of some of the Europeans and the "total ruin of the mission."[59] Yet Tournon interpreted these warnings as yet another example of Jesuit obfuscation and obstructionism and published his own version of the brief on February 7, 1707. In the days before Kangxi arrived at Nanjing on another of his southern tours, the legate left for Macau confident that he had finally asserted his authority over the China mission. But since neither the king of Portugal nor his bishops in Asia, the viceroy of the Estado da Índia, the archbishop of Goa, and the captain of Macau, recognized his authority, Tournon was put under house arrest in the Portuguese colony, where he languished until his premature death in 1710.[60]

The mutually exclusive positions represented by the 1704 brief *Cum Deus optimus* and the imperial *piao* presented the Jesuits with a serious moral dilemma. Should they stay in China and obey the emperor or abandon the mission and obey the pope? Was disobedience to the Holy See an acceptable price to pay in order to remain among the Chinese Christians whom they had labored for over a century to convert? The Jesuits refused to believe that the papacy would terminate their enterprise in the brutal manner that Tournon had chosen, and they were sure that their arguments in favor of the rites had never been given an honest hearing in Rome. They took heart at the Franciscans' similar reluctance to abandon their Chinese Christians. As a result, the Jesuits chose to take the *piao* while they bought time to straighten out affairs back in Europe.

Several factors urged the Jesuits to hurry slowly in conforming to Rome's will. First of all, some of them had accepted the *piao* in the two months between Kangxi's demands and Tournon's decrees. These Jesuits (and a few Franciscans, including the bishop of Peking) had bent before the imperial will, trusting in the former ambiguity of papal pronouncements on the rites. Second, when Tournon confronted José Monteiro and forced him to yield on behalf of the Vice-Province, the legate refused to show the Jesuit superior the original papal documents that underlay his impositions. Therefore the Nanjing Jesuits refused to take the *piao*—but they remained convinced that Tournon's decrees were fabricated. Finally, since the legate was subverting the jurisdiction of the Padroado, the Vice-Province's superiors (along with the Portuguese bishops) viewed his decrees as null and void. Clinging to the hope that the legation had been a passing nightmare, one that had interrupted their work no more than momentarily, the Jesuits lined up to receive their imperial licenses.

The imposition of the *piao* was an exercise in imperial control over the missionaries. Kangxi appointed his son Yinti to conduct the interviews during which the priests were asked two questions: if they had "the intention to return to Europe," and if they "always followed the practices of Matteo Ricci," that is, whether they allowed the rites. These encounters began in December 1706, with groups of provincial missionaries being summoned to the capital by turn to choose their fate. Since the Peking Jesuits—thirteen from the Vice-Province (including four coadjutors) and six from the French mission (including two coadjutors)—were in the "service of the emperor," they were not obliged to take the *piao.* The rest of the European Jesuits—twenty men from the Vice-Province and nineteen from the French mission—accepted their permits and returned to their residences. The four Chinese Jesuit priests and one Chinese coadjutor, possibly unknown to the authorities, were not summoned. Vice-Provincial Monteiro and his four colleagues at Nanjing found themselves in the most difficult situation. They had sworn to abandon the rites before they were offered licenses, and Monteiro refused to go back on his word. Kangxi nevertheless decided to spare them, sending them instead to Canton to await the return of his envoys to Rome.[61]

If the Jesuits had hoped that a higher power would rid them of their rivals, their wish was granted in the form of the *piao.* During the spring and summer months of 1707, the majority of the Dominicans and Augustinians, along with the Vicars Apostolic and their retainers, were sent into exile. In total, forty-one Europeans (thirty-one classifiable as missionaries and the rest as retainers) had been deported by the Qing authorities by December 1708. Only a handful of priests who refused the *piao* remained, hiding in the rural districts of southern China. While they awaited a new response from Rome, twenty-nine priests and four coadjutors from the Vice-Province, twenty-three priests and two coadjutors from the French mission, and eighteen Franciscans remained in China, either at Peking or in the provinces.[62]

The imposition of the *piao* severely damaged the reputation of the Teachings of the Lord of Heaven. The Qing authorities and the members of the imperial household who were charged with carrying out Kangxi's plan to either register or expel the missionaries became privy to the Europeans' divisions. In similar fashion, the mandarins whose duty was to close the churches of recalcitrant priests doubtless began to suspect the intentions of all Europeans seeking converts to Christianity. After all, if the emperor himself had deemed it necessary to monitor the behavior of the missionaries, he would count all the more on his bureaucrats to keep watch over their activities. The repercussions of this public affair constrained the Jesuits' capacity to attract new converts from areas without established Christian communities. Moreover, the glare of official attention likely hastened the falling away of those Christians at the far margins of the mission church, the men and women who had recently converted or those who had suffered through long droughts of pastoral attention due to the limited numbers of priests.

Kangxi's move to assert control over the Europeans, described by one scholar as the "virtual annihilation of the Edict of Toleration," is rightly understood within the context of the power relations between the Chinese state and the Buddhist or Daoist clergy.[63] By dissolving the ambiguity that had framed the Jesuits' (and other Europeans') relations with the Qing state, the emperor set into motion a bureaucratic process of defining and circumscribing missionary activity that could only have negative consequences for the social standing of *Tianzhu jiao* and its adherents. Although Jesuit sources claim that priests who took the *piao* could remain "with the privilege of being exempt from the molestations of mandarins in cities and provinces, and with permission to travel throughout China preaching the faith of Christ," could all Chinese authorities be counted on to grant the missionaries carte blanche in their bailiwicks?[64] Would provincial mandarins be able to separate the wheat from the chaff on the issue of the rites if they were ordered to analyze the practices of the missionaries and their followers, or would they use a heavy hand against all Christians? And how would aspiring climbers on the social ladder of civil service exploit the shifts in the emperor's mood? Might Kangxi eventually accept one of the memorials calling for the proscription of the Jesuits' religion that began to arrive before the throne in 1709 after circulating among provincial literati?[65]

The Society of Jesus also suffered considerable torment in Europe, where it was pilloried by its detractors, both secular and religious, as soon as news of the Tournon legation's failure and the missionaries' decision to accept the *piao* arrived. That Kangxi should appoint Jesuits to act as his emissaries merely made matters worse, since, by representing the emperor, they made clear their insubordination vis-à-vis the pope. Even before learning of the fates of Barros and Beauvollier, Kangxi sent another set of Jesuits to Rome with documents pertaining to the Tournon affair. The group that left Macau in January 1708 included Antonio Provana,

François Noël, and a Chinese assistant who later became a Jesuit priest, Luigi Fan Shouyi (1682–1753). At the Papal Curia they received a rebuke from Clement XI, who maintained that Tournon had acted in accord with his orders. José Ramón Arxó, also in Europe at the time in the capacity of mission procurator, despaired at this new utterance from Rome and "gave up the mission as lost." After reaching Italy, he sent word to his confreres that the pope had become disturbed by letters from China "full of fire against the Society" and blaming the Jesuits for Kangxi's actions. Arxó suspected, however, that there was some reason why testimony acquitting his order had not reached Rome, since, as he claimed, "the Jansenist termite has sapped almost the whole world."[66]

Clashes, Echoes, and Silence, 1710–1724

Despite the momentous turn of events, the majority of the Vice-Province's men remained at their residences ministering to their flocks. With respect to the overall development of Christianity in China, therefore, the fallout of the Tournon legation was not disastrous. Rather it represented a temporary setback in the overall pattern of growth. In addition to the Chinese Jesuits who either escaped detection or were ignored by imperial authorities, there were also priests from other religious orders who lived clandestinely in the provinces. Benefiting from lax supervision at China's maritime frontiers, other European priests managed to infiltrate the empire without taking the *piao* in the eighteenth century. But the events of 1705–1708 had finally dispelled any lingering notions that the Jesuits were synonymous with their religion and that *Tianzhu jiao* was what the men of the Vice-Province declared it to be. The Qing authorities had finally woken up to the fact that Christianity bore faces other than that of the Jesuits.

In contrast to its religious message, the Vice-Province was a tangible entity. It was made of churches, investments, and thousands of dependents who relied on it for spiritual care. At its heart lay a corps of priests whose public image and links to powerful protectors ensured its presence in the empire. Had the China Jesuits forever remained in the shadows, they might not have been concerned about slights to their social standing. They could scurry from clandestine chapel to underground oratory as the "recusant" Dominicans in Fujian and Guangdong did. But theirs was a public enterprise, built on high social visibility at court and in the provinces. That is why the very public imposition of the *piao* forced the Vice-Province into a defensive posture. Its primary task became the preservation of the mission church. The Jesuits continued to travel around their rural mission circuits with the hope of maintaining the fervor they had perceived in the early years. They also continued supervising the demanding schedules of devotions held in their urban churches, seeking to tighten the bonds of solidarity that held their flocks together. In the meantime, the Jesuits made appeals aimed at changing Rome's position on the rites—frustrated attempts that continued for thirty-two years after the reiteration of Tournon's decrees by Clement XI in 1710.

In comparison with earlier periods in the mission's history and in contrast to the copious documentation of the Jesuits' conflicts with their rivals, few descriptions of the mission church during the period from 1708 until 1720 have survived. It is possible that the Vice-Province was avoiding further indictments of its pastoral work by stemming the flow of ink used to celebrate its activities and instead concentrating on the defense of its role in the Tournon affair and its position on the Chinese Rites. Although the members of the French mission continued to supply their colleague Jean-Baptiste du Halde with "edifying and curious letters" about their efforts across China, the men of the Vice-Province maintained an uneasy quiet. So deafening was the silence from East Asia that the Society's procurator in Lisbon felt obliged to beg his confreres to send word of any triumphs of the faith, no matter how small, to share with the order's patrons. After reviewing the letters from Macau in 1714, Francisco de Fonseca claimed he was at a loss to find any news of "even one soul baptized or of one heathen converted." To advance the cause of the Vice-Province, he implored his colleagues to send accounts of conversions, baptisms, and churches and "not just stories of clashes with bishops and friars."[67]

The lack of information from China also slowed the pace of missionary recruitment. The echoes of the Jesuits' many entanglements served as a powerful deterrent for members of the Society in Europe who might have considered petitioning their superiors to be sent to the Qing empire. To be sure, few young Jesuits were able to reconcile their yearning for missionary glory with the moral burden of disobedience to papal authority that all of the members of the Vice-Province had assumed. Even those men who had been specially groomed for the China mission found themselves apprehensive about joining the stigmatized enterprise. For example,

Francisco Cardoso (1677–1723), a Jesuit from Portugal skilled in mathematics, had originally been sent to Asia to help reinforce the Portuguese presence at Peking. But upon hearing of the conflicts in China, he petitioned the Society's superiors in Goa in 1709 to let him remain in India. It was only at the insistence of Miguel de Amaral, at the time Visitor of the Province of Goa, that Cardoso decided to head for the Qing capital after all.[68]

Another reason why the Vice-Province remained mum about its progress in China is that it saw itself confronted with an increasing number of reverses in the mission field. At stake was the issue of control over its religious message, by then a moot question. The kinship networks and connections among villagers that had furthered the spread of Christianity in rural areas had given rise to problems of pastoral oversight as greater numbers of men and women adopted this foreign religion. With so few Jesuits in the cities of the Qing empire, much less in the remote places where they passed on their mission circuits, it was impossible for the Vice-Province to maintain a single image of *Tianzhu jiao* in the minds of plebeian Chinese. The problem was compounded by the fact that many baptisms were administered by catechists, men and women who could err in their perception of who merited that sacrament. Both the catechists and the Jesuits themselves were liable to be taken in by individuals who sought to use the public legitimacy of Christianity as a cloak for their membership in the heterodox sects that flourished in rural areas.

Starting in 1714, but coming to a head in 1717 and 1718, a series of scandals involving members of outlawed sects occurred in rural Shandong Province. According to the bishop of Peking, Bernardino della Chiesa, the local missionaries, their auxiliaries, and their community leaders began to suspect the motivations behind a wave of conversions among rustics. Nevertheless, baptisms carried on apace until authorities began to arrest some of these new Christians on charges of sectarian activity. The villagers in question had come to know *Tianzhu jiao* through Christians living in their area who were nominally under the pastoral supervision of Franciscan missionaries as well as the lone Jesuit at Jinan, Girolamo Franchi (1667–1718). Della Chiesa's report on the events states that not only did these sectarians adopt Christian religious symbols and devotional objects, but also a few of their number even declared themselves to be further incarnations of the Lord of Heaven. One individual even claimed to be the Holy Spirit "come down from heaven to preach the true law of God," since this dubious convert felt that the Europeans had given up the task. The bishop breathed a small sigh of relief on seeing how other Christians were able to identify their false brethren, but not before the local mandarins began their inquiries and punishments, events that further damaged the reputation of Christianity, its preachers, and its adherents.[69]

One story of missionary work that did make its way to Europe in the 1710s was a tale that at first perked up the spirits of the China Jesuits caught under clouds of gloom. This was the conversion of Sunu (ca. 1648–1725), a Manchu from the imperial clan, along with his household. In the years before 1712, one of Sunu's sons, Suerjin, encountered copies of Christian texts at a used book fair in Peking and had been impressed. After circulating these books among his brothers, Suerjin contacted the Peking Jesuits and asked for doctrinal instruction. Missionaries from both the Vice-Province and the French mission built friendships with these Manchu nobles, and at length, starting in 1719, claimed them as converts. Jesuit writings about them go into considerable detail about their pious lifestyles as well as about their fondness for devotional art. Unfortunately for the Vice-Province, most of the news about these Manchu Christians reached Europe only in 1724, after the Sunu clan had been disgraced and sent into exile by the Yongzheng emperor.[70]

Desirous of preserving the Kangxi emperor's benevolence toward them in light of the legation debacle, the Jesuits made displays of faithful service to the throne. As they had maintained since the days of Matteo Ricci, none of their religious ambitions could be achieved without the political legitimacy that the priests at Peking earned for the Vice-Province. Both French and "Portuguese" Jesuits thus made themselves useful to Kangxi during the years from 1708 until 1717 by acting as surveyors for the emperor's cartography projects, including the *Huangyu quanlan tu* (Complete Map of the Empire). From the Vice-Province, Francisco Cardoso, the Bavarian Kaspar Castner (1665–1709), and the Alsatian Romain Hinderer (1668–1744) conducted tours in the southern provinces for this imperial commission. Kangxi rewarded them in 1711 with another example of his calligraphy in honor of the completion of the new sanctuary at the College of Peking *(Nantang)*—this time referring to *Tianzhu* instead of the controversial *Tian.*[71] The Vice-Province's superiors sought to keep up these good relations by sending the artist Giuseppe Castiglione (1688–1766), an Italian coadjutor, to work at court. From his arrival at the Qing capital in 1715 until his death there over fifty years later, he painted well-

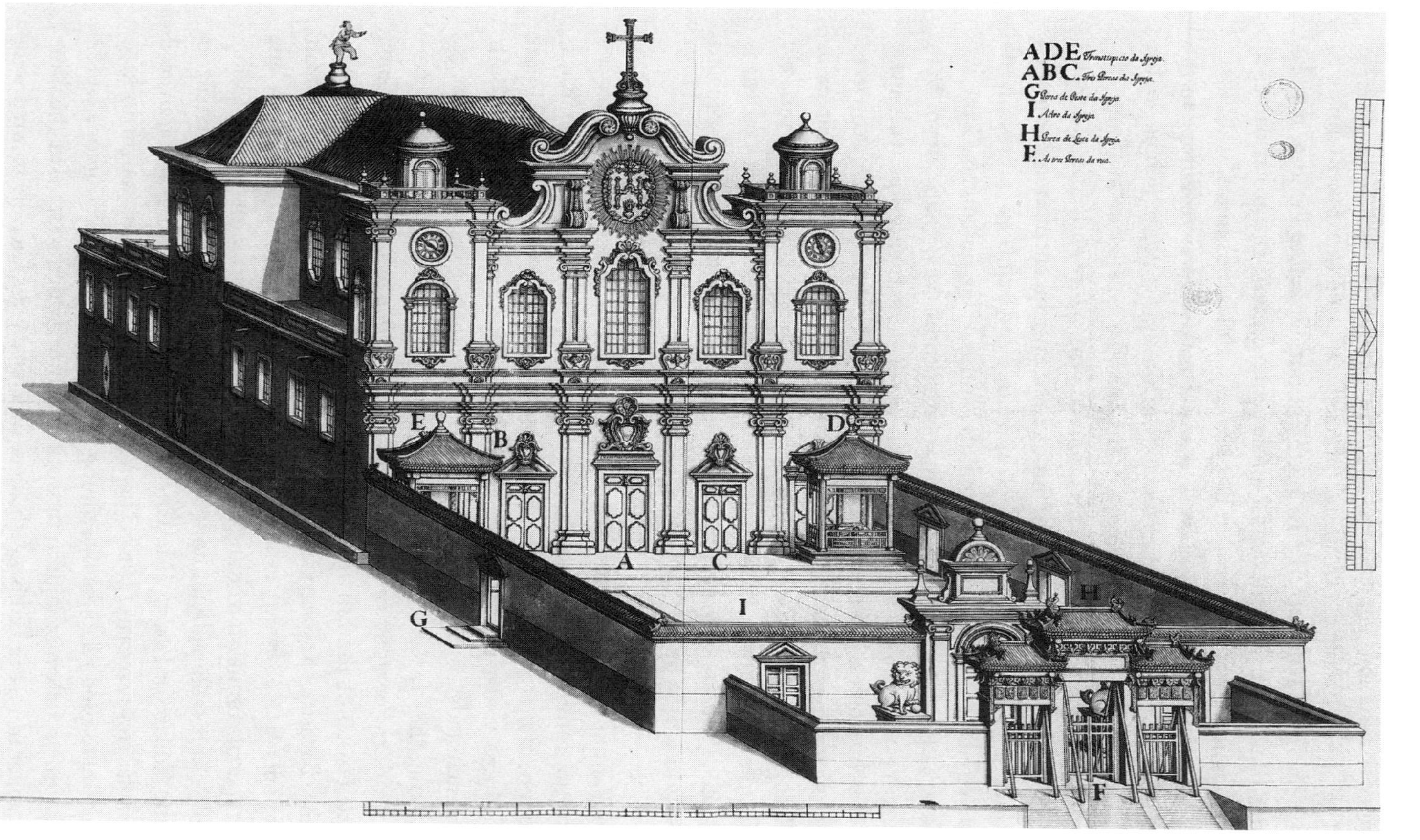

Nantang, or Southern Church, Peking. Depiction of the church at the College of Peking, completed in 1711.

known portraits of court figures, in addition to designing a European-style palace for the Qianlong emperor.

There was also a European prong to the Jesuits' strategy for salvaging their China effort from censure, if not outright destruction by papal fiat. After their futile attempts to resolve their affairs in Europe by themselves, the Society turned to the Portuguese crown and miter for help. The authorities in Lisbon and Goa had a keen interest in the China mission, because part of their own prestige was linked to its fortunes. If blasts from the king's cannons could not keep his European rivals out of Portugal's Asian domains, perhaps the threat of excommunication would keep intruders out of his ecclesiastical territories. Even before the archbishop of Goa received word that Clement XI had confirmed Tournon's condemnation of the rites in 1710, he sent a pastoral letter to the Jesuits in East Asia informing them that any decrees issued by the legate were null and void.[72] The crown also lobbied the pope by sending Rodrigo Anes de Sá, the marquis de Fontes, to Rome in 1712. Although this ambassador spent six years in Italy and was received with considerable pomp in 1716, he was not able to resolve matters in favor of the Society or his royal master. While King João V at least got the reward of having the archbishop of Lisbon raised to the status of cardinal and patriarch, the Jesuits got only a further round of censures: on March 15, 1715, Clement issued an apostolic constitution, *Ex illa die,* that confirmed the prohibition of the rites while demanding obedience from the missionaries in China.[73] Four years later the pope appointed another legate, Carlo Ambrogio Mezzabarba (1685–1741), but this Italian prelate met with no more success at Peking than his predecessor.

At the time of the Kangxi emperor's death in 1722, the missionaries of the Vice-Province were still ministering to their flocks in the provinces, but the rigors of age had eroded much of their ability to sustain the mission church. Their ranks included veterans such as Pieter van Hamme at seventy-one years of age, Manuel Mendes and José Soares at sixty-six, Giampaolo Gozani at sixty-three, Simon Bayard and Francisco Pinto at sixty. Even the Chinese men who had been ordained priests and joined the Society of Jesus were far from being the picture of youth. Francisco Xavier Rosario Ho was fifty-five years old, and Tomé da Cruz (1666–1745) was fifty-six. One might think, therefore, that the members of the Vice-Province would have been wise to extend an olive branch to their confreres in the French mission in the face of dangers that threatened both groups; but no large-scale cooperation between the two enterprises emerged.

Outside of a few instances of priests from the French mission joining the Vice-Province to help staff its residences, relations between the two missions were strained. Doubtless there were legitimate reasons for the mutual recriminations, given that each group of Jesuits had its own ambitions. The Vice-Province's superiors accused the French of appropriating Christian communities in Jiangxi Province—never mind that the Vice-Province could not maintain them. In similar fashion, the French Jesuits at court hinted to Kangxi that the Vice-Province's men had impeded them from carrying out his commissions.[74] Some of the Portuguese priests of the Vice-Province at court moved aggressively against their French brethren, much to the dismay of their more irenic colleagues from German lands. Such was the tenor of their infighting that the bishop of Peking felt obliged to chastise the Jesuits for their lack of fraternal love.[75] Moreover, the French mission itself was rent by divisions between the partisans and opponents (including several members of the Vice-Province at Peking) of figurism, a system of interpretation for texts from Chinese antiquity.[76] At the center of this debate was Joachim Bouvet, whose readings of the *Yijing,* or *Book of Changes,* led him to glimpse veiled references to Christian revelation in this and other obscure works. So the discord between the Vice-Province and the French mission continued. Each carried on as best it could in its own, separate mission districts. The Vice-Province was by far the more burdened enterprise of the two, if only because the French had been conducting missions for only two decades and had a relatively modest range of activity. Without a substantial influx of recruits to carry on its work at court and in the provinces, the Vice-Province had little prospect of enduring.

Into the Shadows, 1724 and Beyond

Afflicted as they were by internal distractions, external worries, and pastoral challenges, the China Jesuits faced their most serious trial when the Yongzheng emperor ascended to the throne in 1723. Recall that since the start of the previous reign, the Jesuits had had no other strategy for defending their enterprise beyond that of entrusting themselves to the safeguard of the emperor's goodwill. While Kangxi had remained friendly with the court Jesuits until his death, he became increasingly frustrated with them after the Tournon legation. In 1717 he even accepted a memorial from a Guangdong mandarin, Chen Mao (ca. 1651–ca. 1719), who called for Christianity to be proscribed. Kangxi, who instructed the petitioner first to "wait several years," expressed a desire in January 1721 to see this order carried out, but no action was taken before his death.[77] Soon after taking up the reins of state, Yongzheng (r. 1723–1735) began where his father had left off, accepting a memorial from the governor general of Fujian and Zhejiang provinces recommending the proscription of Christianity and the expulsion of the missionaries. In the version of the Sacred Edict promulgated in January 1724, *Tianzhu jiao* was included among the "perverse sects and sinister doctrines."[78]

Why did Yongzheng move against Christianity? Some scholars have described his act as an unambiguous response to the failure of diplomatic initiatives between Peking and Rome, while others suggest that he sought to be known to posterity as an adversary of heterodoxy who took similar actions against other religious followings.[79] Other factors may have included Yongzheng's attachment to Buddhism, the Chan school in particular; his determination to impose "law and order"; his suspicious nature; and the feeling that his father had indulged the missionaries far too long. Perhaps the best explanation for his proscription of Christianity has to do with the political struggles that surrounded his rise to the throne. In Erik Zürcher's view, the fact that the Jesuits had friends in the Manchu circles at court—including the Sunu clan, a branch of the imperial household—made their adopted religion a logical target for the emperor's efforts to secure his hold on power. That the Jesuits had other Manchu connections in all likelihood made them even more suspect. The very swiftness of Yongzheng's move against *Tianzhu jiao,* one executed with the same vigor that he employed to eradicate his political rivals, suggests that his motivations were closely linked to his accession to the throne.[80]

Whatever the rationale, Yongzheng's act was a disaster for the Vice-Province. The repressive powers of the Qing state were quickly mustered against the most visible symbols of the Christian religion, church buildings and their resident priests. Just as during the Nanjing affair and the Canton exile, the most intense period of this crackdown occurred soon after edicts were published. In the early months of 1724, all of the Society's edifices—colleges, residences, large and small churches—were seized and designated for other uses. According to José Soares, some of these buildings were "occupied by heathens, and not a few of them were converted into temples of idolatry."[81] Reports that reached Peking from the provinces told of churches being turned into granaries, schools, and hospitals. In Henan, Giampaolo Gozani reported that his sanctuary at Kaifeng was made into a "temple of Baal." And in Fujian Province, the Jesuits were reported to have suffered the ironic indignity of having their churches transformed into clan temples "for honoring ancestors." Members of the French mission in North Zhili witnessed the sacred images from their sanctuaries consigned to the flames, the same fate that befell the religious art in churches belonging to the Society's Province of Japan at Guilin in Guangxi Province.[82]

In October 1724, sixteen years after the Jesuits had chosen to defy Tournon and Clement XI by taking the *piao,* they were rounded up by imperial authorities and transported to Canton for exile to Macau. This time, unlike after the Calendar Case in 1666, the Qing authorities made good on their promise. According to one report of the audience held at court on July 1, 1724, Yongzheng informed Ignatius Kögler (1680–1746), director of the Astronomical Bureau, and two of his confreres from the French mission that the Jesuits were lucky to be expelled alive. After making reference to the Dominicans in Fujian who had incurred the wrath of mandarins for trying to "destroy the doctrine of Confucius," Yongzheng remarked that he had ordered the destruction of many Buddhist temples "and had over a thousand lamas killed."[83] Deportation meant getting off comparatively easy. Men such as Giampaolo Gozani, Manuel Mendes, Vice-Provincial João de Sá (1672–1731), and several members of the French mission lived out their days in Macau. Things went even better for the priests at Peking. They retained their positions (and pensions) at court as artists and technical specialists, enjoying imperial favor for their skills, if not their religion, until the last decade of the eighteenth century.

Despite the rigor of Yongzheng's crackdown, some of the missionaries from the Vice-Province managed to remain in the provinces and continue their pastoral work. Informing the Jiangnan area mandarins that they were too old to make the trek to Canton, and "accompanying their supplications with gifts and silver," at least three Europeans stayed on in Hangzhou and Songjiang. Other Jesuits went undercover to continue their work. Among the most successful of these dwellers in the shadows was João Duarte (1671–1752), a Portuguese priest who remained in Huguang Province until at least 1740. Clandestine missionary work was easiest for the Chinese Jesuits, with Francisco Xavier Rosario Ho, Fan Shouyi, and Tomé da Cruz continuing to visit the Christian communities scattered across the empire. Despite the fact that the Vice-Province had long resisted accepting Chinese priests in its ranks, these men were the Jesuits' best hope for preserving the mission church during the long years of persecution that lay ahead. In September 1726 José Soares could only lament the lost opportunities for preparing an indigenous clergy, calling it a disgrace that "a large number of native priests" was not available to fill the ranks left empty by the departure of "the exiled and the dead."[84]

Of all of those affected by the proscription of Christianity, the Jesuits' flocks fared the best. There were no systematic purges, no squadrons of dragoons sent to flush them out. It does not appear that there were any large-scale episodes of bloodshed against Christians in the provinces, no martyrdoms to add to the lists of those who had given their lives for the faith. In fact, as soon as 1726, the missionaries in Jiangnan reported that they continued in secret to offer the sacraments to thousands. Romain Hinderer visited the mission district centered on Suzhou and Changshu that year and informed his colleagues at Peking that he had heard 5,704 confessions and given the Eucharist to 5,069 men and women. Likewise, Domingos de Brito (1674–1742), a Portuguese priest from the Province of Japan, traveled around the coastal plain and heard 4,270 confessions from women. These activities were not without peril, however, since Brito mentioned that he had been denounced twice to the authorities for holding meetings of women in the Songjiang suburbs. After paying twenty-two taels to *yamen* officials, however, the Jesuit was let go. "In this way," Brito wrote, "we learn to be cautious at our own expense."[85]

No great persecution hit the Jesuits' Chinese Christians in the late 1720s, but their ranks thinned quickly after Yongzheng's edicts. According to José Soares, the year from July 1725 to August 1726 was one of "sterility in the salvation of souls," with few new baptisms to report. Many Christians cowered in fear of the emperor's next move against them, according to the veteran missionary. With each day that passed, Soares asserted, news of the prohibitions reached the ears of more and more members of "the plebs, who are the best disposed to receive the gospel." It did not help that the expulsion of the provincial missionaries and the closing of their churches were a spectacle. As a result, Soares claimed, it had become "very rare" to see people coming to hear the missionaries' teachings.[86]

Perhaps the best indicator of this downward trend can be found in the reported numbers of baptisms. Two years after the 1724 edict, the missionaries at Peking (where both the college and the East Church remained open) claimed to have baptized 305 individuals, including a significant number of deathbed conversions.[87] A quarter of a century earlier, Antoine Thomas had recorded that the average number of yearly baptisms at the capital was 860.[88] Similarly, in Huguang, João Duarte claimed 104 baptisms, fewer than half the average of 260 that he had reported in 1703.[89]

At the heart of the mission church in Jiangnan, the missionaries also recorded drops in the number of baptisms, albeit on a smaller scale. Domingos de Brito and Romain Hinderer provided a breakdown of their tallies according to the age and gender of those who submitted to baptism. Both sets of statistics reveal a large number of baptisms of children under the age of seven (almost half the total in Songjiang), further underscoring the importance of Christianity as a family tradition in the coastal plain. The strong kinship bonds between Chinese Christians and the communal nature of their spiritual activities, revolving around the prayer routines of rural "parishes," would be the central factors in maintaining the vitality of the communities in this area. After all, the sheer numbers of these men and women indicated that they had fostered *Tianzhu jiao* for over a century with only minimal supervision from the missionaries. Unlike the Jesuits' other, smaller flocks, whose religious identities and devotional practices were more closely linked to the presence of their missionary pastors, the Jiangnan communities had relied upon themselves for all of their spiritual needs with the exception of the sacraments, and so would be able to continue long after the Vice-Province disappeared.

The accumulation of reverses in the first three decades of the eighteenth century withered the Society's China enterprise. Despite the fact that its missionaries continued to work in the Qing empire for another fifty years after the proscription of Christianity, the Jesuit mission no longer functioned as it had during the seventeenth century. To be sure, it was only the suppression of the Society of Jesus by papal order in 1773 that finally dismantled the Jesuits' early modern China enterprise. By 1724 the conditions imposed on the Vice-Province by Italian popes and Chinese emperors made it impossible for the Jesuits to conduct their apostolic endeavors with the social visibility and legal freedom necessary for building a mission church on the empire-wide scale that they had envisioned. The Jesuits knew the stakes of the power game being played between Peking and Rome. Giampaolo Gozani, for one, voiced his frustrations when he informed King João V of Portugal in 1725 that the Jesuits' work was impeded "from two sides, the Emperor of China and the Pope."[90] The missionaries were well aware that the effects of high-level diplomacy reached directly to the towns and villages of the mission field where their flocks were found. As José Soares noted in 1726, there could be no hope for the Vice-Province unless the Jesuits kept up good relations with the emperor or, in any event, with influential provincial figures. Without their support, he declared, "little or nothing can be done in China, as experience has always shown."[91]

The Jesuits' move into the shadows negated all the social and political gains that they had made in China over fourteen decades. Clandestine missionary work was the polar opposite of the goal for the mission set out by Alessandro Valignano, Michele Ruggieri, and Matteo Ricci and confirmed again and again by men such as Francisco Furtado, Ferdinand Verbiest, and Tomé Pereira. The linchpin of the Jesuits' success in China had always been their studied image or, in a word, their visibility. To reinforce that image, the men of the Vice-Province added a wide network of political connections meant to ensure their social legitimacy. The ultimate link in this chain—the bond that safeguarded their mission church—was the Jesuits' friendship with successive Chinese emperors. The relationships between the missionaries and the indigenous loci of power had permitted the construction of the mission church, and so when they were forced to become invisible to Chinese authorities, their enterprise crumbled. Absent the political legitimacy they had gained thanks to their visibility, it would have been impossible for the Jesuits to attract so many members of the Chinese lower classes to their religion without calling down the same wrath from the state that was meted out to native sectarian leaders. To be sure, it was the same public image enjoyed by the Jesuits that had enabled them to build a mission church with a dynamism far exceeding the sum of the individual efforts of their paltry numbers. But once they and their religion were relegated to the ranks of heterodox teachings and brought under the heel of imperial justice, the efforts of their most productive confreres, missionaries such as Niccolò Longobardo, Étienne Faber, and José Monteiro, were reduced to naught. These priests would not have been able to recognize the Vice-Province after 1724. The missionary enterprise they had helped to create and sustain had ceased to exist.

II

BUILDING THE CHURCH

6

In the Apostles' Classroom

Good news reached the Jesuit Colégio do Espírito Santo at Évora on April 18, 1622: in a solemn ceremony held at Rome on March 13, Pope Gregory XV declared Ignatius Loyola and Francis Xavier saints. Pealing bells were the first sign of the rejoicing that would last for weeks in the Portuguese city. Processions, high masses, fireworks, and outdoor theater came afterwards. While the Jesuits themselves organized many of these events, their students did not lack initiative. The adolescents in the philosophy classes held muster at the college with harquebuses on April 20, firing salvos in honor of their heavenly protectors. Not to be outdone, the rhetoric students assembled the following day bedecked in martial silks and feathers, bearing cuirasses, swords, daggers, and muskets. The younger boys of the grammar classes also joined in, issuing a challenge to the theology pupils, who responded by "leaving their commentaries and picking up their weapons." These two groups built a fortress on top of the school's fountain and took turns making assaults on it with infantry charges and volleys of musketry. The most elaborate spectacle, however, came in mid-June, when the students staged a reenactment of heroic episodes from the two saints' lives. Francis Xavier's labors in exotic locales were made for impressive tableaux vivants. At one point, the Apostle of the Orient battled Idolatry herself, who was clothed in silk and jewels and riding atop a crocodile. Shortly before the climax, Xavier crossed paths with Buddhist monks who were worshipping a "monstrous idol of Japan twenty-two palms high" and intoning strange chants. He quickly vanquished them all with a burst of the invincible light of the gospel.[1]

Central patio of the University of Évora, Portugal. This courtyard and fountain were formerly part of the Jesuits' Colégio do Espírito Santo. Classrooms were located behind the arcades and the novitiate in a more secluded area.

This pageantry was intended to impress and edify the people of Évora, the college's students in particular. What they beheld in the figure of Francis Xavier was missionary virtue personified, the incarnation of the apostolic ambitions of the Society of Jesus. It was hoped that some of the young men in the audience would be inspired to join the order that had produced such saintly exemplars. The play had the further aim of encouraging those who had already joined the order to petition for service in the overseas provinces of the Portuguese Assistancy. Members of the audience such as theology pupil António de Gouvea and rhetoric student Michel Trigault no doubt found their desire to follow in Xavier's footsteps bolstered by these visions of Jesuit heroism in the East.[2] Both would request assignments to the Indies, and both would have their desires fulfilled. Although fully freighted with zeal, they set sail from Lisbon with little baggage and less knowledge of the rigors of missionary life. The conditions they would find in China were unknown to them, as was the métier of the missionary in Asia. When they reached Macau after the arduous journey on the Cape route and across Maritime Asia, they were surely wizened by exposure to the elements but no great deal wiser about the task before them than they had been at Évora.

One of the most persistent myths about the China Jesuits is that they were a uniquely talented set of men who had been handpicked by their superiors in Europe to confront the challenges of China. It is a tribute to the genius of the Society's publicity enterprise that such interpretations have endured to the present. Yet this notion, like other figments about missionary heroism, consists of much pious fancy coating a grain of truth. In reality, most of the China Jesuits, like their peers who worked in the order's other missions, were no more than junior members of the Society of Jesus who successfully persuaded their superiors of their vocation for missionary work. It is true that they were selected from among a large, pan-European pool of applicants. And it is also true that some of the China Jesuits were known in their homelands for having technical abilities, a factor which may have increased their chances of being chosen. But it is worth remembering that the mission's recruits were selected not by the superiors of the Vice-Province but by Jesuit provincial officers and Superiors General, who had no firsthand knowledge of China. Moreover, many of the China Jesuits sailed to Asia in the middle of their academic formation, too soon for them to have given evidence of genius. It may be superfluous to add that the perilous sea voyage made the final cut; one estimate suggests that only about half of the recruits survived the journey, and many of those who did expired soon after reaching China.[3]

Yet it is undeniable that the men of the Vice-Province showed considerable aplomb in creating and maintaining their China enterprise. Surely this accomplishment was not simply due to chance, or to any master plan drawn up by Alessandro Valignano and Matteo Ricci. A more plausible explanation for the Jesuits' ability to manage their efforts in China for over a century can be found, at least in part, in the skills they brought with them from Europe. But how did the Society of Jesus calibrate its educational apparatus to produce skilled recruits for the China mission? Simply put, it made no attempt to do so. Rather, in the last quarter of the sixteenth century, the Society implemented a largely uniform academic program and probationary experience that outfitted future Jesuits with a diverse set of mental tools, regardless of whether they stayed in Europe or embarked for Asia, Africa, or the Americas. With the exception of the first men to work in the Ming empire, virtually all of the Jesuits received their intellectual and pastoral formation within the Society. Without denying the importance of the individual talents of a substantial number of them, one can see that elements of this common training were crucial in enabling the Jesuits to carry out their apostolic task.

What skills did future missionaries acquire during their European training that would be useful in China? The primary intellectual benefits of a Jesuit education were the ability to analyze linguistic structures, the capacity to engage in logical argumentation, and techniques for dealing with abstract philosophical and theological concepts. But most future missionaries did more than just learn these skills; they taught them to others as part of their training in the Society of Jesus. In this way, they benefited from being on both sides of the lectern. Moreover, as teachers, they learned how to manage large groups of students.

Adolescents typically became novices in the Society of Jesus at the age of sixteen or seventeen, continuing their studies while they went through the order's first two years of training. Living in community with their senior brethren, future China Jesuits gained firsthand knowledge of the order's principal ministries, including missionary work. Their concept of evangelization, however, was a reflection of the standard strategies that worked among Catholics in the European countryside, not of those employed during the Jesuits' ventures in non-Christian lands. What worked for Europe might not be useful in Asia. What, then, was the principal value of the Jesuits' collective European experience for men bound for China? It equipped them with the mental flexibility for drawing appropriate analogies between Chinese culture and their own, at the same time preparing them for guiding the growth of their Christian communities. Any missionary could make use of a store of well-tested pastoral strategies for dealing with rustics and increasing the level of fervor among laymen and women.

Most of the future China missionaries spent the better part of their lives in the controlled environment of the Society's colleges. They were typically ordered to embark shortly after they had finished their training in moral theology and were ordained as priests. Many, however, were sent fresh from the novitiate, before they had taken Holy Orders. When did they learn the practical skills of effective missionaries? Put differently, where did they get the pastoral training they would need to manage their Chinese Christians? Not in colleges but at sea. The months they spent aboard the ships of the Portuguese Carreira da Índia immersed them in a cauldron of human emotions. They witnessed hunger, death, and disease among their confreres. The soldiers, sailors, and adventurers on board added debauchery to this drama, while their vessels were tossed capriciously on the waves. Dealing with these circumstances constituted the first sustained pastoral experience for most of the future China Jesuits. In addition to learning how to minister to others in stressful environments, they gained experience at managing limited material resources. Such skills would be invaluable when they headed into China, to mission stations that were as dissimilar to their former colleges in Europe as they were distant from them.

Aboard the Trojan Horse

In the early months of 1665, António Barradas, the senior officer of the Province of Portugal, sent a personnel catalogue to the Roman curia of the Society of Jesus. Similar reports of men and resources had been composed yearly for over a century. In this account, Barradas recorded the names and personal evaluations of over six hundred priests and coadjutors according to their age and rank within the order. Deep in the document's folios one can catch a glimpse of future China missionaries undergoing their early training. One of the 134 Jesuits at the College of Évora, twenty-year-old Simão Rodrigues, was studying philosophy in his hometown. He had joined the Society six years previously, most likely after studying grammar and rhetoric at the same school. One of Rodrigues's colleagues was José Monteiro, who had traveled from his native Lisbon to join the order at Évora in 1663. Two years later, Monteiro was sixteen and in the final stages of his Latin studies. At the College of Coimbra, Tomé Pereira was completing his novitiate. He had come to the famed university town from the village of São Martinho do Vale in the region of Braga in northern Portugal, and had obtained the degree of Master in Arts. In 1665 Pereira was a face in the crowd, one of the 176 Jesuits in Coimbra. Unbeknownst to him, Rodrigues, or Monteiro, within a decade they would all meet on the far side of the globe, joined in an effort to preach Christianity to Manchus and Chinese.[4]

The three young men were at different points on the common education track followed by Jesuit priests. With the exception of the first few missionaries to work in China, they passed through the same three academic cycles as almost all of their confreres. This curriculum was laid out in the Society's *Ratio Studiorum,* a standardized "Plan of Studies" promulgated in 1599 that was implemented in the order's global network of schools.[5] The normalization of the Society's pedagogical program and the effect that it had on the training of its members contributed, for good or for ill, to the military clichés about the order. For many Jesuits in the early modern period (and beyond), however, rigorous organization was one of their order's primary strengths. In his chronicle of the Society in Portugal, Baltasar Teles, a mid-seventeenth-century provincial officer, likened each Jesuit college to a "Trojan horse filled with soldiers from heaven, which every year produces conquistadors of souls."[6] While this is not the place to synthesize the work of generations of scholars on the subject of Jesuit education in early modern Europe, it is necessary before we proceed to sketch the progression of future missionaries through the Society's academic program.[7]

The initial cycle consisted of two years of study in the humanities. To be sure, these were not the first classes that most students had attended. Rather, these lessons in rhetoric and oratory were the tail end of eight to nine years of Latin classes. Most of the youths who later became Jesuits began their schooling in reading and writing at the age of six or seven. They gradually progressed through the Society's offerings in Latin and, to a lesser extent, Greek grammar. By the time they reached the age of fourteen or fifteen, they would be finished with the grammar classes and ready to start readings in the humanities, that is, in Roman and Greek poetry and prose. The curriculum during these years of study included works from the classical canon—Cicero, Virgil, Homer, Ovid, and Horace. Those who decided to join the Society frequently entered the novitiate at this point, often at the suggestion of instructors who recognized budding academic talent and zeal. The last phase of the Latin cycle thus coincided with their first years as novices, with young Jesuits beginning their spiritual formation as they finished the humanities classes.

The young men who experienced the Society's second and third academic cycles within the order were called scholastics. They were different from their fellows, who, while they underwent the identical novitiate training, were identified as suited for nothing higher than the terminal status of temporal coadjutor. Most of the future China Jesuits became scholastics at about the same time they began the "Arts Course," a program in Greek philosophy. This course of study began with a first year of logic, culminating in a critical examination. The students who passed this test would continue to hear Aristotle's works on natural philosophy and metaphysics in addition to their standard Jesuit commentaries. Those who failed it were often sent to be trained as spiritual coadjutors, that is, priests who were instructed only in moral theology and assigned to say masses or hear confessions. The students who continued in the Arts Course—including all of the China missionaries—would get exposure to mathematics during lectures on Euclid's *Elements* and astronomy from readings in Sacrobosco's works or Aristotle's *De caelo.*

After finishing the philosophy cycle, scholastics were intellectually prepared to begin their theology studies. This final cycle was divided into two sections, an initial two years of moral theology and casuistry, followed by another two years of speculative theology. Scholastics were typically twenty years old when they began this cycle, and had finished the first two years of their order's three-year probationary period. The moral theology courses were the equivalent of their seminary training. There they learned how to hear confessions and resolve cases of conscience, the Society's signature pastoral skill. After completing this initial training, most young Jesuits would be sent to teach parts of the Latin or philosophy cycles for two or three years. These teaching assignments were an integral part of the Society's formational program, and instructors were often sent to teach in colleges other than their own.

It was at this point, when they had reached their mid-twenties, that a significant number of China missionaries sailed for Asia. Others left for India in the midst of the philosophy cycle, which they completed, along with their theology studies, at the Colégio de São Paulo in Goa. A substantial number of China Jesuits went to Asia after completing the entire theology program in Europe. In all these cases, young Jesuits would commence studying Thomistic theology after teaching for a few years. Regardless of where they heard the summas of speculative theology, almost all of the China Jesuits completed this four-year curriculum. Most of them were in their late twenties or early thirties at the time they were ready to join the mission. By that point they would have spent more than half their life residing, learning, and teaching in Jesuit schools.

It should not be surprising that there were minor variations in Jesuit education from one country to another. Such differences were important in China, since the Vice-Province drew recruits from across Europe. To give but one example, the colleges in the Society's Province of Flandro-

Belgica (roughly equivalent to the northern half of what now is Belgium plus the Netherlands) taught the Arts Course in two years instead of three. This fact serves to dispel the impression that one gets by glancing at the Vice-Province's personnel catalogues and seeing men such as Ferdinand Verbiest and Philippe Couplet, both known for their academic achievements, listed as having less philosophy training than their Portuguese, German, French, or Italian confreres.[8] Although such differences were permitted under the flexible pedagogical framework prescribed by the *Ratio Studiorum,* the institutional push toward standardization within the Society meant that they remained the exception rather than the rule. The Vice-Province's catalogues from the early seventeenth through the early eighteenth centuries therefore reveal an impressive consistency. In the overwhelming majority of cases, missionaries are listed with the notation "Studuit in Societate humaniorum litterarum annos 2, philosophiae annos 3, theologiae annos 4."[9]

Which elements of this nine-year course of study were most useful for missionaries in China? To many readers, the answer may seem self-evident in light of the curriculum's strong dose of classical thought. But while the Jesuits' training in rhetoric no doubt made them compelling preachers, the sermons they gave to their Chinese followers did not require the deft manipulation of European literary or biblical allusions. Moreover, the missionaries' writings in Chinese demanded a style vastly different from that of the Ciceronian register. Indeed, the production of Annual Letters was the only rhetorical task in a European mode that was required of the men of the Vice-Province, and this burden often fell to its freshest recruit. So the primary benefit of the Jesuits' education lay in the cultivation of a methodical frame of mind rather than in literary content or prose style.

Naturally, one of the prospective missionary's most important skills was the ability to learn spoken and written Chinese. It is important to underscore the fact that future China Jesuits were predisposed to study languages. Latin grammar was the cornerstone of the Society's educational edifice, and was taught through the dissection of words and phrases. Years of constant drilling made the analysis of prose and poetry routine. The obligation to speak Latin while at school and the frequent composition contests among students further honed their language skills. But the Jesuits' familiarity with foreign tongues did not end with the language of Cicero and Virgil; they also learned Greek and Hebrew in their humanities classes. The fact that they spent so much of their academic training breaking down grammatical and syntactical structures, as well as memorizing declensions, conjugations, and glossaries, gave them the invaluable edge of experience when they were faced with the need to acquire Chinese.

Another aspect of the Society's education program was the atmosphere of "pious competition" that the order's instructors fostered among their students. This technique was one of the hallmarks of Jesuit education, and a spirit of collegial contestation was pervasive in the Society's schools. Pupils were encouraged to compete with one another in displays of erudition as well as piety. (It should not be forgotten that attendance at mass and regular reception of the sacraments were mandatory, or that participation in student devotional confraternities was highly encouraged for all and obligatory for novices as well as those who wished to join collegiate literary academies.) Instructors attempted to gauge every student's abilities, singling out the best pupils in each classroom for rewards and deputizing them to review lessons with the others. At different points during the year, the colleges would hold academic games. Students at each level of study would compete in their discipline, with grammar students composing prose texts, rhetoric pupils writing epigrams and delivering oratory, and philosophy and theology students holding disputations. The advanced philosophy and theology pupils also made presentations of academic reasoning before audiences of local worthies, such as lawyers and prelates. No doubt future missionaries gained much of value from such opportunities for debating and public speaking. In their student years, however, their eyes were fixed on the prizes (typically books or devotional objects) offered to the winners. Not surprisingly, future missionaries brought this pedagogical approach with them to China, using it to foster greater piety and doctrinal knowledge among their Christians.

Here it may be worthwhile to pause and consider the importance of the missionaries' education in the sciences during their training in Europe. No other category of Western erudition is as closely associated with the China Jesuits as natural philosophy or, more specifically, mathematics and astronomy. There are many good reasons for this—not least being the Jesuits' propaganda efforts in the seventeenth century. A voluminous historiography explains their scientific activities in far greater detail than I can afford here. It should be noted, however, that as the chronology of the mission suggests, the Jesuits' "scientific encounters" with the Chinese were, after the mission's first few decades, restricted to the court. Moreover, the vast majority of Chinese Christians had little interest in the Western science and technology that the missionaries used to win friendships among the educated elite. Neither of these factors should detract from the accomplishments of a handful of missionaries who were trained in mathematics and channeled elements of European scientific thought to an enthusiastic Chinese audience. Men such as Johann Terrenz Schreck, a physician, naturalist, mathematician, and member of the Roman Accademia dei Lincei, played important roles in securing the mission's political foundations through their erudition. Yet to assume that the China Jesuits were uniformly capable of discussing mathematics or astronomy with erudite Chinese is to misunderstand the place they attributed to science within their enterprise.

In 1616 mission superior Niccolò Longobardo alerted the Society's hierarchy in Rome about the level of scientific knowledge necessary among recruits for China. He understood the stakes involved in the policy of having some of his subordinates tout their technical expertise at court. This is why he instructed Nicolas Trigault to return to China with "a pair of illustrious mathematicians." As far as the rest of the missionaries were concerned, Longobardo insisted that they only needed to be able to understand the books that were printed by their colleagues at the court.[10] The segment of the philosophy cycle that dealt with Euclid might suffice to give recruits the "mediocre knowledge of mathematics" that he claimed they needed.[11] Those who lacked this background, however, could benefit from the mathematics classes taught at the College of Macau during the 1610s, where Francesco Sambiasi was among the instructors.

Longobardo's plan for using Macau as a training center, however, would not last long. By the mid-1620s the exiled Japan Jesuits had evicted their brethren from the Society's college in the Portuguese colony. But this was no great tragedy for the Vice-Province. By the 1630s the need for mathematics classes was greatly reduced by events inside the Ming empire. The Peking Jesuits' commission work on the imperial calendar in the 1630s, the decline of Ming institutions staffed by the priests' erudite interlocutors, and the growth of plebeian Christian communities outside the court all meant that the Vice-Province could shift its efforts elsewhere. After that point, scientific training came to the Jesuits piecemeal, if at all. Ferdinand Verbiest, for one, gained a significant part of his astronomy training during the initial leg of his journey to Macau in 1656. "Under the stars at night," he wrote, procurator Martino Martini taught him "not superstitious astrology, but the principles of astronomy and about the rising stars."[12]

On the whole, missionaries outside Peking felt little need to keep their scientific skills sharp. José Soares, for one, was surprised when Visitor Francesco Saverio Filippucci ordered him to depart for the capital from his Shanxi Province mission station in 1688. Soares was given the daunting task of educating himself in "astronomical computation" so he could take the place of Verbiest, the recently deceased director of the Astronomical Bureau—a challenge he declined by claiming that the "easy principles" of calculation which he had learned for curiosity's sake in Portugal would serve "for nothing" in Peking.[13] To be sure, this was not the first time that the gulf between the scientific erudition of the court Jesuits and their brethren in the provinces was revealed. In 1649 a Franciscan in Fujian Province wrote to a confrere in Manila about his conflicts with Pietro Canevari. The ignorance of this Italian, wrote Friar Antonio de Santa Maria Caballero, was proof positive that "the Jesuit priests who come to work here as missionaries are not all Solomons in science, as they boast."[14]

"Telling Them the Method"

On May 26, 1602, Álvaro Semedo signed the register of novices at the Colégio do Espírito Santo in Évora. He made a declaration that his parents were Fernão Gomes Semedo and Leonor Vaz Forçada and that he was a native of the town of Nisa in the bishopric of Portalegre in central Portugal. Semedo, a student in the first year of the humanities cycle, had been admitted to probationary status as a scholastic on April 30. During the first weeks of the novitiate, João de Sousa, the local "master of novices," made an examination of the seventeen-year-old postulant's claims about himself and his family origins. Sousa noted that the young man appeared free of any impediments, such as other religious vows, Moorish or Jewish ancestry, or a wife. Semedo also testified that he was willing to undergo the probationary experiences required by the Society of Jesus and that he knew he could be dismissed at any point during that period. Over the next two years the postulant and his superiors added notes to this register on four occasions. The notations were made at intervals of roughly six months, leading up to the last entry on May 1, 1604. About sixty years later a Jesuit superior at Évora returned to Semedo's page to add a comment about the ministries of the former novice. Unlike the entries for the 139 postulants in the register whose declarations were crossed out after their dismissal from the Society of Jesus, the note about Semedo resembled those of his 58 peers who left the novitiate for the overseas missions: "Went to Japan and entered into China."[15]

During the two years that he spent as a novice, Semedo was instructed in the common devotions and corporate behavior of the Society of Jesus. He lived in a cloistered area of the local college with his fellows, proceeding along the order's academic track and partaking in communal religious activities. Similar to the probationary practices of other orders, the Jesuit novitiate included daily devotional routines, attendance at mass, meditative prayer, readings from scripture and Catholic authors, and humble chores. The Society's unique feature was the length of its period of probation. Instead of one year, Jesuits underwent three. This series of experiences, lasting for two initial years of novitiate training upon entry into the order and a third probationary year after completing the academic program, was designed to steel the men of the Society for the rigors of pastoral work beyond the walls of their residences. For Baltasar Teles, the formation of new Jesuits was like the gestation of elephants. Citing Pliny the Elder, he related how these animals spent two years in their mother's womb "in order to gain the strength to suffer future trials, not be intimidated by burdens, and scoff at difficulties." Like elephants whose duties included charging into battle and striking fear in other creatures, the Society had its prolonged probationary period so its men would be ready to "travel the entire world, conversing with the most pertinacious heretics, dealing with the most dissolute sinners, breaching all boundaries regardless of danger to hear confessions, to preach to heathens, to dispute with Lutherans, to work with barbarians, grappling with the dangers of the whole world."[16]

Teles's comments, written to commemorate the centenary anniversary of the Society in 1640, contain no small amount of bombast. Yet they are also a reflection of the reality of the experience of young Jesuits. The first two years of training that future missionaries underwent as novices directly contributed to their ability to confront the task of working in China. It goes without saying that a strong grounding in Catholic devotions was indispensable for those whose chosen ministry was to propagate Christianity. From an institutional perspective, the most enduring legacy of their probationary experience was the Jesuits' powerful sense of corporate unity—their vaunted "way of proceeding." This esprit de corps was first instilled during the novitiate, and would be reinforced during the time spent by young members of the order in the Society's colleges in Europe, India, and Macau. Yet while these legacies of Jesuit novice training were no doubt of great value for the cohesion of the Vice-Province, their actuality is hard to grasp and as difficult to discuss.

In theory, the third year of probation would also have given future China missionaries useful skills. As envisioned by Ignatius Loyola and articulated by successive Superiors General, "tertianship" consisted of activities aimed to enhance the spiritual and pastoral formation of educated Jesuits.[17] Tertians were to devote themselves to duties such as preaching, going on pilgrimage, working in hospitals, teaching doctrine, hearing confessions, performing lowly chores, and doing the Spiritual Exercises. The third year would have introduced mission candidates to the rudiments of the Society's ministries among laymen and women. But it is unclear whether or not the China Jesuits actually underwent the third year of probation.[18] The timing of their departure for Asia, often before the completion of their studies, suggests that they would have been tertians in India, or even in Macau. On at least two occasions in the seventeenth century, however, Jesuit superiors in India were permitted to dispense with this final phase of training.[19] Moreover, sources relating to the backgrounds of the men of the Vice-Province are silent on the subject. It is therefore likely that the Jesuits' activities during their passage to Macau were considered a fitting replacement for a formal tertianship.

For present purposes, it is best to conceive of the China Jesuits' probationary period as the span from the moment they joined the order until their entry into the mission field. At first glance this may look like an overextension of even Baltasar Teles's elephantine metaphor. But from the Vice-Province's perspective, the sum of time that new recruits had spent as Jesuits was what made them effective in China. This period spanned the first two years of the novitiate, the nine years of the academic track, two or more years of teaching, and a year or more on board ship. For instance, in the case of Álvaro Semedo it is clear that although he was no longer a novice after May 1, 1604, he was not yet a missionary either. Earmarked for the Province of Japan and sent to India in 1608, he was not permitted to leave for China until he had completed his four years of theology study. Compared with the other men of the Vice-Province, Semedo was exceptional only in the fact that he did not spend time teaching during the eleven years which elapsed between his entry into the Society and his entry into the Ming empire. That is, he was approved for missionary service only after he had finished the Society's academic track and its probationary hurdles.

Which aspects of Jesuit probation were most relevant to the task of evangelizing in China? Three appear to have been particularly important: the practical experience of assisting in the temporal upkeep of a residence, the organizational skills acquired through teaching, and an awareness of pastoral techniques employed by missionaries in Europe. It is true that unlike their confreres in Europe, the priests of the Vice-Province had few opportunities to engage in these activities once they sailed for Asia—unless they spent time in the Society's colleges at Goa or Macau. Nevertheless, the core skills gained through these experiences were essential for the maintenance of the Vice-Province for nearly a century and a half.

One of the most beneficial elements of the Jesuit novitiate for future China missionaries was also the most mundane. No different from other religious orders, the Society aimed to instill a sense of humility and corporal discipline in its members by obliging them to perform household chores. In an age when one's social status regularly dictated one's profession, such requirements aimed to eliminate lingering sentiments of privilege through obedience and servitude—not to mention banishing idleness through work. To be sure, these chores did little to alleviate the burdens of the staff of Jesuit ministers, temporal coadjutors, cooks, janitors, and slaves who kept the Society's colleges running. Yet by participating in institutional maintenance, future missionaries learned how to manage a domestic economy and how to deal with the exigencies of everyday life outside the chapel and classroom. According to one account of novitiate life in Portugal, typical chores included hanging laundry to dry, sweeping and cleaning living quarters, assisting in the kitchens, helping in the sacristy, nursing the sick in nearby hospitals, and "even doing things repugnant to nature, such as making the beds of the college's blacks."[20]

Reports on the Society's novitiates suggest that "masters of novices" were particularly fond of sending postulants to work in the kitchens of their colleges. One superior in Évora would customarily send the more learned novices directly to toil alongside cooks and scullery boys because it was "the best way to season their knowledge."[21] This was the case with Rodrigo de Figueiredo, who showed academic talent during his studies in Évora and Coimbra. One of his biographies recorded that he could often be found "cleaning and scrubbing the cauldrons and other utensils."[22] Although Figueiredo was doubtless unaware of it at the time, his chores prepared him for the twelve years that he would spend alone in Kaifeng. Since the Vice-Province had no coadjutors to tend to the upkeep of its mission stations, the Jesuits could not hand off their temporal duties. Missionaries had to know how to run their residences, even if that simply meant coordinating the chores of their domestic servants. As François de Rougemont's account book from his years at Changshu makes clear, individual Jesuits were able to conduct their temporal affairs with accuracy, if not dexterity.[23] While a large proportion of these skills were, of course, the fruit of their long years in China, they were amply prepared by their earlier exercises in humility.

The second important aspect of Jesuits' probation, time spent teaching in the colleges, was not prescribed by their order's foundational documents. Rather, it was a custom that emerged in response to the demand for instructors to staff the lower schools (i.e., grammar and humanities classes) and a means of breaking up the final phase of the academic track. The task required youthful energy as well as intelligence, and these were desirable traits for missionaries. An overview of the Vice-Province's personnel catalogues reveals that, with few exceptions, the men listed there had each devoted at least two years to classroom instruction. A handful of examples will suffice. Matteo Ricci spent three years teaching rhetoric and grammar at Cochin and Goa. Niccolò Longobardo taught humanities for three years and Gaspar Ferreira for four. Nicolas Trigault read humanities for eight years in the Southern Netherlands prior to his selection for the mission, while Manuel Dias the younger taught theology for six years at Macau. Simão da Cunha read grammar for six years before requesting a posting overseas, as did António de Gouvea, who gave lessons in that same subject for four years. Michel Trigault, Michael Walta, and Inácio da Costa all taught grammar for two years, while their colleague Gabriel de Magalhães taught grammar, humanities, and philosophy for two years each. Perhaps the most impressive curriculum vitae belonged to Jacques le Faure. This French Jesuit taught humanities for two years, rhetoric for two years, philosophy for four years, moral theology for two years, and speculative theology for four years before sailing to China.[24]

The fact that teaching was not a formal requirement explains, at least in part, the variation in the amount of time different missionaries spent in the classroom. But there were other factors at work. Most important was that candidates for the missions had to petition the Society's superiors for assignments overseas. Many Jesuits wrote their *indipetae,* or Indies petitions, while teaching. This was especially true for the candidates from outside Portugal. Men from the Society's other European provinces often petitioned several times before they were permitted to travel to Lisbon. Antoine Thomas, for instance, taught humanities for five years, rhetoric for one, philosophy for two, and mathematics for two in the Southern Netherlands while he waited for favorable news. During those years Thomas displayed considerable perseverance by writing no fewer than seventeen petitions.[25] By contrast, petitions from candidates at Coimbra or Évora were more readily approved, meaning that Portuguese Jesuits did not typically spend so much time teaching. Their province was considered the natural recruiting pool for all of the overseas missions of the Portuguese Assistancy. When they did teach, it was often in India, where many of them finished their studies. Men slated for the East Asian missions, such as Tomé Pereira, who lived in Goa for six years, typically taught for two years as recompense to their brethren in the Society's South Asian provinces for seeing them through the theology cycle.

In what way was teaching beneficial to the China Jesuits? The teaching experience, in Adrien Demoustier's opinion, was "the most efficient and universally applicable tool for missionary activity."[26] In addition to reviewing academic material, future missionaries learned how to organize and manage groups. These skills would be invaluable to priests in the Vice-Province, whose primary duties included teaching doctrine, coordinating dispersed groups of Christians, and stimulating group piety. After the first half-century of the mission, when the Jesuits' primary task shifted from proselytizing to organizing their Christian communities, such pedagogical techniques became even more useful to the missionaries.

In more than one province, including the Province of Portugal, the Jesuit hierarchy had created a system of teacher training aimed at ensuring that new instructors could manage their classrooms.[27] In 1613 Visitor João Álvares ordered the rectors at the colleges of Coimbra and Évora, the province's two largest schools, to appoint an experienced priest to instruct new teachers, "telling them the method for reading, the ways of teaching, how to govern a class, etc."[28] Faced with large numbers of pupils, Jesuits had to balance their roles as teachers and administrators. They could delegate the teaching of basic concepts to the brighter students in class, thereby freeing up more classroom time to attend to other pupils. By handing out rewards for academic performance, instructors fomented a spirit of "pious competition" among their charges that mimicked the ever-present peer rivalries among adolescent boys.

Other teaching tips were found in the *Ratio Studiorum.* This "Plan of Studies" suggested dividing larger classes into groups of ten students called decuries and appointing a decurion to supervise his peers. In addition to facilitating the correction of academic exercises, this organizational model promoted group discipline.[29] While one should not conclude that the China Jesuits treated their Christians just as they did their pupils in Europe or India, the missionaries did rely on these techniques for structuring their church. It is hard to imagine that a priest such as Manuel Mendes, the superior of the Shanghai residence in the 1690s, would have been able to coordinate the ritual activities of thousands of adherents of *Tianzhu jiao* had he reached China without the organizational skills acquired through teaching.

The third important aspect of probationary training for future China Jesuits was their passive exposure to the pastoral techniques used by missionaries in Europe. In contrast to the heroism of the order's saints and martyrs, the conception of rural missions was more prosaic. Yet therein lay its value. Despite the fact that their Indies petitions were loaded with invocations of holy valor in exotic locales, future China Jesuits could not have been ignorant of the routine tasks proper to missionaries. After all, reports of rural missions were read aloud in the Society's refectories at mealtimes, as were Annual Letters from overseas. In addition, young Jesuits often rubbed elbows with their older confreres whose appointed task was to travel about the countryside preaching repentance and spiritual renewal, filling the pastoral gaps left by an often lax secular clergy, administering the sacraments, and teaching doctrine.[30] While men like Francesco Brancati, Inácio Lobo, and António de Gouvea had had experience preaching and hearing confessions before their departure for China, most of their colleagues left for Asia with only this knowledge of evangelizing strategies. But even a passive engagement with the mundane face of missionary work was valuable, because after the initial phase of conversions, most of the China Jesuits' activities were similar to those of their peers in Europe—with the added burden that the men of the Vice-Province were the primary, rather than the supplementary, clergy.

According to one seventeenth-century commentator, the aim of Jesuit rural missions was to rectify popular morality, confront unorthodox Catholic practices, teach doctrine, administer the sacraments of Penance and of the Eucharist, and make peace between feuding rivals.[31] The goal of provoking a "good reformation of customs and a great shock and movement in the people toward virtue," as one Portuguese superior enunciated it in 1613, reflected the Society's ambitions for such activities across Europe.[32] But what did that mean in concrete terms? First of all, it meant working in concert with the local clergy to reset the tone of rural ritual life. The primary aim of the Jesuits was to teach parish priests how to sustain new devotions, continue doctrine classes, and encourage regular reception of the sacraments. They sought to reinvigorate piety, not replace it. Their strategy was to work within existing structures in order to make lasting changes to popular mores and religious habits. Without falling into a facile parallel between this attitude toward missionary work in Catholic lands and the policy of accommodation in China, we could say that this was one of the most useful techniques future missionaries could learn from their confreres. Perhaps the best example of how the men of the Vice-Province reshaped social practices in China can be found in the *hui,* or associations, used to structure their mission church and foment fervor among the adherents of *Tianzhu jiao.*

Of all the ministries performed by Jesuits on rural missions in Europe, doctrine teaching had pride of place. In sketching out the daily routine for missionaries in rural Portugal in 1610, Visitor João Álvares indicated that a Jesuit's first public exhortation would be on the "need for Christian doctrine." Lessons were to follow each day—a class for women and children in the afternoon and another at night for men.[33] Drawing on the pedagogical techniques commonly used in Jesuit classrooms, missionaries encouraged rural folk to learn prayers correctly. These schoolmasters had a number of tricks up their sleeves, ranging from indulgences for assiduous adults to sacred images and objects for children. During a 1624 mission to Alcácer do Sal in southern Portugal, a Jesuit found the local children "very lacking in the prayers and points of holy doctrine" but open to being "animated with the good prizes they were given." Such was the case with a young boy whose knowledge of doctrine improved from only the Paternoster and Ave Maria to a whole repertoire of prayers when he was promised a nomina and a rosary.[34] Another technique was to organize processions of singing children, events meant to inculcate prayers as well as drown out with pious refrains the bawdy ballads often heard in the streets of early modern towns. For example, one Jesuit's proudest accomplishment during a visit to a provincial Portuguese city in 1594 was the procession "for singing the Ave Maria or the litanies of Our Lady held every day during Lent at dusk."[35] Naturally, the China Jesuits faced with the same problem of inculcating doctrine drew on the Society's store of teaching strategies, including such standbys as composing Christian songs set to popular tunes.[36]

Rural missionaries spent much time hearing confessions. In the European countryside, the visit of an itinerant priest was an opportunity for men and women to make their confessions to someone from outside their close-knit web of relations, unlike their parish priest. For the missionaries, it was a chance to stimulate a desire for the sacrament of penance beyond the yearly minimum of one confession. Moreover, confessions were an effective forum for moral suasion—though hardly a tool for any ambitious project of "social disciplining." To herd rustics into the confessional, one needed both carrot and stick, or, in this case, indulgences and sermons. After announcing the indulgences they carried with them, Jesuits were instructed to apprise the country folk of "the evils of mortal sin, from whence arises the need for the remedy of confession." They were to emphasize "doctrine, confessions, speaking of God, dealing with one's neighbor, and remedying their spiritual needs," instead of delivering discourses marked by "pomp and erudition."[37] Yet this injunction did not mean that Jesuits were barred from using props such as paintings to stir the emotions of their viewers and spur them to confess. One missionary told of how he had related the Via Dolorosa to a rapt audience at Setúbal in 1650, unleashing a flood of "tears of devotion" as soon as he brandished panels showing the Crucifixion.[38] The China Jesuits, too, would have recourse to such methods of increasing lay fervor, especially after they began to urge their Christians to frequent reception of the sacraments in the 1630s. European examples thus taught them how to meet the spiritual needs of plebeian Catholics, that is, how best to teach doctrine and elicit confessions.

Longing to Be Chinese

In 1615 the first editions of Nicolas Trigault's *De Christiana Expeditione apud Sinas* came off the presses at Augsburg. Within months at least one copy made its way to the Colégio de Santo Antão in Lisbon, where Simão da Cunha had a chance to read it. Cunha had been teaching in Lisbon for almost six years by that point, following a path trodden by many a young

Jesuit. Having shown enough natural intelligence to be admitted to the Society as a scholastic, he had proceeded along the academic track in philosophy and theology in Coimbra. Toward the end of his studies Cunha went to the court city, where he taught humanities for five years, spent one year as a substitute in philosophy, and passed some months as a preacher. It was in the midst of this relatively unspectacular career that he experienced an epiphany. Cunha was so moved by the tales of missionary glory described in Trigault's book that he requested to be sent to China. After his petition was approved, Cunha joined the pan-European group of Jesuits escorted by the inspirational author to Lisbon in the early months of 1618. On April 18 that year, Trigault and his recruits set sail for India aboard the *São Carlos.*[39]

Evidently, Simão da Cunha had the right inclination at the right time. Only about a year passed between his decision to write an "Indies petition" and his departure for China. Other missionary hopefuls were not so fortunate. Those who received patents to travel to India often lacked a procurator to escort them to the mission field or arrived at Lisbon only to find that the carracks had already set sail. Moreover, only a fraction of those who applied were selected. Numerous young Jesuits spent years writing letters to the Society's Superiors General in the vain hope of being sent overseas. The voluminous collection of letters preserved at the Society's central archives is a testament to the collective will of generations of Jesuits to serve in the missions. But as the order's superiors no doubt repeated constantly, *multi sunt enim vocati pauci autem electi.*

The selection process for recruits to the China mission remains an enigma. Analyses of the Society's administrative documents have yet to illuminate the steps involved. Nevertheless, the wealth of details found in other sources makes it possible to elaborate an outline of the process, a series of common motivational factors, and a list of the personal qualities considered necessary for prospective missionaries.

Selection for the missions was the fruit of individual initiative. When Jesuits felt the desire to request assignments overseas, they addressed themselves to their local superiors. Since most (though not all) of the petitioners were scholastics or junior members of the order, this meant asking the rectors of their colleges. One missionary hopeful explained how he had spent seven years—from the first month he joined the Society—imploring his superiors for the chance to write to Rome.[40] Another scholastic wrote that he had informed his rector at Coimbra every year for the three years he had been in the order of his "tears and sighs for China."[41] Some did receive permission to try their luck with the Superior General. But authorization to write to Rome was no guarantee of selection. In fact, as one study of the *indipetae* from the Province of Flandro-Belgica for the years 1640 to 1660 has revealed, only eight out of ninety candidates (who together wrote over two hundred letters) were chosen.[42] While the rate of selection was higher for the Province of Portugal (accordingly, so was the number of Portuguese Jesuits in the Vice-Province), only a fraction of its total number of petitioners got a favorable response. Those who were chosen received a patent freeing them from their obligations and instructing them to go to Lisbon to await the departure of the India fleets.

What fueled the desires of so many missionary hopefuls? To start with, tales of heroism overseas were constantly repeated in the novitiates and colleges. Whether during their own readings or at mealtimes in the Society's refectories, Jesuits were continually presented with examples of missionary virtue for emulation. By far the most renowned name in the order's pantheon of the valiant was Francis Xavier, a figure who became doubly important after his beatification in 1609 and canonization in 1622. Many aspirants sought the same "very clear signs" of heaven's will in their own lives that Master Francis had seen in his.[43] Certainly, more than a few Jesuit readers of his many biographies dwelled on the passages that told how God had chosen the Basque priest for the Indies missions. Even in the 1580s, scarcely a generation after Xavier's death, petitioners invoked the "merits of the blessed Father Francisco" in their requests.[44] After his beatification, young Jesuits wrote of their desire to follow in his footsteps, as well as of their prayers for his intercession with hard-hearted Superiors General. One candidate explained how his "many desires to imitate Saint Xavier" had even impelled him to change his surname to that of the Apostle of the Orient.[45] And on at least two occasions Xavier's shade appeared to Italian Jesuits in the throes of mortal illness. After the apparition restored Alessandro Filippucci to health, the young man reciprocated by taking his patron's name, Francesco Saverio, and embarking for China. To Marcello Mastrilli, who was to be martyred at Nagasaki in 1637, Xavier was more direct. At a crucial moment, as Mastrilli was languishing on his sickbed, suffering from a high fever, the saint pointedly asked, "Do you want to die or go to India?"[46]

Beyond imitating Xavier, many petitioners aimed to outdo him. They desired nothing short of martyrdom, a glorious death that the East Asian missions appeared to offer in spades after 1597. Tales of the bloody persecutions in Japan, which began that year, gave rise to chimerical visions of a fast track to sainthood. Passages from the *Martyriologium Romanum* were standard fare at mealtimes, declaimed to Jesuits daily. Perhaps as a natural consequence, the desire to "spill blood and give up life" for the faith was expressed by scores of postulants.[47] As the shadow of persecution grew darker over Japan in the 1630s and 1640s, requests were still made—and assignments given—for service in that country. Men such as Étienne Faber, who left Goa in the late 1620s with the intention of penetrating the Tokugawa realm disguised as a layman, or François Noël, who endeavored to do the same in 1685, were fully aware of their potential fate. Others, however, knew that the Society's superiors were not likely to send many men to certain death and so, in the 1640s, began to request permission to "go to India and from there to pass to Japan, or if that is impossible, to China."[48]

Although the Vice-Province never harvested the crop of martyrs that the Japan mission did, it benefited from the visions of glory associated with East Asia. After all, the China mission was officially an appendage of the Province of Japan. But the minds of young European Jesuits could also accommodate an image of China that was responsible for sparking its own missionary vocations. Annual Letters from the Vice-Province were read aloud in refectories as they made their way from the mission field to the Superior General's desk.[49] Moreover, at least one name from the China mission was added to a manuscript catalogue of "Some Martyrs and Illustrious Men from the Society of Jesus" which was read in Jesuit colleges in Portugal. Surprisingly, it was not Matteo Ricci but Étienne Faber, the tireless missionary from Avignon, who underwent "innumerable labors for the span of twenty-seven years, converting a multitude of infidels to Christ Our Lord."[50]

The arrival of news from China in Europe invariably generated *indipetae.* Just four years after Michele Ruggieri and Matteo Ricci had arrived in Zhaoqing, one petitioner wrote of his desire to serve in the "spacious field of China, where only recently the Society has begun the battle."[51] One of the first recruits to the mission, António de Almeida, recalled wandering about the College of Coimbra saying, "Oh, how I long to be Chinese!" He related his desire to "make great journeys for the love of Christ" in order to transform the Ming empire from "a lake of abominations into a refreshing garden of virtues."[52] Over the course of the sev-

View of the Jesuit College of Coimbra, Portugal. Lithograph, eighteenth century. The novitiate was located in the building on the right-hand side, above some of the college's classrooms.

enteenth century, repeated publicity from the Vice-Province sparked more petitions for China. As the memory of Japan faded, losing its sheen as the dominant image of the Society in Asia, Jesuits began requesting to be sent to the Qing domains. *Indipetae* from at least two postulants in the last quarter of the seventeenth century made it clear that their authors did not want to go to the "Indies" but only to China.[53]

To young Jesuits in Portugal, the presence of foreign confreres en route to the missions was a constant reminder that men were needed overseas. The Province of Portugal was responsible for organizing embarkation at Lisbon for Jesuits from across Europe—or for giving them some form of employment if they missed the customary late March departure of the India fleets. Matteo Ricci, for one, spent the ten months between June 1577 and March 1578 in Coimbra. Ricci's colleagues Lazzaro Cattaneo and Sabatino de Ursis also spent time at the Society's residences in Portugal, as did recruits to the China mission from the Southern Netherlands.[54] For instance, François de Rougemont and a Dutch colleague made it to Lisbon in April 1655, two weeks after the *naus da Índia* had set sail. The pair were then sent to Coimbra to continue their theology studies while they waited for passage east.[55] Their fellow students could not fail to notice the foreign presence in their midst. Naturally, they were stimulated by it, as evidenced by a candidate who wrote to Rome from Coimbra in the hopes of getting a patent of the kind issued to the "Italians staying in this college."[56]

It fell to the Society's senior officers to approve or deny the requests of missionary hopefuls. It was unlikely, however, that the gusts of pathos found in the petitions would suffice to sway Superiors General. They instead consulted the personnel catalogues that were sent to Rome every three years. Provincial officers produced these documents so that the Society's curia would have basic facts about every Jesuit: age, health, time spent in the Society, academic background, and ministries performed. Brief subjective evaluations were made according to five criteria: ingenuity, judgment, prudence, practical experience, and academic proficiency. Finally, the catalogues offered a psychological portrait of each member (i.e., sanguine, melancholic, choleric, or phlegmatic) and a list of ministries for which any one of them was presumed to have talent. Although these notations were succinct, they contained enough information to exclude the unfit. For example, second-year humanities student Manuel Mendes was evaluated in 1675 as having a phlegmatic temperament and "good" ingenuity, judgment, and prudence. Two years after he had entered the novitiate, however, his superiors were still uncertain about his degree of fervor.[57] Three years later they had a clearer picture. According to the 1678 catalogue, the twenty-two-year-old Mendes had transformed his temperament to sanguine and given proof of academic talent. These changes clearly worked in his favor when he sent his petition to Rome. Only two years later he received permission to embark for Asia.[58]

Still, it is unclear which criteria the Society's superiors in Rome considered most important. Concerns over the rigors of the Cape route gave rise to a preference for young men in good health. The fact that the order had a school in Goa permitted the curia to grant patents to willing candidates at the first sign of competence. But there were other factors as well. National origin was important because Rome had to guarantee that the Vice-Province, as part of the Portuguese Assistancy, had a large contingent of Lusitanian Jesuits. Portuguese were therefore expedited to the Asian missions more swiftly than nationals of other countries. Despite the Society's self-image as a cosmopolitan organization, it was still affected by early modern sentiments of national identity. As the crises over the French mission and the Tournon legation made clear, the vital links between crown, empire, and mission demanded loyalty of the sort that was best ensured by common blood. Finally, academic proficiency played an important role, because significant intellectual hurdles lay ahead for those who reached China.

Although the selection process favored sending bright young Jesuits to the missions, talented candidates did not always have their wishes granted. A strong sense of institutional conservatism was found among the Society's provincial hierarchy, making them reluctant to release their best preachers, teachers, and thinkers. The Province of Portugal, with dependent mission fields in Brazil, India, and East Asia, was obliged to supply an average of fifteen candidates per year to other enterprises. While this small number did not greatly reduce the overall tally of Portuguese Jesuits—they averaged 650 in the seventeenth century—it did reduce their total of recognizably talented men. Notions of good governance argued in favor of keeping the best at home, and in 1603 the senior Jesuits resolved "not to send fully educated men and others of particular expectations who can perform greater service in Portugal than in the overseas provinces." Superior General Claudio Aquaviva subtly rebuked this resolution by noting that the Province of Portugal had always shown "great charity to the overseas provinces . . . in giving them some men of higher consideration" when the missions needed them.[59] Nevertheless, the tension between the Society's local priorities and its global needs persisted.

The case of Rodrigo de Figueiredo is a good example of the centripetal forces within the Society that worked to keep its best men in Europe. He joined the order at the age of fourteen in Évora, the city where he had been raised. After completing his novitiate and the humanities cycle, Figueiredo went to study philosophy in Coimbra. According to António de Gouvea, it was then that he began to show "as much talent among his fellow students as piety and fervor among the devout." Figueiredo was known to spend five hours or more at a time on his knees praying. Even so, he enjoyed a reputation for affability. As soon as he began to speak of joining the Japan mission, his superiors attempted to dissuade him. In the hope that his pleas were a passing fancy, they sent him to Italy in 1617 to study theology at the Roman College. Figueiredo made the best of this situation, petitioning Superior General Aquaviva in person. No doubt it helped his case that a procurator for the Province of Japan was in Rome at the same time. In under a year, Figueiredo had secured permission to set sail for Goa, leaving Europe in 1618 to complete his theology studies in that city. On reaching India, he again encountered superiors eager to benefit from his talents. Admiring his eloquence, they assigned him to preach to the local Portuguese population, but Figueiredo's heart was in East Asia. It was only in 1622, after the Goa Jesuits abandoned their designs, that he was able to journey onward to Macau. Frustrated in his desire to continue on to Nagasaki, he entered the Ming empire. Japan's loss was China's gain, wrote Gouvea, that country being "granted the great fortune to receive such a missionary."[60]

As this example suggests, the presence of a procurator could force the curia's hand. These individuals were charged with soliciting recruits and often served as couriers of *indipetae* to Rome. Most important, procurators sped up the selection process by issuing the Vice-Province's perennial call for manpower in person and escorting the chosen to Asia. To give but a few examples, Nicolas Trigault left Lisbon in 1618 with twenty-two recruits; Martino Martini sailed to India in the company of thirty-six missionary hopefuls; and Philippe Couplet started out from Portugal with fifteen companions. During his trip as procurator between 1636 and 1644, Álvaro Semedo gathered petitions from candidates at the Portuguese and Spanish colleges that he visited on his way to Rome. Among them was a letter from a philosophy student at Lisbon who wrote of waiting "with longing eyes for the arrival of Father Semedo from China," so that he might accompany the procurator on his return trip.[61] Another candidate entrusted Semedo to give "a very full report" of his desires in Rome. The procurator apparently relayed the necessary information, since this recruit and forty others left Lisbon for Macau in 1643.[62] As the seventeenth century wore on, the task of soliciting men in northern Europe was left to procurators. Prospective Portuguese missionaries were sought by an "Indies procurator" based in Lisbon who was responsible for sending men to all of the Assistancy's provinces. However efficient this system may have been, it was not the same as having flesh-and-blood missionaries arrive from the far side of the world—a fact proved by the dip in recruits from Portugal for China between the 1660s and the 1690s.

Suffering the Voyage

In April 1628 Étienne Faber stepped aboard one of the three carracks anchored in Lisbon harbor waiting to set sail for India. The ships did not leave Portugal until late that year, missing the winds necessary to propel them into the South Atlantic. The heat and calm on the open sea were oppressive, and many passengers soon succumbed. With the Grim Reaper pacing the deck, the French Jesuit seized the chance to exercise Christian charity. According to Gabriel de Magalhães, Faber circulated among the sick, "serving them day and night, giving them medicine and food with his own hands," and begging those with greater stores of provisions for alms. The future China Jesuit also performed priestly ministries, "animating them, consoling them with pious words, administering the sacraments to them, and helping them die." Apparently Faber was so active that his superior had to curb his zeal lest he, too, fall sick. By the time the ships made it back to Lisbon, the French Jesuit had gained renown for his charity and sanctity. He would confirm this impression when he again embarked for India after some months in Évora, a span "which seemed to him like a thousand years, so great were his desires to suffer." The second voyage went better than the first, giving Faber more opportunities to show his zeal. Not only was he a "veteran soldier" on the 1629 Indies run, but also he had no immediate superior "afraid of his falling ill and limiting his work."[63]

Faber was blessed with good health and zeal to match. Yet like many of his confreres, he walked the razor's edge between life and death at sea. The Society's Asian enterprises saw more men die aboard ship than arrive at their destinations. The seventeenth-century Jesuit chronicler of the overseas missions, Danielo Bartoli, described the numbers of unrealized vocations that ended in burial at sea as "the annual tribute that the Society pays to the ocean."[64] Neptune was brutally exacting on the China Jesuits. One estimate of missionary wastage over the span from 1581 to 1712 suggests that slightly over 50 percent died at sea.[65] Even when they were accompanied by procurators, only a fraction of those bound for China ever set foot in Macau. In fact, Bartoli wrote his comment in reference to five of Nicolas Trigault's twenty-two companions, who died over the course of thirteen days in the equatorial Atlantic. Neither Martino Martini nor Philippe Couplet had better luck: twelve of Martini's thirty-six recruits perished before reaching China, while eight of Couplet's fifteen met a similar fate.[66] Such a continual drain on the Vice-Province's recruitment pool demanded some method for increasing the chances of missionary survival. But despite the Jesuits' best efforts, they had no luck at turning the odds of their gamble with the sea in their favor.

While the death tolls of China-bound Jesuits were no doubt dramatic, drama per se was often wholly absent on the Cape route or on the passage to Macau. Rather, the slow creep of disease and the tedium of months spent at sea were the hallmarks of the voyage. Even for men who were motivated by uncommon zeal, the proposition of spending almost a year in cramped quarters under the shadow of death had little appeal. "Certainly no one who was offered a house, even a regally appointed one, to live shut inside for six months," wrote Alessandro Valignano, "could stay detained or locked in for so long; much less on a ship filled with so many different kinds of inconveniences."[67]

The Visitor was referring to the human spectacle that unfolded aboard the *naus da Índia,* where a cross-section of colonial society was put to a demanding test. The prospect of easy riches drew individuals to climb aboard these vessels with little more than what they could carry. As weeks at sea turned into months, they would eat through their meager provisions and often lose their shirts gambling. The soldiers destined for India were likewise a motley crew, many of them pressed into service by the hand of justice and given to debauchery. As much could be said about the sailors, more than a few of whom were picked up at ports in the Indian Ocean and had little knowledge (if any) of Christianity. The Portuguese nobles who sailed in the service of the king were often no better than their plebeian counterparts. Tensions rose among such individuals at the slightest provocation, unaccustomed as they were to cohabiting with their peers or their betters, and discord was most readily resolved with the pistol or the sword.[68]

Yet it was none other than Ignatius Loyola who first insisted that the Society work in the world, not apart from it. And the world of the Carreira da Índia was replete with opportunities for the Jesuits to exercise their order's basic ministries. For young men who were still engaged in studies or had recently completed the academic track, the journey to India was a chance to undergo the set of experiences prescribed for tertians, Jesuits in their third year of probation. From stem to stern of each carrack lay numerous occasions for preaching, teaching doctrine, caring for the sick, hearing confessions, performing humble chores, and begging for alms. A further similarity to tertianship lay in the fact that traveling Jesuits were barred from studying. If the China-bound missionaries' labors at sea were not a formal tertianship, they were certainly an intensive training course in how to be members of the Society of Jesus. Moreover, by performing these types of duties between Lisbon and Macau, the Vice-Province's recruits gained skills in their order's standard methods of pastoral care. After all, many of them embarked with little or no experience as priests. Those who sailed prior to ordination gained by observing their confreres and working under the supervision of older Jesuits. Aboard ship they often had their first chance to act on the zeal that had driven them to "petition for the Indies," permitting them to confront many of the commonplace chores and challenges of missionary life.

Which ministries did Jesuits perform? One description of a typical three-month voyage from Goa to Macau gives some clues. On May 15, 1686, two priests and a coadjutor embarked on the *Nossa Senhora do Rosário* bound for the China coast. Despite suffering from recurrent fevers, the younger of the two priests "did not cease carrying out the ministries of the Society for his neighbors." Every day he said mass on deck, "and it pleased God that the winds, rains, and rocking of the ship should never interrupt him." Except when he was too ill, he sang the litanies of the Virgin in the afternoon and made spiritual exhortations to his fellow passengers. But according to his companion, his most laudable service was to gather the sailors and African slaves every night, sing doctrine songs with them, and explain the basic prayers. In spite of his weakness, this priest "exercised his great charity with the sick and needy, in their souls as in their bodies." Every morning he awoke early and stationed himself amidships, where, "in a loud and devout voice, he exhorted all to praise God and the Most Holy Virgin."[69]

But this was no typical recruit to the China mission. It was Francisco Nogueira, a veteran of thirty-seven years on the India missions. His colleagues were Simão Martins, the sixty-seven-year-old former provincial officer of the Province of Goa and Visitor-designate, and Brother Luís Pires, a Macanese youth fresh from the novitiate. This trio knew what to do on a ship and had long experience in dealing with the Portuguese and other individuals who by choice or by force had become part of the Estado da Índia. They maintained prayer routines, said daily masses, taught doctrine to the uneducated, sought to reform their neighbors' habits with spiritual sayings, and tended to the sick and the dying. But what of the future China Jesuits who often left Europe straight from the Society's novitiates or colleges? How did they learn the best way to channel their energies at sea?

Two sets of rules were written in the early seventeenth century for regulating Jesuit life on the ships that plied the Cape route. One was elaborated by Visitor João Álvares after his 1610 inspection of the Province of Portugal and the other by Francisco Vieira, Visitor of the Province of Japan, in conjunction with the Provincials of the Goa and Malabar Provinces, in 1616.[70] The two documents drew on the collected experience of senior Jesuits in Asia and laid down a structure of shipboard duties for priests, scholastics, and coadjutors. Their authors intended the rules to be read aloud at several points during the voyage, so that all would be kept aware of the order's expectations. Traveling Jesuits of different ranks were to be apprised of the ministries to be performed and taught how best to handle the trying atmosphere on board the carracks. Both sets of rules contain a mixture of exhortations to Christian charity and warnings about the multifarious snares of the devil.

According to Vieira, Jesuits had three obligations at sea. The first was praying in order to be able "to suffer the voyage with all diligence." The second was guarding their health so that they could be "employed in the missions in India and the salvation of souls." After taking care of these two priorities, they were to fulfill their third obligation, to help their fellow passengers in corporal and spiritual matters. Such, Vieira wrote, "was expected of us, and was what our predecessors always did on these voyages."[71] By invoking the examples of their forebears, Vieira issued a challenge to the young men who had petitioned for a chance to imitate Francis Xavier. Here was a golden opportunity for them to step into the shoes of the Apostle of the Orient. But perhaps this set the bar a bit too high. After all, Xavier had done nothing less than calm raging tempests and turn the salty sea into freshwater.

Jesuits typically embarked at Lisbon in groups of ten or twelve. Their ranks were normally composed one-third of priests and two-thirds of scholastics and coadjutors.[72] One of the priests was appointed superior and accorded the same powers as a college rector or residential superior. Francisco Vieira recommended selecting a good-natured Jesuit for this post, one who would not "make the voyage any more of a burden for his companions."[73] The superior was responsible for organizing his subordinates' routines, assigning chores, serving as the common confessor, and representing the Jesuits in their dealings with the ship's officers. Above all, the appointed leader was entrusted with maintaining a semblance of harmony among the future missionaries. Both Álvares and Vieira enjoined the superiors to defuse any brewing conflicts since, as the former wrote, "besides turning charity and fraternal unity lukewarm, it could cause scandal on the ship if others found out."[74] Vieira underscored this point by insisting that all of the Jesuits' discussions below decks should be restricted to topics which, "if seculars heard, they could be edified, and in no way think there was any immodest bickering or even the shadow of discord." Unfortunately for those scholastics used to the leisure activities of the Society's colleges, this rule also forbade their cherished academic disputations.[75]

A rotating system of duties was to be established among each group. Vieira suggested switching tasks each month, with those who were ordained alternating between preaching and hearing confessions. For scholastics and coadjutors, he enumerated five basic chores: supervising provisions, preparing meals, nursing sick Jesuits, nursing laymen, and acting as a supplementary nurse.[76] For those recruits who were fluent in Portuguese, there was also the task of teaching doctrine to the sailors. In 1583, for instance, João Rodrigues Girão (ca. 1562–1629) was alone among his Flemish, Italian, and Spanish confreres in his capacity to speak to the seamen in their native tongue.[77]

The Jesuits' spiritual ministries among the crew and passengers were, as both Visitors noted, an effective way of "winning souls for God and many friends for the Society." Along with any other priests or brothers who were present, the Jesuits organized religious life on board. In the afternoon they would gather on deck to chant the litanies of the saints, inviting all to sing along. On Saturdays and feast days they would make a more solemn show of intoning the litanies of the Virgin. Individual Jesuits would say masses for small groups regularly, reserving larger masses for major feast days. On a typical March-to-September journey from Lisbon to Goa, these holy days included Easter, Pentecost, the Annunciation, the Holy Trinity, Corpus Christi, Ascension, Assumption, and the Nativity of the Virgin. Vieira recommended that all Jesuits on board devote the days prior to these feasts to exhorting all passengers to confess. The essential task throughout was raising the tenor of piety on board the ship. The Jesuits contributed to it by teaching doctrine, praying and explaining the Rosary, reading devotional books aloud, and instructing others how to make examinations of conscience.[78]

While their shipmates may have viewed the Jesuits' pious practices as an imposition most of the time, their ministries were in high demand whenever the seas stirred. In the rough waters near the Cape of Good Hope, where the South Atlantic meets the Indian Ocean, Jesuits were frequently employed in the attempt to calm anxieties (including their own) by praying aloud for safe passage. A common practice was to say prayers or masses containing invocations of the saints who had given their names to the ships: *São Luís, Santa Ana, Bom Jesus do Carmo, Chagas, Relíquias, Nossa Senhora de Atalaia.* During João Rodrigues Girão's 1583 trip, the Jesuits held a procession on the feast of Saint James since the ship was called the *Santiago.* The festivities included a mass and artillery salvos that contributed to make "everyone happy."[79] Anxious passengers called on the missionaries to lead processions about the ships' decks in times of danger, such as when the winds died down or when the vessels drifted too close to shore. One account remarks that the Jesuits were accustomed on these occasions to turning to "divine remedies, directing frequent prayers to God, to the Virgin most holy, and to all of the saints of heaven, invoking daily the name of every one."[80] When mortal danger threatened, the religious pitch on board trebled. Confessions were heard, relics were carried about, and the saints were implored to calm the wind and waves. One China missionary who sailed in 1629 reported hearing many confessions after he and his colleagues attempted in vain to calm a storm by suspending relics over the towering waves.[81]

These displays of piety were aimed at garnering moral authority for the Jesuits and minting the coin of concord, following João Álvares's injunction to "take great care to keep the ship at peace." In most cases the role of peacemaker fell to senior members of the Society. While other Jesuits might intervene in fights between soldiers and sailors, the superior was to mind the relations among nobles as well as among the ship's officers.[82] As both Visitors observed, dissension between captains (typically noblemen with little knowledge of navigation) and pilots (technical specialists responsible for sailing the vessel) could be fatal. It was crucial, Vieira noted, to make all officers agree on how best to bring the ship to port without appearing "biased or partial toward anyone."[83]

Perhaps the most common Jesuit ministry on board ship was nursing the sick. After overcoming the initial bouts of nausea experienced by many first-time travelers—an affliction that one observer lauded, since it "liberated you from the sad memory of home and the fear of the dangers ahead"—many experienced feverish delirium and the agony of rotting gums, legs, and arms brought on by scurvy.[84] While the Jesuits typically carried sufficient and varied provisions, which made their diet healthier than that of their fellow passengers, they were not impervious to disease. For instance, one Jesuit recorded in 1681 that only five out of 312 passengers aboard one of the Indiamen did not fall ill. During that trip, the missionaries "had the continual experience of the zeal and charity that carried them to India." But such virtues did not grant them immunity. Of nineteen Jesuits, only two escaped the disease that took the lives of four of their confreres (two of whom were slated for the Vice-Province).[85]

Attending to the afflicted was as much a spiritual endeavor as it was a medical one. The Jesuits' first duty was to ensure that all those who fell ill confessed their sins. For safety's sake, Vieira insisted that the priests who knelt to hear these confessions turn their heads so as not to "imbibe the breath" of their penitents.[86] The second priority was to organize an infirmary and ask the ship's master to assign cabin boys to keep it clean. One or two Jesuits were to be appointed to visit all of the sick twice each day with the ship's "doctor, surgeon, or barber" to indicate the treatment for each patient.[87] Besides serving as bedside attendants, missionaries were to make sure that the sick received the stocks of food and medicine known as the King's Provision. While laymen often dispensed these supplies, at times Jesuits were given this hazardous assignment. Agostino Tudeschini (1598–1643) discovered its myriad difficulties in 1629, when sick men were prepared to use force against him to lay their hands on the King's Provision.[88]

The account so far may have given the impression that traveling Jesuits were continually engaged in some form of piety or charity. Not so. Much of their time was spent seeking diversion from the crushing tedium of the voyage. Out of fear that too much *otium* might drain away one's zeal, it was suggested that there be daily readings from devotional books, the Bible, and the *Martyriologium Romanum.* Other leisure activities were encouraged, provided they "served as recreation and entertainment without giving offense to God." João Álvares suggested that Jesuits go up on deck early in the morning and remain there all day, because in addition to "alleviating the head and taking fresh air, it serves as a distraction for the soldiers and passengers." He also recommended that they read stories to their shipmates, and even permitted them to gamble. Playing cards or dice was, as Álvares noted, "a way of avoiding other evils," by which missionaries could intervene to prevent others from "swearing, fights, and the loss of considerable sums of money."[89]

Recall, however, that Jesuits fresh from school were barred from their favorite pastime, studying. In light of the chronic lack of manpower in the China mission, why did the Society forgo the opportunity to expedite the training of its members at sea? After all, there was no shortage of instructors among the senior Jesuits who sailed with almost every fleet. Health concerns dictated this policy. Francisco Vieira and others who had traveled on the Carreira da Índia were convinced that the stagnant air in cabins below deck was lethal. Knowing that young Jesuits might envision their quarters as classrooms, he prohibited his subordinates from beginning philosophy or theology studies or reading "books by saints or preachers and taking notes or writing." His reasons were simple: "In this way we have buried many of our men on these voyages, and even on the mission this past year, 1615, two or three died because they purposely remained in the cabins to study." Vieira conceded one exception to his rule: those preparing sermons to present to the crew and passengers.[90] In spite of these injunctions, other sources reveal that some procurators such as Nicolas Trigault and Martino Martini taught Chinese and astronomy to their recruits—safely topside, though, far from the pestilent air below.

The majority of the missionaries reached the China coast after roughly a year at sea. When conditions were right, Jesuits would spend little time waiting in India for the monsoon winds to carry them across Maritime

Asia. But not all were so fortunate. Manuel Dias the elder, for instance, left Lisbon in 1585 on the ill-fated *Santiago.* He was among a handful of survivors who managed to reach the East African coast in an overloaded skiff after their ship foundered on shoals. They had no better luck on land than at sea. Native raiding parties stripped them of their clothing and goods for bartering, and they were forced to walk for over two months to reach the closest Portuguese settlement.[91] Agostino Tudeschini also experienced the trial of shipwreck on his way to China in 1629.[92] Others found the wait at Goa too much for them to bear and set off for Macau on their own. This was the case of Martino Martini, who walked in 1642 from Goa to Surat, where he found passage to Java aboard an English vessel. News of the acclamation of King João IV had already reached Asia, loosening the tensions between the Portuguese and the Dutch, permitting Martini to sail directly from Java to Macau.[93] François de Rougemont, Philippe Couplet, and a third colleague chose a similar route after reaching Goa in 1656. This trio walked across India as well, but they did Martini one better: they went barefoot.[94]

On January 29, 1659, André Ferrão (ca. 1625–1661) signed his name to the Annual Letter of the Vice-Province of China for 1656. This priest, who was born at Seia on the northern slope of the Serra da Estrela in central Portugal and educated at the College of Coimbra, had sailed from Lisbon aboard the *Bom Jesus de Vidigueira* with Martino Martini in April 1657. He spent six months traveling the Cape route, another half year in residence at the Colégio de São Paulo in Goa, and a further three months sailing to Macau. Ferrão arrived on the China coast on July 14, 1658, and whiled away six months before he was given the task of compressing a pile of three-year-old reports from the Vice-Province into an Annual Letter. He took inspiration in copying the "glorious labors" of his colleagues inside the Qing empire, but felt that he would do them justice only if he related the trials that he had gone through to reach China. Ferrão waxed poetic about the "fruit of tears" reaped across the nautical miles between Lisbon and Macau. These tears had been shed for all the companions who had been left behind "on these long routes and vast seas." Ferrão had parted company with no fewer than twelve confreres. "But they were not all dead," he was pleased to report; only four had died, while three remained in Goa to study theology, and another five were either in India or Macassar "tied down by Galen."[95]

So many tears had he spilled, Ferrão averred, that they were enough to feed another fountain like that famous one in Coimbra, the Fonte das Lágrimas. But, he added, he was not speaking of the tears that each China Jesuit cried for himself, since "being a missionary is not the same as being insensitive." So many diseases and so much misery accompanied the men of the Vice-Province on their way from Europe to East Asia! Moreover, Ferrão noted, those who traveled on the sea were desiccated by the constant winds and salty waves. "So undone and so worn down do we arrive," the missionary wrote about himself and others like him, "that he speaks the truth who calls us relics, not only of the China mission, but of ourselves."[96] It is hard to imagine that such a description would have seemed fitting for an Annual Letter, an account of apostolic labors intended to kindle the vocations of future missionaries. Nevertheless, Ferrão chose to be honest. These were the trials that one had to undergo just to have the opportunity to preach the gospel to the Chinese. But as any veteran of the China enterprise could have said, the journey east was just the beginning.

7

Learning the Language of Birds

THERE WAS NO DOUBT about it, wrote Juan Antonio de Arnedo in the early 1690s. The China enterprise stood out among all of the Jesuits' missions as the one in which erudition and conversion were most intimately linked. The study not just of Western arts and letters but also of indigenous philosophy was indispensable to missionaries working in China, where "books and the preaching of the gospel" were closely intertwined. How could it be otherwise, Arnedo asked, in a land where scholarship reached "the heights of the most learned European nation?" The Jesuits therefore must commit themselves to studying Chinese language and thought.[1]

The missionaries' advances of the preceding century, Arnedo claimed, had revealed the value of their engagement with Chinese intellectual traditions. But how did they gain their entry into the world of indigenous erudition? In other words, how did the Jesuits turn themselves into acceptable interlocutors for late Ming and early Qing literati—those men who stood before the imposing gates of social legitimacy in China? The answer to these questions had been obvious to the men of the Society of Jesus for decades. As João Rodrigues wrote in 1624, the double task of studying Chinese language and thought was hard work. On this score, he claimed, Saint Paul had had it easier than the East Asian Jesuits; after all, the Jesuits were not blessed with a heaven-sent gift of tongues. Rodrigues, the author of the first Western grammars of Japanese, knew something about language study. He understood the predicament faced by the Jesuits who arrived on the China coast worn out by traveling and years of previous schooling but had no choice other than to submit themselves to another course of study "in the manner of children." In addition to learning tongues that were "so confusing and so different from their own," they were obliged to gain familiarity with "the errors of the various ancient sects" found in Asia. If the missionaries did not become well versed in the "symbols and enigmas that constitute the religion and rites of these Asian nations," first passing through the door of language, they could expect no success in their apostolic endeavors.[2]

By the time Rodrigues made this assessment, Jesuits had been engaged in learning Chinese for almost half a century. Beginning with Michele Ruggieri and Matteo Ricci, the missionaries in China had immersed themselves so fully in the language of their hosts that they had gained positions of respect among the erudite elite of the Ming empire. The Jesuits made a strategic decision to focus on learning *guanhua,* the parlance of literati and mandarins. They relied on the techniques of grammatical analysis often used for teaching Latin and Greek in their order's schools so as to understand the syntax of Chinese. Once equipped with an ability to speak and read, they attempted to mimic the basic intellectual formation of their hosts by studying the canonical texts of Confucian thought, that is, *Rujiao,* or the "Teachings of the Literati."

The entry of the Jesuits into the world of Chinese scholarship, sought for the express purpose of finding ammunition for their rhetorical salvos in the battle for souls, produced impressive results. Matteo Ricci became a celebrity in person and in print for his learning, and his shadow loomed over the China enterprise for over a century. But it was not enough for his successors to coast in the wake of their confrere's accomplishments. They had to assume Ricci's mantle of erudition if they were to spread the mission beyond the areas where he was known. Consequently, their primary challenge was to devise a system for transmitting the mission's collective knowledge of indigenous language and thought to each newly arrived priest. Such a training program in spoken Mandarin and Chinese philosophy—especially the aspects of Confucian thought deemed most germane to the Christian message—would permit new Jesuits to build friendships, secure patronage, and gain converts among the great and the good. Because their enterprise was predicated on high social visibility, and because their public image was modeled on that of the elite, this immersion in literati culture was indispensable for the mission's survival and progress.

The slow pace of conversions in the first fifty years of the mission gave the China Jesuits ample time to consider the best way to pass on their knowledge of indigenous language and thought to those who arrived from Europe. By the early 1620s they had already devised the first Western program of Chinese studies, a fusion of traditional Chinese educational methods and Jesuit organizational techniques. This program attempted to equip recruits with the essential tools for their proselytizing activities, and the degree to which the Vice-Province was able to continue it would have a decisive impact on the mission's outcome. In fact, over the course of the seventeenth century, the Jesuits' language skills enabled them to make conversions far in excess of their pastoral capacities. As a result, the training that had made the missionaries so successful was gradually sacrificed as the Vice-Province found itself forced to get new recruits out into the mission field as quickly as possible. The daunting pastoral burdens of those missionaries thus robbed them of the opportunity to devote their first years in China to the study of Confucian thought. There is a certain irony here, because this was a time when the Jesuits were increasingly forced by other Europeans to defend their (allegedly undue) appreciation of native customs. So the fate of the Vice-Province was truly determined by the depth of its members' engagement with the Chinese language—a tongue whose short syllables appeared to make it, according to one of them, "more the language of birds than of men."[3]

The Secret of the Language

The Jesuit mission to China began at a language barrier. The efforts of Francis Xavier and his immediate successors to find a way into Guangdong Province in the second half of the sixteenth century foundered as a result of their inability to enter into a conversation with the local authorities. After nearly three decades of frustration—a feeling that rankled the men of the Society, in view of the inroads they had made in India, Japan, and Southeast Asia—they reached a solution in 1579, when Visitor Alessandro Valignano summoned Michele Ruggieri to Macau. Valignano left orders for his compatriot to dedicate his time to language study, trusting that if a Jesuit could speak for himself at Canton, he might obtain permission to reside within the empire. With knowledge of spoken and written Chinese, Ruggieri could dismiss the interpreters typically employed by the Portuguese traders as well as by his missionary forebears.

This expedient, first used by Xavier himself, had created no small degree of ambiguity and misunderstanding.

Beyond putting Ruggieri in a position to commence the diplomatic overtures that laid the foundations for the China mission, Valignano's orders sought to enhance the status of the Society of Jesus within Macau. Although the Portuguese had been able to establish and maintain their settlement without the help of Jesuit go-betweens, the city's fortunes were bolstered at various moments during the seventeenth century as a result of the missionaries' interventions on its behalf in Canton and Peking. As soon as Ruggieri began to be noticed at the Guangdong emporium by literati for his language abilities, the Portuguese merchants were quick to make a public show of their friendship with him. These encounters at Canton were proof enough that Valignano's investment would pay off. Curiously, his orders had the effect of cooling the initial zeal of his subordinates, some of whom were taken aback by his insistence on a regime of language studies that would precede proselytizing activities. Nevertheless, by 1587, Superior General Claudio Aquaviva confirmed the policy, ordering that "as many missionaries study language as can."[4]

For the first years of his stay in southern China, Ruggieri was left to learn Chinese on his own. As he wrote to his superiors in Rome in 1581, he set to work diligently but soon realized the enormity of the task before him. Ruggieri complained that the Chinese characters were unlike the letters used in Europe "and those of all other nations," and that in fact there was no alphabet, "but as many letters as there are words." Confronted with this daunting plenitude, he inquired into how the Chinese themselves learned to read. Doubtless his spirits were not lifted when he learned that "even the natives spent fifteen years of their lives" in order to be able to tackle written texts.[5] A further difficulty was that he had been ordered to study "the Chinese language of the court"—that is, the Nanjing area form known to the Portuguese traders as Mandarin—but could find no one at Macau who knew both that tongue and Portuguese.

So Ruggieri had to begin his studies in what he called a "ridiculous" manner. The priest found a Chinese master who helped him struggle through a few schoolbooks. He also learned from his teacher through pictures. "For example, when he wanted to teach me how to say and write 'horse' in that language, he drew a horse and above it drew the character that signifies horse and is pronounced 'ma.'" According to a letter that Ruggieri sent the Superior General, the local Jesuits and the Portuguese merchants who heard of his study method thought it impossible that he would learn anything.[6] After these initial lessons in Macau, he consulted with Valignano, who suggested that he might find more favorable conditions for studying Mandarin at Canton. It was in that city that Ruggieri began to study Chinese books in earnest, making his first translations from Chinese into Latin and trying his hand at composing Christian texts in Chinese. Within two years, he claimed in November 1581, divine favor had granted him the ability to memorize fifteen thousand characters, enough to advance "little by little" in reading indigenous writings.[7] A little over a year later, in February 1583, Ruggieri reported that he had started acting on Valignano's desire that he write "a catechism, a *flos sanctorum,* a confessional manual, and a doctrine manual"—although it appears that he produced only a catechism and a set of prayers before beginning to work on a *mappa mundi.*[8]

To be sure, Ruggieri was the only Jesuit who had to learn Chinese in such a painful manner. When Matteo Ricci and Francesco Pasio arrived at Macau in 1582 to join the mission, they benefited from their colleague's experience; they had someone to explain basic grammar and vocabulary to them. They spent little time at Macau, moving quickly to Zhaoqing, where Ruggieri had gained permission to reside for the purpose of language study. Doubtless, Ricci's initial bewilderment on finding out that Chinese had "neither articles, nor cases, nor numbers, nor genders, nor tenses, nor modes" was allayed through his compatriot's explanations.[9] But even if Ruggieri imparted what he knew of Chinese grammar in a short time, an immense problem remained—the need to memorize characters. Between 1583 and 1588 Ruggieri and Ricci did their best to alleviate that problem by compiling a dictionary of Portuguese words, Chinese characters, and their romanizations. This lexicon represents the Jesuits' first systematic attempt to make the Chinese language a common resource for the mission with the provision of a European-style teaching tool for recruits as well as veteran priests.[10]

Perhaps more important than the Jesuits' vocabulary list, however, was their appropriation of indigenous study methods. Ruggieri's comment that Chinese children spent over a decade (in another letter he states "between fifteen and twenty years") learning to read suggests that an analysis of native methods was part of his inquiries into how best to study.[11] Evidence preserved in the Roman Archives of the Society of Jesus shows that some of the first missionaries employed the same texts that Chinese chil-

moderari / temperar — locus amplus planetæ

辰宿列張寒來

暑往秋收冬藏

閏餘成歲律呂

調陽雲騰致雨

辰 sin	宿 siu (stellæ xxviii cores / 28 stellæ)	列 lie (undique ordinate)	張 ciā (patent)	寒 han (frigus)	來 lai (accedit)
暑 sciu (estus)	往 guan (accedit)	秋 ceu (autumnus)	收 sceu (colligit)	冬 tu (Spenis)	藏 çan (servat)
閏 giun (ex lunari)	餘 iu (residu:)	成 cin (fit)	歲 sui (annus)	律 liu (dia sex armonia)	呂 liu (alig sex armonia)
調 tiau (equant)	陽 ia	雲 iun (nubes)	騰 ten (asciendunt)	致 ci (emittunt)	雨 iu (pluviá)

dren learned by rote to increase their vocabulary and practice writing characters. An example of the language primer *Qianzi wen* (Thousand Character Classic), printed in Fujian Province in 1579, has survived with romanizations and Latin translations written in the margins around each character.[12] Given the importance of that coastal province, which had strong trading ties to the Pearl River delta and was a center of printing activity, it is likely that this volume is one purchased by either Ricci or Ruggieri. In any event, it is clear that the Jesuits from early on relied on elements of the native educational canon for learning the language. Moreover, by December 1584 the missionaries at Zhaoqing had invited a Chinese master to board with them, give them daily lessons, and edit Ruggieri's writings.[13] By adopting indigenous study techniques, the missionaries gained a twofold benefit: they saved themselves the trouble of innovation, that is, of newly creating an entire course of study in matters unknown to them; and they gained an awareness of the modes of thought and cultural references inherent in Chinese educational traditions.

Despite the reports of smooth sailing sent by Ruggieri and his colleagues to their superiors in Macau and in Rome, and even if they did manage to memorize scores of characters, there remained a massive stumbling block in the way of their acquisition of Chinese. This obstacle was the tonal nature of the spoken language. Within the first few months of his stay at Macau, Matteo Ricci complained to a fellow Jesuit in Italy that the language was "so equivocal, having many words that mean more than a thousand things." He knew that the difference between homonyms was a matter of their being pronounced "with the voice higher or lower in four variations of tone," but his celebrated memory did not help him in this regard; he was hampered by a tin ear.[14] According to later accounts, it was not until Lazzaro Cattaneo began to study with Ricci at Shaozhou in 1594 that the Jesuits devised a system for identifying the different tones employed in *guanhua* and romanizing them consistently.

Ricci later recorded that his Sicilian confrere made this discovery on the basis of "the music that he knew" and was enabled accordingly to create

---

Annotated folio from *Qianzi wen,* the *Thousand Character Classic* (Fujian, 1579). The romanizations and translations surrounding each character were likely done by Matteo Ricci or one of the other early Jesuits.

a system of accentuation for transcribing Chinese terms that markedly improved the missionaries' learning curve.[15] By the time of his death, Cattaneo was celebrated as having unearthed the "secret of the language." Before they grasped the crucial tonal element, the missionaries often erred in speaking, "since the same word, merely by varying the accents on the syllables and applying one or another tone, could have four, five, or at times more meanings."[16] Once the characters were organized according to sound, the Jesuits found their vocabularies expanding more rapidly. In 1607, describing his lessons with Ricci in a letter, Sabatino de Ursis went so far as to claim, "The challenge posed by these characters and the language is not as great as I had imagined, since all of the difficulty is found in the variety of tones." He asserted that thanks to the efforts of his brethren, learning Chinese was "easy, because by learning a single syllable, one learns fifty or more entirely different things." Ursis even provided his correspondent with an example of the variety of characters and meanings for the syllable "pa," complete with a diagram of musical notes for pronouncing each variation.[17] So important was the mastery of tones to the acquisition of Chinese that later superiors insisted that recruits to the mission bring with them "some fundaments of music for learning the Chinese tones perfectly."[18]

"An Extraordinary Diligence"

During their first decade in the Ming empire, the Jesuits pursued the study of Chinese in an ad hoc manner, with a senior priest (typically Matteo Ricci) instructing new arrivals or scheduling lessons with native masters. But in the late 1590s Ricci left his colleagues behind as he headed north to Peking. This forced the missionaries to develop other methods of passing on their knowledge to new arrivals in what was hoped to be a uniform fashion. A decade of experience had convinced Ricci that recruits needed to acquire a familiarity with spoken Mandarin, written Chinese, and the basic works of the Confucian canon. A trained Jesuit was necessary only for helping new men clear the initial hurdle of speaking. After that, they could rely on hired masters who would teach them writing and guide them through the *Four Books.*

Two significant problems had to be resolved: Which missionaries would do the initial teaching? And where would they do it? In the early 1590s the answers to these questions seemed clear. The College of Macau was spacious enough to accommodate temporarily missionaries heading for Guangdong Province, as well as those bound for Nagasaki. Moreover, part of the stated purpose of the Colégio de Madre de Deus was to provision the East Asian enterprises by teaching "the languages and customs of these kingdoms." Such training would ensure that they departed for Japan or China as men ready for service and not as "greenhorn Portuguese," noted Duarte de Sande, the institution's first rector.[19] Indeed, he himself had taken up the task of instructing two of his compatriots, João Soeiro and João da Rocha, while they completed their theology studies. Sande "knew something of the Chinese language" from his days in Zhaoqing, so he was qualified to teach its rudiments.[20] Nevertheless, Soeiro and da Rocha would have to wait until they entered the Ming empire before they began to study Chinese composition and philosophy.

A number of factors converged to make the Jesuits abandon the idea of using the College of Macau for language training. First of all, the difficulties involved in smuggling men into the empire meant that new missionaries had to be sent as soon as an opportunity presented itself, not necessarily after they were grounded in Chinese. Moreover, once inside the empire, trained priests had few opportunities to return to Macau to teach their colleagues. The cloud of mandarin suspicion that fell over the colony from the 1590s until the 1610s as a result of its links with Japan only served to encourage the China Jesuits to dissociate themselves from Macau. By the time Ming authorities shifted their attention from the Portuguese to the Manchus, relations between the China mission and the Province of Japan had soured. After 1614 the College of Macau became the Japan Jesuits' headquarters in exile and was packed full with distrustful and despondent priests. Finally, the creation of the Vice-Province in 1619 and the end of the Nanjing affair in 1623 led the China Jesuits to move their teaching program away from the Portuguese colony and into the Ming empire for good.

Macau did furnish the China mission with an invaluable resource during the 1590s, however—its sons, the children of either Asian or mixed parentage who had been raised as Christians among the Portuguese-speaking segment of its inhabitants. Borrowing a technique from the Japan Jesuits, who had since the early 1580s been accepting Japanese men into their ranks as coadjutors charged with teaching their European confreres, Alessandro Valignano assigned two youths, Francisco Martins and Sebastião Fernandes, to Matteo Ricci, who began the task of training them in 1591 at Shaozhou. After almost two years of study, the pair were reported to have a "mediocre knowledge of the Chinese language and letters."[21] The initial progress of these native coadjutors encouraged Ricci to accept a few other "sons of Macau" during the following two decades and subject them to a language training program of their own. Yet because of the small size of the mission, the China Jesuits enlisted the services of only a handful of them, despite Ricci's contention that the colonial upbringing of these Chinese coadjutors made them far more trustworthy and secure in their faith than their Japanese peers who had been "born amid heathens."[22]

There is little evidence regarding the curriculum followed by Jesuit students of Chinese in the mission's first decades, the period before the Nanjing affair in 1616. A 1598 letter written by Niccolò Longobardo at Shaozhou suggests that the program consisted of two phases, the first focused on speaking and the second dedicated to studying the *Four Books.* After his arrival in late December of the previous year, the Sicilian priest had begun to hear lessons from what he called "speech books," texts meant to prepare one for learning composition. Two Macanese coadjutors, António Leitão (ca. 1581–1611) and Domingos Mendes (1582–1652), joined Longobardo in his studies, while Lazzaro Cattaneo and Francisco Martins began a course of study on the "Quin"—that is, *Jing,* the classics of the Chinese tradition.[23]

This course of study appears to have been repeated in later years, but instead of studying at Shaozhou, the Jesuits ran more of their training classes at Nanjing or Peking. In March 1605 Alfonso Vagnone wrote from the southern capital that he was busily engaged in his studies alongside two other recent arrivals, Feliciano da Silva and Pedro Ribeiro. In an excerpt from a letter to his superiors in Rome, Vagnone expressed his frustration at not being able to acquire the language faster: "In this house, there is only one priest and a native brother who know the language, as well as we three priests who are studying, meaning that only a fraction gets done of what should if we were all trained hands."[24] Doubtless the Italian Jesuit took solace in the fact that by 1608, he and his colleagues had brought about the conversion of the Chinese master who visited the residence to read lessons.[25] At the same time that these lessons were taking place at Nanjing, Sabatino de Ursis and Diego de Pantoja were studying at Peking alongside Matteo Ricci and Sebastião Fernandes.

The reference to the *Jing* as part of the Jesuits' program of study and the intimation that they spent years under the tutelage of indigenous instructors is as intriguing as it is enigmatic. What specific texts did they read? One can safely assume that their readings included the *Sishu,* or *Four Books,* the central works of the Confucian tradition (the *Doctrine of the Mean,* the *Great Learning,* the *Analects,* and the *Mencius*). But it remains unclear if all of the missionaries during this early period also read the *Wujing,* or *Five Classics,* that is, the *Documents Classic,* the *Record of Rites,* the *Book of Changes,* the *Book of Odes,* and the *Spring and Autumn Annals.* And what of other works of philosophy, literature, or religion? A catalogue of the texts seized from the library at their Nanjing residence in 1616 suggests that the missionaries' collection was one that might be considered typical for Chinese scholars, but it does not reveal any penchant for collecting rare or valuable works.[26] More likely their studies during these first decades were organized along utilitarian lines with the aim of giving new arrivals access to a literary register that they would attempt to reproduce in their own writings. Whatever the precise content of their studies may have been, according to Diego de Pantoja, several literati expressed their admiration at the Jesuits' engagement with the works of the Confucian canon. The knowledge acquired by the foreign priests in their journey along the Way of the Sages, their Chinese peers suggested, made them so superior to their compatriots that they would no doubt be elected pope if they ever returned to Europe.[27]

In the second decade of the seventeenth century, as both Jesuit enterprises in East Asia underwent dramatic crises, the missionaries sequestered at Hangzhou and Macau had time to ponder the language training methods they had employed thus far. The contrast between the techniques used in Japan and those employed in China was stark, and João Rodrigues, the famed interpreter, spelled out the differences in his *Arte Breve da Lingoa Iapoa* (Macau, 1620). In this invaluable book, which is at once a Japanese grammar, a reference work, and a cultural treatise, Rodrigues defended the use of a program rooted in the study of rules and "grammatical precepts with good masters, listening to lessons from books in which the pure and elegant language is contained, composing and doing other appropriate exercises."[28] His notion of proper study was formed with regard to the methods used by the Society in its colleges for teaching Latin, Greek, and Hebrew—not to mention the methods employed by the Japan mission, where the substantial numbers of men who arrived between 1576 and 1614 permitted a similar type of classroom study.[29] Moreover, Rodrigues argued that this was the ideal method for teaching languages to missionaries since their maturity and familiarity with studying made their task easier. To be sure, he conceded, those who studied in this manner often sacrificed elegance and fluency; almost all of them were prone to "many improprieties" in their speech.[30]

But there was another way of learning Asian languages, according to Rodrigues—the way that had been used by the China Jesuits. This method involved total immersion in a foreign environment, where one would learn the tongue by living alongside native speakers and "diligently noting various phrases and ways of speaking of diverse subjects." As a result, one would learn vocabulary easily, although writing and composing would continue to be a challenge. In sum, Rodrigues conceded that this way of learning led to developing a more natural speaking ability than was possible by following classroom instruction, but deemed it inappropriate for members of religious orders since it involved "constant dealings with the natives, being always in their midst." Even if a student was not restrained by the bonds of community life, Rodrigues insisted, this way of studying demanded "at the very least an extraordinary diligence."[31]

But should one assume that the China Jesuits were indeed possessed of such uncommon capacities? Surely not, given the fact that during the first fifty years of the mission they spent an average of four years each studying Chinese language and literature. The slow pace of conversions during that period ensured that they had plenty of time to spare for this endeavor, and so they slowly worked their way toward fluency and familiarity with the Confucian canon. Moreover, the China mission never received enough recruits to warrant the type of classroom teaching that Rodrigues prescribed. Nor had any Chinese-speaking missionaries taken the time to compose an *arte* of their adopted tongue à la *Arte Breve da Lingoa Iapoa*—and they may even have doubted whether such a task was possible. Also, since the Jesuits were spread thin among their far-flung residences, they had no choice but to immerse themselves fully in Chinese society. Nevertheless, the missionaries did retain the impulse—so typical of their order—to form classes for language study, and they would attempt to implement a plan of studies as soon as they had enough new arrivals at one time to permit it.

Even if the China Jesuits were forced to rely on teaching methods that contained a stronger imprint of indigenous techniques than their order's standard practices, they did more than seek a passing fluency in Mandarin. It is worth noting that the years spent by the Jesuits on their studies imbued them with a tangible sense of admiration for the complexity of Chinese thought. Modern scholars are aware of the appreciation that men such as Matteo Ricci had for Confucian philosophy (though the same cannot be said for East Asian religious thought), but less well known is that their successors, in general, shared this sentiment. To be sure, since the Jesuits had spent their formative years in academic environments where humanistic inquiry was common coin, the task of studying the Chinese philosophical canon spoke directly to their talents. It is therefore no surprise that during the mission's early decades, when prudence, persecution, or politics demanded that they keep a low profile, the Jesuits repeatedly returned to their studies to refine their strategies for introducing Christianity into the native cultural framework.

Even a minor figure such as João Monteiro rhapsodized in an Annual Letter about how the study of Chinese texts served as an intellectual refuge from the hardships of missionary work. In them, he claimed, it was possible to find "pearls of wisdom so full of honey and so covered with the sugar of divine consolation" that all of the dangers and drudgery of life in China seemed to disappear. Monteiro opined that the years of language study required of the missionaries seemed to be "brief months." He also contended that the priests who took up the study of Chinese books derived more pleasure than "the Poets in the lessons of their Homer or Virgil, the Rhetoricians in their Cicero and Lucian, the Philosophers in their Plato and Aristotle, and the Mathematicians in their Euclid and Archimedes." What made this academic endeavor so engaging, in Monteiro's view, were the Chinese characters. These "enigmatic hieroglyphics" had many varieties of meaning, a characteristic that made them "pleasing and amusing."[32] Although Monteiro's words were in part destined to disabuse potential recruits in Europe who held Chinese to be an impossible language—a tactic employed by the China Jesuits on previous occasions to boost their numbers—they no doubt reflect commonly held views of the missionaries in late Ming and early Qing China.[33]

A *Ratio Studiorum* for China

When news of the founding of the Vice-Province reached Macau in 1619, the China Jesuits began to feel a true enthusiasm about their enterprise. The end of their troubles at Nanjing and the return of Nicolas

Trigault with a crop of recruits were cause for celebration. In this heady atmosphere they made ambitious plans for the mission's future, devising strategies about how best to proceed after years of sequestration. Taking their cue from past experience no less than from the suggestions of their mandarin protectors, the Jesuits reaffirmed their commitment to the study of Chinese language and thought. These were the keys, they believed, to avoiding future persecutions and expanding the mission's geographic reach.

The orders from Rome that mandated severing their new administrative unit from the withering Province of Japan encouraged the China Jesuits to standardize the techniques they used for training new arrivals. More specifically, the foundational rules for the Vice-Province that Superior General Muzio Vitelleschi sent to Visitor Gabriel de Matos (1572–1634) in 1621 prohibited individual missionaries from deciding "the books, the method, or the amount of time of their studies" as they saw fit. Instead, the elders of the mission were instructed to consult on how best to produce a *ratio studiorum,* a plan of studies, for teaching *guanhua* and Chinese thought.[34]

The concept of a *ratio studiorum* would have been clear to all members of the Vice-Province. What Vitelleschi wanted the senior China Jesuits to produce was a set of rules organized in the same fashion as the pedagogical framework that structured the personnel and curriculum of the Society's colleges throughout the world. In an effort to homogenize the teaching methods of its educational establishments, various members of the order from across Europe had worked for years to produce a model curriculum that could be applied universally to all Jesuit colleges. The *ratio studiorum* that was promulgated throughout the Society's provinces in 1599 was flexible enough to accommodate the cultural variations of the different countries where it was to be employed, but structured enough to ensure a high degree of curricular uniformity and standard mechanisms for evaluating the teaching at any given school. The same goals were set for the *ratio studiorum* that was commissioned for the China mission, with the expectation that the curriculum laid down in the early 1620s would last for decades.

The consultations that produced the Vice-Province's *ratio studiorum* most likely took place from 1622 until 1624 under the direction of Manuel Dias the elder. Dias had been deputized by Visitor Matos to conduct an inspection of the mission in the wake of the Nanjing affair. On his tour he had the opportunity to speak with almost all Jesuits who had "some experience with the study of Chinese letters and language," including Niccolò Longobardo, Manuel Dias the younger, Alfonso Vagnone, Giulio Aleni, Álvaro Semedo, Pedro Ribeiro, Nicolas Trigault, and Gaspar Ferreira. Most of the information regarding the subject material to be used during the proposed course of study, as well as the timing and order of its reading and writing components, likely originated with this group. Dias, a man with more than ten years of experience as rector of the College of Macau, was almost certainly the one responsible for giving the curriculum its structure and apportioning the rules and obligations to each participant in the teaching process, from the Vice-Provincial on down to the coadjutors.

Dias's program consisted of four years of study, divided into three phases. The initial stage of the course, the first six months, was for training missionaries how to speak *guanhua* correctly. The second, lasting a year and a half, was for reading texts from the Confucian canon with a fellow Jesuit (often a Macanese coadjutor) for a master. The third stage consisted of two years of lessons with a Chinese master. This instructor was to give lessons on composition and readings from the texts used in the preceding stage of the program, explaining them as they were understood by literati. By laying out a course of study that was equal in length to the amount of time devoted by Jesuits to the study of moral and systematic theology, Dias made clear the conviction that the language program was crucial for the mission's development. He went so far as to say that such a plan of study was just as indispensable "for the service of God, the good of the Society, and the conversion of souls as that of philosophy in Europe." Dias charged the Vice-Provincial with providing the broadest level of oversight for the program, making sure that it was practiced and preserved in its entirety. He also warned against shortening the program from its full four years—a considerable span for priests to be inactive once in China, given the mission's chronic manpower shortages—"without a very urgent reason," since he saw the future of the Vice-Province hanging in the balance.[35]

The primary aim of the *ratio studiorum* was to produce missionaries qualified to assume the erudite scholar-priest's mantle bequeathed to them by Matteo Ricci. They were expected to be able to engage in dialogue with prospective converts from different levels of Chinese society and to sustain amicable relations with the governing elite of the cities where they resided. Put another way, they were to turn themselves into ersatz literati, adopting the dominant fashions of the Jiangnan region. The Vice-Provincial was instructed to emplace his aspiring scholars of Chinese in an area best suited for studying, one with the optimal "shelter, climate, and other things beneficial" to that purpose. To the Jesuits in late Ming China, this was shorthand for Jiangnan, since that was where they maintained the most residences and where intersecting trade routes kept the area awash with provisions. Moreover, the dialect spoken there—at least among literati—was *guanhua.* Not for nothing was this dialect called Mandarin; it was the form of speech most widely used by the members of the bureaucracy. While the events of 1616 removed Nanjing from the list of possible training sites, the mission had nearby residences where the Jesuits could find an abundance of masters who spoke Mandarin as "purely and clearly" as they desired.[36]

To be sure, the question of what form of spoken Chinese the missionaries were taught raises its corollary: How did they penetrate the profusion of local dialects that would have barred them from communicating with popular milieux? The missionaries realized almost from the start that the greatest numbers of potential converts were to be found among poor rustics. Educated converts, the ones who spoke *guanhua,* were comparatively few, although they could be found throughout the empire. Could it be that the Jesuits simply did not speak to their flocks, or that they addressed them only though interpreters? Missionary sources are ambiguous about the issue, offering few references to local dialects. One exception is the testimony of Francisco Simões regarding a mission circuit in North Zhili, which suggests that some priests had considerable trouble with local dialects, at least in their first years in China. Most, if not all, of the area's villages seemed to have their "own particular ways of speaking, tantamount to different languages," Simões lamented. Such diversity could be found even in hamlets separated by "one league or less," he complained, making it appear that "the Devil mixed the language up in such a way as to make preaching the Holy Gospel more difficult."[37]

It seems ironic that the Jesuits devoted so much time to studying a form of Chinese that would offer them so little capacity to carry out the task of communicating the Christian gospel to the masses. But there was a certain rationality in the choice of *guanhua.* Mandarin, as the priests learned early on, was widely understood even outside literati circles, if only because even the most remote village had some form of intercourse with the imperial bureaucracy. Moreover, the extreme diversity of spoken dialects from province to province was countered by the uniformity of the written language. His lament about the confusion sowed by the Devil notwithstanding, Francisco Simões recognized that Chinese characters facilitated his interactions with the populace, "since the letters and hieroglyphs, in spite of their being pronounced in one way or another, do not vary in meaning and everywhere signify the same thing." Yet another consideration speaks more to the academic capacities of the Jesuits than to the logic of their training program. Individuals who were capable of mastering Latin during their schooling, the Portuguese language during their passage eastward, and Mandarin during their early study years in China would surely have been able, given time, to learn the dialects of areas around their residences. After all, a Jesuit assigned to an area with a distinct variant of Chinese, such as Cantonese or Shanghainese, faced the same predicament that an imperial official sent to the same area confronted—except for the likelihood that the Jesuit would stay in that place longer and have more frequent dealings with plebeians. Although their Mendicant detractors might fault the Jesuits in Fujian for not being able to speak the local dialect (the Dominicans and Franciscans spent their formative years amid the Fujianese sojourners in Manila), surely this final linguistic hurdle was not insuperable.[38]

Just like its European counterpart, the *ratio studiorum* for the China mission prescribed a structured learning environment. Each academic year was divided into semesters, with two classes to be held every day, six days a week. On any given day, students would hear one hour of lessons in the morning and forty-five minutes in the afternoon, with recitations required each day. The superior of the residence where lessons were held was to assume the role of rector, moderating the pace of the program where necessary. Such moderation often meant controlling the ambitions of the missionaries, men with long years of training behind them who were eager to begin their apostolic endeavors. As a result, the *ratio studiorum* contains more injunctions about how to slow the students' progress than how to speed it up. In light of the perceived health risks of excessive exertion, the superior should "not let the priests study during rest time, nor during the time allotted for sleep." Some form of recreation "used by the Society, but not strange to the Chinese," was also mandated for Sunday afternoons and feast days with the goal of keeping those studying "sane and happy." During the summer, a two-month vacation was imposed on the missionary-pupils; during the first week of each month, all studies were prohibited. In the other weeks of vacation, the residential superior might encourage his charges to hone their reading comprehension by studying selected Chinese texts written by Jesuit authors.[39]

The first two years of the program were to be conducted by a "master who reads in Portuguese," that is, either a European missionary or a Chinese coadjutor. For the authors of the *ratio studiorum,* the "Portuguese" master was the linchpin of the program's success, since his "diligence and way of reading" would determine whether his students learned "the language and literature poorly or well." To underscore this claim, Manuel Dias the elder asserted that teaching one Jesuit correctly was equivalent to catechizing many Chinese. One of the duties reserved for the Vice-Provincial was selecting the right man. He was told to pick the most effective teacher even if it meant removing this individual from "another occupation, from which he derived more consolation."[40] The *ratio studiorum* suggests that the assignment of teachers caused consternation among talented missionaries, frustrations that were directly addressed in admonitions to would-be instructors. These men were urged to be tolerant toward their pupils and warned against belittling them. Dias reminded the instructors that their students—whose ranks included musicians, astronomers, physicians, and theologians—were often "already masters of higher sciences," mature men who "should not be treated like children." They were told to treat their pupils charitably "and neither get annoyed nor irritate them if they ask about the same thing or character many times."[41]

At the base of the educational edifice erected by the *ratio studiorum* were, of course, the students themselves. They were forewarned that constancy and dedication were indispensable if they were to attain their goal, because the "lack of an *arte,* the variety of tones, the ambiguity of words, and the multitude of characters" were formidable difficulties.[42] Yet Dias reassured them that they would benefit from divine protection during this "heavy labor" for the conversion of Asian souls. He also enjoined them to respect the orders of their masters and residential superiors, observing the intended structure and content of the program. Most important, students were instructed to pay attention to learning the correct pronunciation of the tones used in *guanhua,* the keys to learning spoken Mandarin. They were encouraged to repeat their lessons aloud every day to ensure proper pronunciation, "because as difficult as the tones are to grasp at first, they are as helpful for the rest of your life for speaking and writing Chinese words in Portuguese."[43]

During the initial six months of the course, Jesuit pupils were supposed to acquire a familiarity with spoken *guanhua* and to begin learning to read and write characters. Their first task was to start memorizing characters from a vocabulary list organized "as a *bifolio*," that is, with the Chinese terms and their definitions laid out in parallel columns of text. Manuel Dias also recommended using "the indices that Diego de Pantoja made." Vocabulary lists such as these can be found in European libraries, but it is not clear to which texts these instructions refer.[44] Jesuit masters could avail themselves of Nicolas Trigault's *Xiru ermu zi,* or "Western Scholars' Aid for the Ear and the Eye in Reading Characters" (first edition Hangzhou, 1626), for building their pupils' vocabularies. This text contains diagrams of Chinese characters organized according to the Western alphabet, presenting a phonetic method for memorizing characters and their correct pronunciation. Using a romanization and phonetization system modeled on Matteo Ricci's *Xizi qiji,* or "Miracle of Western Characters" (first edition Peking, 1605), Trigault's vocabulary was well received by Jesuits and literati alike, as evinced by its subsequent reprintings.[45] Students following the course of study outlined in the *ratio studiorum* were instructed to make use of accepted lexicons such as these. They were specifically warned against making their own lists, compositions which were alleged to be "nothing but a waste of time," since they "accustomed one to using inelegant style."[46]

The second component of the first stage of the program was designed to introduce students to speaking *guanhua* fluently. Just as students in the Society's European colleges were required to speak Latin to one another, so the *ratio studiorum* mandated that students speak Chinese at all times, except during their recreation periods.[47] But as João Rodrigues claimed in his *Arte Breve da Lingoa Iapoa,* true facility in a foreign tongue could come only if one enjoyed daily interactions with native speakers. Here the China Jesuits' limited numbers worked in their favor, since they were forced to employ servant boys at their residences who performed the duties apportioned to the order's temporal coadjutors elsewhere. In fact, the *ratio studiorum* recommended that residential superiors assign a domestic to each student so that they might practice speaking together in their free time. Manuel Dias also suggested that students be given "superintendence over the chores of the house," obliging them to engage with the servants at the residence on a daily basis about a variety of subjects related to managing a domestic economy—something they would all later do when they moved on to their own residences.[48]

One of the most important aspects of the initial training in spoken

Chinese was teaching indigenous forms of etiquette. The residential superiors were to provide the example of their own public comportment, gradually introducing the pupils to the "courtesies used when dealing with and speaking to the Chinese," as well as the accepted forms of table manners, the proper way to drink tea, "the way to arrange one's hair," and other culturally specific practices.[49] Students were also introduced to etiquette during their lessons by using "speech books" of the type employed by the missionaries since the 1590s. These texts consisted of dialogues designed to make Jesuits familiar with handling public interactions, such as with their literati friends or the members of their flocks. One such text was written by José Monteiro as an example of a polite exchange between a priest and a Chinese Christian:

Priest:
  What is your family name? = Kiaò yeù guèi sìm.
Christian:
  My family name is *Cham* = Çùi gîn çièn sìm *Chām* [Chang].
P: What is your Christian name? = Kiào çò xìn mŏ xìm mîm.
C: My Christian name is *Paulo* = Xìm mîm *Paò Lŏ.*
P: How old are you? = Yeù leào tō xào niên kì.
C: I am eighty-five years old = Yeù pă xĕ ù sùi.
P: What a beautiful age! = Haò cāo xeù.
C: I'm too old to be good for anything = Çùi gîn laò leaò mŏ cān.
P: How long have you been a Christian? = Fūm tiēn chù kiaò. Yèu leaò kì tō niên kì.
C: I've been a Christian since I was a child = Çûm yeù fūm kiaò.
P: Then the whole family is Christian = Yĕ kiā tū fūm kiaò leaò.
C: My wife is not Christian = Pì fâm mŏ yeu lîm sì.
P: Why don't you exhort her? = Çèm mŏ pù kiuèn lìm chìm.
C: I exhort her, she doesn't want to. She's got the Devil in her head = Kiuèn, pù kēm. Xì mò guèi tĭe têu.[50]

The authors of the *ratio studiorum* intended that by memorizing the intricacies of Chinese salutations and having the students reenact them, such mundane interchanges might become spontaneous. Other dialogues were also drawn up to teach the standard questions and responses to Chinese queries on points of Christian doctrine, or how to make small talk about travel, food, or the weather. Since the implicit goal of this program was to enable missionaries to make friends and influence people, it should come as no surprise that today's language programs employ, mutatis mutandis, the same type of teaching techniques.

The third part of the initial phase of the language program consisted of writing characters. For half an hour of each class day for these six months, the "Portuguese" instructor was to teach his pupils the correct order for making the brush strokes of each new character. The goal of these lessons was to learn "how to write them like the Chinese," and for this a native method of instruction was employed.[51] Students were instructed to use a text such as *Qianzi wen* (Thousand Character Classic), just as Matteo Ricci and Michele Ruggieri had done, and trace the characters on sheets of fine paper. Pupils were reminded how important it was for them to develop a "great facility in writing Chinese well," and were instructed to pay close attention to learning the accepted method of romanizing Chinese terms "with aspirations and accents." At this phase, the authors of the *ratio studiorum* thought that writing short texts would be a "waste of time" and suggested that the students should rather translate "part of their past lessons into Portuguese or Latin" for an hour on Sundays or feast days. The aim of such exercises was not to produce literal translations but to prove that the students had understood the meaning of the Chinese phrases.[52]

Confucian Canon Fodder

Once equipped with a basic knowledge of the language, students entered the second phase of the program prescribed in the *ratio studiorum.* This phase consisted of a year and a half of lessons with a "Portuguese" master on Chinese thought, that is, reading texts from the Confucian canon. During their lessons, pupils would come to understand the structure of classical Chinese and how it differed from spoken *guanhua,* while being introduced to the foundations of Chinese history, philosophy, and law. As they worked their way through the various parts of the *Sishu,* or *Four Books,* their "Portuguese" master would discourse on style and grammar while offering glosses on the textual content. Students were issued copies of the works read during their lessons and encouraged to make notes in the margins of these texts to keep for later reference. As Manuel Dias did not fail to comment, annotating readily available texts was less expensive and time-consuming than copying out the works by hand.[53]

The *ratio studiorum* clearly outlines the structure of the "Portuguese" master's lessons. The primary template for the teaching techniques employed in China was that used by the Society elsewhere to teach Latin or Greek literature, a model that was familiar to all the missionaries. Each lesson consisted of readings from sequential passages in a given Chinese text, with the instructor explaining "not only the meaning of each individual character, but especially the meaning of the whole phrase and what it corresponds to in Portuguese or Latin." He would also elaborate on the grammatical construction of each sentence. Particular attention was to be paid to characters that appeared in the text for the first time. Lessons would end each day with explanations of the more confusing parts of each passage and with a few selected phrases. Twice each week the master was to assign compositions for homework, typically on subjects found in that week's readings. When the students had progressed to the end of the text they had been analyzing, the instructor would reread the text aloud, "as Latin books are read in our schools for the benefit of the listeners."[54]

As might be expected, given the attention to detail that marks the *ratio studiorum,* Dias and his consultors also specified the texts to be taught. The Vice-Provincial was charged with making sure that the approved curriculum for the first two years of the program was limited to the dialogue books mentioned in the previous section, the *Sishu,* and the *Shujing,* meaning that a year and a half was devoted to the *Great Learning,* the *Doctrine of the Mean,* the *Analects,* the *Mencius,* and the *Documents Classic.* The last of these titles belongs to the *Wujing,* or *Five Classics,* and deals primarily with historical events from China's remote antiquity. But if residential superiors were to purchase copies of the *Five Classics* for their students, the pupils might be tempted to read on through the other texts found there. The *ratio studiorum* permitted that for the *Yijing,* or *Book of Changes,* and even suggested using the *Changes* for lessons—albeit sparingly, because "this book has little for us," as Dias put it. But when it came to others of the *Five Classics,* that is, the *Book of Odes,* the *Record of Rites,* and the *Spring and Autumn Annals,* Dias was emphatic. They were "useless for our men," was his verdict, and were to be kept out of the missionaries' classrooms.[55]

The works selected for this curriculum reveal that by the 1620s the Jesuits had reached some conclusions about how much engagement with indigenous intellectual traditions was necessary for making successful missionaries. The choice of the *Four Books,* works read by every contemporary schoolboy, indicates their desire to be versed in the standard literary referents, philosophical precepts, and cultural register used by many of their prospective interlocutors. The prescribed use of the "ordinary gloss," in all probability referring to the commentaries by Zhu Xi (1130–1200) that were found in most editions of the *Sishu* in the seventeenth century, further confirms their intent to enter the common contemporary frame of reference.[56] Passages from these texts would enable the Jesuits—with no small amount of logical and rhetorical gymnastics—to suggest to educated Chinese that their traditions (when stripped of their Buddhist and Daoist accretions) were at least congenial to Christian teachings and at best contained traces of divine revelation. The principle of utility can likewise be observed in their selection of the *Documents Classic* and parts of the *Book of Changes.* In the *Documents,* the Jesuits discovered descriptions of Chinese civilization before the birth of Christ that they could compare to the accounts of Western society found in the Old Testament or classical antiquity. More specifically, they found the terms *Tian* (Heaven) and *Shangdi* (Lord on High) used to refer to a deity who responded to human pleas.[57] The cryptic style of the *Changes,* rich in symbolism, offered a wealth of possibilities for analogy with elements of Christian revelation—opportunities for suggesting that China had known the Judeo-Christian God before the advent of Buddhism.

The last phase of the language program involved a systematic review of the materials taught in the first two years. That review was to be undertaken from a different perspective, lest the misunderstandings of one generation of missionaries be passed on to the following one. Fearing just that, the authors of the *ratio studiorum* planned for pupils to spend two full years under a Chinese master who was not one of their confreres. On the one hand, a native master would give students a true insider's view of indigenous culture. On the other, he would be able to teach composition and style far better than someone who was not a native speaker. Such masters were not hard to find, especially in the Jiangnan region, where unemployed literati and failed civil service candidates abounded during the late Ming and early Qing periods. Although Manuel Dias stipulated that these masters be "well versed" in Chinese books, the content of this part of the program set the bar for prospective teachers low. In late imperial China it was not hard to find someone who could read the *Four Books,* the *Documents Classic,* and the *Book of Changes,* as well as teach the elements of style and composition.

Before hiring a Chinese master, however, the Jesuits needed to negotiate a favorable contract and make sure they got the most for their money. The expenses for language teachers were paid out of the Vice-Province's meager financial reserves, and that fact encouraged the missionaries to find masters who not only were diligent but also agreed to serve for a fair, if not discounted, wage.[58] It appears that whenever possible, they preferred to hire literati converts. Once a Chinese master was hired, the residential superior had the duty of maintaining good relations between him and the students. The superior was to model his approach to the master according to native employment practices, so that the instructor enjoyed his teaching and "did not complain." On occasion, however, attempting to force the European academic calendar onto the pattern of Chinese life proved difficult—for example, when the residential superiors sought to discourage the master from taking a long holiday break at the time of the Chinese New Year celebrations.[59]

The structure of the lessons to be given by the Chinese master was similar to the one prescribed for the "Portuguese" master. The missionary-students were to go through the *Four Books* and the *Documents Classic* in order. There would be two hours of lessons each day. The Chinese master was to respond to any questions that might arise about his explanations of the texts and expound the significance of every character. Pupils were meant to get a solid grounding in the teachings of the "sect of the literati," paying attention to the way they understood the creation of the world, its eventual end, the nature of man and of the soul, "and all the rest that pertains to Chinese philosophy." It was hoped that in the process of learning about these topics from a literatus, missionaries would be able to hone their rhetoric in anticipation of objections to their arguments that they might face during their proselytizing activities. The master was instructed to use the "ordinary gloss," that is, Zhu Xi's commentary, but could also make use of the "gloss of *Cham Colao*."[60] This text, the *Sishu jizhu zhijie,* was written by Grand Secretary Zhang Juzheng (1525–1582) in colloquial style as a primer for the young Wanli emperor. From it, students would obtain a brief introduction to state orthodoxy as understood by their near contemporaries in the Ming era.[61]

The Chinese master was also charged with training his pupils in elegant composition. But while the *ratio studiorum* stipulated two weekly lessons on writing style, it also specified that these lessons were not to teach the "style of *Vem Cham,*" that is, the style used for writing (*bagu*) *wenzhang,* or eight-legged essays, for the civil service examinations.[62] The Jesuits intended to mimic literati only up to a point. They were uninterested in acquiring the techniques of test-taking, the sine qua non for climbing onto the ladder of success in the imperial bureaucracy. It was far more important for them to learn the art of writing books persuasively, since it was expected that after completing their course of studies they would spend much of their free time composing apologetic tracts to further the cause of the Christian religion. In teaching composition, the Chinese master was to assign topics for essays that he would later correct. To acquaint students more fully with forms of social intercourse, the Chinese master was also to teach pupils how to write correspondence, both short notes and longer letters. Once they had completed the language program and headed off to their assigned residences, such skills in conducting public affairs would be a great boon to the missionaries, who were often obliged to deal with members of the social elite on their own.

This discussion has assumed that the pupils in the course sketched in the *ratio studiorum* were both European Jesuits and Macanese coadjutors. Yet since those in the latter group were to be freighted with the duty of serving as language instructors in the future, the *ratio studiorum* concludes with a series of additional obligations for them. Whereas priests were entrusted with learning and remembering the lessons on their own, coadjutors were to memorize the contents of the *Four Books* and the *Documents Classic* and recite what they had learned to the master each day. During the summer recess of the second year of the program, these students were to be drilled on part of the contents of the Jesuits' apologetic works, "at least enough to make them able to speak about the books with the Chinese who ask about them."[63]

In order to become more useful auxiliaries, coadjutors were also to learn from a trained missionary how to catechize Chinese Christians. This instruction was to take place during the holidays of the third year of the program, when they were in the middle of their lessons with the Chinese master. According to the *ratio studiorum,* the content of the catechetical message was of central importance, and the aim of these lessons was to make sure that the brothers knew precisely what Chinese terms to use. In light of the controversies current in the 1620s over the use of certain phrases to signify Christian concepts, it is not surprising that the instructor who taught these lessons was also charged with making clear which terms were not to be used "since they do not match the truth of each mystery." Finally, each student was to learn how to present an abbreviated catechism to prospective converts on their deathbeds, "when there is not time to catechize perfectly."[64] Equipped with the same competency in language (if not in performing rituals) as priests, coadjutors became an integral part of the Vice-Province's division of labor. On reaching an acceptable level of fluency, priests were to begin preaching to the domestics in their residences once every two weeks and hearing the confessions of the local Christians.[65] Coadjutors, by contrast, were assigned the more routine and repetitive task of teaching doctrine, a chore for which priests would have increasingly less time as the seventeenth century went on.

Sapientia Sinica

In 1624 Manuel Dias submitted the *ratio studiorum* to Visitor Jerónimo Rodrigues for evaluation and implementation. It remains unclear if the Visitor ever ordered the Vice-Province's superiors to use the program exactly as it was proposed, since subsequent documents from the mission do not specifically mention the plan of studies. Nevertheless, evidence found in Annual Letters, administrative orders and reports, and epistolary sources makes a detailed reconstruction of the language program employed by the Vice-Province after 1624 possible. From these documents, one can see that the Jesuits initially adhered to the program outlined in the *ratio studiorum*. Over the remaining decades of the seventeenth century, however, that program was subjected to alterations in response to a number of factors. The most important of these was the Vice-Province's chronic lack of recruits. The skills gained by the missionaries from their training program made them far more effective in their work of conversion than could have been expected from their numbers. Paradoxically, this success created pastoral burdens that forced a reduction in the amount of time later recruits were allotted for studying. By the beginning of the eighteenth century, the Jesuits of the Vice-Province, with the exception of the missionaries at Peking, had all but abandoned the systematic study of Chinese thought in favor of sending new arrivals to minister to native Christians as rapidly as possible.

When the Jesuits left their secluded quarters in Hangzhou and Macau in 1623 to return to the mission field, they needed a new site for holding their language courses. After all, with a shift in the political winds in Peking, a change in the status of the mission, and an infusion of new blood from Europe thanks to Nicolas Trigault, the missionaries could rightfully anticipate that their ranks would swell. Yet their list of possible locations was not extensive. Neither Macau nor Nanjing would do, and the Peking house was too public an environment for training students. Of the residences in Jiangnan, the Hangzhou and Shanghai houses were busy centers of religious activity, places where pupils might easily become distracted from their studies. The best choice appeared to be the town of Jiading, a short distance from Shanghai, where Inácio Sun Yuanhua had offered the missionaries part of his palace as a residence in 1621. At once in the Jiangnan region, at close proximity to the Society's other establishments, and without the demands and distractions of a substantial local Christian community, Jiading was an ideal setting.

Perhaps the best aspect of the Jiading residence was that it was situated within the private compound of an imperial official. This fact ensured that the students enjoyed protection and seclusion, as well as spacious grounds for recreation. The Vice-Province had earmarked the Jiading house for language training as early as 1623; it is known that Álvaro Semedo was training a priest, Johann Terrenz Schreck, and a coadjutor, Pascoal Mendes, there that year.[66] Writing in the Annual Letter for the following year, Francisco Furtado had little to say about the residence, which did "not attend to conversions" but rather accommodated "the class of language and letters." By 1624 the Vice-Province's superiors had sent a total of three priests and three brothers to study at Jiading. The house was described as "very commodious" for the purpose of teaching Chinese but not nearly as serviceable if there were "a crowd of catechumens and cultivation of Christians" for the missionaries to handle. The students made considerable progress in the calm of Sun's palace, and it was claimed that in just over two years, one of the priests could read Chinese books and "understand them as well as Latin ones." Those who had commenced their studies in the late summer of 1623 had allegedly learned "more than five thousand characters" in eight months of lessons and were able to reproduce them "by heart without going to see the vocabulary."[67]

With a sufficient number of students and a proper teaching environment, the Jesuits were able to enact the *ratio studiorum* at Jiading. Reports from 1625 and 1626 indicate that the residence was run like a small college, with a Jesuit instructor teaching three priests and six students from Macau. It was duly noted that this concentration of missionaries lived in community "without making many Christians."[68] As the 1620s drew to a close, it appeared that the Vice-Province had successfully put its classroom-style teaching program on a solid footing. Indeed, it appeared that the creation of the "college" at Jiading would meet the training needs of the mission for decades to follow.

But those appearances were deceptive, and a change in the political climate forced the Jesuits to abandon this residence. By 1631 the missionaries were no doubt aware of the trouble that might arise from their links to Sun Yuanhua, their patron who stood accused of treason. When Licentiate Inácio was condemned for fomenting revolt against the Chongzhen emperor and beheaded in 1632, the missionaries left Jiading. This move was meant to protect them from an official backlash and, as Francesco Brancati later recorded, to forestall any potential persecution against the local Christians.[69] In any event, the Vice-Province lost its dedicated teaching facility. Jiading was the last residence to be used almost exclusively for conducting missionary training.

The loss of Jiading must have came as a blow to the Jesuits' hopes of giving their Chinese enterprise more solid institutional foundations. But in fact, the mission's expansion, beginning in the 1630s, quickly rendered the idea of that type of group training impracticable. By 1636 the Vice-Province had eleven residences, all of which needed men. With only twenty-five European priests and four Macanese coadjutors, it was impossible for the mission superiors to consider bringing even four or five Jesuits together in one house.[70] This exigency did not mean a radical departure from the teaching methods prescribed by the *ratio studiorum,* because the rules laid down in that document were flexible enough to conform to any class size or location. For example, in 1631 one priest was responsible for teaching another at Hangzhou, while at Nanchang another missionary was charged with giving lessons to two recent arrivals.[71] So the shift from a "college" model of teaching to one in which newly arrived priests were assigned to live with experienced missionaries who doubled as their instructors does not appear to have jeopardized the curriculum. In 1631 Visitor André Palmeiro reiterated the main lines of the teaching program put forth seven years previously. After reviewing and approving the content and structure of the current course of studies, Palmeiro exhorted the students to diligence and ordered them not to distract themselves with "curiosities and instruments," although he conceded that missionaries with technical skills could use such implements in moderation "to alleviate their studies."[72]

The shift away from a system of language teaching at a centralized location to a method of teaching by apprenticeship at dispersed mission stations had its costs and its benefits. While it spread the teaching burden from the shoulders of one to those of several missionaries, it diminished the uniformity and, indeed, the quality of the instruction. Even as the Vice-Province was enabled by the change to distribute its manpower more evenly, the trained missionaries at each residence were obliged to divide their time between their pastoral or proselytizing activities and their teaching duties. Given the pace of the mission's expansion, however, the Jesuits had no choice but to dilute their resources among their residences and hope that new arrivals would learn the language quickly enough to take on their part of their pastoral responsibilities. It is possible that the change in teaching methods had the effect of raising morale among new recruits, who surely found the prospect of having to commit themselves to years of language study frustrating. Involving the language students in the routine activities of mission station life soon after their arrival instead of sequestering them meant that they would acquire a new tongue, gain experience in dealing with Chinese Christians, and begin to realize their vocations as missionaries all at the same time.

How the change was carried out in the 1630s can be reconstructed from the Vice-Province's personnel catalogue for 1634. This document shows that senior Jesuits had been assigned to guide each of the students in the acquisition of Chinese. For example, at the Kaifeng residence in Henan Province, Rodrigo de Figueiredo, described as "very skilled in the language and letters," was entrusted with teaching Pietro Canevari. In Jiangzhou, Shanxi Province, Étienne Faber received his lessons from two confreres, Alfonso Vagnone and Brother Francisco de Lagea (1585–1647). Similarly, Francisco Furtado and Brother Francisco Ferreira (1604–1652) were responsible for teaching Chinese to Michel Trigault at Xi'an. At Fuzhou, in Fujian Province, Inácio Lobo had three teachers to learn from, namely, Simão da Cunha, Bento de Matos (1600–ca. 1657), and Brother Manuel Gomes. At Nanchang, Álvaro Semedo taught Tranquillo Grassetti; at Jianchang, Gaspar Ferreira taught Inácio da Costa; and at Shanghai, Pedro Ribeiro taught Agostino Tudeschini.[73] At least one consequence of this type of training is worth noting. In general, Jesuits stayed in the areas where they studied the language, suggesting that their simultaneous dealings with instructors and local Christians enabled them to acquire *guanhua* as well as the regional dialect at the same time. Once they were capable of speaking to both the elite and the plebeians in a given region, it would have been counterproductive to shift them to other areas.

But was the *ratio studiorum* indeed preserved after the shift to decentralized teaching? Given the pressures created by the mission's expansion, was it possible for the Jesuits to maintain their goal of giving each new arrival years of lessons in Chinese thought? The notebooks kept by Francesco Brancati during his language training in the late 1630s illuminate the issue. This Sicilian Jesuit arrived at Macau in 1636. Early the next year, Vice-Provincial Francisco Furtado escorted him and three other recent arrivals, Ludovico Buglio, João Monteiro, and Girolamo Gravina, into China. On their trek northward, Furtado left Buglio and Monteiro at Nanchang in Jiangxi Province to hear lessons from Brother Francisco Ferreira. The Vice-Provincial entrusted Gaspar Ferreira with teaching Gravina at Jianchang in the same province and brought Brancati to the Shanghai residence for his training, leaving the Sicilian in the company of veteran missionary Pedro Ribeiro and Brother Manuel Gomes. It was Gomes who was responsible for conducting the lessons. Francisco Furtado claimed that this coadjutor, the son of a Javanese father and a Chinese mother who had been raised in Macau speaking Portuguese, knew the Chinese "language and letters well." By the time he began to teach Brancati, Gomes was almost thirty years old. He had spent half his life working with the China Jesuits. Confident in the combination of the priest's abilities and the coadjutor's experience, Furtado informed Visitor Manuel Dias the elder of his certainty that in "one or two years" Brancati would be able to contribute to the mission.[74]

Brancati's progress may be traced from a series of annotations in his personal editions of the *Four Books,* today preserved in the central archives of the Society of Jesus in Rome. Recall that the *ratio studiorum* permitted missionary-students to write in their copies of the Chinese texts. The Sicilian filled the margins—and almost every free space in each of the six volumes—with comments in Latin, Portuguese, romanized *guanhua,* and at times Italian. From the way Brancati wrote his annotations, it appears that Gomes gave his explanations of the texts in Portuguese (the definitions interspersed among the characters are most often in this language). At times, however, Brancati also jotted down notes in other languages. Key passages are often highlighted in the text with "index hands" pointing to specific characters; occasionally, there are references to works from the

Western canon. After digesting the content of each chapter, Brancati would write a summary in Latin in the margin above the Chinese text.[75]

Most important for our purposes here are the dates recorded by Brancati at various intervals in the text. In the lower margin of the first page of the *Da Xue,* or *Great Learning,* he wrote, "We began 8 May 1637, *ad maiorem Dei gloriam.*"[76] This springtime date suggests that the priest had already gained the prescribed familiarity with spoken *guanhua* during his travels with Francisco Furtado (a gifted linguist who translated parts of Aristotle's works and their associated commentaries into Chinese) and during the first months he spent at Shanghai. Each of the six volumes that Brancati read consisted of approximately seventy double-sided pages, with nine columns of text on each page (Zhu Xi's commentaries were printed in double columns). By June 4, 1637, Brancati and Gomes had proceeded through the first volume of their text (including the *Zhongyong,* or *Doctrine of the Mean*) and were beginning the second chapter of the *Lunyu,* or *Analects.*[77] Over the course of the following month and a half, they would continue to read that work until they paused for a summer vacation between August 6 and September 24.[78] When Francesco Brancati recommenced his studies in the early autumn of 1637, he spent a month finishing his lessons on the *Analects* and started to read the *Mencius,* the longest of the *Four Books,* on October 28.[79] This text would take more than three months to read, with a minor break at Christmastime, lasting until January 11, 1638.[80] It can safely be assumed that the pair of Jesuits completed their reading of the *Sishu* around the time of the Chinese New Year celebrations. It is unclear whether Brancati and Gomes continued to read the *Documents Classic* and passages from the *Book of Changes* during the spring months of 1638, but in light of their swift progress through the *Four Books,* it seems likely that they did.

Brancati's notebooks offer a number of insights into the way the Jesuits conducted their language training in the seventeenth century's middle decades. They confirm the basic outline of the *ratio studiorum,* that is, an initial immersion in spoken *guanhua* followed by a series of guided readings from the Confucian canon. Brancati evidently finished his lessons with Gomes in a year and a half, or six months less than the prescribed two years of study with the "Portuguese" master. One reason for this expeditious pace may have been that they skimmed over the "ordinary gloss," something that may be inferred from the fact that the Sicilian priest left few annotations among the columns of commentary by Zhu Xi. Did

Dixit in quo consistat humana ac mundana perfectio, posuitque illas tria, scilicet lumen naturale, renovare populum, et in vero vel summo bono seu tranquillitate ultimatus terminus eius perfectionis. Nunc vero in hoc cap. tradit modum quomodo ad illa tria pervenire possimus.

Cognito fine illico habetur in operibus determinatio; cum si quis operetur et nullum habeat in operando finem, nullam potest habere in suis operibus determinationem. Determinatione iam cognita quod tale vel tale opus nobis agendum est ad finem consequendum, tunc possumus animo minime in varias res distrahi. Dum vero quieto animo fuerimus, tranquilla quidem illico fruemur pace. In hac tranquillitate positi optime poterimus speculari; speculando vero ac discurrendo illud summum bonum assequi poterimus.

Cum ipsae res omnes (velut arbores) suas habeant radices ac ramos, omnesque item et originem et [illegible] si quis noverit quod est in re prius, quod [illegible] poterit, iam proximus est ad bonum [illegible]

當推以及人。使之亦有以去其舊染之汙也。止者，必至於是而不遷之意。至善，則事理當然之極也。言明明德、新民，皆當止於至善之地而不遷。蓋必其有以盡夫天理之極，而無一毫人欲之私也。此三者，大學之綱領也。

知止而后有定，定而后能靜，靜而后能安，安而后能慮，慮而后能得。

后與後同，後倣此。止者，所當止之地，即至善之所在也。知之，則志有定向。靜，謂心不妄動。安，謂所處而安。慮，謂處事精詳。得，謂得其所止。

物有本末，事有終始。知所先後，則近道矣。

明德為本，新民為末。知止為始，能得為終。本始所先，末終所後。此結上文兩節之意。

古之欲明明德於天下者，先治其國；欲治其國者，先齊其家；欲齊其

Aristotelica doctrina 7 phys. t. 19
Anima sedendo et quiescendo fit prudens

Brancati continue his studies with a Chinese master in the two years after finishing with Gomes, as he was supposed to? No evidence suggests that. If indeed the missionary had to forgo the final component of his studies, he would have benefited from only half the recommended program. In either case, Brancati would have had little time for academic pursuits after finishing up with Gomes. By midsummer 1638, both Pedro Ribeiro and the Macanese coadjutor had moved on to Hangzhou, leaving Brancati in charge of the largest Christian community in China.[81]

Other Jesuits who began their studies in the late 1630s also experienced acceleration in the pace of their training. Descriptions of how Lodovico Buglio, Brancati's compatriot, studied Chinese suggest that much of the moderation considered necessary for healthy study by the authors of the *ratio studiorum* had been abandoned. According to Buglio's necrology, he allowed nothing to impede his progress, going to the point of decorating the walls and bookshelves of his cubicle with characters to facilitate memorizing them.[82] It does not appear that he spent any more time than Brancati on his studies. In October 1639, less than three years after he first entered China, he was assigned to open a new mission in Sichuan Province by himself. In contrast with Brancati, whose pastoral burdens were and remained onerous, however, in later decades Buglio enjoyed comparative ease at Peking, permitting him to engage in further study.

The abbreviated course of study followed by Francesco Brancati and Lodovico Buglio in 1637 and 1638 was representative of a trend in the evolution of the Jesuits' language teaching over the course of the seventeenth century. As the stream of recruits from Europe was reduced to a trickle and the numbers of new Christians swelled to a flood, newly arrived priests could not be kept out of the action for years of lessons. Instead, the Vice-Province's superiors sacrificed the academic integrity of the missionaries' language training for the spiritual good of their expanding flock. To be sure, by the late 1630s the political position of the mission had changed to such an extent that not every priest needed to be a carbon copy of Matteo Ricci. With a handful of men ensconced at Peking, ensuring the

---

Annotated folio from the *Great Learning (Daxue),* in the *Four Books (Sishu),* printed ca. 1630. Francesco Brancati wrote the commentaries on this folio during his lessons with Manuel Gomes in 1637.

protection of their colleagues in the provinces, the heaviest academic burden fell on the former, while the latter could content themselves with training in Christian vocabulary and a basic knowledge of the Confucian canon. Such skills sufficed for proselytizing, mostly among plebeians, and dealing with the growing numbers of Christians.

For all that, the cost of shortening the missionary training program was high. As the Jesuits reduced the amount of time they devoted to study, they necessarily diminished their capacity to compose books in Chinese. From Ricci's day until the middle of the seventeenth century, almost all of the missionaries were involved in the production of apologetic, devotional, or scientific texts. For example, his multiple responsibilities notwithstanding, Manuel Dias the younger, who served as Visitor in 1614–15 and as Vice-Provincial from 1623 until 1635 and again from 1650 until 1654, composed a number of Chinese works during his years in Jiangxi, Fujian, and Zhejiang. In addition to his fourteen-volume *Shengjing zhijie* (1636–1642), a partial translation of a set of commentaries on the gospel readings used during the liturgical year, Dias wrote an explanation of the Ten Commandments (*Tianzhu shengjiao shijie zhiquan,* 1659); a treatise responding to doubts about Christian doctrine *(Taiyi lun);* a text on astronomy called *Catechism on the Heavens* (*Tianwen lüe,* 1615); an explanation of the Nestorian stele unearthed near Xi'an and of other Christian monuments found in Fujian, titled *Tang jingjiao beisong zhengquan* (Commentary on the Laudatory Inscription of the Luminous Religion of the Tang, 1644); and a translation of Luis de Granada's version of *Contemptus Mundi (Qingshi jinshu).*[83] According to his necrology, Dias also left a translation of Granada's catechism and an explanation of the sacraments in terms of scholastic theology among other works "which could not be printed owing to the poverty of the mission."[84]

Later generations of priests would, on the whole, have neither the training nor the opportunity for sustaining this sort of publication effort. The general decline in the numbers of converts from the elite meant that there were fewer patrons willing to shoulder the costs of printing new books, and the general penury of the mission meant that the Jesuits could not afford to pay for more than the reprinting of old works or the publication of short new tracts. But the fact that the missionaries were no longer trained in composition was also an integral factor. An overview of the surviving collections of texts written by the Jesuits in Chinese reveals that after the Canton exile, the production of new works (both religious and scientific) was largely monopolized by the priests at Peking, such as Ferdinand Verbiest and Lodovico Buglio. The court Jesuits enjoyed significant advantages over their brethren in the provinces. Their sphere of activity was circumscribed, that is, largely limited to the capital city itself, and they had comparatively few pastoral burdens. Moreover, those priests who worked at the Astronomical Bureau carried out tasks that were more academic in nature than those shouldered by their confreres, whose pastoral duties gradually consumed ever greater amounts of time.

One should not assume that the overall decrease in the number of compositions meant that later generations of Jesuits were somehow incapable of comprehending indigenous thought or expressing their own conceptions in Chinese. Instead, this trend reflected the evolving demands of the Vice-Province as the focus of the missionaries' efforts shifted away from currying favor among the elite and toward evangelizing the ranks of the unlettered. The cases of Philippe Couplet and Prospero Intorcetta, both of whom reached China in 1659 and worked in the Jiangnan region, cast light on the language program experienced by the generation of missionaries who followed that of Francesco Brancati. Couplet's first assignment was the study of language at Ganzhou in Jiangxi Province under the direction of Brother António Fernandes (1620–1670). The most pressing demands on the missionaries at that residence were pastoral, and local superior Jacques Le Faure was no doubt pleased that after only one year Couplet was "well enough versed in the language to attend to baptisms, confessions, and preaching."[85] Once he had acquired linguistic skills sufficient for handling duties of this type, the Flemish Jesuit could take up the study of the Confucian canon. Although it remains unclear if Fernandes instructed Couplet as Gomes taught Brancati, there is no doubt that Couplet was familiar with the *Four Books* and the *Documents Classic;* after all, he compiled a chronology of Chinese dynasties titled *Tabula Chronologica Monarchiae Sinicae* and was one of the translators who worked on the Latin edition of the *Four Books,* called *Confucius Sinarum Philosophus.*

As Couplet was studying at Ganzhou, Prospero Intorcetta was also engaged in a language program not far away at Jianchang. He took lessons from Vice-Provincial Inácio da Costa, at the same residence where Costa himself had learned from Gaspar Ferreira. The Vice-Provincial had escorted Intorcetta to Jianchang with the purpose of introducing him to the local mandarins and Christians—another invaluable aspect of the "apprenticeship" style of teaching—and instructing him in native philoso-

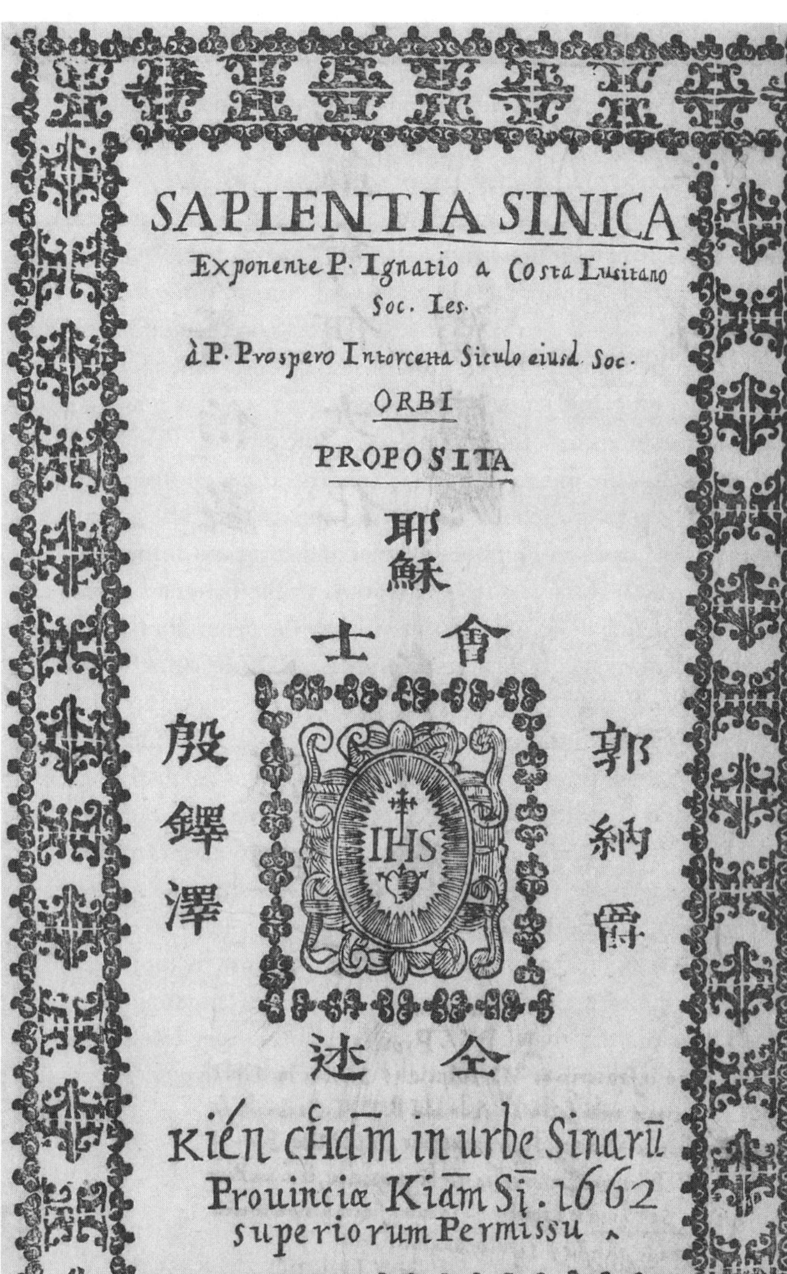

SAPIENTIA SINICA

Exponente P. Ignatio a Costa Lusitano Soc. Ies.

à P. Prospero Intorcetta Siculo eiusd. Soc.

ORBI

PROPOSITA

耶穌會士

郭納爵

殷鐸澤

全述

KIÉN CHĀM in urbe Sinarū

Prouinciæ Kiām Sī. 1662

superiorum Permissu

phy.[86] While undergoing instruction, Intorcetta kept detailed notes on his readings. A synopsis of what he had learned about the *Four Books* was published in 1662. This text, called *The Meaning of Chinese Wisdom as explained by Fr. Ignacio da Costa, Portuguese, of the Society of Jesus, and made public by Fr. Prospero Intorcetta, Sicilian, of the same Society,* contained Latin versions of the *Great Learning* and the *Analects* along with Costa's glosses and key terms in romanization. It was the first translation of selections from the *Sishu* to be printed in a European language.[87]

Perhaps the most telling aspect of Intorcetta's *Chinese Wisdom* is that it was intended to serve as a teaching tool. According to its dedicatory preface, Intorcetta published his explanation of the two texts for the use of other missionaries not just in China but throughout the Confucian cultural sphere, from Southeast Asia to Korea. Ostensibly, his purpose was to encourage his peers to engage with the dominant native philosophical tradition so that they could see how well it conformed to "natural law and Christian wisdom."[88] Yet it is undeniable that the strains felt by the Vice-Province spurred the Jesuits to produce textual substitutes for the personal training they had previously afforded new recruits. When they were confronted with the pressing need to keep the Society's residences occupied, the superiors of the Vice-Province took the option of sending recent arrivals off to mission stations by themselves after no more than a crash course in speaking Chinese.

The new recruits could be issued a copy of Intorcetta's *Sapientia Sinica* or the translation he produced of the *Doctrine of the Mean,* printed with the title *Sinarum Scientia Politico-Moralis* (Canton, 1667; Goa, 1670), and told to learn about Chinese philosophy on their own. Before the 1660s, the Jesuits were not yet in such dire straits. The Calendar Case of 1664 and their ensuing confinement at Canton spared them from having to confront this issue for the better part of a decade. That circumstances would drive them to adopt such a drastic expedient, however, remained all too distinct a possibility in the offing.

Frontispiece to the first printed translation into a Western language of part of the Confucian *Four Books.* From Prospero Intorcetta, *Sapientia Sinica* (Jianchang, 1662).

"The Only Brief Way"

The Jesuits who left their confinement at Canton in 1671 found themselves overwhelmed by pastoral burdens created by the expansion of the Christian communities in their absence. The years that followed saw the situation grow worse, as few recruits arrived to replace the dead or join the efforts of the living. If there was a silver lining to this cloud, however, it was that not much of the veterans' time had to be devoted to teaching new confreres.

When new missionaries did arrive, the Vice-Province turned to its standard pool of instructors, its coadjutors. By the 1680s some of these were poised to be ordained as priests, but one responsibility still rested squarely on their shoulders: after completing the novitiate, they were to serve as "masters of Chinese language and letters" for the new missionaries.[89] The men selected for ordination were all literati; presumably they were more qualified teachers than the "sons of Macau" who had learned the Chinese classics from Europeans. After all, the first component of the language program that was stripped from the course outlined in the *ratio studiorum* was the time spent with a Chinese master. So the Vice-Province's reliance on its first Chinese priests to provide language instruction represents a significant change of course. Indeed, so important was Paulo Banhes Wan Qiyuan considered for this task that when he mysteriously disappeared in 1691, other Jesuits voiced their greatest concerns not so much over his deserting his mission station as over his decamping before he had finished teaching Francisco Pinto.[90]

To be sure, the Chinese men who became Jesuit priests in 1688 were not the only ones responsible for language teaching. Senior missionaries trained younger men who were to assist them in their old age. This was the case with Jean Valat, the French superior of the Jinan residence in Shandong Province, who died in 1696 at the venerable age of eighty-two. During the last decade of his life Valat was assisted by a number of young recruits, turning his residence into a "school from which issued excellent missionaries."[91] Among his pupils were men such as Miguel de Amaral, Francisco Pinto, and Antonio Faglia (1663–1706), all of whom spent time as missionaries in Shandong or North Zhili provinces.

If there was anywhere in the Vice-Province where the need to study language and literature had grown over the course of the seventeenth century, it was Peking. Not only were the court Jesuits obliged to master the essentials of Chinese philosophy, but their high visibility and frequent dealings with the Kangxi emperor and members of the imperial clan of the Qing dynasty meant that they also had to learn the Manchu tongue, and the Vice-Province contracted with Manchu masters and Chinese masters to take care of facets of instruction that were dispensed with in the provinces.[92] But despite the favorable conditions for language training found at Peking, it was no easy task for newly arrived Jesuits to match the standards of erudition set by such predecessors as Johann Adam Schall and Ferdinand Verbiest. That it was hard going indeed can be surmised from the words of Antoine Thomas, who reported within a year of arriving in China in 1686 that he was pushing himself because unless he demonstrated dexterity in handling "the Chinese characters and books," the mandarins would find him "incapable of filling the place of Father Verbiest."[93] Peking missionaries such as Thomas appear to have spent so much time on their studies that they ignored other duties. During an inspection of the capital's residences in 1689, Jean Valat felt compelled to remind the court Jesuits to engage actively with their spiritual charges, citing the benefits of greater interaction "both for helping to learn the language quickly and for increasing the fervor and level of instruction of the Christians."[94]

In the two decades from the 1670s until the 1690s, the Vice-Province received so few recruits that the training of provincial missionaries was gradually reduced to the bare minimum, that is, a short course in spoken *guanhua* supplemented by readings in the *Four Books*. Even when a fresh influx of priests arrived in China (between 1688 and 1697 the number of priests in the Vice-Province jumped from nineteen to forty-two), the challenges posed by the coming of the French Jesuits and members of other religious orders were too serious for the Vice-Province to contemplate holding language classes in the manner prescribed by the *ratio studiorum*.[95] Of paramount importance for the mission were the tasks of occupying the territories claimed by Jesuits in the past and assuming a pastoral presence in as many Christian communities as possible to impede the arrival of competitors. The situation of the Vice-Province was precarious, giving it little choice but to accelerate its training program, abandoning all pretense of matching the formation given to previous generations of missionaries, including those who had learned Chinese in little over a year.

New solutions to the old problem were not lacking, however. An excellent example of the Vice-Province's effort to expedite the formation of its new members is a text written by José Monteiro around the turn of the eighteenth century. As a clear indication of its purpose, Monteiro called his work "The True and Only Brief Method for Quickly Learning to Speak the Chinese Language which by its nature is very difficult . . . For Use in Training Missionaries."[96] Its contents were a grammar textbook, vocabulary lists, and confessional manual, and its primary objective was to enable priests to dispense with those aspects of training that did not directly pertain to their pastoral responsibilities, the duties of baptizing and confessing Christians in particular. A newly arrived missionary armed with this type of book could head directly to a provincial mission station where the number of Christians was greatest and the demand for the sacraments most intense. He would learn how to speak (not read or write) *guanhua* by memorizing the grammatical patterns and romanized terms found in the text and would have at his disposal a number of stock phrases for exhorting his spiritual charges to piety, but little else.

Monteiro was well aware of the predicaments faced by the Vice-Province around 1700. As a missionary in Fuzhou and the representative of the bishop of Macau in Fujian Province, he was on the front line of the Jesuits' battles against the Vicars Apostolic, an experience that no doubt contributed to his appointment to the post of Vice-Provincial from 1698 until 1702 and again from 1704 to 1707. His text appears to have been the closest that the China Jesuits ever came to producing an *arte* for *guanhua* after the fashion of João Rodrigues's *Arte Breve da Lingoa Iapoa.*[97]

To be sure, Monteiro observed a degree of brevity that makes Rodrigues's work seem prolix by comparison. The "prologue" to the "True and Only Brief Way" consists of a single sentence: "The Chinese language which is called Mandarin is like Latin among the Europeans since it is universally used in this most vast empire, and people who understand this language can be found in all parts of it." From here, Monteiro plunges into explanations of the sounds used in *guanhua* with reference to contemporary Portuguese and Latin pronunciation. He remarks that Mandarin "totally excludes the use of the letters B, D, and R," and that no Chinese word begins with the letters A or E: "To say *Amen,* the Chinese says yá mên; and to say *Ecclesia,* they say Nge ke le si ya."[98] Monteiro includes a description of the five tones of contemporary *guanhua* and an explanation of his system of romanization. The last parts of the grammar section present rules and examples for pronouns, adverbs, adjectives, and quantities, with lists of romanized terms attached. A dialogue between a Chinese Christian and a Jesuit completes this section (partially cited earlier), serving as a grammar exercise and an additional vocabulary list.

It is no small irony that more than a century after the Society of Jesus had begun training men in Chinese language and thought, Monteiro concluded that the "True and Only Brief Way" for becoming fluent quickly was by studying vocabulary lists, much in the manner of Michele Ruggieri and Matteo Ricci. To be sure, the Jesuits had always made use of such lists and had always counted on the ability of their brethren to memorize large numbers of terms. Yet Monteiro's method is crude and the phrases it presents are inelegant. His "Brief Way" leads not to fluency but to stilted speech. That said, however, it must be granted that a newly arrived missionary needed to know what to say to the members of his flock if he was to act as a pastor. In this instructional text, Christian vocabulary occupies a central place by necessity, and readers are exposed to such basic elements of doctrine as "God created heaven, earth, and all things from nothing = Tiēn chù çùm vû sēm tiēn tì vàn vĕ . . . Our merits are not enough for reaching eternal glory = Ngò mèn tiè cūm laô pù keù tĕ tiēn tâm tiĕ fŏ . . . Even the Devil obeys God = Liên mŏ guèi tìm Tiēn chù mìm."[99] Monteiro also treats such topics as the obligations of a Christian, the attributes of the rational soul, and other spiritual matters.

In addition, he directs attention to more practical, mundane affairs. Since his text was designed for use by men going off to residences by themselves, it necessarily had to teach recruits the words needed for managing a domestic economy. In the sections dealing with residences, one finds short phrases for addressing concerns to household servants. More expressions of this type can be found in the section relating to the kitchen and cooking, since it is clear that the missionaries always delegated this task to others. To give the appearance of fluency, Monteiro's text suggests, priests had to be able to complain about the food they were served:

This meat is not cooked enough = Chècò jŏ mŏ chù tĕ làn
It is half raw, or half cooked = Jŏ puòn sēm, puòn xŏ
These greens have no taste = Chècò çài mŏ ùi
They are too salty = Chècò çài hiên tĕ kìn
I cannot chew these greens = Chècò çài yāo pù tùm
The rice is poorly cooked = Fàn pù làn; pù xŏ, mŏ chù te xŏ
The rice has stones in it = Fàn yeù xĕ teû

This tea was made a while ago = Chècò châ pào tĕ kieù leaò
You used too few leaves = Fàm châ yĕ xaò leaò
This tea is poorly made = Chècò châ xaò pú haò[100]

Subsequent sections of Monteiro's manual take the reader from inside the mission station to society at large. Here, the organizing themes include clothing, family relationships, studies, provinces and cities, levels of officialdom, courts and law, soldiers and arms, professions, and food. One particularly useful part of the text for solitary missionaries is devoted to the human body and health, instructing sick Jesuits on the terms to use when describing their symptoms to Chinese doctors. The last part of the text, occupying a quarter of the whole work, consists of a series of dialogues in the form of a confessional manual. From this manual of casuistry, readers not only gained insight into how to interrogate penitents in the confessional but also learned which sins were typical of Chinese Christians, at least according to Monteiro.[101]

If one were to judge by Monteiro's "True and Only Brief Way" alone, it would appear that under the pressure of external challenges, the Jesuits had abandoned teaching their newly arrived colleagues the foundations of Chinese philosophy. Other sources, however, suggest that a connection between the missionaries and the *Four Books* persisted, even if it was the faintest shadow of what it had been in the halcyon days of the first half of the seventeenth century. One vocabulary list of Chinese terms contains at its end a short section titled "Sentences from the *Sishu* that a Priest should know in order to use them when arguing with Chinese Heathens." Here, on five sheets of paper, one finds excerpts from the *Great Learning* and the *Doctrine of the Mean,* transcribed in Chinese characters and Portuguese romanizations and accompanied by an explanation in Portuguese.[102]

The arguments presented in these "Sentences," based on those found in other Jesuit writings, were designed to show that the Confucian canon contained implicit and explicit references to the Christian God. To give but one example, the citations begin with the first line of the *Great Learning:* "What the Great Learning teaches, is—to illustrate illustrious virtue; to renovate the people; and to rest in the highest excellence."[103] According to the attached gloss, one can "clearly deduce" from this phrase that there is "an ultimate end where man must come to rest." Such is the case, the argument continues, "because it says that the true law and doctrine consist in making one able by following his understanding and natural inspiration to reach and rest at his ultimate end, which is the greatest goodness." The argument concludes that this *suma bondade,* translated earlier as "highest excellence," can be none other than God.[104] It is hard to believe that a missionary would willingly have entered into a debate with a Chinese literatus armed only with a handful of bons mots, but perhaps this was an indication of the priests' level of confidence in their religious message—or of their degree of resignation at the slim prospects of gaining new literati converts without more powerful rhetorical weapons at their disposal.

The use of "brief" methods for learning Chinese or lists of "choice phrases" plucked from the Confucian canon may have enabled the men of the Vice-Province to muster some form of control over their territorial gains in the mission field, but these were in reality a factor that would later contribute to the collapse of their enterprise. The veteran missionaries who had arrived in China before the 1690s knew that by reducing the duration of the language training afforded to recent arrivals, the mission inched closer to the edge of the precipice. From their perspective, the 1692 Edicts of Toleration notwithstanding, the Jesuits had to maintain their public image as erudite men trained in both Western and Chinese thought. For the mission to continue to expand, it had to be staffed by men who were familiar with native intellectual traditions, in addition to the pastoral skills required for managing communities of Christians spread over large areas.

Perhaps the most important factor of this equation for continued growth was the need to produce new texts in Chinese rather than rely on the books that had been reprinted time and again since the 1620s and 1630s. But without a system for teaching new missionaries the elements of Chinese written style, it was unlikely that new texts would be written to fill this void. The Vice-Province's superiors were aware of this problem, and they sought to resolve it by issuing exhortations to their subordinates, since they had no other means available. After a visit to the mission's residences in the early 1690s, Visitor Francisco Nogueira sent out a series of directives that gave voice to the veteran Jesuits' complaints that their younger confreres did "not apply themselves to the study of Chinese letters" and that as a result few among them could "write a letter or compose Chinese books," with obvious negative consequences for the mission. Nogueira asserted that the priests of old offered a good example on this score, since of their number "only one can be found who did not write and compose." In an attempt to spur his subordinates to greater diligence, he urged them not to content themselves with "only learning the language" but recommended that they take up the study of Chinese philosophy. As if to underscore the importance of this order, Nogueira requested that the Vice-Provincial inform him of the names of those who were unable to commit themselves to this task so he could transfer them elsewhere, "where the study of letters is not so necessary."[105]

This call for a return to the academic virtues of times past came too late for the Vice-Province to stave off the encroachment of its rivals from other orders and from Rome. In fact, Francisco Nogueira's exhortation to study the Chinese classics was a glaring understatement of the challenges facing the mission in the years around 1700. It would have required a superhuman effort for the Jesuits to meet their crushing pastoral obligations and still have time left for engaging in intellectual pursuits.

Yet in the view of at least one missionary, if the Jesuits had committed themselves to delving more deeply into native philosophical texts, they might have found there the ammunition necessary for fighting their battles over the Chinese Rites. This was the opinion voiced by José Soares, one of the missionaries at the imperial court, in 1705, after he had realized what the potential consequences of the Tournon legation might be. At the very moment when the Jesuits confronted the need to uncover sufficient evidence from indigenous sources to defend their interpretations of the rites, few men were up to the task, Soares lamented. He made particular reference to the documents of the communities of Chinese Jews and Muslims that would give credence to the Jesuits' claim that the terms *Tian* and *Shangdi* referred to the Semitic God—airtight proof, sure to convince their detractors that the *Jing Tian* inscriptions displayed in the churches of the Vice-Province were not idolatrous. "There is no doubt," Soares wrote, "that in this most vast and most ancient empire there are many other monuments of the True Vigil where they speak of the true God. But the missionaries' want of curiosity means that we lack many documents through which we could dispel the ill-founded scruples of our adversaries."[106] By 1705, however, Tournon was already on his way to Asia with orders from the papacy to bring the China Jesuits to heel. After that point, the degree of the Jesuits' engagement with Chinese language and Confucian thought would become irrelevant, since none of their communication skills would suffice to convince either the emperors or the popes who would judge their fate.

8

The Business of Conversion

One day in the early spring of 1604, while João Soeiro was recovering from a serious spell of consumption in Nanchang, he received a visit from a young man from neighboring Fujian Province. Despite the fact that the youth's family, the Lin clan, was renowned for its members' successes in the civil service examinations, and even though his father was a wealthy mandarin, he had spent his days like the prodigal son, "in youthful pleasures, traveling about and seeking to learn the alchemy for making silver." Drawn to Soeiro because of a clock at the Nanchang residence, Lin spoke to the missionary about mathematics. The Jesuit slipped various references to the Law of God into their discussion—"as he and the rest of the priests usually do"—and gradually they turned to the subject of religion. Seeing that Lin was becoming interested, Soeiro presented him with a catechism "to mull over slowly." During the following weeks, the man made daily visits to Soeiro, peppering him with questions about Christianity. So content was he with the Jesuit's responses that he "stamped his feet and clapped his hands, carried away by his pleasure."[1]

When Manuel Dias the elder arrived at Nanchang as part of an inspection tour later that year, Lin took the opportunity to ask the missionaries more questions about their religion. According to the Jesuits, his doubts mirrored those of the Prophet Jeremiah, who asked "*quare via impiorum prosperatur,* etc."[2] Lin wanted to know why God gave "good things to the bad, and bad things to the good," and why He did not kill the evildoers who wrought so much destruction on the world. "Why," he asked, "did

God create those who He knew would not be saved?" Lin also inquired about good works. What use were they if God had foreknowledge of those who were destined for heaven and those who were slated for hell? The prospective convert also sought to know why the Almighty did not make all of His creatures virtuous and save Himself the trouble of being offended by some of them. More mundanely, Lin was puzzled about the Jesuits' insistence that sick individuals pray to God for healing. "If everything happens according to His will, how can we ask Him for health since it was He who gave us the illness in the first place?" Moreover, Lin continued, why did God grant health to those who prayed and made sacrifices at Buddhist or Daoist temples? Their recovery would obviously be attributed to the deities they worshipped, and not to the Lord of Heaven. Although their account of Lin's doubts does not include the missionaries' rejoinders, they asserted that their answers "went down so well with him, showing that he had as much good sense as skill in coming up with doubts."[3]

This is an evocative if somewhat quirky vignette of the process of conversion. To be sure, most of the Jesuits' colloquies with people who presented similar doubts did not end in the same way as the Nanchang missionaries' talks with Lin, that is, with baptism—though Lin himself was obliged to present his sons for baptism in his stead since he had two wives and was thus barred from the sacrament. Yet for those who chose to adopt Christianity, especially before the middle of the seventeenth century, when *Tianzhu jiao* began to be transmitted mainly through kinship networks, the road to conversion commenced with an encounter. In Lin's case, it came when he sought out Soeiro's clock, but for others it occurred when they perused the Jesuits' publications or spoke with one of their compatriots who was a Christian. For still others, the process began when they first happened to meet a missionary, either at a Jesuit residence or while a priest conducted a countryside mission.

Once attracted to the missionary's religious message, the prospective convert was drawn into a dialogue about the teachings, obligations, and practices of followers of the Lord of Heaven. These discussions, the Jesuits hoped, would end with baptism and the integration of another neophyte into the ranks of the mission church. But just how did this process take place? How did the missionaries introduce their teachings to the Chinese? What did they say or do to persuade men and women in the late Ming and early Qing periods to accept their religion? What rituals or paraphernalia did the Jesuits employ to make their faith understood to individuals whose experience of religion was vastly different from the European one? And, once these men and women decided to become Christians, what signs or symbols did they adopt to identify themselves as adherents of *Tianzhu jiao?* In short, how did the Jesuits involved in the "business of conversions" purvey their "divine merchandise" in China?[4]

Despite the wealth of detail found in the mission's archival legacy about the march of the faith in China—including accounts of miraculous healings, virtuous Christians, confounded Buddhists, vexed Daoists, and, on occasion, converts "gone cold"—one finds few specific answers to these questions. This lack of information is unsurprising, given that the most vivid descriptions of missionary work are found in the Vice-Province's Annual Letters, documents destined primarily for internal consumption within the Society of Jesus. It appears that among the members of the order, a common understanding of the norms and practices of missionaries—be they at the Mughal court, in the forests of the Amazon, or in the villages just beyond the city walls of Lisbon or Évora—was taken for granted, since all Jesuits were to have served at least some months as missionaries during their novitiate training. In that context, the Annual Letters from overseas had two purposes: to transmit information about the temporal and spiritual status of each of the Society's enterprises and to offer examples of the virtues of the missionaries and their Christians. Nevertheless, in the lulls of this celebratory symphony, the Vice-Province's scribes inserted enough descriptions of their proselytizing routines to paint a reasonably clear picture of the China Jesuits' commonly used techniques.

Before we commence a discussion of those methods, it is important to clarify two points. First, the term "missionary strategy" has been used in a number of different ways by other scholars, with a general—although, from the view of this study, mistaken—emphasis on conversion "from the top down."[5] The overwhelming majority of Chinese Christians were of plebeian extraction. In light of that fact and other reasons already discussed, it is difficult to avoid the conclusion that the Jesuits developed techniques they considered to be efficacious for converting members of the lower ranks of society. The following analysis deals with the methods they used to claim this type of convert, leaving aside the more familiar theme of Jesuit interactions with the elite through books or learned discussions.

A second issue has to do with the character of the sources used in this analysis. It would be foolish to attempt to draw definite conclusions solely from missionary testimonials about why lower-class people living in late Ming and early Qing China chose to become Christians or how they conceived of their religious identity. Those who have treated well-documented members of the elite, such as Xu Guangqi or Yang Tingyun, have found it difficult enough to answer such questions.[6] Scholarship on Chinese sources has as yet failed to come up with more than a handful of substantial descriptions of popular Chinese Christianity that are not filtered through an elite lens.[7] Whoever wants to find out how missionaries interacted with prospective converts and discover what practices endowed Chinese Christians with a recognizable religious identity must therefore turn to Jesuit sources. To be sure, missionary accounts often reveal more about the Jesuits than about their converts, but for present purposes that is precisely why they are useful. One confronted with the silence of the majority of Chinese Catholics hopes to learn something from a few stage whispers of their missionary pastors regarding the course of conversion and the form of Catholic practice—even if that something is no more than what Jesuit direction intended it to be rather than what it actually was.

Holy Men from the Distant West

For all his immense importance to the history of the China mission, the towering figure of Matteo Ricci left behind a mixed legacy for his successors, not to speak of historians. The mark that he impressed on the Society's enterprise was so deep that scholars can be forgiven for confusing his personal actions with his confreres' strategies in China or with Jesuit evangelization methods in general. To be sure, Ricci's dealings with Ming era individuals were multifaceted, and it is difficult to separate his religious tactics clearly from his political or humanistic ones. Yet most of the things for which the mission founder has been remembered fall clearly into the category of diplomatic or intellectual actions rather than what are properly termed missionary activities. This is not to say that Ricci did not propagate Christianity while he was in China or to imply that he did not dedicate all his actions *ad maiorem Dei gloriam.* Rather, it is to redefine terms by pointing out that his most important legacy (both to his contemporaries and to modern scholars) was that he made it possible for his successors to propagate the gospel. Nicolas Trigault's adaptation of Ricci's diaries, titled *De Christiana Expeditione apud Sinas,* had a lot to say about the Italian's progress toward Peking, his dealings with mandarins, and his writings in Chinese. There are, however, far fewer passages in this book or in other sources from the mission's first decades that speak in more than summary fashion of the methods used by its founding father to persuade his interlocutors to submit to baptism.

Yet the lack of a clearly explicated missionary method is not a confirmation of its absence in actuality. On the contrary, Ricci's actions, whether political, religious, or intellectual, can be understood as a passive means of promoting Christianity by drawing others to himself, and Trigault was quite clear in casting Ricci's actions as integral parts of the journey of the faith into China. But in contrast to the more active means of proselytization that his successors would employ, the mission founder worked slowly in building up an attractive image of himself and the other Jesuit representatives of *Tianzhu jiao.* It is no surprise that even that most trenchant critic of Ricci's methods, the Japan missionary João Rodrigues, acknowledged that the Italian's "great fame for sanctity" led many Chinese to an awareness of the Christian message. In the "dense thicket of superstition" that was the Ming empire, Rodrigues wrote after Ricci's death in 1610, it was hard to find anyone "who had not heard of him, or does not speak of him as if he were a saint." Wafts of Ricci's "sweet odor of virtue" had spread across China, carried about on the currents of correspondence linking literati who had met him and drifting from province to province in the books that he wrote on scientific, religious, or moral themes.[8]

The passive method employed by Ricci and his confreres in the mission's first decades centered on the Jesuits' urban residences. From the start, the priests sought to make their houses poles of attraction for curiosity seekers. Their residences were places for distributing Christian tracts, sites for viewing scientific instruments and other European objects, and vantages for observing the priests while they conducted Catholic rituals. The missionaries hoped that after being exposed to the composite image of Christianity that was presented there, interested Chinese would alert others and spread news of this foreign religion. Willing players of the Jesuits' game did not take long to appear. By the summer months of 1584, the priests at Zhaoqing had already been joined by a literatus from Fujian Province. When this man, who was christened Paul, left for his home in early December that year on his way to Peking, he carried copies of

Michele Ruggieri's first catechism with him. As he parted company with the Jesuits, he promised "to make his wife and children Christians, and to teach the Law of God to others."[9]

As ever more individuals visited the missionaries at their residences in Guangdong Province, news of the priests spread throughout southern China. By the early 1590s, the constant movement of officials, traders, and other travelers—just the type most readily drawn to the Jesuits—along the empire's main north-south axis of communication had carried Ricci's renown into Jiangxi Province. The mission founder recorded how a merchant from that region had come to the border town of Nanxiong on business and learned from an acquaintance of the "foreign priests who had come from the West." Given his ripe age of sixty, the merchant had been encouraged to seek out Ricci at Shaozhou to prepare himself for the hereafter by learning "the true road for reaching heaven." Upon meeting the missionaries, he listened to a presentation of Christian doctrine and decided to remain with the priests for a month. During his stay, the merchant was baptized Joseph and even participated, under Ricci's direction, in the meditations prescribed by Ignatius Loyola in the *Spiritual Exercises.*[10] The Jesuit's use of the central work of Ignatian spirituality within a month of first explaining the essence of Christianity set the bar for neophyte devotions high—far too high, it would appear, since other missionaries made only sparing use of this method of pious introspection among their Chinese Christians in later years.

By the late 1590s, Ricci had shifted the focus of his actions to making his way to Peking. On his journey north, he left the residences that he had founded in Shaozhou, Nanchang, and Nanjing in the hands of his confreres. Reassured by Ricci's fame—but perhaps frustrated by the general lack of conversions in almost two decades of work—these men began to develop more active evangelization tactics to complement the passive strategy employed at their residences. Instead of waiting for the curious to seek them out, some of the missionaries decided to sally forth with their religious message. To be sure, there was no absolute division between passive and active missionary tactics, and all of the Jesuits would use a combination of both methods depending on their target audience. In any case, the transition to public preaching was a risky venture, since it involved altering the image of the demure scholar that Ricci had cultivated for himself and his colleagues. In order to stave off potential repercussions, the first priests to use more active strategies first deployed them in social settings different from those of their urban haunts. They headed to the countryside, where members of the elite were few. There, the symbolic power of the wandering holy man (especially when he was visually linked by his dress to the political power of the mandarins) was greater than it was in the cities, where temples and other religious institutions abounded.

Niccolò Longobardo pioneered the active method in the villages around Shaozhou in the summer of 1599. Building on an initial experience from the previous autumn, when he had gone to confess a sick Christian in a village, Longobardo developed a way of going on a "spiritual hunt."[11] First, he would send one of his assistants (a coadjutor or a catechist) ahead to a given hamlet to alert its inhabitants to the arrival of "a preacher from the distant West who would speak to them about religious matters." The assistant would encourage the villagers to gather before a table at which Longobardo sat. The Jesuit then began to announce "the true religion of God, the Lord of Heaven, through whom alone man could achieve salvation." After this preamble, he explained each of the Ten Commandments. The final step in this introduction to Christianity was to unveil a portrait of "God the Savior who had taught this holy law" and place lighted candles and incense by it.[12] One should not underestimate the power of these ritual gestures, especially among the unlettered, who were as apt to be impressed by Longobardo's studied Chinese-style gravitas as by the theatricality of his presentation.

Once he had introduced the Supreme Being, Longobardo would exhort the villagers to abandon their other religious habits and accept initiation as Christians. To the literate few, he distributed catechetical tracts. These individuals would also be summoned to hear the catechism from the missionary, lessons that they would be entrusted to repeat to others. The Jesuit conceded a further reward to these men, allowing them to be present for parts of the mass which he celebrated on a portable altar. When Longobardo considered his villagers sufficiently trained in the precepts of their new faith, he administered baptism. Before moving on to the next village, the Jesuit gave his neophytes rosaries and medallions to serve as "the spiritual arms of the militia in which they had just begun to profess membership."[13]

Longobardo's use of words, gestures, and devotional objects stands in marked contrast to the form of Catholicism that is typically associated with the China Jesuits in general. The faith preached and witnessed here is not the esoteric religion of literati converts seeking to reconcile Western concepts with Confucian philosophy. Rather, it is a reflection of the tangible devotions of ordinary Christians in early modern Catholic Europe. As far as the rural folk who learned of *Tianzhu jiao* from an itinerant missionary such as Longobardo were concerned, Christianity was a religion which along with the promise of salvation bore the obligation to abide by a strict moral code. The practice of this faith consisted of frequent prayer, typically assisted by devotional images or objects, and occasional participation in rituals. As presented by the Jesuits in Chinese villages, the basic teachings of the Lord of Heaven were concise and simple; even children could learn them. The missionaries, however, took on an assignment that was far from simple: they were responsible for getting the converts to live by the moral strictures of their adopted religion and ensuring that they had a basic knowledge of doctrine and the primary Catholic prayers.

But even if the challenge of guaranteeing rudimentary indoctrination for all neophytes was not an easy task, means of solving the problem were available. Those solutions drew on the pastoral techniques employed by the Society in Europe. After all, the China Jesuits emanated from Post-Tridentine milieux in Catholic Europe where their order, as well as other members of the secular and regular clergy, was engaged in a massive project of doctrinal education among children and the unlettered. The distribution of broadside doctrine primers was a common method used for inculcating basic prayers such as the Ave Maria and Paternoster as well as teaching the Nicene Creed, the Seven Deadly Sins, the Corporal and Spiritual Works of Mercy, the Ten Commandments, and the Cardinal and Theological Virtues.[14]

Taking his cue from his order's standard practices, Longobardo distributed doctrine pamphlets to his prospective converts. Unlike the apologetic treatises written for cultivated audiences by Matteo Ricci and others, these were texts intended for less erudite segments of the population. One of the first such manuals to be distributed widely in China was João Soeiro's *Tianzhu shengjiao yueyan,* first published circa 1600. This short text (in some versions thirteen pages and in others seven) consisted of dialogues between a missionary and a prospective convert about prayers and points of faith.[15] Apparently such brief tracts achieved their purpose of ensuring a basic level of doctrinal knowledge among the Chinese Christians in the mission's early years. By 1612, mission superior Longobardo insisted that the Jesuits could not alter the Chinese wording of the prayers found in the doctrine pamphlets, and especially not the indispensable and inalterable formula used in administering the sacrament of baptism, that is, the translation of the timeless phrase "Ego te baptizo in nomine Patris et Filii et Spiritus Sancti." When some of the priests began to question the way that formula had been rendered into Chinese (according to them, the current version contained unacceptable ambiguities about the Trinity), Longobardo countered that the primers had made the true doctrine "known to everyone."[16]

To Longobardo, the assertion that all Chinese Christians had learned their doctrine by using printed primers was proved by his experiences of baptizing women. Few women would have been present at one of the Jesuits' presentations; they would have had to learn about *Tianzhu jiao* from their husbands, sons, or other male relatives. With primers in hand, and especially by using texts structured in dialogue form, Chinese men were able to carry out the missionaries' exhortation that all members of a household should learn doctrine and convert. In 1602 Longobardo wrote of how impressed he was by the way Christian men in the Shaozhou area took to the task of indoctrinating their female relations. He described being invited to perform women's baptisms in the presence of their husbands and relations, but only after each woman had taken a turn at reciting the whole catechism from memory. After this initial recitation, candidates for baptism would answer questions about "what they had heard regarding the most important mysteries of the holy faith." Longobardo insisted that he was unsure what was more impressive about these encounters, the "diligence that they employ in learning and memorizing doctrine, as well as in practicing for this test," or the "spirit and confidence that they show, unafraid of being seen and examined by foreign men."[17]

When all was said and done, a combination of active and passive tactics was the best method. To be sure, even when the political situation in a given area urged the missionaries to use caution (that is, to work in a passive fashion), they still needed to make an initial active gesture to open a new residence. That this was the case can be seen in the account of the Jesuits' first visit to Shanghai. In September 1608 Lazzaro Cattaneo was assigned to make the journey from Nanjing to the hometown of Xu Guangqi. The Christian mandarin sent a sedan chair to meet the Jesuit at the riverside and lodged him in his palace for three days. Clearly the public endorsement of a local worthy paid off, for during that initial period Cattaneo claimed that many "mandarins, as well as other literati and honorable friends of Doctor Paulo," came to visit. During the weeks that followed, Cattaneo stayed in Xu's study, a small building separated from his palace. There the Jesuit received "all manner of people," including the city governor, one of Xu's close friends, who arrived "with all the solemnity and pomp due his office." Another group that came to visit Cattaneo were members of the Buddhist and Daoist clergy. According to the missionary, one high-ranking Daoist priest was "so satisfied" with the Jesuit's message that he intended to return to hear further elaborations on Christianity. But instead of simply waiting for this parade of visitors to end, Cattaneo also went about the city, "coming to the aid of those who asked for Christian doctrine and desired to be informed about the Law of God." In two months of exhausting effort, he claimed forty-two converts, among them five *xiucai,* or minor degree holders. This success gave him "hope, with the help of divine favor, for a copious harvest."[18]

Vendors in the Spiritual Marketplace

The reference to the Buddhist and Daoist priests who came to meet Cattaneo in Shanghai is a reminder that the China Jesuits did not work in a vacuum. The Europeans were merely one group among many in a spiritual marketplace where different teachings competed for attention. The most intense competition in late Ming and early Qing China appears to have taken place at the popular level, where the Jesuits squared off against other purveyors of religious ceremonial. In a society in which rituals were judged for their ability to channel the favor of supernatural beings or keep them at bay, the Europeans had to devise ways of promoting their religion in a manner that would make it appear valuable to prospective converts. The bulk of their interactions with Buddhism and Daoism therefore took place not in the rarefied air of cosmological discourse (especially since, on the whole, the China Jesuits refused to enter into dialogue with these Asian traditions and appear to have remained largely ignorant of their complexities), but rather on the pragmatic ground of plebeian piety.[19]

That Christianity demanded the exclusive attention of its adherents, instead of letting them participate in its ceremonies or not at their pleasure, made the Jesuits' task doubly difficult. They knew full well that they were not in Catholic Europe, where the combination of royal and ecclesiastical power enforced religious exclusivity. They were also aware that the Ming empire presented challenges unlike those faced by their brethren who worked in the Amazonian jungle or the baronies of the Japanese daimyo. In those regions, conversions among the elite had led to forced transformations of the religious landscape. In China, however, there was no official religion outside of the Confucian state orthodoxy, a complex of teachings considered atheistic by the Jesuits. Despite their connections to the governing elite in some regions, the missionaries could summon no coercive power to increase the size of their flocks. Instead, they had to join in the profusion of religious traditions that existed side by side, competing for adherents and patrons on a largely equal footing. They had to rely on their powers of persuasion to convince prospective converts that their teachings were better than the widespread Buddhist-Daoist-Confucian syncretism or the popular salvationism of the Pure Land school.[20] For the Jesuits, the encounter with indigenous traditions produced no end of frustrations. From their perspective, a host of features on the Chinese religious landscape conspired against them in their apostolic endeavors, and the Buddhist and Daoist clergy's resistance was by no means the least of the vexations that plagued them.

From the early years of the mission, the Jesuits identified the "bonzes," that is, Buddhist clergy, as their primary rivals. At first they seemed to be courting a paradoxical similarity with these adversaries by dressing in garments cut after the fashion of the native religious. To be sure, Michele Ruggieri, who was certainly aware of the ambiguity created by his use of this type of clothing, tried to make things clear in verse. "If you ask me about the things of the Western Paradise," he explained, "my explanation is not that of Buddha Sakya."[21] Matteo Ricci went a step further; on becoming mission superior, he abandoned any vestimentary connection between the Jesuits and the Buddhist clergy, adopting instead the garb of the literati.

Yet this change of image did not make the missionaries' task easier. By enlisting the visual referents of state officials through their clothing and attracting the curiosity of some segments of the elite, the Jesuits raised the level of competition between themselves and their rivals. First of all, the priests actively denounced indigenous traditions to members of the elite. Their attempts to win friends and followers among Chinese literati thus made them different from representatives of other minority religions. For instance, the local Jewish and Muslim communities did not engage in missionary efforts and largely kept their religious teachings to themselves. And, while the leaders of millenarian cults and other secret sects did seek adherents in popular milieux, they avoided contact with the bureaucracy for fear of persecution (although they did attract members among eunuchs and *yamen* clerks). Therefore, by engaging with influential figures in a quest for social legitimacy, political protection, and patronage, the Jesuits publicly entered the lists against representatives of entrenched traditions.

The conversion of a handful of Jiangnan literati at the start of the seventeenth century induced criticism from the indigenous clergy and in turn incited antagonism at the popular level. The events surrounding Lazzaro Cattaneo's first visit to Shanghai are a good example of how such conflicts began. In the year before the priest's arrival in 1608, Xu Guangqi's father had died. When it came time for the funeral ceremony, Xu insisted on a Christian burial, and Cattaneo made it known that he would not permit the presence of "either Bonzes or Tausus [*Daoshi,* or Daoist priests]." Seeing how much they stood to lose by not conducting this funeral, the native clergy "began to spread the notion that the Law of God denied the honors and suffrages due to ancestors." This was a powerful denunciation because the ritual manifestation of respect for the deceased was a deeply rooted practice, one that had originated in primordial Chinese culture and was an integral part of Chinese religion. In spite of the displays of friendship that Cattaneo received from many quarters, he lamented that the slanderous opinions "deterred many of those who had wanted to hear of our Holy Law."[22]

It was not only in the shadow of mandarins that the Jesuits encountered resistance to their message on religious grounds. In the countryside, too, they clashed with established notions of sanctity and ritual power. According to one account, individuals who had seen Niccolò Longobardo distribute his concise doctrine primers to villagers in Guangdong Province mocked the fact that Christianity could be "summed up on four sheets of paper." The brevity of the Jesuits' teachings, these opponents claimed, was proof that they were only "a law for foreigners." Such brief statements could not compare with the "the tomes of doctrines, exorcisms, and prayers of the idols."[23] Lacking the logistical capacity to endow every mission station with weighty volumes—in Latin or other European languages, of course—on theology, philosophy, or other Western sciences, the Jesuits could do little to confront this criticism. In sending Nicolas Trigault to Europe in 1613, mission superior Longobardo instructed him to acquire books to be used for "giving satisfaction to the Chinese."[24] In the following years, the Jesuits launched a vigorous publishing effort to make translations of more substantial and complex explanations of Christian theology and Aristotelian philosophy available in China.

No matter what they did to respond to their critics, the Jesuits could not negate the daunting challenges rooted in the millennial presence of Buddhism and Daoism in China. So entrenched were these traditions in Chinese society that seeking to cancel them out was the equivalent of attempting to divorce the myriad manifestations of Christianity from early modern European society. One of the first to express his frustration at the built-in resistance of the Chinese religious landscape was Niccolò Longobardo—not a surprise, since it was he who pioneered the practice of missionizing at the popular level. This Jesuit dismissed Daoism as no more than a grab bag of divining and fortune-telling techniques. The pervasive presence of Buddhism was his primary stumbling block.

Longobardo gave four reasons for his opinion that "the adoration of the *pagodes,*" that is, Buddhist deities or their representations, would be more difficult to uproot in China than in other "heathen lands." First, he lamented, icons of the Buddhist pantheon could be found everywhere. The Chinese "surpass all other heathens" in idolatry, he claimed, given that the *pagodes* abounded not only in temples but also in private homes; one could not even find a "boat or shack" that lacked them.[25] Longobardo's other three reasons were more closely linked to the intertwining of Confucian thought and popular Buddhism. He noted that many individuals were reluctant to abandon the religion of their forebears to adopt *Tianzhu jiao.* In popular circles, devotional objects were considered family patrimony that could not be alienated without provoking scandal. Another reason why native traditions presented such a challenge was, according to Longobardo, that the moral standards of Buddhism and Confucianism ran parallel to each other. Moreover, since "the false gods lived well in moral terms" and were known for their miracles, it proved hard to denounce them convincingly. Comparing his task to that of early Christian apologists, he asserted that the Jesuits would make more converts if they could only illustrate Christianity's moral superiority. What was needed were stories about Buddhist deities involving them in "plundering, adulteries, and other abominations," activities for which the gods of Greek and Roman antiquity were notorious. The Jesuit's final reason touched on the imperial approbation with which Buddhism had been received in China during the later Han dynasty. Referring to the patronage bestowed on the Buddhist community at Luoyang in Henan Province by the

Huan emperor (r. AD 147–167), Longobardo informed his readers that the *pagodes* had come to China "sixteen hundred years ago from India or Siam." And since Buddhism had been accepted by a sovereign, it could only be "completely removed by order of the king."[26] Taking his cue from this precedent, Longobardo later suggested that the Jesuits, too, seek an acknowledgment of *Tianzhu jiao* from the Wanli emperor.[27]

These were not the only impediments to the spread of Christianity in China. The Jesuits were aware that certain elements of their religion did little to attract new members. In fact, as Erik Zürcher has noted, the imported religion's moral strictures were considered to be particularly rigorous by Chinese standards.[28] The key sticking point appears to have been the missionaries' insistence on observance of the Ten Commandments. For instance, when Feliciano da Silva traveled to Hangzhou in 1612 at the insistence of Li Zhizao and Yang Tingyun, he recorded only eighteen baptisms. (Four of these were of abandoned babies.) Attempting to explain this paucity of conversions in that year's Annual Letter, Longobardo claimed that despite the public endorsement of Christianity by influential men such as Li and Yang, "many come to bite, but few end up taking the bait of life." He went on to explain that he felt the Chinese were sincere in their desire to "love our God, since they truly understand Him to be great and incomparably better than any of their idols." But they lost interest, Longobardo said, when they understood Christianity's moral strictures. All of a sudden they would find "many difficulties that they had not previously envisioned." Among the negative consequences of conversion as far as they were concerned was that they would have to "dismiss their concubines, lose the profits of usury, abandon the use of fortune-telling, cast out their idols." In short, they resisted having "to order their lives according to our precepts."[29]

The primary obstacle to Christianizing wealthy individuals was polygamy. The practice of taking more than one wife was the most serious of the "impediments of the rich" that kept members of the late Ming elite from baptism. Here again, the Jesuits ran up against Chinese standards of moral behavior. The Confucian conception of filial piety put a premium on the birth of (male) heirs in every family and permitted polygamy for that reason. But the missionaries' attitude on this transgression of the Sixth Commandment was inflexible. Prospective converts had to send all but one wife away before they could be baptized. This is not to say, however, that the early Jesuits did not try to find a loophole in canon law that might permit more members of the elite to convert. In 1592, only a decade after the mission had been founded, Francesco de Petris asked the Society's Superior General to secure a papal dispensation for baptizing such men. Those who promised to restrict themselves to having carnal relations with only one of their wives should not be obliged to send the others away before being admitted to the sacrament, de Petris argued. If no such provision was granted, he claimed, "the door to the faith will remain locked for a great multitude of people."[30] Yet no dispensation was forthcoming from Rome. The Jesuits resigned themselves to the prospect that few wealthy Chinese would become Christians and duly celebrated those men who were "freed of their impediments" and subsequently baptized.[31]

At the popular level, the exclusivity of the Jesuits' message directly conflicted with the pervasive religious pragmatism of the Chinese peasantry. To be sure, many individuals were drawn to the missionaries because they appeared to be powerful masters of ritual whose presence added to the existing plethora of means for dealing with the supernatural. Yet these men and women chafed at the Jesuits' denunciations of Buddhism and Daoism, and resisted the obligation that prospective converts rid themselves of any traces of "idolatry." This meant having one's *pagodes* consigned to the flames at the time of baptism. No doubt the missionaries' audacity in making this stipulation gave pause to many. Surely the missionary cannot be serious in his demands, the people of the Shaozhou area evidently thought when Longobardo came to preach among them. Writing about his rural missions in 1602, he reported that some of the villagers were initially taken by the gospel of *Shangdi* (this was a decade before the terms controversy). They willingly accepted images of the Almighty to put in their domestic oratories, but arranged their *pagodes* "like vassals, setting them in some other corner of the house without throwing them out." When these individuals found out that the "truly converted" did not want these objects "even in the filthiest part of their homes," the spread of Christianity slowed. Little by little, Longobardo complained, "they backed off, shutting their ears to this new doctrine."[32]

A further aspect of plebeian religiosity that vexed the Jesuits was the tradition of *zhai,* fasting or abstinence. This practice differed from the Catholic obligation to abstain from eating meat during certain periods of the year. While in Confucian thought it was related to notions of ritual purity when performing sacrifices, at the popular level, abstention from meat was linked to the Buddhist commandment that proscribed killing.

Members of sectarian groups were especially known for their commitment to fasting.[33] So widespread was the practice of *zhai* that the Jesuits were bound to confront it sooner or later. As early as 1592 Francesco de Petris complained to his superiors about the prevalence of fasting.[34] Another account from a missionary in the Nanjing area, written a decade later, commented on the many peasants who observed a Buddhist-inspired fast. Some practiced *zhai* because "they believed that they would gain pardon for their sins," while others maintained the hope that "they would be reborn in rich households." Everyone, this report asserted, thought that the killing of animals was sinful.[35]

The missionaries objected not to fasting per se but to the beliefs that drove Chinese men and women to fast. In order to ensure that their converts understood the reasons for the Christian fasting regime, the Jesuits insisted that all prospective converts who practiced *zhai* had to eat meat in anticipation of baptism. Forcing converts to change the eating habits they had maintained for years was a formidable challenge. Many were dissuaded from converting when faced with this fundamental alteration of their lifestyle, not to mention the less foreseeable consequences of adhering to a new religion. The Jesuits were not afraid of employing ruses to test the resolve of their catechumens. During a visit to the countryside near Nanjing, one missionary cajoled a farmer who had been a Buddhist devotee into breaking his fast by a show of deference. When the man invited the priest for a meal, he offered his guest "delicacies of meat and fish" while reserving "herbs and beans" for himself. Espying a golden opportunity, the Jesuit begged his host to partake of the food first. The man was cornered, "thinking up a thousand courtesies and solutions" to avoid eating the meat or fish. After all, it had been "thirty years" since he had last eaten such things. With "his hand trembling and his face pale," though, the farmer gave in, taking a nibble, and submitted to baptism soon after.[36]

"What Happens on These Missions"

In the mid-1620s, after seven years in seclusion, the Jesuits fanned out across the Ming empire with renewed vigor. Looking back over the history of their mission since its inception, they moved decisively to expand their activities in the provinces where they had seen the most significant growth in the number of converts. Taking their cue from the techniques elaborated by veteran missionaries such as Niccolò Longobardo, the men of the Vice-Province took their religious message to rural towns and villages. It came as no surprise to them that after initial efforts to publicize Christianity in new areas, they began to see the size of their flocks expand. While their Annual Letters attributed this turn of events to the hand of the Almighty, the Jesuits were aware that the collective experience of fifty years of proselytizing in China had engendered some techniques that were more useful than others for propagating *Tianzhu jiao.*

That the Jesuits should have found their evangelization tactics too routine to record in detail for posterity dismays the historian of the Society's overseas missions. It is only in rare instances that the missionaries explained in writing how they worked among plebeian Chinese. One of the exceptions is the 1627 Annual Letter composed by Manuel Dias the younger, who found it desirable to transcribe an account of a missionary's visit to a rural area, claiming that "eyewitness testimony" would help readers gain a better understanding of "what happens on these missions."[37] Dias's source was a letter from Rodrigo de Figueiredo to a confrere stationed at Jiading (possibly João Fróis), which describes a journey to several hamlets in the periphery of Ningbo in Zhejiang Province. This trip lasted "eighteen or nineteen days" and resulted in eighty baptisms. Moreover, Figueiredo recorded with satisfaction, "many hundreds" more had listened to his expositions of doctrine and resolved to submit to baptism at a later date, and "many thousands" were made aware of *Tianzhu jiao* for the first time.[38]

The occasion for Figueiredo's visit to that corner of Zhejiang arose when a Christian tailor surnamed Wang stopped at the Hangzhou mission station on his way home from Peking. The man had been baptized Francisco by the court Jesuits, who assured him that a priest would be willing to travel with him in order to baptize his household and kin. When the convert showed up in Hangzhou in March 1627 with his baptismal certificate in hand, he insisted that one of the Jesuits accompany him to his home district. After overcoming his initial reluctance, Figueiredo went along to see if the man could make good on his promise to introduce him to "enough people to wear him out preaching."[39] While this individual appears to have been more persistent than most of the Jesuits' converts who clamored for pastoral attention, such invitations often determined the areas where the Jesuits would evangelize. By acceding to such demands, they gained local contacts who could serve, if necessary, as translators between *guanhua* and the regional dialect.

天主降生聖像

諸神瞻仰聖容四聖記錄靈蹟

聖史若望

聖史瑪竇

立天地之主宰
肇人物之根宗
推之于前無始
引之于後無終
彌六合兮無間
超庶類兮非同
本無形之可擬
乃降生之遺容
顯神化以溥愛
昭勸懲以大公
位至尊而無上
理微妙而無窮

聖史路加

聖史瑪爾訶

Before leaving Hangzhou, Figueiredo assembled the necessary paraphernalia for carrying out his proselytizing activities. Along with the equipment he used for saying mass, he packed a set of devotional objects and images, doctrine primers, prayer books, and other writings in Chinese. The kit that Figueiredo put together followed the rules that had been issued to members of the Vice-Province in 1624, titled "Reminder for the Priests Who Go on Brief Missions to Attend to the Christians."[40] These directives instructed missionaries to travel with baptismal and liturgical apparatuses, as well as "rosaries and paper images to distribute to those they baptize." Their baggage was also to include devotional objects, such as nominas, veronicas, or agnus dei, for converts who were perceived as being more fervent than the average, or were simply of higher social standing. It goes without saying that these rules also encouraged missionaries to bring Jesuit texts, and to "hand them out readily, since they greatly help give notice of the Law of God." In order to facilitate their proselytizing work among the unlettered, the missionaries were also advised to bring texts with engravings of biblical or devotional scenes, such as João da Rocha's *Song nianzhu guicheng,* or "Rules for Reciting the Rosary" (first edition 1619). Another exemplary tract was Giulio Aleni's *Tianzhu jiangsheng chuxiang jingjie,* or "Illustrated Explanation of the Incarnation of the Lord of Heaven," which first appeared in 1637.

When Figueiredo left for the Ningbo district, he sailed from Hangzhou on one of the innumerable boats that swarmed on the rivers of the Ming empire. This was a common mode of travel for the missionaries, especially in coastal areas. In the mountains and plains of northern China, though, the Jesuits often relied on mules or donkeys for transportation. On occasion, they even employed sedan chairs—even if admissions of this indulgent mode of travel are rarely found in Annual Letters. The Jesuits were not afraid to admit, however, that they were usually accompanied by domestics who acted as porters, or even bodyguards.[41] To be sure, priests who decided to forgo these conveniences soon earned a reputation for sanctity, one validated by their displays of poverty and humility. Such was

---

Woodcut print of Christ with orb of the universe. Frontispiece to Giulio Aleni, *Illustrated Explanation of the Incarnation of the Lord of Heaven (Tianzhu jiangsheng chuxiang jingjie),* 1637. This image is similar to the standard depictions of Jesus used in China by the Jesuits.

the case of Étienne Faber, who traveled for years in the remote fastness of southern Shaanxi Province. According to his necrology, Faber carried his "sweet cargo of holy images" on his back and his baggage atop a mule or in a wheelbarrow. And when fording rivers, he would not take off his shoes, but always waded in the water fully dressed, "never letting his servants or his Christians carry him across on their shoulders or in their arms."[42]

Figueiredo's first stop in the virgin mission territory of coastal Zhejiang was one of that area's numerous clusters of farmhouses, each belonging to a different clan. His guide led him to a schoolhouse, where the Jesuit found a crowd of young boys and a master. Soon after, Figueiredo was visited by a group of literati who engaged him in a discussion on the Teachings of the Lord of Heaven and asked if he had "any images of that god." Selecting an appropriately impressive painted scroll, the missionary unrolled it and with tailor Wang's help hung it on a wall. According to the Jesuit's account, at that moment "all of the boys and their master began to kowtow and pray to it." They chanted in unison, "We adore you Lord, we ask you to help us, please grant us understanding for our studies." Taking advantage of this propitious beginning, the next day Figueiredo set up an altar beneath the image, replete with an ornate altar cloth and a separate table for burning incense.[43]

By unrolling his devotional painting in public with a certain degree of pomp, Figueiredo was employing a standard Jesuit tactic for inaugurating a mission. Given the profusion of Buddhist and Daoist iconography in China, the Jesuits knew the ritual power that images possessed, especially among rustics. Very few specimens of this type of art have survived, although missionary sources contain numerous descriptions of the visual resources that the Jesuits employed.[44] For instance, when Inácio Lobo invited villagers to a clan temple in the Pescadores Islands in 1637, he set up an altar with candles and incense before unveiling a devotional painting. After giving a brief talk on the afterlife, he revealed a portrait of Jesus that was "well painted and adorned with red silk." According to this account, the villagers were so struck by seeing "such a beautiful painting that they did not take their eyes off it."[45]

As this last remark suggests, the combination of Western painting techniques and subject matter made the Jesuits' images noteworthy in China. But what did they represent? According to missionary sources, the most commonly used subjects were the Savior (a half-length portrait of Christ with orb and scepter) and the Virgin and Child (based on the portrait attributed to Saint Luke, called the *Salus Populi Romani,* at the basilica of Santa Maria Maggiore in Rome). It appears that the Jesuits did not employ depictions of the Crucifixion when explaining Christian teachings to new audiences, something that their missionary rivals never tired of repeating. This is not to say that they omitted the Passion from their preaching—as evinced by the fact that the crucifix was a topos in Chinese anti-Christian literature—but rather they felt that the use of such images was not the best introduction to their religious message. In fact, the rules issued for the Vice-Province in 1621 temporarily barred the missionaries from displaying the crucifix "in public or in cubicles in places where heathens enter."[46] The Jesuits ran into enough problems even without recourse to images sure to scandalize the uninitiated. When Gaspar Ferreira traveled around North Zhili in 1607, his detractors circulated a rumor that his depiction of the Lord of Heaven was his own portrait or that of one of his ancestors. "Under the pretext of teaching a new law," the accusation ran, Ferreira himself was "seeking to be adored."[47]

But to return to Rodrigo de Figueiredo. Once he had his altar set up and his devotional painting displayed, he commenced proselytizing. His exotic presence was reason enough for many men and women to come visit him. According to Figueiredo, everyone "for a league and a half around" was aware of his arrival, and all stopped in at his lodgings for a look. The Jesuit made sure to keep his cubicle door open at all times, even during his meals, noting how his numerous callers "noticed everything about him and enjoyed seeing it all." Once a crowd had gathered, he stood before his altar, prepared to discourse on Christianity. Before he launched into his standard six-point lecture, he kowtowed repeatedly before the image of the Savior and invited his listeners to do the same. Then Figueiredo told them about the portrait, explaining that it depicted "the Creator of everything, neither a *pagode* nor an idol, but the true and living God." The Jesuit informed his audience about how this Supreme Being created heaven and earth, and enjoined them "not to worship other gods or to fear demons, but to serve the one true Lord."[48]

Figueiredo then moved into an explanation of the human condition, giving an account of the fall of the rebel angels, the creation of Adam and Eve, and the reasons for the Incarnation. He outlined the central mysteries of the faith and gave "a brief explanation of the Credo." After sketching the theological foundations of Christianity, he introduced his listeners to the Ten Commandments. Figueiredo's penultimate point identified the prerequisites for baptism, such as the "will to follow this Law, and contrition for one's sins." He concluded by intoning the Jesuits' habitual refrain about the altruistic reasons for their self-exile in China, explaining that his only ambition was "to propose these truths." He insisted that he could guarantee nothing beyond "blessings in the other life" to those who adopted Christianity and warned them that they "would not lack labors in this one," although they could count on divine succor in their travails or at least on "the patience to suffer them with joy and merit." After issuing this disclaimer, Figueiredo provided instruction on the principal Catholic prayers, on how to use rosary beads, and on the proper display of the nominas and images given to neophytes.[49]

After making an initial presentation, missionaries naturally concentrated on those men and women who desired baptism. Figueiredo reported that he spent an average of two days in each hamlet he visited. Inculcating Catholic obligations and practices in neophytes consumed most of this time. To facilitate this task he used a doctrine primer, most likely the catechism in dialogue form by João da Rocha called *Tianzhu shengjiao qimeng*.[50] This text was a Chinese adaptation of *Christian Doctrine* by the Portuguese Jesuit theologian Marcos Jorge (1524–1571), a standard work translated into several languages.[51] By presenting catechumens with a scripted dialogue on the basic prayers and points of the faith, the missionaries could make sure that their converts knew a minimum of doctrine prior to receiving baptism—even if their catechumens showed little engagement with their adopted religion beyond parroting the stock phrases of a doctrine primer.

Even children could repeat the simple phrases found in catechetical dialogues, a characteristic that made such texts invaluable. Long years of experience in Europe, as well as in China, had taught the Jesuits the benefits of enlisting the young as a fifth column in their army of indoctrination. Children could be counted upon to repeat prayers and mimic ritual gestures to their mothers or other women who were prevented from dealing directly with the missionaries because of gender taboos. Although Figueiredo appears to have faced far fewer difficulties in addressing women personally in the backwaters of Zhejiang Province than in Hangzhou, he still relied on their children as effective, albeit unwitting, catechists. He lingered in one hamlet for the sole purpose of "perfecting some children in the prayers"; in another, he made "the children repeat the prayers many times."[52]

Figueiredo illustrated his technique of using children to teach their parents in three episodes from his trip. In one, he described how he had a room full of men and women trying to learn prayers and make the sign of the cross. "The children, who had learned them quicker," he reported, "walked around laughing at their mothers and fathers." Upon seeing that his mother made the sign of the cross incorrectly, one boy darted to her side to guide her hand.[53] In a different village, children who had heard Figueiredo's presentation of the prayers "walked around repeating them, some out of mockery, some because they found those unknown words to be amusing."[54] Yet another story relates how a group of children were scolded for making "that invocation of the *pagodes, O Mi To Fe,*" at a similar gathering.[55] To Figueiredo's delight, their parents instructed them to use the Jesuits' preferred phrase, "Lord of Heaven help me [*Tianzhu jiu wo*]." The salutary ejaculation having been impressed on the children in this way, "they did not cease making this holy invocation while the lesson lasted."[56]

"See How It Slips into Lies"

Rodrigo de Figueiredo gave a candid assessment of his mission to the Zhejiang countryside. He claimed few baptisms and reported incidents in which his tactics had failed to produce the desired result. On occasion he won converts by the sheer force of his presence and his theatrical ritual gestures. Most of the time, however, Figueiredo relied on his rhetorical skills in attempting to undo native beliefs and supplant them with Christian teachings. The work of persuasion was not easy. The Jesuits were aware that their Christian truths were not self-evident to the Chinese. How, then, did they enter into dialogue with illiterate or semiliterate rustics on religious matters? They had to undermine the foundations of popular belief by employing an appropriate register of discourse that obeyed their interlocutors' patterns of logic. The missionaries' primary challenge was therefore to argue against Buddhism and Daoism as they were understood in plebeian circles; it was, as Figueiredo put it, to explain "why one should not adore the *pagodes,* or observe the fasts, or practice any of the other superstitions which fill these lands."[57]

There is no doubt that the China Jesuits were skilled in the art of persuasion. Rhetoric and casuistry were the Society's celebrated talents. All of the Vice-Province's missionaries had been schooled in their order's logic, rhetoric, and theology curricula. But this did not guarantee that they could successfully engage with the modes of thought of the unlettered. Priests such as Figueiredo, who had spent over ten years studying Latin grammar and rhetoric, Aristotelian philosophy, and Thomistic theology, were surely able to best any peasant in a test of wits. Such subtlety was of little use, however, since it would only drive away potential neophytes, embarrassed and frustrated. The fact that Figueiredo was a talented orator, whose gift for preaching almost won him a permanent assignment to the viceregal chapel in Goa instead of a journey to China, was surely helpful.[58] But it appears that the principal skill called on for dealing with peasants was an ability to make comparisons and draw analogies without relying, as one missionary noted, "on philosophical demonstrations that they cannot penetrate or understand."[59]

The Jesuits structured their presentations of Christian doctrine around the figure of *Tianzhu,* the Lord of Heaven. Figueiredo's starting point for his introduction to Christian doctrine echoed the Book of Genesis, but "the beginning" that he described was radically different from the Chinese understanding of the creation of the world. There was no single creation myth in traditional China, but rather a set of complementary stories relating to primordial events.[60] The Jesuits confronted these myths head-on. Lacking demonstrable proof of their own version of the story, they instead sought to reveal the perceived inconsistencies of the Chinese accounts.

Figueiredo's report offers an especially revealing look at how the missionaries dealt with Chinese cosmogony. He transcribed a debate that he had had with a farmer who expressed doubts about his teachings in the presence of other peasants. The Jesuit claimed that this individual was the most perceptive of his clan, although he conceded that this particular group was "so learned" that it amazed him. The farmer's first doubt came with Figueiredo's dismissal of the story of Pangu, the offspring of Yin and Yang, or the heavenly chiseler, who carved the two spheres of heaven and earth from the primordial mass.[61]

> The farmer said to me: "You say that this god of yours made heaven and earth. So what did our Pangu do? Our books say that he was the one who divided them, but it seems that for you there was no Pangu."
>
> I responded: "Not a whiff of him. The one who made earth and separated it from heaven was the True God whom I preach to you."
>
> To this he responded: "Wait right there, I am going to bring you a book where you will see this very clearly." And shortly after leaving,

he returned with a handwritten ledger. He began to read the beginning of the General Chronicle where it claims that before there was heaven or earth, Pangu divided them.[62]

I then said to him: "I have seen other larger and more respected books than the one you have there which say the same thing, and I believe those books as much as yours. Wasn't your book written by a man? Couldn't he lie?"

He responded to me very sharply, grabbing the doctrine primer that was on the table: "That's quite a tall order. So you'd have me believe what it says in this little book when you don't want me to believe what my book says or those other larger books?"

To which I replied: "If you think that book is big, than you should believe what it says in my other book here which is much bigger than all of yours" and pointed to one of our books that happened to be on the table.[63]

After reaching an impasse on the size and relative importance of their books, Figueiredo tried a different tack. He attempted to poke holes in the Pangu story and other Chinese creationist traditions, drawing analogies with the realities of peasant life.

I continued: "Doesn't that book of yours say that Pangu was a man?"

"Yes," replied the farmer.

And I: "See then how it slips into lies. Tell me, when this man divided heaven and earth, he was first on earth, and if so, how did he get to heaven? Either that, or he was first in heaven, and if so, how did he get to earth to divide them? And if he was between one and the other, how was he not crushed to death? Moreover, if you cannot split a log in three days, how could one man split heaven and earth?" To this, I added: "And what did this man eat while he worked?"

The farmer was silenced with these reasons, and his companions stared at him. But since he was confident, he flipped ahead in his book and said: "So, you also don't believe that the Three Kings created all things?"[64]

"True," I said, "because that is a bigger lie, since it follows that if these kings were men like us and lived before things were created, they would have died of hunger before they had begun to create anything."

At this point, one of the farmer's friends helped him: "They ate grass and fruit."

To which I replied: "That would have been enough for them not to starve, but whoever made the grass and fruit they ate would have made everything else, so the Three Kings wouldn't have been necessary for making them."

With this, his companion went mute while the farmer returned to his book, saying: "So what can you tell me of the ten suns that appeared during the time of King Yao?"[65]

"It's a lie," I said, "because if you read further on you will find that when this happened, this king sent an archer to shoot them down with an arrow, making them disappear. It may seem to you unlikely that there ever could have been such an archer, but if you look further on in your book you will find that the same king sent a valiant man to tie up the winds in a grove so they wouldn't blow down so many houses and trees."[66]

Upon hearing this he began to think that I knew more about his books than he had thought at first. He then closed his tome, saying: "You are right in what you say, but by the same token I want to know where your god was and what he ate while he created heaven and earth?"

"You ask most beautifully," I said, "and very perceptively, but first you will want to know who this god of mine is, because you will learn that since he doesn't have a body, he doesn't need space and doesn't eat or drink." And so I went on telling him such things, explaining how God is unique and true, and must be adored rather than the *pagodes.*[67]

No sooner had Figueiredo touched on the subject of the Chinese pantheon than his discussion with the farmer turned to basic Buddhist beliefs. Since these deities were held to be especially powerful—in plebeian circles and not, as the Jesuits claimed, among the literati, who refused to worship "the *pagodes,* or adore any supreme lord other than heaven and earth"—the missionaries faced the challenge of proving their impotence and *Tianzhu*'s strength.[68] When Figueiredo denounced the *pagodes,* his interlocutor immediately retorted: "What can you tell me of the miracles they have done? Or the power that they have to help those who serve them or harm those who spurn them?" Here the missionary encountered one of the difficulties enumerated by Niccolò Longobardo in discussing popular Buddhism, namely, the moral rectitude of its gods. Clearly aware of this problem, Figueiredo questioned the *pagodes'* power to mete out punishment. He told the farmer that he had traveled thousands of miles from Portugal to China with the sole purpose of "denouncing them, and persuading people to stop worshipping them." If the Chinese gods were omniscient and judgmental, the Jesuit claimed, why did they not do him harm "in the midst of so many dangers in strange lands?" Although he admitted that this argument was "very crude," Figueiredo was content that it cooled another of the farmer's doubts.[69]

The transmigration of souls, or reincarnation, was another belief fostered by popular Buddhism that frustrated the missionaries. One well-worn argument they deployed in rural areas was aimed squarely at the sensibilities of peasants and their routine dealings with animals. The Jesuits asked their interlocutors to consider the variety of living things of all sorts and species, and to ponder the fact that "thousands of living creatures swarmed in one dead body alone." It was evident that these beings far outnumbered humans, the missionaries contended; therefore it was not possible for human souls to occupy all of those animals. Following similar logic, the Jesuits attacked the vegetarianism of Buddhist devotees. They argued that it was futile to try to improve one's chances of being reborn as a "docile animal," such as a cow or a horse. The missionaries argued that the limited number of such animals and the fact that they were herbivores meant that their souls would never be condemned to descend the chain of being. It was therefore useless for any human to observe a vegetarian diet solely in the hope of attaining such a prized reincarnation.[70]

The farmer who challenged Figueiredo does not appear to have been satisfied with the priest's explanations. He wanted to know why the Lord of Heaven created so many different creatures if not for the purpose of punishing or rewarding humans.

> He said: "You say that God created everything, but what about the tigers and wolves that devastate our fields, or the rats and other vermin that we have? What purpose do they serve? Why did God create them?"
>
> He asked this question because I had asked him: "If pigs, fish, and the other things in the world were useless, as the *bonzes* say, what other reason would God have had for creating them if not to be food?"
>
> I answered that his doubt was not an easy one but I freed him

from it without difficulty. We were . . . in a farmer's house filled with a thousand gadgets and tools needed for his profession. Pointing to them, I said: "Look at all of those things there. I'll have you know that yesterday I was wondering what they could be used for and nothing came to mind. I'm sure that since you know all about farming, you'll laugh at my ignorance."

He was greatly pleased by my saying that I didn't know how those tools were used. I added: "But I never thought that they didn't have a purpose, because why would the owner of the house have them if they didn't?" Then I told him to wait a moment, and opened up one of the drawers on my portable desk. I took out a host press that I had brought with me for sealing letters and asked him if he could tell me what it was, or what purpose it served.

He laughed at the idea that such a thing had a function. So I responded: "Either you think it is useless or, despite the fact that you don't know what it is, you think I had a reason for bringing it here?"

"That's right," he said.

I answered: "Then you should accept that God did not make his creatures, as you said, in vain. Rather, they do not lack benefits or uses in the world just because you don't know which ones they are. They may even have numerous benefits or important uses."[71]

It goes without saying that the work of destroying native beliefs by using simple logic caused problems for the missionaries. The notion of a single omnipotent God was perhaps more readily understandable to Chinese peasants than other points of *Tianzhu jiao.* Figueiredo said nothing in his report to deny this, noting instead that the same farmer who had raised so many doubts was particularly puzzled by the ideas of virgin birth and clerical celibacy. He pressed the Jesuit to tell him who Jesus' father was, and if Mary was vilified for her shameful pregnancy. "Who would take care of a girl like this," he asked. "Who would keep her and feed her?" The priest was no doubt relieved when the farmer desisted, admitting that he "could not fathom such mysteries."[72] Figueiredo stood on firmer ground with his response to the farmer's questions as to why he did not have a house or a wife. He invoked his vocation as a missionary: "Do you think I could have brought a wife and a house with me the way I've come here, roaming about the world?"[73]

Not only did the peasants react to some tenets of Christianity with incredulity, but also at times they chafed at the moral strictures of the Ten Commandments. The version of Christian morality preached by the Jesuits was rigorous by Chinese standards. Whereas the Sixth Commandment stood in the way of many members of the elite who kept concubines, other prohibitions dissuaded peasants from submitting to baptism. Such was the case with the farmer in Figueiredo's story. He admitted to the Jesuit that while he was "resolved not to believe in the idols or worship them any longer," he held back from converting when he learned of the Second Commandment. The farmer informed Figueiredo that he would be unable to avoid offending *Tianzhu,* since at times he was obliged to swear oaths at temples. One of the farmer's colleagues likewise demurred, admitting that he had "some affairs with merchandise that were not compatible with the Commandments." It seems that the Jesuit heard many such comments—to the point, he claimed, where his servants became despondent "upon seeing so little fruit for so much work."[74]

Forging a Chinese Christian Identity

Rodrigo de Figueiredo claimed to have made eighty new Christians during his trip to Ningbo district. That is, he administered eighty baptisms. It is unlikely that these men and women learned more than the rudiments of *Tianzhu jiao* in the short weeks the missionary spent among them. Having decided to submit to baptism, however, they had to assume a new and largely unknown religious identity. By studying prayers, acquiring devotional objects or other symbols of their adopted faith, and joining a larger community of believers, they became recognizable as Christians to their peers and their pastors. One illustration of the tentative beginnings of this process of identity formation comes in Figueiredo's account of the final hours of preparation before he administered baptism to a group of villagers:

> I have been in this house for two days now. At the other end of the table where I write these words, the owner of the house is reading over the prayers that I taught him in a doctrine primer. His son, who learned them more quickly, is doing the same for the women in the house next door. . . . In the morning, Palm Sunday, I am to give them baptism, and I do not know how many people there will be. There are lots of children in this house. Just now they are grabbing

> my arms and saying, "Master, teach us," and so I shall repeat the prayers together with them.[75]

In addition to learning basic Christian prayers, prospective converts were required to show their resolve to abandon their previous beliefs by making an act of contrition. According to the 1621 rules issued to the nascent Vice-Province, all baptismal candidates were to be examined on their knowledge of the central Christian teachings as well as their degree of remorse at their past practices.[76] There existed indigenous traditions of declaring repentance (the Confucian-inspired "self-indictment" or "self-reproach" treatises written by late Ming literati are an example) that smoothed the introduction of such demands by the Jesuits.[77] In discoursing to his catechumens on the value of Christian statements of contrition, Figueiredo underscored their use in channeling the grace of baptism more effectively. The missionary spoke of one woman who made an exuberant display of remorse by beating her breast so harshly that all those who were present "were obliged to tell her to stop."[78]

Perhaps the most dramatic moment on the path to baptism traced by the China Jesuits was the destruction of non-Christian devotional objects. Consignment to the flames was the prescribed fate for statues, scrolls, books, and other objects proper to Buddhist or Daoist piety. Annual Letters from the Vice-Province are filled with accounts of Christian jubilation at these burnings. Figueiredo gives a good example. When one catechumen showed up at the Jesuit's door with a large sack, the priest thought at first that it might be a gift of rice. When it was revealed to contain a hoard of Buddhist objects, including a "very expensive doctrine manual," the missionary handed the sack to the children of the house where he was staying. "They entertained themselves," Figueiredo wrote, "by burning it all with as much glee as a group of schoolboys from Macau would have displayed."[79]

To be sure, encouraging public burnings of religious objects was risky business. In order to avoid sparking new persecutions, Visitor André Palmeiro instructed his subordinates in 1629 to urge their neophytes to discretion. Restraint was needed on the part of catechumens and missionaries alike to lower the level of commotion caused when they torched "the *pagodes,* books, and other superstitious things at the time of conversion."[80] It does not appear, however, that the Visitor's injunction had much effect on tempering the zeal of either the Jesuits or their followers, since the pyres raged unabated. For example, Simão da Cunha described how he was summoned by a group of Christians in upland Fujian Province in 1653 to oversee the destruction of their *pagodes.* "Not even on the feast of Saint John"—a reference to the Midsummer Eve bonfires of his homeland—"is so much wood burned in the streets of Portugal."[81] After a rural mission in Jiangxi Province in 1688, Manuel Mendes reported that the practice continued. When his converts offered him their wooden statues, he passed them on to his cooks for use as firewood. By the end of his stay in one town, Mendes claimed to have assembled "a beautiful mound of heads" as well as devotional books and other objects. So large was his trove that "it appeared that the devil made several shipments to deceive these poor people." Naturally, Mendes ordered his trophies to be burned.[82]

In contrast to the level of detail that Rodrigo de Figueiredo lavished on the proselytizing process in his 1628 account, he gave little information about how he administered baptism. Other missionaries were similarly tight-lipped on this topic. Insights into the way this ceremony was performed in China must therefore be extracted from the compendia of rules issued by the Vice-Province's superiors. The Jesuits were forced to adapt the various ritual gestures that typically accompanied baptisms in Europe to conform to Chinese cultural and gender taboos. While the Latin formula for baptizing remained the same one prescribed by the Roman Ritual, missionaries were warned against touching the newly baptized, especially the women. For instance, at the point in the ceremony where the priest handed salt to a female catechumen, he was instructed to have her husband, parents, or godparents make this gesture. In similar fashion, the missionaries were enjoined to omit the part of the ritual where spittle was applied to the nose and ears of adults, "since they find it very strange."[83]

As one would expect in a ritual of religious initiation, one of the climactic moments came with the bestowal of a new name. Upon completion of the baptismal ceremony, the priest would issue each neophyte a slip of red paper with his or her Christian name written on it.[84] Here the European appellation was transposed into its Chinese phonetic equivalent; "Miguel" became "Mi-ke-er," and so forth. To ensure that the missionaries' rendition of Christian names into Chinese followed a uniform standard, in 1629 Visitor André Palmeiro ordered that his subordinates produce a common list of saints' names. He also insisted that every priest keep a baptismal roll, recording in both Portuguese and Chinese the name of the baptized as well as the date of the ceremony and the names of their godparents. Palmeiro considered it desirable for the missionaries to appoint godparents for each catechumen. But in light of the fact that these were often recent converts themselves, the Visitor noted that they need not be told of their obligation to ensure the indoctrination of their spiritual kin.[85]

Those who submitted to baptism also received new devotional objects from the missionaries. After working so hard to destroy the outward signs of their converts' previous beliefs, the Jesuits felt obliged to replace them with some tangible means of religious expression. They were aided by the customs fostered by popular religiosity in Catholic Europe, where all manner of devotional objects were employed. Many of the images, rosaries, nominas, veronicas, and agnus dei that they distributed to their converts were similar, at least superficially, to the Buddhist and Daoist objects that the Jesuits so readily threw into the fire. The missionaries, of course, were aware of this fact and made a good thing of it; they were glad that their devotional objects fit so readily into the symbolic context of Chinese religious practice. For example, in one of the numerous accounts of the adoption of Christian paraphernalia by neophytes found in the Jesuits' correspondence, Simão da Cunha described a convert who showed up at his baptism wearing Buddhist beads around his neck. "Now he wears the beads of the Holy Law," wrote the Portuguese missionary in 1653, "and with a beautiful cross attached to them, he preaches in his town."[86]

Evidently the Chinese Christians believed their devotional objects to have considerable power for warding off evil, healing the sick, and driving away demons. The Vice-Province's Annual Letters are replete with accounts of miraculous events that occurred with the timely imposition of these talismans. Chinese Christian writings from the first half of the seventeenth century contain similar episodes, confirming that the missionaries' flocks invested their devotional objects with great importance.[87] One report from Zhejiang Province in the 1620s tells of a man who brought "an image of the Savior, a few crosses, and some printed names of Jesus" to his home to replace his *pagodes.* For three nights after he installed these new icons in his house, the neophyte heard loud noises of stomping feet at midnight. It was as if a crowd were storming out of his house. To the Christians in the area, this was nothing other than the devil tramping off, now that "a new lord, stronger than he, ruled the house."[88] In another report, António de Gouvea told of a fire that was about to consume a village near Changshu in the Jiangnan region in 1636. As the flames began to lick the walls of a neophyte's house, the pious owner risked all to hang an agnus dei from the rafters. "The respect that the fire showed was marvelous," writes Gouvea. "All the nearby houses burned down, leaving only the Christian's house standing."[89]

Even if ironclad logic characterized the Jesuits' doctrine presentations, as their reports intimate, it is likely that many Chinese peasants adopted Christianity for no other reason than the perceived power of the new religion's devotional objects. The sheer quantity of accounts of the magic performed by rosary beads, nominas, holy water, and other paraphernalia suggests that these items played an increasingly important role in spreading *Tianzhu jiao* in popular circles from the 1630s onward. For example, António de Gouvea reported in 1636 that after "seeing some of his Christian neighbors praying the rosary before an image of the Savior," a boy from Nanjing expressed the wish to be baptized. His parents would not permit it. Soon after, the boy fell ill and, in a state of delirium, insisted that devils had come to carry him off. It was only after he managed to invoke "the holy name of *Tianzhu*" that he regained his health and persuaded his parents to let him convert. A similar turn of events occurred when a pregnant woman in rural Fujian found herself in the midst of a dangerous delivery. After swearing to become Christian if the Lord of Heaven helped her in her time of need, she was given an agnus dei to wear just as she gave birth. When both mother and child came through safely, the woman and her husband "fulfilled their vow, and the whole household became Christian."[90]

The Jesuits also introduced their Chinese followers to the Catholic tradition of relics. To be sure, they did not engage in importing human remains from Europe and India to China to distribute to their Christians (although they doubtless had some quantity of saintly flesh and bones in their churches). Instead, they fostered devotions to certain saints—in particular the Society's own, Ignatius Loyola and Francis Xavier—and employed derivative relics associated with them. For instance, the Jesuits made use of slips of paper bearing an imprint of Loyola's signature. These items were either real autographs cut from the thousands of documents signed by the Basque mystic during his tenure as the Society's Superior General or printed copies. According to one report from Jiangzhou in Shanxi Province in the mid-1630s, this relic was so venerated by local Christians that it "always travels from one Christian house to the next, and from town to town." Ignatius's mark was used most often in cases of

demonic possession, as well as during deliveries when the lives of the mother and child were at risk.[91]

Xavier's relics also circulated in China. The fact that the Apostle of the Orient had actually trod on Asian soil meant that physical traces of him might still be found locally. In 1643 the missionaries at Shanghai had in their possession a flask of water that had been filled in the puddles that accumulated at the feet of Xavier's coffin in India. Sips from this relic, possibly brought to China by Martino Martini, were reported to have healed three moribund Christians that year alone.[92] Other missionaries visited the site of the saint's first tomb on Shangchuan Island and collected handkerchiefs full of dirt (they even "ripped up the nearby bushes") for themselves and their flocks.[93] The desire for such relics had not abated half a century later, when Francisco Simões wrote of giving a Xaverian relic to a woman in North Zhili. The Jesuit offered her a thread from a piece of cloth that he had cut from the saint's corpse. As soon as rumors began to spread that the priest was distributing relics, he found scores of makeshift reliquaries awaiting him in each village that he visited.[94]

The Vice-Province faced a considerable logistical challenge in attempting to provide devotional objects to its neophytes. In the best of circumstances, the missionaries could rely on regular shipments from Macau filled with items from that Portuguese colony, from elsewhere in the Estado da Índia, or even from Europe. It appears that the bulk of the objects that were sent to China by Jesuit procurators beyond the mission's borders came from the Portuguese territories in western India. But the tenuous nature of the link between Goa and Macau, especially after the fateful period from 1639 to 1641, which saw the end of the Japan trade and the fall of Malacca, made it difficult for the Society to keep the Vice-Province stocked with religious paraphernalia. The chaos of the dynastic transition in China merely added to the problem of finding adequate supplies of imported Christian objects.

But the missionaries had the option to acquire materials locally, and at times they commissioned artisans for this purpose. When the priests at

---

Painting of Madonna and Child, Chinese (Shaanxi Province), seventeenth century. This scroll is one example of the devotional art produced in China by the Jesuits and their Christian followers.

Xi'an exhausted their supply of nominas in 1634, they had a wooden tablet carved with the words "Jesus" and "Maria," which they stamped on special paper. Since these objects were more perishable than their metal equivalents, some Christians took to wearing them "not around their necks, but sewn into their caps and bonnets very prettily."[95] When the mission's finances were depleted, the Jesuits asked their Christians to produce their own objects for the priests to bless. While in Huai'an in 1640, Francesco Sambiasi relied on the local Christians to make "a great quantity" of nominas by hand. Although he conceded that the improvised items were not as ornate or embellished as those made in Europe, all the same they served "to make up for the lack."[96] And as the Pax Tartarica settled over northern China in 1647, Inácio da Costa remarked on his flock's ingenuity in finding substitutes for imported rosaries. "No one lacks something to pray with in this penury of beads," he wrote. "Some buy beads of the *pagodes,* restring them our way, and bring them to be blessed, some string together wild seeds, some align balls of dough made of fragrant flour, some tie knots of straw, and some just pray with their fingers."[97]

The symbolic vocabulary of the Jesuits' Chinese Christians was not restricted to the use of European devotional objects or their native equivalents. One example of how they contributed to fashioning their own religious identity can be seen in the widespread use of Christian *duilian.* The custom of making these sheets of red paper adorned with auspicious couplets was an ancient Chinese practice with Daoist origins. Pasting them around doorways was held to be an effective means for warding off evil spirits.[98] Native Christians adapted this custom for their own purposes by decorating their homes with the names of Jesus and Mary. A report from the early 1620s describes such public displays as acts of defiance against the decrees of Shen Que, the impetus behind the Nanjing affair. "At the very time when following the Law of God was prohibited with great penalties," wrote Francisco Furtado, "many folks had the holy name of Jesus printed in large letters on red paper and posted above their doors as if to say, 'If you want me I am here, *non recuso mori.*'"[99] In Shanghai two decades later, the Jesuits reported that a Christian had made a similar defense of the practice of displaying the *shenghao,* or holy names, above his door. During an interrogation he told a mandarin that his *duilian* were "arms against the devil." Just as the city walls served to keep enemies at bay, the Christian averred, "the holy name of God on these papers defends our houses from the devil so he does not enter and disturb our souls."[100]

It goes without saying that the devotional objects described here constituted the most superficial level of the Chinese Christian's religious identity. To be sure, the Jesuits preferred to envision their converts as true believers who relied on such items for establishing regular prayer habits or moderating the rhythms of personal devotions rather than as simpletons equipped with new talismans. The missionaries therefore had to find ways of encouraging their neophytes to engage in forms of spiritual expression that were not limited to the constant recitation of a few prayers. To this end, they wrote devotional texts that replicated the form and content of European spiritual literature for the laity. In addition to circulating Christian calendars listing all the feasts and fasts to be observed during the year, the Jesuits distributed compendia of prayers, works of hagiography, and elaborations on the various mysteries of the faith.

As one might expect, prayer manuals circulated widely in the mission church. Among the plethora of such texts were included Giulio Aleni's discussion of how to attend mass, *Misa jiyi;* João Fróis's explanation of the Passion and its accompanying litanies, *Tongku jingji;* and the collaborative volume of prayers called *Tianzhu shengjiao nianjing zongdu.* Whereas Aleni's text taught its readers how to comport themselves during rituals, Fróis's treatise presented its readers with material for individual devotions. According to the 1628 Annual Letter, it related episodes from the lives of Christ and the Virgin and contained the Litanies of the Saints and of the Virgin with the intention of introducing Christians "to the pious practice of praying in their homes at night." Another such book presented meditations by Gaspar Ferreira that included examples drawn from the lives of the saints, special prayers for various occasions, and a summary of what "the Church teaches about the saints and other mysteries." According to this source, these texts were "greatly celebrated by the Christians," to the point that they would bring them along when they came to mass or traveled.[101] No book, however, circulated more widely among the adherents of *Tianzhu jiao* than *Nianjing zongdu* or *Rike* (Daily Exercises). The first edition of this work was printed at Hangzhou in 1628. In addition to prayers, it contained a number of smaller devotional texts by different Jesuit authors. According to António de Gouvea, there was "no other book that the Christians carried in their hands so frequently."[102]

"Unlike the Dark Temples"

The creation of Christian sanctuaries was the final transaction in the missionaries' "business of conversion." Only after they had claimed success in sparking conversions and equipping their neophytes with Christian symbols would they attempt to create physical focal points for their Christian communities. To be sure, the Jesuits began this task as soon as they offered devotional images to the newly baptized, by encouraging their neophytes to set up oratories in their homes. But the presence of household sanctuaries did not preclude the need for larger worship spaces, especially in areas with large numbers of converts. The first centers of Christian activity were the Jesuits' urban residences. Each of these had a sanctuary complete with altar, images, incense, and hortatory inscriptions, including the Ten Commandments and lists of the Works of Mercy. These buildings were either purchased by the Vice-Province or donated to the mission by wealthy Christians (or by emperors, as in the case of the Peking residences).

Beyond their urban residences, the Jesuits worked together with their flock to improvise ritual spaces. The general poverty of rural neophytes made this a difficult task. Many village sanctuaries were simply "oratories," that is, rooms in Christian homes that were emptied of furniture during group devotions. Some villages had "chapels," or designated sanctuaries that did not revert to other uses when religious activities ceased. Such was the case with the chapel consecrated by Pedro Ribeiro in the town of Zhuanshu near Shanghai in 1636. According to that year's Annual Letter, a widow had offered part of her house as a sanctuary and quarters for visiting priests. Ribeiro responded by installing above the altar an image of the Savior, "to whose holy name the widow dedicated her chapel." The missionary was very pleased with this gesture toward the widow's coreligionists, noting that the space was "very commodious for the Christians to gather, to pray, and to hear spiritual talks."[103]

The Jesuits and their Christians occasionally benefited from acts of pious largesse, whether from Chinese or external sources, that allowed them to acquire new sanctuaries. Within China, donations of real estate or funds came from wealthy Christians. For instance, members of the Xu clan, in particular Paulo Xu Guangqi's granddaughter Candida, were responsible for the purchase of several village sanctuaries in the Shanghai-Songjiang area. In other areas, Christian communities often coalesced around chapels established in households of the elite. One report from 1643 describes how a lower-level literatus from a town near Changshu offered "one of the best rooms in his house" for installing an altar and an image. What made this case especially noteworthy was that the local

Christians organized a procession as part of the chapel's consecration ceremony, passing through the streets, with candles in hand, behind a carriage bedecked with silk drapery that bore the devotional image.[104]

The Vice-Province also used funds from outside China to establish sanctuaries in places that were not properly mission stations, where individual Jesuits negotiated for the purchase of secular buildings or disused religious structures, transforming them into churches with room to lodge a visiting priest or catechist. Before 1639, when Portuguese trade with Japan was abruptly severed, the China mission received donations from the traders at Macau partly for this purpose. But thanks to the Society's sustained publicity efforts, pious legacies from farther afield also made their way to China. For instance, Jacques le Faure purchased a decrepit temple near the Jiangxi Province town of Ji'an in the late 1650s with "some alms that arrived from Europe." According to the Jesuit, the temple's keepers were in such dire straits that they did not object to his plan for converting it into a *Tianzhu tang.* (Note that the term *tang* was also used to denote administrative or judicial buildings, not Buddhist or Daoist sanctuaries—a further semantic step from any lingering associations between the Jesuits and their non-Christian rivals.)[105] Le Faure's first step was to send away "the bonzes who lived in it, along with all their golden *pagodes.*" He was happy to report to his superiors that he completed this move "with no uproar from the heathens, who instead were pleased to have such heavenly protection for their town."[106]

So the Jesuits made use of existing structures in much the same way that they christened Buddhist prayer beads as rosaries. By transforming temples into churches, the missionaries appropriated loci associated with the sacred in the popular mind. This practice should not be considered yet another example of the singular capacity for tolerance and cultural accommodation that has long been ascribed to the China Jesuits but rather should be seen as a shrewd financial move necessitated by the limited financial resources of the missionaries and their followers. To erect new churches was a far more costly endeavor than to purchase decaying temples from cash-strapped religious communities. Moreover, it is unclear precisely how many of the Jesuits' church buildings were actually former temples rather than secular buildings.

This is not to say that the conversion of temples into churches never provoked popular resistance, or that the consecration of new churches always facilitated the Jesuits' proselytizing efforts. Rather, these were convenient ways for the mission church to make its physical (and spiritual) presence felt. For instance, during his visits to the Wuyi Mountains in Fujian Province in 1645, Simão da Cunha reported how a "famous temple" had been converted into a church. After the local Christians (perhaps with the Jesuit's help) purchased the building, a neophyte named Lucas took the initiative to cast out its Buddhist icons, pausing only to smash the head of each statue. Cunha blessed the sanctuary, much to the "joy of all of the Christians, as also to the sadness of its former devotees, who used to come every month on pilgrimage."[107] At some point during the following decade, the Wuyi Christians acquired another temple that they dedicated to the Virgin and reserved for the use of women.[108]

Although it may sound paradoxical, the creation of ritual spaces for the worship of the Lord of Heaven did not necessarily mean that the Jesuits and their Christians engaged in the public practice of their religion. It was one thing to rededicate a temple in the remote Fujian wilderness to *Tianzhu* but a vastly different task to attempt the same thing in Peking or even a relative backwater like Shanghai. The public practice of *Tianzhu jiao* would have been the clearest possible sign that Christianity had become part of the Chinese religious landscape. It would have been explicit confirmation that the missionaries' traffic in "divine merchandise" was legitimate in the eyes of the authorities and that their followers were viewed as a group which practiced a nonthreatening minority religion. Short of the conversion of the emperor himself, the establishment of recognizable and tolerated Christian communities centered on identifiable sanctuaries was the sum of the Jesuits' aspirations for their mission.

It was only in the middle decades of the seventeenth century, in the midst of the chaos of the dynastic transition, that the Jesuits and their followers felt confident enough to move the practice of their religion into the public eye. In the last decades of Ming rule, as the mission laid its foundations from north to south, it had done so under a veil. In spite of the renown of figures such as Matteo Ricci, the practice of *Tianzhu jiao* in Peking took place behind closed doors. As Visitor André Palmeiro learned during his stay there in 1629, the city's male Christians attended masses and heard sermons on Sundays and holy days in a sanctuary which was "very pretty and gilded, but not open to the public."[109] It could not have been too private, though, since the Peking church was described alongside brief explanations of Christian doctrine in indigenous guides to the scenic sites of the capital printed in the 1630s.[110]

By the time the dust had settled at the new Qing court in 1644, the Jesuits and their followers were part of the pattern of Chinese life, and their churches were the largest signs of the Christian thread in the fabric of Chinese religion. At Peking, the repeated gestures of friendship made by the Shunzhi emperor toward Johann Adam Schall emboldened the missionaries to make changes in the outward display of their faith. One of the clearest manifestations of this shift could be seen in the design of the new residence, called the Eastern Church, which Shunzhi granted to Gabriel de Magalhães and Lodovico Buglio in 1655. On the building's façade, above the courtyard of the new church, the Jesuits commissioned a set of sculptures and a large cross to complement the gold-lettered panel reading "Gift of the Emperor" that hung over the main door. All of these Christian symbols were clearly visible to passersby above the residence's walls, proclaiming the presence of the missionaries and their religion in no uncertain terms.[111]

Elsewhere in China the missionaries also took advantage of the changed political climate to promote the crystallization of a Chinese Christian identity. Taking their cue from the events at Peking, the Jesuits in the provinces embellished their urban churches with palpable signs of the presence of *Tianzhu jiao,* making statements in stone and wood. Shedding the inhibitions of the past, they even introduced architectural forms of European inspiration into the design of the churches that they opened in the late 1650s and early 1660s.[112] Work on two new sanctuaries in European style commenced at Hangzhou and Yangzhou in the Jiangnan region as the 1650s drew to a close. And when Jacques le Faure inaugurated a new residence in Ganzhou, Jiangxi Province, in January 1658, he was keen to add Western features to its sanctuary. Taking advantage of the good relations that he maintained with governor Tong Guoqi (*juren* 1648, d. 1684) and other mandarins, and putting the sum of one hundred taels given him by the governor to good use, he commissioned a cruciform church. While the building was of modest size ("five fathoms at its length, and three and a half at its crossing"), its two rows of windows near the roofline let daylight stream inside, filling the space. According to le Faure, this characteristic made his church "noticeably unlike the dark temples of the Chinese."[113] What the local Christians did inside their sanctuaries also differed from what took place in Buddhist and Daoist sanctuaries, as we shall see in the next chapter.

9

A Good Method and Order

In early 1655 Manuel Jorge raised a cry of alarm over the state of the Vice-Province of China. Seventeen priests and three coadjutors, he lamented, were all that was left to staff the mission church. "Such a small number," exclaimed Jorge, "to garrison so many fortresses!" Every member of this paltry band was entrusted with a Chinese province, "each as big as a kingdom." To make matters worse, the "troubles of old age and gray hair" had greatly limited the missionaries' capacities. Some Jesuits, such as Manuel Dias the younger and Álvaro Semedo, were in their seventies, while others like Simão da Cunha, Johann Adam Schall, and António de Gouvea were in their sixties. Several were over fifty, and only two men—Feliciano Pacheco and Jorge himself—were in their thirties. Citing the mission's chronic shortage of manpower and the burgeoning number of neophytes, Jorge wondered what the future might hold for the Society's China enterprise. Logic dictated that if this situation continued, those twenty men would pass away leaving tens of thousands of Christians "without masters to teach them, without pastors to govern them, without examples to animate them."[1]

Jorge hoped to attract a wave of new recruits to the mission. His remarks were meant to engender the pity and resolve of his intended audience—his confreres in Europe, many of whom, he claimed, were "occupied with only one lesson, only one sermon each month or, at times, only one confession outside their residences each week." But Jorge's plaint on the number of missionaries and his lament for the Vice-Province's future obscured one of the China Jesuits' primary accomplishments, the internal organization of the mission church. His rhetoric was illogical. Jorge voiced fears for the mission's future, not its present, leaving the question of how seventeen priests and three coadjutors could manage a body of believers that counted tens of thousands of souls. How was it possible that the missionaries did not fold under the crushing weight of these pastoral burdens? To be sure, it was only in the late 1690s (and then only in the Shanghai area, the region that far outstripped all others in numbers of Christians) that the Jesuits began to admit that they no longer knew the true size of their mission church. But they had devised effective techniques for looking after their flocks with the minimum of pastors years before that.

Growth posed challenges of two distinct orders. The first was organizational, demanding more calculation than zeal. In contrast to the images of heroism that captured the fancy of early modern hagiographers and even some modern scholars, the work of missionaries after the initial phase of conversion was essentially identical to that of parish priests. As one Jesuit commentator explained in reference to missions outside European colonial rule—and therefore beyond the control of the secular church, its bishops, secular clergy, and inquisitors—"since there are not enough priests in those parts to serve as the pastors and vicars of those Christians who newly convert and receive baptism, the Society is entrusted with their cultivation."[2] Put differently, the lack of diocesan structures that might have given fuller institutional articulation to the practice of Catholicism in China made each mission station a de facto cathedral and every subordinate Christian community a de facto parish.

The China Jesuits' vocations, however, were clearly not the same as those of parish priests (or other members of the secular clergy) in Europe or its overseas empires. The mission church was therefore not drawn along diocesan lines. Rather, it was structured according to the Society's tried and tested methods of shaping lay piety and organizing students in its colleges. Its building blocks were groups of laymen, called sodalities, confraternities, or brotherhoods, and *hui,* meaning "association" or "society," in Chinese. Seeking to dispel ambiguities, one missionary felt compelled to explain: "By confraternities we do not mean groups of the kind commonly formed in Europe. They are like classes that we divide the Christians into so we can attend to them by turns."[3] The groups' resemblance to parishes was limited to their being localized bodies of believers who converged on a specific sanctuary for receiving the sacraments and conducting devotions. Beyond this aspect, the organizational units of the mission church had none of the legal or political qualities of their counterparts outside the Vice-Province.[4]

Even in the realm of lay piety, the Jesuits' organizational sodalities were only distant reflections of parishes. To start with, the missionaries themselves were far from being the overseas equivalents of European benefice holders. They did not envision their ministry in China in the same way that even a reform-minded parish priest in Catholic Europe conceived of his cure of souls. The spiritual life of the Jesuits' "parishes" centered on certain pious activities that often made them more dynamic, at least in terms of their devotional practice, than a significant fraction of their European coevals. The Chinese units, typically called *Shengmu hui,* Brotherhoods of the Holy Mother, mandated weekly prayer routines for members, encouraged community solidarity, and made the reception of the sacraments obligatory. Such demands made them watered-down versions of the devotional confraternities to be discussed in the next chapter, yet while setting the bar for lay piety among Chinese Christians higher than it was for most European Catholics. That this should be the case among the Society's spiritual charges is not surprising. After all, the Jesuits were representatives of a reforming impulse among the Catholic clergy which sought to transform the nature of lay piety from passive attendance at rituals to active desire for the sacraments. Whereas in Europe the Jesuits relied on their example of fervor to inspire the laity, offering spiritual direction only to those who attended their schools or became members of their lay brotherhoods, in China they made such ideals of religious practice the expected norm for their flock.

Even if organizational brotherhoods enabled the Jesuits to devolve much of the responsibility for communal devotions onto the Chinese Christians, the missionaries still needed to supervise the religious activities of the mission church. As the number of adherents of *Tianzhu jiao* increased and the number of priests stagnated, the challenge of oversight increasingly fell to the missionaries' auxiliaries. These individuals, often referred to as catechists, were drawn from the ranks of the neophytes who had shown zeal and willingness to serve as doctrine teachers, local leaders, and intermediaries between the priests and their far-flung communities.[5] The Jesuits gave them the power to baptize, to exhort their fellow Christians, and to teach catechism to the children who had been born into the faith. In short, they were responsible for supervising, indoctrinating, and expanding the mission church, taking on the tasks the Jesuits could no longer perform if they wanted to make it possible for all of their followers to say confession and receive the Eucharist at least once each year. To ensure that catechists maintained their zeal, the missionaries elaborated a system of mutual oversight based on the confraternity model. By the end of the seventeenth century they were, as one missionary put it, "like the nerves or the arms" used by the priests for cultivating their Chinese church.[6]

"The Holy Use of Confraternities"

When Matteo Ricci was forced from Zhaoqing in 1589, he exhorted his converts to persevere "in the midst of a pagan nation" and informed them of the trials of the Primitive Church. While promising to return as soon as he could, he urged them not to forget what it had taken them "seven whole years to learn" and left a set of instructions to govern their communal spiritual life in his absence. Ricci told them to gather at the home of one of their number on appointed days to "speak of divine matters and commend themselves to God." To assist them in planning their activities, he supplied them with a calendar of Catholic feasts organized according to the lunar months.[7] It is unclear what happened to this group of Christians in the decades that followed, since the Jesuits, it appears, did not return to Zhaoqing for decades. Nevertheless, the creation of this conventicle was their first attempt to equip their followers with the institutional means for practicing Catholicism in their absence.

As their enterprise got more fully under way, the Jesuits experimented with various techniques for managing their communities of converts. One of the first substantial groups of neophytes was centered on the Nanchang mission station in Jiangxi Province. By 1605 João Soeiro and Manuel Dias the elder claimed to have over two hundred souls in their care, far too many to gather at the small chapel at once. The missionaries therefore divided their Christians into three groups. Each of these was assigned a different day each month to gather at the sanctuary for prayers and a sermon or a doctrine lesson from a priest. All of the Christians were encouraged to assist at mass on Sundays and feast days, despite the suspicions that such gatherings might arouse.[8]

In dividing their flock, the Jesuits were relying on organizational techniques drawn from their experience in their order's colleges. Virtually all of the China missionaries had years of experience as schoolmasters in the Society's well-subscribed grammar and rhetoric classes. They knew how to deal with large groups and were skilled at dividing students for mutual encouragement and "pious competition." The Jesuits' methods in the mission field recalled their use of decuries (groups of ten students led by an appointed decurion) in the classroom, as discussed in Chapter 6. They were clearly aware of the parallels between their indispensable organizational activities in China and their order's customary pedagogical practices, and they took advantage of those similarities.

It is nevertheless worth noting that forms of communal organization had a rich pedigree in Chinese society. The Jesuits thought they could rely on their order's standard educational methods and they were correct, because late Ming society was fertile ground for their initiatives. In rural as in urban settings, there was a profusion of *hui* serving all manner of purposes, religious and secular. Nicolas Standaert asserts that the Jesuits did little more than encourage the impulse among their followers to form associations.[9] Such a claim is especially apt with regard to the organizational confraternities, since the primary value of these groups was the cohesion they offered to the mission church. Thus the fact that Chinese men and women from all levels of society were familiar with forms of communal religious activity mitigated the Jesuits' organizational challenge.

The division of Christian communities into smaller units did more than facilitate pastoral care; it provided a means of defense from persecution. Since the majority of Christians came from plebeian ranks, there was a distinct possibility that their gatherings would attract unwanted attention from the authorities. Part of the common litany of complaints against secret religious sects in late imperial China invoked fears of sedition and popular uprisings incited by unorthodox teachings. To mandarins who had only a superficial knowledge of *Tianzhu jiao,* Christianity seemed similar to outlawed sects such as the White Lotus, something the Nanchang Jesuits found out to their peril in 1607. This sect was a perennial target of (unsuccessful) crackdowns, because its leaders were suspected of fomenting peasant rebellions. The Jesuits appear to have bought the official line on the White Lotus movement, which they asserted was "like that of the Anabaptists in Europe," in that it obliged its devotees to engage in practices reminiscent of "those horrendous stories from Münster in Germany."[10] Christianity had to avoid being lumped in with heterodox sects at all costs, as Matteo Ricci and his confreres knew only too well. One tactic was to publicize *Tianzhu jiao* by circulating books about its religious message. Another was to keep a low profile, disguising Christian assemblies as much as possible by dividing larger ones into smaller units—although this was precisely the same tactic used by the White Lotus sectarians and other outlawed groups.

A further impetus for the development of a fragmented system of church organization came from the presence of female Christians. The existence of social taboos against interactions between unrelated men and women did not dissuade the missionaries from attempting to provide pastoral care to all of their converts. As the number of Christian women increased, the Jesuits had to devise a way for dealing with them in a socially acceptable manner. Whereas in the countryside there was greater intermingling of the sexes, and the missionaries therefore were able to bring men and women together for rituals, things were different in the cities where the Society maintained residences. Since urban mission stations doubled as living quarters, discretion demanded that their sanctuaries be restricted to men only. Experience had cautioned the Jesuits against transgressing gender taboos, and in 1621 the Vice-Province's foundational statutes mandated the separation of male and female neophytes. Missionaries were ordered to "seek to create a few oratories in the homes of some Christians where women can be baptized, mass can be said, and talks can be given to them."[11] So important was gender separation for preserving the Jesuits' good name that Visitor André Palmeiro reiterated this order verbatim just eight years later.[12]

In addition, the missionaries took care in shaping the way that female neophytes would practice their religion, making reference to familiar European models of group piety. In the decades since their order was founded in 1540, the Jesuits had created scores of devotional groups for lay Catholics. During their formative years, all the priests who worked in China had belonged to their order's flagship archconfraternity, a group primarily for students that was dedicated to Our Lady of the Annunciation and had branches in all of the Society's colleges. The Annunciadas, as they were called in the Portuguese world, will be discussed in detail in the next chapter, but it is important to note now that, to a man, the missionaries were fully experienced in the coordination of group piety. In the Ming empire they relied on this experience for structuring the devotional life of their neophytes, institutionalizing prayer routines and reception of the sacraments by writing them into each group's statutes.

Starting in the 1620s, but increasing in pace in the 1630s, the Jesuits organized their female followers into confraternities dedicated to the Blessed Virgin, *Shengmu hui.* The sanctuaries where women met for communal devotions were labeled *Shengmu tang,* or Chapels of the Holy Mother, in contrast to the residence churches used by men, which typically invoked the Savior. In 1634, for example, five women's groups that met in different neighborhoods could be found in Hangzhou. According to João Fróis, the women of each quarter would gather in oratories at private homes on appointed days in order "to be cultivated, and so that those wishing to be baptized can become Christians." The same year, another women's group was founded at a town in Shaanxi Province. The members of this confraternity met "once or more times" each month for prayers and for discussing matters of the faith. "Those who understand better and know more," wrote Fróis, "were entrusted with instructing and indoctrinating those who are less proficient."[13] Three years later, Gaspar Ferreira took a similar approach at Jianchang in Jiangxi Province. The town's Christians, he claimed, were "very given to confraternities"; the women had their own *Shengmu hui.* Four times during the course of the year they would gather in a private home "to hear mass, confess, and take communion and to spend the day hearing good talks and performing their devotions." Much to Ferreira's consolation, these activities were not limited to urban women. In rural villages, the "holy use of confraternities" had been successfully introduced as well.[14]

The primary aim of founding women's confraternities was to provide a focal point for devotions, a space where individuals benefited more from their peers than from their pastors. This is not to say that the priests who assisted in the pious exercises of each group were not important, but rather that the Christians themselves were primarily responsible for their communal spiritual life. So the confraternity mode of organization was an ideal model for coordinating various groups of Christians whom the Jesuits could not continuously cultivate. It worked particularly well among the dispersed pockets of converts claimed by the missionaries in rural areas. The Jesuits dedicated those groups to the Virgin as well, calling them *Shengmu hui.*

As the number of rural converts grew in the late 1620s and early 1630s, so did the number of new confraternities. For instance, Alfonso Vagnone oversaw the creation of several such groups around Jiangzhou in Shanxi Province. The 1630 Annual Letter reports that in four or five different villages, he designated chapels where Christians would "gather to pray their devotions and read spiritual books, exhorting one another how to keep the Commandments." These sanctuaries had space for lodging the missionaries, although the Jesuits' visits typically lasted for only a few days each year. To make up for the lack of resident priests, Vagnone appointed "some of the more fervent and devout" as community leaders, or *huizhang.* These individuals were entrusted with "inciting the others to exercises of piety and devotion."[15] A similar organizational system was employed among the Christians living in the countryside around Peking. By 1637 Niccolò Longobardo reported that there were fourteen oratories in different towns and villages where neophytes gathered to hold their confraternity meetings. A priest would visit these groups by turn to offer them the sacraments of the Eucharist and penance. According to the Jesuits, some outsiders were so impressed with the Christians' group devotions that they, too, asked for baptism.[16]

While all of the China Jesuits undertook the task of establishing women's groups or rural confraternities regardless of geographical region, the priests at Shanghai faced the greatest logistical challenges. Their flock was, bar none, the largest and would remain so until long after the end of the period discussed here. In the 1630s Pedro Ribeiro became the first missionary to experience the burden of having to "walk in circles almost all year long" in order to attend to the Christians in his care.[17] Faced with even greater pastoral burdens, Ribeiro's successor Francesco Brancati rationalized his approach to the Shanghai church. After all, he was the only priest in an area with thousands of Christians, all of whom needed to have their confessions heard and take communion every year. Therefore, by 1643 Brancati had organized the Christians residing in the city's outlying villages into thirty men's groups dedicated to the Virgin.[18] As the number of adherents of *Tianzhu jiao* grew, so did the number of confraternities. In 1647, only four years later, Brancati reported that he managed forty confraternities meant to ensure that all Christians would be able to confess "at least once or twice during the year." (He ministered to women during annual visits to their villages.) Each of these groups had its own leader, who coordinated prayers and served as the intermediary with the Jesuit. Each year during Advent and Lent, Brancati invited the sodalities by turn to the Shanghai church to receive the sacraments. "With this plan," read the Annual Letter in 1647, "the work proceeds more smoothly and the missionary's conscience is calm, since he reports that all of his parishioners confess."[19]

Brancati was convinced that he had discovered the ideal method for structuring the spiritual life of his numerous charges. In 1648 he sent another description of the Shanghai area men's confraternities to the Annual Letter's compiler. Brancati explained how he had started another five *Shengmu hui,* bringing the total number to forty-five. Twelve of these bodies had their own chapels, or dedicated structures, while the rest met in oratories, that is, special rooms in Christian homes. On the first Sunday of the month, every group would gather at its sanctuary to pray, hear readings from spiritual books, or "perform other devout works" until midday. On All Saints' Day (November 1), Brancati would announce the schedule according to which the different confraternities would visit Shanghai's Church of the Savior during the following Advent and Lent. On each group's appointed day, its members would awake at midnight to begin their trek to the sanctuary. Upon arriving, they would set many candles upon a bier placed in the middle of the church. Brancati would say mass, after which he would lead the group in saying prayers for the Christian villagers who had died that year. Then the priest would retire to the church's sacristy, leaving the congregation kneeling and praying the Litanies of the Virgin. Brancati would later return to give a sermon and after that would hear confessions. As a means of keeping attendance, all wrote down their names, and the *huizhang* compiled a list of those absent, assuming the responsibility for telling those who had not come, those who were sick, and those who were away on business to report for confession on another day.[20]

However effective Brancati's system was, it could not replace the type of pastoral care that came from continual contact with a priest. But in light of the Vice-Province's chronic lack of manpower, it was the best possible solution. Reports from the 1640s reveal that Brancati was aware of this predicament, suggesting that even the mutual supervision of village Christians through their confraternities was not enough to keep all from "going cold." In one case he told how a venomous snake had bitten a Christian woman who had "because of her laziness one day stopped going to Our Lady's Confraternity that was held in her village."[21] In another instance he described a man who had gradually lost his faith. "Finding himself in the midst of profits and merchandise," wrote Brancati, "little by little he saw the capital of Christian devotion and the profit of his many merits suffer, making him cold and unconcerned for his soul."[22] So lax did this Christian become that he tried to hang himself three times. Yet each time he began to tighten the noose, he "remembered Our Lady and that he was a member of her brotherhood," and felt the knot loosen. During a fourth attempt, when he was about to drown himself in a river, he had an even more vivid vision of his divine protectress. His "diabolical intention" was so pernicious, she informed him, "that by fleeing from the passing labors of life in this way he was only setting himself up for an eternity of suffering." Upon hearing this warning, we are told, the Christian came to his senses, returning to his *Shengmu hui* to participate with "diligence and fervor."[23]

The organizational strategies developed during the final years of Ming rule proved their worth during the cataclysm of the dynastic transition. Not only did the *Shengmu hui* offer a degree of mutual psychological support during this time of great anxiety, but also they ensured a modicum of security for the Jesuits' Christians. The fact that new converts were easily integrated into existing groups also meant that the missionaries could take advantage of the climate of crisis for publicizing their religious message instead of having to focus on teaching the practice of Catholicism to new converts. For instance, when rebel armies overran the city of Xi'an in the early 1640s and prevented large gatherings, the Jesuits were forced to reorganize the community. They divided the women's confraternity into four smaller groups according to neighborhoods and appointed days for each group to visit the local *Shengmu tang*. "In this way there was no one who was not cultivated in the things of God," reported Inácio da Costa, "and the danger that could have arisen if they all gathered at once was avoided." Nevertheless, he claimed, there was no controlling the fervor of some women who insisted on coming to all four meetings "and were not even satisfied with that."[24]

By the time Qing rule was established across most of China in the 1650s, the confraternity model of organization had become the dominant form of communal piety. This meant that, in effect, the Vice-Province's manpower needs left an indelible mark on the practice of Catholicism in China. In coastal Jiangnan, where the numerical strength of *Tianzhu jiao* was greatest, the vast majority of Christians practiced their religion in Confraternities of the Holy Mother. During the two and a half decades that Francesco Brancati spent at Shanghai, he made sure that the *hui* was the locus of almost all ordinary communal piety. Between 1643 and 1658 he increased the number of confraternities from 30 to 120.[25] So expansive had his *hui* network become that when he sent a list of the churches, chapels, and oratories that he administered to Visitor Francisco Furtado in 1653, he referred to it as "this diocese of mine." Beyond the two main churches, the catechumen house, and mortuary chapel within the city walls, Brancati circulated among at least thirty-three sanctuaries each year. At the time, his flock was divided into seventy confraternities, and the aim of all was to "conserve and augment" the mission church. "Your Reverence can see from this report," pleaded the overburdened Sicilian, "the great necessity I have for companions who can help me cultivate and carry forward this Christian community."[26]

The priests' increased reliance on confraternity structures at mid-century inevitably provoked negative responses from the more zealous members of the mission church, men and women who were not satisfied with the routines of their "parishes" and preferred more frequent access to the sacraments and more interaction with their pastors. While devotional brotherhoods with especially rigorous practices, designated to provide outlets for that type of fervency, could be established in areas with greater concentrations of Christians, not every village could muster enough people to make such groups practicable. A complicated case was cited from the Hangzhou region by Feliciano Pacheco, who reported that the *Shengmu hui,* "both those inside and outside the city walls," were true examples of "fervor and edification," making up for the fact that most of the rural Christians lived too far from the church to attend mass in the city. But he added that some of his flock were "not content with the brotherhoods." These men (one assumes) came from "two or more leagues distant," waking at midnight to begin their trek to Hangzhou.[27] Impassioned Christians even came part of the way from their villages—"half a league"—on their knees, performing this self-mortification not only on major holy days but also on those of secondary importance.[28]

In spite of the dissatisfaction of a handful of Christians, the Jesuits had little reason to experiment with different ways of administering the mission church in the second half of the seventeenth century. The missionaries' exile to Canton in the late 1660s confirmed the worth of the system that had been implemented thus far. The *Shengmu hui* had met the task of maintaining the dispersed groups as effectively during the years that the Jesuits spent in their confinement as they had under normal circumstances, when the missionaries were around the proverbial corner from their flocks. In fact, the missionaries' exile created the conditions for expanding the modes of group piety that had previously been limited to women and rural men. In the absence of their pastors, urban male Christians organized themselves in the manner of their rural counterparts, coordinating their devotions just like the *Shengmu hui.* This system, with its strong emphasis on lay coordination and limited pastoral oversight, would continue long after the end of the Canton exile. The numbers of missionaries did not increase and even decreased in the 1670s and 1680s, and the Jesuits, intent at all costs on preserving the church they had created, accordingly stuck to tried-and-true methods, relegating innovation to the back burner.

Brothers and Sisters of the Holy Mother

The upshot of the Jesuits' determination to spread the use of organizational groups throughout the mission church was that certain forms of piety and specific devotions took precedence over others. But which ones? Their insistence on communal piety meant that the practice of Catholicism in China was largely restricted to the Society's interpretation of proper lay religious activities. Just as the Jesuits themselves were virtually the sole representatives of the Catholic clergy in the country until late in the seventeenth century, the devotions of Chinese Christians in their organizational confraternities were synonymous with the practice of *Tianzhu jiao.* But what was it like to belong to one of these brotherhoods? What were the members' obligations? And what were their rewards, spiritual and temporal?

A Chinese manuscript that lays down the statutes for setting up a *Shengmu hui,* or Marian Confraternity, provides answers to these questions. This text is found at the Roman Archive of the Society of Jesus along with two other sets of confraternity statutes in Chinese (to be examined later on). Although the document is anonymous and contains no internal references to the Vice-Province, it was most likely composed either by a Jesuit or by one of the Society's lay auxiliaries.[29]

The rules commence with a preamble about the reasons for starting such a group and the benefits of membership. There follow eleven points regarding the group's practices and structure. The organizational character of the statutes is revealed in the initial declaration: this type of group was instituted for Christians who "live in the remote countryside and may be unable to come to the church." Missionaries created *Shengmu hui* "in various places" throughout their districts to facilitate prayer gatherings in a given area on Sundays and feast days. Members were informed that "all of the brotherhoods" were called Brotherhoods of the Holy Mother because Mary was "the perfect virgin, whom the Lord of Heaven chose to conceive the Holy Son." The invocation of the Virgin made these Chinese groups similar, as far as their devotional aspects were concerned, to the Society's lay brotherhoods in Europe (for instance, the previously mentioned brotherhoods of Our Lady of the Annunciation). While the Jesuits could not claim exclusivity in this universal Catholic devotion, most of their brotherhoods had an explicitly Marian character, in much the same way that those founded by the Dominicans often invoked the rosary.[30]

The preamble suggests that the body of the statutes was the only structure holding Chinese Christian communities together. The rules sought to ensure group cohesion by reminding members that they were constantly in danger of making a wrong turn onto the road to perdition. Mary "most merciful" was invoked as the "mother of us all," the ideal guide to the sacred teaching who led the way to Heaven. True devotion to her was needed for Christians to avoid "the lure of Satan," so that they might gain eternal happiness rather than earn the unending pains of hell. Spiritual commitment to the Virgin involved observance of the Ten Commandments and regular participation in confraternity activities.

These exhortations to assiduity and piety were, in effect, the only strictures that the Jesuits were able to place on their Christians. (Even after *Tianzhu jiao* became a faith that was passed from one generation to another through kinship networks, the missionaries repeatedly lamented that family ties were scarcely more effective than exhortations for binding Chinese Christians to their religion.) But perhaps this was the Jesuits' way of ensuring that only the truly committed would remain loyal. The statutes do not stipulate mechanisms for enforcing attendance; they only permit repeated exhortations to those who do not "abide by the regulations, or skip meetings without an excuse." Total recalcitrants were to be "left alone."[31]

The principal activity of these Marian brotherhoods was communal prayer. The first point of the statutes clearly outlines the order of the recitations to take place at each meeting. Members were to kneel, make the sign of the cross, and say an introductory prayer (found in *Nianjing zongdu,* the standard prayer manual). They then recited nine Ave Marias and nine Paternosters. This set of prayers was repeated nine times, each time with a different invocation in the following order: the Holy Trinity;

the Passion of Christ and the Eucharist; Mary, mother of mercy; Saint Joseph, patron saint of China; angels and guardian angels; saints and personal patron saints; and the souls in Purgatory. The final two repeats invoked the spiritual benefit of the mission church: the eighth invocation was for the Lord's blessing to descend upon "the family of each member and the community," while the ninth was for *Tianzhu* to "enlighten the hearts and minds of all people to accept the Holy Teaching." The ritual was sealed with the sign of the cross, and then a selected member of the group read "a few passages from a sacred book."[32]

Other Jesuit sources, such as Philippe Couplet's biography of Candida Xu, also outline sequences of prayers. Couplet's description of communal devotions in the Shanghai-Songjiang area in the 1670s contains some interesting details. Evidently, the confraternity members chanted responsorial prayers under the guidance of their president, the *huizhang*. The organizational confraternity statutes do not specify this particular aspect of lay devotion, but it appears to have been the standard way of reciting prayers—and remained so until the early twentieth century. According to Couplet, the first set of devotions began with the sign of the cross. The assembled Christians would then "slowly sing" the Litanies of the Saints. After these initial prayers, the *huizhang* intoned a series of orations, first for "the Emperor, for the magistrates, for peace in the empire, and for the fruits of the earth," and then for "the Emperor of the Holy Law (as the pope is called in China), for the priests, and for the whole church." Further prayers were said for causes similar to those found in the *Shengmu hui* statutes, namely, for "the propagation of the faith, for the extirpation of heresies, for the preachers of the Gospel," and for the Chinese faithful, both living and deceased.[33]

The *Shengmu hui* statutes, being intended to strengthen Christian solidarity, fostered ideas of community that differed from the standard Chinese understanding of *hui* membership. For instance, while it was common practice for social gatherings to include a meal or banquet, the statutes expressly forbade eating at meeting times. "Keep in mind," reads the second rule, "that enjoyment of the flesh will spoil the well-being of the spirit."[34] From the missionaries' perspective, this injunction served two purposes. First, it kept the prayer meetings from becoming occasions of drunkenness or gluttony. It also preempted the inevitable tensions that would arise if people felt forced to compete with one another in offering food at meetings. It is likely, however, that the first reason alone provided

sufficient justification for the missionaries to bar banqueting. After all, one of the greatest transformations of popular piety in Catholic Europe in the early modern period was the shift from occupational-based confraternities to devotional groups as the principal loci of collective lay piety. As a result, there was a dramatic decrease in the amount of feasting that was typically associated with confraternity activities, something for which the reforming Catholic clergy duly congratulated itself.[35]

The statutes made provisions for a *huizhang,* who was to be elected by the group's members, along with two deputies, "so that things may be handled properly and efficiently." Apart from the community's general approbation, there appear to have been no prerequisites for this office. It is tempting to assume that the same marks of prestige that distinguished individuals in late Ming and early Qing villages helped to narrow down the pool of candidates for the post of *huizhang.* For instance, the Jesuits recorded that the Confraternity of the Holy Mother in the village of Nanfeng in Jiangxi Province elected a "literatus of much knowledge and virtue" as president in August 1692.[36] Not enough biographical data about the membership of the mission church have been uncovered as yet to permit definite conclusions. There can be no doubt, however, that the title of *huizhang* conferred a degree of respect among Chinese Christians that made it a desirable position for pious men.

Few special functions for the *huizhang* are outlined in the *Shengmu hui* statutes. It can be inferred that the president was responsible for recording the name of each family that belonged to the group (although, for reasons of safety, not the names of "everyone in the family"). Likewise, the *huizhang* was to serve as the group's moral censor, expelling those members who were "known to have sinned" until they reconciled themselves. Keeping Christians apprised of the calendar of major feast days so that they could meet for prayers was among the *huizhang*'s primary duties. Another responsibility was acting as an intermediary between the community and the closest missionary. It was, moreover, the president's duty to identify children who had gleaned some bits of doctrine so that the priest

---

Woodcut print of the Annunciation in *Method for Reciting the Rosary (Song nianzhu guicheng),* appended to João da Rocha, *Instruction for the Young on the Holy Religion of the Lord of Heaven (Tianzhu shengjiao qimeng),* 1619.

might bestow devotional objects on them during his periodic visits and "encourage them to make further efforts."[37]

Perhaps the most important of the *huizhang's* tasks was to coordinate prayers for the sick and the dying. The president was responsible not only for contacting the priest to offer the sacraments to the infirm, but also for ensuring that those at death's door would benefit from the continual prayers of other Christians. Just as members of devotional confraternities in Europe were obliged to pray for the sick, the dying, and the dead of their number, so the members of the *Shengmu hui* were entrusted with praying for the souls of their confreres in times of mortal crisis. When a Chinese Christian fell ill, the *huizhang* was to assemble the brothers to exhort the infirm "to repentance and remorse" for his sins, invoking both the pains of hell and the rewards of heaven. If it was impossible to summon a priest, the president was to lead the others in prayer, "crying out the name of the Holy Trinity, invoking the Holy Names of Jesus and Mary," and praying to the guardian angels and patron saints to intercede with God on behalf of the afflicted. When the soul was called to its eternal reward, the *huizhang* was to organize a burial in strict observance of a prescribed set of funeral norms.[38]

The capability to rally prayers at such moments was considered one of the greatest benefits of participation in a *Shengmu hui.* Another important reward was the assurance of a dignified funeral. China was a society that placed considerable emphasis on the proper conduct of burial rituals and respect for the dead. The pomp mandated by Chinese tradition was often beyond the reach of plebeians, and those who made exuberant displays of filial piety during burials could lead their households into bankruptcy. It must have come as a great relief to the less prosperous Christians that they could count on having their brethren at their funerals—without significant expenditure.[39] While the Jesuits often organized specialized funerary confraternities at their urban residences, in the countryside the Christian duty of burying the dead fell directly to the members of the organizational groups.

Appended to the manuscript containing the statutes for the *Shengmu hui* is a set of rules to be used in conducting Christian funerals. While it is not clear if they were meant specifically for the *Shengmu hui,* these rules give a good general picture of the funeral practices of Chinese Christians in the later seventeenth century.[40] The principal duties were split between the eldest son of the deceased's family and the *huizhang.* In keeping with

Confucian traditions, the son was responsible for laying out the corpse and providing a coffin "according to the financial means of the family." He was also to select the burial date and make the initial ritual gestures on behalf of the soul of the deceased, which included lighting incense, saying prayers, and inviting the confraternity to assist in the funeral. The role of the president was to lead the others in saying the prayers listed in the ritual, all of them drawn from the common prayer manual. He was also to coordinate the ceremonies, putting the corpse into its coffin and organizing the burial procession. The president would also appoint individuals to keep vigil over the coffin, making sure that they avoided all "drinking, amusement, and idle talk" during their watch. If the family's representative was so inclined, he could offer a meal for the confraternity, but the rules cautioned that he should not exceed his means in making such a gesture. Even if a meal was provided after the funeral, "one need not offer wine."[41]

The funerals of Chinese Christians needed to be handled delicately. On these occasions, the millennial traditions of indigenous culture, which had Confucian, Daoist, and Buddhist roots, impinged most forcefully on the practices of *Tianzhu jiao.* While not all Chinese customs were offensive to the missionaries' notion of orthopraxis, it was imperative for them to set clear boundaries to distinguish Christian conceptions of due funeral pomp from native practices. The Jesuits' insistence on a strict and specific order of prayers and rituals reveals how intent they were on ensuring that funerals which took place beyond their gaze were conducted properly. Here again, the missionaries relied on organizational brotherhoods to check the intrusion of unacceptable customs, playing the supervisory role that they themselves could not. All were exhorted to recall the Christian teachings about the afterlife and consequently to eschew excessive displays of grief. They were also reminded of the Jesuits' "moderate" stance on the Chinese Rites, namely, the custom of keeping ancestral tablets that recorded the names of the deceased. While the bereaved family and the members of the confraternity were permitted to make gestures of respect and were even allowed to place offerings before these tablets, it was made clear that such gestures were merely symbolic. "How," ask the rules pointedly, "can the soul of the deceased really enjoy them?"[42]

Funerals also offered the *Shengmu hui* opportunities to make public demonstrations of piety. To be sure, by denouncing Daoist and Buddhist practices as forcefully as they did, the Jesuits drastically reduced the number of individuals who could be summoned to participate in Christian funeral processions. Forbidden to pay for the services of non-Christian ritual masters and their attendants, adherents of *Tianzhu jiao* had only one another to rely on for staging burial pomp. It appears, however, that the Jesuits and their Christians came up with a norm that balanced the missionaries' requirements for orthopraxis with their flocks' demands for display. The burial cortège envisioned by the rules included musicians, flags, banners with pious slogans, and processional carriages, one bearing the Holy Name and another a cross. The members of the confraternity came next, "in order of seniority," followed by the bereaved family and the coffin. The carriage of the cross was the focus of devotions at the gravesite, as the brotherhood recited prayers and performed the burial. The role of the *huizhang,* standing in for a priest, was to sprinkle both the grave and the coffin with holy water and lead the others in prayer. The ceremony ended when the family's representative knelt to thank the confraternity members for their prayers and assistance.[43]

Teaching the Angels

So far, the focus has been on the devotional activities of adult Christians, or, more specifically, adult male Christians. The analytical scope should now be expanded, because Chinese Christianity was—and became even more predominantly so as the seventeenth century wore on—a family religion. New organizational challenges arose when the mission church shifted from a body of converts to a community in which *Tianzhu jiao* was passed from mother to daughter and from father to son. The Jesuits needed to ensure that all children of Christian parents would be educated in the rudiments of their inborn faith. Compared to the challenge of persuading adults to abandon the religion of their forebears, this task was relatively easy. Children came to the missionaries as tabulae rasae, free of the encrustation of religious customs that would have to be chipped away by argumentation. Teaching doctrine to children was therefore something that could readily be delegated to auxiliaries.

There was no lack of adult Chinese Christians willing to take up the task of indoctrinating children. In order to channel their good intentions effectively, the Jesuits had to elaborate new teaching methods appropriate to the mission field. This came to them naturally, in view of their experience as educators and their skills at structuring lessons. In Europe their order enjoyed renown for teaching doctrine to children; indeed, Jesuits whose primary assignment was to hold impromptu doctrine classes in town squares and city streets could be found across the Catholic world. They used songs to inculcate prayers and encouraged their pupils to memorize points of faith by distributing devotional objects to those who gave correct answers. To be sure, the Jesuits neither invented nor monopolized doctrine teaching in Europe. They were one force among a host of clerical and lay catechetical initiatives in the massive pan-European surge in religious education that occurred in the early modern period.[44] In China, however, the Society's methods of indoctrination were clearly the first and foremost. It was no coincidence that when João da Rocha translated a doctrine dialogue *(Tianzhu shengjiao qimeng)*, he selected a text that had been written specifically for teaching children—and popularized by a Portuguese Jesuit who left the most important theology chair at the University of Coimbra, no less, to spend years leading doctrine-singing children around the city of Lisbon.[45]

Seeing the success of the *Shengmu hui* in structuring communal devotions, the Jesuits employed a confraternity model for doctrine teaching as well. Starting as early as the 1640s, they began to establish *Tianshen hui*, Confraternities of the Angels, to provide a uniform structure for children's spiritual education. It is somewhat of an exaggeration to call these groups of children and teachers "brotherhoods," rather than merely "classes," but the name itself seems to have been part of the Jesuits' strategy for encouraging participation. It does not appear that the missionaries had written statutes for these groups, at least not ones with the same degree of complexity as those issued to the organizational *hui* or devotional groups. But by using a special title and motivational tactics for children to learn their lessons, the missionaries hoped to turn the memorization of the catechism into a cause for "pious competition" among the younger followers.

It ought to be no surprise that the first *Tianshen hui* were founded by Francesco Brancati to handle the pastoral challenges found in the Shanghai area. The Sicilian missionary published a catechism titled *Tianshen huike* for use by the laymen and women who ran these groups. This book, written in simple dialogue form, contains prayers and points of doctrine.[46] Missionaries in other areas took their cue from Brancati and began forming similar groups in the 1650s and early 1660s. For instance, the Jesuits in two other Jiangnan cities, Yangzhou and Changshu, had founded *Tianshen hui* by 1660. That year Jean Valat created similar doctrine groups at Tai'an in Shandong Province. This Jesuit reported creating confraternities for boys and girls, "giving them all of the statutes and rules appropriate for their capacities." Valat could hardly contain his joy at seeing how well the groups fulfilled their task. "Most of the boys and girls," he noted, "already know how to pray not only the Paternoster, Ave Maria, Credo, and the Commandments, but also many other prayers from the daily prayer book, and the Litanies of the Angels and of the Virgin."[47]

One of the best descriptions of the *Tianshen hui* comes in a letter that Simão da Cunha sent to Visitor Francisco Furtado from the mountainous interior of Fujian Province in 1653. Cunha commented on how dismayed he had been when he visited Dingzhou and found many children "who had received holy baptism at a tender age but knew nothing of the Law." He was exasperated by the fact that parents did not teach doctrine to their children: "It seems that they have imbibed a heresy found here in China, which holds that fathers should not be masters for their sons." His solution was to create a Confraternity of the Angels, which was to meet on the third Sunday of each month. Cunha himself conducted the group's first meetings, and then passed on the teaching duties to a Christian adult. Satisfied by the results in Dingzhou, the Jesuit proceeded to create such *hui* throughout his mission district.[48]

The *Tianshen hui* that met at Cunha's residence in Yanping convened once a month on a Sunday afternoon. First, the children would report to the church in the company of their parents and make prostrations before the devotional images. Cunha noted that there was always an adult on hand to teach them the appropriate prayers to say when bowing to the icons of the Lord of Heaven and instruct them how to bless themselves with holy water. When all of the children were quietly assembled in the mission station's reception hall, the priest would recite prayers for the pupils to repeat. After this initial exercise, the Jesuit would ask individual children questions about prayers and points of doctrine. In order to inspire them, Cunha set up a table with "prizes that they can see, such as images, veronicas, books, rosaries." Those who responded correctly received prizes, while the others were told they would be rewarded when they had memorized their prayers. At the end of *Tianshen hui* meetings, two children would stand on a bench and recite the doctrine dialogue found in their primer. Just before going home, all would say an act of contrition. A further benefit of these classes was that they contributed to indoctrinating adults. "The children teach many things to their parents," wrote Cunha, "which they take like pills covered in sugar that otherwise cannot be swallowed."[49]

The satisfactory results produced by Confraternities of the Angels during the 1650s and early 1660s led the Jesuits to mandate them throughout the mission church. This move came in the late 1660s, when the missionaries' exile forced them to delegate virtually all of their pastoral work to their lay auxiliaries. In the rules and exhortations dispatched to Christian communities from Canton, Vice-Provincial Feliciano Pacheco reminded adults that those who loved their "children or younger brothers must love their souls above all, and after that care for their bodies." He encouraged them to create *Tianshen hui,* insisting on the benefits that adult Christians would receive from having children who knew Catholic prayers and doctrine in their midst. God was more likely to hear the prayers of children at the bedside of a sick elder, he claimed, because "He is pleased with them, as they have had very little contact with the world and are only lightly contaminated with sin."[50]

Pacheco's instructions also included tips for setting up such teaching groups. Each community should designate a fervent Christian, he suggested, choosing an individual who belonged to a devotional confraternity (not an organizational brotherhood). This person would be charged with making sure that children attended *Tianshen hui* meetings and that all families took turns at making snacks "for attracting and stimulating the children," that is, providing incentives likely to hold their attention. Pacheco cautioned doctrine teachers "not to do too much, but to attempt primarily to explain the principal truths of the religion to the children, and the observance of the Ten Commandments." Solid grounding in the precepts of the Decalogue would inculcate the basic Christian notions of morality, and that was essential. As if to underscore this sentiment, Pacheco concluded his remarks on the *Tianshen hui* with the following exhortation: "Mind their moral formation, that is the most important thing."[51]

By the early 1670s the mission church was a multigenerational body in which *Tianshen hui* were an integral part of Christian life. This situation was especially clear in the Jiangnan region, the cradle of innovation in pastoral strategies. The response of François de Rougemont was to purchase devotional objects periodically for the doctrine groups convened in Changshu. His account book from the early 1670s contains entries of expenditures for "sweets" and prizes intended for distribution at their meetings.[52] In the Shanghai-Songjiang area, Candida Xu paid for the scores of devotional objects used by *Tianshen hui.* According to her biographer, Philippe Couplet, Xu donated "rosaries, agnus dei, images, crosses, medals, and other similar items of devotion to be distributed among the children." Each year the priests would hold a ceremony on the feast of Saint Michael (September 29) at Shanghai's Church of the Savior to distribute these prizes to the area's doctrine teachers.[53] The presence of such groups, however, was also felt in remote rural areas. In 1686 José Soares formed a Confraternity of the Angels which met once each month in a village in Shanxi Province. Evidently the country boys and girls took to the question-and-answer method, "responding with much dexterity about the prayers and mysteries of the Holy Law."[54]

"Apostles for This Kingdom"

As the mission church began to expand significantly in the 1630s, the Jesuits made greater use of lay catechists for ministering to their Christians. To be sure, they had long relied on eunuchs and women to catechize segments of the population with whom they could not deal in person. But the reality of burgeoning numbers of Christians made the employment of catechists a general phenomenon. These individuals took on the tasks of teaching doctrine, providing oversight for local communities, maintaining sanctuaries, and, at times, preaching to other Christians. Catechists also engaged in proselytizing in the Jesuits' stead—to the point that, by 1700, they were the primary motor of the mission church's expansion. In light of this range of activities, the use of the term "catechists" is perhaps misleading. Yet from the missionaries' perspective, their primary task was to provide instruction to other men, women, and children in basic Christian doctrine, regardless of whether the objects of their attention were already baptized. The other responsibilities that they accumulated should be understood as outgrowths from this principal function as the Jesuits were forced to hand over an ever greater proportion of their duties to their lay auxiliaries.

Visualize the organization of the mission church as a pyramid with a handful of priests and coadjutors at its topmost level. At the second layer of management extends the network of catechists. At the bottom one finds the *huizhang,* the presidents of the organizational confraternities. The distinction between the lower two levels is not entirely clear. It appears that the social standing of the *huizhang* was higher than that of the catechists, and that their positions within their local communities reflected the positions of respect they commanded. But while catechists often had responsibilities similar to those of the *huizhang*, they were deputized by the missionaries for a greater range of duties. It is likely that while most *huizhang* performed catechetical duties, catechists were not necessarily entrusted with community organization.[55] The primary differences between the two offices were the catechists' doctrine teaching tasks, their greater range of movement among a given set of Christian communities, and the more personal nature of their relationship with the missionaries. The same qualities distinguished them from the Vice-Province's coadjutors. Whereas catechists shared many tasks with Jesuit brothers, they were not bound by the Society's vows. Moreover, there were far more catechists in the service of the mission than there were coadjutors, especially after the 1630s.

The Vice-Province's Annual Letters include numerous accounts of the catechists' activities. Unfortunately, the sources shroud these men and women in a cloud of anonymity, revealing more about their duties than their identities. For instance, the 1636 Annual Letter speaks of a catechist who happened upon a prospective convert while traveling through the Shanghai countryside. When the Christian came across a woman who was burning spirit money for her deceased husband, he entered her home "and asked the woman what the useless fire was." The woman reportedly stated that she was merely obeying her spouse's testament, but that had not stopped "the devil from entering her house and making her child sick." Seizing the opportunity, the catechist told her of the Teachings of the Lord of Heaven, healed the child with holy water, and was rewarded with the conversion of the whole household.[56] Another report from Hangzhou in 1644 eulogized Paulo Li, a catechist who lived to be more than eighty years old. Li had two principal tasks, namely, "to travel constantly in search of new souls to baptize and to cultivate those of the Christians." In the missionaries' estimation, he was most effective with women of the elite, whom he addressed "with great energy and propriety in the local tongue, using such apt comparisons that he always convinced them."[57]

As this last comment suggests, catechists were most valuable to the missionaries as native speakers of China's myriad dialects. In addition to helping the Jesuits address women, catechists often accompanied the priests through rural areas. In both cases they were indispensable intermediaries. One revealing account of a missionary's bond of friendship with his catechist is found in the deathbed exhortation that Rodrigo de Figueiredo made to a longtime auxiliary in 1639. The Portuguese Jesuit averred that the man would soon reach paradise because of the years he had spent "teaching and preaching to women about matters relating to Christ and His mother." Figueiredo then posed a set of rhetorical questions about the catechist's activities to prove his point: "Didn't you preach and tell those women that they should strive to gain glory? Were you not aware this only comes after death? Well, now your time has come, be happy. You served me and accompanied me all these years. What fruit did we cull from all that wandering? By any chance, were we banqueted at the homes we went to? Did you get money from those we visited? Did you wear silk? Did you eat better, or were you better off because more people heard you and learned from you? This was the hour you worked for, the one that comes next is what you were striving to reach."[58]

Figueiredo worked in Henan Province with more than one assistant of this type. He was one of the first missionaries to create a confraternity designed to train and supervise catechists. Figueiredo organized his group in 1639, dedicating it to Saint Thomas with the purpose of nourishing "preachers and catechists to serve as apostles for this province and for this kingdom, just as Thomas did for the Orient." The brotherhood's twenty members met twice each month at the house of one of their number for praying, preaching, and discussing points of doctrine, as well as speaking of "ways of moving the Christian community forward and spreading the word of God." On each occasion the catechists would draw up a schedule of meetings with Figueiredo at his residence. The whole of the appointed day was to be spent at the church, hearing mass, praying, and listening to the missionary's elaborations on different points of doctrine. Figueiredo even wrote a textbook of sorts for his catechists, with lessons on themes such as "the life of Christ, that of Our Lady, and the propagation of the Law from the first day of the creation of the world until the present." Figueiredo's disciples were entrusted with passing on the content of these lessons to the rest of the flock at Kaifeng on Sundays, while individual Christians awaited their turn to confess. According to him, groups would form in the church to listen to the catechists talk—"one over here about the practices and virtues of Our Lady; another over there about the torment and passion of her blessed son; this one listing the sons and descendants of Jacob; that one telling of the punishments He inflicted on Pharaoh to free His people from captivity, the miracles and marvels of Moses when he crossed the Red Sea, what happened the rest of the way to the Promised Land, the life of Joseph, and the stories of Tobias, Judith, and Daniel." In Figueiredo's opinion, all who heard these lessons derived great benefit from them. Even the children present were so well versed in these stories that he was at pains to recall if more could be expected from their peers in "any patio of students in Europe."[59]

Missionaries in other parts of China tried similar strategies to coordinate their catechists. Reports from the 1650s and 1660s reveal a general impulse toward this sort of organization as the mission church expanded. For example, in 1658 Girolamo Gravina created a Confraternity of the Twelve Apostles at Changshu. He restricted membership to twelve catechists whose goal was "to seek their own salvation with all their strength and inclination." More important, members were to channel their fervor toward helping their neighbors spiritually. They set about this task by proselytizing non-Christians and supervising their local coreligionists, seeking the conversion of entire households where one or more members had been baptized, and urging all Christians to confess at least once each year. While their general goal was to "seek the conversion of heathens, especially their relatives and friends," these Twelve Apostles had a special monthly obligation either to "reinvigorate a lukewarm Christian or convert a heathen." Gravina claimed considerable success with this group, telling of how a member took his task so seriously that one month he brought in some thirty people to be baptized.[60] Evidently the Changshu Christians were also satisfied with the Twelve Apostles, since the confraternity still met regularly in the 1670s, when François de Rougemont was the local pastor.[61]

The valuable role of the Vice-Province's catechists was confirmed during the Canton exile. With the exception of the Dominican Luo Wenzao and a handful of Jesuit coadjutors, catechists—even if acting in no more than a surrogate, semiofficial capacity—were the only representatives of the Catholic clergy among the Chinese Christians. Missionary sources are agreed that they were responsible for bringing new members to the church, yet the Jesuits were clearly worried about the way they carried out their apostolic endeavors. Among the topics discussed by the men of the Vice-Province in January 1668 was the need to ensure that all regional churches (that is, the agglomerate of Christian communities administered by the priests at a given residence) had a catechist confraternity. It can be inferred from this rule that the Jesuits hoped to devise some common method of organizing and supervising their auxiliaries. In the late 1660s they clearly saw the need to regularize Chinese Catholic practice and therefore sought to impose conformity on the different forms of catechist activity that had developed over the three preceding decades.[62]

A clear solution to that diversity would emerge fully only in the 1670s, after the Jesuits returned to their residences to resume control of their communities. By that time, however, the overburdened missionaries needed more help than ever before from their doctrine-teaching auxiliaries. The catechists had proved their worth in supervising the religious activities of their fellow Christians in the preceding years, and the return of the priests confirmed them in their role as community overseers. In areas with larger Christian communities, such as coastal Jiangnan, the Jesuits elaborated a new system for regulating their auxiliaries. They instituted groups called Confraternities of Saint Francis Xavier, or *Sheng Fangjige hui,* to instill a sense of solidarity as well as to ensure mutual oversight among the catechists. By bringing them together for periodic meetings with the priests, the Jesuits also afforded themselves a certain degree of quality control; they could verify that all of their catechists were teaching doctrine correctly and were acting as proper representatives of the missionaries and their religion.

The most vivid account of the catechists' confraternities is found in Philippe Couplet's description of the Shanghai church in the 1670s. In that decade, the Flemish missionary states, he and his colleagues relied on sixty catechists. All of these belonged to the Confraternity of Saint Francis Xavier, which held its meetings in the presence of the priests at the city's main church. According to Couplet, this group was the "most important of all" the congregations in the area. Its primary task was to make sure that children born into Christian families were properly indoctrinated. Each catechist was charged with visiting all the Christian households in his district four times a year. Once each season the catechists would gather in Shanghai to present written accounts of the state of each family. They were to inform the priests whether or not there were devotional images and holy water in every home and also to tell him if any of the Christians had relapsed into "their old superstitions." They were also responsible for reporting any children who needed to be baptized and any elderly or infirm individuals who needed "the remedies of the Church." The catechists' most difficult task is likely to have been their role as moral censors. In their written evaluations, they were to inform the priest "precisely about the behavior of every individual Christian."[63]

The Shanghai Jesuits also employed a Confraternity of Saint Ignatius Loyola to assist them in cultivating their Christians. Couplet records that this group was composed of "bachelors, literati, and students" who sought to inspire their peers with rhetoric. (While it is unclear whether missionaries in other areas relied on their more educated Christians in the same manner, it seems likely.) The Shanghai group met on the first day of each month at the missionaries' residence to pray and exercise their apologetical skills by raising doubts about their religion that they would resolve together. The Jesuits would then supply them with tracts and books for use in writing compositions and instruct them on matters relating to the "principal truths of the faith, its mysteries, and the most famous feasts of the church." Members would then produce treatises that they would read aloud to the assembly, taking corrections from the missionaries. Once they were equipped with approved texts, the Jesuits would send them to preach on the following Sunday at the churches that they themselves were unable to visit. Couplet was particularly fond of this group, noting that "the Chinese are greatly inclined to produce texts and recite their compositions," and that such exercises were good for "cultivating the talents" of educated Christians.[64]

The increased reliance on lay auxiliaries inevitably created new challenges. The way catechists went about teaching doctrine was one of the Jesuits' main preoccupations. While the missionaries themselves all had teaching experience and knew how to structure lessons, the same could not necessarily be said for their surrogates. In the late 1670s they began to air their frustrations on the matter. Ferdinand Verbiest lamented to a confrere that the catechists at the capital did "not usually keep much order" during their explanations.[65] To be sure, his view of their disorganization was in all likelihood a corollary of his general appraisal of indigenous forms of reasoning. Verbiest wrote to another colleague that, just as in the canonical texts of indigenous philosophy, the Chinese typically explained things using "backwards maxims, without a linked discourse."[66] Verbiest's solution to this problem was straightforward. In 1677 he published an "order of catechizing" for his auxiliaries, called *Tianzhu jiaoyao xulun*.[67]

Verbiest's concerns were echoed by the hierarchy of the Society's Asian missions in the 1680s. Prompted by events in Tonkin, where French

Vicars Apostolic had rushed to transform native catechists into priests, Visitor Andrea Lubelli (1628–1685) sent a circular letter to his subordinates in 1681. Fearing that the Vicars appointed to China might try the same tack in the Qing empire, he urged his confreres to educate their auxiliaries thoroughly. Insisting that the training of "good and fervent catechists" was the "first of our cares and the greatest of our tasks," Lubelli outlined the skills that all of them had to be taught. In addition to a solid grounding in doctrine, all needed to know necessary arguments to deploy when addressing prospective converts, using "comparisons that suited the capacities of their listeners."[68]

Lubelli sought to ensure that Chinese catechists presented doctrine in a logical fashion. They were to start by affirming the existence of God, the eternal soul, and the divine punishment and rewards for human behavior. After this preamble they were to discuss "the divine precepts which conform to reason" and refute the "superstitious errors and idols." Only after having persuaded their interlocutors of these basics were catechists to venture into more speculative territory and broach the topic of the mysteries of the faith, such as the "Trinity, Incarnation, and Life and Death of the Lord." Like Verbiest, Lubelli insisted on thorough training for all auxiliaries, especially the more educated ones. Recalling his experiences with literati catechists at Canton, the Visitor remarked that "almost all" of them spoke in an impenetrable manner. "In a half hour they want to say everything," Lubelli wrote, "but they do it in such a confusing way that those who already know the mysteries leave their classes with muddled heads, and those who come to hear the holy law for the first time even more so." And all this, he continued, "because we trust them since they are literati!"[69]

The catechists' assistance to the mission church was not necessarily gratis. In addition to offering them lodgings, the Jesuits paid them a wage to cover their living expenses. François de Rougemont's account book from the 1670s reveals emoluments to a number of catechists who worked with him in the Changshu area. He employed male and female catechists, who performed largely the same duties as the members of Shanghai's Confraternity of Saint Francis Xavier. They made periodic visits to Christian households, acted as interpreters in areas with different dialects, and maintained village churches. They did not, however, all come from the same social stratum or have the same financial wherewithal. Their number included minor literati and physicians no less than individuals who were blind and destitute. The Jesuit's ledger indicates that he paid his catechists' travel expenses ("I gave the catechist Francisco Fang Yuwang, who was ordered to go to various locations, as travel money 0.720 tael") and gave some of them charity ("For Kin Martha, the catechist, as alms 0.600 tael").[70]

To be sure, by mixing money into their transactions with catechists, the Jesuits knew that they might draw a few bad pennies. The more optimistic, such as José Soares, downplayed the significance of the financial aspect of human relations. He insisted that the catechists' sense of "charity for their neighbors weighs more in their hearts than their interest or temporal necessity." If not, Soares argued, they would surely "spend their time in some service or contract where they could draw a profit."[71] Men such as Francisco da Veiga (1631–1703), a Portuguese Jesuit who spent part of his career on Hainan Island, were more wary of the auxiliaries on their payroll. While Veiga recognized the worth of a good catechist, he approved only of those who esteemed "the office more than the benefice." Those who did not were a plague on the mission. "With their right eye on the silver and their left eye on the doctrine," he wondered, "what kind of teaching can one expect?"[72]

Delegating the Power to Convert

By the last quarter of the seventeenth century, the crushing weight of the Jesuits' pastoral burdens made it impossible for them to carry out proselytizing tasks in the manner of their predecessors. Since the performance of the sacraments was their exclusive and inalienable duty, the Jesuits delegated the task of evangelization and indoctrination to their auxiliaries. They nevertheless aimed to retain a degree of control by grouping catechists into Confraternities of Saint Francis Xavier. To be sure, by endowing their auxiliaries with the authority to expound the principles of their religion as well as perform ceremonies such as baptism, the missionaries ceded an important part of their ritual power. One need only recall the fierce resistance mounted by certain Jesuits to the idea of a native clergy to be reminded how dangerous such moves were seen to be in some quarters. In order to make sure that renegade catechists would not carry off *Tianzhu jiao* in unorthodox directions, the missionaries opted for formalism. They instituted special brotherhoods in which auxiliaries would be examined on matters of doctrine and held to high standards of personal piety and morality.

One of the best ways of understanding how the Jesuits employed the confraternity model to monitor their catechists is to look at the statutes of one such brotherhood. In the same set of manuscripts containing the *Shengmu hui* statutes and the funeral ritual previously discussed, one finds a set of rules for a Confraternity of Saint Francis Xavier.[73] Similar in format to the statutes of the organizational brotherhood, these rules consist of a short preamble followed by eighteen points. Befitting a confraternity of catechists, Xavier was presented as the paragon of evangelizing. Members were reminded that the Basque missionary was a member of the Society of Jesus "sent by order of the pope to preach the doctrine to Eastern peoples." God had endowed Xavier with the power to show others the way to paradise, and He worked many miracles to corroborate the missionary's message. Those who endeavored to honor *Tianzhu* and "save all people" were therefore encouraged to emulate "the virtue of the saint." More important, they were heartily enjoined to "abide by the regulations."[74]

Prospective members of this catechist confraternity had to meet certain conditions and undergo a probationary period. The group's first rule set the bar for the moral conduct of all brothers: they were to be models of probity in their observance of the Ten Commandments and "all the other rules of the Holy Teaching." Postulants had to attend the group's four seasonal meetings and could join only after a year. They were urged to consider the pious actions of the group's members as "food for the soul" and were warned that those who strayed into sin or experienced a crisis of faith would suffer after they lost this divine nourishment. Those who joined the group were instructed to "watch their words as if they were guarding a treasure." Since the essence of Christianity was to pass over their lips, they were strictly forbidden to speak any "useless or idle words" to others. According to the statutes, the best way to avoid falling into disgrace was to maintain an active spiritual life. Members ought to ensure that not only they but all the members of their household as well "respectfully serve the Lord day and night, recite prayers, say their confession, abide by the Ten Commandments, and perform Holy Works properly."[75]

In contrast to the *Shengmu hui* statutes, the catechist group's rules give little information about how the four yearly meetings were to be held. Rather, they present a set of evangelizing techniques, with special focus on the minimum criteria for admitting adults to baptism. By spelling out these procedures in detail, the Jesuits hoped that their auxiliaries would rely more on their discretion than their zeal. In other words, they wanted their catechists to make a careful examination of the reasons why individuals sought baptism. Under ideal circumstances, catechists would let a priest interview all potential converts to make sure they had been properly indoctrinated. It was the auxiliaries' job to verify that those whom they presented to the missionaries expressed remorse for their sins and were determined "to reject all pagan teachings." They were to insist that submitting to baptism without a sincere desire to obey Christian precepts "would do no good." Although only the Jesuits themselves were supposed to perform this ritual, they granted confraternity members the privilege of baptizing people who were "critically ill." Another provision permitted catechists to perform secret baptisms in order to accommodate those who sought to convert against their families' wishes. All baptisms performed by auxiliaries were to be reported to the missionaries, with the details of the date of the ceremony, the hometown of the converts, and their family name duly noted.[76]

Once the Jesuits endowed their catechists with ritual powers, the need for discretion was even greater. Missionary sources suggest that the baptismal ceremony was often understood in popular circles as a healing ritual. Chinese sources also reveal that the sprinkling of holy water, whether or not during the rite of baptism, was considered thaumaturgic.[77] Jesuits often doubted the urgent pleas uttered by potential converts in the throes of disease. "I am reluctant to baptize some sick people unless they are moribund," wrote one veteran, "since they only want to enter the Holy Law after spending what they had to implore the *pagodes.*" Too many begged to be baptized so they might "attain bodily health, but they do not heal their souls." Their subsequent loss of fervor was proof enough for this Jesuit: "They say they want it with their mouth, but they do not say it with their heart."[78] But if the missionaries themselves had trouble gauging converts' sincerity, how much more so their catechists?

The rules of the Confraternity of Saint Francis Xavier contain straightforward exhortations to caution when dispensing the rite of baptism. Two rules warn against haste when dealing with the sick and dying. Catechists were told that in these cases, baptism "cannot be given lightly." Even at times of mortal danger, they were to present a synopsis of Christian doctrine and wait for positive acknowledgment from the prospective convert. Catechists were reminded that "holy water is medicine for healing the spirit, not the physical body," a tidbit that they surely passed on to their afflicted interlocutors. The auxiliaries were urged to exercise greater caution if they were summoned to the bedside of a sick individual and found members of the Buddhist and Daoist clergy present. According to the statutes, this was a sure sign that the diseased considered the Lord of Heaven "an equal to a bodhisattva" and therefore did not deserve any of the Christian's prayers.[79]

Another important duty of the catechists was to supervise the religious and moral behavior of the Christians in their appointed districts. Confraternity members were instructed to "guide and watch" the souls of all the children they baptized, in an attempt to ensure that their parents lived up to the baptismal promises. Catechists were also given the power to rebuke adult Christians who had "gone cold." It is important to note that the statutes provided for the members' mutual supervision as well. If a catechist knew of another who had done "something bad," he was instructed to admonish the transgressor "secretly and tactfully." Those who repeatedly refused such fraternal correction were to be reported to missionaries.

There was more than one way for the catechists to abuse the powers accorded them by the missionaries. The men of the Vice-Province were acutely concerned about the public image of *Tianzhu jiao* and knew full well the stakes involved in letting zealous laymen speak on their behalf. But how were the missionaries to monitor the way their auxiliaries presented Christianity? While the Jesuits trusted the members of the Confraternity of Saint Francis Xavier to watch their mouths "as if guarding a treasure," making sure that they did not circulate any unorthodox writings was another matter entirely. Here again, however, the missionaries could only rely on trust and moral injunctions. Catechists were warned against using "any unpublished writings" and were obliged to make notations of all sources for the materials used in their compositions. Considering that the Jesuits themselves had each of their Chinese publications reviewed by three readers, their vigilance vis-à-vis would-be apologist authors who lacked even basic education in theology is scarcely surprising. Just as in the case of the literati confraternity at Shanghai described by Philippe Couplet, catechists were to submit their writings for evaluation at the group's meetings. Yet the limits of this attempt at message control were patently evident in the statutes' final word on the matter. If presumption drove a member to distribute unapproved texts, his behavior was to be considered "not in accordance with the rules," with the inferred punishment of expulsion.[80]

The Universal Congregation

Writing to his European confreres in the early 1690s, Juan Antonio de Arnedo presented an unflattering picture of the realities of missionary life in China. He enumerated the routine burdens shouldered by the men of the Vice-Province, especially at the larger mission stations, such as Shanghai. Particularly arduous, according to Arnedo, was being "shackled to the confessional until midday" and afterwards being obliged to say mass, "followed by a sermon and prayers." He also mentioned "having to attend to so many neophytes," as well as being required to make laps around rural circuits "in the cold and under the sun, all the while incurring many expenses and molestations." These, however, were among the more positive aspects of missionary life. Arnedo also complained about having to manage the temporal affairs of a mission station, "the impertinence of the Chinese, the unhappiness of some servants, and the disdain of many of this nation." Even more distressing were the "anxiety of being in charge of so many churches, the laxity of many Christians, the apostasies of others, and the opposition from the heathens." Such drudgery, Arnedo insisted, required "much spirit" of the missionaries since even the pluckiest often became "bored with their lives."[81]

Arnedo's derogatory sketch is surprising—and not simply because it appeared in an Annual Letter. His litany of complaints makes no mention of the complex workings of the mission church. In fact, the loudest chord that Arnedo strikes is a lament about the stultifying nature of his routines: hearing confessions, saying mass, caring for a residence. He did not raise his voice against the confusion of disorganized Christian communities. Rather, his complaints were a veiled indictment of the very structures that permitted the propagation of *Tianzhu jiao* in Qing China. If it were not for the intricate organization of the mission church, Arnedo and his colleagues would not have been immersed in such dulling routines. They would have faced a monstrous agglomeration of Chinese Christians and might never have come to grips with the real problem of keeping them indoctrinated. But such a reality was unthinkable to those on the spot. By the time the Jesuits' China enterprise had passed its centenary mark in the 1680s, its Christian communities constituted an intricate system of interdependent parts reminiscent of the European clocks the missionaries repeatedly laid before the Dragon Throne.

The Jesuits were the key that gave the initial impulse to the mission church, and they were the weights that kept its mechanism balanced. They laid down its organization, provided their Christians with periodic access to the sacraments, and, in their spare time, supplied at least a minimum of pastoral supervision to their flocks. But most of the dynamism behind the workings of the mission church came from the Jesuits' auxiliaries. They were the ones who carried out the supervisory tasks that would have been the local clergy's responsibility, had there been more priests in China. To give but one example, the forty-two village confraternities attached to the Songjiang mission station strained the capacities of its resident Jesuit, Emmanuele Laurifice. The Italian priest therefore identified eight doctrinally well-versed individuals from each of these *Shengmu hui* and appointed them to supervise the comportment of their peers. The selectees were obliged to visit the Christian households of their appointed districts every three months. According to the Annual Letter for the late 1680s, they were to "ask about each family's health in the name of the priest, console the sick, make sure those in danger received the sacraments, and exhort all to observe the Holy Law."[82] During their visits, the deputies were to instruct children in doctrine. They were also told to baptize all infants, even those who appeared healthy, because it was impossible for the priest to make trips to the countryside for administering the sacrament to newborns, and "experience had shown that if they were not cared for with this degree of punctuality, many would die without baptism."[83]

So the task of community oversight was delegated to catechists. According to one report, by the early 1690s there existed a congregation of these auxiliaries "in almost all of the missions."[84] As should be expected, the most intricate system of catechist coordination was found in coastal Jiangnan. It appears that in the final years of the seventeenth century, the standards had been raised. In order to join the Confraternity of Saint Francis Xavier, one had to be of "known zeal, accompanied by good letters and preaching talent." But this was not all. Prospective catechists had to pass an examination, given by the priests, which required them to deliver an extemporaneous sermon or apologetic discourse on some aspect of *Tianzhu jiao.* Only those who defended their discourses "with dexterity" were permitted to join the group. It was imperative that they not cede ground in arguments with their non-Christian rivals or those who doubted their truths. At least the Jesuits were pleased with the catechists' work. "They can be called the root and flower," enthused one missionary, "from whence sprouts the copious fruit that is harvested every year in this most vast Christian community."[85]

The indispensable cogs in the clockwork of the mission church were its organizational confraternities. These groups were the Jesuits' response to the challenge of having to provide all of their Christians with access to the confessional and the Eucharist at least once a year. Of the two sacraments, confession was the more time-consuming by far for the priests, since it required individual encounters. It was the tens of thousands of men and women requiring that kind of attention in the Shanghai area alone that led Juan Antonio de Arnedo to lament that his confreres were "shackled to the confessional." It would have been impossible for the local priests based in Shanghai to attend to this multitude had they lacked "a good method and order," the Spanish Jesuit noted. This particular community was split into "more than one hundred confraternities," each with its appointed superior whose duties were to visit Christians in nearby villages and to attend monthly *hui* meetings.[86]

In other words, the Shanghai area had a plethora of Christian meeting places where these organizational confraternities converged to say prayers and receive the sacraments. According to a report from 1697, Francesco Brancati's former "diocese" had not ceased to expand, and its number of sanctuaries grew apace. In addition to the three churches within the city walls (one for men and two for women), there was also a church at the cemetery where the Jesuits were buried, as well as sixty churches scattered about nearby villages. There were also nineteen oratories, some of which were "larger than the churches." Another thirty hamlets with resident Christians lacked "decent conditions" for saying mass. Those who lived in them were instructed to head for the nearest sanctuaries "to hear the Divine Word and fulfill their obligations," that is, to confess and take communion. These sacraments were administered by one of the four local missionaries. In order to make them available to women, the elderly, and the infirm, a priest would visit each of the sanctuaries once a year. Female catechumens who had already been indoctrinated would also be baptized on such occasions. The Shanghai Jesuits spent an average of four months each year on these visits and another three months attending to the various male confraternities by turn at the city's residence church.[87]

While such elaborate systems of "parish" organization and visitations were not uniformly necessary throughout the Vice-Province, each missionary was obliged to devise ways of dealing with female Christians.

Their standard practice was to create separate sanctuaries for women, most often called *Shengmu tang,* Churches of the Holy Mother, which were located in close proximity to the Jesuits' residences but not directly connected to them. Often, the women's churches were sizable structures, reflecting the spread of Christianity among females. For instance, the one in Nanjing, dedicated to the Immaculate Conception, was a substantial building that had formerly been the principal church for male Christians.[88] In 1693 the Christian women of the Qing capital paid for the construction of a new church, one dedicated to the Annunciation and located on the grounds of the Jesuits' College of Peking. According to José Soares, they funded the new church by "depriving themselves of their rings, pendant earrings, buttons, and other gold and silver ornaments."[89] Twice each year, the capital's Christian women would gather for "universal congregations," attending mass together. During the rest of the year, they met monthly (or, in some cases, weekly) in one of twenty-six different women's confraternities affiliated with chapels and oratories throughout the city. In order to "avoid confusion," each of these groups visited the Church of the Annunciation in a predetermined order so that its members could confess and take communion.[90]

By the turn of the eighteenth century, the mechanism of the mission church had attained its ultimate degree of development. The springs (the catechists), gears (the doctrine teaching groups), and cogs (organizational confraternities) that maintained the dynamism of the practice of *Tianzhu jiao* operated with a vigor that made the function of the missionaries themselves seem negligible. To be sure, this was a community of Catholics and could not be sustained solely by the actions of the laity, regardless of their level of zeal. It needed priests, but the Jesuits knew that it did not need many of them. In the flush of confidence that led Vice-Provincial Antoine Thomas to petition his Roman superiors for a mere twenty-four extra priests in 1703 was an implicit acknowledgment of the ingenious method of organization that his confreres had used to structure their church.[91] Thomas and his brethren were well aware that the Chinese Christians themselves were the driving force behind Chinese Christianity. In contrast to the trend toward greater clerical influence in the lives of early modern European Catholics, most of the Jesuits' Chinese flocks were responsible for their own piety. Thanks to the *Shengmu hui,* the *Tianshen hui,* and especially the lay auxiliaries, the mission church could sustain itself, and even expand, without the missionaries. This is the reason why the Teachings of the Lord of Heaven did not disappear from China when the Vice-Province was fatally transformed in the 1720s. It is no coincidence that when a pair of European Jesuits were seized at Suzhou in 1748, they were condemned to death for plotting sedition on the basis of a particularly damning piece of evidence: Qing officials had discovered Tristano d'Attimis (b. 1707) and António José Henriques (b. 1707) wandering around the Jiangnan countryside with a map listing the local Christian *hui*.[92]

10

Brothers of Passion and Mercy

Martino Martini spent the better part of his years as a missionary creating images of China for Europeans. In his richly illustrated *Novus Atlas Sinensis,* as well as in his vivid *De Bello Tartarico,* he illuminated the grandeur and tragedy of the world's greatest empire. And at the end of his life, he presented an equally dramatic vision of Europe to the Chinese. In 1660 Martini oversaw the completion of a new sanctuary in the heart of Hangzhou. During two years of construction, Chinese artisans shaped local materials into a foreign-looking edifice. They erected an imposing façade to dominate the Jesuits' walled compound, whose height was pierced by three arched doorways. Inside the church, the artisans raised soaring vaults atop thirty thick columns, each with a pedestal and capital in the style of ancient Greece and Rome. Martini ordered the builders to leave room for fifteen lancet windows, then had craftsmen fill them with mother-of-pearl panels carved so delicately "that they are transparent and lustrous." An altar was set up in each of the church's three naves. Above the high altar hung an imposing gilt-framed retable of Christ the Savior. The lateral chapels on either side of the transept contained portraits of the Madonna and the Archangel Michael, paintings most likely imported from Macau or Goa. According to the Jesuits, Chinese visitors were particularly taken with the triumphal arches that connected the interior columns. Like the church's other features, they claimed, this was "something never seen before in China."[1]

That the beauty of their sanctuary drew the attention of connoisseurs in the Jiangnan region must have pleased the missionaries, but the primary reason for their satisfaction with the new church derived, no doubt, from observing how the city's Christians used it. Just like Catholic churches in Europe, the Hangzhou sanctuary was at once the focal point of a community and a composite of ritual spaces claimed by a number of devotional groups. At one side of the church was a secluded chapel dedicated to the Holy Crucifix and used by a penitential group. Its members, described by the Jesuits as the "most devout and fervent" of their flock, gathered on Fridays to hear mass, say prayers, and sing the Litanies of the Passion. Afterwards they performed flagellation "with such contrition as to provoke tears of devotion even in the most stubborn and taciturn." Another group, a Marian sodality, gathered on Saturdays at the altar of the Blessed Virgin located in the main sanctuary to attend mass amid billows of incense. A third brotherhood, dedicated to dispensing charity, also claimed a part of the church. This group kept a locked coffer in the sanctuary, where its members put their obligatory donations. Once each month, its leaders withdrew funds for assisting poor Christians while a missionary kept watch. The donations were meant to succor the community's less affluent members in times of illness or to buy coffins for them and "meet the other expenses of their funerals."[2]

While Martini's church stood out among the Vice-Province's other sanctuaries for its beauty, it was hardly unique in the number and variety of devotional groups that it housed. Across China, the Jesuits' mission stations were meeting points for a host of congregations aimed at fostering piety. It should come as no surprise that specialized devotional groups were formed among the urban adherents of *Tianzhu jiao.* After all, they enjoyed almost continual pastoral care from the missionary who lived in their midst, and they heard masses and said their confessions with far greater frequency than rural Christians. The practice of Christianity for those who lived in the shadow of the Jesuits' residences was therefore far more varied than in the countryside. On top of the standard prayer routines that were proper to their organizational confraternities, urban Christians might also channel their fervor through other, more demanding forms of piety, such as the obligation to confess and receive the Eucharist regularly, the public exercise of charity, or the practice of communal self-mortification—all beneath the gaze of the priests. For the Jesuits, such expressions of fervor were the clearest reward for their missionary labors. They encouraged the cream of their crop to serve as models of piety to the rest of their followers, hoping that the example of the few would act as leaven for the spiritual progress of the many.

The best way for the Jesuits to supervise and direct intense expressions of piety was through *hui,* associations. In this regard, too, they benefited from that same Chinese penchant for social organization that had enabled them to use Brotherhoods of the Holy Mother as building blocks for the mission church. Whether at the missionaries' suggestion or of their own volition, the more fervent Christians created devotional confraternities from the first decades of the mission onward. The Jesuits' initial outreach to the educated elite, especially in the cities where they opened their first residences, made this a logical development. The social ground had been more than sufficiently prepared for the burgeoning of Christian confraternal activity through the profusion of charitable groups and literary academies—not to speak of the devotional groups of Buddhist or Daoist inspiration that also flourished in late Ming China, drawing members from all levels of society. Indeed, the creation of mutual interest associations or religious brotherhoods was, in the apt phrase of Nicolas Standaert, a Ming "national pastime."[3] As Standaert has noted, with their devotional groups the Jesuits were not creating new forms of religious expression in China ex nihilo but rather reinforcing an indigenous tradition that suited their religious goals.[4]

Yet one should not insist exclusively on the Chinese character of these devotional groups and thereby risk obscuring the parallels between the practice of confraternal piety in Catholic Europe and its counterpart in the mission church. The China Jesuits were products of a spiritual milieu in which devotional confraternities were the premier form of communal piety. They belonged to a religious order known for its strong predilection toward this form of lay religious activity. Moreover, the Society of Jesus insisted that its novices participate in student confraternities during their academic formation. The confraternal movement—or, more specifically, the push to replace occupational groups with devotional ones in the late sixteenth century—was one of the hallmarks of the Catholic Reformation, and the Jesuits were among its greatest proponents. Not only did the Society seek to transform existing modes of piety through its confraternities, but its members aimed to carry out the ambitious project of the "spiritual reformation of the republic" as well by propagating new forms of lay religiosity.[5] They were sure that the best way to bring about such a change in the greatest number of people was to organize confraternities which obliged members to rigorous prayer routines and frequent reception of the sacraments. Just as they regimented students in their classrooms, the Jesuits charged the members of these groups with mutual moral supervision. Here, too, they hoped that a spirit of "pious competition" would take hold and gradually ratchet up the degree of fervor.[6]

The confraternities that gathered in the Hangzhou church in 1660 were therefore the products of the intertwining of two distinct cultural strands, one Chinese and the other European. If one conceives of early modern Catholicism as the mixture of equal parts devotion, doctrine, and ritual, then the activities of the Jesuits' Chinese brotherhoods represent that religious compound in full. But what were the devotions conducted by these groups? In what ways did their forms of piety give outward expression to specific Christian teachings? In short, how did their piety make them an example for their coreligionists? The various forms of confraternal piety that were practiced in the Hangzhou church and other sanctuaries like it were the product of a process of evolution that stretched back five decades. They did not, however, represent the final stage in the development of group devotions sponsored by the China Jesuits. By the end of the seventeenth century, according to some of the missionaries, the level of communal spirituality achieved by their Chinese Christians was comparable to that of the "most devout congregations of Europe." For José Soares, this was nothing short of a miracle. After all, he wrote from Peking in 1697, the Jesuits' devotional groups had cultivated mature "fruits of piety from tender plants sprouting amid thorns," reaping a crop of the type usually produced after a long time by seedlings "grown in good earth."[7]

Drawing up the Rules

The emergence of devotional confraternities was a natural result of the slow growth of the mission church in the early seventeenth century. For three decades after 1582, the Jesuits' flock barely breached the one thousand–member mark. But while this lack of quantity disturbed the missionaries and their superiors, it permitted the priests to focus on the quality of their converts' religious practices. That the earliest devotional groups should appear in the cities where the Jesuits opened their first residences is not surprising. It was a logical development in Peking, where Matteo Ricci gave uninterrupted pastoral care to a handful of converts from his arrival in 1601 until his death nine years later. Such continual interaction sparked a desire for more complex forms of devotional expression. After all, Ricci had not been shy in encouraging his early converts to engage in meditative prayer—to the point of directing some of them through part of Ignatius Loyola's *Spiritual Exercises,* a challenge for many if not most contemporary European Catholics.

The first devotional group was a Marian sodality instituted at Peking on September 8, 1609, the feast of the Nativity of the Virgin. According to Ricci's diary, a court attendant named Lucas Li voiced his desire to start a *hui* in which he and his coreligionists might make public acts of charity. "For many days he discussed this work with his companions, drawing up rules according to their custom," recorded the Jesuit, "which he showed to Father Matteo for him to emend and accommodate to Christian norms." Among the stipulations that Ricci added to Li's statutes were "some points about confessing, praying, and receiving new members into the congregation." As was fitting for a charitable group in the late Ming period, one of the principal aims of Li's brotherhood was to bury deceased church members "with pomp and solemnity." Another was to offer alms to poor Christians; each member was required to make monthly donations to a fund for such expenses. The group had a further obligation to decorate the city's sanctuary with "wax, perfume, and flowers" on feast days throughout the year. On the first Sunday of every lunar month, the sodality members gathered at Li's house to hear a sermon from one of the Jesuits and be given answers to their questions about *Tianzhu jiao.*[8]

The description of this Peking brotherhood clearly reveals its twin Chinese and European sources of inspiration. Lucas Li likely conceived of his confraternity as a Christian version of the other *hui* which were legion in late Ming China. The Jesuits recognized this impulse as typical for their converts, especially the members of the elite. In 1602 Diego de Pantoja informed his confreres in Spain that many high-ranking mandarins "like nothing better than to speak of virtuous things, and so gather, in groups like confraternities, to discuss them." During these meetings, some would give talks and others would debate the best ways "to govern, and to attain virtue."[9] Pantoja was referring to literati groups, such as the *Tongshan hui* (Society for Sharing Goodness) or the *Guangren hui* (Association for Spreading Benevolence), which were inspired by traditional Confucian ideals and contemporary morality books. Myriad *Renhui* (benevolent societies) could be found across China. They were especially thick on the ground in areas with concentrations of literati, such as Peking and the

Jiangnan region. Without question, they were responsible for an increase in social awareness among members of the elite and a reinvigoration of charitable giving.[10] Other literati groups were more explicitly dedicated to sharing the pleasures of erudition through recitations of poetry or prose. In either case, their worthy actions dismayed Pantoja. It "breaks the heart," he insisted, to witness such talk of virtue among individuals who lacked "the necessary remedy" for their souls.[11]

No doubt Lucas Li was also partly inspired by indigenous forms of communal religious expression. In late Ming times there was a widespread revival of Buddhism, both at the monastic level and in popular milieux, where Buddhist associations flourished.[12] Groups such as the *Nianfo hui* (Society for Reciting the Name of the Buddha) and the *Fangsheng hui* (Association for Releasing Life) could be found throughout China. Similar to their counterparts among Catholic confraternities, these groups followed specific devotions and invoked different aspects of religious teachings: the *Nianfo hui* stressed the continual invocation of Amida Buddha; the *Fangsheng hui* sought to prevent the killing of animals by purchasing and freeing them.[13] Astute observers that they were, the missionaries were aware of the profusion of religious groups. Their reports describe groups such as one in Jiangzhou, Shanxi Province, which counted more than one hundred members who gathered to fast and pray "with special superstitions" to a Buddhist deity.[14] The members of another *hui* assembled on certain days "to recite their doctrines and prayers." The Jesuits were forced to acknowledge at least one praiseworthy aspect of these non-Christian religious activities. Prayers were sung at these meetings, they wrote, "with such order and harmony that they seem like the choruses of our European religious."[15]

Li's Peking confraternity also had characteristics proper to devotional congregations in Europe. Nicolas Trigault recorded that Matteo Ricci had appended to Li's statutes some rules "taken from the Roman sodality of the Annunciation."[16] This organization was the Society's flagship confraternity, the Prima Primaria of an archconfraternity with branches in every Jesuit college throughout the world. Its formal name was the Congregation of the Annunciation, and its first chapter had been founded by Jan Leunis at the Society's Roman College in 1563.[17] In the *caput mundi* it was known under its colloquial name, the Annunziata, and in Portuguese domains as the Annunciada. As former students and teachers in their order's schools, the China Jesuits were familiar with the rules of this congregation and were quick to adapt them for the purposes of shaping communal piety in the Ming empire. The flexibility of the confraternity model had long been proven by the Jesuits in Europe, where it was employed not only for students but for ordinary laymen and women as well.[18]

What was the nature of devotional confraternities in early modern Europe? Marc Venard has defined them according to a set of criteria that distinguishes them from the occupational confraternities of the late medieval period. The goal of the devotional groups was to stimulate individual and collective piety, that is, to serve as a forum for mutual moral and spiritual encouragement. Banqueting and nondevotional activities were therefore prohibited. In order to encourage people to join, no financial or occupational restrictions were placed on membership, and members were not constrained to stay in the group under pain of sin. In addition to praying, fasting, and receiving the sacraments, members at times engaged in various forms of self-mortification, including flagellation.[19] The branches of the Jesuits' Prima Primaria had all of these qualities; indeed, they were conceived as "seminaries of all virtue and sanctity," according to the preamble to the statutes of the Annunciada at the Colégio de Espirito Santo in Évora. The students who belonged to it (among whom were included more than a few future China Jesuits) were to benefit from "the company of many good people" whose example would spread the ardor for virtue throughout the group. Annunciada members were obliged to participate in weekly prayer meetings, attend mass daily, take communion at least once per month, and confess every other week—pious exercises designed to make members "a light to others," permitting them to lead their peers on "the path to heaven."[20]

The principal European element introduced by Matteo Ricci into Lucas Li's *hui* was an insistence that its members receive the sacraments regularly. As in Europe, this requirement aimed to encourage individuals to pray often, lead pious lives, and submit to the spiritual direction of their pastors. The members' duty to confess often enabled the Jesuits to verify that their moral and spiritual demands were met, while the obligation to take communion frequently was a prod to introspection. According to Ricci, these demands paid off. He averred that it was the Peking sodality's prayer meetings and reception of the sacraments that caused the spiritual state of its forty members to improve every day. Once they saw how successful the group at the northern capital was, the Nanjing Jesuits worked with the more devout members of their flock to create a similar congregation in 1610.[21]

It did not take long, however, for some of the Chinese aspects of the court confraternities to begin to trouble the missionaries. After all, Ricci had merely introduced devotional criteria into the Peking group's charter. He and his colleagues had no clear picture of what their Christians would do at their meetings. But the court sodalities were committed to their charitable vocation, and so demanded regular financial contributions, just like Confucian benevolent societies. Moreover, in keeping with Chinese traditions of conviviality, the brothers held banquets at their meetings. It was not long before the Jesuits set about "reforming" the two groups in the same way that occupational confraternities in Europe had been either extinguished or transformed into devotional brotherhoods over the course of the sixteenth century.[22] As early as 1612, Niccolò Longobardo reported that the Peking sodality had been "reduced to the style of the congregations in Europe." He further noted that the members did not "collect money or bring things to eat." But as confirmation of their commitment, Longobardo added that they had not lost fervor as a result of these changes, nor did they stop coming to meetings. The Nanjing group, however, resisted any immediate changes, since its members "thought it well to collect money and eat something like a collation on meeting days." Nevertheless, the brothers promised the Jesuits that they would adopt the ways of the Peking sodality before long.[23] In the end, the combination of these changes and the spiritual demands on sodality members made the Jesuits' devotional confraternities different from their Chinese counterparts of Confucian and Buddhist inspiration.[24]

A "Holy Envy"

If the Jesuits had any doubts about the value of their first confraternities for sustaining and inspiring the rest of the mission church, these were dispelled in the wake of the Nanjing affair. During the years when the missionaries were in seclusion, the two sodalities continued their prayer routines and charitable activities. Jesuits who visited Peking and Nanjing after 1618 reported that although their members were forced to keep a low profile, the groups continued to meet in private homes "to discuss the things of God." Periodically, a Jesuit coadjutor would attend these meetings to respond to questions about *Tianzhu jiao* and "offer consolation with a spiritual talk." In Nanjing, where the memory of persecution was still fresh, the sodality played an even more important role. Francisco Furtado claimed in 1620 that its members were wholly responsible for "conserving and carrying forward" the local church.[25] The brothers showed their mettle again during the final flare-up of persecution in 1622. They gathered regularly for prayers and, in addition, visited sick Christians and organized funerals.[26]

Although the Jesuits were impressed by the vitality and durability of these groups, they were not in a hurry to establish them everywhere. In fact, the political climate of the mid-1620s was unfavorable to creating *hui,* especially among literati Christians. The Ming crackdown against the reforming mandarin faction known as the Donglin Academy in 1625 affected the Jesuits' plan to encourage new devotional groups. For the remaining years of the Ming era and on into Qing rule, the term *hui* had connotations of sedition and rebellion. As the missionaries informed the readers of their Annual Letter in 1626, the Tianqi emperor had expressly banned literati gatherings, "which have always been suspect in China."[27] It would therefore take a considerable effort at public relations for the Jesuits to disabuse suspicious authorities of the notion that their *hui,* many of which had literati members, were different from those behind the internecine bureaucratic strife of the 1620s.

But threats from on high did little to curb the Chinese Christians' urge to create new confraternities. For instance, in 1625 Gaspar Ferreira grudgingly acceded to demands from some members of his Jiangxi Province flock to start up a new confraternity for praying the rosary. His condition was that the group not call themselves a *hui* since the term was "so hated, thanks to the revolts in the South that surround the court."[28] Three years later a group of Christians at Peking instituted a charitable congregation, dedicated to Our Lady of Piety, which distributed funds to poor church members for medical or funeral expenses.[29] Even prominent Christians such as Yang Tingyun founded Christian discussion groups during this period—perhaps not all that surprising a gesture, as this mandarin had already shown his willingness to buck official decrees by sheltering the Jesuits during the Nanjing affair.[30]

In the end, the Chinese Christians' desire to form new devotional groups gradually wore down the Jesuits' fears of an official backlash. By the time Visitor André Palmeiro's final directives to the missionaries were issued in 1631, his stipulation that priests in the provinces not "institute confraternities without special orders from the Vice-Provincial" was moot.[31] The collapse of Ming authority, especially severe outside the imperial capitals, was as obvious to the Jesuits as the rumblings of war from beyond the Great Wall. Rather than deny their Christians the opportunity to engage in communal devotions, in the 1630s the Jesuits actively began to encourage the creation of new groups throughout the mission church.

These new bodies were clearly different from the organizational *Shengmu hui* that began to appear around the same time, since devotional confraternity members were obliged to receive the sacraments more often. For instance, Pedro Ribeiro founded one group for men and another for women at Shanghai in 1636. Both were dedicated to the Virgin; hence, in all likelihood, they were called *Shengmu hui.* Members were required to attend mass, hear sermons, and confess monthly. The two prefects of the men's group were charged with visiting sick Christians and distributing alms to the poor. The first members of the women's group were four granddaughters of Xu Guangqi along with their female children and domestics. They too gathered monthly to confess, attend mass, and listen to a sermon. Both confraternities shared the Jesuit devotional practice of selecting the name of a saint whose feast day fell in a particular month to serve as a temporary patron.[32]

The 1630s also saw the beginning of the spread of penitential groups throughout the mission church. These congregations typically invoked the Passion and provided a venue for the practice of bodily mortification, such as flagellation. Resurrecting the memory of the first such group, one that had been founded by Lazzaro Cattaneo in Yang Tingyun's chapel in 1618, Francisco Furtado instituted a penitential confraternity at Hangzhou in 1636.[33] He dedicated a special chapel inside the city's main church where its members could conduct their exercises beyond public view. The group met once a month on a Friday to attend mass, hear a sermon, and practice discipline. According to that year's Annual Letter, the members (whose number included some women) competed among themselves for devotional rigor, making displays of penitential zeal with instruments that were "severe enough to be frightening." The Hangzhou Jesuits had to intervene at times "to apply a brake to the fervor," seizing their fearsome lashes.[34]

Christians elsewhere in China practiced other forms of penitential piety. In Kaifeng, for instance, Rodrigo de Figueiredo administered a Brotherhood of the Holy Cross that had been founded in 1639 by the "eight principal and most devout" men of that city. The group's leader was a rich youth who brought a large wooden cross with him every time he attended mass. On Sunday mornings he would emplace it in the church courtyard,

where he and his confreres would kneel to pray the Litanies of the Passion, take turns kissing the foot of the cross, and lash themselves in unison. When they had finished these pious exercises, one of them would give a short talk on some aspect of the Passion. According to Figueiredo, each of the brothers would carry the "heavy and holy wood of Our Redemption" by turns while the priest said mass.[35]

The mission church's most widespread form of confraternal activity was perhaps the structured exercise of charity. To analyze charitable groups together with devotional groups is, however, somewhat problematic, since they do not explicitly meet the definitions of communal piety as they have been presented here. Charitable confraternities during the 1630s were, by and large, cut according to the Chinese mold; many were, in effect, traditional groups whose members happened to be Christians. Charitable confraternities from that period do not appear to have demanded a significant degree of devotional rigor. Nevertheless, the public practice of the corporal works of mercy (a standard element in Jesuit catechetical teaching) was a demonstration of personal piety that went beyond the bounds of what was expected from members of organizational confraternities. While the missionaries reserved their highest praise for the members of their penitential groups, they did not pass over the contributions made by members of charitable confraternities for ensuring church cohesion. To be sure, the activities of the latter were directed outward rather than inward. The purpose they espoused was to distribute alms and attend the funerals of poor Christians, or, to put it differently, to ensure that poverty was no barrier to the proper practice of *Tianzhu jiao.*

The Jesuits were not blind to the manifestations of confraternal charity rooted in native traditions. Chinese forms of social assistance constituted the framework for the development of Christian charitable groups, even if the missionaries described those groups in terms of European models of public piety. The Jesuits were familiar with *Renhui,* benevolent societies inspired by commonplace notions of morality as well as by the explicit standards of Confucian ethics. For example, António de Gouvea wrote in

---

Woodcut print of the Agony in the Garden in *Method for Reciting the Rosary (Song nianzhu guicheng),* appended to João da Rocha, *Instruction for the Young on the Holy Religion of the Lord of Heaven (Tianzhu shengjiao qimeng),* 1619.

the 1640s about a Zhejiang literati association called "Tum Xen Hoei" (one of the multitude of *Tongshan hui* in contemporary China) that was devoted to acts of charity. Four times during the year, the literati and retired mandarins who made up the *hui* would meet to discuss virtue and make their donations. A roll of the group's expenditures was printed seasonally. What impressed Gouvea most was the "order, fidelity, and punctuality" of this accounting system, a method that made its financial officer seem like "a diligent head of the Holy Misericórdia."[36]

The Jesuit's comparison of the *Tongshan hui* to this Portuguese charitable institution makes sense, since the Misericórdias were lay-run societies responsible for a host of activities that ranged from providing dowries to poor girls and paying for the funerals of the destitute to administering the estates of deceased members. While membership in this Portuguese group was not the same as being in a European devotional confraternity, it did come with a number of semiannual sacramental requirements attached. Moreover, the Misericórdia's activities were performed with clerical oversight and repeated exhortations to greater piety.[37] For the Vice-Province's Portuguese priests, this was the principal model of charitable activity, but they did not consider it problematic to build on native foundations. After all, as Gabriel de Magalhães wrote about another literati group in Zhejiang, indigenous works of mercy such as "giving coffins for the destitute to be buried in" were but one step removed from what adherents of the *Tianzhu jiao* were encouraged to do. In his eyes, a group with such laudable aims had to have been founded by a Christian, or at least "one who would soon be."[38]

Chinese Christians, especially those from the ranks of the elite, found ready parallels between late Ming patterns of social assistance and Christian teachings on charity. The Confucian ideal of benevolence *(Ren)* was linked with the corporal works of mercy. The statutes Wang Zheng wrote for a *Renhui* combined the streams of Chinese and Western morality, directing its members toward contributing to "the highest *Ren* through which the Lord of Heaven loves man" by performing "the meritorious work of loving others."[39] While it is unclear if Wang actually instituted a group based on these rules, there is no doubt that Christians elsewhere in China did establish charitable confraternities. One was founded at Peking in 1636 by a group of wealthy church members. According to that year's Annual Letter, this group was a fountain of charity whereby "the poor and needy are helped, with great edification and glory of Our Lord."[40] The calamities of the late 1630s and 1640s offered more opportunities for the exercise of charity elsewhere in China. For example, at Nanchang a Confraternity of Piety had its hands full feeding the hungry (one of the Seven Corporal Acts of Mercy) in 1643, "as much for the lack of rations due to drought as with the revolts of the rebels who entered the province again over the border with Huguang."[41]

Charitable groups also attended to burying the dead, assisting the dying with their prayers and exhortations, and making dignified funerals possible for all Christians. This form of charity was particularly important in China, where the cult of the dead figured so prominently.[42] It is worth recalling that one of the principal duties assigned to Lucas Li's Peking brotherhood in 1609 was to participate in Christian funerals. Similar obligations were written into the statutes of charitable groups in later decades as both a consolation for destitute church members and a shield against outside criticism. When Simão da Cunha became aware of the rumors circulating in the inland districts of Fujian Province that the followers of *Tianzhu jiao* employed inadequate ritual at funerals, he responded by creating Confraternities of Piety. The members of these groups were to attend burials, making a show of singing the litanies and wearing mourning attire. "In this way," wrote Cunha in 1653, "the relatives of the deceased, even if they are heathens, remain quiet, seeing how we commemorate the dead, because until now they thought that we kicked them into the grave without any ceremony, like dogs."[43]

As suggested earlier, many of the devotional confraternities that were created in the 1630s, 1640s, and 1650s were sisterhoods formed for the communal exercise of charity, penitence, or piety. It is unclear, however, if the devotional initiatives of Christian women were not merely outgrowths of the activities of the organizational *Shengmu hui*. In any event, missionary sources frequently record the creation of new groups with distinct spiritual or charitable aims that went beyond the standard prayer routines and sacramental obligations of the Jesuits' female "parishioners." For instance, in the 1640s a group of women at Xi'an instituted a confraternity to succor those Christians most affected by the upheaval in the northwestern provinces. Among its other pious works, this group regularly "gave food to thirteen poor women."[44]

So eager were the women of Xi'an to manifest new forms of communal religious expression that their pastor, Inácio da Costa, accused them of being afflicted with "a holy envy." Whenever they saw the local men creating any new confraternity—"or making any act of devotion out of the ordinary"—they conspired among themselves to do the same. Costa cited the three groups of elderly women who met, as the title of their *hui* made clear, in "preparation for death." Members of these groups fasted before meetings and performed other acts of mortification. All of them had lashes with which they whipped themselves, and, what impressed the missionary even more, some made examinations of conscience.[45] Women's groups with similar devotional practices were established in other Chinese provinces. A female *hui* administered by Simão da Cunha at Yanping in Fujian Province met regularly to "read lessons from holy books in public, hold spiritual lectures, and conduct many penitences." In short, the Jesuit averred, the women "appeared to be a convent of well-reformed religious."[46]

"Such Decency and Composure"

The flowering of confraternal devotional activity in the mission church during the years of the imperial transition was a mixed blessing for the Jesuits. On the one hand, they were pleased to see a nucleus of fervent men and women form in each of their Christian communities. On the other, the missionaries could not entirely regulate either the spread or the form of these *hui.* No doubt they found it easier to extend pastoral care to the devout in groups rather than individually. But the urge to create *hui* among the members of the mission church appears to have been stronger than the Jesuits' capacity to exercise control over them, as revealed in the description of the Shaanxi Province mission station in the 1656 Annual Letter. Whereas the missionaries at Xi'an were clearly pleased with the different brotherhoods they administered, they could not offer much information about "the many and varied ones that both men and women hold by themselves."[47]

Another logical—if not natural—consequence of the Jesuits' limited pastoral capabilities was the potential of these groups for sliding into temporal excesses. After all, the primary impulse among the Chinese Christians was to form *hui,* not necessarily Jesuit-patterned sodalities. While the missionaries may have been able to monitor the brotherhoods that met in their residence churches, the same degree of supervision was not possible elsewhere. How, one might ask, could Francesco Brancati regulate the fervor of the twenty-two penitential brotherhoods that he claimed were part of his Shanghai "diocese" in the early 1650s?[48] Only the Jesuits who tended smaller flocks stood a good chance of supervising devotional groups. For instance, the priests at Hangzhou discovered a confraternity outside the city walls in 1656 that paid no more than lip service to prayer. The greater part of its activities, claimed the missionaries, consisted of "a feast of the body, eating and drinking." Obviously, reform was imperative—changes of the type imposed by the Catholic clergy upon European brotherhoods that went astray. "This laxity was removed," the Jesuits reported, "and in its place was put a mass and sermon that the priest goes to offer on meeting days."[49]

One of the primary tactics used in the Vice-Province to control the sodalities was to pay close attention to their statutes. The missionaries tried to impress upon their Christians the need to have the rules for their *hui* approved. Perhaps, the Jesuits reasoned, if members were apprised of the statutes and aware that the priests had produced them, then a collective will to conformity and observance would manifest itself—especially if the priests aroused another form of "holy envy" by setting limits on the number of individuals who could join. When Jean Valat was implored by some Christian men at Tai'an in Shandong Province in 1658 to institute a Marian sodality, he agreed only on the condition that its membership be limited to twenty. After selecting these worthies himself, Valat wrote a list of "rules and customs that they were to observe."[50] Satisfied with this group's piety, he issued similar statutes for a women's group the following year. In this case, however, the Jesuit was less strict with regard to the prerequisites for membership. His one stipulation was that only those properly schooled in doctrine so as to be eligible for taking the Eucharist could join. One hundred and fifteen women became members in the first year alone.[51]

The Jesuits' attempts at reforming some of their devotional groups while creating others with stronger checks on excess had a salutary effect. As far as the missionaries were concerned, the mission church's devotional elite showed signs of heightened spirituality. Their observance of the norms of piety laid down in their confraternities' statutes put them on the way to reaching the ideal forms of lay religious expression envisioned by the Society of Jesus. In the opinion of some Jesuits, not a few Chinese Christians had attained even higher levels of personal zeal than could be expected of their European counterparts. On the eve of the Canton exile, Gabriel de Magalhães wrote of how the manners of Peking's *hui* members were a model for all lay Catholics. He was especially impressed by the way they assisted at mass with "such decency and composure," kneeling for the entire ceremony and standing only during the gospel; unlike European Christians, they did not "look one way or the other, speak, tell stories, or act indecently" during the service. Moreover, Magalhães noted, they behaved reverently, "not even daring to spit, but when they feel compelled to do so, they go and do it outside the church."[52]

This type of pious example, the Jesuits hoped, would inspire all Chinese Christians. The devotional confraternities were implicitly charged with sustaining the level of fervor within the mission church at large. They faced their first (and greatest) challenge while the missionaries were detained in the late 1660s. The set of rules dispatched by the Jesuits from Canton for governing their dispersed flocks in effect posted the devotional groups to the mission church's vanguard. The Marian sodalities and the penitential confraternities received special attention; the day they were to meet at their local church each month was specified. To avoid attracting notice, these groups were advised against saying "long prayers" during their meetings. Similarly, men's and women's congregations were warned not to meet on the same day. Those who wished to practice flagellation, to fast, or to wear a cilice—common activities for the Confraternities of the Passion—were urged to continue. Nevertheless, the Jesuits forbade their female followers to "take discipline" in groups. They also stipulated that penitential practices be avoided by "the old, the poor, the sick, and people not able to endure them." Without due pastoral oversight, the missionaries felt that it was better for such individuals to "do other good spiritual works as compensation."[53]

While at Canton the Jesuits reflected on how confraternal piety had spread throughout the mission church. They found the proliferation of *hui* with a host of different saintly patrons and pious practices to be a vexing problem. Over the preceding decades, individual Jesuits had spurred the formation of brotherhoods without any apparent attempt at uniformity. Problems would necessarily arise when those men were replaced by others who were unfamiliar with the style of a given confraternity. For example, the Jesuits at Fuzhou ministered to a Brotherhood of the Guardian Angel that had no equivalent elsewhere in China.[54] A similar idiosyncrasy was reported from the Shanghai area in 1661, when the Sicilian-born Francesco Brancati told a confrere that the fifty-three penitential groups under his care performed "all of the exercises of the secret congregations of

Palermo and Naples."[55] Would such practices be readily understood by his successors from Évora and Mechelen? The standardization of confraternal piety was the wisest course of action. The Jesuits therefore agreed to transform their confraternities into four standard types: one Marian, another penitential, a third doctrinal (for children), and the last for catechists. In each church, one group was to begin "seeking, raising, and baptizing foundlings."[56]

Another question the Jesuits faced was how to ensure that participation in devotional confraternities was restricted to the most fervent. As we saw in the previous chapter, the mode of communal piety characteristic of the organizational *Shengmu hui* involved ordinary Chinese Christians in prayer routines and sacramental obligations that were less intense forms of those practiced by the devotional groups. There was nothing to keep these men and women from being touched by the same spirit of "pious competition" that was found among their more fervent brethren. Unless they were given orders to the contrary, ordinary Christians might mimic the practices of the restricted sodalities.

In order to draw a clear dividing line between different levels of communal piety, the Jesuits reserved one activity for their confraternities alone, the privilege of selecting "saints of the month." This devotion had originated with Saint Francis Borja (1510–1572), the Society's third Superior General, who had experienced it during his childhood in the Aragonese city of Gandía.[57] By the end of the sixteenth century, this practice had spread throughout the order's colleges and brotherhoods. During meetings of Jesuit sodalities, members would draw slips of paper from a bowl, each bearing the name of a saint whose feast day fell during that month and a verse of scripture. This saint was to serve as a temporary patron. According to one set of Annunciada statutes from Portugal, each brother was to pray to his saint daily, "doing him some special service, either as a work of charity toward others or as an act of penance." Further devotions were expected on the saint's feast day.[58] According to Philippe Couplet, the use of "saints of the month" was first used among the Chinese Christians at the direction of Giacomo Rho.[59] By the 1660s, this custom was popular among the mission church's devout members. Through their attempt to restrict the "saints of the month" to a fraction of their flock, the Jesuits aimed to keep the practice from becoming a banal commonplace while at the same time making it a reward for those who showed the piety necessary for joining a devotional confraternity.

The move toward standardization came to fruition only after the Jesuits returned to their flocks in the early 1670s. It would appear that the confraternities created then adhered to the plans drawn up during the missionaries' exile. When Couplet arrived in the Shanghai-Songjiang area in 1675, he set about reconstituting the region's Marian sodalities and penitential brotherhoods.[60] François de Rougemont, too, made an effort to create similar groups when he took up residence in Changshu in the early 1670s.[61] The rules adopted at Canton gave guidance to missionaries outside the Jiangnan area as well. During a visit to Jianchang, Jiangxi Province, in 1686, Manuel Mendes approved the creation of a new Marian sodality reserved for the city's female spiritual elite.[62]

The fact that charitable brotherhoods were not mentioned in the Jesuits' list of approved groups does not mean that the missionaries ceased to encourage communal charity or that Chinese Christians lost their urge to form *hui* dedicated to altruism. The members of their flock were for the most part poor and lived "by the work of their hands," wrote the Peking Jesuits in the early 1670s. Even so, some of those who were "more amply provisioned in heavenly than in earthly goods" started a confraternity that obliged them to donate one tael a month toward buying clothes for poor Christians.[63] Recall that the Jesuits decided at Canton to insist that the other devotional groups perform works of social assistance, such as the task of gathering foundlings. By the late 1680s, at least one Christian group had been formed with the purpose of attending to the thousands of abandoned children who died each year in Chinese cities because of "the cold, or for lack of milk, or because they are bitten by dogs." This Peking brotherhood, whose members were all "well versed in the baptismal formula," scoured the capital's streets in search of infants. The lucky few who showed vital signs were taken to orphanages, while the others were baptized before they expired. As a result of this charitable activity, claimed one missionary, the Peking church "grew more in heaven than on earth."[64]

The Full Flower of Communal Piety

Across the decades from 1609 until the 1690s, the principal trend in the development of confraternal piety in the mission church was toward the models of piety fostered by the Society of Jesus in Europe. This gradual but ultimately incomplete shift saw the proportional reduction of properly Chinese forms of *hui* activity (such as banqueting and regular contributions) in favor of European types of group practices (such as mandated devotional cycles). From the Jesuits' perspective, by the end of the seventeenth century, some of their Chinese brotherhoods had begun to resemble European pious associations. But the final stage in this evolution occurred only in the areas where the missionaries could offer uninterrupted attention to the local spiritual elite. In regions where the Jesuits were obliged to spend most of the year on mission circuits, they could not provide such supervision. It is therefore not surprising that the push to reach the Society's ideal for communal piety occurred in Peking, the same city where the first devotional group was formed.

In the 1690s the Jesuits ministered to four principal devotional congregations at the capital city. All met at least once a month, and all required their members to confess and take communion regularly. The spiritual reward for participation in these groups went beyond the obvious recompense for sacramental assiduity, since the Jesuits had the authority to award indulgences to diligent confraternity members. The Eastern Church (*Dongtang,* or Church of Saint Joseph), which had been shuttered from the 1660s until the 1690s, was home to a Congregation of Saint Joseph. This group's distinguishing feature was its distribution of alms to poor Christian families "in honor of the Glorious saint, the Holy Virgin, and the Holy Child." The College of Peking (*Xitang,* called *Nantang* after about 1703) was where the Confraternity of Souls was based. This group was entrusted with conducting Christian burials with appropriate pomp, as well as maintaining the banners and processional carts used during funeral cortèges. Its members included a few "dexterous catechists," whose function was to engage with passersby who were attracted by these pious displays. The third brotherhood was devoted to the Passion, and was similar to the penitential groups found elsewhere in the mission church. When this group met at the college church, the members would lie prostrate before an image of the crucified Christ and chant the Litanies of the Passion "in alternating voices in a sad song." After an hour of prayer and "no lack of tears," the brothers would subject themselves to "a rigorous discipline on their backs for the length of a Miserere."[65]

The most illustrious devotional group, in the opinion of José Soares, was the one that he himself had created in 1694, the Congregation of the Annunciation of Our Lady, *Shengmu lingbao hui.* This group initially consisted of forty male members.[66] Within three years, however, it counted seventy-six professed members and fifty-five probationary novices. Multiple women's groups were also formed at the capital with the same invocation of the Annunciation. According to Soares, their members represented the "flower of the entire Christian community, of both sexes, and from both inside and outside the city walls." The statutes for these groups consisted of a translation of the common rules of the Roman Prima Primaria completed by Soares. With minor variations, the Chinese members were obliged to keep the same sacramental schedules and prayer routines as their counterparts in Europe. At Peking, their weekly devotions included singing the litanies, collecting alms for the poor, and attending mass. Soares's praise for their displays of devotion knew few limits; they attended mass with "singular modesty, reverence, and devotion." It was possible to say "without exaggeration," Soares insisted, that their comportment exceeded that of the "most well-instructed and circumspect Europeans."[67]

Once a month the men's Annunciada gathered to sing responsorial prayers and hear a mass for the souls of deceased brothers and their relatives. The assembled congregation also chanted the litanies of the Virgin and heard a short sermon on an aspect of her life. After these rituals, members chose a "saint of the month," said a rosary, and held talks on spiritual matters. They ended their meetings by reporting to the supervising priest on affairs pertaining to the confraternity and the Christian community in general. These meetings lasted two and a half hours, wrote Soares, and were conducted with an "order and decency" that would incite the envy of European sodalities. On two occasions each year, at the feasts of the Annunciation and the Assumption, the brotherhood held its principal ceremonies. (The women's groups held their "universal congregations," that is, the general assembly of all of the women's Annunciadas, at the same times of the year.) According to Soares, these festivities were a cause for great joy, "not only at the holy table of Communion but also at the one used during the solemn banquet that the president and his assistants offer to the whole congregation on those days." While the Jesuits permitted banquets at these feasts in acknowledgment of Chinese customs of conviviality, normal meetings did not include meals. The two celebrations were also the occasions for electing officials and inducting new members. Novices had to make general confessions to qualify for entry and accept that those who broke the group's statutes would be punished publicly or even expelled.[68]

The Peking Annunciadas' members were encouraged to make charitable contributions, and, according to Soares, they gave freely and generously. Part of the congregation's funds was spent on maintaining its church, part on alms for needy Christians (including the gift of clothes to the poor, so they could attend mass), and part on "other pious works." The female groups made donations toward the construction of a new women's church, dedicated to the Annunciation, at the college in 1694. For Soares, however, the Annunciadas' most valuable public service came through the expenditures they made, "part on books of the Holy Law to distribute to Christians and heathens, part on printing and painting sacred images, part on rosaries and reliquaries." Such activities seem to have been unique to the Peking congregations. Their publishing venture supplied many of the images and texts, both Chinese and Manchu, which were used throughout the mission church. And although, in the missionaries' words, these sacred objects "did not match those of Europe," they appear to have been satisfactory as far as the Chinese Christians were concerned.[69]

If there was one missionary who felt that some Chinese Christians had reached a level of spiritual engagement equal to that of Europeans, it was José Soares. He was convinced that the Peking Annunciadas were clear reflections of the Marian sodalities he had known in his native Portugal. In order to gain recognition for this pastoral accomplishment, Soares petitioned the Society's Superior General to have the groups enrolled on the register of affiliates of the Roman Archconfraternity of the Annunciation.[70] In addition to attracting renewed attention to the efforts of the men of the Vice-Province, this gesture also made sure that the members of the Peking Annunciadas received the same indulgences for their prayers and pious works that were granted to similar Marian sodalities around the globe.

To what extent, however, should one trust the claims that Soares—the spiritual director of the Annunciadas—made about his confraternities? Did these groups really meet European standards of piety? Some of the Vice-Province's most bitter critics certainly thought so. When Jean de Fontaney wanted to marshal evidence that the "Portuguese" Jesuits were conspiring against the French mission, he wrote to the Society's executive secretary for the French provinces with extracts from the rules of Soares's Marian sodalities. Instead of dismissing the groups out of hand as some hybrid form of confraternal piety, Fontaney compared them to "our congregations in Europe." His complaint did not concern any of the groups' devotional aspects or sacramental requirements. Rather, focusing on the men's Annunciada, he insisted that its statutes accorded excessive power to its prefect and that the group's main aim was to collect money. Fontaney viewed the prefect's capacity to dismiss members and impose punishments as coercive tactics designed to keep the Peking Christians from seeking pastoral care from the French. His complaint against obligatory donations, offerings made upon joining the group and as fulfillment of *ex voto* promises, stood on less solid ground. "In Europe," Fontaney wrote, "members donate for the expenses of the congregation, but they have not yet made it into a rule."[71]

In general, the devotional confraternities of the mission church did not reach the European standards of lay piety held by the Society of Jesus. While the Annunciada model was replicated at Fuzhou "in imitation of the court" by Fujian Christians as early as 1695, most of the Jesuits' brotherhoods were structured like the ones created in the 1660s.[72] That was the moment when the broad lines of communal devotions were set. Devotional congregations fell into three principal categories: Marian sodalities, charitable confraternities, and penitential brotherhoods. These three modes of group religiosity had the same basic goal, namely, to channel the fervor of Chinese Christians. All of them stressed pastoral oversight, collective moral supervision, charitable works, reception of the sacraments, and regular prayer routines. A look at a set of statutes from each type of confraternity will reveal how they functioned.

Awaiting the Blessings of the Virgin

The most common type of devotional confraternity was the Marian sodality, typically called *Shengmu hui.* A pious dedication to Mary was in keeping with the common devotions to the Virgin fostered by the Society in Europe and elsewhere. This general predilection explains why the Vice-Province's organizational units were also labeled *Shengmu hui,* although the differences between those groups and the devotional confraternities of the same name were clear. For one, the devotional sodalities were most often found in urban milieux where they could receive pastoral oversight and access to the sacraments from resident missionaries. Moreover, they included a range of devotional activities that went beyond the spiritual obligations demanded of ordinary Chinese Christians. It is nevertheless the case that many devotional *Shengmu hui* bore close resemblances to their organizational counterparts and that the available sources do not make the dividing line between the two categories perfectly clear.

In the 1630s, reports from across the Vice-Province began to mention the creation of devotional *Shengmu hui.* For instance, in 1637 Gaspar Ferreira reported adding an altar at the residence church in Jianchang, Jiangxi Province, where a Marian sodality gathered to attend mass on meeting days. This group also stayed to receive the Eucharist and listen to one of their number give a "spiritual lesson for a quarter of an hour."[73] António de Gouvea claimed in 1645 that the members of the *Shengmu hui* in Fuzhou were a clear example of piety. They far outdid their coreligionists in "frequenting the Holy Sacraments of Confession and Communion, in attending mass, and in fasts."[74] The Jesuits likewise claimed that the Marian sodality at Yanping in Fujian Province was responsible for making the local Christians "much more fervent and zealous for the conversion of their relatives, friends, neighbors, and acquaintances." This group's members would meet in the house of one of their number to "spend a good part of the day making their devotions to the sound of flutes." This music attracted onlookers, who left with "more than an awareness of the Law of God," claimed the missionaries, since they were "edified by the fervor and devotions of the Christians."[75]

In order to structure these expressions of communal piety, the Jesuits and their Christians produced *hui* statutes. When their rules were written out, or, in some cases, printed, the groups took on an air of formality. This was the case of the Marian sodality created by Jean Valat at Tai'an, Shandong Province, in 1658. The formal gesture of selecting the twenty most "capable, expert, and exemplary" Christians and issuing a set of written statutes no doubt contributed to the group's sense of cohesion.[76] Humbert Augery drew up rules for a similar sodality, most likely the group that gathered in Martino Martini's Hangzhou church. Although it is unclear when this text was written, it seems likely that it was produced in either the early 1660s or the early 1670s. Augery's text is a printed booklet intended to be given to new members upon joining the *Shengmu hui.* It consists of a preamble followed by seventeen points touching on procedural matters as well as the order of prayers at meetings and on feast days.[77]

To set the tone for the group's activities, Augery began with a brief discussion of the benefits of devotion to the Virgin. He noted that although Christians were to focus on the Lord of Heaven, their numerous sins made them "strong in body but weak in spirit." Even those who appealed to *Tianzhu* "with all their might" did not always have their prayers answered. They needed a heavenly intercessor, and there was none better than Mary, "whose virtue surpasses that of all the other saints." Augery cited Saint Augustine to contrast the figure of Eve with that of the Virgin. "One inflicts pain," he remarked in reference to original sin, "and the other cures." By praying to Mary, the Jesuit contended, one could expect "peace and happiness during one's lifetime and eternal blessings after death." Those who joined the *Shengmu hui* clearly merited the Virgin's special blessing. And the Lord of Heaven, Augery added, would not abandon anyone who was devoted to the Holy Mother.[78]

Augery also described how he came to devise the statutes for this sodality. He noted that upon his arrival in Wulin (another name for Hangzhou), some Christians inquired about the "right way to pay homage to the Holy Mother, with the intention to do it in the manner of her devotees in the West." Acceding to their wishes, Augery translated and adapted the statutes for a European sodality, most likely the rules of the Prima Primaria. He then gave this text to the Chinese aspirants "so that they could practice and abide by the rules." Augery made it clear that those in the West who observed the rules of their sodalities received "special favor from the Holy Mother." What he was referring to were the indulgences granted to members of sodalities that were officially recognized by the papacy. In Europe, Augery explained, when *hui* members displayed "diligence and prudence" that pleased the Holy Mother, the priest in charge of their group would ask for a plenary indulgence from the pope. The Holy See usually granted such requests, and he would surely do the same for the members of this *Shengmu hui* if they followed Augery's exhortation to "do your best."[79]

The prescription for the Hangzhou brotherhood reveals that it was inspired by European models of confraternal piety. The first and second statutes place primary importance on treating all members as equals. Augery exhorted them to "love one another unswervingly" and never discriminate. Moreover, they were to elect a prefect by secret ballot on the basis of "virtue and not age." The only deference that members were to show was to their priest, requesting his judgment on any matters relating to Christian teachings, as well as seeking his approval for group activities. The elected prefect was, however, accorded a central role within the brotherhood. He was charged with supervising the moral conduct of the group, exhorting members to remain strong in faith, and comforting those who fell ill. The prefect was also enjoined to advise those members who were "successful in life" to give to charity. He was responsible for requesting masses when members died and for organizing prayers for the sick, the dying, and the dead. Along with these duties came the power to chastise or dismiss those who repeatedly disobeyed his orders. This last feature diverged from European patterns of confraternity governance but, in light of the small number of missionaries, made the *hui* less dependent on clerical oversight.[80]

The membership of the *Shengmu hui* was to be drawn from the ranks of the especially devout. In order to join, petitioners had to submit to a probationary period, during which the group's members would examine the postulant's conduct, inform him of the rules, and report his name to the priest for approval. Those admitted were to say a special prayer in which the novice implored Christ and Mary for their blessings and in particular for their guidance toward proper moral conduct, "whether in action or in repose." This prayer was a spiritual counterpart to Augery's encouragement that members mind one another's business, especially when they disobeyed the statutes or Christian precepts. Further, the brothers were charged with caring for their families' moral and spiritual welfare, being told to "mind their moral conduct as you take care of their food and clothing." The charge to survey morals did not stop, however, at the members' doorsteps. They were also instructed to encourage non-Christians to submit to baptism and exhort lax adherents of *Tianzhu jiao* to "repent and reform."[81]

The practices mandated for this sodality were much more rigorous than those prescribed for organizational groups. Since the devotional *hui* was predicated on the idea of regular contact between its members and their priest, Augery could raise his standards. All in the *Shengmu hui* were to make a daily examination of conscience, pray the Salve Regina three times, and recite the Paternoster and the Ave Maria five times each day. They were required to fast one day every month in remembrance of their parents and benefactors. Members were to confess once a month and make a general confession on the Feast of the Assumption (August 15). The sodality observed four Marian feasts: Purification (February 2), Annunciation (March 26), Assumption, and Nativity (September 8). Its members were to receive the Eucharist on all of these occasions as well as at Easter and Christmas, three times more often than ordinary Chinese

Christians. When the feasts fell on Saturdays, the *hui* was instructed to meet for special devotions, chanting prayers to the Virgin before the displayed host while holding candles.[82]

The Hangzhou brotherhood was to hold its meetings on the first Saturday of every month at church. First, the members would attend mass in order "to pray to the Holy Mother to request the Lord's blessing upon the brethren." The priest was to remain present for the duration of the gathering, answer questions about doctrine, and hear the members give accounts of their behavior. They were urged to avoid "concealment or partiality" during these moments of self-denunciation. At each stage of their meetings, the members would recite prayers such as the Litanies of the Saints, the rosary, and the Credo. Other prayers found in the common prayer manual, *Nianjing zongdu,* were said for "all people," the pope, "the spread of Catholic teachings," and relatives living and deceased. Not surprisingly, orations for "peace and harmony among Christian princes" said by Marian sodalities in Europe were replaced with prayers for the Qing emperor and the Chinese government. The selection of "saints of the month" was the concluding activity. Members were to take turns reading the name of their temporary patron as well as the scripture verse on their slip of paper, offering exegesis extempore for those who did not understand the meaning of the biblical passage.[83]

The Workings of Mercy

Perhaps no part of the Jesuits' religious message was so warmly received in China as the call for corporal works of mercy. This part of Christian teaching enjoyed such resonance because it harmonized well with indigenous patterns of social action inspired by the Confucian notion *Ren,* benevolence. Understandably, some of the first Christian *hui* were created by literati converts seeking to channel their faith through familiar conduits. António de Gouvea related how Yang Tingyun founded a literati group at Hangzhou in the 1610s. This brotherhood was modeled on examples found in the "ancient books" of the Confucian canon, he wrote, and called a "gin hoei [*Renhui*], which means Monte de Piedade." Gouvea here used the Portuguese term for the community chest, a phrase more often linked to the medieval Italian institutions called Monti di Pietà. This group had two aims: to convert those who joined it and to provide alms to poor Christians. Gouvea claimed that Yang's friends joined his brotherhood, making contributions that went to succor the poor "in their illnesses, as well as at the hour of death and burial."[84]

The alacrity with which Chinese Christians created charitable brotherhoods presented the Jesuits with ideal conditions for coaxing this indigenous model of confraternal social action into more devotional molds. The missionaries accomplished this task by insisting that the brothers say prayers at their meetings and obliging them to receive the sacraments. They also placed emphasis on certain forms of Christian charity that involved more spiritual than material gestures, such as conducting funeral processions and praying for the souls of the dead. This is where the Peking Jesuits attempted to steer their Confraternity of Piety during the early 1630s. In addition to assisting at burials, the group would hear mass when it held meetings and afterwards proceed to the "two common graveyards of the Christians to pray their rosaries for the dead."[85] A generation later, Gabriel de Magalhães described a similar group called "*Kim mo,* Respect and Remembrance for the Last Things." According to him, this group's actions were equivalent to the corporal works of mercy. The group attended to "the needy poor, orphans, and widows" and sent members to console the sick. Its most important activity, however, was to help bury the dead. For this activity, the group kept carriages for transporting coffins and had a store of banners and candles.[86]

The Roman Archives of the Society of Jesus preserve a manuscript containing a set of statutes for a *Renhui.* Although the group described in the text has the same name as the myriad benevolent associations of the late Ming and early Qing periods, it bears little resemblance to the charitable groups founded by contemporary literati or even Christian converts. As Erik Zürcher has shown in his analysis of Wang Zheng's *Renhui,* such groups could be no more than reflections of their Confucian parallels, barely suggesting that *Tianzhu jiao* was their inspiration.[87] Moreover, neither Wang's group nor Yang Tingyun's *hui* excluded non-Christians from its activities. By contrast, the manuscript statutes are explicitly Christian, with repeated references to central doctrines, the Virgin, and devotional obligations matching their demands for social action—making it clear that membership was restricted to Christians.[88]

Before listing nineteen organizational points, the statutes contain a preamble reminding participants that the Teachings of the Lord of Heaven can be boiled down to two main points: love of God and love of neighbor. In the elaboration on the first precept, members were exhorted to "listen attentively to the explanations" of Christian doctrine and avoid the "heretical teachings" of other religions. In the explanation of the second theme, they were encouraged to perform works of mercy, not just because they pertain to "universal virtue" but because the group's heavenly patron was "none other than the Holy Mother." The *Renhui* was to imitate her boundless mercy by taking action "wholeheartedly, and not just with spoken words."[89] The tone of this discussion suggests that this brotherhood was designed for Christians who showed less inclination to devotional rigor than their peers in the Marian sodalities. Whereas those who joined the *Shengmu hui* were offered theological reflections on the intercessory nature of the Virgin, postulants for the *Renhui* were reminded of basic Christian teachings. Without any overemphasis on the differences in their intended audiences, it is worth noting that the *Renhui* statutes include explanations of how to perform certain devotions, such as group prayers and examinations of conscience, presumably so familiar to members of the Marian sodality that there was no need to expatiate on them in the rules.

The fundamental aim of the charitable brotherhood was to apportion alms and prayers to the Christian community. Accordingly, the initial statutes outline how the group was to manage its financial resources. All donations, the first rule indicated, were to be disbursed according to the common consent of the *hui,* regardless of the amount contributed by each brother. In order to ensure probity, the group was to have four elected officials: one president, two vice presidents, and a treasurer. As a further security measure, the collection box was to be kept in the church and shut with three locks. Each of the three presiding members was to have a key, while the treasurer was to keep the account book with "all debits and credits recorded clearly by date." For all of this attention to the collection of funds, it is curious that there are no suggestions as to the types of charitable work that the group was to perform. In fact, the statutes imply that the group would develop its own preferred forms of public piety over time. Nevertheless, they do note that the "first priority will be given to the Funeral Liturgy," that is, the group's participation in burials. Since funeral processions were among the most visible acts of Christian devotion in China, members were reminded to do everything "in accord with the rites of the Holy Teaching." Moreover, they were to pay special attention to the way they sang the prayers, whether in responsorial or in unison. "There should be no confusion," read the statutes, "nor should vulgar words be used."[90]

The outward expression of virtue was not limited to the moments when the *Renhui* acted as a group. Individual members were charged with being models of piety for the rest of their community. As was the case with the Marian sodality, they were urged to start their work of charity at home "and then extend it to others." This charge entailed supervising the moral conduct of those in their households and caring for the physical and spiritual welfare of their parents, wives, and children. Outside the home, brothers were instructed to have *Tianzhu* always on their minds and warned "never to forget the Lord of Heaven in their speech."[91]

Whether or not those who joined this brotherhood saw themselves among the spiritual elite of their communities, they were obliged to engage in devotional routines that were more intense than those prescribed for ordinary Christians. Upon joining, all members were to confess. Afterwards, they were to receive the sacrament of penance once a month. Although the statutes had no provisions for how to conduct meetings, participants were to report to the church on the first Sunday of the month to select a "saint of the month." On their patron's feast day, they were to attend mass. Members were also required to pray part of the rosary and sing a Litany of the Virgin in the morning and the evening, as well as another three Paternosters and Ave Marias each day in honor of their "saint of the month." All of these prayers, of course, were in addition to the numerous orations made at the bedsides of sick brothers or the gravesides of deceased Christians. As a further prod toward rectitude, members were required to reflect on their "thoughts, words, and deeds" before retiring each night. This introspection was nothing short of an examination of conscience, one of the Society's preferred meditative techniques. When, on reflection, one's actions appeared to be good, *Renhui* members were told, they were to give thanks to *Tianzhu.* When they did not, however, the brothers were to "pray for pardon."[92]

Passionate Discipline

In contrast to the charitable brotherhoods which rested firmly on indigenous moral foundations, the mission church's penitential groups clearly revealed their European origins. In spite of the widely held (though false and repeatedly denied) notion that the China Jesuits wasted little breath on the doctrine of the Incarnation, the missionaries were so insistent on teaching their followers about Christ's Passion that they managed to displace deeply rooted traditions against self-mortification. As Erik Zürcher has shown, the idea that the inclinations of the soul might be in conflict with the desires of the body was at odds with Chinese thought. In some of their publications, however, the Jesuits made a radical extrapolation from the benign Confucian exhortation to moral self-cultivation. They understood the notion of "subduing" the body as a call to corporal mortification—an exaggeration exposed by their critics as well as their admirers.[93] On another level, the common understanding of filial piety in Chinese culture considered hurting or mutilating one's body an insult to progenitors. The Jesuits themselves were surprised that their followers so willingly acted on their suggestions to practice fasting and discipline. Their penitential zeal was "something to give thanks to God for," wrote Feliciano Pacheco, "since although the Chinese are such friends of their bodies, they resolve to punish them so bitterly and severely."[94] Philippe Couplet, for one, chanced an explanation. He claimed that the novelty of the doctrine of the Passion in China was responsible for making "a greater impression on the hearts of these new Christians."[95]

Whatever the reason for the reception of Christian notions of self-mortification, the fact is that in the 1630s the Jesuits began to encourage the creation of penitential groups throughout the mission church. Like other devotional confraternities, these groups were founded primarily in urban settings where their members could benefit from the continual supervision of spiritual directors. They met to meditate on the Passion at the missionaries' residence churches on Fridays, often at night and in secluded chapels in order to avoid raising suspicions. One report about Shanghai in the early 1640s told how penitents displayed their fervor "all year long" through prayers, meditations, and flagellation. Their piety climaxed during Lent, when they would meet every Friday "in the morning and afternoon to practice self-discipline and pray."[96] A similar group met in the mid-1650s under the guidance of Étienne Faber and Inácio da Costa at Xi'an, gathering on Saturday nights to pray, listen to saintly exempla, and lash themselves. The missionaries claimed that the custom of fasting prior to these bouts of flagellation was well established, as was attendance at mass. Some of the group's married men refrained from sex on meeting days, a display of zeal that, while not required by Catholic convention, was duly lauded by the Jesuits as a "holy custom."[97]

The missionaries wrote extensively about their followers' self-mortification rituals because they were visible proof of the tenor of fervor among the mission church's spiritual elite. Yet the dividing line between extreme empathy for Christ's suffering and the will to practice flagellation was a substantial one, and the Jesuits knew that even their most fervent followers needed coaxing over that frontier. Therefore, they encouraged intense routines of prayer and meditation, performed both individually and as a group. The best way to understand how the missionaries guided their followers to that critical threshold is to examine the statutes for a penitential brotherhood, such as the set of rules prepared by Humbert Augery for Hangzhou Christians joining the *Tianzhu Yesu kuhui,* Confraternity of the Passion of Lord Jesus. This printed booklet most likely dates from either the early 1660s (prior to 1664) or the early 1670s and consists of a brief preamble followed by ten rules for structuring group activities.[98]

The primary intention of Augery's *kuhui* was to foster its members' internal spirituality. His preamble invokes the biblical account of the Transfiguration as a divine injunction to imitate the example of Christ. Although he does not state it explicitly, members were to obey this "command of *Tianzhu*" literally. Their activities were reenactments of the human suffering of Christ's Passion, complete with mortifying scourges. Augery encouraged the confraternity to meditate on four themes; in addition to the precepts of love of God and love of neighbor, he added the need to be "humble and yielding" as well as to tolerate the faults of others. Curiously, Augery included no other theological cogitations in his preamble. In contrast to the lengthy discussion found in his *Shengmu hui* statutes, he ended with a brief order for the group to pray to the Virgin to intercede on behalf of deceased Christians.[99]

The regulations for this confraternity are markedly different from those of the Jesuits' other devotional groups. They place far more emphasis on individual piety than on group organization or cohesion. There is no indication of how the confraternity was to select a president or any mechanisms for regulating membership. The only prerequisite for joining the group was a general confession, that is, an accounting of all sins since baptism with the goal of identifying recurring faults. Likewise, the statutes make but one reference to a form of group discipline. Latecomers at meetings were to kneel in prayer "holding a bunch of incense" before the sacred image.[100] This lack of provisions regarding organization and discipline underscores the purely devotional nature of the group, since the Jesuits worked under the assumption that penitential activities were individual manifestations of piety. No statutes barred the devout from entering the group at will, and perhaps more important, none prevented members from leaving it. Nevertheless, the same spirit of "pious competition" fostered by the Jesuits in their other sodalities undoubtedly bound the penitential groups together and impelled them to greater degrees of devotional rigor.

As should be expected for a group that emphasized individual piety, Augery's group had the most demanding spiritual requirements of all the Jesuits' brotherhoods. Members were to confess and take communion every month—an obligation that meant receiving the Eucharist six times more frequently than ordinary Christians and twice as often as members of the devotional *Shengmu hui.* Each day, members of the penitential group were to recite a prayer of "the Five Wounds." They were also to pray a *coroa* (Portuguese for "crown") of Paternosters, that is, a rosary with thirty-three beads commemorating the number of barbs in the crown of thorns as well as the years in Christ's life. Moreover, members were instructed to meditate on the Passion when they woke up each day and to "resolve not to violate any of the Ten Commandments."[101]

The statutes are intentionally vague about the group's meetings and penitential activities. Whereas the rules for the other sodalities prescribe a sequence of prayers at gatherings, this group was simply instructed to "go to the church and pray in the morning" of the third Friday of each month. Every Friday, however, held special significance for members, since on that day they were to "perform one penitential act at will" in honor of Christ's suffering.[102] This is the statutes' only reference to self-mortification; there are no references to flagellation, fasting, or wearing the cilice. While this seems a paradoxical omission, it was in keeping with the Jesuits' ideas on the nature of penitential piety. For displays of fervor to be genuine, they could not be prescribed—especially since by making rules about penitential devotions, one might imply that there were certain preferential ways of manifesting piety. With regard to self-mortification, the missionaries left the method and the duration up to their Christians. In this respect, the China Jesuits borrowed a refrain from the statutes of the Society's European sodalities, where brothers were to perform penitential acts "each according to his devotion."[103]

Despite their central focus on internal piety, Augery's statutes were also concerned with channeling members' piety toward other Christians. In keeping with their general ambition to imitate Christ, their first duty was to act as peacemakers. Augery urged them to "conscientiously exhort" quarreling adherents of *Tianzhu jiao* to abandon their feuds. Members were also to succor the anxious and the infirm, encouraging their brethren to confess. It is possible to interpret this injunction to visit the sick as encouragement to persuade non-Christians to submit to baptism in times of mortal crisis. Members were reminded that they would earn "more merit" if they were the ones who reported potential converts and sick Christians to the priest.[104]

The Transmission of Piety

The three forms of confraternal piety sketched in this chapter represent the advanced stage of the development of the mission church. These groups constituted the engine of fervor that provided much of the dynamism for the spread of *Tianzhu jiao* in the seventeenth century and supplied the energy for its preservation, albeit among smaller numbers of Christians, after 1724. What made these groups such an important part of the mission church? First of all, they created effective outlets for the practice of piety, whether it was expressed in an external or an internal manner. Harnessing the indigenous impulse to create *hui,* the Jesuits fostered forms of group activity that contributed to maintaining the neophyte's zeal long past the moment of baptism. Moreover, the confraternal model worked to sustain the fervor of individuals who had been born—not converted—into their faith. On another level, the devotional confraternities created a new series of social distinctions within the mission church. To qualify for membership in a brotherhood was, in one sense, to rise above other Christians—a crucial morale boost in view of the fact that the majority of the Jesuits' followers were from the lowest ranks of society. Of course, the missionaries would not have admitted to creating such distinctions merely with the aim of social mobility in the Christian community. For them, the display of confraternal piety was an ideal for laymen and women to express the depth of their commitment to the Teachings of the Lord of Heaven. So much the better if the side effect of such manifestations of devotion was that others got infected with similar desires.

Another reason why the devotional brotherhoods were important was that they were, in the short term, a way to make up for the lack of missionaries. To be sure, all these forms of group piety demanded the presence of priests for saying masses, hearing confessions, and distributing the Eucharist. But instead of having to provide individual guidance to the

聖母端冕居諸神聖之上

甲聖三加冕于
聖母定爲諸
聖人及天神
之母皇

乙九品天神欽
崇聖母

丙諸國帝王士
民祈望聖母
爲萬世主保
恩母

丁天下萬方恭
建殿宇崇奉
聖母受其種
種恩庇

spiritual elite of the mission church, the Jesuits could entrust their confraternities with setting the general direction for the development of Catholic piety. And since the groups met on scheduled days, the priests could better calibrate their pastoral routines. While the Grim Reaper, of course, still visited the Chinese Christians at unpredictable hours, they could rest assured that members of various confraternities were keeping watch, ready to offer prayers and conduct burials if the Jesuits were off on a mission circuit or otherwise detained. To the men of the Society of Jesus, however, the devotional confraternities of their Chinese church represented something else. These groups were the most mature, tangible fruit of their labors in the "vineyard of the Lord." The Jesuits had come to China with the intent of converting its people to Catholic Christianity. They did not, however, set the end of the process of conversion at the baptismal font. Rather, they conceived of a period of evangelization and spiritual development in which baptism was a crucial early moment. The end point—if there was such a thing before one beheld *Tianzhu* in the court of heaven—came in the understanding and practice of orthodox forms of lay piety. This was, to be sure, the same benchmark that was set for lay Catholics in Europe. When the Peking and Fuzhou Jesuits created Annunciadas at the end of the seventeenth century, they saw their goal becoming a reality. They had taken the raw materials of Chinese social and religious behavior and had molded them into an approximation of their European ideal—just as Martino Martini had done by building his church at Hangzhou. Through the soft pressure of pastoral care, the Jesuits had stood the standard model of cultural transmission into China on its head. Before the Yongzheng reign and under ideal conditions, Catholicism in the Qing empire was manifested in increasingly European—and Jesuit—forms. It was the odor of piety emanating from their mission church that galvanized the men of the Vice-Province to fight unceasingly in the eighteenth century against their enemies, both Roman and Manchu.

Woodcut print of the Coronation of the Virgin, in Giulio Aleni, *Illustrated Explanation of the Incarnation of the Lord of Heaven (Tianzhu jiangsheng chuxiang jingjie),* 1637. Note the presence of both Chinese and European figures in the lower half of the picture.

Conclusion

In the summer heat of 1670, Manuel de Saldanha, the ambassador extraordinary of the king of Portugal and viceroy of the Estado da Índia, journeyed across China to Peking on a mission to seek a renewal of trade between the city of Macau and the Qing empire. After being forced to cool his heels in Canton for two years and then traveling up China's waterways for six months, Saldanha was received by the Kangxi emperor. In the ambassador's suite was Francisco Pimentel (1629–1675), a Portuguese Jesuit belonging to the Society's Province of Japan, who was traveling under the guise of a layman while serving as Saldanha's confessor. Pimentel was a keen observer who freely recorded his thoughts on China, reporting on the embassy's interactions with Manchus and mandarins as well as describing its relations with the missionaries at Peking.[1]

This was one Jesuit who was unimpressed by what he saw, and he was not shy about sharing his opinions with the old China hands Ferdinand Verbiest, Gabriel de Magalhães, and Lodovico Buglio. The Qing capital, Pimentel informed them, lagged far behind its counterparts in Europe, such as Rome, Paris, and Lisbon. In stark contrast to the impression of grandeur created by the accounts of Jesuit authors, he complained, the reality of China left much to be desired. In his opinion, a visitor to Peking would be justified in thinking that he had been transported to "any of the poorest villages in Portugal." The city's buildings, just like those he had seen elsewhere in the empire, were made of poor materials and had oppressively low rooflines. The palaces of the rich were no exception; in any event, they had no outstanding features save a few pretty courtyards and painted chambers. What thoroughly fixed Pimentel's opinion was that even the wealthy lacked comfort, their homes being insulated from Peking's severe climate only by rice paper.[2]

"The priests were unhappy that I had such a low impression of Chinese buildings," he wrote. "To sway me they said that I had not seen everything, that I had not been to the house of mandarin so-and-so in such-and-such a city, an edifice on a par with those in any other part of the world." Yet Pimentel remained skeptical. He informed his confreres that he was certain what they said was true, but they could not change his opinion. Sniffing at their effusive paeans to China's marvels, Pimentel wondered why, of all the cities in their dominions, its emperors had chosen to hold court at Peking, "the worst one of them all."[3]

Pimentel resented the Peking Jesuits' dismissal of his observations. "They owe me some credit on this subject," he contended, "because I traveled through five provinces during the two and a half years it took me to get from Canton to the court." One thing Pimentel encountered, however, was not at odds with his confreres' descriptions of China. As he put it, he was constantly "chased by the Christians" during his travels.[4] When those who lived along his route learned that a priest was passing through on his way to Peking, many of them rushed to intercept Pimentel so they could confess their sins to him. In short, he found tangible evidence of a large and widely disseminated mission church. Or, put another way, from the point of view of a missionary, China was not such a miserable edifice after all.

Recall that Pimentel's progress across the Qing empire occurred at a time when most of the Jesuits were confined in Canton and only the Dominican Luo Wenzao was able to circulate freely about the country. Yet he was unprepared to minister to the Chinese Christians. "They were utterly disconsolate," he wrote, "when they found out that I did not speak their language." So great was the press of penitents that Pimentel commissioned a special confessional manual from a native Christian literatus whom the Canton Jesuits had attached to the embassy. This handbook consisted of a list of sins in Portuguese and Chinese, accompanied by another list of the numbers one to five. Christians could thus confess in silence, "pointing to the species of sin and then finding the character which indicated the number of times." Both men and women sought out the priest, and those who could not read confessed with the help of his interpreter. Knowing that Pimentel could not speak Mandarin, the captive missionaries had not given him a list beforehand of their Christian communities. Despite that, word of his imminent arrival traveled quickly enough. And when the speed of the embassy's barges outpaced the currents of rumor, local Christians were alerted to his presence by the adherents of *Tianzhu jiao* in his company or simply by the flags on the ships that bore the red crosses of Portugal's Order of Christ.[5]

Pimentel put considerable stock in his observations. He knew about Chinese architecture because, as a member of the ambassadorial train, he had been lodged in several mandarin palaces along his route. The conditions he had endured at Peking were, from his point of view, far from being the image of Oriental splendor that his mind's eye beheld after he read the accounts of Nicolas Trigault, Álvaro Semedo, and Martino Martini. But he had met throngs of Christians and observed their desire for the sacraments, an experience that stirred his soul. He wrote of being overjoyed by how his servant, a young man from the island of Timor who had been raised in Macau, challenged the religious beliefs of the local boatmen who steered them across the Yangzi. He gladly performed more than two hundred baptisms of adults and children at the insistence of Christian men and women. And although he could not speak to them in their native tongue, Pimentel was certain of the piety of Agueda Tong and her husband, Tong Guoqi, the high-ranking mandarin who housed the priest during his visit to Nanjing. Although Tong had not yet submitted to baptism in 1670, he had long been an ally of the missionaries thanks to his Christian wife. Even if Pimentel refused to believe a word of what the China Jesuits told him about Tong's pious inclinations, he had prima facie evidence of them in the church at Ganzhou that the mandarin had paid to build. And while staying in Tong's palace, where he said daily masses in a small chapel, Pimentel saw before him the fruit of the Qing official's willingness to convert all members of his household to the Teachings of the Lord of Heaven.

Predilection for cultural contrasts and disregard (surely not ignorance) of the widely invoked early modern adage "comparisons are odious" lay at the heart of Francisco Pimentel's doubts. Over the months he had spent traveling by ship from Lisbon to Macau, his mind had conjured up images of China derived from his confreres' writings in order to dissolve the oppressive weight of the horizon line at sea. When he finally beheld the fraction of the Qing empire that he could glimpse from the ambassadorial barges, his fancies jarred against the reality before him—yet only partially. When Pimentel used a European scale of cultural and artistic grandeur to gauge the level of Chinese magnificence, he failed to register indigenous achievements. But when he turned his gaze to things more proper to his own cultural frame—that is, when he looked for the fruits of missionary work that he himself had been trained to cultivate as a religious professional—he saw clearly the accomplishments of his colleagues. Pimentel would take that awareness with him to Tonkin, where his destiny lay, using it to compare the results of his own apostolic labors in that mission field with those he had witnessed in China.

Pimentel was surprised by what he found in China in 1670. It is only natural for historians, looking back from a distance of three centuries, to raise questions about the similarities and differences between the Jesuits' efforts in China and their enterprises elsewhere in the early modern world. After all, the Society of Jesus conducted missionary projects simultaneously in Africa, Asia, Europe, and the Americas, staffing them all with men drawn from the same pool of recruits as those who were assigned to the Vice-Province. In the preceding chapters I have shown how the China Jesuits relied on evangelizing techniques and pastoral strategies that their confreres employed among European Catholics. It is therefore unsurprising that the Society's men in other overseas mission fields would rely on similar methods. Bearing in mind the obvious differences in the conditions for missionary work between areas as disparate as the Amazonian rainforest, the North American woodlands, the South India coast, and the Chinese empire, one can identify a series of characteristics that unified Jesuit efforts around the globe. Such commonalities include the problem of learning indigenous languages, the confrontation with other religious traditions, the strategies employed for indoctrination and creating new Christian identities, and the modes of organization used to structure neophyte communities. While the pursuit of detailed comparisons between the China mission and the Society's other missions lies beyond the scope of this study, in the following pages I sketch some general similarities between them.

Unity amid Diversity

Before embarking on a journey, however brief, around the Jesuit world, one needs to suggest some parameters for this exercise in comparison.

First of all, one must recognize the Society of Jesus itself as the constant element among the variables found in different missionary environments. Without ignoring the variations between the order's provinces in Europe (which served as the primary recruiting ground for its missionaries), one discerns a formidable sense of corporate unity rooted in the Jesuits' shared training experiences, organizational structure, and pastoral ministries. Yet that bond of internal cohesion was itself the product of a process of evolution that took place over the decades following the order's establishment in 1540. It is therefore possible to speak of a pan-European Jesuit identity only after the order had articulated common patterns of activity and administration, a development roughly dating to the late 1570s and early 1580s. Before then, the character of the order had been dominated by the charisma of its founding generation (Ignatius Loyola, Peter Canisius, Simão Rodrigues)—a phenomenon replicated in the overseas missions (Francis Xavier, Matteo Ricci, Manuel da Nóbrega). The most promising terms for comparing missionary enterprises can thus be found chronologically after the first generations of Jesuits had forged their order's identity and the pioneers of each mission reached their first conclusions about how best to conduct their apostolic endeavors. While the vicissitudes of the early missions to India, Brazil, Japan, Syria, Ethiopia, Morocco, Kongo, and the Indonesian archipelago certainly contributed to the development of Jesuit strategies and attitudes, they reflect the flux of the Society of Jesus itself in its first decades. Further contrasts can be detected between the policies of mission founders and those of their successors. In the case of the China mission, the administrative and evangelical strategies elaborated under Niccolò Longobardo offer better terms for comparison with other missions than those created under Matteo Ricci's leadership.

A second consideration has to do with the presence of European colonial power as a factor in missionary activity. While the East Asian missions were carried out without the coercive force of Spanish or Portuguese armies, this was not the case in the Jesuits' other enterprises. But the imperial eye saw far more than its hand could grasp, and the reach of Iberian or French power often extended only scant miles from those nations' fortified settlements.[6] Jesuits whose bases were properly within the bounds of empire often conducted missions to areas far beyond the limits of colonial coercion, in lands where indigenous rulers retained a high degree of control over their affairs. Accordingly, one should not posit an absolute divide between those missionary activities conducted in proximity to European outposts and those developed in contested areas. To be sure, before the eighteenth century, few colonial armies followed behind the Jesuits who traveled with Huron bands about the snowy fastness of Canada, and only slave-seeking *bandeirantes* dared penetrate the highlands of Paraguay to raid the Society's reductions there. In those areas, as in many others, missionaries carried out their evangelization projects with the cooperation of indigenous groups. Without at least the tacit approval of native peoples, the Jesuits could entertain no hope of realizing their goals. Moreover, there was a continual ebb and flow of personnel between colonial colleges and mission territories, with the former serving as staging posts for the latter as well as safe havens for missionaries in times of trouble.

One of the best avenues for comparing Jesuit missions emanates from their common starting point, the language barrier between the priests and their intended converts. In the Vice-Province, the missionaries' degree of engagement with Chinese language and thought had a decisive impact on their ability to create and sustain their image as worthy interlocutors for the indigenous elite. It took the combined efforts of individuals such as Matteo Ricci and Lazzaro Cattaneo to uncover the rudiments of *guanhua* and organize what they had learned according to grammatical rules with which they and their confreres were familiar. Elsewhere, the linguistic challenge was just as formidable, and Jesuits used similar techniques for deconstructing languages and reassembling them in forms understandable to Europeans. This endeavor is exemplified by João Rodrigues's *artes* for the Japanese language, as well as by the Jesuits' pioneering grammars of the languages of Angola, Chile, and southern India—not to mention the missionaries' more ambitious projects of creating a new lingua franca for use across areas with what they deemed excessive linguistic diversity, such as the "general language" they devised in Brazil for the peoples of the Tupi-Guaraní cultural area.[7]

The production of linguistic treatises represents an advanced point on the path from ignorance to fluency. Earlier along that course, other Jesuits had experiences similar to those of Michele Ruggieri and his "painting" classes with his first Chinese master. The Tyrolean missionary Eusebio Francisco Kino (1645–1711), who spent decades in the high deserts of northern Mexico and on the parched coast of Baja California, went "with ink-well in hand whenever the Indians were present," acquiring their tongue as best he could by listening to his interlocutors and quickly jotting down the correct pronunciation.[8] Kino's urge to compile and organize native languages was similar to that of Paul le Jeune (1591–1664), superior of the Society's mission to New France in the 1630s. Reflecting on the challenge of acquiring Montagnais and Algonquin, le Jeune averred that "before knowing a language, it was necessary for me to make books from which to learn it." For him, the key to picking up any of the indigenous peoples' tongues resided in "composing it often, in learning a great many words, and in acquiring their accent." Despite his claim that European languages differed greatly from the tongues of the people of the Eastern Woodlands, le Jeune claimed consolation in one crucial fact: "People may call them barbarians as much as they please, but their language is very regular."[9]

Even for the Jesuits, some language barriers remained insurmountable. In those instances, missionaries had to rely on auxiliaries to bridge the communication gap between a lingua franca and the local dialect—even if this meant sacrificing precision, not to mention the moral problems posed by hearing confessions through intermediaries. In China, realizing that it did no good merely to lament that their Mandarin was often of little use beyond the urban centers where their mission stations were located, the men of the Vice-Province pragmatically relied on a corps of catechist-interpreters. While years of residence in a given area surely gave the Jesuits familiarity with the seven major regional tongues in China, their travels along rural circuits continually suggested that they were in a veritable Babel.[10] Similarly, the transatlantic slave trade created daunting linguistic challenges for Jesuits intent on curing the greatest possible number of souls. Such was the case at Cartagena de Indias, where Alonso de Sandoval (1576–1652) coordinated the Society's efforts to baptize and indoctrinate the hundreds of African slaves who were disembarked there each year. The sheer variety of linguistic groups and the drifting population of slaves in the Colombian port made Sandoval believe that it was impossible to learn all the necessary languages. Not only was there "no one who could teach them," he pointed out, but also the priests' dealings with slaves did not "suffice for them to stick to us naturally." To remedy the situation, the Cartagena Jesuits tried to keep up contacts with slaves from different African regions, whom they would summon (if, that is, their masters permitted it) to act as interpreters in seeking to communicate with the moribund survivors of the Middle Passage.[11]

It goes without saying that the Jesuits' goal in their language studies was to equip themselves with the means for transmitting the Christian message. But the capacity to communicate is not always equivalent to the ability to persuade. Where allies bearing the gun and the lash were not present, rhetoric was one of the missionaries' only means of claiming souls. In East Asia, the Jesuits engaged in publication efforts to cast their words farther into the realm of Chinese and Japanese discourse than their voices could carry. But their printing enterprise would have floundered if not for the help they received from learned *indigènes* about elegant form and style, as well as how to intone proper cultural resonances. In other areas they employed whichever form of communication carried the degree of authority to which they aspired. Among the Hurons and Iroquois, missionaries aimed to develop their language skills to the point where they could be accepted as orators. Once they were deemed worthy of addressing elite assemblies, they acquired a degree of social respect that no language course or grammar study could afford them.[12] Moreover, the Jesuits were not averse to adapting the images and metaphors that they used to explain Christian concepts to fit their hosts' cultural contexts: whereas in China they linked Confucian moral norms to the Ten Commandments, in Japan they associated loyalty to the feudal lord with duty to Deus, and in the Great Lakes region they endowed divine personages with the fearsome attributes of Iroquois warriors.[13]

Persuasion implies confrontation, and Jesuits sallied forth into battle against other religious traditions and their representatives across the globe. Their antagonism toward the Buddhist clergy in China has been amply adduced throughout this book, as well as their attempts to undermine the spiritual certainties of prospective converts. But neither in the case of the men of the Vice-Province nor elsewhere were missionaries well versed in their opponents' theologies and cosmologies prior to arriving in the mission field. They had to acquire ways to argue against the foundations of non-Christian practices in situ if they were to supplant them with Catholicism. They also had to identify who their religious rivals were in any given mission field. Every series of Annual Letters contains accounts of bugbears, such as "bonzes" in Japan, mullahs in the Moluccas, yogis in India, or Andean religious specialists in Peru. But the Jesuits appear to have invested in the study of other religions only in proportion to the degree of antagonism they perceived from the representatives of those traditions. Compare, for example, their blanket dismissal of Daoism and the *Daoshi* in China to their tactics of engagement toward Buddhism and the bonzes.

When Jesuits confronted other religious professionals, they sought opportunities to make public displays of their skills, whether prophylactic, ritual, rhetorical, or scientific. After all, their capacity to predict, explain, or deliver the miraculous better than their rivals largely determined their ability to gain social legitimacy as well as their capacity to provoke conversions. In China, the Jesuits' showdown with indigenous astronomers ensured the political protection of the mission, while, according to their reports, the performance of Catholic ceremonies that alleviated epidemics or droughts where other rituals had failed won new adherents of *Tianzhu jiao.* Jesuits elsewhere also made use of such skills. For instance, the Society's missions to the Guaraní in Paraguay often became stages for contests between priests and shamans over the mastery of effective rituals, healing techniques, and moral teachings.[14] In southern India in the early 1680s, one Jesuit found himself caught between two war parties bent on capturing the village where he had his residence and church. One of the rival captains brought soldiers, retainers, and Brahmins to hear the missionary speak of the origin of Hindu deities. "I proved to him by reason, and by arguments drawn from their own stories," claimed the Jesuit with an eye to both self-preservation and the conversion of the other, "that the 'First Cause' alone was God and that his gods were not."[15]

But besting opponents in cosmological confrontations was only half the battle for claiming souls. Recall that Rodrigo de Figueiredo moved from one set of problems to another the moment his Chinese peasant interlocutors conceded defeat and asked for an explanation of Christian teaching. A general tactic used by the Jesuits for building a new theological edifice in the minds of prospective converts was derived from the long tradition of catechesis teaching in Europe. They would start, in the biblical sense, with the beginning, first introducing the notion of a single God, then discoursing on the elements of Judeo-Christian morality, and afterwards explaining the Incarnation and Passion of Christ. Missionaries considered this pattern of instruction equally applicable in other parts of Asia as well as in the Americas. During his attempts to set up missions in the Indonesian archipelago at the same time Islam was spreading over that area, Manuel Ferreira (1586–1625) would present himself to a local ruler as the ambassador of "the King of the Heavens who sent him to offer His divine law . . . and the salvation for his soul that he would find in none other."[16] And António de Andrade gave a summary of Christian teachings to a group of lamas at Tsaparang in the 1620s, explaining the notion of the Trinity in halting Tibetan and without translations for terms such as "person, nature, to proceed, faith, grace, etc."[17] Among the Iroquois in North America, French Jesuits used a similar approach by introducing God, the Great Voice, who made "the many things we see when we move our eyes from side to side."[18]

Much as the Jesuits tended to order their own learning processes according to "plans of studies," so they organized their catechetical efforts in a logical order. In fact, it is only the modern observer who discerns a division between the Society's sacred and secular pedagogical activities. The same impulse toward educational uniformity that made texts such as Manuel Álvares's *De Institutione Grammatica* (first edition 1572), Cipriano Suárez's *De Arte Rhetorica* (first edition 1562), and the *Commentarii Collegii Coninmbricensis* (first edition 1593) the standard textbooks for the different phases of the Jesuit academic program throughout Europe also gave rise to widely used doctrine manuals such as Marco Jorge's *Doutrina Christã* (first edition 1566). It should come as no surprise that missionaries who were trained on such texts should attempt to replicate them in the overseas missions. João da Rocha's *Tianzhu shengjiao qimeng,* a Chinese version of Jorge's doctrine dialogue, has already been mentioned, and other adaptations were made for use in regions as far distant as Brazil, India, and eastern Europe. In 1624 Mateus Cardoso published a Kikongo translation of this text at Lisbon and promptly shipped it off to the mission field for distribution. During his trek overland from the coastal enclave of Luanda to the Kongolese capital São Salvador the following year, Cardoso (ca. 1584–ca. 1626) was pleased with how this *cartilha* helped him to cement his friendship with local potentates. After giving a copy to one lord—as a substitute for a Portuguese primer that the missionary had left on a previous visit—the Jesuit implored him to teach doctrine to others, commenting that "he could perform the office of master well since he knew how to read."[19]

While the distribution of doctrine manuals was an effective means for spreading the Christian message, one should not assume that the Jesuits were at a loss when it came to teaching the illiterate. To start with, Marcos Jorge's catechism and its translations were written in simple dialogue form; moreover, the Society's missionaries made extensive use of song for inculcating doctrine. Drawing on proven methods used among rustics in Europe, the China Jesuits and their lay auxiliaries combined Christian themes with popular tunes and encouraged especially women and children to sing along. But the missionaries' use of music in East Asia was less developed than it was in other mission fields in Africa and the Americas, where song was the most important means of indoctrination. For instance, Mateus Cardoso records that he was met by a group of children outside São Salvador in 1625 who took him the final mile into the capital "in a procession with flags hoisted, singing the prayers in the language of the Kongo."[20] And in the coastal mountains of Brazil, António Vieira (1608–1697) reported that his colleagues gathered groups of Indian children to sing the catechism which the priests had composed "in verses and very appropriate tones." Recording the growing numbers of youths at each successive doctrine class, Vieira saw proof of the assertion of Brazil mission founder Manuel da Nóbrega (1517–1570) that "with music and vocal harmony he dared to summon to himself all of the heathens in America."[21]

As I have demonstrated, the China Jesuits envisioned and tracked the spiritual path of their converts far beyond the baptismal font and the doctrine class. After passing through the catechumenate, adult Christians were expected to consider themselves part of a community of believers and participate in group rituals. In the Vice-Province there were two basic forms of collective spirituality: organizational brotherhoods and devotional sodalities. While the former served to structure the Jesuits' mission church, the latter permitted the exercise of more intense and varied forms of piety for those possessed of higher levels of fervor. Yet while the confraternity model was especially appropriate in Ming and Qing society in light of the strong indigenous impulse to create *hui,* such forms of group piety were not limited to China. In Paraguay, Jesuits instituted Marian sodalities in their reductions as a way to provide specific channels for the more devout among their Guaraní Christians. Antonio Ruiz de Montoya (1585–1652) described how in the late 1630s confraternity members were entrusted with special roles in respect to the dying and the dead; they were to keep prayer vigils and summon the priest when the time for Last Rites drew near.[22] Elsewhere, brotherhoods sought to provide a measure of group solidarity for some of the Christians who received pastoral care from the Jesuits, as in Bogotá, where the Society's priests organized a confraternity for African slaves with the invocation of Saint Mary Major.[23] And when their spiritual charges faced mortal danger, as on the Japanese island of Kyushu during the Tokugawa era persecutions, other Jesuit-inspired groups showed their utility for enhancing the bonds of group solidarity and mutual protection.[24]

Another manifestation of lay piety—fostered by necessity in many missions as a result of a lack of priests—is found in the activities of the Jesuits' native auxiliaries. Just as the men of the Vice-Province relied on catechists and *huizhang* for coordinating rituals and maintaining the cohesion of the mission church, Jesuits in other mission fields also had recourse to lay assistants. Having lost hope that they would ever receive enough recruits to meet their needs, the missionaries in southeastern India pleaded in their 1667 Annual Letter for catechists. After a training period, these individuals could go "into the towns and suburbs, into villages and marketplaces, in the countryside and the forests, using their time according to our instructions, like hunters skilled in not only making fresh captures, but also in domesticating the inhabitants of the forest."[25] In the case of the longhouse societies of New France, the task of leading collective prayers and indoctrinating new church members often fell to clan mothers. These women had taken over this important activity from the Iroquois men whom the Jesuits had originally appointed to the task with the title of "prayer captains" or "dogiques"—a term that made its way around the world from Japan, where *dojuku* (literally "cohabitant") was the label used to denote the priests' lay auxiliaries.[26]

Yet a further indication of the Jesuits' intended evolution for their mission churches across the globe can be found in their attempts to introduce new devotions into the standard set of Catholic ritual activities (prayer routines, attendance at mass, reception of the sacraments). Starting in earnest in the 1630s, the men of the Vice-Province encouraged the use of penitential discipline among some Chinese Christians, instructing them in the proper modes of corporal mortification and organizing Brotherhoods of the Passion for collective exercises. Since these practices often formed a central part of the Jesuits' personal devotions during their academic and pastoral training in Europe, it is not surprising that missionaries brought a penchant for this type of devotion with them overseas. Mateus Cardoso described how he placed a flagellant's lash in the hand of Garcia I of Kongo and informed him that it was for use during Advent and Lent. The Jesuit also offered him a cilice and encouraged the king to wear it next to his skin "for doing penance."[27] Priests from the Province of Paraguay also encouraged corporal mortification as a correct manifestation of shame and penitence, remarking how some men took readily to "bloody disciplines . . . not even sparing the face its own special punishment." Indian women practiced similar pious rigors, although they did them in secret since the Jesuits did not admit them to "the public disciplines of the men."[28] One wonders, however, if the task of instilling such forms of devotion was as difficult elsewhere as it was in China, where indigenous moral teachings ran counter to valorizations of corporal mortification. At least in Canada, missionaries had little trouble encouraging their spiritual charges to practice discipline. Jesuit accounts report the incorporation of native practices such as immersion in freezing water or burning flesh with coals into the standard European repertoire of hair shirts, fasting, and lashings.[29]

In spite of all these manifestations of zeal, experienced missionaries knew that the work of creating Christian communities was a long-term effort. For all of the military metaphors found in the Jesuits' reports from their mission fields, they were committed to a war of attrition, not to engaging their foes in skirmishes and raids. Herein lay the basic contradiction at the heart of all early modern missionary endeavors: missionary vocations were the product of fervor bred from tales of miracles and heroism, heightened emotional states that often degenerated into impatience at the real difficulties involved in attaining bona fide conversions and instilling Catholic devotional habits in non-Christian lands. Stories from some mission fields, such as Japan, told of hundreds of converts in relatively short spans, spurring great expectations elsewhere. But when similar tallies failed to materialize, frustrations were felt at both the individual and the institutional level. In the case of the Vice-Province of China, the sluggish pace of conversions led to decades of hand-wringing at the Society's headquarters in Rome and the appointment of more than one Visitor. Some Jesuit superiors chose to deflate their correspondents' hopes for rapid apostolic triumphs before similar pressures were felt in their appointed territories. In 1633, less than a decade after the first missionaries arrived in the St. Lawrence valley, Paul le Jeune compared his incipient mission to others that were slow to develop. "It was thirty-eight years," he asserted, "before anything was accomplished in Brazil. How long have they been waiting at the gates of China?" Fittingly, le Jeune drove home his point with a metaphor drawn from nature: "Let it be remembered that mushrooms spring up in a night, while it requires years to ripen the fruits of the palm."[30]

Diversity amid Unity

While the themes suggested here indicate a great deal of commonality among Jesuit missions in different corners of the early modern world, one should not overstate the possibilities for comparison. After all, the wide spectrum of cultures in which the missionaries worked poses a number of problems for those seeking to establish a unified vision of the Society's activities. Even the Jesuits themselves were aware of the perils of subsuming all of their pastoral efforts in non-Christian lands under the rubric of "missionary activity." José de Acosta (1540–1600), for one, was clearly aware of the challenges that faced the Society's men in civilizations as disparate as those of Peru and China. This Spanish missionary in the Andes pointed to the problems of language and how the use of characters rather than words created terminological ambiguity: "For the Indian, with twenty-four letters that he knows how to write and join together, can write and read all the words in the world, and the mandarin with his hundred thousand letters will be hard put to it to write any proper name such as Martín or Alonso, and much less to write the names of things that he does not recognize."[31] Recall that the path to the discovery of such incommensurability in China led the Jesuits to the point of rupture, and even tragedy, as in the case of Nicolas Trigault's suicide during the Terms Controversy. Elsewhere, the adoption or imposition of European tongues largely obviated the need to tax the missionaries' capacities as interpreters—or their health.

The physical conditions of missionary work in different regions also varied to such an extent as to make easy comparison impossible. While the men of the Vice-Province frequently complained of poverty and even hunger, the most trying experience for many was their journey along the Cape route. Those who survived the trip to the mission field often enjoyed conditions of luxury, compared to the hardships suffered by their confreres (excepting, of course, the thousands of Jesuits who staffed the order's colleges throughout the world). Leaving aside the handful of China missionaries who were swept up in the tumult of the Manchu invasions, the majority of the Society's men in the Ming and Qing empires busied themselves with pastoral and proselytizing duties in the calm environment of cities and villages. Traveling their mission circuits was a far cry from António de Andrade's trek to Tibet, during which he had to make headway across the Himalayan snow lying down, "as when one swims, so as not to sink into it."[32] Likewise, while José Monteiro was keen to tell recruits to the Vice-Province how to express their disgust at their domestics' gastronomic missteps, at least he did not have to lament a lack of rats to eat, as Luís Figueira (ca. 1574–1643) did during a trip through the mountains of northern Brazil in 1607.[33] And although the Jesuits' compounds in cities such as Peking, Shanghai, and Hangzhou may have had only rice paper to keep the cold from flowing through their windows, that was surely nothing compared to the rigors of a winter spent in a low-slung Huron longhouse cramped between smoldering embers within and snowdrifts without.[34]

One final order of considerations about the limits of comparison among the Society's missions worldwide has to do with the Jesuits' links to European imperial projects. As mentioned earlier, the degree to which colonial armies exercised control over the vast dominions claimed by their sovereigns is easy to overestimate. But that fact did not prevent the Jesuits who worked beyond the farthest shadow of European power from considering their efforts to be in concert with other imperial objectives. A handful of examples will suffice. The coincidence of colonial and missionary aims was certainly evident in southern India, where the Jesuits' apostolic efforts among the inhabitants of the Fishery Coast strengthened the commercial links between the Portuguese and native pearl traders.[35] Further illustrations can be found in the numerous *reducciones, aldeias,* and *réserves* scattered across the colonial hinterlands of the Americas. In Japan, the Jesuits managed to establish their mission on a firm footing by acting as intermediaries between the local lords and the Portuguese traders. And in the case of the Vice-Province of China, the reciprocal relationship between the Jesuits and the city of Macau offers a clear case of the melding of secular and religious goals. The colony was at once the missionaries' safe haven, staging post, and conduit for salaries and supplies. These favors gave the Jesuits ample reason to rise repeatedly to the defense of Macau's interests—and even the Portuguese enclave's very existence—before the Dragon Throne.

In some instances, the physical proximity between the men of the Society and colonial officials and settlers led to a conflation of aims and attitudes. The degree of confidence expressed in some Jesuit writings borders on folly, if only because the missionaries themselves exaggerated their ability to summon force to carry out their own projects. Recall how Alonso Sánchez traveled from Asia to Europe intent on selling his idea of an easy conquest of China to Philip II of Spain. Similar episodes of missionary bluster seem in proportion to the degree of hostility that the Jesuits perceived in the mission field and what they imagined their compatriots could do about it. For example, although Paul le Jeune expressed his concerns about the difficulty of the conversion enterprise in Canada in the 1630s, he did not shy away from suggesting that some gesture be made toward the Iroquois akin to the "great show of power made at first by the Portuguese in the East and West Indies."[36] Nearly thirty years later he again insisted that the war drum was the best instrument for setting the tone for the missions in the Great Lakes region: "The Iroquois are worse than the bonzes and Brahmins. They are not to be defeated by the pen, but by force of arms; and there are no pirates on the China Sea so dangerous."[37]

But the relationships between the Society's missionary enterprises and European overseas empires were not always symbiotic. The Jesuits often worked at cross-purposes to secular European interests. At times they pursued their own worldly aims with an eye to prestige (if not profit). For instance, the missionaries' conflicts with Spaniards and Paulistas over the Guaranís in Paraguay in the 1630s and 1640s displayed a degree of institutional independence, assertion, and ambition on par with their takeover of temporal control over the port of Nagasaki in the 1580s. Moreover, the oftentimes tense relationship between the Society and other ecclesiastical institutions, such as the Inquisition or the Mendicant orders, in different colonial societies offers further evidence of the contradictory aims of these different imperial agents despite their common goal of implanting Christianity.[38] Such contradictions were no less glaring than the commonplace divergences of purpose between crown officials, private merchants, and representatives of the secular church hierarchy overseas. They were the coarse texture of the loose-knit web of empire that the Europeans cast over the early modern globe.

In China, however, many of the questions raised here about the relations between missionary activity and imperial projects were moot. The Jesuits could not summon a European army to force a change of heart among those who rebuked them or denied the veracity of their theological arguments. Once inside the domains of the Ming and Qing emperors, they severed their ties to the solid institutional reputation that the Society enjoyed among Europeans. From the standpoints of indigenous language, law, and learning, the Jesuits found themselves at the bottom of the cultural heap at the beginning of their enterprise. While they did gain prestige over the course of the decades surveyed in this book, they remained no more than diplomats in China; they could influence the powerful only through friendship or persuasion. One of the best indicators of the tenuousness of the Jesuits' position in that country was their hesitancy about enrolling native priests in their ranks. Not only were they anxious about their ability to make Chinese recruits live up to their vows, but also they feared that no mandarin would force a renegade priest to submit to the correction of the Vice-Province's superiors.

The fact that the China Jesuits were able to mount a missionary enterprise and sustain it for almost a century and a half in the Ming and Qing empires is a testament to the Society's ability to train its men and coordinate its proselytizing and pastoral efforts effectively. In their efforts to create a mission church deeply rooted in Chinese society, however, the men of the Vice-Province were virtually alone for most of the period surveyed here. Had European soldiers and settlers rather than other missionaries joined them, perhaps their spiritual legacy would have been as enduring in China as it was in other lands where they established missions. Even so, vestiges of the Jesuits' presence can still be found from the foot of the Great Wall to the mouth of the Pearl River. Atop a bastion in the old walls of Peking, the instruments used by Ferdinand Verbiest to calculate the imperial calendar sit beneath the same sun and stars. Visitors to the Forest of Stele Museum at Xi'an can inspect a great stone slab carved with Nestorian teachings, the same eighth-century monument to which Li Zhizao and Manuel Dias the younger drew attention in print to demonstrate the long pedigree of Christianity in China. Amid the bustle of Shanghai, a Catholic cathedral can be found at the site of the former family compound of Xu Guangqi, appropriately dedicated to Ignatius Loyola. In a tomb located in a secluded grove not far from the shores of the famed West Lake of Hangzhou, ossuaries containing the bones of Martino Martini and other missionaries sit undisturbed by the passage of time. And in Macau, the imposing façade of the Jesuit church rises majestically above the old city, despite the fact that the last Portuguese flag has been lowered from above the governor's residence. Curiosity impels most modern visitors up the steep stone staircase at this last site to see what are known as the Ruins of St. Paul's. There they spend a few moments contemplating the carvings of ships, dragons, and saints set in stone four centuries ago, or perhaps they glance at the vista of sampans in the city's inner harbor. For these travelers, a voyage has ended on the very spot where the Jesuits' journey into China began.

Bibliographic Note

This study relies primarily on archival materials in Portugal and Italy, in particular those found in the Ajuda Palace library in Lisbon and the central archive of the Society of Jesus in Rome, the two principal repositories for sources relating to the Jesuits' Asian missions. Ajuda houses the Jesuítas na Ásia collection, consisting of sixty-one volumes and more than thirty thousand manuscript pages, eighteenth-century copies of documents once found in the Society's archive in Macau and related to both the Vice-Province of China and the Province of Japan. A catalogue of this collection was published by Francisco Cunha Leão in 1998 under the title *Jesuítas na Ásia: Catálogo e Guia* (Lisbon, 2 vols.), but it contains little more than the titles and subheadings of each text as they are found in the documents themselves. While such information is a useful general guide to the collection, it is often misleading. Anyone seeking to use the Jesuítas na Ásia documents should read this catalogue closely, check the typescript indices at Ajuda, and consult the archivist. Since the Ajuda Library has no recent catalogue (its card catalogue is old and incomplete), consultation is often the only way to identify sources.

The central archive of the Society of Jesus in Rome, known by its Latin name Archivum Romanum Societatis Iesu (ARSI), was reconstructed at its present site on Borgo Santo Spirito adjacent to St. Peter's Square after the order was suppressed in 1773 and its possessions dispersed across Europe. It is the central repository for the Society's administrative documents. The Japonica-Sinica collection, those sources relating to the Province of Japan and the Vice-Province of China, was the compendium used most in this study. To a lesser extent, documents in the Lusitanica (Province of Portugal) and Goana (Province of Goa) collections were also used. Other sources, such as letters which touch on sensitive administrative issues and "Indies Petitions," are in the Fondo Gesuitico collection. While there are a number of general sketches of the holdings at ARSI, there is no complete descriptive catalogue of the archive. A list of the contents of each volume can be found in the typescript catalogue at the archive, and individual volumes of documents often contain lists of their documents. The director of the archive, and the staff at ARSI, however, know their collections well and can help researchers find materials.

Other Portuguese and Italian archives also house valuable materials. In Portugal, the manuscript collection of the Biblioteca Nacional in Lisbon contains a handful of codices (bound volumes of manuscripts) containing papers from the China mission. In this library are also to be found two of the volumes that originally belonged to the Jesuítas na Ásia collection. Other sources are scattered about the Biblioteca Nacional's holdings and can be discovered only by chance or through references in scholarly publications. The staff of this library has been producing, piecemeal, a catalogue of its manuscripts for over two centuries with no end in sight. Nevertheless, there is a serviceable card catalogue and an Internet-based search engine which often contains information not found in other reference tools available at the Biblioteca Nacional. The same can be said for the Portuguese national archive, the Torre do Tombo. This study makes use of documents found in the Cartório Jesuítico and the Armário Jesuítico, two collections made up from sources seized upon the orders of the marquis of Pombal after 1759. Their catalogues are very old and imprecise. Persistence is essential for consulting these collections, which contain administrative and financial information on the Province of Portugal, as well as sources relating to overseas missions in the Portuguese Assistancy. Further materials for this study were found at the Arquivo Histórico Ultramarino in Lisbon, the Biblioteca da Academia das Ciências in Lisbon, and the Biblioteca Pública/Arquivo Distrital in Évora.

Outside the central archive of the Society of Jesus, there are four main Italian repositories for documents relating to the China mission. The most important for this study by far was the Archivo della Propaganda Fide, now located at the Pontificia Università Urbaniana close to the Vatican. The collection of materials found in the Scritture Riferite nei

Congressi, Indie Orientali e Cina, is indispensable for understanding the Rites Controversy and the arrival of the Propaganda bishops in the late seventeenth century. Documents found at the Biblioteca Nazionale Centrale, the Biblioteca Apostolica Vaticana, and the Biblioteca Casanatense also proved of value. Only the first of these, the Biblioteca Nazionale, has a specific catalogue of its holdings related to the Society of Jesus. The Vatican Library has few reference guides to its Jesuit sources or, indeed, to its other early modern collections. The documents at the Casanatense Library related to China touch on the clashes between the Jesuits and the Dominicans in Fujian, and contain sources on the Rites Controversy and the Tournon legation.

To say more about the archival sources available to scholars interested in working on the topic of the Jesuit mission to China would be redundant. A comprehensive overview of the collections in Europe, Asia, and America can be found on pp. 113–237 of the *Handbook of Christianity in China,* published in 2001 by E. J. Brill (Leiden). Moreover, it would be superfluous to include a list of the relevant secondary works on the Jesuits in China since the *Handbook* is essentially an exhaustive bibliography of the mission. Nicolas Standaert's volume consists of almost one thousand pages of citations of articles, monographs, and archival sources, divided thematically. Each section of this massive work on Chinese Christianity and Sino-Western relations contains a short essay and the relevant bibliographical references. The international team contributing to the *Handbook* was made up of some of the best scholars working in the field today, and both the essays and the bibliography are uniformly of high quality. Readers seeking further information on aspects of the China mission, such as the Jesuits' scientific activity or their Chinese writings, should consult the *Handbook.*

References to the secondary literature on topics not covered in the *Handbook* can be found in the endnotes. These subjects include works on the Society of Jesus, its development in Europe, and its expansion overseas. Other studies of the history of early modern Europe and, in particular, of early modern Catholicism are also cited in the notes. While it would be impossible to give a full bibliography of this rich and expanding field, interested readers should consult John O'Malley, *Catholicism in Early Modern History: A Guide to Research* (St. Louis, 1988), and R. Po-Chia Hsia, ed., *A Companion to the Reformation World* (Oxford, 2004), for introductory information and guides to past and present literature.

Notes

Abbreviations

AHSI	*Archivum Historicum Societatis Iesu*
AHU	Arquivo Histórico Ultramarino, Lisbon
AL	Annual Letter
Alden	Dauril Alden, *The Making of an Enterprise: The Jesuits in Portugal, Its Empire, and Beyond, 1540–1750* (Stanford, 1996)
Álvares Orders	João Álvares, Visita da Provincia de Portugal, [Coimbra?], 1613, ARSI FG 1540, bundle 6
AN/TT	Arquivo Nacional/Torre do Tombo, Lisbon
APF	Archivo della Propaganda Fide, Rome
ARSI	Archivum Romanum Societatis Iesu, Rome
BA	Biblioteca da Ajuda, Lisbon
BACL	Biblioteca da Academia das Ciências, Lisbon
BNL	Biblioteca Nacional, Lisbon
BPADE	Biblioteca Pública e Arquivo Distrital, Évora
CCT	Nicolas Standaert and Ad Dudink, eds., *Chinese Christian Texts from the Roman Archives of the Society of Jesus,* 12 vols. (Taibei, 2002)
Chan	Albert Chan, *Chinese Books and Documents in the Jesuit Archives in Rome: A Descriptive Catalogue* (Armonk, N.Y., 2002)
Charity CS	Renhui huigui (Charity Confraternity Statutes), ARSI *Jap-Sin* II 169.1
CHC	D. Twitchett and F. W. Mote, *The Cambridge History of China,* 15 vols. (Cambridge, 1976–)
Dehergne	Joseph Dehergne, *Répertoire des Jésuites de Chine de 1552 à 1800* (Rome, 1973)
DI	Josef Wicki, ed., *Documenta Indica,* 17 vols. (Rome, 1948–1988)
Dunne	George Dunne, *Generation of Giants: The Story of the Jesuits in China in the Last Decades of the Ming Dynasty* (Notre Dame, Ind., 1962)

East West	Charles Ronan and Bonnie Oh, eds., *East Meets West: The Jesuits in China, 1582–1773* (Chicago, 1988)
FG	Fondo Gesuitico Collection at ARSI
Figueiredo Ningbo	Rodrigo de Figueiredo, Report of Mission to Ningbo District, in Manuel Dias the younger, AL Vice-Province 1627, Shanghai, 9 May 1628, ARSI Jap-Sin 115-I:144r–153v.
FR	Pasquale d'Elia, ed., *Fonti Ricciane: Documenti Originali Concernanti Matteo Ricci e la Storia delle Prime Relazione tra l'Europa e la Cina (1579–1615),* 3 vols. (Rome, 1942–1949)
Funeral Ritual	[Francesco Saverio Filippucci and António Li], Lin sang chu bin yi shi (Ritual Sequence for Attending Funerals and Organizing the Procession), [Canton, ca. 1685], ARSI Jap-Sin II 169.4
Goa	Goana Collection at ARSI
Gouvea	António de Gouvea, *Cartas Ânuas da China,* Horácio P. Araújo, ed. (Lisbon, 1998)
Guerreiro	Fernão Guerreiro, *Relação Anual das Coisas que fizeram os Padres da Companhia de Jesus nas Partes da Índia Oriental,* ed. Artur Viegas (pseud.), 3 vols. (Lisbon, 1605; reprint, Coimbra, 1930–1942)
Handbook	Nicolas Standaert, ed., *Handbook of Christianity in China,* vol. 1, *635–1800* (Leiden, 2001)
Informação	Niccolò Longobardo, Informação da Missão da China, Nanxiong, 28 November 1612, ARSI Jap-Sin 113:265r–281r
JA	Jesuítas na Ásia Collection at Biblioteca da Ajuda
Jami et al.	Catherine Jami, Peter Englefriet, and Gregory Blue, eds., *Statecraft and Intellectual Renewal in Late Ming China: The Cross-cultural Synthesis of Xu Guangqi (1562–1633)* (Leiden, 2001)
Jap-Sin	Japonica-Sinica Collection at ARSI
Lus	Lusitanica Collection at ARSI
Marian CS	Shengmu huigui (Marian Confraternity Statutes), ARSI Jap-Sin II 169.3
Masini	Federico Masini, ed., *Western Humanistic Culture Presented to China by Jesuit Missionaries (XVII–XVIII Centuries)* (Rome, 1996)
Matos Orders	Gabriel de Matos, Ordens dos Vizitadores e Superiores Universais da Missão da China com Algumas Respostas do Nosso Reverendo Padre Geral, Macau, 1621, BAJA 49-V-7:217r–232r
Monteiro Praxis	José Monteiro, Vera et Unica Praxis breviter ediscendi, ac expeditissime loquendi Sinicum idioma, suapte natura adeo difficile . . . In Usum Tyronum Missionariorum [Fujian?, ca. 1700], BACL Mss. Azul 421
OS	Pietro Tacchi-Venturi, ed., *Opere Storiche del P. Matteo Ricci S.I.*, 2 vols. (Macerata, 1911–1913)
Palmeiro Orders	André Palmeiro, Ordens que o Padre André Palmeiro Visitor de Japão e China deixou a Vice-Provincia da China vizitandoa no anno de 1629 aos 15 de Agosto, Macau, 15 January 1631, ARSI Jap-Sin 100:20r–39v
Ratio China	Manuel Dias the elder, Ratio Studiorum para os Nossos que ham de Estudar as letra e lingua da China, [Macau?], 1624, BAJA 49-V-7:310v–319v

Ratio Studiorum	Society of Jesus, *Ratio Studiorum, Plan Raisonée et Institution des Études dans la Compagnie de Jesus,* ed. Adrien Demoustier and Dominique Julia (Paris, 1997)
Ross	Andrew Ross, *A Vision Betrayed: The Jesuits in Japan and China, 1542–1742* (Maryknoll, N.Y., 1994)
SF	Anastasius van de Wyngaert, ed., *Sinica Franciscana,* 9 vols. in 14 bks. (Quaracchi-Florence, 1929–1997)
SWCRJ	*Sino-Western Cultural Relations Journal*
Vieira Orders	Francisco Vieira, Regimento pera os Padres e Irmãos da Companhia que se embarcão de Portugal pera a India, Goa, January 1616, ARSI FG 721/II, folder 3
Xavier CS	Sheng Fengshike huigui (Confraternity of St. Francis Xavier Statutes), ARSI Jap-Sin II 169.2

Introduction

1. António Leite, AL College of Macau 1621, Macau, 30 December 1621, BAJA 49-V-5:341v–343r.

2. See Andrew Plaks, *Four Masterworks of the Ming Novel* (Princeton, 1987), 183–276.

3. "Early modern Catholicism" is a phrase coined by John O'Malley to replace terms such as "Catholic Reformation" and "Counter-Reformation," as well as the more recent notion of "Confessionalization." The subject of the China mission does not fit easily into such categories, since they all imply forms of dialogue with a shared Christian past and specific features of European society, culture, and history. See John O'Malley, *Trent and All That: Renaming Catholicism in the Early Modern Era* (Cambridge, Mass., 2000), 119–143.

4. Three surveys offer synoptic overviews of the evolution of early modern Catholicism: Jean Delumeau, *Le Catholicisme entre Luther et Voltaire* (Paris, 1971); R. Po-Chia Hsia, *The World of Catholic Renewal, 1540–1770* (Cambridge, 1998); and Robert Bireley, *The Refashioning of Catholicism, 1450–1700: A Reassessment of the Counter Reformation* (Washington, D.C., 1999).

5. William Bangert, *A History of the Society of Jesus* (St. Louis, 1986), 22, 45, and 46.

6. An overview of the Society's early years can be found in John O'Malley, *The First Jesuits* (Cambridge, Mass., 1993).

7. For a general view of missionary activity in Europe with special emphasis on the Jesuits, see Louis Châtellier, *The Religion of the Poor: Rural Missions and the Formation of Modern Catholicism, c. 1500–c. 1800,* trans. Brian Pearce (Cambridge, 1997).

8. An excellent analysis of a Jesuit college in Europe can be found in R. Po-Chia Hsia, *Society and Religion in Münster, 1535–1618* (New Haven, 1984), 59–92.

9. For a survey of the historiography of the Society of Jesus and the currents of European historical thought that impinged upon it, see John O'Malley, "The Historiography of the Society of Jesus: Where Does It Stand Today?" in O'Malley, Gauvin Alexander Bailey, Steven Harris, and T. Frank Kennedy, eds., *The Jesuits: Cultures, Sciences, and the Arts, 1540–1773* (Toronto, 1999), 3–37.

10. A persuasive interpretation of these repressive forces in Europe is Adriano Prosperi, *Tribunali della coscienza: inquisitori, confessori, missionari* (Turin, 1996).

11. Two studies are particularly helpful for understanding the early modern papacy: A. D. Wright, *The Early Modern Papacy: From the Council of Trent to the French Revolution, 1564–1789* (New York, 2000); and Paolo Prodi, *The Papal Prince, One Body and Two Souls: The Papal Monarchy in Early Modern Europe* (Cambridge, 1987).

12. An analysis of the push toward conformity in ritual can be found in Simon Ditchfield, *Liturgy, Sanctity, and History in Tridentine Italy: Pietro Maria Campi and the Preservation of the Particular* (Cambridge, 1995).

13. Matteo Ricci and Nicolas Trigault, *De Christiana Expeditione apud Sinas* (Augsburg, 1615).

14. E.g., Álvaro Semedo, *Imperio de la China* (Madrid, 1642), and the compendium of late-seventeenth- and early-eighteenth-century Jesuit missionary reports edited by Jean-Baptiste du Halde, *Lettres Édifiantes et Curieuses écrites des Missions Étrangères,* 34 vols. (Paris, 1702–1776).

15. The representative work of this genre is Dunne. A more recent example is Ross.

16. E.g., Arnold Rowbotham, *Missionary and Mandarin: The Jesuits at the Court of China* (Berkeley, 1942); Joseph Needham, "Chinese Astronomy and the Jesuit Mission: An Encounter of Cultures," in *Science and Civilization in China,* 7 vols. (Cambridge, 1954–), 3:437–458; and Pasquale d'Elia, *Galileo in China: Relations through the Roman College between Galileo and the Jesuit Scientist-Missionaries (1610–1640),* trans. Rufus Suter and Matthew Sciascia (Cambridge, Mass., 1960).

17. Two pioneering works reinvigorated the field: Jonathan Spence, *The Memory Palace of Matteo Ricci* (New York, 1984); and Jacques Gernet, *Chine et Christianisme: Action et Réaction* (Paris, 1982). Two other important studies, written in dialogue with Gernet, are Nicolas Standaert, *Yang Tingyun, Confucian and Christian in Late Ming China: His Life and Thought* (Leiden, 1988); and Erik Zürcher, *Bouddhisme, Christianisme et Société Chinoise* (Paris, 1990).

18. E.g., Benjamin Elman, *On Their Own Terms: Science in China, 1550–1900* (Cambridge, Mass., 2005).

19. A synopsis of the Jesuit presence in the Portuguese empire is in Alden.

20. The same cannot be said about scholars of the Jesuit mission to Japan. E.g., Georg Schurhammer, *Francis Xavier: His Life, His Times,* trans. M. Joseph Costelloe, 4 vols. (Rome, 1973–1982); and Charles Boxer, *The Christian Century in Japan, 1549–1640* (Berkeley, 1951).

21. By force of numbers, the Jesuits were the dominant group in China during this

period. Charts of the numbers of missionaries from different religious orders are in Claudia von Collani, "Missionaries," in *Handbook,* 307–308 and 322–354.

1. An Uneasy Foothold

1. On Xavier's last days, see Georg Schurhammer, *Francis Xavier: His Life, His Times,* trans. M. Joseph Costelloe, 4 vols. (Rome, 1973–1982), 4:567–591, 601–644.

2. Xavier to Francisco Pérez and Gaspar Barzaeus, Shangchuan, 13 November 1552, ibid., 639.

3. Melchior Nunes Barreto, Enformação de algumas cousas acerca dos Custumes e Leis do Reyno da China, Malacca (1554), in Raffaela d'Intino, ed., *Enformação das Cousas da China: Textos do Século XVI* (Lisbon, 1989), 63–76.

4. Joseph Sebes, "The Precursors of Ricci," in *East West,* 19–61.

5. Antonio Monserrate to Everard Mercurian, Goa, 26 October 1579, in *DI* 11:645. Valignano's original order is in Ruy Vicente to Everard Mercurian, Goa, 29 March 1579, ibid., 552; and Rui Vicente to Everard Mercurian, Goa, 13 November 1579, ibid., 695.

6. Valignano first asked for Bernardino Ferrario (1537–1584), a Jesuit two years his elder. See Michele Ruggieri to Everard Mercurian, Cochin, 12 November 1581, ARSI Jap-Sin 9-I:58r.

7. Matteo Ricci and Francesco Pasio, two future China Jesuits who had sailed to India with Ruggieri, were twenty-seven and twenty-five years old, respectively, in 1579.

8. Alessandro Valignano, Summario de las Cosas que Pertencen a la Provincia de la India Oriental y al Govierno della, Shimo (Japan), August 1580, in *DI* 13:200–201.

9. Ibid., 199.

10. Ruggieri to Claudio Aquaviva, Zhaoqing, 7 February 1583, in *OS* 2:412.

11. Francesco Pasio to Claudio Aquaviva, Zhaoqing, 5 February 1583, ARSI Jap-Sin 9-I:135r.

12. Ruggieri to Everard Mercurian, Macau, 12 November 1581, in *OS* 2:404.

13. Ruggieri to Claudio Aquaviva, Zhaoqing, 7 February 1583, in *OS* 2:413.

14. Ibid.

15. Francesco Pasio to Claudio Aquaviva, Macau, 15 December 1582, in *OS* 2:409.

16. Ruggieri to Claudio Aquaviva, Macau, 14 December 1582, in *OS* 2:407.

17. Ruggieri to Claudio Aquaviva, Zhaoqing, 7 February 1583, in *OS* 2:416.

18. Ibid.

19. Ruggieri to Claudio Aquaviva, Zhaoqing, 7 February 1583, in *OS* 2:418.

20. Matteo Ricci to Claudio Aquaviva, Zhaoqing, 30 November 1584, in *OS* 2:51.

21. Valignano to Claudio Aquaviva, Goa, 1 April 1585, in *DI* 14:4–5.

22. *FR* 1:195–196.

23. Valignano to Gil Gonzalez Davila, Goa, 23 December 1585, in *DI* 14:140.

24. *FR* 1:196.

25. Ibid.

26. Ibid., 203–204.

27. On Chinese attitudes toward the Portuguese, see John Wills Jr., "Relations with the Maritime Europeans, 1514–1662," in *CHC* 8:301–332 and 333–375.

28. Valignano to Claudio Aquaviva, Cochin, 20 December 1586, in *DI* 14:439–440.

29. One Zhejiang literatus, Xu Wei (1521–1593), wrote poems about Ruggieri. See Albert Chan, "Two Chinese Poems Written by Hsü Wei (1521–1593) on Michele Ruggieri, S.J. (1543–1607)," *Monumenta Serica* 44 (1996): 317–337.

30. Léon Bourdon, "Un Projet d'Invasion de la Chine par Canton à la Fin du XVIe Siècle," in *Actas do III Colóquio Internacional de Estudos Luso-Brasileiros, Lisboa 1957* (Lisbon, 1960), 97–121.

31. Albert Chan, "Michele Ruggieri, S.J., and His Chinese Poems," *Monumenta Serica* 41 (1993): 129–176, esp. 132.

32. Matteo Ricci to Fabio de Fabii, Shaozhou, 12 November 1589, in *OS* 2:93.

33. Ricci to Alessandro Valignano, Shaozhou, 9 September 1589, in *OS* 2:82.

34. On the relations between China, Japan, and Korea, see Jurgis Elisonas, "The Inseparable Trinity: Japan's Relations with China and Korea," in John Whitney Hall and James McClain, eds., *The Cambridge History of Japan,* 6 vols. (Cambridge, 1988–1999), 4:235–265.

35. These two individuals also had Chinese names; Fernandes's was Zhong Mingren and Martins's Huang Mingshao. Yet while both were of Chinese or mixed ancestry, they identified themselves culturally with the Portuguese in Macau. For instance, on joining the Society, Fernandes renounced any inheritance from his parents, Pedro Fernandes and Leonor Fernandes, a couple he further noted had been "legitimately married" according to Portuguese custom. See Sebastião Fernandes, Carta de Renunciação, Nanjing, 16 January 1600, BAJA 49-V-16:5v–6v.

36. Ricci to Duarte de Sande, Nanchang, 29 August 1595, in *OS* 2:161.

37. On Ricci's humanistic writings, see Howard Goodman and Anthony Grafton, "Ricci, the Chinese, and the Toolkits of Textualists," *Asia Major,* 3d ser., 2.2 (1990): 95–148.

38. Although Pasquale d'Elia suggests that Scielou was Shi Xing, the president of the Ministry of War during the Japanese invasion of Korea in the 1590s, Jonathan Spence contests that attribution. See *FR* 1:339, n. 1; and Spence, *The Memory Palace of Matteo Ricci* (New York, 1985), 287, n. 107.

39. Ricci to Duarte de Sande, Nanchang, 29 August 1595, in *OS* 2:128.

40. Ibid., 135.

41. On the symbolic importance of the Jesuit use of Chinese dress, see Willard Peterson, "What to Wear? Observation and Participation by Jesuit Missionaries in Late Ming Society," in Stuart Schwartz, ed., *Implicit Understandings: Observing, Reporting, and Reflecting on the Encounters between Europeans and Other Peoples in the Early Modern Era* (Cambridge, 1994), 403–421. On the Buddhist clergy, see Chün-Fang Yü, *The*

Renewal of Buddhism in China: Chu-hung and the Late Ming Synthesis (New York, 1981), 138–191.

42. Ricci to Duarte de Sande, Nanchang, 29 August 1595, in *OS* 2:136–137.

43. Erik Zürcher, "Bouddhisme et Christianisme," in *Bouddhisme, Christianisme et Société Chinoise* (Paris, 1990), 11–42, esp. 35–36.

44. Sande, AL College of Macau 1595, Macau, 16 January 1596, ARSI Jap-Sin 52:121r.

45. Ricci to Duarte de Sande, Nanchang, 29 August 1595, in *OS* 2:145–146.

46. Ibid., 148–149.

47. Ibid., 154.

48. After a cordial first reception, Ricci changed his opinion of the *wangfu* clans, labeling them "turbulent and seditious men." See *FR* 2:333.

49. Ricci to Girolamo Benci, Nanchang, 7 October 1595, in *OS* 2:164.

50. Manuel Dias the elder, AL College of Macau 1598, Macau, 1598, ARSI Jap-Sin 52:269r.

51. On the distinction between the rendering of *Tianxue* as "Learning from Heaven" versus "Heavenly Studies," see Willard Peterson, "Learning from Heaven: The Introduction of Christianity and Other Western Ideas into Late Ming China," in *CHC* 8:789–839, esp. 789–793.

52. Diogo Antunes, AL College of Macau 1602, Macau, 29 January 1603, ARSI Jap-Sin 46:322v.

53. On this text and a translation, see Gail King, "For the Instruction of Those Aspiring to Be Christians: João Soeiro's *Tianzhu shengjiao yueyan,*" *SWCRJ* 29 (2004): 59–67.

54. Guerreiro 1:256 and 2:114. A letter from Nanchang in 1604 claims that more than two hundred conversions had been made that year, while Guerreiro's published text puts the figure at close to three hundred. See Manuel Dias the elder to João Álvares, Nanchang, 29 November 1604, in *OS* 2:482.

55. Guerreiro 1:257–258.

56. See, for example, Claudia von Collani, "Missionaries," in *Handbook,* 286–354, esp. 310–311.

57. Nicolas Standaert arrived at this conclusion through statistical analysis of the Chinese Christian community. See Standaert, "Chinese Christians," in *Handbook,* 380–398, esp. 386–393.

58. Letter by Niccolò Longobardo, Shaozhou, 13 November 1604, in Guerreiro 2:126.

59. For example, the Jesuits reported that fifty-eight people were baptized at Nanchang in 1609, including only one *xiucai* or *shengyuan,* the lowest level of civil service exam graduate. See [Niccolò Longobardo?], AL China Mission 1608, Shaozhou, 21 December 1609, ARSI Jap-Sin 113:113v.

60. *FR* 1:253.

61. [António de Gouvea?], AL Fuzhou Residence 1646, Fuzhou, 1646, BAJA 49-V-13:434r.

62. Guerreiro 1:246.

63. Ibid., 248–249.

64. Pantoja to Luís de Guzman, Peking, 9 March 1602, in Pantoja, *Relacion de la Entrada de Algunos Padres de la Cõpañia de IESVS en la China* (Seville, 1605), 77v.

65. *FR* 2:328–329.

66. Ad Dudink, "Opponents," in *Handbook,* 503–533, esp. 509; and *FR* 2:448–461.

67. Guerreiro 2:99.

68. João da Rocha to [Manuel Dias the elder?], Nanjing, 5 October 1602, BAJA 49-V-5:10v.

69. See, for example, Arnold Rowbotham, *Missionary and Mandarin: The Jesuits at the Court of China* (Berkeley, 1942), 60–118; and Ross, 136–140 and 155–190.

70. *FR* 2:347.

71. Informação, 274v.

72. *FR* 2:347

73. Informação, 274r.

74. FR 2:482.

75. Guerreiro 2:90.

76. Manuel Dias the elder to João Álvares, Nanchang, 22 November 1604, ARSI Jap-Sin 14-I:178r.

77. Anon., Partial AL Japan Province, Nagasaki, 25 October 1600, BAJA 49-IV-59:3r and 5v.

78. Manuel Dias the elder to João Álvares, Macau, 17 January 1601, ARSI Jap-Sin 14-I:46v.

79. On July 31, 1611, news of the creation of the Province of Japan reached Macau. The official patents for its separation from the former Province of the East Indies had been issued on December 9, 1608. See Dehergne, 327.

80. Alessandro Valignano, Regimento . . . dos Negocios que o Padre Francisco Rodrigues leva a cargo em Portugal, Macau, 1604, BAJA 49-V-18:265v.

2. In the Shadow of Greatness

1. Willard Peterson, "Why Did They Become Christians? Yang T'ing-yün, Li Chih-tsao, and Hsü Kuang-ch'i," in *East West,* 129–152. On Xu, see Nicolas Standaert, "Xu Guangqi's Conversion as a Multi-faceted Process," in Jami et al., 170–185.

2. [Niccolò Longobardo?], AL China Mission 1608, Shaozhou, 21 December 1609, ARSI Jap-Sin 113:111v. On late Ming Shanghai, see Timothy Brook, "Xu Guangqi in His Context: The World of the Shanghai Gentry," in Jami et al., 72–98; and Linda Cooke Johnson, *Shanghai: From Market Town to Treaty Port, 1074–1858* (Stanford, 1995), 66–95.

3. [Niccolò Longobardo?], AL China Mission 1608, Shaozhou, 21 December 1609, ARSI Jap-Sin 113:112r.

4. Feliciano da Silva to Gaspar Ferreira, Hangzhou, [November? 1612], in Niccolò Longobardo, AL China Mission 1612, Nanxiong, 20 February 1613, ARSI Jap-Sin 113:238r.

5. On Yang's Buddhist critics, see Nicolas Standaert, *Yang Ting-yun, Confucian and Christian in Late Ming China: His Life and Thought* (Leiden, 1988), 162–182.

6. Informação, 276v.

7. On Pantoja's petitions for Ricci's gravesite, see *FR* 2:564–619.

8. Rodrigues to Claudio Aquaviva, Macau, 22 January 1616, ARSI Jap-Sin 16-I:287v.

9. See, for example, Dunne, 106; and Nicolas Standaert, "The Creation of Christian Communities," in *Handbook,* 543–575, esp. 546.

10. A 1610 report claimed that thirty years' work had gleaned 2,500 converts. See *FR* 2:483.

11. Martin Heijdra estimates that the Chinese population ranged between 231 million and 289 million in 1600, and rose to between 268 million and 353 million in 1650. See Heijdra, "The Socio-economic Development of Rural China during the Ming," in *CHC* 8:436–439.

12. Nicolas Standaert, "Chinese Christians," in *Handbook,* 380–393, esp. 382.

13. Longobardo, AL China Mission 1612, Nanxiong, 20 February 1613, ARSI Jap-Sin 113:217r–218r.

14. Informação, 266r.

15. For further discussion, see Timothy Brook, "The Early Jesuits and the Late Ming Border: The Chinese Search for Accommodation," in Wu Xiaoxin, ed., *Encounters and Dialogues: Changing Perspectives on Chinese-Western Exchanges from the Sixteenth to Eighteenth Centuries* (Sankt Augustin, 2005), 19–38.

16. Informação, 266r and 268r.

17. Longobardo, Appontamentos acerca da Ida do Nosso Padre Procurador a Roma, Nanxiong, 8 May 1613, ARSI Jap-Sin 113:301r.

18. On Trigault's voyage, see Edmond Lamalle, "La Propagande du P. Nicolas Trigault en faveur des Missions de Chine (1616)," *AHSI* 9 (1940): 49–120.

19. Longobardo to Claudio Aquaviva, Nanxiong, 28 November 1612, ARSI Jap-Sin 15-II:195r.

20. See Jurgis Elisonas, "Christianity and the Daimyo," in John Whitney Hall and James McClain, eds., *Cambridge History of Japan,* 6 vols. (Cambridge, 1988–1999), 4:365–372.

21. Cattaneo to Claudio Aquaviva, Hangzhou, 19 July 1615, ARSI Jap-Sin 16-II:203v.

22. Niccolò Longobardo, Appontamentos acerca de Pedirse a Licentia del Rey, Nanxiong, 19 February 1615, ARSI Jap-Sin 113:461v–462v.

23. See Erik Zürcher, "The First Anti-Christian Movement in China (Nanking,

1616–1621)," *Acta Orientalia Neerlandica* (Leiden, 1971), 188–195; and Ad Dudink, "*Nangong shudu* (1620), *Poxie ji* (1640), and Western Reports on the Nanjing Persecution, 1616/1617" *Monumenta Serica* 48 (2000): 133–265.

24. Zürcher calls the religion of Christian literati "Confucian Monotheism." See Erik Zürcher, "Confucian and Christian Religiosity in Late Ming China," *Catholic Historical Review* 83.4 (October 1997): 614–653.

25. On elite anxiety in the late Ming period, see Timothy Brook, *Praying for Power: Buddhism and the Formation of Gentry Society in Late Ming China* (Cambridge, Mass., 1993), 311–321.

26. Dudink, *"Nangong shudu,"* 241–248.

27. Edward Kelly, "The Anti-Christian Persecution of 1616–1617 in Nanking" (Ph.D. diss., Columbia University, 1971), 277.

28. Ad Dudink, "Opposition to the Introduction of Western Science and the Nanjing Persecution (1616–1617)" in Jami et al., 191–224.

29. Dudink, *"Nangong shudu,"* 164–165.

30. Ibid., 241.

31. Vieira to Aleixo de Meneses, Macau, 10 December 1617, BAJA 49-V-5:217r.

32. English translation in Kelly, "Anti-Christian Persecution," 303–307.

33. Vieira to Muzio Vitelleschi, Macau, 10 July 1617, ARSI Jap-Sin 17:84r.

34. Manuel Dias the younger to Manuel Severim de Faria, Macau, 18 November 1618, BNL Mss. 29, no. 22.

35. Francisco Vieira to [Nuno Mascarenhas?], Macau, 17 December 1617, ARSI Jap-Sin 17:113v.

36. Francisco Furtado, AL Vice-Province 1624, Hangzhou, 17 April 1625, BAJA 49-V-6:180r.

37. Álvaro Semedo, *Relatione della Grande Monarchia della Cina* (Rome, 1643), 279. The 1643 Rome edition varies from the 1642 Madrid edition and, most likely, the since lost Portuguese manuscript written in 1640. On the Nanjing confraternities, see Semedo, *Imperio de la China* (Madrid, 1642), 301.

38. Manuel Dias the younger, AL China Mission 1618, Macau, 7 December 1619, BAJA 49-V-5:239v.

39. Ibid., 250r–264v.

40. Standaert, *Yang Tingyun,* 93.

41. Manuel Dias the younger to Manuel Severim de Faria, Macau, 18 November 1618, BNL Mss. 29, no. 22.

42. Vagnone to Nuno Mascarenhas, Macau, 10 November 1619, ARSI Jap-Sin 161-I:42r.

43. Dias the elder to Manuel Severim de Faria, Macau, 15 January 1619, BNL Mss. 29, no. 24.

44. The eighth member was Manuel de Figueiredo (1589–1663), a coadjutor who served as procurator in Macau.

45. Claudio Aquaviva created the Vice-Province in 1615 as a semi-independent appendage to the Province of Japan, with its own superiors and consultors. But his death that year obliged Trigault to petition Muzio Vitelleschi anew. The separation therefore dates to 1619. See Dehergne, 328.

46. On mission revenues from royal pensions, lay benefactors, and land rents, see Alden, 298–401.

47. On internal Jesuit administration, see Adrien Demoustier, "La Distinction des Fonctions et l'Exercice du Pouvoir selon les Règles de la Compagnie de Jésus," in Luce Giard, ed., *Jésuites à la Renaissance: Système Éducatif et Production du Savoir* (Paris, 1995), 3–33. On the case of the Portuguese Assistancy, see Alden, 233–235 and 241–247.

48. Francisco Vieira to Nuno Mascarenhas, Macau, January 1617, ARSI Jap-Sin 17:63r–64r.

49. Matos Orders.

50. Compare Dunne, 282–302; Claudia von Collani, "Missionaries," in *Handbook,* 286–354, 311.

51. Ursis to Nuno Mascarenhas, Canton, 2 December 1617, ARSI Jap-Sin 17:110r–110Ar.

52. The 1621 text mentions building scientific instruments and revising mathematical treatises in Chinese. See Matos Orders, 223r and 231v.

53. Ibid., 228v–229v. João da Rocha's *Tianzhu shengjiao qimeng* (Instruction for the Young on the Holy Religion of the Lord of Heaven, 1619) echoed the sentiment that Chinese Christians could gradually adapt themselves to their religion's moral strictures. See Chan, 71.

54. Matos Orders, 231v–232r.

55. Ibid., 232r.

56. Dias the elder to Jerónimo Rodrigues, Hangzhou, 3 April 1623, ARSI Jap-Sin 161-II:81v.

57. Excerpt from Manuel Dias the elder, Hangzhou, 1 March 1625, in Francisco Furtado, AL Vice-Province 1624, Hangzhou, 17 April 1625, BAJA 49-V-6:167r.

58. The consequences of this memorial are discussed in Charles Boxer, "Portuguese Military Expeditions in Aid of the Mings against the Manchus, 1621–1647," *T'ien-hsia Monthly* 7.1 (August 1938): 24–50.

59. António Leite, AL College of Macau 1621, Macau, 30 December 1621, ARSI Jap-Sin 114:267r.

60. On Sun, see Huang Yi-Long, "Sun Yuanhua (1581–1632): A Christian Convert Who Put Xu Guangqi's Military Reform Policy into Practice," in Jami et al., 225–259.

61. Francisco Furtado, AL Vice-Province 1621, [Jiading?], 8 September 1622, BAJA 49-V-5:331r.

62. Erik Zürcher, "Christian Social Action in Late Ming Times: Wang Zheng and His 'Humanitarian Society,'" in Jan de Meyer and Peter Engelfriet, eds., *Linked*

Faiths: Essays on Chinese Religions and Traditional Culture in Honour of Kristofer Schipper (Leiden, 1999), 269–286, esp. 273.

63. Francisco Furtado, AL Vice-Province 1623, Hangzhou, 10 April 1624, BAJA 49-V-6:122v.

64. Manuel Dias the younger, Triennial Catalogue, Vice-Province, 1626, ARSI Jap-Sin 134:303r–304v.

65. Dias the elder to Jerónimo Rodrigues, Hangzhou, June 1623, ARSI Jap-Sin 161-II:83r.

66. According to the 1652 Annual Letter, Longobardo (b. 1565) died in early September 1654. See Manuel Jorge, AL Vice-Province 1652, Hangzhou, 7 May 1655, BAJA 49-IV-61:205v. Compare to Dehergne, 153–154.

67. Ibid.

68. On the Xi'an stele, see Paul Pelliot, *L'Inscription Nestorienne de Si-Ngan-Fou,* ed. Antonino Forte (Kyoto and Paris, 1996), 5–94.

69. Francisco Furtado, AL Vice-Province 1623, Hangzhou, 10 April 1624, BAJA 49-V-6:119v.

70. Ad Dudink and Nicolas Standaert, "Apostolate through Books," in *Handbook,* 600–631, esp. 628.

71. Dias the elder to Jerónimo Rodrigues, Hangzhou, 3 April 1623, ARSI Jap-Sin 161-II:82r.

72. Anon., AL Vice-Province 1626, [n.p., 1627?], BAJA 49-V-6:329v.

73. Ibid., 331r/v. Examples in Jonathan Chaves, "Gathering Tea for God," *SWCRJ* 24 (2004): 6–23.

74. On late Ming political thought and literati factions, see Willard Peterson, "Confucian Learning in Late Ming Thought," in *CHC* 8:708–788; and Benjamin Elman, "Imperial Politics and Confucian Societies in Late Imperial China: The Hanlin and Donglin Academies," *Modern China* 15.4 (October 1989): 379–418.

75. Anon., AL Vice-Province 1626, [n.p., 1627?], BAJA 49-V-6:308v–314v, esp. 315r.

76. Manuel Dias [the younger?], AL Vice-Province 1625, Jiading, 1 May 1626, BAJA 49-V-6:221r.

77. Figueiredo, AL Vice-Province 1628, Hangzhou, 22 August 1629, BAJA 49-V-6:590v.

78. Palmeiro to Muzio Vitelleschi, Macau, 20 December 1629, ARSI Jap-Sin 161-II:109r.

79. Ibid., 109r/v.

80. Palmeiro Orders, 23r–24r.

81. Rodrigues to Claudio Aquaviva, Macau, 22 January 1616, ARSI Jap-Sin 16-I:285v.

82. Jurgis Elisonas, "Acts, Legends, and Southern Barbarous Japanese," in Jorge dos Santos Alves, ed., *Portugal e a China: Conferências nos Encontros de História Luso-Chinesa* (Lisbon, 2001), 15–50, esp. 28.

83. Anon., Rol dos Papeis guardados na Secretaria da Vice-Provincia, Canton, 1669, BAJA 49-IV-62:558r.

84. António de Gouvea to Domingo de Navarrete, Canton, 3 December 1669, BA 44-XII-40:164.

85. A partial autograph copy of Longobardo's text, titled "Resposta breve sobre as Controversias do Xamty, Tienxin, Limhoen e outros nomes e termos sinicos," Peking, [1624?], is in APF, Scritture Riferite nei Congressi, Indie Orientali Cina, vol. 1, 145r–168v. On Yang's testimony, see Standaert, *Yang Tingyun,* 183–203.

86. André Palmeiro to Muzio Vitelleschi, Macau, 16 January 1631, ARSI FG 730-I: 12v.

87. André Palmeiro to Muzio Vitelleschi, Macau, 18 May 1628, ARSI FG 730-I:3r/v.

88. André Palmeiro to Muzio Vitelleschi, Macau, 16 January 1631, ARSI FG 730-I:13r.

89. Palmeiro to Muzio Vitelleschi, Macau, 20 December 1629, ARSI Jap-Sin 161-II:117r.

90. Muzio Vitelleschi seconded this decision in a letter dated 6 August 1632. See Anon., Rol dos Papeis guardados na Secretaria da Vice-Provincia, BAJA 49-IV-62:558v.

91. Palmeiro Orders, 37v–39v.

92. Dias the younger to Muzio Vitelleschi, Peking, 1 October 1634, ARSI FG 730-I:21v.

93. Lazzaro Cattaneo, AL Vice-Province 1630, Hangzhou, 12 September 1631, BAJA 49-V-8:667r.

94. Ibid., 721v and 727v.

95. João Fróis, AL Vice-Province 1631, Hangzhou, 1632, BAJA 49-V-10:37r.

96. Semedo, *Imperio de la China,* 303.

97. Dunne, 226–244; and Ross, 205–206.

98. David Mungello, *The Great Encounter of China and the West, 1500–1800* (New York, 1999), 18.

99. John Wills Jr., "Brief Intersection: Changing Contexts and Prospects of the Chinese-Christian Encounter from Matteo Ricci to Ferdinand Verbiest," in John Witek, ed., *Ferdinand Verbiest (1623–1688): Jesuit Missionary, Scientist, Engineer, and Diplomat* (Nettetal, 1994), 383–394, esp. 394.

3. Witnesses to Armageddon

1. António de Gouvea, AL Vice-Province 1636, Hangzhou, 20 November 1637, in Gouvea, 57–58.

2. Michel Trigault, AL Jiangzhou Residence 1639, Jiangzhou, [1639?], BAJA 49-V-12:431r.

3. António de Gouvea, AL Vice-Province 1636, Hangzhou, 20 November 1637, in Gouvea, 76.

4. João Monteiro, AL Vice-Province 1637, Nanchang, 16 October 1638, BAJA 49-V-12:39v.

5. António de Gouvea, AL Vice-Province 1636, Hangzhou, 20 November 1637, in Gouvea, 104–106 and 112–117.

6. João Monteiro, AL Vice-Province 1637, Nanchang, 16 October 1638, BAJA 49-V-12:18v.

7. Ibid., 55r–56r.

8. A veronica is a specific type of devotional pendant bearing an image of Christ's face. Nominas, name medals, were glass or metal pendants bearing the name of Jesus or Mary.

9. António de Gouvea, AL Vice-Province 1636, Hangzhou, 20 November 1637, in Gouvea, 91.

10. João Monteiro, AL Vice-Province 1637, Nanchang, 10 October 1638, BAJA 49-V-12:40r.

11. In 1640 Michel Trigault claimed that the Jiangzhou Christians numbered eight thousand. See Trigault, AL Jiangzhou Residence 1640, Jiangzhou, [1641?], BAJA 49-V-12:584r.

12. Francisco Furtado to Manuel Dias the elder, Nanchang, 1 January 1638, BAJA 49-V-12:199r.

13. António de Gouvea, "Asia Extrema," Fuzhou, 10 April 1644, BAJA 49-V-2:498.

14. João Monteiro, AL Vice-Province 1637, Nanchang, 10 October 1638, BAJA 49-V-12:37r.

15. Francisco Furtado to Manuel Dias the elder, Nanchang, 1 January 1638, BAJA 49-V-12:205v.

16. António de Gouvea, AL Vice-Province 1636, Hangzhou, 20 November 1637, in Gouvea, 71.

17. Gabriel de Magalhães, Partial AL Vice-Province 1640, Hangzhou, 30 August 1641, BAJA 49-V-12:489r.

18. Furtado to Manuel Dias the elder, Nanchang, 1 January 1638, BAJA 49-V-12:202r.

19. According to Álvaro Semedo, Macau was "almost depopulated and totally fallen" by 1650. See Semedo to Vincenzo Caraffa, Canton, 25 October 1650, ARSI Jap-Sin 161-II:353v.

20. Furtado to Muzio Vitelleschi, [Peking?], 2 February 1641, ARSI Jap-Sin 161-II:228v.

21. On the Mendicants in Fujian, see Eugenio Menegon, "Ancestors, Virgins, and Friars: The Localization of Christianity in Late Imperial Mindong (Fujian, China), 1632–1863" (Ph.D. diss., University of California, Berkeley, 2002), esp. 94–164.

22. Vagnone to Nuno Mascarenhas, Macau, 10 November 1619, ARSI Jap-Sin 161-I:42v.

23. Vieira to Nuno Mascarenhas, Macau, January 1617, ARSI Jap-Sin 17:63v.

24. The rapid spread of Christianity in Fu'an district provoked reprisals from local mandarins as early as 1634, but especially in 1637–38. See Eugenio Menegon, "Jesuits, Franciscans, and Dominicans in Fujian: The Anti-Christian Incidents of 1637–38," in Tatiana Lipiello and Roman Malek, eds., *"Scholar from the West": Giulio Aleni, S.J. (1582–1649), and the Dialogue between Christianity and China* (Brescia and Nettetal, 1997), 219–262.

25. Caballero to Juan Pastor, Jinan, 24 January 1652, in *SF* 2:413.

26. Schall to Alexandre de Rhodes, Peking, 8 November 1637, ARSI Jap-Sin 161-II:196r.

27. Francisco Furtado to Manuel Dias the elder, Peking, 8 [September?] 1637, BAJA 49-V-12:182v–183r.

28. See Dunne, 269–302; Ross, 118–200; J. S. Cummins, *A Question of Rites: Friar Domingo Navarrete and the Jesuits in China* (Aldershot, 1993), 1–168.

29. Furtado to Manuel Dias the elder, Peking, 8 [September?] 1637, BAJA 49-V-12:182r.

30. João Monteiro, AL Vice-Province 1641, Hangzhou, 7 September 1642, BNL Reservados 722:1r. The reference is from Wisdom 5:21, "And the whole world shall fight with him against the unwise."

31. Ibid., 1v.

32. Gouvea, "Asia Extrema," BAJA 49-V-2:334.

33. João Monteiro, AL Vice-Province 1637, Nanchang, 16 October 1638, BAJA 49-V-12:19r.

34. Gouvea, "Asia Extrema," BA JA 49-V-2:573–579.

35. Ibid., 582–584.

36. See Erik Zürcher, "In the Yellow Tiger's Den: Buglio and Magalhães at the Court of Zhang Xianzhong, 1644–1647," *Monumenta Serica* 50 (2002): 355–374.

37. António de Gouvea, AL Vice-Province 1646, Fuzhou, 30 August 1647, in Gouvea, 302.

38. [Inácio da Costa?], AL Northern Residences, Vice-Province 1643, 1644, and 1645, [Xi'an?, 1646?], BAJA 49-V-13:119r.

39. António de Gouvea, AL Southern Residences, Vice-Province 1644, Fuzhou, 16 August 1645, in Gouvea, 188.

40. Ibid., 148–149.

41. Frederic Wakeman Jr., *The Great Enterprise: The Manchu Reconstruction of Imperial Order in Seventeenth-Century China,* 2 vols. (Berkeley, 1985), 1:18.

42. [Inácio da Costa?], AL Northern Residences, Vice-Province 1643, 1644, and 1645, [Xi'an?, 1646?], BAJA 49-V-13:111v.

43. [Álvaro Semedo?], Relação das Guerras e Levantamentos . . . desdo Anno de 1642 athé o de 1647, Macau, 1648, BAJA 49-V-13:12v–13r.

44. See Lynn Struve, *The Southern Ming, 1644–1662* (New Haven, 1984), 75–94 and 125–138.

45. Sambiasi, AL Nanjing Residence 1645, [Canton?, 1645], BAJA 49-V-13:320v–340r.

46. Anon., Relação do Estado Prezente do Imperio da China, Macau, 1645, ARSI Jap-Sin 123:141v.

47. Sambiasi, AL Nanjing Residence 1645, [Canton?, 1645], BAJA 49-V-13:339v.

48. Dunne, 344–347; and Albert Chan, "A European Document on the Fall of the Ming Dynasty (1644–1649)," *Monumenta Serica* 35 (1981–1983): 75–109.

49. Anon., Relação das couzas que aconteçerão e aconteçem na pessoa do Padre Francisco Sambiasi no Reino da China e em Macau, [Macau?, 1646?], ARSI Jap-Sin 123:152v.

50. Manuel Jorge, AL Vice-Province 1651, [Hangzhou, 1652?], BAJA 49-IV-61:82r–83v.

51. António de Gouvea, AL Vice-Province 1646, Fuzhou, 30 August 1647, in Gouvea, 290.

52. Anon., Relação do Estado Prezente do Imperio da China, ARSI Jap-Sin 123:141v.

53. Triennial Catalogue, Vice-Province 1645, ARSI Jap-Sin 134:325r–326v.

54. Semedo to Vincenzo Carraffa, Canton, 25 October 1650, ARSI Jap-Sin 161-II:353r.

55. Cunha to Francisco Furtado, Yanping, 25 January 1653, BNL Reservados 722:46v.

56. Feliciano Pacheco, AL Central Residences, Vice-Province 1660, Huai'an, 19 July 1661, BAJA 49-V-14:718v–719r.

57. Gabriel de Magalhães, AL Vice-Province 1640, Hangzhou, 30 August 1641, BAJA 49-V-12:511v.

58. Brancati, AL Shanghai Residence 1647, Shanghai, [1647?], BAJA 49-V-13:459r.

59. Brancati, AL Shanghai Residence 1648, Shanghai, [1648?], BAJA 49-V-13:479r; and Brancati to Francisco Furtado, Shanghai, [1653?], BA 50-V-38:97r.

60. Cunha to Francisco Furtado, Yanping, 25 January 1653, BNL *Reservados* 722:43r and 50v–51v. Compare Cummins, *Question of Rites,* 110.

61. Andre Ferrão, AL Vice-Province 1656, Macau, 29 January 1659, BAJA 49-V-14:68v–69r.

62. Feliciano Pacheco, AL Central Residences, Vice-Province 1660, Huai'an, 19 July 1661, BAJA 49-V-14:708v.

63. Gabriel de Magalhães, AL Northern Residences, Vice-Province 1658, Peking, 20 September 1659, BAJA 49-V-14:237v.

64. André Ferrão, AL Vice-Province 1656, Macau, 29 January 1659, BAJA 49-V-14:64r.

65. Manuel Jorge, AL Vice-Province 1657, Nanjing, 12 May 1658, BAJA 49-V-14:152v–154r.

66. Gabriel de Magalhães, AL Northern Residences, Vice-Province 1660, Peking, 20 July 1662, BAJA 49-V-14:692r.

67. Ibid., 697r.

68. Triennial Catalogue, Vice-Province 1651, ARSI Jap-Sin 134:338r–339r.

69. Faure, AL Ganzhou Residence 1658, 1659, and 1660, Ganzhou, n.d, BAJA 49-V-14:648r.

70. Motel, AL Wuchang Residence 1661 and 1662, Wuchang, [1662?], BAJA 49-V-15:138r.

71. Magalhães, AL Northern Residences, Vice-Province 1658, Peking, 20 September 1659, BAJA 49-V-14:237v.

72. Luís da Gama, Triennial Catalogue, Vice-Province 1663, ARSI Jap-Sin 134:345r–346r.

73. Compare David Mungello, *The Great Encounter of China and the West, 1500–1800* (New York, 1999), 22.

4. The Problem of Success

1. Manuel Jorge, Breve Relação. . . . de como foy perseguida a Ley de Deus na China e seos pregadores desterrados nestes proximos annos de 1664, 1665, Canton, 28 January 1667, BAJA 49-V-15:197v, 206r, and 211r.

2. On Magalhães's denunciations of Schall, see Antonella Romano, "Observer, Vénérer, Servir: Une Polemique Jésuite autour du Tribunal des Mathématiques à Pékin," *Annales: Histoire, Sciences Sociales* 59.4 (July–August 2004): 729–756.

3. Francesco Brancati to Vincenzo Caraffa, Shanghai, 27 September 1650, ARSI Jap-Sin 142:125r–128v.

4. Ad Dudink, "Opponents," in *Handbook,* 503–533, 513–514.

5. On the Calendar Case, see Harriet Zurndorfer, "'One Adam having driven us out of paradise, Another has driven us out of China': Yang Kuang-hsien's Challenge of Adam Schall von Bell," in Leonard Blussé and Harriet T. Zurndorfer, eds., *Conflict and Accommodation in Early Modern East Asia* (Leiden, 1993), 141–168.

6. Jorge, Breve Relação,BAJA 49-V-15:427r–431r.

7. Ibid., 212v–214r.

8. Zurndorfer, "'One Adam,'" 164.

9. Domingo Fernández de Navarrete, *Tratados Historicos, Politicos, Ethicos, y Religiosos de la Monarchia de China* (Madrid, 1676), 350.

10. Jorge, Breve Relação, BAJA 49-V-15:432v–435r.

11. François de Rougemont, *Relaçam do Estado Politico e Espiritual do Imperio da China, pellos annos de 1659 até o de 1666* (Lisbon, 1672), 193.

12. Navarrete, *Tratados,* 350.

13. Andrea Lubelli, Breve Relação da Persiguição Geral, Canton, [26 December 1666?], BAJA 49-V-15:287v.

14. Navarrete, *Tratados,* 351.

15. Rougemont, *Relaçam do Estado Politico,* 193–194.

16. Pacheco, Praxes quadam discussae in pleno eotus 25 patrum statutae et decreta ad servandum inter nos in Sinica Missione uniformitatem, Canton, [January 1668?], ARSI Jap-Sin 162:253r–255v.

17. Da Gama to Giovanni Paolo Oliva, Macau, 10 December 1668, ARSI Jap-Sin 162:239r.

18. Santa Maria (possibly thanks to Jean Valat) found Longobardo's "Resposta breve" at the Jesuits' Shandong residence in the early 1660s. Two-thirds of the treatise had been burned, but the introduction—a discussion of Chinese cosmology and Longobardo's interviews with literati on the disputed terms—was intact. Santa Maria sent a Latin translation to the cardinals of the Propaganda Fide, the Roman ecclesiastical organ responsible for missionary affairs. This text was printed in several languages in Europe by the Society's rivals—yet the volumes lacked Longobardo's caveats alerting the reader that its arguments could be correctly understood only in the context of the other treatises by João Rodrigues, Sabatino de Ursis, Alfonso Vagone, and Diego de Pantoja. For Santa Maria's letter, see Antonio de Santa Maria to Cardinals of the Propaganda Fide, [Jinan?], 29 March 1662, APF Scritture Riferite nei Congressi, Indie Orientali Cina, 1:23r/v.

19. In 1669 the papacy further confused the matter when it reaffirmed the two conflicting decrees on the rites (1645 and 1656). On the Canton conference, see J. S. Cummins, *A Question of Rites: Friar Domingo Navarrete and the Jesuits in China* (Aldershot, 1993), 413–424.

20. Hubert Verhaeren, trans. and ed., "Les Ordonnonces de la Sainte Eglise," *Monumenta Serica* 4 (1939–1940): 451–477.

21. Da Gama to Giovanni Paolo Oliva, Macau, 25 October 1667, ARSI Jap-Sin 162:196v.

22. Lubelli, Breve Relação da Persiguição Geral, BAJA 49-V-15:287v.

23. Jorge, Breve Relação, 435r.

24. Luís da Gama to Giovanni Paolo Oliva, Macau, 25 October 1667, ARSI Jap-Sin 162:196v.

25. Bartholomeu de Espinoza to Giovanni Paolo Oliva, Macau, 9 December 1670, in Rougemont, *Relaçam do Estado Politico,* 228.

26. Noël Golvers, *François de Rougemont, SJ, Missionary in Ch'ang-shu (Chiang-Nan): A Study of the Account Book (1674–1676) and the Elogium* (Leuven, 1999), 27–28.

27. Translation in H. Bosmans, ed., "Les Lettres Annuelles de la Vice-Province de la Compagnie de Jésus en Chine, Année 1669 par Adrien Grelon," *Revue Trimestrielle pour l'Étude des Antiquités de la Flandre* 62 (1912): 15–61, 58–61.

28. Monica Esposito, "Qing Daoism," in Livia Kohn, ed., *Daoism Handbook* (Leiden, 2001), 623–658, 625.

29. Gabriel de Magalhães to João Cardoso, Peking, 6 September 1675, BAJA 49-IV-16:159r–160v. The date of the inscription has caused confusion. Magalhães tells that Kangxi visited on July 12, 1675, but wrote "the Chinese year *sin hay*" on the text that

he sent to the Jesuits the next day. The missionary claimed that Kangxi had written the inscription "four years prior" (in 1671) but delayed giving it to them.

30. Tomé Pereira, Relação Breve da Morte e Enterramento do Padre Gabriel de Magalhães, Peking, 25 June 1677, BAJA 49-V-17:565r–568v.

31. Triennial Catalogue, Vice-Province 1678, 1680, and 1688, ARSI Jap-Sin 134:362r–371v.

32. See François de Rougemont's spiritual diary from 1674 to 1676, in Golvers, *François de Rougemont,* esp. 186–204.

33. Philippe Couplet, *Historia de una Gran Señora Christiana de la China, llamada Doña Candida Hiù* (Madrid, 1691), 88–90.

34. Ibid., 85, 146, and 36.

35. Ibid., 44, 41, 86, and 138.

36. Martini, Partial AL Hangzhou Residence 1648, Hangzhou, [1648?], BAJA 49-V-13:609r.

37. [Adrien Grelon?], Rol das Christandades que tenho a minha conta, [Ganzhou?, 1681?], ARSI Jap-Sin 112:39r.

38. Nicolas Standaert, "Chinese Christians," in *Handbook,* 380–403, 382.

39. Juan Antonio de Arnedo, AL Vice-Province 1685–1690, Ganzhou, 30 November 1691, ARSI Jap-Sin 117:238r.

40. Soares to Antoine Thomas, Jiangzhou, 29 April 1687, BAJA 49-V-20:69v.

41. Juan Antonio de Arnedo, AL Vice-Province 1685–1690, Ganzhou, 30 September 1691, BAJA 49-V-19:669v.

42. In 1617 twelve Jesuits signed a report asserting that the time was not ripe for ordaining Chinese priests. Niccolò Longobardo, Informação dos Irmãos Chinenses Naturaes de Macau, Hangzhou, 4 October 1617, ARSI Jap-Sin 17:91r–92v.

43. The most spectacular case of apostasy among Japanese Jesuits was Fabian Fucan (1565?–1621?), a master apologist who wrote a treatise called "Deus Destroyed" after turning against his former confreres. See George Elison, *Deus Destroyed: The Image of Christianity in Early Modern Japan* (Cambridge, Mass., 1991), 142–184 and 257–291.

44. Dunne, 167; Alden, 262–266.

45. Nicolas Standaert and John Witek, "Chinese Clergy," in *Handbook,* 462–470, esp. 462.

46. Alden, 262–263.

47. This was the reason Manuel de Sequeira (1633–1673), the first Chinese Jesuit, left Macau for Europe in 1645. Sequeira joined the order in Rome and was ordained after studying theology at Coimbra. He returned to China in 1668 only to find his colleagues detained in Canton. A biography is Francis Rouleau, "The First Chinese Priest of the Society of Jesus: Emmanuel de Siqueira, 1633–1673 (Cheng Ma-no, Wei-hsin)," *AHSI* 28 (1959): 3–50.

48. Buglio to Filippo de Marini, Peking, 16 May 1680, BAJA 49-V-17: 316r.

49. On the debates over the Chinese liturgy in Europe and China, see François

Bontinck, *La Lutte autour de la Liturgie Chinoise aux XVIIe et XVIIIe siècles* (Leuven and Paris, 1962), 21–159.

50. Lodovico Buglio, Ferdinand Verbiest, and Gabriel de Magalhães, Alguns Pontos pella Conservaçam e Augmento deste Christandade, Peking, [1668?], ARSI Jap-Sin 124:112v.

51. Motel to Sebastião de Almeida, Wuchang, 1678, ARSI Jap-Sin 124:111Br.

52. Ibid., 111Br/v.

53. Jacques le Faure and Adrien Grelon complained that they were maltreated by Feliciano Pacheco, António de Gouvea, and Luís da Gama. Le Faure asserted that his countrymen were "born free, and by their nature incapable of suffering the yoke of foreign domination." Fearing that the Canton exile would lead to expulsion from China, he added that French Jesuits should go to mission territories administered by France rather than Portugal. Grelon was more direct: he asked for reassignment to Syria or Madagascar if the China mission was extinguished. He consented to remain in the Vice-Province only if he could return to the isolation of his mission station. See Le Faure to Claude Boucher, Canton, 1 November 1668, ARSI FG 730-I:79r–80v; and Adrien Grelon to Claude Boucher, Canton, 1 November 1668, ARSI FG 730-I:81r–82v.

54. Navarrete, *Tratados,* 361. Navarrete numbers Humbert Augery among these "French Fathers."

55. Brancati to Giovanni Paolo Oliva, Canton, 23 October 1668, ARSI Jap-Sin 162:219v.

56. Motel to Sebastião de Almeida, Wuchang, 1678, ARSI Jap-Sin 124:111r/v. Motel lists the following priests as those who objected to the idea: Manuel Dias the younger, Álvaro Semedo, Simão da Cunha, Johann Adam Schall, Inácio da Costa, Francesco Brancati, Francesco Ferrari (1609–1671), Pietro Canevari, and António de Gouvea. Motel himself arrived in China at the same time as the Moderns.

57. Buglio, Verbiest, and Magalhães, Alguns Pontos pella Conservaçam e Augmento deste Christandade, ARSI Jap-Sin 124:112r/v.

58. Intorcetta, Memorial . . . ao Padre João Cardoso, Provincial de Japão, Macau, 12 September 1674, ARSI Jap-Sin 23:365r.

59. Motel to Sebastião de Almeida, Wuchang, 1678, ARSI Jap-Sin 124:111r.

60. Pereira to Sebastião de Almeida, Peking, 3 January 1678, ARSI Jap-Sin 124:116r.

61. Verbiest to Sebastião de Almeida, Peking, 8 January 1678, ARSI Jap-Sin 124:120r.

62. Buglio to Sebastião de Almeida, Peking, 11 January 1678, ARSI Jap-Sin 124:117r.

63. Sebastião de Almeida, with concern, forwarded a note from Couplet agreeing to the proposal. See Philippe Couplet to Sebastião de Almeida, [Songjiang?], 1678, ARSI Jap-Sin 124:114v.

64. Valat to Sebastião de Almeida, Jin'an, 15 January 1678, ARSI Jap-Sin 124:118r.

65. Wan inherited the rank of *jiansheng,* a status purchased in order to enable its

holder to bypass local examinations and present himself directly for provincial ones, along with other legal and tax exemptions. See Prospero Intorcetta to Francesco Saverio Filippucci, Hangzhou, 16 January 1689, BAJA 49-IV-63:435v.

66. Gabiani to Francesco Saverio Filippucci, Peking, 14 May 1688, BAJA 49-IV-63:306v.

67. Prospero Intorcetta to Francesco Saverio Filippucci, Hangzhou, 27 September 1688, BAJA 49-V-20:91v–92r.

68. José Monteiro to António de Rego, Fuzhou, 12 February 1690, ARSI Jap-Sin 199-I:65v.

69. Giandomenico Gabiani to Francesco Saverio Filippucci, Nanjing, 19 February 1690, BAJA 49-IV-64:98v; Gabiani to Francesco Saverio Filippucci, Nanjing, 6 April 1690, BAJA 49-IV-64:107r/v.

70. Pereira to Simão Rodrigues, Peking, 5 December 1688, BAJA 49-IV-63:563r.

71. Intorcetta to Francesco Saverio Filippucci, Hangzhou, 5 October 1689, BAJA 49-IV-63:540r.

72. Couplet's staged exoticism was not universally well received. Vice-Provincial Gabiani disapproved of his excessive baggage and Chinese assistants. António dos Reys, the Portuguese Assistant, wrote to Visitor Joseph Tissanier in Macau that future procurators should not bring "Indians or Chinese as companions nor so many cases of things, all of which were Father Couplet's fancy." See Theodore N. Foss, "The European Sojourn of Philippe Couplet and Michael Shen Fuzong, 1683–1692," in Jerome Heyndrickx, ed., *Philippe Couplet, S.J. (1623–1693): The Man Who Brought China to Europe* (Nettetal, 1990), 121–142, esp. 126–127; and Dos Reys to Tissanier, Rome, 22 January 1686, BAJA 49-V-19:871r/v.

73. These editions were printed at Lyon (1616), Lille (1617), Paris (1618), Augsburg (1617), Seville (1621), Naples (1622), and London (1626).

74. Semedo's text appeared at Rome (1643 and 1653), Paris (1645), Lyon (1667), and London (1655).

75. For instance, Martini claimed 150,000 Chinese Christians in 1651, though other estimates from over a decade later claimed only 105,000. See Martino Martini, *Brevis Relatio de Numero et Qualitate Christianorum apud Sinas* (Rome, 1654), 5.

76. A modified version of this text was reprinted as *Historica Relatio de Ortu et Progressu Fidei Orthodoxae in Regno Chinensi per Missionarios Societatis Jesu* (Regensburg, 1672).

77. A Latin version of this text appeared at Rome in 1672.

78. Gabriel de Magalhães, preface to *Nouvelle Relation de la Chine,* trans. Barnout (Paris, 1690).

79. On this book's publication, see Cummins, *Question of Rites,* 193–215.

80. Marini to Manuel Fernandes, Macau, 21 November 1680, BAJA 49-V-17:41r.

81. Marini to Manuel Fernandes, Macau, 3 December 1681, BAJA 49-V-17:45r.

82. See Anastase van den Wyngaert, "Mgr. Fr. Pallu et Mgr. Bernardin della Chiesa:

Le Serment de Fidelité aux Vicaires Apostoliques 1680–1688," *Archivum Franciscanum Historicum* 31 (1938): 17–47.

83. Andrea Lubelli to Alessandro Cicero, Macau, [1681?], BAJA 49-V-19:34v.

84. Noël Golvers, "Lettre du P. Ferdinand Verbiest, vice-provincial de la mission de Chine, à ses confrères de la Société en Europe, le 15 août 1678, de la résidence impériale de Beijing," *Courrier Verbiest* 5 (December 1993): 5–9.

85. Intorcetta to António de Rego, Hangzhou, 25 May 1688, ARSI Jap-Sin 164:58v.

86. On the French Jesuits' relations with Kangxi, see John W. Witek, *Controversial Ideas in China and Europe: A Biography of Jean-François Fouquet, SJ (1665–1741)* (Rome, 1982), 58–72.

87. Prospero Intorcetta to Simão Martins, Hangzhou, 31 October 1687, BAJA 49-IV-63:92v.

88. Intorcetta to Francesco Saverio Filippucci, Hangzhou, 21 February 1688, BAJA 49-IV-63:146r/v.

89. Fontaney to Ferdinand Verbiest, Ningbo, 13 August 1687, BAJA 49-IV-63:102r.

90. Filippucci to Prospero Intorcetta, Canton, 28 April 1688, BAJA 49-IV-63: 297r. Compare Witek's irenic assessment of Filippucci in his *Controversial Ideas,* 52.

91. Fontaney to Francesco Saverio Filippucci, Nanjing, 9 August 1688, BAJA 49-IV-63:211r/v.

92. See Dunne, 8–15; Ross, 205–206; Alden, 157; and David Mungello, "A Confucian Echo of Western Humanist Culture in Seventeenth Century China," in Masini, 279–292, 282.

93. Filippucci to Tomé Pereira, Canton, 30 March 1688, BAJA 49-V-20:101r.

94. Fontaney, Extrait des Lettres, Canton, 26 October 1690, ARSI Jap-Sin 132:62r.

95. Filippucci to Sebastião de Magalhães, Macau, 19 October 1690, BAJA 49-IV-64:212r.

96. Manuel Ferreira to Tirso González, Lisbon, 27 March 1690, ARSI Jap-Sin 164:234v.

97. Brief Catalogue, Vice-Province 1691, ARSI Jap-Sin 134:375r.

5. Between Tolerance and the Intolerable

1. Emanuele Laurifice to Tirso González, Songjiang, 11 November 1691, ARSI Jap-Sin 165:121v. For further discussion, see David Mungello, *The Forgotten Christians of Hangzhou* (Honolulu, 1994), 59–66.

2. [Francisco Pinto?], AL Hangzhou Residence 1691–1693, Hangzhou, [1693?], BAJA 49-V-22:178v.

3. See Joseph Sebes, *The Jesuits and the Sino-Russian Treaty of Nerchinsk (1689): The Diary of Thomas Pereira* (Rome, 1962).

4. Pereira's memorials and the corresponding edicts are in Lo-Shu Fu, ed., *A Documentary Chronicle of Sino-Western Relations (1644–1820),* 2 vols. (Tucson, Ariz., 1966), 1:104–106.

5. Erik Zürcher, "Emperors," in *Handbook,* 492–502, esp. 497.

6. Fu, *Documentary Chronicle,* 1:105–106.

7. Ad Dudink, "Opponents," in *Handbook,* 503–533, esp. 516.

8. [Francisco Pinto?], AL Hangzhou Residence 1691–1693, Hangzhou, [1693?], BAJA 49-V-22:179v.

9. Anon., AL College of Macau and Canton Residences 1692, Macau, [1693?], BAJA 49-V-22:103r.

10. [Francisco Pinto?], AL Hangzhou Residence 1691–1693, Hangzhou, [1693?], BAJA 49-V-22:178v–180r.

11. José Soares translated the edicts into Latin at Peking. Spanish, French, and Italian editions followed: *La Liberdad de la Ley de Dios en el Imperio de la China,* trans. Juan de Espinola (Valencia, 1696); Charles Le Gobien, *Histoire de l'Édit de la Chine, en faveur de la Religion Chrestienne* (Paris, 1696); and *Istoria dell'Editto dell'Imperatore della Cina in favore della Religione Cristiana* (Turin, 1699).

12. Anon., AL College of Macau and Canton Residences 1692, Macau, [1693?], BAJA 49-V-22:103r–104r.

13. Brief Catalogue, Vice-Province 1692, ARSI Jap-Sin 134:375; Triennial Catalogue, Vice-Province 1699, ARSI Jap-Sin 134:385r–386r.

14. José Soares, Draft AL Vice-Province 1697, Peking, 30 July 1697, BAJA 49-V-21:78r/v.

15. Pieter Van Hamme, AL Wuchang Residence 1692, Wuchang, [1693?], BAJA 49-V-22:165v–166r.

16. José Soares, Partial AL Vice-Province July 1694–July 1697, Peking, 30 July 1697, BAJA 49-V-22:636r.

17. Tomé Pereira to Tirso González, Peking, 30 April 1693, ARSI Jap-Sin 165:394v; Simão Rodrigues, AL Changshu Residence 1692, Changshu, [1692?], BAJA 49-V-22:167r.

18. [Juan Antonio de Arnedo?], AL Nanchang Residence 1692, Nanchang, [1693?], BAJA 49-V-22:170v; José Soares, Partial AL Vice-Province July 1694–July 1697, Peking, 30 July 1697, BAJA 49-V-22:644v.

19. José Soares, Partial AL Vice-Province July 1694–July 1697, Peking, 30 July 1697, BAJA 49-V-22:642r; Soares to Tirso González, Peking, 28 September 1694, ARSI Jap-Sin 166:29r; José Monteiro to Tirso González, Fuzhou, 15 September 1695, ARSI Jap-Sin 166:80r.

20. José Soares, Partial AL Vice-Province July 1694–July 1697, Peking, 30 July 1697, BAJA 49-V-22:634r.

21. Ibid., 633r/v.

22. [Francisco Simões], Breve Relação das Missoens de . . . Pecheli no principio deste anno de 1693, [Zhending?, March?] 1693, BAJA 49-V-22:165v.

23. Pieter Van Hamme, AL Wuchang Residence 1692, Wuchang, [1693?], BAJA 49-V-22:166r.

24. José Soares, Partial AL Vice-Province July 1694–July 1697, Peking, 30 July 1697, BAJA 49-V-22:636v.

25. [Francisco Pinto?], AL Hangzhou Residence 1691–1693, Hangzhou, [1693?], BAJA 49-V-22:177v.

26. Francisco Nogueira, Ordens para as Residencias da China, Macau, [1694?], BAJA 49-V-23:338r. This order was reiterated in a 1704 circular letter by Vice-Provincial Antoine Thomas. See Fortunato Margiotti, *Il Cattolicismo nello Shansi dalle origini al 1738* (Rome, 1958), 309.

27. Triennial Catalogue, Vice-Province 1699, ARSI Jap-Sin 134: 385r–386r; José Monteiro, Triennial Catalogue, Vice-Province 1702, ARSI Jap-Sin 134:397r–400r.

28. Antoine Thomas, Triennial Catalogue, Vice-Province 1703, Peking, 25 September 1703, ARSI Jap-Sin 134:408Fv.

29. Ibid.

30. Ibid., 408Er.

31. Ibid., 408Fv.

32. José Monteiro, Reddius Collegiorum et Residentiarum Vice Provinciae Sinensis Societatis Iesu, [Ganzhou?], 1699, ARSI FG 722, bundle 16.

33. [Carlo Turcotti?], Breve Relação da Missão da China até o anno de 1700, [Canton?], 1700, BAJA 49-V-23:504r/v.

34. Soares to José Monteiro, Peking, 8 January 1705, BAJA 49-V-24:524r.

35. [Turcotti?], Breve Relação da Missão da China até o anno de 1700, BAJA 49-V-23:504v.

36. Pereira to Tirso González, Peking, 30 August 1693, ARSI Jap-Sin 165:394r.

37. Brief Catalogue, Vice-Province (including non-Jesuit missionaries) 1701, ARSI Jap-Sin 134:392Ar–392Cv.

38. Anon., Relação Sincera e Verdadeira do que fez, pertendeo, e ocazionou na Missão da China, e em Macao o Patriarca de Antioquia Carlo Thomaz Mailard de Tournon, Macau, [early 1708?], BAJA 49-V-25:718r.

39. Brief Catalogue, Vice-Province (including non-Jesuit missionaries) 1701, ARSI Jap-Sin 134:392Ar–392Cv.

40. Pereira to Tirso González, Peking, 30 August 1693, ARSI Jap-Sin 165:394v.

41. José Soares, Partial AL Vice-Province July 1694–July 1697, Peking, 30 July 1697, BAJA 49-V-22:641v.

42. Francisco Nogueira to [Tirso González?], Macau?, 20 November 1695, AHU Macau Series, box 2:27.

43. Pereira to Tirso González, Peking, 10 August 1694, ARSI Jap-Sin 166:14r.

44. Cicero to Jean-Baptiste Maldonado, [Peking?], 11 June 1695, ARSI Jap-Sin 166:64r.

45. Louis Le Comte, *Nouveaux Memoires sur l'État Présent de la Chine,* 2 vols. (Paris, 1699, 1701), 2:175–176.

46. French Mission Catalogue, [after 1706], ARSI Jap-Sin 134:390r.

47. Fontaney to Jean-Joseph Guibert, Canton, 28 September 1701, ARSI Jap-Sin 167:160r–161r. On the French Jesuits' provincial missions, see John Witek, *Controversial Ideas in China and Europe: A Biography of Jean-François Fouquet, SJ (1665–1741)* (Rome, 1982), 72–145, esp. 101–125.

48. Grimaldi to Portuguese Assistant, Peking, 15 October 1700, BAJA 49-V-23:534r–535r.

49. Anon., Noticias de Pekim do anno de 1703, [Peking?, 1703?], BAJA 49-V-24:267v.

50. Anon., Novas de Pekim desde Novembro de 1701 até os 18 de Fevreiro de 1702, Peking, [18 February 1702?], ARSI Jap-Sin 128:118r.

51. Gozani to José Monteiro, Fuzhou, 20 June 1701, BAJA 49-V-25:16r.

52. For more on this European polemical literature, see René Étiemble, *L'Europe Chinoise*, 2 vols. (Paris, 1988), 241–369; and Paul Rule, *K'ung-tzu or Confucius? The Jesuit Interpretation of Confucianism* (Sydney, 1986), 70–149.

53. Cicero to Pedro II, Nanjing, 26 September 1702, AHU Macau Series, box 2:32.

54. On the Tournon legation, see Francis Rouleau, "Maillard de Tournon, Papal Legate at the Court of Peking: The First Imperial Audience (31 December 1705)," *AHSI* 31 (1962): 264–323; and Antonio Sisto Rosso, *Apostolic Legations to China in the Eighteenth Century* (South Pasadena, Calif., 1948), 149–186.

55. Anon., Tragica Relação dos Successos mais notaveis que acontecerão nas Missoens da China e na cidade de Macao desdo anno de 1706 athé 1707, [Macau?, 1707?], BAJA 49-V-25:173v.

56. Rouleau, "Tournon," 296.

57. Rosso, *Apostolic Legations*, 136–146; Zürcher, "Emperors," in *Handbook*, 498.

58. On the aftermath of Tournon's audiences, see Edward Malatesta, "A Fatal Clash of Wills: The Condemnation of the Chinese Rites by the Papal Legate Carlo Tommaso Maillard de Tournon," in David Mungello, ed., *The Chinese Rites Controversy: Its History and Meaning* (Nettetal, 1994), 211–246.

59. [José Monteiro?], Relação do que se tem passado nesta missão da China desde Dezembro de 1706 até o Prezente, Canton, 1 December 1707, BAJA 49-V-25:197v.

60. On Tournon in Macau, see Rouleau, "Tournon," 265–267.

61. [Monteiro?], Relação do que se tem passado nesta missão da China, BAJA 49-V-25:202r–203r.

62. Anon., Catalogo dos Missionarios que foram lançados da China nos annos 1706, 1707, e 1708 e dos que forão nella athé Dezembro de 1708, [Canton?, December 1708?], BAJA 49-V-25:205v; José Monteiro, Catalogue of Missionaries in China, Canton, December 1708, ARSI FG 722, bundle 5.

63. Dudink, "Opponents," 517–518.

64. Anon., Relação Sincera e Verdadeira, BAJA 49-V-25:765r.

65. Dudink, "Opponents," 518.

66. Letter from José Ramón Arxó, Rome, 30 November 1709, BAJA 49-V-26:410r/v.

67. Fonseca to [José Monteiro], Lisbon, 15 March 1714, BAJA 49-V-27:453v.

68. Amaral to Manuel Saraiva, Goa, 23 November 1709, ARSI Goa 9-II:446r–448v.

69. Bernardino della Chiesa to Juan Fernández Serrano, Linqing, 10 May 1720, in *SF* 5:757–771. For more on this theme, see Lars Peter Laamann, "Memories of Faith: The 'Christian Sutras' of Eighteenth-Century China," in R. N. Swanson, ed., *The Church and the Book* (Woodbridge, England, 2004), 279–302.

70. Domingos Pinheiro, Compendio da Historia de como Varias Pessoas da Familia Imperial Tartaro Sinica abraçaram a Religiam Christam, Peking, [September?] 1724, BNL Reservados 32:7r. On the Sunu clan, see John Witek, "Manchu Christians," in *Handbook,* 445–447; and Pasquale D'Elia, *Il Lontano Confino e la Tragica Morte del P. João Mourão S.I., Missionario in Cina (1681–1726),* (Lisbon, 1963), 51–181.

71. [José Soares?], Declarão-se, e Provão-se livres de toda a Censura as Inscrições, que o Imperador da China deo em 2 de Mayo de 1711 à Nova Igreja do Collegio da Companhia de Jesus em Pekim, Peking, [May?] 1711, BAJA 49-V-27:86r–96v.

72. Pastoral letter from Agostinho da Anunciação, Goa, 29 April 1710, BAJA 49-V-26:565r.

73. ARSI holds files organized by year (starting in 1716) containing sworn oaths signed by each China missionary. See ARSI FG 722, bundle 15.

74. Giampaolo Gozani to José Monteiro, Peking, 9 January 1714, BAJA 49-V-27:435v–436r.

75. Bernardino della Chiesa to Giampaolo Gozani, Linqing, 18 January 1714, in *SF* 5:591–593.

76. Claudia von Collani, "Figurism," in *Handbook,* 668–679, esp. 671.

77. Dudink, "Opponents," 518–519.

78. Nicolas Standaert, "Creation of Chinese Communities," in *Handbook,* 534–575, esp. 564.

79. Dudink, "Opponents," 521.

80. Zürcher, "Emperors," 499.

81. José Soares, Continuaçam dos Successos na Missão da China, Peking, 30 September 1726, BNL Reservados 8123:6v.

82. Letter from Joseph de Moyriac de Mailla, Peking, 16 October 1724, in Jean-Baptiste du Halde, ed., *Lettres Édifiantes et Curieuses écrites des Missions Étrangères,* 34 vols. (Paris, 1702–1776), 17:245–247 and 282–284.

83. Anon., Relaçam e Substancia da Pratica q*ue* o Emperador Tartaro Sinico Yumchim teve ao 1 de Julho de 1724 com tres padres da Companhia de Jesus, Peking, [1724?], AN/TT Mss. Liv. 1096:1r–2v.

84. Soares, Continuaçam dos Successos na Missão da China, BNL Reservados 8123:7r.

85. Roman Hinderer, AL Hangzhou College 1726, Hangzhou, 3 September 1726; Domingos de Brito, AL Songjiang Residence 1726, Songjiang, 3 September 1726, BNL Reservados 8123:8r/v.

86. Soares, Continuaçam dos Successos na Missão da China, BNL Reservados 8123:2r.

87. Ibid., 8r.

88. Thomas, Triennial Catalogue, Vice-Province 1703, Peking, 25 September 1703, ARSI Jap-Sin 134:408Cv.

89. Ibid., 408Fv; Soares, Continuaçam dos Successos na Missão da China, BNL Reservados 8123:7r.

90. Gozani to João V, Macau, 21 November 1725, BAJA 49-V-28:156r.

91. Soares, Continuaçam dos Successos na Missão da China, BNL Reservados 8123:2r.

6. In the Apostles' Classroom

1. André Gomes, *Relaçam Geral das Festas . . . na canonização dos gloriosos Sancto Ignacio de Loyola . . . & S. Francisco Xavier . . . no anno de 1622* (Lisbon, 1623), 77r–78v and 83r–84v.

2. Brief Catalogue, Province of Portugal 1622, ARSI Lus 39:125v.

3. Nicolas Standaert, "The Jesuit Presence in China (1580–1773): A Statistical Approach," *SWCRJ* 12 (1991): 4–17, esp. 4–5.

4. António Barradas, Triennial Catalogue, Province of Portugal 1665, ARSI Lus 45:315v–319r.

5. On the *Ratio Studiorum,* with a French translation, see *Ratio Studiorum.*

6. Balthasar Teles, *Chronica da Companhia de Iesu da Provincia de Portugal,* 2 vols. (Lisbon, 1647), 2:24.

7. On Jesuit education, see John O'Malley, *The First Jesuits* (Cambridge, Mass., 1993), 200–242; and Adrien Demoustier, "Les Jésuites et l'enseignement à la fin du XVIe Siècle," in *Ratio Studiorum,* 12–28.

8. Feliciano Pacheco, Triennial Catalogue, Vice-Province 1666, ARSI Jap-Sin 134:348r–349r.

9. The Vice-Province's catalogues are in ARSI Jap-Sin 134:300r–414r. Over the course of the seventeenth century, the novices' average age increased, meaning that fewer finished their humanities studies as Jesuits.

10. Informação, 267v.

11. Longobardo, Appontamentos a cerca da Ida do nosso Padre Procurador a Roma, Nanxiong, 8 May 1613, ARSI Jap-Sin 113:303r.

12. Verbiest to Ignace Malgaert, Genoa, February 1656, in H. Josson and L. Willaert, eds., *Correspondance de Ferdinand Verbiest, SJ, Directeur de l'Observatoire de Pékin* (Brussels, 1938), 9.

13. Soares to Filippucci, Peking, 6 August 1688, BAJA 49-IV-63:207v–208r.

14. Caballero to Antonio de San Gregorio, Anhai, 15 October 1649, in *SF* 2:374.

15. Anon., Livro Segundo das Entradas deste Novicado de Évora, 1596–1619, BPADE Mss. CXXX/1–1:47v. The questions posed to novices are in the order's *Gen-*

eral Examen. See Ignatius Loyola, *Constitutions of the Society of Jesus,* trans. and ed. George Ganss (St. Louis, 1970), 85–91. Further questions for scholastics are on 110–112 and 115–117.

16. Teles, *Chronica,* 2:68.

17. On tertianship, see Manuel Ruiz Jurado, "La Tercera Probación en la Compañia de Jesús," *AHSI* 60 (1991): 265–351.

18. In 1610 Visitor João Álvares dispensed Indies-bound Jesuits from tertianship, despite repeated orders from Superiors General that no Jesuit forgo those experiences. See Álvares, Visita da Provincia de Portugal, [Coimbra?], 1613, AN/TT Armário Jesuítico, bk. 5:4; and Jurado, "La Tercera Probación," 322.

19. Josef Wicki, "Dois Compêndios das Ordens dos Padres Gerais e Congregações Provinciais de Provínica de Goa feitos in 1664," *Studia* 43–44 (1980): 343–532, esp. 511.

20. António Franco, *Imagem da Virtude em o Noviciado da Companhia de Jesus no Real Collegio de Jesus de Coimbra,* 2 vols. (Évora and Coimbra, 1719), 1:10–11.

21. Manuel Severim de Faria, *Promptuario Espiritual* (Lisbon, 1651), 147r.

22. António Franco, *Imagem da Virtude em o Noviciado da Companhia de Jesus do Real Collegio do Espirito Santo de Évora do Reyno de Portugal* (Lisbon, 1714), 879.

23. Noël Golvers, *François de Rougemont, SJ, Missionary in Ch'ang-shu (Chiang-Nan): A Study of the Account Book (1674–1676) and the Elogium* (Leuven, 1999), 93–237 and 553–630.

24. Triennial Catalogue, Vice-Province 1621–1666, ARSI Jap-Sin 134:301r–349v.

25. Thomas's letters from 1663 to 1675 are in ARSI Jap-Sin 148:1r–17r; and ARSI FG 753:115, 121, and 127.

26. Adrien Demoustier, "Les Catalogues du Personnel de la Province de Lyon en 1587, 1606, et 1636," *AHSI* 43 (1974): 3–84, esp. 68.

27. A form of teacher training was also used in the French provinces. See François de Dainville, *Les Jésuites et l'Education de la Société Française: La Naissance de l'Humanisme Moderne* (Paris, 1940), 344–346.

28. Álvares Orders, 24.

29. Demoustier, "Les Jésuites et l'enseignement," 22–23; Dainville, *Les Jésuites et L'Éducation,* 142–155; Society of Jesus, "*Ratio Studiorum,*" trans. Léone Albrieux and Dolorès Pralon-Julia, ed. Marie-Madeleine Compère, in *Ratio Studiorum,* 161.

30. On Jesuit missions in Europe, see, for example, Louis Châtellier, *The Religion of the Poor: Rural Missions and the Formation of Modern Catholicism, c. 1500–c. 1800,* trans. Brian Pearce (Cambridge, 1997), 7–183; and Adriano Prosperi, *Tribunali della Coscienza: Inquisitori, Confessori, Missionari* (Turin, 1996), 551–684.

31. Teles, *Chronica,* 1:339.

32. Álvares Orders, 43.

33. Ibid., 45.

34. João Pereira, Report of Mission to Alcácer do Sal, [Évora?], April 1624, BNL Mss. 30, no. 213:3r.

35. [António Mascarenhas?], Mission Report, Coimbra, 1594, ARSI Lus 106:186r.

36. Jonathan Chaves, "Gathering Tea for God," *SWCRJ* 24 (2004): 6–23.

37. Álvares Orders, 44 and 48.

38. Bartolomeu de Britto, Report of Mission to Setúbal, Setúbal, 20 April 1650, BNL Mss. 30, no. 214:1v.

39. Mathais de Maya, AL Japan Province 1659 and 1660, Macau, [1661?], BAJA 49-V-14:725v.

40. António de Lessa to Muzio Vitelleschi, Coimbra, 13 April 1642, ARSI Lus 74:288r.

41. Estêvão Collasso to Tirso González, Coimbra, 22 November 1694, ARSI FG 757, no. 45.

42. Noël Golvers, "Les *Litterae Indipetae* et les Raisons Profondes des Vocations en Chine aux Pays-Bas du Sud en 1640–1660," pt. 1, *Courrier Verbiest* 12.3 (2000): 4–5; pt. 2, ibid., 13.2 (2001): 6–7.

43. João de Lucena, *Historia da Vida do P. Francisco Xavier* (Lisbon, 1600), 25–26.

44. Francisco de Betancor to Claudio Aquavivia, Coimbra, 10 April 1587, ARSI Lus 70:322r.

45. António de Lessa to Muzio Vitelleschi, Coimbra, 13 April 1642, ARSI Lus 74:288r.

46. [Pietro Possini?], *Relatione della Sanità Miracolozamente Ricuperata per Intercessione di S. Francesco Saverio da Alexandro Filippucci de la Compagnia di Giesu alli 12 de Marzo 1658* (Macerata, 1658); Marcello Mastrilli, *Relaçam de hum Prodigioso Milagre que o Glorioso S. Francisco Xavier Apostolo do Oriente obrou na Cidade de Napoles no anno de 1634* (Goa, 1636), trans. Manuel de Lima, ed. Manuel Cadafaz de Matos (Lisbon, 1989), 18.

47. Francisco de Betancor to Claudio Aquavivia, Coimbra, 10 April 1587, ARSI Lus 70:322r.

48. António de Lessa to Muzio Vitelleschi, Coimbra, 13 April 1642, ARSI Lus 74:288r.

49. See, for instance, the 1620 Annual Letter from the Vice-Province with the notation "read at the College of Évora and in Lisbon," in Francisco Furtado, AL Vice-Province 1620, Hangzhou, 24 August 1621, ARSI Jap-Sin 114:234r.

50. Anon., Catalogo de Alguns Martyres e Outros Varoens Illustres da Companhia de Jesus, [Lisbon?, after 1695], BNL Reservados 4283:14r/v.

51. Brás Luis to Claudio Aquaviva, Évora, 6 June 1587, ARSI Lus 70:333r.

52. Almeida to Manuel Rodrigues, Canton, 5 November 1585, in *OS* 2:438 and 441.

53. Joachim Calmes to Giovanni Paolo Oliva, Coimbra, 6 January 1681, ARSI FG 757, no. 22; Estêvão Collasso to Tirso González, Coimbra, 22 November 1694, ARSI FG 757, no. 45.

54. Cattaneo to Nuno Mascarenhas, Shanghai, 22 April 1619, ARSI Jap-Sin 161-I:33r; Brief Catalogue, Province of Portugal 1601, ARSI Lus 39:36r.

55. Golvers, *François de Rougemont,* 14–15.

56. António de Lessa to Muzio Vitelleschi, Coimbra, 13 April 1642, ARSI Lus 74:288r.

57. Triennial Catalogue, Province of Portugal 1675, ARSI Lus 45:449r and 467v.

58. Triennial Catalogue, Province of Portugal 1678, ARSI Lus 46:5v and 27r.

59. Claudio Aquaviva, Responses to 1603 Provincial Congregation Resolutions (Province of Portugal), BNL Reservados 753:43r/v.

60. António de Gouvea, "Ásia Extrema," Fuzhou, 10 April 1644, BAJA 49-V-2:575r/v.

61. António Rebello to Muzio Vitelleschi, Lisbon, 8 August 1638, ARSI FG 757, no. 51.

62. Adriano Pestana to Muzio Vitelleschi, Coimbra, 26 August 1640, ARSI FG 757, no. 58.

63. Gabriel de Magalhães, Vida e Morte do Padre Estevão Fabro, Peking, 21 March 1658, BAJA 49-V-14:304r–305r.

64. Danielo Bartoli, *Dell'Historia della Compagnia de Giesu: La Cina* (Rome, 1663), 699.

65. Joseph Dehergne, citing an imprecise source, claims that of the 249 sent to China via Portugal, 127 died en route. Nicolas Standaert gives more data but can only speculate on the high rate of missionary wastage at sea. See Dehergne, 324; and Standaert, "Jesuit Presence in China," 4.

66. Ibid., 5.

67. [Alessandro Valignano and] Duarte de Sande, *Diálogo sobre a Missão dos Embaixadores Japoneses à Curia Romana,* ed. and trans. Américo da Costa Ramalho (Macau, 1997), 66.

68. On the Carreira da Índia, see Charles Boxer, "The Carreira da India (Ships, Men, Cargoes, Voyages)," in *From Lisbon to Goa, 1500–1700* (London, 1984), 33–82.

69. Simão Martins, Successos da Viagem . . . de Goa para Macao, Malacca, 18 December 1686, BAJA 49-V-19:834v.

70. Álvares Orders, 50–54; Viera Orders.

71. Vieira Orders, 14r.

72. Josef Wicki, "Liste der Jesuiten-Indienfahrer 1541–1758," *Aufsätze zur Portugiesischen Kulturgeschichte* 7 (1967): 252–450.

73. Vieira Orders, 13v–14r.

74. Álvares Orders, 50.

75. Vieira Orders, 16v.

76. Ibid., 15v.

77. Girão to João Correia, Goa, 1 December 1583, in *DI* 12:866.

78. Vieira Orders, 16v.

79. Girão to João Correia, Goa, 1 December 1583, in *DI* 12:867–868.

80. [Valignano and] Sande, *Diálogo,* 41.

81. Anthony Disney, "Getting to the China Mission in the Early Seventeenth Cen-

tury," in Artur de Matos and Luís Thomaz, eds., *Actas do VI Seminário Internacional de Historia Indo-Portuguesa* (Lisbon, 1993), 95–109, esp. 105.

82. Álvares Orders, 53.

83. Vieira Orders, 15v.

84. [Valignano and] Sande, *Diálogo,* 33.

85. Adrião Pedros to Giovanni Paolo Oliva, Lisbon, 7 October 1681, ARSI Goa 9-II:323r.

86. Vieira Orders, 17r.

87. Ibid., 19v.

88. Disney, "Getting to the China Mission," 103.

89. Álvares Orders, 51–52.

90. Vieira Orders, 17v.

91. Manuel Godinho Cardozo, *Relação do Naufragio da Nao Santiago,* in Bernardo Gomes de Brito, ed., *História Trágico Marítima* (Lisbon, 1736); reprint, ed. Fernando Ribeiro de Mello and Neves Águas, 2 vols. (Lisbon, 1971), 2:433–506.

92. Disney, "Getting to the China Mission," 105–106.

93. António de Gouvea, AL Southern Residences, Vice-Province 1644, Fuzhou, 16 August 1645, in Gouvea, 197–198.

94. Golvers, *François de Rougemont,* 15–18.

95. André Ferrão, AL Vice-Province 1656, Macau, 29 January 1659, BAJA 49-V-14:62v.

96. Ibid., 63r.

7. Learning the Language of Birds

1. Arnedo, AL Vice-Province 1685–1690, Ganzhou, 30 November 1691, ARSI Jap-Sin 117:648r.

2. João Rodrigues to Muzio Vitelleschi, Macau, 28 January 1624, BAJA 49-V-6:153v.

3. Feliciano Pacheco, AL Central Residences, Vice-Province 1660, Huai'an, 19 July 1661, BAJA 49-V-14:704r.

4. Aquaviva to Valignano, Rome, 28 December 1587, ARSI Jap-Sin 3:13v.

5. Ruggieri to Everard Mercurian, Macau, 12 November 1581, in *OS* 2:401.

6. Ruggieri to Claudio Aquaviva, Zhaoqing, 7 February 1583, in *OS* 2:411.

7. Ruggieri to Everard Mercurian, Macau, 12 November 1581, in *OS* 2:401.

8. Ruggieri to Claudio Aquaviva, Zhaoqing, 7 February 1583, in *OS* 2:412.

9. Ricci to Martino de Fornari, Macau, 13 February 1583, in *OS* 2:27.

10. Ruggieri and Ricci, *Dicionário Português-Chinês,* ed. John Witek (Lisbon, 2001).

11. Ruggieri to Claudio Aquaviva, Zhaoqing, 7 February 1583, ARSI Jap-Sin 9-I:137v. A discussion of Chinese pedagogical traditions in the Ming-Qing period is in Benjamin Elman, *A Cultural History of Civil Examinations in Late Imperial China* (Berkeley, 2000), 260–292.

12. *Qianzi wen* (Fujian, 1579), ARSI Jap-Sin I 58a. See Chan, 112–114.

13. Francisco Cabral to Alessandro Valignano, Macau, 5 December 1584, in *OS* 2:429.

14. Ricci to Martino de Fornari, Macau, 13 February 1583, in *OS* 2:27.

15. *FR* 2:32–33.

16. Gabriel de Magalhães, Partial AL Hangzhou Residence 1640, Hangzhou, 30 August 1641, BAJA 49-V-12:479r.

17. Ursis to [Italian Assistant?], Peking, 23 August 1608, ARSI Jap-Sin 14-II:316v.

18. Niccolò Longobardo, Appontamentos a cerca da Ida do nosso Padre Procurador a Roma, Nanxiong, 8 May 1613, ARSI Jap-Sin 113:303r.

19. Sande, AL China Mission 1594, Macau, 28 October 1594, ARSI Jap-Sin 52:42v.

20. [Alessandro Valignano], Catalogue of Men and Residences, Macau, November 1592, in Josef Franz Shütte, *Monumenta Historica Japoniae,* vol. 1, *Textus Catalogorum Japoniae (1549–1654)* (Rome, 1975), 285.

21. Alessandro Valignano, Catalogue for Japan Province, Macau, 1 January 1593, ibid., 325.

22. Ricci to Claudio Aquaviva, Peking, 8 March 1608, in *OS* 2:340.

23. Longobardo to Girolamo Centimano, Shaozhou, 5 February 1598, in *OS* 2:468.

24. Vagnone to [Portuguese Assistant?], Nanjing, 16 March 1605, ARSI FG 730-I:1r.

25. Sabatino de Ursis to [Italian Assistant?], Peking, 23 August 1608, ARSI Jap-Sin 14-II:316r.

26. Ad Dudink, "The Inventories of the Jesuit House at Nanking," in Masini, 145–157, esp. 156.

27. Pantoja to Luis de Guzman, Peking, 9 March 1602, in Diego de Pantoja, *Relacion de la Entrada de Algunos Padres de la Cõpañia de Jesus en la China* (Seville, 1605), 116r.

28. João Rodrigues, *Arte Breve da Lingoa Iapoa* (facsimile, transcription, and Japanese translation), trans. and ed. Hino Hiroshi (Tokyo, 1993), 360.

29. João Paulo Oliveira e Costa, "Os Jesuítas no Japão (1549–1598): Uma Análise Estatística," in *O Japão e o Cristianismo no Século XVI: Ensaios de História Luso-Nipónica* (Lisbon, 1999), 17–47, esp. 44–45.

30. Rodrigues, *Arte Breve,* 361.

31. Ibid., 360.

32. Monteiro, AL Vice-Province 1641, Hangzhou, 7 September 1642, ARSI Jap-Sin 117:44v.

33. João Fróis assured the readers of the 1631 Annual Letter that "the fears that they have in Europe about the language and letters of China are greater than the difficulties." See Fróis, AL Vice-Province 1631, [Hangzhou?], 1632, BAJA 49-V-10:36v.

34. Matos Orders, 223r/v.

35. Ratio China, 311r.

36. Ibid., 311r/v.

37. [Francisco Simões], Breve Relação das Missões de . . . Pechili no principio deste anno 1693, [Zhending?], 1693, BAJA 49-V-22:156v.

38. Eugenio Menegon, "Ancestors, Virgins, and Friars: The Localization of Christianity in Late Imperial Mindong (Fujian, China), 1632–1863" (Ph.D. diss., University of California, Berkeley, 2002), 287–288.

39. Ratio China, 312r.

40. Ibid., 311v.

41. Ibid., 313r/v.

42. Ibid., 313v.

43. Ratio China, fols. 313v–314r.

44. Examples of these lists are in ARSI Jap-Sin IV 7, BNL Reservados 3306, and BNL Reservados 7974.

45. Chan, 430–432.

46. Ratio China, 314v.

47. Ibid.

48. Ibid., 312r.

49. Ibid., 311r–312r.

50. Monteiro Praxis, 14.

51. Ratio China, 313r.

52. Ibid., 314r.

53. Ibid., 313v–314r.

54. Ibid., 313r.

55. Ibid., 311r.

56. Ibid., 313r. Compare to David Mungello, "The Seventeenth-Century Jesuit Translation Project," in *East West,* 252–272, esp. 254.

57. Willard Peterson, "Learning from Heaven: The Introduction of Christianity and Other Western Ideas into Late Ming China," in *CHC* 8:789–839, esp. 805.

58. One of the few references to payments made to Chinese masters indicates, in 1623, that the cost per year ranged from 16 to 18 taels. See Manuel Dias the elder to Jerónimo Rodrigues, Hangzhou, 3 April 1623, ARSI Jap-Sin 161-II:81r.

59. Ratio China, 312v.

60. Ibid., 314v.

61. On the Jesuits' use of Zhang, see Henri Bernard, *Sagesse Chinoise et Philosophie Chrétienne* (Leiden and Paris, 1935), 131; and Dudink, "Inventories," 147, n. 50. Compare Mungello, "Jesuit Translation Project," 254.

62. Ratio China, 312v.

63. Ibid., 314v.

64. Ibid., 314v–315r.

65. Ibid., 312r.

66. Francisco Furtado, AL Vice-Province 1623, Hangzhou, 10 April 1624, BAJA 49-V-6:106v.

67. Francisco Furtado, AL Vice-Province 1624, Hangzhou, 17 April 1625, BAJA 49-V-6:184v.

68. Manuel Dias the younger, AL Vice-Province 1625, Jiading, 1 May 1626, BAJA 49-V-6:230r; anon., AL Vice-Province 1626, [n.p., n.d.], BAJA 49-V-6:322r.

69. Brancati to Francisco Furtado, 1653, BNL Reservados 722:58v.

70. Francisco Furtado, Triennial Catalogue, Vice-Province 1636, ARSI Jap-Sin 134:311r–312v.

71. João Fróis, AL Vice-Province 1631, [Hangzhou?], 1632, BAJA 49-V-10:55v and 65r.

72. Palmeiro Orders, 37r.

73. [Manuel Dias the younger?], Brief Catalogue, Vice-Province, [1634?], ARSI Jap-Sin 134:309r/v.

74. Furtado to Dias the elder, Nanchang, 1 January 1638, BAJA 49-V-12:200v.

75. *Sishu,* 6 vols., notations by Francesco Brancati, 1637–38, ARSI Jap-Sin I 10.

76. Ibid., 1:9r.

77. Ibid., 2:81r.

78. Ibid., 3:150r

79. Ibid., 4:237r.

80. Ibid., 6:397r.

81. Triennial Catalogue, Vice-Province 1639, ARSI Jap-Sin 134:316r; Gabriel de Magalhães, AL Hangzhou Residence 1640, Hangzhou, 30 August 1641, BAJA 49-V-12:479r.

82. Claudio Filippo Grimaldi, Breve Relação da Vida e Morte do Padre Luis Bulho, Peking, 24 October 1682, BAJA 49-V-19:219v.

83. See Chan, 120–123 and 193.

84. Feliciano Pacheco, AL Central Residences, Vice-Province 1660, Huai'an, 19 July 1661, BAJA 49-V-14:718r.

85. Le Faure, AL Ganzhou Residence 1658, 1659, and 1660, Ganzhou, n.d., BAJA 49-V-14:657v.

86. [André Ferrão?], Partial AL Fujian and Jiangxi Residences 1660, [n.p., 1661?], BAJA 49-V-14:743r.

87. The translations made by Matteo Ricci in the early 1590s were never printed. See *FR* 2:33. Henri Bernard suggests that the translation published by Intorcetta was done by André Ferrão in 1660 and joined to Costa's commentaries. See Bernard, *Sagesse Chinoise,* 128–129.

88. Intorcetta, *Sapientia Sinica,* 2r.

89. Prospero Intorcetta, Memorial . . . ao P. João Cardoso Provincial de Japão, Macau, 12 September 1674, ARSI Jap-Sin 23:365r.

90. José Monteiro to Francisco Nogueira, Puching, 9 July 1695, BAJA 49-V-23:12r/v.

91. José Soares, Partial AL Vice-Province July 1694–July 1697, Peking, 30 July 1697, BAJA 49-V-22:628v.

92. The two masters were each paid two taels monthly. See Jean Valat, Carta e Ordenações do Padre Jean Valat depois da Visita de Pekim, Peking, 14 March 1689, ARSI Jap-Sin 164:50r.

93. Thomas to Joseph Tissanier, Peking, 16 September 1686, BAJA 49-V-19:870v.

94. Valat, Carta e Ordenações do Padre Jean Valat depois da Visita de Pekim, Peking, 14 March 1689, ARSI Jap-Sin 164:49r.

95. Triennial Catalogue, Vice-Province 1688, ARSI Jap-Sin 134:370r; Triennial Catalogue, Vice-Province 1697, ARSI Jap-Sin 134:380r.

96. Monteiro Praxis.

97. Francisco Varo, a Dominican who worked in Fujian Province, wrote a grammar in the 1680s, titled *Arte de la Lengua Mandarina,* that was published at Canton in 1703. See W. South Colbin and Joseph Levi, eds. and trans., *Francisco Varo's Grammar of the Mandarin Language (1703)* (Philadelphia and Amsterdam, 2000).

98. Monteiro Praxis, 1.

99. Ibid., 17–19.

100. Ibid., 38–39.

101. Ibid., 61–78.

102. Anon., Chinese-Spanish Dictionary, BNL Reservados 11611:172v–174v.

103. Translation from James Legge, trans. and ed., *The Four Books* (New York, 1966), 308.

104. Anon., Chinese-Spanish Dictionary, BNL Reservados 11611:172v.

105. Francisco Nogueira, Ordens para as Residencias da China, Macau, [1694?], BAJA 49-V-23:340r/v.

106. Soares to José Monteiro, Peking, 8 January 1705, BAJA 49-V-24:543r.

8. The Business of Conversion

1. Guerreiro 2:114–115.

2. The passage is Jeremiah 12:1, "Why doth the way of the wicked prosper? Why is it well with all them that transgress, and do wickedly?"

3. Guerreiro 2:116.

4. These euphemisms are in Gabriel de Magalhães, Partial AL Vice-Province 1640, Hangzhou, 30 August 1641, BAJA 49-V-12:511v.

5. Nicolas Standaert, "Chinese Christians," in *Handbook,* 380–391, esp. 386.

6. See, for example, Willard Peterson, "Why Did They Become Christians? Yang T'ing-yün, Li Chih-tsao, and Hsü Kuang-ch'i," in *East West,* 129–152; and Nicolas Standaert, "Xu Guangqi's Conversion as a Multi-faceted Process" in Jami et al., 170–185.

7. See Erik Zürcher, "The Jesuit Mission in Fujian in Late Ming Times: Levels of Response," in E. B. Vermeer, ed., *Development and Decline of Fukien Province in the 17th and 18th Centuries* (Leiden, 1990), 417–457; and Erik Zürcher, "The Lord of

Heaven and the Demons: Strange Stories from a Late Ming Christian Manuscript," in G. Naundorf, K. H. Pohl, and H. H. Schmidt, eds., *Religion und Philosophie in Ostasien* (Würzburg, 1985), 359–375.

8. Rodrigues to Claudio Aquaviva, Macau, 22 January 1616, ARSI Jap-Sin 16-I:287v.

9. Francisco Cabral to Alessandro Valignano, Macau, 5 December 1584, in *OS* 2:430.

10. *FR* 1:314–315.

11. Longobardo to João Álvares, Shaozhou, 4 November 1598, in *OS* 2:475.

12. *FR* 2:193–194.

13. Ibid., 195.

14. On European doctrine teaching, see Sara Nalle, *God in La Mancha: Religious Reform and the People of Cuenca, 1500–1650* (Baltimore, 1992), 104–133; and Paul Grendler, *Schooling in Renaissance Italy: Literacy and Learning, 1300–1600* (Baltimore, 1989), 333–362.

15. For more, see Chan, 159 and 236.

16. Informação, 270r.

17. Guerreiro 1:257.

18. Cattaneo to Alfonso Vagnone, cited in Niccolò Longobardo, AL China Mission 1608, Shaozhou, 21 December 1609, ARSI Jap-Sin 113:111r–112r.

19. On Buddhist and Daoist critiques of Christianity, see Jacques Gernet, *Chine et Christianisme: Action et Réaction* (Paris, 1982), 91–142; and Nicolas Standaert, *Yang Tingyun, Confucian and Christian in Late Ming China: His Life and Thought* (Leiden, 1988), 161–182.

20. On Ming era Buddhism and Daoism, see Yü Chün-fang, "Ming Buddhism," in *CHC* 8:893–952; and Judith Berling, "Taoism in Ming Culture," in *CHC* 8:953–986.

21. Albert Chan, "Michele Ruggieri, S.J., and His Chinese Poems," *Monumenta Serica* 41 (1993): 129–176, esp. 159.

22. Cattaneo to Alfonso Vagnoni, cited in Niccolò Longobardo, AL China Mission 1608, Shaozhou, 21 December 1609, ARSI Jap-Sin 113:112r.

23. *FR* 2:229–230.

24. Informação, 276r.

25. Diogo Antunes, AL China Mission and AL College of Macau 1602, Macau, 29 January 1603, in João Paolo Oliveira e Costa and Ana Fernandes Pinto, eds., *Cartas Ânuas do Colégio de Macau (1594–1627)* (Macau, 1999), 99.

26. Ibid., 99–100. Longobardo's chronology corresponds to Kenneth Chen, *Buddhism in China: A Historical Survey* (Princeton, 1964), 40–42.

27. Longobardo, Appontamentos acerca de pedirse a licentia del Rey pera a Nossa Estada e pera a Pregação da Lei de Deos na China, Nanxiong, 19 February 1615, ARSI Jap-Sin 113:461r–463v.

28. Erik Zürcher, "Bouddhisme et Christianisme," in *Bouddhisme, Christianisme et Société Chinoise* (Paris, 1990), 11–42, esp. 32.

29. Longobardo, AL China Mission 1612, Nanxiong, 20 February 1613, ARSI Jap-Sin 113:238v and 239v.

30. Petris to Claudio Aquaviva, Shaozhou, 15 November 1592, in *OS* 2:464.

31. António de Gouvea, *Asia Extrema,* ed. Horácio Araújo, 3 vols. (Lisbon, 1995–), 2:173.

32. Diogo Antunes, AL China Mission and AL College of Macau 1602, Macau, 29 January 1603, in Oliveira e Costa and Pinto, *Cartas Ânuas,* 100.

33. Daniel Overmyer, *Folk Buddhist Religion: Dissenting Sects in Late Traditional China* (Cambridge, Mass., 1976), 186; Susan Naquin, "The Transmission of White Lotus Sectarianism in Late Imperial China," in David Johnson, Andrew Nathan, and Evelyn Rawski, eds., *Popular Culture in Late Imperial China* (Berkeley, 1985), 255–291.

34. Petris to Claudio Aquaviva, Shaozhou, 15 November 1592, in *OS* 2:464–465.

35. João da Rocha to Manuel Dias the elder, Nanjing, 5 October 1602, BAJA 49-V-5:14r.

36. Ibid., 15r.

37. Figueiredo Ningbo, 144r.

38. Ibid., 153r.

39. Ibid., 144v.

40. [Manuel Dias the elder?], Lembrança para os Padres que vam em Missam Breve cultivar os Christãos, [Macau?, 1624?], BAJA 49-V-7:317r/v.

41. Palmeiro Orders, 33v.

42. Gabriel de Magalhães, Vida e Morte do Padre Estevão Fabro, Peking, 21 March 1658, BAJA 49-V-14:315v–316r.

43. Figueiredo Ningbo, 145r/v.

44. A discussion of Jesuit iconography in China is found in Hui-Hung Chen, "Encounters in Peoples, Religions, and Sciences: Jesuit Visual Culture in Seventeenth-Century China" (Ph.D. diss., Brown University, 2004).

45. João Monteiro, AL Vice-Province 1637, Nanchang, 16 October 1638, BAJA 49-V-12:55v.

46. Matos Orders, 230v.

47. Ferreira to Matteo Ricci, cited in Ricci to Claudio Aquaviva, Peking, 18 October 1607, in *OS* 2:323.

48. Figueiredo Ningbo, 145v.

49. Ibid., 146r.

50. Figueiredo claimed that this text had "greatly helped the Christian community." See Figueiredo, AL Vice-Province 1628, Hangzhou, 22 August 1629, BAJA 49-V-6:597v. Compare to Chan, 71.

51. A Portuguese edition of Jorge's text printed at Augsburg in 1616 noted that it had been translated into "German, Latin, Greek, French, Italian, English, Bohemian,

Slavic, Hungarian, and Spanish." Later versions appeared in Indian, East Asian, African, and Native American tongues. See Marcos Jorge, *Doutrina Christam . . . Representada por Imagens,* ed. Georg Mayr (Augsburg, 1616), 3.

52. Figueiredo Ningbo, 147r/v.

53. Ibid., 147v.

54. Ibid., 152v.

55. *A Mi Tuo Fo,* or Amitabha Buddha. Invoking this Buddha's name is one of the central practices of the Pure Land school. For further discussion, see Chen, *Buddhism in China,* 342–350.

56. Figueiredo Ningbo, 147v.

57. Ibid., 153r.

58. António de Gouvea, Asia Extrema, Fuzhou, 10 April 1644, BAJA 49-V-2:574.

59. Mathias de Maya, AL Japan Province 1659 and 1660, Macau, [1661?], BAJA 49-V-14:735v.

60. Erik Zürcher, "'In the beginning': 17th Century Chinese Reactions to Christian Creationism," in Zürcher and Chun-Chieh Huang, eds., *Time and Space in Chinese Culture* (Leiden, 1995), 132–166; Derk Bodde, "Myths of Ancient China," in Charles Le Blanc and Dorothy Borei, eds., *Essays on Chinese Civilization* (Princeton, 1981), 45–84.

61. On Pangu, see E. T. C. Werner, *A Dictionary of Chinese Mythology* (Shanghai, 1932; reprint, Boston, 1977), 355.

62. This "Chronicle" may be one of the *lei shu,* compendia of myth and history frequently written in less-than-erudite Chinese. It may also refer to the *Shanhai jing,* the "Classic of Mountains and Seas," where the story of Pangu appears. See Bodde, "Myths," 65.

63. Figueiredo Ningbo, 149v.

64. These Three Kings created the world: *Tianhuang* (king of heaven), *Dihuang* (king of earth), and *Renhuang* (king of humans). For further discussion, see Bodde, "Myths," 65–79.

65. *Zhuangzi* and *Spring and Autumn Annals* record that in antiquity ten suns shone in succession each day. Confusion in heaven during King Yao's reign caused all ten suns to appear at once, making many think the world would burn up. See ibid., 70.

66. In *Huainan zi,* an archer named Yi, or Hou Yi, saved the world by shooting all but one of the suns. The figure who gathered the winds is likely Shen Yi, another semi-divine archer. See ibid.; and Werner, *Chinese Mythology,* 159 and 418.

67. Figueiredo Ningbo, 149v–150r.

68. Mathias de Maya, AL Japan Province 1659 and 1660, Macau, [1661?], BAJA 49-V-14:736r.

69. Figueiredo Ningbo, 150r/v.

70. Mathias de Maya, AL Japan Province 1659 and 1660, Macau, [1661?], BAJA 49-V-14:735v–736r.

71. Figueiredo Ningbo, 150v.

72. Ibid. For more on the Jesuits' problems explaining the virgin birth, see Eugenio Menegon, "Child Bodies, Blessed Bodies: The Contest between Christian Virginity and Confucian Chastity," *Nan Nü: Men, Women, and Gender in Early and Late Imperial China,* 6.2 (2004): 177–240, esp. 207.

73. Figueiredo Ningbo, 151r.

74. Ibid., 151r and 153r.

75. Ibid., 151v.

76. Matos Orders, 229r.

77. On these practices, see Pei-yi Wu, "Self-examination and Confession of Sins in Traditional China," *Harvard Journal of Asiatic Studies* 39.1 (June 1979): 5–38, esp. 22–34.

78. Figueiredo Ningbo, 147r. On how the conversion process and baptism ritual were understood by Chinese converts, see Erik Zürcher, "Confucian and Christian Religiosity in Late Ming China," *Catholic Historical Review* 83.4 (October 1997): 614–653, esp. 635–638.

79. Figueiredo Ningbo, 151v.

80. Palmeiro Orders, 26v.

81. Cunha to Francisco Furtado, Yanping, 25 January 1653, BNL Reservados 722:47r.

82. Mendes to Miguel de Amaral, Nanchang, 8 February 1688, ARSI Jap-Sin 164:34r.

83. [Manuel Dias the elder?], Algumas Cousas Que se hão de guardar na Igreja, Missas, Baptismos, e Enterramentos para em todas as Casas aver Conformidade, [Macau?, 1624?], BAJA 49-V-7:315r/v.

84. Lazzaro Cattaneo, AL Vice-Province 1630, Hangzhou, 12 September 1631, BAJA 49-V-8:717r.

85. Palmeiro Orders, 26r–27r.

86. Cunha to Francisco Furtado, Yanping, 25 January 1653, BNL Reservados 722:46r.

87. Zürcher, "Levels of Response," 445–449; Zürcher, "Strange Stories," 362–371.

88. Francisco Furtado, AL Vice-Province 1623, Hangzhou, 10 April 1624, BAJA 49-V-6:128v.

89. António de Gouvea, AL Vice-Province 1636, Hangzhou, 20 November 1637, in Gouvea, 72.

90. Ibid., 69 and 113.

91. Ibid., 93.

92. António de Gouvea, AL Southern Residences, Vice-Province 1643, Fuzhou, 15 August 1645, in Gouvea, 135.

93. Baldassare Citadella, Relação . . . da Viagem de Macao a Ilha de Sanchoam, Macau, 8 October 1644, ARSI Jap-Sin 64:244v–245r.

94. [Francisco Simões], Breve Relação das Missoens de . . . Pecheli no principio deste anno de 1693, [Zhending?, March?] 1693, BAJA 49-V-22:164v.

95. João Fróis, AL Vice-Province 1634, Hangzhou, 8 September 1634, BAJA 49-V-10:426v.

96. Gabriel de Magalhães, AL Vice-Province 1640, Hangzhou, 30 August 1641, ARSI Jap-Sin 122:86v.

97. Costa, AL Northern Residences, Vice-Province 1647, Xi'an, [1648?], BAJA 49-V-13:443r.

98. On *duilian,* see Ronald Knapp, *China's Living Houses: Folk Beliefs, Symbols, and Household Ornamentation* (Honolulu, 1999), 81–101.

99. Furtado, AL Vice-Province 1623, Hangzhou, 10 April 1624, BAJA 49-V-14:127r. The reference is Acts 25:11, "I refuse not to die."

100. António de Gouvea, AL Southern Residences, Vice-Province 1644, Fuzhou, 16 August 1645, in Gouvea, 191.

101. Rodrigo de Figueiredo, AL Vice-Province 1628, Hangzhou, 22 August 1629, BAJA 49-V-6:598r.

102. Gouvea, Ásia Extrema, Fuzhou, 10 April 1644, BAJA 49-V-2:576. A translation and analysis of the *Rike* is in Paul Brunner, *L'Euchologe de la Chine: Editio Princeps 1628 et Développements jusqu'à nos Jours* (Münster, 1964).

103. António de Gouvea, AL Vice-Province 1636, Hangzhou, 20 November 1637, in Gouvea, 76.

104. António de Gouvea, AL Southern Residences, Vice-Province 1643, Fuzhou, 15 August 1645, in Gouvea, 126.

105. Ad Dudink, "Church Buildings," in *Handbook,* 580–586, esp. 580.

106. [Jacques le Faure], AL Ganzhou Residence 1658, 1659, and 1660, Ganzhou, [1661?], BAJA 49-V-14:653v.

107. Cunha, AL Jianning Residence 1645, Jianning, 1645, BAJA 49-V-13:348v–349r.

108. Simão da Cunha, Rol da Igrejas e Christandades, Yanping, 25 January 1653, BNL Reservados 722:51r.

109. Palmeiro, Itinerario, Macau, 8 January 1630, BAJA 49-V-8:523v.

110. Susan Naquin, *Peking: Temples and City Life, 1400–1900* (Berkeley, 2000), 211.

111. Magalhães, AL Northern Residences, Vice-Province 1658, Peking, 20 September 1659, BAJA 49-V-14:237v.

112. Directives issued in 1621 and 1629 stipulated that churches be erected in Chinese style. See Matos Orders, 221r; and Palmeiro Orders, 32r.

113. [Le Faure], AL Ganzhou Residence 1658, 1659, and 1660, Ganzhou, [1661?], BAJA 49-V-14:648v–650r.

9. A Good Method and Order

1. Jorge, AL Vice-Province 1652, Hangzhou, 7 May 1655, BAJA 49-IV-61:206r/v and 228v.

2. Guerreiro 1:3.

3. André Ferrão, AL Vice-Province 1656, Macau, 29 January 1659, BAJA 49-V-14:82v.

4. For further discussion, see Nicolas Standaert, "Social Organisation of the Church," in *Handbook,* 456–461; and Fortunato Margiotti, "Congregazioni Mariane della Antica Missione Cinese," in *Das Laienapostolat in den Missionen* (Supplement X), J. Specher and P. W. Bühlmann, eds., *Neue Zeitschrift für Missionswissenschaft* (1961): 131–151, esp. 132–137.

5. For more, see Nicolas Standaert and John Witek, "Catechists," in *Handbook,* 470–473; and Robert Entenmann, "Chinese Catholic Clergy and Catechists in Eighteenth-Century Szechuan," in *Actes du VIe Colloque International de Sinologie, Chantilly, 1989: Images de la Chine, Le Contexte Occidental de la Sinologie Naissante* (Taipei, 1995), 389–410.

6. José Soares, Draft AL Vice-Province 1697, Peking, 30 July 1697, BAJA 49-V-21:61v.

7. *FR* 1:270.

8. Ibid., 2:339.

9. Standaert, "Social Organisation," 456–457.

10. Feliciano Pacheco, AL Central Residences, Vice-Province 1660, Huai'an, 19 July 1661, BAJA 49-V-14:717r. On the White Lotus sect in the Ming era, see Barend Ter Haar, *The White Lotus Teachings in Chinese Religious History* (Leiden, 1992), 114–246.

11. Matos Orders, 229v.

12. Palmeiro Orders, 23v–24r.

13. Fróis, AL Vice-Province 1634, Hangzhou, 8 September 1634, BAJA 49-V-10:394v and 426v.

14. João Monteiro, AL Vice-Province 1637, Nanchang, 16 October 1638, BAJA 49-V-12:39v.

15. Lazzaro Cattaneo, AL Vice-Province 1630, Hangzhou, 12 September 1631, BAJA 49-V-8:716v.

16. João Monteiro, AL Vice-Province 1637, Nanchang, 16 October 1638, BAJA 49-V-12:6v.

17. António de Gouvea, Ásia Extrema, Fuzhou, 10 April 1644, BAJA 49-V-2:437.

18. António de Gouvea, AL Southern Residences, Vice-Province 1643, Fuzhou, 15 August 1645, in Gouvea, 129.

19. António de Gouvea, AL Southern Residences, Vice-Province 1647, Fuzhou, 20 January 1649, in Gouvea, 371.

20. Francesco Brancati, AL Shanghai Residence 1648, Shanghai, 1648, BAJA 49-V-13:479r/v.

21. António de Gouvea, AL Vice-Province 1649, Fuzhou, 15 November 1650, in Gouvea, 412.

22. Francesco Brancati, AL Shanghai Residence 1644, Shanghai, 12 March [1645?], BNL Reservados 722:266v.

23. António de Gouvea, AL Southern Residences, Vice-Province 1644, Fuzhou, 16 August 1645, in Gouvea, 189–190.

24. [Francisco Furtado?], AL Northern Residences, Vice-Province 1643, 1644, and 1645, [Peking?, 1646], BAJA 49-V-13:119v.

25. Brancati, AL Shanghai Residence 1658, Shanghai, 1658, BAJA 49-V-14:472v.

26. Brancati to Francisco Furtado, Shanghai, [1653?], BA 50-V-38:92v and 97r.

27. Feliciano Pacheco, AL Central Residences, Vice-Province 1660, Huai'an, 19 July 1661, BAJA 49-V-14:715v.

28. André Ferrão, AL Vice-Province 1656, Macau, 29 January 1659, BAJA 49-V-14:91v.

29. Marian CS. Translation by Chen Huihung and Tang Haitao. For more on this text, see Chan, 459–460. Reproduction in *CCT* 12:489–494.

30. Marian CS, 10r.

31. Ibid., 10r, 11r/v.

32. Ibid., 10v–11r.

33. Philippe Couplet, *Historia de una Gran Señora Christiana de la China, llamada Doña Candida Hiù* (Madrid, 1691), 88–89.

34. Marian CS, 11r.

35. On confraternity reform in Catholic Europe, see Marc Venard, "Les Confréries dans l'Espace Urbain: L'Exemple de Rouen," in *Le Catholicisme à l'Épreuve dans la France du XVIe Siècle* (Paris, 2000), 221–235.

36. [Juan Antonio de Arnedo?], AL Nanchang Residence 1692, Nanchang, [1693?], BAJA 49-V-22:170r.

37. Marian CS, 11r/v.

38. Ibid., 12r/v.

39. On Chinese funeral practices, see J. J. M. de Groot, *The Religious System of China: Its Ancient Forms, Evolution, History, and Present Aspect, Manners, Customs, and Social Institutions Connected Therewith,* 6 vols. (Leiden, 1892), 1:3–240.

40. Funeral Ritual. Translation by Chen Huihung and Tang Haitao. On this text, see Chan, 460. Reproduction in *CCT* 5:439–446.

41. Funeral Ritual, 13r–16v.

42. Ibid., 13r, 16v.

43. Ibid., 15r/v.

44. On Jesuit doctrine teaching in early modern Europe, see Alain Lottin, "La Catechese en Milieu Populaire au XVIIe Siècle: L'Exemple de l'École Dominicale de Valenciennes et du Père Marc (1584–1638)," in *Être et Croire à Lille et en Flandre, XVIe–XVIIIe siècle* (Arras, 2000), 405–417.

45. Inácio Martins (1531–1598), the Jesuit who revised the doctrine primer originally written by Marcos Jorge.

46. For further discussion, see Chan, 155–156.

47. Gabriel de Magalhães, AL Northern Residences, Vice-Province 1660, Peking, 20 July 1662, BAJA 49-V-14:697v.

48. Cunha to Francisco Furtado, Yanping, 25 January 1653, BNL Reservados 722:47v.

49. Ibid., 48r.

50. Hubert Verhaeren, trans. and ed., "Les Ordonnonces de la Sainte Église," *Monumenta Serica* 4 (1939–40): 451–477, esp. 466 and 458.

51. Ibid., 466.

52. Noël Golvers, *François de Rougemont, SJ, Missionary in Ch'ang-shu (Chiang-Nan): A Study of the Account Book (1674–1676) and the Elogium* (Leuven, 1999), 427–428.

53. Couplet, *Gran Señora,* 41.

54. Soares to Antoine Thomas, Jiangzhou, 29 April 1687, BAJA 49-V-20:70v.

55. Standaert and Witek, "Catechists," 471.

56. António de Gouvea, AL Vice-Province 1636, Hangzhou, 20 November 1637, in Gouvea, 77.

57. António de Gouvea, AL Southern Residences, Vice-Province 1644, Fuzhou, 16 August 1645, in Gouvea, 201.

58. Rodrigo de Figueiredo to Francisco Furtado, Kaifeng, [1639?], in Gabriel de Magalhães, Partial AL Vice-Province 1640, Hangzhou, 30 August 1641, BAJA 49-V-12:490v.

59. Ibid., 489r/v.

60. Feliciano Pacheco, AL Central Residences, Vice-Province 1660, Huai'an, 19 July 1661, BAJA 49-V-14:708v–709r.

61. Golvers, *François de Rougemont,* 424.

62. Feliciano Pacheco, Ordens feitos em Consultas Plenas Extraordinarias, Canton, [January 1668?], ARSI Jap-Sin 162:255v.

63. Couplet, *Gran Señora,* 40–41.

64. Ibid., 38–39.

65. Verbiest to Filippo Marini, Peking, 24 August 1678, BAJA 49-V-17:504r.

66. Verbiest to Francesco Saverio Filippucci, Peking, 7 January 1684, BAJA 49-V-19:473r.

67. See Chan, 350–351.

68. Lubelli to the Jesuits of the Japan Province and the Vice-Province, Macau, 6 March 1681, BAJA 49-V-19:51v.

69. Ibid., 52r.

70. Golvers, *François de Rougemont,* 412–421, 140, and 137.

71. José Soares, Draft AL Vice-Province 1697, Peking, 30 July 1697, BAJA 49-V-21:61v.

72. Veiga, AL Hainan Residence, June 1686–July 1687, Qiongzhou, 22 August 1687, BAJA 49-V-19:843v.

73. Xavier CS. Translation by Chen Huihung and Tang Haitao. For more on this text, see Chan, 458–459. Reproduction in *CCT* 12:479–487.

74. Xavier CS, 5r.

75. Ibid., 5v–6r.

76. Ibid., 6r/v, 8r/v.

77. Erik Zürcher, "The Lord of Heaven and the Demons: Strange Stories from a Late Ming Christian Manuscript," in G. Naundorf, K. H. Pohl, and H. H. Schmidt, eds., *Religion und Philosophie in Ostasien* (Würzburg, 1985), 359–375, esp. 366–370.

78. Francisco da Veiga, AL Hainan Residence, June 1686–July 1687, Qiongzhou, 22 August 1687, BAJA 49-V-19:845v.

79. Xavier CS, 6v–8r.

80. Ibid., 8v.

81. Arnedo, AL Vice-Province 1685–1690, Ganzhou, 20 September 1691, BAJA 49-V-19:672r/v.

82. Juan Antonio de Arnedo, AL Vice-Province 1685–1690, Ganzhou, 30 November 1691, ARSI Jap-Sin 117:238v.

83. Juan Antonio de Arnedo, AL Vice-Province 1685–1690, Ganzhou, 20 September 1691, BAJA 49-V-19:670r.

84. Ibid., 671v.

85. José Soares, Partial AL Vice-Province, July 1694–July 1697, Peking, 30 July 1697, BAJA 49-V-22:633v.

86. Juan Antonio de Arnedo, AL Vice-Province 1685–1690, Ganzhou, 30 September 1691, BAJA 49-V-19:671v.

87. José Soares, Partial AL Vice-Province, July 1694–July 1697, Peking, 30 July 1697, BAJA 49-V-22:632v–633r.

88. Giandomenico Gabiani to Simão Martins, Nanjing, 4 March 1688, BAJA 49-V-20:202v–203r.

89. Soares, Draft AL Vice-Province 1697, Peking, 30 July 1697, BAJA 49-V-21:60r.

90. Ibid., 64v.

91. Antoine Thomas, Triennial Catalogue, Vice-Province 1703, Peking, 25 September 1703, ARSI Jap-Sin 134:408Fv.

92. Anon., *Relação Summaria da Prizam, Tormentos, e Glorioso Martyrio dos Veneraveis Padres António Joseph Portuguez e Tristam de Attamis Italiano* (Lisbon, 1751), 12.

10. Brothers of Passion and Mercy

1. Feliciano Pacheco, AL Central Residences, Vice-Province 1660, Huai'an, 19 July 1661, BAJA 49-V-14:715r.

2. Ibid., 716r.

3. Nicolas Standaert, *Yang Tingyun, Confucian and Christian in Late Ming China: His Life and Thought* (Leiden, 1988), 63.

4. See Standaert, "Social Organization," in *Handbook,* 456–461, esp. 457.

5. This goal is stated in Álvares Orders, 49.

6. On Jesuit Marian sodalities in Europe, see Louis Châtellier, *The Europe of the Devout: The Catholic Reformation and the Formation of a New Society,* trans. Jean Birrelli (Cambridge, 1989), 3–46.

7. Soares, Draft AL Vice-Province 1697, Peking, 30 July 1697, BAJA 49-V-21:63v.

8. *FR* 2:482.

9. Pantoja to Luís de Guzman, Peking, 9 March 1602, in Diego de Pantoja, *Relacion de la Entrada de Algunos Padres de la Cõpañia de IESVS en la China* (Seville, 1605), 54r.

10. Joanna Handlin Smith, "Benevolent Societies: The Reshaping of Charity during the Late Ming and Early Ch'ing," *Journal of Asian Studies* 46.2 (1987): 309–337.

11. Pantoja to Luis de Guzman, Peking, 9 March 1602, in Pantoja, *Relacion,* 54r.

12. Yü Chün-fang, *The Renewal of Buddhism in China: Chu-hung and the Late Ming Synthesis* (New York, 1981), 9–27 and 192–222.

13. Standaert, *Yang Tingyun,* 64–65.

14. Manuel Dias the younger, AL Vice-Province 1627, Shanghai, 9 May 1628, BAJA 49-V-6:480v.

15. Niccolò Longobardo, AL Vice-Province 1613, Nanxiong, 1 August 1614, ARSI Jap-Sin 113:360r/v.

16. Matteo Ricci and Nicolas Trigault, *De Christiana Expeditione apud Sinas* (Augsburg, 1615), 589.

17. On the 1587 Common Rules, and a translation, see Elder Mullan, *History of the Prima Primaria Sodality of the Annunciation and Sts. Peter and Paul* (St. Louis, 1917), 74–76 and 325–340.

18. Châtellier, *The Europe of the Devout,* 49–109.

19. Marc Venard, "Qu'est ce qu'une Confrérie de Dévotion? Réflexions sur les Confréries Rouennais du Saint Sacrement," in *Le Catholicisme à l'Épreuve dans la France du XVIe Siècle* (Paris, 2000), 237–247, esp. 246.

20. Anon., *Regra dos Estudantes Congregados da Virgem Nossa Senhora da Annunciada na sua Confraria sita na Universidade de Evora da Companhia de Jesus* (Évora, 1662), 1.

21. *FR* 2:482 and 492.

22. Marc Venard, "La Crise des Confréries en France au XVIe Siècle," in *Catholicisme à l'Épreuve,* 249–268.

23. Informação, 274v and 275v.

24. Contemporary Buddhist groups apparently used a less stringent regime of devotional activities than their Christian counterparts. See Timothy Brook, *Praying for Power: Buddhism and the Formation of Gentry Society in Late Ming China* (Cambridge, Mass., 1993), 105 and 44.

25. Furtado, AL China Mission 1620, Hangzhou, 24 August 1621, ARSI Jap-Sin 113:245v and 255v.

26. Francisco Furtado, AL Vice-Province 1624, Hangzhou, 17 April 1625, BAJA 49-V-6:180r.

27. Anon., AL Vice-Province 1626, [n.p., 1627?], BAJA 49-V-6:314v–315r.

28. Manuel Dias the younger, AL Vice-Province 1625, Jiading, 1 May 1626, BAJA 49-V-6:220v.

29. Rodrigo de Figueiredo, AL Vice-Province 1628, Hangzhou, 22 August 1629, BAJA 49-V-6:585v.

30. Standaert, *Yang Tingyun,* 60–62.

31. Palmeiro Orders, 23v–24r.

32. António de Gouvea, AL Vice-Province 1636, Hangzhou, 20 November 1637, in Gouvea, 74–75.

33. Philippe Couplet, *Historia de una Gran Señora Christiana de la China, llamada Doña Candida Hiù* (Madrid, 1691), 36.

34. António de Gouvea, AL Vice-Province 1636, Hangzhou, 20 November 1637, in Gouvea, 78–79.

35. Figueiredo to Francisco Furtado, Kaifeng, [1639?], in Gabriel de Magalhães, Partial AL Vice-Province 1640, Hangzhou, 30 August 1641, BAJA 49-V-12:489v.

36. António de Gouvea, "Asia Extrema," Fuzhou, 10 April 1644, BAJA 49-V-2:432.

37. On the Misericórdias, see Isabel dos Guimarães Sá, *Quando o Rico se faz Pobre: Misericórdias, Caridade e Poder no Império Português, 1500–1800* (Lisbon, 1997), 49–86; and A. J. R. Russell-Wood, *Fidalgos and Philanthropists: The Santa Casa da Misericórdia of Bahia, 1550–1755* (Berkeley, 1968), 1–41.

38. Magalhães, AL Hangzhou Residence 1640, Hangzhou, 30 August 1641, BAJA 49-V-12:483v.

39. Erik Zürcher, "Christian Social Action in Late Ming Times: Wang Zheng and His 'Humanitarian Society,'" in Jan de Meyer and Peter Engelfriet, eds., *Linked Faiths: Essays on Chinese Religions and Traditional Culture in Honour of Kristofer Schipper* (Leiden, 1999), 269–286, esp. 278.

40. António de Gouvea, AL Vice-Province 1636, Hangzhou, 20 November 1637, in Gouvea, 61.

41. Ibid., 149.

42. Standaert, *Yang Tingyun,* 65.

43. Cunha to Francisco Furtado, Yanping, 25 January 1653, BNL Reservados 722:45r.

44. [Inácio da Costa?], AL Northern Residences, Vice-Province 1643, 1644, and 1645, [Xi'an?, 1646?], BAJA 49-V-13:116r.

45. Costa, AL Northern Residences, Vice-Province 1647, [Xi'an?, 1648?], BAJA 49-V-13:442v.

46. Manuel Jorge, AL Vice-Province 1651, [Hangzhou, 1652?], BA 50-V-38:165v.

47. André Ferrão, AL Vice-Province 1656, Macau, 29 January 1659, BAJA 49-V-14:68v.

48. Brancati to Francisco Furtado, Shanghai, [1653?], BA 50-V-38:97r.

49. André Ferrão, AL Vice-Province Northern Residences, Vice-Province 1656, Macau, 29 January 1659, BAJA 49-V-14:91r.

50. Gabriel de Magalhães, AL Northern Residences, Vice-Province 1658, Peking, 20 September 1659, BAJA 49-V-14:261r.

51. Gabriel de Magalhães, AL Northern Residences, Vice-Province 1659, Peking, 20 November 1661, BAJA 49-V-14:547r/v.

52. Gabriel de Magalhães, AL Northern Residences, Vice-Province 1658, Peking, 20 September 1659, BAJA 49-V-14:241v.

53. Hubert Verhaeren, trans. and ed., "Les Ordonnonces de la Sainte Église," *Monumenta Serica* 4 (1939–40): 451–477, esp. 462 and 465.

54. António de Gouvea, AL Southern Residences, Vice-Province 1644, Fuzhou, 16 August 1645, in Gouvea, 217.

55. Brancati to Luis Espineli, Suzhou, 9 October 1661, ARSI Jap-Sin 124:19r. Further discussion of the Jesuits' encouragement of corporal mortification in southern Italy is in Jennifer Selwyn, *A Paradise Inhabited by Devils: The Jesuits' Civilizing Mission in Early Modern Naples* (Aldershot and Rome, 2004), 227–242.

56. Feliciano Pacheco, Ordens feitos em Consultas Plenas Extraordinarias, Canton, [January 1668?], ARSI Jap-Sin 162:255v.

57. Juan Eusebio Nieremberg, *Vida del Santo Padre . . . Francisco de Borja* (Madrid, 1644), 9.

58. Anon., *Regra dos Estudantes,* 10.

59. Couplet, *Gran Señora,* 87.

60. Ibid., 35.

61. Noël Golvers, *François de Rougemont, SJ, Missionary in Ch'ang-shu (Chiang-Nan): A Study of the Account Book (1674–1676) and the Elogium* (Leuven, 1999), 424–430.

62. Mendes to Miguel de Amaral, Nanchang, 8 February 1688, ARSI Jap-Sin 164:32r.

63. Gabriel de Magalhães, AL Peking Residence 1673 and 1674, Peking, [1675?], BAJA 49-V-16:185v.

64. Juan Antonio de Arnedo, AL Vice-Province 1685–1690, Ganzhou, 30 September 1691, BAJA 49-V-19: 652r/v.

65. José Soares, Draft AL Vice-Province 1697, Peking, 30 July 1697, BAJA 49-V-21:66v–68v.

66. José Soares to Tirso González, Peking, 28 September 1694, ARSI Jap-Sin 166:29r.

67. José Soares, Draft AL Vice-Province 1697, Peking, 30 July 1697, BAJA 49-V-21:62v–63r.

68. Ibid., 63v–64r.

69. Ibid., 65r/v.

70. Soares to Tirso González, Peking, 28 September 1694, ARSI Jap-Sin 166:29r.

71. Jean de Fontaney, Remarques sur les Regles de la Congregation de N.D. etablie a Pekin . . . dont le Pere Suares a soin, Amoy, 14 November 1697, ARSI Jap-Sin 166:256r–257v.

72. José Soares, Partial AL Vice-Province, July 1694–June 1697, Peking, 30 July 1697, BAJA 49-V-22:642r. The Fuzhou Jesuits also petitioned the Society's superiors to recognize their group. See José Monteiro to Tirso González, Fuzhou, 15 September 1695, ARSI Jap-Sin 166:80r.

73. João Monteiro, AL Vice-Province, 1637, Nanchang, 16 October 1638, BAJA 49-V-12:39v.

74. António de Gouvea, AL Southern Residences, Vice-Province, 1645, Fuzhou, 15 June 1646, in Gouvea, 238.

75. João Monteiro, AL Vice-Province, 1641, Hangzhou, 7 September 1642, BNL Reservados 722:29r.

76. Gabriel de Magalhães, AL Northern Residences, Vice-Province, 1658, Peking, 20 September 1659, BAJA 49-V-14:261r.

77. Augery, *Statutes for the Sodality of the Blessed Virgin (Shengmu huigui),* Hangzhou, [1660–1672?], ARSI Jap-Sin II, 173.2a. Translation by Chen Huihung and Tang Haitao. For more on this text, see Chan, 233–234. Reproduction in *CCT* 12:441–462.

78. Augery, *Shengmu,* 1–2.

79. Ibid., 3.

80. Ibid., 4–6 and 8.

81. Ibid., 9–10 and 6.

82. Ibid., 6–8.

83. Ibid., 6–7 and 11.

84. António de Gouvea, "Asia Extrema," Fuzhou, 10 April 1644, BAJA 49-V-1:437r/v; and Standaert, *Yang Tingyun,* 65.

85. João Fróis, AL Vice-Province, 1632, Hangzhou, 1 August 1632, BAJA 49-V-10:82v.

86. Magalhães, AL Northern Residences, Vice-Province, 1659, Peking, 20 November 1661, BAJA 49-V-14:530r.

87. Zürcher, "Social Action," 276–277. Also, Standaert, *Yang Tingyun,* 65–66.

88. Charity CS. Translation by Chen Huihung and Tang Haitao. For more, see Chan, 457–458. Reproduction in *CCT* 12:473–487.

89. Charity CS, 1r/v.

90. Ibid., 1v–2v.

91. Ibid., 3v.

92. Ibid., 3r/v.

93. Erik Zürcher, "Confucian and Christian Religiosity in Late Ming China," *Catholic Historical Review* 83.4 (October 1997): 614–653, 629–630, and 639.

94. Pacheco, AL Central Residences, Vice-Province, 1660, Huai'an, 19 July 1661, BAJA 49-V-14:711v.

95. Couplet, *Gran Señora,* 36.

96. António de Gouvea, AL Southern Residences, Vice-Province, 1644, Fuzhou, 16 August 1645, in Gouvea, 188.

97. André Ferrão, AL Vice-Province, 1656, Macau, 29 January 1659, BAJA 49-V-14:69r.

98. Augery, *Statutes for the Confraternity of the Passion (Tianzhu yesu kuhui),* Hangzhou, [1660–1672?], ARSI *Jap-Sin* I 173.2b [hereafter *Kuhui*]. Translation by Chen Huihung and Tang Haitao. For more, see Chan, 234. Reproduction in *CCT* 12:463–469.

99. Augery, *Kuhui,* 12–13.

100. Ibid., 13–15.

101. Ibid., 14.

102. Ibid., 13–14.

103. Anon., *Regra dos Estudantes,* 9.

104. Augery, *Kuhui,* 15.

Conclusion

1. For more on Saldanha's embassy, see John Wills Jr., *Embassies and Illusions: Dutch and Portuguese Envoys to K'ang-hsi, 1666–1687* (Cambridge, Mass., 1984), 82–126.

2. Pimentel, Breve Relação da Jornada que fes a Corte de Pekim o Sr. Manoel de Saldanha, Macau, [1672?], BNL Mss. 10, no. 1:88v–89r. Although these passages were translated by the author, a full translation of Pimentel's text is in Wills, *Embassies,* 193–236.

3. Pimentel, Breve Relação, 89r.

4. Ibid., 88v and 103v.

5. Ibid., 103v–104r.

6. For more on the limits of colonial power in the Americas, see Christine Daniels and Michael V. Kennedy, eds., *Negotiated Empires: Centers and Peripheries in the Americas, 1500–1820* (New York, 2002).

7. Pedro Dias, *Arte da Lingua de Angola* (Lisbon, 1697); Luis de Valdivia, *Arte y Gramatica General de la Lengua que corre en todo el Reyno de Chile* (Lima, 1606); Tomé Estêvão (Thomas Stephens), *Arte da Lingoa Canarim* (Rachol, 1640). On the creation of the *lingua geral* in Brazil, see Charlotte de Castelnau-L'Estoile, *Les Ouvriers d'une Vigne Stérile: Les Jésuites et la Conversion des Indiens au Brésil, 1580–1620* (Lisbon and Paris, 2000), 141–169.

8. Ernest Burrus, ed. and trans., *Kino Writes to the Duchess: Letters of Eusebio Francisco Kino, S.J., to the Duchess of Aveiro* (Rome and St. Louis, 1965), 163–164.

9. Ruben Gold Thwaites, *The Jesuit Relations and Allied Documents,* 73 vols. (Cleveland, 1896–1901), 5:113 and 117.

10. On the differences among Chinese dialects, see Jerry Norman, *Chinese* (Cambridge, 1988), 181–244.

11. Alonso de Sandoval, *Un Tratado sobre la Esclavitud,* ed. Enriqueta Vila Vilar (Madrid, 1987), 370–375.

12. James Axtell, *The Invasion Within: The Contest of Cultures in Colonial North America* (Oxford, 1985), 81–88.

13. John Steckley, "The Warrior and the Lineage: Jesuit Use of Iroquois Images to Communicate Christianity," *Ethnohistory* 39.4 (Autumn 1992): 478–509.

14. Dot Tuer, "Old Bones and Beautiful Words: The Spiritual Contestation between Shaman and Jesuit in the Guaraní Missions," in Jodi Bilinkoff and Allan Greer, eds., *Colonial Saints: Discovering the Holy in the Americas, 1500–1800* (New York, 2003), 77–97.

15. S. Jeyaseela Stephen, ed. and trans., *Letters of the Portuguese Jesuits from Tamil Countryside, 1666–1688* (Pondicherry, 2001), 270.

16. Hubert Jacobs, ed., *The Jesuit Makasar Documents (1615–1682)* (Rome, 1988), 25.

17. Hugues Didier, ed., *Os Portugueses no Tibete: Os Primeiros Relatos dos Jesuítas (1624–1635),* coord. Paulo Lopes Matos, trans. Lourdes Júdice (Lisbon, 2000), 126.

18. John Steckley, trans. and ed., *De Religione: Telling the Seventeenth-Century Jesuit Story in Huron to the Iroquois* (Norman, Okla., 2004), 51.

19. António Brásio, ed., *Monumenta Missionaria Africana,* 15 vols. (Lisbon, 1952–), 7:372.

20. Ibid., 7:379.

21. António Vieira, *Obras Varias,* ed. J. M. C. Seabra and T. Q. Antunes, 2 vols. (Lisbon, 1856), 2:72–73.

22. Antonio Ruiz de Montoya, *The Spiritual Conquest Accomplished by the Religious of the Society of Jesus in the Provinces of Paraguay, Paraná, Uruguay, and Tape,* ed. C. J. McNaspy, trans. C. J. McNaspy, John Leonard, and Martin Palmer (St. Louis, 1993), 118.

23. Sandoval, *Tratado,* 264.

24. Kawamura Shinzo, "Making Christian Lay Communities during the 'Christian Century' in Japan: A Case Study of Takata District in Bungo" (Ph.D. diss., Georgetown University, 1999), 118–219; Peter Nosco, "Secrecy and the Transmission of Tradition: Issues in the Study of 'Underground' Christians," *Japanese Journal of Religious Studies* 20.1 (1993): 3–29, esp. 3–10.

25. Stephen, *Letters,* 6.

26. Allan Greer, "Conversion and Identity: Iroquois Christianity in Seventeenth-Century New France," in Kenneth Mills and Anthony Grafton, eds., *Conversion: Old Worlds and New* (Rochester, N.Y., 2003), 175–198, esp. 182.

27. Brasio, *Monumenta Missiologica,* 7:383.

28. Ernesto J. A. Maeder, *Cartas Anuas de la Provincia de Paraguay, 1637–1639* (Buenos Aires, 1984), 103 and 106.

29. Greer, "Conversion and Identity," 188–189.

30. Thwaites, *Jesuit Relations,* 6:25.

31. José de Acosta, *Natural and Moral History of the Indies,* ed. Jane Mangan and Walter Mignolo, trans. Frances López-Morillo (Durham, N.C., 2002), 339.

32. Didier, *Portugueses no Tibete,* 86.

33. Serafim Leite, *Luiz Figueira: A Sua Vida Heróica e Sua Obra Literária* (Lisbon, 1940), 115.

34. Axtell, *Invasion Within,* 74–75.

35. Ines Županov, *Missionary Tropics: The Catholic Frontier in India (16th–17th Centuries)* (Ann Arbor, 2005).

36. Thwaites, *Jesuit Relations,* 6:145

37. Ibid., 46:291 and 293.

38. One example is the Jesuits' hesitant participation in the Andean extirpation campaigns in the later seventeenth century. See Kenneth Mills, *Idolatry and Its Enemies: Colonial Andean Religion and Extirpation, 1640–1750* (Princeton, 1997), 162–164.

Illustration Credits

Maps on pages 26-27, 88, 122, and 175 by Christopher L. Brest

Page

38–39	Image courtesy Biblioteca Pública de Évora, códex cxv/2-1, map no. 47.
72	The Metropolitan Museum of Art, Purchase, Carl Selden Trust, several members of The Chairman's Council, Gail and Parker Gilbert, and Lila Acheson Wallace Gifts, 1999 (1999.222). Photograph, all rights reserved, The Metropolitan Museum of Art.
120–121	Princeton University Library.
131	Universitätsbibliothek München, 2° P.or.33.
146	The Scheide Library at Princeton University.
196	Image courtesy of the Instituto de Investigação Científica Tropical—Arquivo Histórico Ultramarino, Lisbon.
208	Photograph by author.
229	Museu Nacional de Machado de Castro, Coimbra. Photograph by José Pessoa, Divisão de Documentação Fotográfica—Instituto Português de Museus.
248	ARSI Shelfmark Jap-Sin I-58a, fol. 27r. Image courtesy Archivum Historicum Societatis Iesu—Institutum Historicum Societatis Iesu, Rome.
274	ARSI Shelfmark Jap-Sin I-10, fol. 9v. Image courtesy Archivum Historicum Societatis Iesu—Institutum Historicum Societatis Iesu, Rome.
278	Rare Books Division, The New York Public Library, Astor, Lenox, and Tilden Foundations.
304	Courtesy Lilly Library, Indiana University, Bloomington, Indiana.

320	© The Field Museum, Chicago (negative no. CSA33288).
342	Research Library, The Getty Research Institute, Los Angeles (1365–379).
376	Research Library, The Getty Research Institute, Los Angeles (1365–379).
400	Courtesy Lilly Library, Indiana University, Bloomington, Indiana.

Index